MW01504326

Microsoft®
Windows® 2000
Server
Internetworking Guide

IT Professional

PUBLISHED BY
Microsoft Press
A Division of Microsoft Corporation
One Microsoft Way
Redmond, Washington 98052-6399

Library of Congress Cataloging-in-Publication Data
Microsoft Windows 2000 Server Resource Kit / Microsoft Corporation.
     p. cm.
    Includes index.
    ISBN 1-57231-805-8 (Resource Kit)
    ISBN 0-7356-1797-X
    1. Microsoft Windows 2000 Server.   2. Operating systems (Computers).   I. Microsoft
Corporation.
    QA76.76.O63 M5241328   2000
    005.4'4769--dc21   99-045616

Printed and bound in the United States of America.

1 2 3 4 5 6 7 8 9   QWT   7 6 5 4 3 2

Distributed in Canada by Penguin Books Canada Limited.

A CIP catalogue record for this book is available from the British Library.

Microsoft Press books are available through booksellers and distributors worldwide. For further information about international editions, contact your local Microsoft Corporation office or contact Microsoft Press International directly at fax (425) 936-7329. Visit our Web site at www.microsoft.com/mspress. Send comments to *rkinput@microsoft.com*.

Acquisitions Editor: Juliana Aldous Atkinson
Project Editor: Aileen Wrothwell

Body Part No. X08-78662

Thank you to those who contributed to this book:

Department Managers: Paul Goode, Ken Western
Documentation Managers: Laura Burris, Martin DelRe, Peggy Etchevers
Resource Kit Program Managers: Chris Hallum, Martin Holladay,
Louis Kahn, Ryan Marshall, Paul Sutton

Internetworking Guide

Technical Writing Lead: Martin DelRe
Routing and Remote Access Technical Writing Lead: Joseph Davies
Writers: Wolfgang Baur, Joseph Davies, Martin DelRe, Grant Fjermedal,
Glenn Geignetter, Victor Goltsman,
Leo Gruzman, Mario Matiev, Judith Meskill

Editing Leads: Deborah Annan, Jennifer Hendrix, Kate O'Leary
Book Editing Lead: Susan F. Sarrafan
Developmental Editor: Gary W. Moore
Copy Editors: Kate McLaughlin, Mary Rose Sliwoski,
Scott Somohano, Debbie Uyeshiro
Glossary: Daniel Bell

Resource Kit Tools Software Developers: Dan Grube,
Michael Hawkins, Darryl Wood, Zeyong *Xu*
Documentation Tools Software Developers: Amy Buck, Tom Carey,
Ryan Farber, Mark Pengra, Fred Taub

Production Leads: Sandy Dean, Jane Dow, Keri Grassl, Jason Hershey
Production Specialists: Michael Faber, Dani McIntyre, Lori Robinson

Indexing Leads: Jane Dow, Veronica Maier
Indexers: Kumud Dwivedi, Cheryl Landes

Lead Graphic Designer: Flora Goldthwaite
Designers: Chris Blanton, Siamack Sahafi

Art Production: Blaine Dollard, Jenna Kiter, Amy Shear, Gabriel Varela

Test Lead: Jonathan Fricke
Testers: Brian Klauber, Jeremy Sullivan

Windows 2000 Lab Manager: Edward Lafferty
Administrators: Deborah Jay, Grant Mericle, Dave Meyer,
Dean Prince, Robert Thingwold, Luke Walker, Joel Wingert, Frank Zamarron
Lab Partners: Cisco Systems, Inc., Compaq, Inc.,
Hewlett-Packard Corporation, Intel Corporation

A special thanks to the following technical experts who contributed to and supported this effort:

Bernard Aboba, Mohammad (Shabbir) Alam, Anoop Anantha, Zubair Ansari,
David Baldridge, Vijay Baliga, Adam Bargmeyer, Stephen Bensley, Boyd Benson,
Hakan Berk, David Brooks, Evan C. Cacka, Ting Cai, Anil Cakir, Ross Carter,
Mike Cerceo, Rakesh Chanana, Frank Chidsey, John Claugherty, Larry Cleeton,
Ken Crocker, Carl DaVault, Joseph Davies, Gulsen Demiroz, William Dixon,
David Eitelbach, Scott Emmons, Kyril Faenov, Pat Fetty, Peter Ford,
Kevin Forsythe, Tom Fout, Nick Gage, Tony Gaston, Alexandru Gavrilescu,
Abolade Gbadegesin, Narendra Gidwani,Stephen Hui, Rich Hagemeyer,
David Janson, George Jose, Kevin Kean, Jawad Khaki, Chaitanya Kodeboyina,
Shirish Koti, Deepak Kumar, Mark Larusso, Brian Lieuallen, David S. Loudon,
Don Lundman, Richard Machin, Rhonda Marshall, Jeremy Martin, Paul Mayfield,
Kelley McGrew, Randy McLaughlin, Paul Miner, Tim Moore, Vivek Nirkhe,
Chris Olson, Ashwin Palekar, Gurdeep Singh Pall, Paolo Phan,Amritansh Raghav,
Marc Reynolds, Kenny Richards, David Roundtree, Rao Salapaka,Walter Schmidt,
Joseph Seifert, Mark Sestak, Alan Shen, Vesa Suomalainen, Dave Thaler,
Chuck Timon, Rob Trace, Blake Underwood, Sean Wheeler, Kevin Willems,
David C. Winkler, Jon Wojan, Glen Zorn, Suzanne Zwick

Contents

Part 4   Media Integration

Chapter 14   Asynchronous Transfer Mode   723

Part 5   Other Protocols

Part 6   Appendixes

Introduction

Welcome to the *Microsoft® Windows® 2000 Server Resource Kit Internetworking Guide*.

The *Microsoft® Windows® 2000 Server Resource Kit* consists of seven volumes and a single compact disc (CD) containing tools, additional reference materials, and an online version of the books. Supplements to the *Windows 2000 Server Resource Kit* will be released as new information becomes available, and updates and information will be available on the Web on an ongoing basis.

The *Internetworking Guide* describes the services and protocols that allow you to extend Microsoft® Windows® 2000 networks across a variety of local area network (LAN), wide area network (WAN), and remote network connections. This guide explains how to manage and troubleshoot all facets of Windows 2000 internetworking technologies including:

- Windows 2000 Routing and Remote Access services, including virtual private networking technologies.
- Windows 2000 interoperability with other operating systems.
- Windows 2000 advanced media technologies, including support for Asynchronous Transfer Mode and telephony integration services.

This information supplements the online documentation included with Microsoft® Windows® 2000 Server and builds on the information contained in the *Microsoft® Windows® 2000 Server Resource Kit TCP/IP Core Networking Guide*.

Document Conventions

The following style conventions and terminology are used throughout this guide.

Element	Meaning
bold font	Characters that you type exactly as shown, including commands and switches. User interface elements are also bold.
Italic font	Variables for which you supply a specific value. For example, *Filename.ext* could refer to any valid file name for the case in question.
`Monospace font`	Code samples.
`%SystemRoot%`	The folder in which Windows 2000 is installed.

Reader Alert	Meaning
Tip	Alerts you to supplementary information that is not essential to the completion of the task at hand.
Note	Alerts you to supplementary information.
Important	Alerts you to supplementary information that is essential to the completion of a task.
Caution	Alerts you to possible data loss, breaches of security, or other more serious problems.
Warning	Alerts you that failure to take or avoid a specific action might result in physical harm to you or to the hardware.

Resource Kit Compact Disc

The *Windows 2000 Server Resource Kit* companion CD includes a wide variety of tools and resources to help you work more efficiently with Windows 2000.

Note The tools on the CD are designed and tested for the U.S. version of Windows 2000. Use of these programs on other versions of Windows 2000 or on versions of Microsoft® Windows NT® can cause unpredictable results.

The *Resource Kit* companion CD contains the following:

Windows 2000 Server Resource Kit Online Books An HTML Help version of the print books. Use these books to find the same detailed information about Windows 2000 as is found in the print versions. Search across all of the books to find the most pertinent information to complete the task at hand.

Windows 2000 Server Resource Kit Tools and Tools Help Over 200 software tools, tools documentation, and other resources that harness the power of Windows 2000. Use these tools to manage Active Directory™, administer security features, work with the registry, automate recurring jobs, and many other important tasks. Use Tools Help documentation to discover and learn how to use these administrative tools.

Windows 2000 Resource Kit References A set of HTML Help references:

- **Error and Event Messages Help** contains most of the error and event messages generated by Windows 2000. With each message comes a detailed explanation and a suggested user action.

- **Technical Reference to the Registry** provides detailed descriptions of Windows 2000 registry content, such as the subtrees, keys, subkeys, and entries that advanced users want to know about, including many entries that cannot be changed by using Windows 2000 tools or programming interfaces.

- **Performance Counter Reference** describes all performance objects and counters provided for use with tools in the Performance snap-in of Windows 2000. Use this reference to learn how monitoring counter values can assist you in diagnosing problems or detecting bottlenecks in your system.

- **Group Policy Reference** provides detailed descriptions of the Group Policy settings in Windows 2000. These descriptions explain the effect of enabling, disabling, or not configuring each policy, as well as explanations of how related policies interact.

Resource Kit Support Policy

The software supplied in the *Windows 2000 Server Resource Kit* is not supported. Microsoft does not guarantee the performance of the *Windows 2000 Server Resource Kit* tools, response times for answering questions, or bug fixes to the tools. However, we do provide a way for customers who purchase the *Windows 2000 Server Resource Kit* to report bugs and receive possible fixes for their issues. You can do this by sending e-mail to rkinput@microsoft.com. This e-mail address is only for *Windows 2000 Server Resource Kit* related issues. For issues relating to the Windows 2000 operating system, please refer to the support information included with your product.

PART 1

Routing

Routing services provide reachability of network locations for IP and IPX traffic for intranets, extranets, branch offices, and the Internet. This section details the basics of routing and the routing protocols and facilities of the Microsoft® Windows® 2000 Routing and Remote Access service.

In This Part

CHAPTER 1

Unicast Routing Overview

Unicast routing is the process of forwarding unicasted traffic from a source to a destination on an internetwork. Unicasted traffic is destined for a unique address. To understand the details of routing protocols, such as Routing Information Protocol (RIP) and Open Shortest Path First (OSPF), and their implementation in Microsoft® Windows® 2000 Server, it is important to have a solid foundation in the principles of unicast routing. Because Windows 2000, with the Routing and Remote Access service, is an open platform that can conceivably host any internetworking protocol and routing protocol, this chapter provides an overview of protocol-independent unicast routing principles. The Internet Protocol (IP) and the Internetwork Packet Exchange (IPX) protocol are used as the example protocols where appropriate.

In This Chapter

Related Information in the Resource Kit

- For more information about unicast IP routing support, see "Unicast IP Routing" in this book.

- For more information about IPX routing support, see "IPX Routing" in this book.

- For more information about virtual private networks, see "Virtual Private Networking" in this book.

Internetwork Routing

The following terms are essential to your understanding of routing:

End Systems. As defined by the International Standards Organization (ISO), end systems are network devices without the ability to forward packets between portions of a network. End systems are also known as hosts.

Intermediate Systems. Network devices with the ability to forward packets between portions of a network. Bridges, switches, and routers are examples of intermediate systems.

Network. A portion of the networking infrastructure (encompassing repeaters, hubs, and bridges/Layer 2 switches) that is bound by a network layer intermediate system and is associated with the same network layer address.

Router. A network layer intermediate system used to connect networks together based on a common network layer protocol.

Hardware Router. A router that performs routing as a dedicated function and has specific hardware designed and optimized for routing.

Software Router. A router that is not dedicated to performing routing but performs routing as one of multiple processes running on the router computer. The Windows 2000 Server Router Service is a software router.

Internetwork. At least two networks connected using routers. Figure 1.1 illustrates an internetwork.

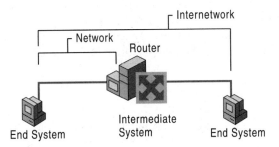

Figure 1.1   An Internetwork

Addressing in an Internetwork

The following internetwork addressing terms are also important to your understanding of routing:

Network address. Also known as a network ID. The number assigned to a single network in an internetwork. Network addresses are used by hosts and routers when routing a packet from a source to a destination in an internetwork.

Host address. Also known as a host ID or a node ID. Can either be the host's physical address (the address of the network interface card) or an administratively assigned address that uniquely identifies the host on its network.

Internetwork address. The combination of the network address and the host address; it uniquely identifies a host on an internetwork. An IP address that contains a network ID and a host ID is an internetwork address.

For detailed information about how IP implements network ID and host ID addressing, see "Introduction to TCP/IP" in the *Microsoft® Windows® 2000 Server Resource Kit TCP/IP Core Networking Guide*.

When a packet is sent from a source host to a destination host on an internetwork, the Network layer header of the packet contains:

- The Source Internetwork Address, which contains a source network address and source host address.
- The Destination Internetwork Address, which contains a destination network address and destination host address.
- A Hop Count, which either starts at zero and increases numerically for each router crossed to a maximum value, or starts at a maximum value and decreases numerically to zero for each router crossed. The hop count is used to prevent the packet from endlessly circulating on the internetwork.

Routing Concepts

Routing is the process of transferring data across an internetwork from a source host to a destination host. Routing can be understood in terms of two processes: host routing and router routing.

Host routing occurs when the sending host forwards a packet. Based on the destination network address, the sending host must decide whether to forward the packet to the destination or to a router. In Figure 1.2, the Source Host forwards the packet destined for the Destination Host to Router 1.

Router routing occurs when a router receives a packet that is to be forwarded. The packet is forwarded between routers (when the destination network is not directly attached to the router) or between a router and the destination host (when the destination network is directly attached). In Figure 1.2, Router 1 forwards the packet to Router 2. Router 2 forwards the packet to the Destination Host.

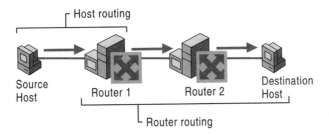

Figure 1.2   The Routing Process

Host Routing

When a host using a routable protocol wants to send data to another host, it must first obtain the internetwork address of the destination. The destination internetwork address is obtained through an address resolution process whereby the sending host obtains the destination internetwork address by referencing its logical name. For example, TCP/IP hosts use Domain Name System (DNS) name resolution to resolve a DNS domain name to an IP address. Novell NetWare workstations query the bindery (a database stored on a NetWare server) or directory tree of their default server to resolve a server name to its Internetwork Packet Exchange (IPX) internetwork address.

Once the destination internetwork address has been obtained, the source network and the destination network addresses are compared. When the source and destination hosts are on the same network, the packets are sent directly to the destination host by the source without the use of a router (see Figure 1.3). The source host sends the packet to the destination by addressing the packet to the destination's physical address. This is known as a direct delivery. In a direct delivery, the destination internetwork address and the destination physical address are for the same end system.

Conversely, when the source and destination hosts are on different networks, the packets to the destination cannot be directly delivered by the source. Instead, the source delivers them to an intermediate router (see Figure 1.3) by addressing the packet to the router's physical address. This is known as an indirect delivery. In an indirect delivery, the destination internetwork address and the destination physical address are not for the same end system.

During an indirect delivery, the sending host forwards the packet to a router on its network by determining the router corresponding to the first hop or by discovering the entire path from the source to the destination.

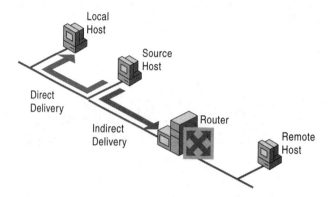

Figure 1.3   Host Routing Process

Host Determination of the First Hop

IP and IPX sending hosts determine the physical address of the first hop router using one of the following processes:

Host routing table   A routing table on the host yields the forwarding address of the router to be used to reach the desired destination network ID. An example is the IP routing table on a Microsoft TCP/IP host. See "Routing Tables" later in this chapter for a detailed definition of a routing table.

Dynamic updates of host routing table   TCP/IP has a facility to dynamically update the host routing table with better routes, as packets are sent to destinations. The Internet Control Message Protocol (ICMP) Redirect message is sent by an IP router to a sending host informing it of a better route to a destination host. The better route becomes a host route in the routing table. TCP/IP for Windows 2000 supports the dynamic update of the IP routing table based on the receipt of the ICMP Redirect message.

Eavesdropping   TCP/IP hosts have the ability to listen to the routing protocol traffic used by routers. This is known as eavesdropping or wiretapping. Eavesdropping hosts have the same routing information as the routers. An example of eavesdropping is Silent RIP. Silent RIP is the ability of a TCP/IP host to listen to RIP for IP routing traffic exchanged by RIP routers and update its routing table. Microsoft® Windows NT® Server 3.51 and Service Pack 2 and later, Microsoft® Windows NT® Workstation 4.0 and Service Pack 4 and later support Silent RIP.

Default route To simplify the configuration of hosts and routers and to reduce the overhead associated with each host having routes for all the networks in the internetwork, a sending host is configured with a single default route. The default route and its forwarding address to the default router are used when no other routes to the destination network are found. The Default Gateway for TCP/IP hosts is a default router.

Querying the network for the best route For hosts without a routing table or a configured default router, the sending host can determine the physical address of the first hop router by querying the routers on the network. A query for the best route to a specified destination network address is sent as a broadcast or multicast packet. The responses from the routers are analyzed by the sending host, and the best router is chosen. An example of this querying process is the RIP GetLocalTarget message sent by an IPX host. The Routing Information Protocol (RIP) GetLocalTarget message contains a desired destination IPX network ID. IPX routers on the sending host's network that can reach the destination IPX network ID send a response to the sending host. Based on the RIP responses from the local routers, the sending host chooses the best router to forward the IPX packet.

Host Determination of the Entire Path

When using some routable protocols, the sending host does more than determine the first hop. The source host goes through a route discovery process and determines the path between the sending host and the destination. The list of networks or routers is then included in the Network layer header and is used by the routers to forward the packet along the indicated path. This process is known as source routing.

In source routing, the routers are only acting as store and forward devices because the routing decisions have already been made by the sending host. Source routing is not typically implemented as a method of routing because the path either needs to be known or discovered. Source route discovery processes tend to be traffic intensive and slow. IP routing is normally done through routing decisions made by sending hosts and IP routers based on local routing tables. However, in network testing and debugging situations, it is sometimes desired to specify an exact route through the IP internetwork that overrides the path that would normally be taken. This is known as IP source routing.

In IP source routing, the entire route is specified by the sending host through the IP addresses of successive IP routers between the source and destination. At each IP router, the IP datagram is addressed to the next router using the Destination IP address field of the IP header.

IP supports two types of source routing. The first type is loose source routing, in which the IP address of the next router can be one or more routers away (multiple hops). The second type is strict source routing, in which the next router must be a neighboring router (single hop).

Note Token Ring source routing is a Media Access Control (MAC)–sublayer routing scheme and does not apply to the internetwork-based source routing discussed earlier.

Router Routing

When a router is forwarded a packet that is not destined for that router, the router must either deliver it to the destination host or to another router, as shown in Figure 1.4.

- If the destination network matches a network to which the router is attached, the router forwards the packet to the destination host by addressing the packet to the destination host's physical address. The router performs a direct delivery to the destination.

- Conversely, if the destination network is not directly attached, the router forwards the packet to an intermediate router. The intermediate router chosen is based on the forwarding address of the optimal route in the routing table. The router forwards the packet by addressing the packet to the intermediate router's physical address. The router performs an indirect delivery to the next router in the path to the destination.

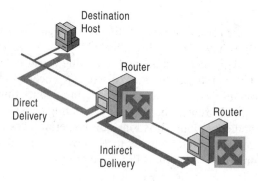

Figure 1.4   Router Routing Process

Routing Tables

During the routing process, the routing decisions of hosts and routers are aided by a database of routes known as the routing table. The routing table is not exclusive to a router. Depending on the routable protocol, hosts may also have a routing table that may be used to decide the best router for the packet to be forwarded. IP hosts have a routing table. IPX hosts do not have a routing table.

The types of possible entries in a routing table include:

Network Route. A route to a specific Network ID in the internetwork.

Host Route. A route to a specific internetwork address (Network ID and Host ID). Instead of making a routing decision based on just the network ID, the routing decision is based on the combination of network ID and host ID. Host routes allow intelligent routing decisions to be made for each internetwork address. Host routes are typically used to create custom routes to control or optimize specific types of internetwork traffic.

Default Route. A route that is used when no other routes for the destination are found in the routing table. For example, if a router or end system cannot find a network route or host route for the destination, the default route is used. Rather than being configured with routes for all the Network IDs in the internetwork, the default route is used to simplify the configuration of end systems or routers.

Note In many router implementations including the Windows 2000 Routing and Remote Access service, there is a routing table and a forwarding table. The routing table is used to store all the routes from all possible sources. The forwarding table is what is used by the routable protocol when forwarding the packet. For example, for a Windows 2000 router, the Routing and Remote Access service maintains the IP routing table using a component called the Route Table Manager. The IP forwarding table is contained within the TCP/IP protocol. The Route Table Manager updates the IP forwarding table based on incoming route information from multiple sources. The contents of the routing table do not necessarily match the contents of the forwarding table. For the purposes of discussion in this introductory chapter, the routing table and the forwarding table are the same.

Routing Table Structure

As illustrated in Figure 1.5, entries in the routing table usually consist of the following fields:

Network ID The Network ID field contains the identification number for a network route or an internetwork address for a host route.

Forwarding Address The Forwarding Address field contains the address to which the packet is to be forwarded. The forwarding address can be a network interface card address or an internetwork address. For network IDs to which the end system or router is directly attached, the Forwarding Address field may be blank.

Interface The Interface field indicates the network interface that is used when forwarding packets to the network ID. This is a port number or other type of logical identifier. For example, the interface for a 3COM EtherLink III network interface card may be referred to as ELNK3 in the routing table.

Metric The Metric field indicates the cost of a route. If multiple routes exist to a given destination network ID, the metric is used to decide which route is to be taken. The route with the lowest metric is the preferred route. Some routing algorithms only store a single route to any Network ID in the routing table even when multiple routes exist. In this case, the metric is used by the router to decide which route to store in the routing table.

Metrics can indicate different ways of expressing a route preference:

Hop Count. A common metric. Indicates the number of routers (hops) in the path to the network ID.

Delay. A measure of time that is required for the packet to reach the network ID. Delay is used to indicate the speed of the path—local area networks (LAN) links have a low delay, wide area network (WAN) links have a high delay—or a congested condition of a path.

Throughput. The effective amount of data that can be sent along the path per second. Throughput is not necessarily a reflection of the bit rate of the link, as a very busy Ethernet link may have a lower throughput than an unutilized 64-Kbps WAN link.

Reliability. A measure of the path constancy. Some types of links are more prone to link failures than others. For example, with WAN links, leased lines are more reliable than dial-up lines.

Lifetime   The Lifetime field indicates the lifetime that the route is considered valid. When routes are learned through the exchange of information with other routers, this is an additional field that is used. Learned routes have a finite lifetime. To keep a learned route in the routing table, the route must be refreshed through a periodic process. If a learned route's lifetime expires, it is removed from the routing table. The timing out of learned routes provides a way for routers to reconfigure themselves when the topology of an internetwork changes due to a downed link or a downed router.

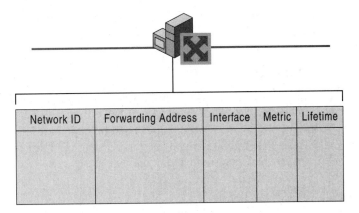

Network ID	Forwarding Address	Interface	Metric	Lifetime

Figure 1.5   Routing Table Structure

Note   The Lifetime field is typically not visible in routing tables.

This list of fields is a representative list in the routing tables. Actual fields in the routing tables for different routable protocols may vary. For information about the IP routing table, see "Introduction to TCP/IP" in the *TCP/IP Core Networking Guide*. For information about the IPX routing table, see "IPX Routing" in this book.

Locality of the Routing Table

All the routing decisions made by the end system or the router are based on information in a local routing table that physically resides in the random access memory (RAM) of the system making the routing decision. There is no single, holistic view of the internetwork that is being gathered by a server and downloaded to each end system and router so that all users have the same view of the internetwork and all traffic flows along predictable pathways.

Each router in a path between a source and destination makes a local routing decision based on its local routing table. The path taken from the source to the destination may not be the same as the path for response packets from the destination back to the source. If the information in the local routing tables of the end systems or routers is incorrect due to misconfiguration or changing network conditions, then routing problems can result. Troubleshooting routing problems may involve the analysis of the routing tables of the end systems (source and destination) and all the routers forwarding packets between them.

For information about the operation and troubleshooting of IP routing, see "Unicast IP Routing" in this book. For information about the operation and troubleshooting of IPX routing, see "IPX Routing" in this book.

Static and Dynamic Routers

For routing between routers to work efficiently in an internetwork, routers must have knowledge of other network IDs or be configured with a default route. On large internetworks, the routing tables must be maintained so that the traffic always travels along optimal paths. How the routing tables are maintained defines the distinction between static and dynamic routing.

Static Routing

A router with manually configured routing tables is known as a static router. A network administrator, with knowledge of the internetwork topology, manually builds and updates the routing table, programming all routes in the routing table. Static routers can work well for small internetworks but do not scale well to large or dynamically changing internetworks due to their manual administration.

Static routers are not fault tolerant. The lifetime of a manually configured static route is infinite and, therefore, static routers do not sense and recover from downed routers or downed links.

A good example of a static router is a multihomed computer running Windows 2000 (a computer with multiple network interface cards). Creating a static IP router with Windows 2000 is as simple as installing multiple network interface cards, configuring TCP/IP, and enabling IP routing.

Dynamic Routing

A router with dynamically configured routing tables is known as a dynamic router. Dynamic routing consists of routing tables that are built and maintained automatically through an ongoing communication between routers. This communication is facilitated by a routing protocol, a series of periodic or on-demand messages containing routing information that is exchanged between routers. Except for their initial configuration, dynamic routers require little ongoing maintenance, and therefore can scale to larger internetworks.

Dynamic routing is fault tolerant. Dynamic routes learned from other routers have a finite lifetime. If a router or link goes down, the routers sense the change in the internetwork topology through the expiration of the lifetime of the learned route in the routing table. This change can then be propagated to other routers so that all the routers on the internetwork become aware of the new internetwork topology.

The ability to scale and recover from internetwork faults makes dynamic routing the better choice for medium, large, and very large internetworks.

A good example of a dynamic router is a computer with Windows 2000 Server and the Routing and Remote Access Service running the Routing Information Protocol (RIP) and Open Shortest Path First (OSPF) routing protocols for IP and RIP for IPX.

Routing Problems

Routing problems can occur when either the host's or router's routing tables contain information that does not reflect the correct topology of the internetwork.

Routing Loops

During the router routing process, the packets are forwarded in the optimal direction according to the information in the local routing table. If the routing table entries on all the routers are correct, the packet takes the optimal path from the source to the destination. However, if any routing table entries are not correct, either through a misconfiguration or through learned routes that do not accurately reflect the topology of the internetwork, then routing loops can form. A routing loop is a path through the internetwork for a network ID that loops back onto itself.

Figure 1.6 illustrates a routing loop in which:

- According to the routing table on Router 1, the optimal route to Network 10 is through Router 2.

- According to the routing table on Router 2, the optimal route to Network 10 is through Router 3.

- According to the routing table on Router 3, the optimal route to Network 10 is through Router 1.

The hop count in the network layer header is used to prevent the packet from perpetually looping. Each time a router passes the packet from one network to another, it either increases or decreases the hop count. If the hop count reaches its maximum value (when increasing) or is 0 (when decreasing), the packet is discarded by the router.

For example, IPX hosts send IPX packets with a 0 hop count. Each RIP for IPX router increases the hop count by one. When it reaches 17, the packet is silently discarded. When IP hosts send IP packets, they set a maximum link count in the Time-to-Live (TTL) field in the IP header. Each IP router encountered decreases the TTL by one. When the TTL is 0, the IP router discards the packet and sends an ICMP Time Exceeded message back to the sending host. By default, Windows NT version 4.0 and later TCP/IP hosts set the TTL to the value of 128.

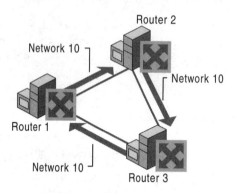

Figure 1.6   A Routing Loop

Black Holes

Common internetworking protocols such as IP and IPX are connectionless, datagram-based protocols. They do not guarantee a successful delivery. IP and IPX attempt a best effort, unacknowledged delivery to the next hop or the final destination. This behavior can lead to conditions on the internetwork in which data is lost.

If a downstream router goes down and is not detected by the upstream router, the upstream router still forwards the packets to the downed router. Because the failed downstream router does not receive them, the packets forwarded by the upstream router are dropped from the internetwork. The upstream router is sending packets to a black hole, a condition of an internetwork where packets are lost without an indication of the error. In Figure 1.7, Router 1 has not been informed that Router 2 has failed and continues to forward packets to Router 2. The failed Router 2 creates a black hole.

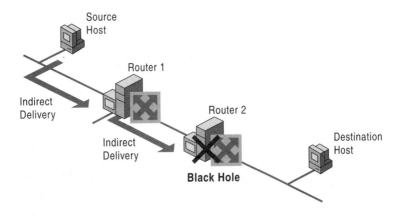

Figure 1.7   Routing Black Hole

Black holes can form when a link or router fails, and the failure is not yet detected. In a static routing environment, black holes persist until the link or router is brought back up or the static routers are reconfigured by the network administrator. In a dynamic routing environment, routers sense downed links or routers through the expiration of the lifetime of learned routes in their routing tables.

Black holes can also form when an active router discards packets without indicating the reason why the packets are being discarded. A good example is a Path Maximum Transmit Unit (PMTU) black hole router that discards IP packets that must be fragmented without sending a message to the sender indicating the error. PMTU black hole routers can be difficult to detect because packets of smaller sizes are forwarded. For more information about this specific issue, see the "TCP/IP Troubleshooting" chapter in the *TCP/IP Core Networking Guide*.

Routers and Broadcast Traffic

Internetwork-level broadcasts are Media Access Control (MAC)-level broadcast frames with a special destination internetwork address that informs the router that the packet is to be forwarded to all other networks except the network on which it was received. Routers must be configured to pass internetwork-level broadcast traffic. A MAC-level broadcast frame is used to reach all the hosts on a network. Routers, unlike bridges, do not forward MAC-level broadcast traffic. However, to reach all the hosts on an internetwork, some routable protocols support the use of internetwork-level broadcasts.

The inherent danger of forwarding internetwork-level broadcasts is the possibility of an internetwork-level broadcast storm in which a host malfunctions and continuously sends out the same internetwork-level broadcast packet. If the routers forward this traffic, the result is that all the hosts on the internetwork process each broadcast frame, possibly crippling the entire internetwork.

The NetBIOS over IPX broadcast is an internetwork-level broadcast. NetBIOS applications on an IPX internetwork use a NetBIOS over IPX broadcast to perform name registration, resolution, and release. When the NetBIOS over IPX broadcast packet is received by an IPX router, the router records the network on which the packet was received in the NetBIOS over IPX header. Thus, the internetwork path is recorded in the NetBIOS over IPX header as it traverses the IPX internetwork.

Before being forwarded, the IPX router checks the internetwork path information to prevent the forwarding of the NetBIOS over IPX broadcast onto a network on which it has already traveled. This prevents the broadcast from looping and causing more broadcast traffic. As an additional safeguard, NetBIOS over IPX broadcast packets can only propagate across eight networks using seven routers. At the eighth router, the packet is discarded without notifying the sending host. This is known as a silent discard. For more information about NetBIOS over IPX broadcasts, see "IPX Routing" in this book.

Note An IPX internetwork path is recorded in a similar fashion to the MAC-sublayer routing information in a Token Ring source routing Explorer frame. However, unlike Token Ring source routing, the IPX internetwork path is not used in the subsequent communication. The IPX internetwork path is only used to prevent the broadcast packet from being forwarded on the same IPX network more than once.

Tunneling

Tunneling, also known as encapsulation, is a method of using an internetwork infrastructure of one protocol to transfer a payload. Typically, the payload is the frames (or packets) of another protocol (see Figure 1.8). Instead of being sent as it is produced by the originating host, the frame is encapsulated with an additional header. The additional header provides routing information so the encapsulated payload can traverse an intermediate internetwork (also known as a transit internetwork). The encapsulated packets are then routed between tunnel endpoints over the transit internetwork. Once the encapsulated payload packets reach their destination on the transit internetwork, the frame is de-encapsulated and forwarded to its final destination.

The entire process of encapsulation, transmission, and de-encapsulation of packets is known as tunneling. The logical path through which the encapsulated packets travel through the transit internetwork is called a tunnel.

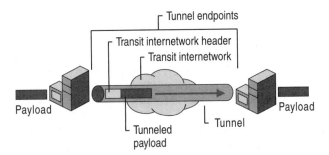

Figure 1.8   Tunneling

The transit internetwork can be any internetwork. The Internet is a good example as the most widely known public internetwork. There are also many examples of tunnels that are carried over corporate internetworks.

Some common types of tunneling:

SNA Tunneling over IP Internetworks To send System Network Architecture (SNA) traffic across a corporate IP internetwork, the SNA frame is encapsulated with a User Datagram Protocol (UDP) and IP header. This is known as Data Link Switching (DLSw) and is described in RFC 1795.

IPX Tunneling for Novell NetWare IPX packets are sent to a NetWare server or IPX router that wraps the IPX packet with a UDP and IP header and sends them across an IP internetwork. The destination IP router removes the UDP and IP header and forwards them to the appropriate IPX destination.

Point-to-Point Tunneling Protocol Point-to-Point Tunneling Protocol (PPTP) allows IP, IPX, or NetBEUI traffic to be encrypted and encapsulated in an IP header to be sent across a corporate IP internetwork or public internetworks like the Internet. For more information, see "Virtual Private Networking" in this book.

Layer 2 Tunneling Protocol Layer Two Tunneling Protocol (L2TP) allows IP, IPX, or NetBEUI traffic to be encrypted and then sent over any medium that supports point-to-point datagram delivery such as IP, X.25, Frame Relay, or ATM. For more information, see "Virtual Private Networking" in this book.

IP Security (IPSec) Tunnel Mode IPSec Tunnel Mode allows IP payloads to be encrypted and then encapsulated in an IP header to be sent across a corporate IP internetwork or public internetworks like the Internet. For more information about IPSec, see "Internet Protocol Security" in the *TCP/IP Core Networking Guide*.

Note Windows 2000 Server only ships with support for PPTP, L2TP, and IPSec tunneling.

Foundations of Routing Protocols

Dynamic routers use routing protocols to facilitate the ongoing communication and dynamic updating of routing tables. Routing protocols are used between routers and represent additional network traffic overhead on the network. This additional traffic can become an important factor in planning WAN link usage. RIP and OSPF for IP, and RIP and NLSP for IPX are all routing protocols. In some cases, such as RIP for IP (version 1) and RIP for IPX, the routing information is exchanged using MAC-level broadcasts.

An important element of a routing protocol implementation is its ability to sense and recover from internetwork faults. How quickly it can recover is determined by the type of fault, how it is sensed, and how the routing information is propagated through the internetwork.

When all the routers on the internetwork have the correct routing information in their routing tables, the internetwork has converged. When convergence is achieved, the internetwork is in a stable state and all routing occurs along optimal paths.

When a link or router fails, the internetwork must reconfigure itself to reflect the new topology. Information in routing tables must be updated. Until the internetwork reconverges, it is in an unstable state in which routing loops and black holes can occur. The time it takes for the internetwork to reconverge is known as the convergence time. The convergence time varies based on the routing protocol and the type of failure (downed link or downed router).

Routing protocols are based either on a distance vector or link state technology. The main differences between distance vector and link state routing protocols include the following:

- What routing information is exchanged.
- How the information is exchanged.
- How quickly the internetwork can recover from a downed link or a downed router.

Distance Vector

Routers use distance vector–based routing protocols to periodically advertise the routes in their routing tables. Routing information exchanged between typical distance vector–based routers is unsynchronized and unacknowledged. Table 1.1 lists some distance vector–based routing protocols.

Table 1.1   Distance Vector–Based Routing Protocols

Routable Protocol	Distance Vector–Based Routing Protocols
IP	Routing Information Protocol (RIP) Interior Gateway Routing Protocol (IGRP)
IPX	Routing Information Protocol (RIP)
AppleTalk	Routing Table Maintenance Protocol (RTMP)

Advantages of Distance Vector–Based Routing Protocols

- Simpler.

   Distance vector–based routing protocols are simple router advertisement processes that are easy to understand.

- Easy to configure.

   In its simplest incarnation, configuring a distance vector–based routing protocol is as easy as enabling it on the router interfaces.

Disadvantages of Distance Vector–Based Routing Protocols

- Large routing tables.

   Multiple routes to a given network ID can be reflected as multiple entries in the routing table. In a large internetwork with multiple paths, the routing table can have hundreds or thousands of entries.

- High network traffic overhead.

   Route advertising is done periodically even after the internetwork has converged.

- Does not scale.

   Between the size of the routing table and the high overhead, distance vector–based routing protocols do not scale well to large and very large internetworks.

- High convergence time.

   Due to the unsynchronized and unacknowledged way that distance vector information is exchanged, convergence of the internetwork can take several minutes. While converging, routing loops and black holes can occur.

Link State

Routers using link state–based routing protocols exchange link state advertisements throughout the internetwork to update routing tables. Link state router advertisements consist of a router's attached network IDs and are advertised upon startup and when changes in the internetwork topology are sensed. Link state updates are sent using directed or multicast traffic rather than broadcasting. Link state routers build a database of link state advertisements and use the database to calculate the routing table. Routing information exchanged between link state–based routers is synchronized and acknowledged. Table 1.2 lists some link state routing protocols.

Table 1.2   Link State–Based Routing Protocols

Routable Protocol	Link State–Based Routing Protocol
IP	Open Shortest Path First (OSPF)
IPX	NetWare Link Services Protocol (NLSP)

Advantages of Link State–Based Routing Protocols

- Smaller routing tables.

    Only a single optimal route for each network ID is stored in the routing table.

- Low network overhead.

    Link state–based routers do not exchange any routing information when the internetwork has converged.

- Ability to scale.

    Between the smaller routing tables and low overhead, link state–based routing protocols scale well to large and very large internetworks.

- Lower convergence time.

    Link state–based routing protocols have a much lower convergence time and the internetwork is converged without routing loops.

Disadvantages of Link State–Based Routing Protocols

- Complex.

    Link state–based routing protocols are much more complex and difficult to understand than distance vector–based routing protocols.

- More difficult to configure.

    A link state–based routing protocol implementation requires additional planning and configuration.

- Resource intensive.

    For very large internetworks, the database of link state advertisements and the calculation of routing table entries can be memory and processor intensive.

Routing Infrastructure

The routing infrastructure is the entire structure of the routed internetwork. The infrastructure has important attributes to consider when you are deciding on which routable protocols and routing protocols to use.

Single Path vs. Multipath

In a single-path routing infrastructure, only a single path exists between any two networks in the internetwork. While this may simplify the routing tables and the packet flow paths, single-path internetworks are not fault tolerant. A fault can be sensed with a dynamic router, but the networks across the failure are unreachable for the duration of the fault. A downed link or a downed router must be brought back up before packets can be delivered successfully across the downed link or router.

In a multipath routing infrastructure, multiple paths exist between networks in the internetwork. Multipath internetworks are fault tolerant when dynamic routing is used, and some routing protocols, such as OSPF, can balance the load of network traffic across multiple paths with the same metric value. Multipath internetworks, however, can be more complex to configure and can have a higher probability of routing loops during convergence when using distance vector–based routing protocols.

Flat vs. Hierarchical

In a flat routing infrastructure, each network ID is represented individually in the routing table. The network IDs have no network/subnet structure and cannot be summarized. RIP-based IPX internetworks use flat network addressing and have a flat routing infrastructure.

In a hierarchical routing infrastructure, groups of network IDs can be represented as a single routing table entry through route summarization. The network IDs in a hierarchical internetwork have a network/subnet/sub-subnet structure. A routing table entry for the highest level (the network) is also the route used for the subnets and sub-subnets of the network. Hierarchical routing infrastructures simplify routing tables and lower the amount of routing information that is exchanged, but they require more planning. IP implements hierarchical network addressing, and IP internetworks can have a hierarchical routing structure.

In hierarchical routing infrastructures, the internetwork can be divided into routing domains (also known as regions or areas). A routing domain is a collection of contiguous networks connected by routers that share the routing information for the routes within the domain. Routing domains are connected by a common routing domain called the backbone. Intra-domain routing is performed by the routers within the domain. Inter-domain routing is performed by domain routers connected to the backbone.

Autonomous Systems

In very large internetworks, it is necessary to divide the internetwork into separate entities known as autonomous systems, as shown in Figure 1.9. An autonomous system (AS) is a portion of the internetwork under the same administrative authority. The administrative authority can be an institution or corporation but can also be defined by the use of a routing protocol such as OSPF. The contiguous portion of an IP internetwork that is using OSPF to distribute routing information is under OSPF administrative authority and is, therefore, an OSPF AS. The AS may be further divided into regions, domains, or areas that define a hierarchy within the AS.

The protocols used to distribute routing information within an AS are known as Interior Gateway Protocols (IGPs). The protocols used to distribute routing information between ASs are known as Exterior Gateway Protocols (EGPs).

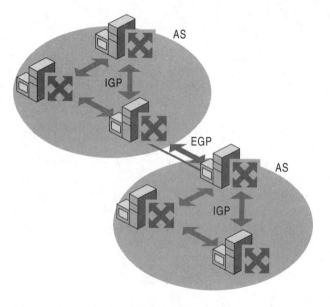

Figure 1.9   Autonomous Systems with IGPs and EGPs

Interior Gateway Protocols

Interior Gateway Protocols (IGPs) are intra-AS routing protocols. IGPs distribute routes within the AS in either a flat or hierarchical manner.

The following are IGPs for IP internetworks:

RIP for IP. An RFC-based distance vector IGP.

OSPF. An RFC-based link state IGP.

Interior Gateway Routing Protocol (IGRP). A distance vector IGP developed by Cisco Systems, Inc.

Exterior Gateway Protocols

Exterior Gateway Protocols (EGPs) are inter-AS routing protocols. EGPs define the way that all of the networks within the AS are advertised outside of the AS. This can include a list of network routes in a flat routing infrastructure or a list of summarized network routes in a hierarchical routing infrastructure. EGPs are independent of the IGPs used within the AS. EGPs can facilitate the exchange of routes between ASs that use different IGPs.

The following are EGPs for IP internetworks:

Exterior Gateway Protocol (EGP). An RFC-based EGP that was developed for use between ASs on the Internet. EGP is no longer used on the Internet due to its lack of support for complex, multipath environments and Classless Inter-Domain Routing (CIDR).

Border Gateway Protocol (BGP). An RFC-based EGP that is currently used between ASs on the Internet. BGP overcomes the weaknesses of EGP.

Additional Resources

- For more information about routing, see *Routing in the Internet* by Christian Huitema, Englewood Cliffs, NJ: 1995, Prentice Hall.
- For more information about routing, see *Interconnections: Bridges and Routers* by Radia Perlman, Reading, MA: 1992, Addison-Wesley.

CHAPTER 2

Routing and Remote Access Service

Microsoft® Windows® 2000 includes the Routing and Remote Access service, a component originally supplied for Microsoft® Windows NT® version 4.0, which provides integrated multiprotocol routing and remote access, and virtual private network server services for Microsoft® Windows® 2000 Server–based computers.

In This Chapter

Related Information in the Resource Kit

- For more information about unicast IP routing support, see "Unicast IP Routing" in this book.

- For more information about IP multicast support, see "IP Multicast Support" in this book.

- For more information about IPX routing support, see "IPX Routing" in this book.

- For more information about demand-dial support, see "Demand-Dial Routing" in this book.

- For more information about remote access, see "Remote Access Server" in this book.

- For more information about virtual private networking support, see "Virtual Private Networking" in this book.

Introduction to the Routing and Remote Access Service

Multiprotocol routing support for the Windows NT family of operating systems began with Microsoft® Windows NT® 3.51 Service Pack 2, which included components for the Routing Information Protocol (RIP) for IP, RIP for IPX, and the Service Advertising (SAP) for IPX. Windows NT 4.0 also included these components. In June 1996, Microsoft released the Routing and Remote Access Service (RRAS) for Windows NT 4.0, a component that replaced the Windows NT 4.0 Remote Access Service, RIP for IP, RIP for IPX, and SAP for IPX services with a single integrated service providing both remote access and multiprotocol routing.

RRAS for Windows NT 4.0 added support for:

- RIP version 2 routing protocol for IP.
- Open Shortest Path First (OSPF) routing protocol for IP.
- Demand-dial routing, the routing over on-demand or persistent WAN links such as analog phone, ISDN, or using the Point-to-Point Tunneling Protocol (PPTP).
- ICMP Router Discovery.
- Remote Authentication Dial-In User Service (RADIUS) client.
- IP and IPX packet filtering.
- Point-to-Point Tunneling Protocol (PPTP) support for router-to-router VPN connections.
- A graphical user interface administrative program called Routing and RAS Admin and a command-line utility called Routemon.

Windows 2000 Routing and Remote Access Service

The Routing and Remote Access service for Windows 2000 Server continues the evolution of multiprotocol routing and remote access services for the Microsoft Windows platform. New features of the Routing and Remote Access service for Windows 2000 include:

- Internet Group Management Protocol (IGMP) and support for multicast boundaries.
- Network address translation with addressing and name resolution components that simplify the connection of a small office/home office (SOHO) network to the Internet.
- Integrated AppleTalk routing.

- Layer Two Tunneling Protocol (L2TP) over IP Security (IPSec) support for router-to-router VPN connections.
- Improved administration and management tools. The graphical user interface program is the Routing and Remote Access administrative utility, a Microsoft Management Console (MMC) snap-in. The command-line utility is Netsh.

All of the combined features of the Windows 2000 Routing and Remote Access service make a Windows 2000 Server–based computer function as the following:

- Multiprotocol router

  A Routing and Remote Access service computer can route IP, IPX, and AppleTalk simultaneously. All routable protocols and routing protocols are configured from the same administrative utility.

- Demand-dial router

  A Routing and Remote Access service computer can route IP and IPX over on-demand or persistent WAN links, such as analog phone lines or ISDN, or over VPN connections using either PPTP or L2TP over IPSec.

- Remote access server

  A Routing and Remote Access service computer can act as a remote access server providing remote access connectivity to dial-up or VPN remote access clients using IP, IPX, AppleTalk, or NetBEUI.

The combination of routing and remote access services on the same computer create a Windows 2000 remote access router.

An advantage of the Routing and Remote Access service is its integration with the Windows 2000 Server operating system. The Routing and Remote Access service works with a wide variety of hardware platforms and hundreds of network adapters; the result is a lower cost solution than many mid-range dedicated router or remote access server products.

The Routing and Remote Access service is extensible with application programming interfaces (APIs) that third-party developers can use to create custom networking solutions and that new vendors can use to participate in the growing business of open internetworking.

Combining Routing and Remote Access

One question that is commonly asked about the Routing and Remote Access service is: Why combine both routing and remote access into a single service? Both services worked fine separately in the original version of Windows NT 4.0.

The reason for combining the two services lies in the Point-to-Point Protocol *(PPP)*, which is the protocol suite that is commonly used to negotiate point-to-point connections for remote access clients. PPP provides link parameter negotiation, the exchange of authentication credentials, and network layer protocol negotiation. For example, when you dial an Internet service provider (ISP) using PPP, you agree to the size of the packets you are sending and how they are framed (link negotiation), you log on using a user name and password (authentication), and you obtain an IP address (network layer negotiation).

Demand-dial routing connections also use PPP to provide the same kinds of services as remote access connections (link negotiation, authentication, and network layer negotiation). Therefore, the integration of routing (which includes demand-dial routing) and remote access was done to leverage the existing PPP client/server infrastructure that existed for the remote access components.

The PPP infrastructure of Windows 2000 Server includes support for:

- Dial-up remote access (remote access over dial-up equipment such as analog phone lines and ISDN) as either the client or server.

- VPN remote access (remote access over VPN connections using either PPTP or L2TP over IPSec) as either the client or server.

- On-demand or persistent dial-up demand-dial routing (demand-dial routing over dial-up equipment such as analog phone lines and ISDN) as either the calling router or the answering router.

- On-demand or persistent VPN demand-dial routing (demand-dial routing over VPN connections using either PPTP or L2TP over IPSec) as either the calling router or the answering router.

Authentication and Authorization

The distinction between authentication and authorization is important for understanding how connection attempts are either accepted or denied.

- *Authentication* is the verification of the credentials of the connection attempt. This process consists of sending the credentials from the remote access client to the remote access server in either a cleartext or encrypted form using an authentication protocol.

- *Authorization* is the verification that the connection attempt is allowed. Authorization occurs after successful authentication.

For a connection attempt to be accepted, the connection attempt must be both authenticated and authorized. It is possible for the connection attempt to be authenticated using valid credentials, but not authorized. In this case, the connection attempt is denied.

If the remote access server is configured for Windows authentication, Windows 2000 security verifies the credentials for authentication and the dial-up properties of the user account, and locally stored remote access policies authorize the connection. If the connection attempt is both authenticated and authorized, the connection attempt is accepted.

If the remote access server is configured for RADIUS authentication, the credentials of the connection attempt are passed to the RADIUS server for authentication and authorization. If the connection attempt is both authenticated and authorized, the RADIUS server sends an accept message back to the remote access server and the connection attempt is accepted. If the connection attempt is either not authenticated or not authorized, the RADIUS server sends a reject message back to the remote access server and the connection process is denied.

If the RADIUS server is a Windows 2000 server–based computer running the Internet Authentication Service (IAS), the IAS server performs authentication through Windows 2000 security and authorization through the dial-up properties of the user account and the remote access policies stored on the IAS server.

The configuration of the Routing and Remote Access service authentication provider is done from the **Security** tab from the properties of a remote access router in the Routing and Remote Access snap-in or by using the **netsh ras aaaa set authentication** and **netsh ras aaaa set authserver** commands.

Accounting

The Routing and Remote Access service can be configured to log accounting information in the following locations:

- Locally stored log files when configured for Windows accounting. The information logged and where it is stored are configured from the properties of the Remote Access Logging folder in the Routing and Remote Access snap-in.

- At a RADIUS server when configured for RADIUS accounting. If the RADIUS server is an IAS server, the log files are stored on the IAS server. The information logged and where it is stored are configured from the properties of the Remote Access Logging folder in the Internet Authentication Service snap-in.

The configuration of the Routing and Remote Access service accounting provider is done from the **Security** tab from the properties of a remote access router in the Routing and Remote Access snap-in or by using the **netsh ras aaaa set accounting** and **netsh ras aaaa set acctserver** commands.

Installation and Configuration

Unlike with RRAS for Windows NT 4.0 and most network services of Windows 2000, you cannot elect to install or uninstall the Routing and Remote Access service through **Add/Remove Programs** in Control Panel. The Windows 2000 Routing and Remote Access service is automatically installed in a disabled state.

▶ **To enable and configure the Routing and Remote Access service**

1. Run **Routing and Remote Access** from the Administrative Tools folder.

2. For the local computer, right-click the server icon and select **Configure and Enable Routing and Remote Access**.

    For a remote computer, right-click the **Server Status** icon and click **Add Server**. In the **Add Server** dialog boxes, select the server you want to add.

3. To configure your remote access router, in the Routing and Remote Access Server Setup Wizard, select the appropriate options.

Once the wizard has finished, the remote access router is enabled and configured based on your selections in the wizard. To do further configuration, use the Routing and Remote Access snap-in.

Refreshing the Configuration

You cannot remove the Routing and Remote Access service using **Add/Remove Programs** in **Control Panel**; however, you can refresh the configuration by disabling the Routing and Remote Access service and then reconfiguring it. Disabling the service removes all Routing and Remote Access registry settings.

▶ **To refresh the configuration of the Routing and Remote Access service**

1. Run **Routing and Remote Access** from the Administrative Tools folder.

2. For the appropriate computer, right-click the server icon and select **Disable Routing and Remote Access**.

3. When prompted with the warning dialog box, select **Yes**.

4. To configure the Routing and Remote Access service configuration, use the enable and configure procedure.

Note If you disable the Routing and Remote Access service, all current configuration for the service, including routing protocol configuration and demand-dial interfaces, is removed and all currently connected clients are disconnected.

Features of the Routing and Remote Access Service

The Routing and Remote Access service for Windows 2000 includes a wide variety of features for unicast and multicast IP routing, IPX routing, AppleTalk routing, remote access, and VPN support.

Unicast IP Support

Unicast IP support consists of the following:

- Static IP routing

  With this inherent function of the TCP/IP protocol for Windows 2000, you can manage static routes using the Routing and Remote Access snap-in rather than the Route tool.

- Routing Information Protocol (RIP) versions 1 and 2

  A distance vector-based routing protocol commonly used in small and medium IP internetworks.

- Open Shortest Path First (OSPF)

  A link state-based routing protocol commonly used in medium to large IP internetworks.

- DHCP Relay Agent

  An agent that relays Dynamic Host Configuration Protocol (DHCP) messages between DHCP clients and DHCP servers on different network segments.

- Network address translation

  A network address translator component that creates a translated connection between privately addressed networks and the Internet.

- IP packet filtering

  The ability to define what traffic is allowed into and out of each interface based on filters defined by the values of source and destination IP addresses, TCP and UDP port numbers, ICMP types and codes, and IP protocol numbers.

- ICMP router discovery

  The ability to periodically advertise and respond to host router solicitations to support ICMP router discovery by hosts on a network segment.

For more information, see "Unicast IP Support" in this book.

IP Multicast Support

IP multicast support consists of the following:

- Multicast forwarding

  With this inherent function of the TCP/IP protocol for Windows 2000, you can view the multicast forwarding table using the Routing and Remote Access snap-in.

- Internet Group Management Protocol (IGMP) versions 1 and 2

  The TCP/IP protocol to track multicast group membership on attached network segments.

- Ability to support limited multicast forwarding and routing

  When you use the IGMP routing protocol and configure interfaces for IGMP router mode and IGMP proxy mode, the Windows 2000 router can support multicast forwarding and routing for specific configurations.

- Multicast boundaries

  Multicast boundaries (barriers to the forwarding of IP multicast traffic) can be based on the IP multicast group address, the Time-To-Live (TTL) in the IP header, or on the maximum amount of multicast traffic in kilobytes per second.

For more information, see "IP Multicast Support" in this book.

IPX Support

IPX support consists of the following:

- IPX packet filtering

  The ability to define what traffic is allowed into and out of each interface based on filters defined by the values of source and destination IPX network, node, socket numbers, and packet type.

- RIP for IPX

  A distance-vector-based routing protocol commonly used on IPX internetworks. The Routing and Remote Access service also provides the ability to configure static IPX routes and RIP route filters.

- SAP for IPX

  Service Advertising Protocol (SAP) is a distance-vector-based advertising protocol commonly used on IPX internetworks to advertise services and their locations. The Routing and Remote Access service also provides the ability to configure static SAP services and SAP service filters.

- NetBIOS over IPX

  NetBIOS over IPX is used by Microsoft networking components to support file and printer sharing components. The Routing and Remote Access service can also forward NetBIOS over IPX broadcasts and configure static NetBIOS names.

For more information, see "IPX Routing" in this book.

AppleTalk

AppleTalk consists of supporting the forwarding of AppleTalk packets as an AppleTalk router and the use of the Routing Table Maintenance Protocol (RTMP). For more information about AppleTalk routing, see "Services for Macintosh" in this book.

Demand-Dial Routing

IP and IPX traffic can be forwarded over demand-dial interfaces over persistent or over on-demand WAN links. For on-demand connections, the Routing and Remote Access service automatically creates a PPP-based connection to the configured endpoint when traffic matching a static route is received.

For more information, see "Demand-Dial Routing" in this book.

Remote Access

The Routing and Remote Access service enables a computer to be a remote access server, accepting remote access connections from remote access clients using traditional dial-up technologies such as analog phone lines and ISDN.

For more information, see "Remote Access Server" in this book.

VPN Server

The Routing and Remote Access service enables a computer to be a virtual private network (VPN) server, supporting both PPTP and L2TP over IPSec and accepting both remote access and router-to-router (demand-dial) VPN connections from remote access clients and calling routers.

For more information, see "Virtual Private Networking" in this book.

RADIUS Client

The Routing and Remote Access service can be configured as a Remote Authentication Dial-In User Service (RADIUS) client for authentication, authorization, and accounting. Parameters of all PPP-based connection attempts are sent to the configured RADIUS server for authentication and authorization. Information about connections is sent to the configured RADIUS server for accounting.

Windows 2000 also includes the Internet Authentication Service (IAS), an implementation of a RADIUS server. For more information, see "Internet Authentication Service" in this book.

SNMP MIB Support

Windows 2000 and the Routing and Remote Access service provide Simple Network Management Protocol (SNMP) version 1 agent functionality with support for Internet MIB II as documented in RFC 1213. SNMP management stations can be used to manage a Windows 2000 remote access router. Beyond Internet MIB II support, the Routing and Remote Access service also provides MIB dynamic-link libraries (DLLs) for the following:

- IP Forwarding Table MIB

  Objects in the IP Forwarding Table MIB are documented in RFC 1354, "IP Forwarding Table MIB."
- Microsoft RIP version 2 for Internet Protocol MIB
- Wellfleet-Series7-MIB for OSPF
- Microsoft BOOTP for Internet Protocol MIB
- Microsoft IPX MIB
- Microsoft RIP and SAP for IPX MIB

- Internet Group Management Protocol MIB

  Objects in the Internet Group Management Protocol MIB are documented in the Internet draft titled "Internet Group Management Protocol MIB."

- IP Multicast Routing MIB

  Objects in the IP Multicast Routing MIB are documented in the Internet draft titled "IP Multicast Routing MIB."

Extensive LAN and WAN Support

The Routing and Remote Access service can run over any of the network adapters supported by Windows 2000 Server, including WAN cards from Eicon, Cisco, SysKonnect, Allied and US Robotics. For more information about supported network adapters, see the Windows 2000 Hardware Compatibility link at http://windows.microsoft.com/windows2000/reskit/webresources.

Graphical and Command-Line Management Utilities

The Routing and Remote Access service includes the Routing and Remote Access snap-in, a Windows 2000 administrative utility that provides easy viewing and configuration of local or remote Windows 2000 remote access routers, and Netsh.exe, a command-line utility that can also run scripts for local automated configuration. For more information, see "Routing and Remote Access Service Tools and Facilities" later in this chapter.

API Support for Third-Party Components

The Routing and Remote Access service has fully published API sets for unicast and multicast routing protocol and administration utility support. Routing protocol developers can write additional routing protocols and interface directly into the Routing and Remote Access service architecture. Other software vendors can also use Routing and Remote Access service administration APIs to provide their own management utilities.

Architecture of the Routing and Remote Access Service

The architecture of the Routing and Remote Access service is shown in Figure 2.1.

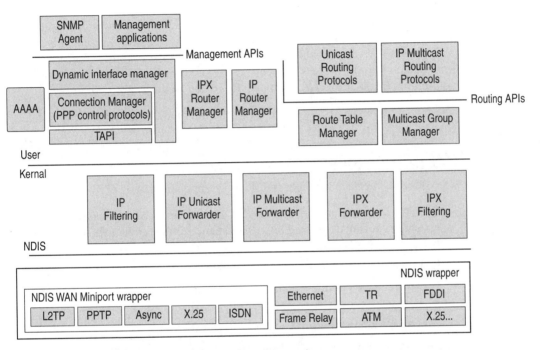

Figure 2.1   Architecture of the Routing and Remote Access Service

---

Note   The Network Address Translation (NAT) component of the Routing and Remote Access service is not shown in Figure 2.1. NAT is not a routing protocol. For more information about how the NAT component interacts with Routing and Remote Access components and the TCP/IP protocol, see "Unicast IP Routing" in this book.

SNMP Agent

The Windows 2000 Routing and Remote Access service supports the Simple Network Management Protocol (SNMP) management information bases (MIBs) previously described in the "Features of the Routing and Remote Access Service" section earlier in this chapter.

Management Applications

Management applications for the Routing and Remote Access service include the Routing and Remote Access snap-in, available from the Administrative Tools folder and the Netsh command-line utility.

AAAA

A set of components that provides authentication, authorization, auditing, and accounting (AAAA) for the Routing and Remote Access service when it is configured for Windows authentication and Windows accounting. When the Routing and Remote Access service is configured for RADIUS authentication and accounting, the local AAAA components are not used.

The AAAA components are also used by the Internet Authentication Service (IAS).

DIM (Mprdim.dll)

The dynamic interface manager (DIM) is a component that:

- Supports a remote procedure call (RPC) interface for SNMP-based management functions used by management utilities such as the Routing and Remote Access snap-in.
- Loads configuration information from the Windows 2000 registry.
- Communicates with the Connection Manager for demand-dial connections.
- Communicates configuration information to the router managers (such as the IP Router Manager and IPX Router Manager).
- Manages all routing interfaces including LAN, persistent demand-dial, and IP-in-IP interfaces.

Connection Manager

A set of components that:

- Manages WAN devices.
- Establishes connections using TAPI.
- Negotiates PPP control protocols, including Extensible Authentication Protocol (EAP).
- Implements Multilink and Bandwidth Allocation Protocol (BAP).

TAPI

The Telephony Application Programming Interface, also known as Telephony API (TAPI), provides services to create, monitor, and terminate connections in a hardware-independent manner. Connection Manager uses TAPI to create or receive demand-dial connections. For more information about TAPI, see "Telephony Integration and Conferencing" in this book.

IP Router Manager (Iprtmgr.dll)

A component that:

- Obtains configuration information from the DIM.

- Communicates IP packet filtering configuration to the IP filtering driver.

- Communicates IP routing configuration information to the IP forwarder in the TCP/IP protocol.

- Maintains an interface database of all IP routing interfaces.

- Loads and communicates configuration information to IP routing protocols (such as RIP for IP and OSPF supplied with Windows 2000).

- Initiates demand-dial connections on behalf of routing protocols by communicating with the DIM.

IPX Router Manager (Ipxrtmgr.dll)

A component that:

- Obtains configuration information from the DIM.

- Communicates IPX packet filtering configuration to the IPX filtering driver.

- Communicates IPX routing configuration information to the IPX forwarder driver.

- Maintains an interface database of all IPX routing interfaces.

- Loads and communicates configuration information to IPX routing protocols (RIP for IPX, SAP for IPX).

- Initiates demand-dial connections on behalf of routing protocols by communicating with the DIM.

Unicast Routing Protocols

The Routing and Remote Access service provides the following unicast routing protocols.

RIP for IP (Iprip2.dll)

A component that:

- Communicates RIP for IP learned routes with the Route Table Manager.
- Uses Windows Sockets to send and receive RIP for IP traffic.
- Exports management APIs to support MIBs and management applications through the IP Router Manager.

OSPF Routing Protocol (Ospf.dll)

A component that:

- Communicates OSPF learned routes with the Route Table Manager.
- Uses Windows Sockets to send and receive OSPF traffic.
- Exports management APIs to support MIBs and management applications through the IP Router Manager.

RIP for IPX (Ipxrip.dll)

A component that:

- Communicates RIP for IPX learned routes with the Route Table Manager.
- Uses Windows Sockets to send and receive RIP for IPX traffic.
- Exports management APIs to support MIBs and management applications through the IPX Router Manager.

SAP for IPX (Ipxsap.dll)

A component that:

- Communicates SAP for IPX learned services with the Route Table Manager.
- Uses Windows Sockets to send and receive SAP for IPX traffic.
- Exports management APIs to support MIBs and management applications through the IPX Router Manager.

IP Multicast Protocols

The Routing and Remote Access service provides the following IP multicast protocol.

IGMP Version 1 and 2

A component that:

- Communicates multicast group membership information to the Multicast Group Manager.
- Uses Windows Sockets to send and receive IGMP traffic.
- Exports management APIs to support MIBs and management applications through the Multicast Group Manager.

Route Table Manager (Rtm.dll)

A component that:

- Maintains a user mode route table for all routes for those protocols being routed (IP and IPX). The route table includes all routes from all possible route sources.
- Exposes APIs for adding, deleting, and enumerating routes that are used by the routing protocols.
- Ages learned routes.
- Communicates only the best routes to the appropriate forwarder driver. The best routes are the routes with the lowest preference level (for IP routes) and lowest metrics. The best routes become the routes in the IP forwarding table and the IPX forwarding table.

Multicast Group Manager

A component that:

- Maintains all multicast group memberships.
- Communicates multicast forwarding entries (MFEs) in the IP multicast forwarder.
- Reflects group membership between IP multicast routing protocols.

IP Filtering Driver (Ipfltdrv.sys)

A component that:

- Obtains configuration information from the IP Router Manager.
- Applies IP filters after the IP forwarder has found a route.

IP Unicast Forwarder

A component of the TCP/IP protocol (Tcpip.sys) that:

- Obtains configuration information from the IP Router Manager.
- Stores the IP forwarding table, a table of the best routes obtained from the route table manager.
- Can initiate a demand-dial connection.
- Forwards unicast IP traffic.

IP Multicast Forwarder

A component of the TCP/IP protocol (Tcpip.sys) that:

- Stores multicast forward entries (MFEs) obtained from IP multicast routing protocols through the Multicast Group Manager.
- Based on multicast traffic received, communicates new [source, group] information to the Multicast Group Manager.
- Forwards IP multicast packets.

IPX Filtering Driver (Nwlnkflt.sys)

A component that:

- Obtains configuration information from the IPX Router Manager.
- Applies IPX filters after the IPX forwarder driver has found a route.

IPX Forwarder Driver (Nwlnkfwd.sys)

A component that:

- Obtains configuration information from the IPX Router Manager.
- Stores the IPX forwarding table, a table of the best routes obtained from the route table manager.
- Can initiate a demand-dial connection.
- Forwards IPX traffic.

Unicast IP Components and Processes

The unicast IP components of the Routing and Remote Access service are shown in Figure 2.2.

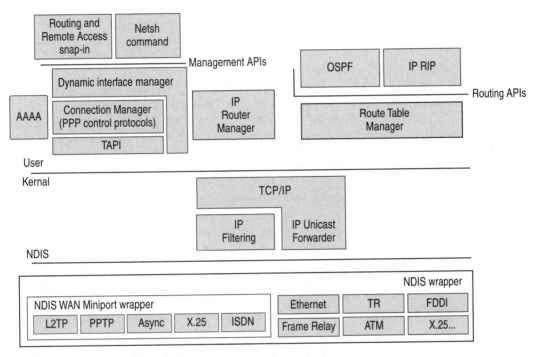

Figure 2.2   Unicast IP and the Routing and Remote Access Service

The following sections describe typical unicast IP routing processes in terms of the Routing and Remote Access service unicast IP routing components.

Incoming and Outgoing Packet (Transit Traffic)

An incoming packet is handed first to the IP forwarder, which finds a route and then hands it to the IP filtering driver to check for input filters and output filters. If approved for acceptance by the input filters and for forwarding by the output filters, the packet is handed back to the IP forwarder driver, which forwards the packet over the appropriate interface using Network Driver Interface Specification (NDIS). If the input or output filters do not permit the packet to be forwarded, the packet is silently discarded. If a route is not found, an ICMP Destination Unreachable-Host Unreachable message is sent back to the source of the packet.

Incoming Packet (Local Host Traffic)

An incoming packet is handed first to the IP forwarder, which notes that the packet is not to be routed (destination IP address is the router or a broadcast address). The IP forwarder then hands it to the IP filtering driver to check for input filters. If accepted by the input filters, the packet is handed up to the TCP/IP driver, which processes the packet. If the packet is not accepted by the input filters, the packet is silently discarded.

Outgoing Packet (Local Host Traffic)

An outgoing TCP/IP packet is handed by the TCP/IP driver to the IP filtering driver, which checks for output filters. If approved for sending by the output filters, the packet is handed to the IP forwarder, which sends the packet using the best route over the appropriate interface using NDIS. If the packet is not approved by the output filters, the packet is silently discarded. If a route is not found, an IP routing error is indicated to the source application of the packet.

Routing Protocol Network Communication

The RIP for IP and OSPF routing protocols operate like any other Windows Sockets application sending and receiving IP packets.

Routing Table Updates

RIP for IP and OSPF update routes in the Route Table Manager. Based on the best route and route source ranking, the table of best routes is updated in the IP forwarder.

IP Multicast Components and Processes

The IP multicast components of the Routing and Remote Access service are shown in Figure 2.3.

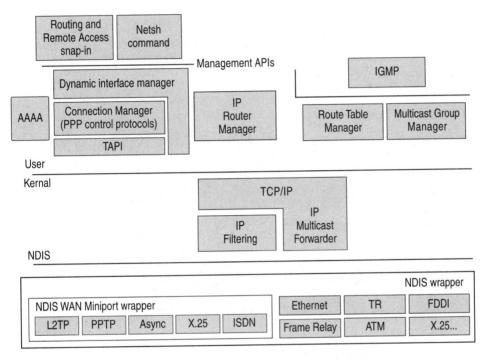

Figure 2.3   IP Multicast and the Routing and Remote Access Service

The following sections describe typical IP multicast forwarding processes in terms of the Routing and Remote Access service IP multicast components.

Incoming Multicast Packet (MFE Not Present)

An incoming IP multicast packet's source address and group address are compared to the MFEs to the IP multicast forwarding table. If an entry for the [source, group] is not found, an inactive MFE for the [source, group] is added to the multicast forwarding table and communicated to the Multicast Group Manager. The packet is placed in a buffer awaiting the change from an inactive MFE to an active MFE.

Incoming Multicast Packet (Active MFE Present)

An incoming IP multicast packet's source address and group address are compared to the MFEs in the IP multicast forwarding table. If an active entry for the [source, group] is found, the multicast traffic is forwarded out the appropriate interface(s).

Multicast Routing Protocol Network Communication

The IGMP v2 IP multicast routing protocol operates like any other Windows Sockets application sending and receiving IP packets.

Multicast Forwarding Table Updates

Based on the ongoing IGMP traffic on interfaces on which IGMP router mode is enabled, the IGMP v2 multicast routing protocol updates [source, group] entries in the Multicast Group Manager. The Multicast Group Manager then updates the IP multicast forwarding table.

IPX Components and Processes

The IPX components of the Routing and Remote Access service are shown in Figure 2.4.

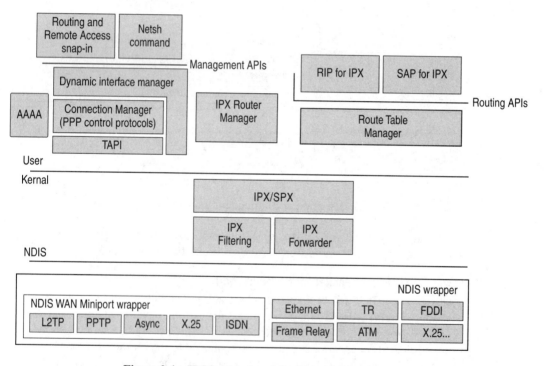

Figure 2.4   IP Multicast and the Routing and Remote Access Service

The following sections describe typical IPX routing processes in terms of the Routing and Remote Access service IPX routing components.

Incoming and Outgoing Packet (Transit Traffic)

An incoming packet is handed first to the IPX forwarder driver, which finds a route and then hands it to the IPX filtering driver to check for input filters and output filters. If approved for acceptance by the input filters and for forwarding by the output filters, the packet is handed back to the IPX forwarder driver, which forwards the packet over the appropriate interface using NDIS. If the input or output filters do not permit the packet to be forwarded or if a route is not found, the packet is silently discarded.

Incoming Packet (Local Host Traffic)

An incoming packet is handed first to the IPX forwarder driver, which notes that the packet is not to be routed (the destination IPX internetwork address is the router or a broadcast address) and then hands it to the IPX filtering driver to check for input filters. If accepted by the input filters, the packet is handed up to IPX/SPX, which processes the packet normally. If the packet is not accepted by the input filters, the packet is silently discarded.

Outgoing Packet (Local Host Traffic)

An outgoing IPX packet is handed by the IPX/SPX driver to the IPX filtering driver, which checks for output filters. If approved for sending by the output filters, the packet is handed to the IPX forwarder driver, which sends the packet using the best route over the appropriate interface using NDIS. If the packet is not approved by the output filters, the packet is silently discarded. If a route is not found, a RIP GetLocalTarget message is sent. For more information about IPX routing processes, see "IPX Routing" in this book.

Routing Protocol Network Communication

The RIP for IPX and SAP routing protocols operate like any other Windows Sockets application sending and receiving IPX packets.

Routing Table Updates

Based on information received by the routing protocol, the routing protocol updates routes in the Route Table Manager and, based on the best route, the table of best routes is updated in the IPX forwarder driver.

Registry Settings

When the Routing and Remote Access service is enabled, it creates and maintains its settings in the Windows 2000 registry. For performance reasons, most of the Routing and Remote Access service configuration information is stored in binary in large configuration blocks, not as separate registry entries that can easily be viewed and changed. All configuration of the Routing and Remote Access service should be done through the Routing and Remote Access snap-in or through the Netsh command-line utility described later in this chapter.

Routing and Remote Access service and router interface configuration information is stored in HKEY_LOCAL_MACHINE\System\CurrentControlSet\Services\RemoteAccess.

Router component configuration information is stored in HKEY_LOCAL_MACHINE\Software\Microsoft\Router.

Router phone book settings are stored in HKEY_LOCAL_MACHINE\Software\Microsoft\RouterPhonebook.

Routing and Remote Access Service Tools and Facilities

The following utilities and facilities are provided with the Routing and Remote Access service to aid in configuration and amassing information for accounting, auditing, or troubleshooting:

- Routing and Remote Access snap-in
- Netsh command-line tool
- Authentication and accounting logging
- Event logging
- Tracing

Routing and Remote Access Snap-In

The Routing and Remote Access snap-in is available from the Administrative Tools folder and is the primary management utility for configuring Windows 2000 local and remote access servers and routers.

Routing and Remote Access Floating Windows

Within the Routing and Remote Access snap-in is a series of floating windows that display table entries or statistics. Once displayed, a floating window can be moved anywhere on the display and remains on top of the Routing and Remote Access snap-in when the snap-in is the foreground application. Table 2.1 lists the floating windows in the Routing and Remote Access snap-in, and their location.

Table 2.1   Routing and Remote Access Floating Windows

Floating window	Location	Description
TCP/IP information	IP Routing/General IP Routing/General/Interface	Global TCP/IP statistics, such as the number of routes, packets received, and packets forwarded.
Multicast forwarding table	IP Routing/General	The contents of the TCP/IP multicast forwarding table.
Multicast statistics	IP Routing/General	Statistics per group, such as the number of multicast packets received.
Address translations	IP Routing/General/Interface	The contents of the Address Resolution Protocol (ARP) cache.
IP addresses	IP Routing/General/Interface	The IP addresses assigned to routing interfaces.
IP routing table	IP Routing/General/Interface IP Routing/Static Routes	The contents of the IP routing table.
TCP connections	IP Routing/General/Interface	The list of TCP connections, including local and remote addresses and TCP ports.
UDP listener ports	IP Routing/General/Interface	The list of UDP ports on which the router is listening.
Areas	IP Routing/OSPF	The list of configured OSPF areas.
Link state database	IP Routing/OSPF	The contents of the OSPF link state database.
Neighbors (OSPF)	IP Routing/OSPF	The list of neighboring OSPF routers and their state.
Virtual interfaces	IP Routing/OSPF	The list of configured virtual interfaces and their state.
Neighbors (RIP)	IP Routing/RIP	The list of neighboring RIP routers.
DHCP Allocator information	IP Routing/Network Address Translation	Statistics on the number of types of DHCP messages sent and received.
DNS Proxy information	IP Routing/Network Address Translation	Statistics on the number of types of DNS messages sent and received.
Mappings	IP Routing/Network Address Translation/Interface	Contents of the network address translation mapping table.

continued

Table 2.1 Routing and Remote Access Floating Windows *(continued)*

Floating window	Location	Description
Group table	IP Routing/IGMP	Global list of groups detected using IGMP routing protocol.
Interface group table	IP Routing/IGMP/Interface	Interface list of groups detected using IGMP routing protocol.
IPX parameters	IPX Routing/General	Global IPX statistics such as the number of routes and services, packets received, and packets forwarded.
IPX routing table	IPX Routing/General IPX Routing/Static Routes	The contents of the IPX routing table.
IPX service table	IPX Routing/General IPX Routing/Static Services	The contents of the SAP service table.
RIP parameters	IPX Routing/RIP for IPX	Global statistics on the RIP for IPX protocol.
SAP parameters	IPX Routing/SAP for IPX	Global statistics on the SAP for IPX protocol.

Netsh Command-Line Tool

Netsh is a command-line and scripting tool for Windows 2000 networking components for local or remote computers. Netsh is supplied with Windows 2000. Netsh also provides the ability to save a configuration script in a text file for archival purposes or for configuring other servers.

Netsh is a shell that can support multiple Windows 2000 components through the addition of Netsh helper DLLs. A Netsh helper DLL extends Netsh functionality by providing additional commands to monitor or configure a specific Windows 2000 networking component. Each Netsh helper DLL provides a context (a group of commands for a specific networking component). Within each context, subcontexts can exist. For example, within the **routing** context, the subcontexts **ip** and **ipx** exist to group IP routing and IPX routing commands together.

Netsh command-line options include the following:

–a *AliasFile* Specifies that an alias file be used. An alias file contains a list of Netsh commands and an aliased version so that the aliased command line can be used in place of the Netsh command. Alias files can be used to map commands to the appropriate Netsh command that might be more familiar in other platforms.

–c *Context* Specifies the context of the command corresponding to an installed helper DLL.

Command Specifies the Netsh command to carry out.

–f *ScriptFile* Specifies that all of the Netsh commands in the file ScriptFile be run.

–r *Remote Computer Name or IP Address* Specifies that Netsh commands are run on the remote computer specified by its name or IP address.

Commands can be abbreviated to the shortest unambiguous string. For example, issuing the command **ro ip sh int** is equivalent to issuing **routing ip show interface**. Netsh commands can be either global or context specific. Global commands can be issued in any context and are used for general Netsh functions. Context-specific commands vary according to the context.

Table 2.2 lists the netsh global commands.

Table 2.2   Global Netsh Commands

Command	Description
..	Moves up one context level.
? or **help**	Displays command-line Help.
add helper	Add a Netsh helper DLL.
delete helper	Removes a Netsh helper DLL.
show helper	Displays the installed Netsh helper DLLs.
online	Sets the current mode to online.
offline	Sets the current mode to offline.
set mode	Sets the current mode to online or offline.
show mode	Displays the current mode.
flush	Discards any changes in offline mode.
commit	Commits changes made in offline mode.
show machine	Displays the computer on which the Netsh commands are carried out.
exec	Executes a script file containing Netsh commands.
quit or **bye** or **exit**	Exits Netsh.

continued

Table 2.2   Global Netsh Commands *(continued)*

Command	Description
add alias	Adds an alias to an existing command.
delete alias	Deletes an alias from an existing command.
show alias	Displays all defined aliases.
dump	Writes configuration.
popd	A scripting command that pops a context from the stack.
pushd	A scripting command that pushes the current context on the stack.

Netsh has the following command modes:

- Online

  In online mode, commands issued at a Netsh command prompt are carried out immediately.

- Offline

  In offline mode, commands issued at a Netsh command prompt are accumulated and carried out as a batch by issuing the **commit** global command. Accumulated commands can be discarded by issuing the **flush** global command.

You can also run a script (a text file with a list of Netsh commands) by using either the **–f** command-line option or by issuing the **exec** global command at a Netsh command prompt.

To create a script of the current configuration, use the global **dump** command. The **dump** command generates the current running configuration in terms of Netsh commands. You can then use the script created by this command to configure a new server or to reconfigure the existing server. If you are making extensive changes to the configuration of a component, it is recommended to begin the configuration session with the **dump** command, in case you need to restore the configuration prior to changes being made.

For the Routing and Remote Access service, Netsh has the following contexts:

- **ras**

  Use commands in the **ras** context to configure remote access configuration.

- **aaaa**

  Use commands in the **aaaa** context to configure the AAAA component used by both Routing and Remote Access and Internet Authentication Service.

- **routing**

  Use commands in the **routing** context to configure IP and IPX routing.

- **interface**

  Use commands in the **interface** context to configure demand-dial interfaces.

For more information about context-specific commands, see Windows 2000 Server Help and the help provided by the Netsh tool.

Authentication and Accounting Logging

The Routing and Remote Access service supports the logging of authentication and accounting information for PPP-based connection attempts when Windows authentication or accounting is enabled. This logging is separate from the events recorded in the system event log. You can use the information that is logged to track remote access usage and authentication attempts. Authentication and accounting logging is especially useful for troubleshooting remote access policy issues. For each authentication attempt, the name of the remote access policy that either accepted or rejected the connection attempt is recorded.

The authentication and accounting information is stored in a configurable log file or files stored in the *%SystemRoot%*\System32\LogFiles folder. The log files are saved in Internet Authentication Service (IAS) 1.0 or database format, meaning that any database program can read the log file directly for analysis.

You can configure the type of activity to log (accounting or authentication activity) and log file settings from the properties of the Remote Access Logging folder in the Routing and Remote Access snap-in.

If the remote access router is configured for RADIUS authentication or accounting and the RADIUS server is a computer running Windows 2000 and the Internet Authentication Service (IAS), the same information is recorded on the IAS server computer.

Event Logging

The Windows 2000 Router performs extensive error logging in the system event log. You can use information in the event logs to troubleshoot routing or remote access processes.

Four levels of logging are available:

1. Log errors only (the default)
2. Log errors and warnings
3. Log the maximum amount of information
4. Disable event logging

For example, if an OSPF router is unable to establish an adjacency on an interface, you can:

1. Disable OSPF on the interface.
2. Change the level of logging for OSPF to log the maximum amount of information.
3. Enable OSPF on the interface.
4. Examine the system event log for information about the OSPF adjacency process.
5. Change the level of logging for OSPF to log errors only.

You can then troubleshoot the adjacency problem by analyzing the OSPF entries in the system event log.

Setting the level of event logging is available from the **General** tab of the following dialog boxes:

- **IP Routing Properties** and **General Properties**
- **IP Routing Properties** and **Network Address Translation Properties**
- **IP Routing Properties** and **RIP Properties**
- **IP Routing Properties** and **OSPF Properties**
- **IP Routing Properties** and **IGMP Properties**
- **IPX Routing Properties** and **General Properties**
- **IPX Routing Properties** and **RIP for IPX Properties**
- **IPX Routing Properties** and **SAP for IPX Properties**

Logging consumes system resources and should be used sparingly to help identify network problems. After the event has been logged or the problem is identified, you should immediately reset logging to its default value (log errors only).

When logging the maximum amount of information, the logging information can be complex and very detailed. Some of this information is useful only to Microsoft support engineers or to network administrators who are very experienced with the Windows 2000 Routing and Remote Access service.

Tracing

The Windows 2000 Routing and Remote Access service has an extensive tracing capability that you can use to troubleshoot complex network problems. Tracing records internal component variables, function calls, and interactions. Separate routing and remote access components can be independently enabled to log tracing information to files (file tracing). You must enable the tracing function by changing settings in the Windows 2000 registry.

Caution Do not use a registry editor to edit the registry directly unless you have no alternative. The registry editors bypass the standard safeguards provided by administrative tools. These safeguards prevent you from entering conflicting settings or settings that are likely to degrade performance or damage your system. Editing the registry directly can have serious, unexpected consequences that can prevent the system from starting and require that you reinstall Windows 2000. To configure or customize Windows 2000, use the programs in Control Panel or Microsoft Management Console (MMC) whenever possible.

You enable tracing for each routing protocol by setting the registry values described later in this section. You can enable and disable tracing for routing protocols while the router is running. Each installed routing protocol or component is capable of tracing and appears as a key (such as OSPF and RIPV2).

Tracing consumes system resources and should be used sparingly to help identify network problems. After the trace is captured or the problem is identified, you should immediately disable tracing. Do not leave tracing enabled on multiprocessor computers.

The tracing information can be complex and very detailed. Most of the time this information is useful only to Microsoft support engineers or to network administrators who are very experienced with the Windows 2000 Routing and Remote Access service.

File Tracing

To enable file tracing for each component (represented as *Component* below), you must set the value of the **EnableFileTracing** registry entry in HKEY_LOCAL_MACHINE\SYSTEM\SOFTWARE\Microsoft \Tracing*Component* to **1**. The default value is **0**.

To set the location of the trace file for each component, you must set the value of the **FileDirectory** registry entry in HKEY_LOCAL_MACHINE\SYSTEM\SOFTWARE \Microsoft\Tracing*Component*. The location of the log file is entered as a path. The file name for the log file is the name of the component for which tracing is enabled. By default, log files are placed in the *systemroot*\Tracing directory.

To set the level of file tracing for each component, you must set the value of the **FileTracingMask** registry entry in HKEY_LOCAL_MACHINE\SYSTEM\SOFTWARE\Microsoft \Tracing*Component*. The tracing level can be from **0** to **0xFFFF0000**. By default, the level of file tracing is set to **0xFFFF0000**, the maximum level of tracing.

To set the maximum size of a log file, you must set the value of the **MaxFileSize** registry entry in HKEY_LOCAL_MACHINE\SYSTEM\SOFTWARE\Microsoft\Tracing *Component*. You can change the size of the log file by setting different values for **MaxFileSize**. The default value is **10000** (64 KB).

C H A P T E R   3

Unicast IP Routing

Microsoft® Windows® 2000 provides extensive support for unicast Internet Protocol (IP) routing (routing to a unicast destination IP address) with the unicast IP routing protocols and features of the Windows 2000 Router. Your implementation of unicast routing can be simple or complex depending on the size of your IP internetwork, the use of Dynamic Host Configuration Protocol (DHCP) to allocate IP address configuration, connectivity to the Internet, the presence of non-Microsoft or legacy hosts on your internetwork, and other factors.

In This Chapter

Related Information in the Resource Kit

- For more information about unicast routing, see "Unicast Routing Overview" in this book.

- For more information about Windows 2000 and IPX routing, see "IPX Routing" in this book.

- For more information about the Windows 2000 Routing and Remote Access service, see "Routing and Remote Access Service" in this book.

Windows 2000 and IP Routing

An Internet Protocol (IP) router is an IP node that can forward IP packets that are not addressed to the router. Microsoft® Windows NT® version 4.0 and earlier provided a static IP router for simple IP routing. Microsoft® Windows NT® version 3.51 (Service Pack 2 and newer) and Microsoft® Windows NT® Server 4.0 provided a Routing Information Protocol (RIP) for IP service using RIP for IP version 1 (v1). The Routing and Remote Access Service (RRAS) for Windows NT 4.0 (Service Pack 3 and later) provided an integrated IP router with support for RIP for IP (v1 and v2), Open Shortest Path First (OSPF), IP packet filtering, demand-dial routing, and other features.

Windows 2000 Server provides the Routing and Remote Access service with support for RIP for IP, OSPF, IP packet filtering, demand-dial routing, and network address translation. For more information about the components in Windows 2000 that make up the IP router, see "Routing and Remote Access Service" in this book.

Windows 2000 Router Features for IP Routing

The Windows 2000–based computer running the Routing and Remote Access service, known as a Windows 2000 Router, provides a rich set of features to support IP internetworks:

RIP for IP   Support for version 1 and version 2 of RIP for IP, the primary routing protocol used in small to medium IP internetworks.

OSPF   Support for the industry standard Open Shortest Path First (OSPF) routing protocol used in large and very large IP internetworks.

DHCP Relay Agent   Support for an RFC 1542–compliant Dynamic Host Configuration Protocol (DHCP) Relay Agent, also known as a Boot Protocol (BOOTP) Relay Agent, that transfers messages between DHCP clients and DHCP servers located on separate networks.

Network Address Translator (NAT)   Support for network address translation to translate private and public addresses to allow the connection of small office or home office (SOHO) networks to the Internet. The network address translator (NAT) component also includes a Dynamic Host Configuration Protocol (DHCP) allocator and a Domain Name System (DNS) proxy to simplify the configuration of SOHO hosts.

IP Packet Filtering   Support for separately configured input and output filters for each IP interface based on key fields in the IP, Transmission Control Protocol (TCP), User Datagram Protocol (UDP), and Internet Control Message Protocol (ICMP) headers.

ICMP Router Discovery Support for ICMP Router Advertisements messages to allow the automated discovery of default routers by hosts using ICMP router discovery.

Platform to Support Other IP Routing Protocols Application Programming Interface (API) support that provides a platform to support additional routing protocols such as the Border Gateway Protocol (BGP) for IP. The Windows 2000 Router does not provide BGP, but BGP can be written by third-party independent software vendors. For more information about the API support for third-party routing protocols, see the Windows 2000 Software Development Kit.

Preference Levels

When there are multiple sources of routing information, it becomes necessary to define which route sources are better sources than others. For example, when exchanging routes between RIP and OSPF portions of an intranet, the definition of the metric differs between RIP and OSPF. Rather than trying to reconcile the metrics for two routes to the same destination network ID from different route sources, the route learned from the more preferred route source is used and the route from the less preferred route source is ignored, regardless of the metric.

For example, if a router is configured to use both RIP and OSPF, then both RIP and OSPF-learned routes are added to the Route Table Manager (RTM) IP routing table. If the metric of an OSPF learned route is 5 and the metric of the corresponding RIP learned route is 3 and OSPF is the preferred routing protocol, then the OSPF route is added by RTM to the IP forwarding table.

Preference levels for route sources can be configured from the **Preference Levels** tab on the properties of the **IP Routing\General** container in the **Routing and Remote Access** snap-in. The **Preference Levels** tab allows you to set preference levels for all routes from a specific route source. To set a specific preference level for a static route, use the **netsh routing ip add rtmroute** command.

RIP for IP

RIP for IP is a distance vector routing protocol that facilitates the exchange of IP routing information. Like RIP for IPX, RIP for IP has its origins in the Xerox Network Services (XNS) version of RIP and became a popular routing protocol due to its inclusion in Berkeley UNIX (BSD 4.2 and later) as the *routed* server daemon (a daemon is similar to a Windows 2000 service). There are two versions of RIP. RIP version 1 (v1) is defined in RFC 1058. RIP version 2 (v2) is defined in RFC 1723. In this chapter, information about RIP for IP applies to both versions of RIP. Additional information about the differences between RIP v1 and RIP v2 is also included in this chapter.

RIP and Large Internetworks

While simple and well supported in the industry, RIP for IP suffers from some problems inherent to its original LAN-based design. The combination of the these problems makes RIP a desirable solution only in small to medium-sized IP internetworks.

RIP and Hop Counts

RIP uses a hop count as the metric for the route stored in the IP routing table. The hop count is the number of routers that must be crossed to reach the desired network. RIP has a maximum hop count of 15; therefore, there can only be 15 routers between any two hosts. Networks 16 hops and greater away are considered unreachable. Hop counts can be customized so that slow links are set to multiple hops; however, the accumulated hop count between any two networks must not exceed 15.

The RIP hop count is independent of the Time-to-Live (TTL) field in the IP header. On an internetwork, a network 16 hops away would normally be reachable for an IP packet with an adequate TTL; however, to the RIP router, the network is unreachable and attempts to forward packets to hosts on the network result in ICMP Destination Unreachable–Network Unreachable messages from the RIP router.

RIP and Routing Table Entries

RIP allows for multiple entries in the routing table for a network if there are multiple paths. The IP routing process chooses the route with the lowest metric (lowest hop count) as the best route. However, typical RIP for IP router implementations, including Windows 2000, only store a single lowest metric route for any network. If multiple lowest hop count routes are received by RIP, the first lowest metric route received is stored in the routing table.

If the RIP router is storing a complete list of all the networks and all of the possible ways to reach each network, the routing table can have hundreds or even thousands of entries in a large IP internetwork with multiple paths. Because only 25 routes can be sent in a single RIP packet, large routing tables have to be sent as multiple RIP packets.

RIP Route Advertising

RIP routers advertise the contents of their routing tables every 30 seconds on all attached networks through an IP subnet and MAC-level broadcast. (RIP v2 routers can be configured to multicast RIP announcements.) Large IP internetworks carry the broadcasted RIP overhead of large routing tables. This can be especially problematic on WAN links where significant portions of the WAN link bandwidth are devoted to the passing of RIP traffic. As a result, RIP-based routing does not scale well to large internetworks or WAN implementations.

RIP Convergence

By default, each routing table entry learned through RIP is given a timeout value of three minutes past the last time it was received in a RIP announcement from a neighboring RIP router. When a router goes down due to a hardware or software failure, it can take several minutes for the topology change to be propagated throughout the internetwork. This is known as the slow convergence problem.

Convergence in RIP Internetworks

RIP for IP, like most distance vector routing protocols, announces its routes in an unsynchronized and unacknowledged manner. This can lead to convergence problems. However, you can enable modifications to the announcement algorithms to reduce convergence time in most situations.

Count-to-Infinity Problem

The classic distance vector convergence problem is known as the count-to-infinity problem and is a direct result of the asynchronous announcement scheme. When RIP for IP routers add routes to their routing table, based on routes advertised by other routers, they keep only the best route in the routing table and they update a lower cost route with a higher cost route only if is being announced by the same source as the current lower cost route. In certain situations, as illustrated in Figures 3.1 through 3.5, this causes the count-to-infinity problem.

Assume that the internetwork in Figure 3.1 has converged. For simplicity, assume that the announcements sent by Router 1 on Network 1 and Router 2 on Network 3 are not included.

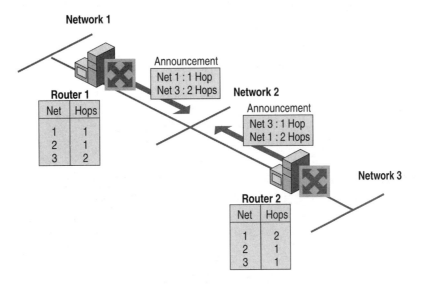

Figure 3.1   Converged Internetwork

Now assume that the link from Router 2 to Network 3 fails and is sensed by Router 2. As shown in Figure 3.2, Router 2 changes the hop count for the route to Network 3 to indicate that it is unreachable, an infinite distance away. For RIP for IP, infinity is 16.

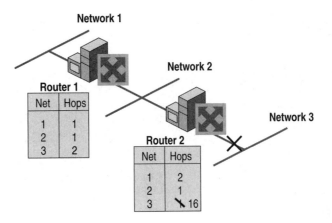

Figure 3.2   Link to Network 3 Fails

However, before Router 2 can advertise the new hop count to Network 3 in a scheduled announcement, it receives an announcement from Router 1. The Router 1 announcement contains a route to Network 3 which is two hops away. Because two hops away is a better route than 16 hops, Router 2 updates its routing table entry for Network 3, changing it from 16 hops to three hops, as shown in Figure 3.3.

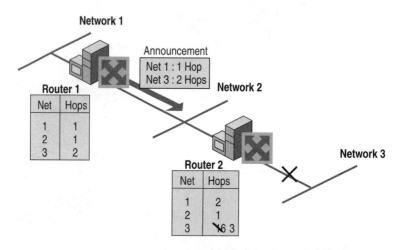

Figure 3.3   Router 2 After Receiving Announcement From Router 1

When Router 2 announces its new routes, Router 1 notes that Network 3 is available three hops away through Router 2. Because the route to Network 3 on Router 1 was originally learned from Router 2, Router 1 updates its route to Network 3 to four hops. (See Figure 3.4.)

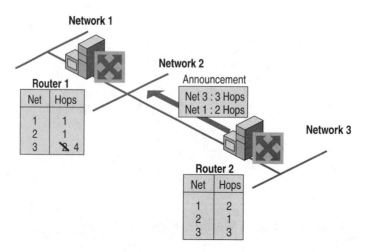

Figure 3.4   Router 1 After Receiving Announcement From Router 2

When Router 1 announces its new routes, Router 2 notes that Network 3 is available four hops away through Router 1. Because the route to Network 3 on Router 2 was originally learned from Router 1, Router 2 updates its route to Network 3 to five hops. (See Figure 3.5.)

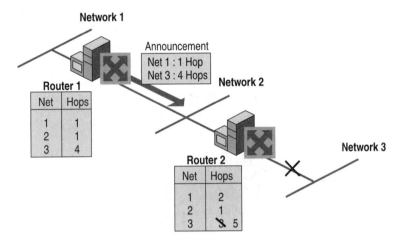

Figure 3.5   Router 2 After Receiving Another Announcement from Router 1

The two routers continue to announce routes to Network 3 with higher and higher hop counts until infinity (16) is reached. Then, Network 3 is considered unreachable and the route to Network 3 is eventually timed out of the routing table. This is known as the count-to-infinity problem.

The count-to-infinity problem is one of the reasons why the maximum hop count of RIP for IP internetworks is set to 15 (16 for unreachable). Higher maximum hop count values would make the convergence time longer when count-to-infinity occurs. Also note that during the count-to-infinity in the previous example, the route from Router 1 to Network 3 is through Router 2. The route from Router 2 to Network 3 is through Router 1. A routing loop exists between Router 1 and Router 2 for Network 3 for the duration of the count-to-infinity problem.

Reducing Convergence Time

To help reduce the convergence time of RIP for IP internetworks and to avoid count-to-infinity and routing loops in most situations, you can enable the following modifications to the RIP announcement mechanism:

- Split horizon
- Split horizon with poison reverse
- Triggered updates

Split Horizon

Split horizon helps reduce convergence time by not allowing routers to advertise networks in the direction from which those networks were learned. The only information sent in RIP announcements are for those networks that are beyond the neighboring router in the opposite direction. Networks learned from the neighboring router are not included.

Split horizon eliminates count-to-infinity and routing loops during convergence in single-path internetworks and reduces the chances of count-to-infinity in multi-path internetworks. Figure 3.6 illustrates how split horizon keeps the RIP router from advertising routes in the direction from which they were learned.

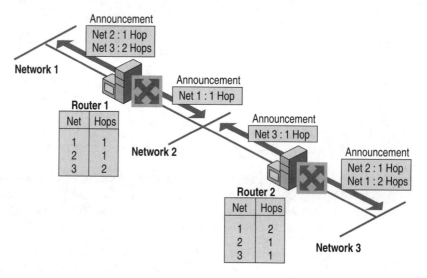

Figure 3.6   Split Horizon

Split Horizon with Poison Reverse

Split horizon with poison reverse differs from simple split horizon because it announces all networks. However, those networks learned in a given direction are announced with a hop count of 16, indicating that the network is unreachable. In a single-path internetwork, split horizon with poison reverse has no benefit beyond split horizon. However, in a multipath internetwork, split horizon with poison reverse greatly reduces count-to-infinity and routing loops. Count-to-infinity can still occur in a multipath internetwork because routes to networks can be learned from multiple sources.

In Figure 3.7, split horizon with poison reverse advertises learned routes as unreachable in the direction from which they are learned. Split horizon with poison reverse does have the disadvantage of additional RIP message overhead because all networks are advertised.

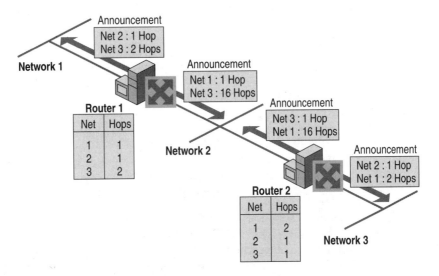

Figure 3.7   Split Horizon with Poison Reverse

Triggered Updates

Triggered updates allow a RIP router to announce changes in metric values almost immediately rather than waiting for the next periodic announcement. The trigger is a change to a metric in an entry in the routing table. For example, networks that become unavailable can be announced with a hop count of 16 through a triggered update. Note that the update is sent *almost immediately*, where a time interval to wait is typically specified on the router. If triggered updates were sent by all routers immediately, each triggered update could cause a cascade of broadcast traffic across the IP internetwork.

Triggered updates improve the convergence time of RIP internetworks but at the expense of additional broadcast traffic as the triggered updates are propagated.

RIP for IP Operation

The normal operation of a RIP for IP router consists of an initialization process, during which the router learns the routes of the internetwork from neighboring routers; an ongoing periodic advertisement process; and the proper advertisement of unreachable routes when the router is brought down through an administrative action.

Initialization

Upon startup, the RIP for IP router announces its locally attached networks on all of its interfaces. The neighboring RIP routers process the RIP announcement and add the new network or networks to their routing tables as appropriate.

The initializing RIP router also sends a General RIP Request on all locally attached networks. The General RIP Request is a special RIP message requesting all routes. The neighboring RIP routers receive the General RIP Request and send a unicast reply to the requesting router. The replies are used to build the initializing RIP router's routing table.

Ongoing Maintenance

By default, every 30 seconds the RIP router announces it routes on all of its interfaces. The exact nature of the routing announcement depends on whether the RIP router is configured for split horizon or split horizon with poison reverse. The RIP router is also always listening for RIP announcements from neighboring routers in order to add or update the routes in its own routing table.

Administrative Router Shutdown

If a RIP for IP router is downed properly through an administrative action, it sends a triggered update on all locally attached networks. The triggered update announces the networks available through the router with a hop count of 16 (unreachable). This topology change is propagated by neighboring RIP routers throughout the IP internetwork using triggered updates.

As dynamic routers, RIP for IP routers also react to changes in the internetwork topology from downed links or downed routers.

Downed Link

If a link goes down corresponding to one of the router's interfaces and this failure is detected by the interface hardware and indicated to the router, this change is sent out as a triggered update.

Downed Router

If a router goes down due to a power outage or other hardware or software failure, it does not have the ability to inform neighboring routers that the networks available through it have become unavailable. To prevent the lingering existence of unreachable networks in routing tables, each route learned by RIP for IP has a maximum lifetime of 3 minutes (by default). If the entry is not refreshed by the receipt of another announcement in 3 minutes, the entry's hop count is changed to 16 and it is eventually removed from the routing table.

Therefore, if a RIP for IP router goes down, it takes up to 3 minutes for the neighboring routers to mark the routes learned from the downed router as unreachable. Only then do they propagate the topology change throughout the internetwork using triggered updates.

RIP for IP Version 1

RIP version 1 (v1) is defined in RFC 1058 and is widely deployed in small to medium-sized intranets.

RIP v1 Message Format

RIP messages are encapsulated in a User Datagram Protocol (UDP) datagram sent from the router interface IP address and UDP port 520 to the subnet broadcast IP address. The RIP v1 message consists of a 4-byte RIP header and up to 25 RIP routes. The maximum size of the RIP message is 504 bytes. With the 8-byte UDP header, the maximum size of the RIP message is a 512-byte IP payload. Figure 3.8 illustrates the RIP v1 message format.

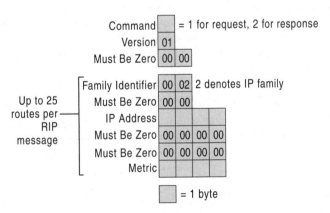

Figure 3.8   RIP Version 1 Message Format

Command A 1-byte field containing either 0x01 or 0x02. 0x01 indicates a RIP request for all (a General RIP Request) or part of the routing tables of neighboring routers. 0x02 indicates a RIP response consisting of all or part of a neighboring router's routing table. A RIP response can be sent in response to a RIP request or as the periodic or triggered update message.

Version A 1-byte field set to the value of 0x01 for RIP v1.

Family Identifier A 2-byte field identifying the protocol family. This is set to the value of 0x00-02 to indicate the IP protocol family.

IP Address A 4-byte field set to the IP network ID which can be a class-based network ID, a subnetted network ID (advertised only within the subnetted network), an IP address (for a host route), or 0.0.0.0 (for the default route). For a General RIP Request, the IP Address is set to 0.0.0.0.

Metric A 4-byte field for the number of hops to the IP network that must be a value from 1 to 16. The metric is set to 16 in a General RIP Request or to indicate that the network is unreachable in a RIP response (announcement).

Problems with RIP v1

RIP v1 was designed in 1988 to suit the dynamic routing needs of LAN technology–based IP internetworks. Shared access LAN technologies like Ethernet and Token Ring support Media Access Control (MAC)–level broadcasting where a single packet can be received and processed by multiple network nodes. However, in modern internetworks, the use of MAC-level broadcasts is undesirable because all nodes must process all broadcasts. RIP v1 was also designed in a time when the Internet was still using network IDs based on the Internet address classes. Today, however, the use of Classless Inter-Domain Routing (CIDR) and variable length subnetting is almost required to conserve IP addresses.

Broadcasted RIP Announcements

All RIP v1 route announcements are addressed to the IP subnet (all host bits are set to 1) and MAC-level broadcast. Non-RIP hosts also receive RIP announcements. For large or very large RIP internetworks, the amount of broadcast traffic on each subnet can become significant.

While producing additional broadcast traffic, the broadcast nature of RIP v1 also permits the use of Silent RIP. A Silent RIP computer processes RIP announcements but does not announce its own routes. Silent RIP could be enabled on non-router hosts to produce a routing table with as much detail as the RIP routers. With more detailed routes in the routing table, a Silent RIP host can make better routing decisions.

Subnet Mask Not Announced with Route

RIP v1 was designed for class-based IP internetworks where the network ID can be determined from the values of the first 3 bits of the IP address in the RIP route. Because the subnet mask is not included with the route, the RIP router must determine the network ID based on a limited set of information. For each route in a RIP v1 message, the RIP v1 router performs the following process:

- If the network ID fits the address classes (Class A, Class B, or Class C), the default class-based subnet mask is assumed.
- If the network ID does not fit the address class, then:
  - If the network ID fits the subnet mask of the interface on which it is received, the subnet mask of the interface on which it was received is assumed.
  - If the network ID does not fit the subnet mask of the interface on which it is received, the network ID is assumed to be a host route with the subnet mask 255.255.255.255.

As a result of the assumptions listed previously, supernetted routes might be interpreted as a single network ID rather than the range of network IDs that they are designed to represent and subnet routes advertised outside of the network ID being subnetted might be interpreted as host routes.

As a mechanism for supporting subnetted environments, RIP v1 routers do not advertise the subnets of a subnetted class-based network ID outside the subnetted region of the IP internetwork. However, because only the class-based network ID is being advertised outside the subnetted environment, subnets of a network ID in a RIP v1 environment must be contiguous. If subnets of an IP network ID are noncontiguous, known as disjointed subnets, the class-based network ID is announced by separate RIP v1 routers in different parts of the internetwork. As a result, IP traffic can be forwarded to the wrong network.

No Protection from Rogue RIP Routers

RIP v1 does not provide any protection from a rogue RIP router starting up on a network and announcing false or inaccurate routes. RIP v1 announcements are processed regardless of their source. A malicious user could use this lack of protection to overwhelm RIP routers with hundreds or thousands of false or inaccurate routes.

RIP for IP Version 2

RIP version 2 (v2) as defined in RFC 1723 seeks to address some of the problems associated with RIP v1. The decision to refine RIP was controversial in the context of newer, smarter routing protocols such as OSPF. However, RIP has the following advantages over OSPF:

- RIP for IP is easy to implement. In its simplest default configuration, RIP for IP is as easy as configuring IP addresses and subnet masks for each router interface and then turning on the router.
- RIP for IP has a large installed base consisting of small and medium-sized IP internetworks that do not wish to bear the design and configuration burden of OSPF.

Features of RIP v2

To help today's IP internetworks minimize broadcast traffic, use variable length subnetting to conserve IP addresses, and secure their routing environment from misconfigured or malicious routers, several key features were added to RIP v2.

Multicasted RIP Announcements

Rather than broadcasting RIP announcements, RIP v2 supports sending RIP announcements to the IP multicast address of 224.0.0.9. Non-RIP nodes are not disturbed by RIP router announcement traffic.

The disadvantage of this new feature is that Silent RIP nodes must also be listening for multicast traffic sent to 224.0.0.9. If you are using Silent RIP, verify that your Silent RIP nodes can listen for multicasted RIP v2 announcements before deploying multicasted RIP v2.

The use of multicasted announcements is optional. The broadcasting of RIP v2 announcements is also supported.

Subnet Masks

RIP v2 announcements send the subnet mask (also known as a network mask) along with the network ID. RIP v2 can be used in subnetted, supernetted, and variable-length subnet mask environments. Subnets of a network ID do not have to be contiguous (they can be disjointed subnets).

Authentication

RIP v2 supports the use of authentication mechanisms to verify the origin of incoming RIP announcements. Simple password authentication was defined in RFC 1723, but newer authentication mechanisms such as Message Digest 5 (MD5) are available.

Note Windows 2000 supports only simple password authentication.

RIP v1 Routers Are Forward Compatible with RIP v2

RIP v1 was designed with forward compatibility in mind. If a RIP v1 router receives a message and the RIP version in the RIP header is not 0x01, it does not discard the RIP announcement but processes only the RIP v1 defined fields.

Also, RIP v2 routers send a RIP v1 response to a RIP v1 request except when configured to send only RIP v2 announcements.

RIP v2 Message Format

To ensure that RIP v1 routers can process RIP v2 announcements, RIP v2 does not modify the structure of the RIP message format. RIP v2 makes use of fields that were defined in RIP v1 as Must be Zero.

The use of the Command, Family Identifier, IP Address, and Metric fields is the same as previously defined for RIP v1. The Version field is set to 0x02 to indicate a RIP v2 message. Figure 3.9 illustrates the RIP v2 message format.

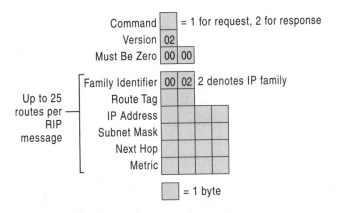

Figure 3.9   RIP Version 2 Message Format

Route Tag

The Route Tag field is used as a method of marking specific routes for administrative purposes. Its original use as defined by RFC 1723 was to distinguish routes that were RIP-based routes (internal to the RIP environment) from non-RIP routes (external to the RIP environment). The Route Tag is configurable on routers that can support multiple routing protocols.

Note   Windows 2000 supports the configuration of the Route Tag for RIP v2 interfaces.

Subnet Mask

The 4-byte Subnet Mask field contains the subnet mask (also known as a network mask) of the network ID in the IP Address field.

Next Hop

The 4-byte Next Hop field contains the forwarding IP address (also known as the gateway address) for the network ID in the IP Address field. If the next hop is set to 0.0.0.0, the forwarding IP address (the next hop) for the route is assumed to be the source IP address of the route announcement.

The Next Hop field is used to prevent non-optimal routing situations. For example, if a router announces a host route for a host that resides on the same network as the router interface advertising the route and the Next Hop field is not used, the forwarding IP address for the host route is the IP address of the router's interface, not the IP address of the host. Other routers that receive the announcement on that network forward packets destined for the host's IP address to the announcing router's IP address rather than to the host. This creates a non-optimal routing situation.

Using the Next Hop field, the router announces the host route with the host's IP address in the Next Hop field. Other routers receiving the announcement on that network forward packets destined for the host's IP address to the host's IP address rather than forwarding them to the announcing router.

Because the Next Hop field becomes the Gateway Address field in the IP routing table, the IP address in the Next Hop field should be directly reachable using a router interface.

Authentication in RIP v2

The authentication process for RIP v2 announcements uses the first route entry in the RIP message to store authentication information. The first route entry must be used, leaving a maximum of 24 routes in a RIP v2 authenticated announcement. To indicate authentication, the Family Identifier field is set to 0xFF-FF. The Authentication Type field, normally used as the Route Tag field for a route, indicates the type of authentication being used. Simple password authentication uses the Authentication Type value of 0x00-01.

The 16 bytes after the Authentication Type are used to store the authentication value. For simple password authentication, the 16-byte Authentication Value field stores the left-justified, null-padded, case-sensitive, clear-text password. Figure 3.10 illustrates the RIP v2 authentication message.

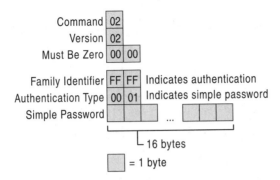

Figure 3.10   RIP v2 Message Format Using Authentication

RIP v1 routers disregard the first route in a RIP v2 authenticated announcement because the Family Identifier for the route is unknown.

Note Simple password authentication for RIP v2 prevents unauthorized or misconfigured RIP routers from being placed on the network. The simple password is not secure, however, because it is sent on the network in clear text. Anyone with a protocol analyzer such as Microsoft Network Monitor can capture the RIP v2 packets and view the authentication password.

Mixed RIP v1 and RIP v2 Environments

RIP v2 routers and RIP v1 routers should be used together with caution. Because RIP v1 routers do not interpret the Subnet Mask field in the route, RIP v2 routers must not announce routes which can be misinterpreted by a RIP v1 router. Variable length subnet masks (VLSM) and disjointed subnets cannot be used in mixed environments.

For an interface using RIP v2 to make announcements such that RIP v1 routers can process the announced routes, the RIP v2 routers must summarize subnet routes when announcing outside a subnetted environment. A specific subnet route announced to a RIP v1 router can be misinterpreted as a host route. Also, the RIP v2 routers cannot announce supernet routes. A RIP v1 router would misinterpret the route as a single network, rather than as a range of networks.

If RIP v2 routers are on the same network as RIP v1 routers, the RIP v2 router interface must be configured to broadcast its announcements. Multicasted RIP v2 announcements are not processed by the RIP v1 routers.

Windows 2000 as a RIP for IP Router

Windows 2000 RIP for IP is RFC 1058 and 1723 compliant and has the following features:

- Split horizon, poison reverse, and triggered updates convergence algorithms.
- Ability to modify the announcement interval (default is 30 seconds).
- Ability to modify the routing table entry timeout value (default is 3 minutes).
- Ability to be a Silent RIP host.
- Peer Filtering: Ability to accept or discard updates of announcements from specific routers identified by IP address.
- Route Filtering: Ability to accept or discard updates of specific network IDs or from specific routers.
- RIP Neighbors: Ability to unicast RIP announcements to specific routers to support nonbroadcast technologies like Frame Relay. A RIP neighbor is a RIP router that receives unicasted RIP announcements.
- Ability to announce or accept default routes or host routes.

Note When a Windows 2000 Router advertises a non-RIP learned route, it advertises it with a hop count of two. Non-RIP learned routes include static routes (even for directly attached networks), OSPF routes, and SNMP routes.

You can view the current RIP neighbors in the **Routing and Remote Access** snap-in by right-clicking the **RIP** routing protocol and clicking **Show Neighbors**.

Troubleshooting RIP for IP

If a RIP environment is properly configured, RIP routers learn all the best routes from neighboring routers after convergence. The exact list of routes added by RIP to the IP routing table depends, among other factors, on whether or not the router interfaces are inside a subnetted region, whether or not RIP v2 is being used, and whether or not host routes or default routes are being advertised.

Problems with RIP can occur in a mixed RIP v1 and v2 environment, with the use of Silent RIP hosts, or when all the appropriate RIP routes are not being received and added to the IP routing table.

Improper routes in a mixed RIP v1 and RIP v2 environment

On networks containing RIP v1 routers, verify that RIP v2 is configured to broadcast its announcements on networks containing RIP v1 routers.

On networks containing RIP v1 routers, verify that the RIP v2 router interfaces are configured to accept both RIP v1 and RIP v2 announcements.

Silent RIP hosts are not receiving routes

If there are Silent RIP hosts on a network that are not receiving routes from the local RIP router, verify the version of RIP supported by the Silent RIP hosts. For example, if the Silent RIP hosts only support listening for broadcasted, RIP v1 announcements, you cannot use RIP v2 multicasting.

If you are using the RIP listener component available on Microsoft® Windows NT® Workstation version 4.0, Service Pack 4 and later, you must configure your RIP routers for RIP v1 or RIP v2 broadcasting.

RIP routers are not receiving expected routes

- Verify that you are not deploying variable length subnetting, disjointed subnets, or supernetting in a RIP v1 or mixed RIP v1 and RIP v2 environment.
- If authentication is enabled, verify that all interfaces on the same network are using the same case-sensitive password.
- If RIP peer filtering is being used, verify that the correct IP addresses for the neighboring peer RIP routers are configured.
- If RIP route filtering is being used, verify that the ranges of network IDs for your internetwork are included or are not being excluded.
- If RIP neighbors are configured, verify that the correct IP addresses are configured for the unicasted RIP announcements.
- Verify that IP packet filtering is not preventing the receiving (through input filters) or sending (through output filters) of RIP announcements on the router interfaces enabled for RIP. RIP traffic uses UDP port 520.
- Verify that TCP/IP filtering on the router interfaces is not preventing the receiving of RIP traffic.
- For dial-up demand-dial interfaces using auto-static updates, configure the demand-dial interfaces to use RIP v2 multicast announcements. When a router calls another router, each router receives an IP address from the other router's IP address pool, which are on different subnets. Because broadcasted RIP announcements are addressed to the subnet broadcast address, each router does not process the other router's broadcasted request for routes. Using multicasting, RIP requests and announcements are processed regardless of the subnet for the router interfaces. For more information about demand-dial interfaces and auto-static updates, see "Demand-Dial Routing" in this book.
- For RIP over demand-dial interfaces, verify that the packet filters on the remote access policy profile of the answering router are not preventing the receipt or sending of RIP traffic. TCP/IP packet filters can be configured on the profile properties of the remote access policies on the answering router (or the Internet Authentication Service (IAS) server if RADIUS is used) that are used to define the traffic that is allowed on the remote access connection.

Host or default routes are not being propagated

- By default, host routes and default routes are not announced using RIP. You can change this behavior from the **Advanced** tab of the properties of a RIP interface in the **Routing and Remote Access** snap-in.

OSPF

Open Shortest Path First (OSPF) is a link-state routing protocol defined in RFC 2328. It is designed to be run as an Interior Gateway Protocol (IGP) to a single Autonomous System (AS). In a link-state routing protocol, each router maintains a database of router advertisements called Link State Advertisements (LSAs). LSAs for routers within the AS consist of a router, its attached networks, and their configured costs. An OSPF cost is a unitless metric that indicates the preference of using a link. There are also LSAs for summarized routes and routes outside of the AS.

The router distributes its LSAs to its neighboring routers. LSAs are gathered into a database called the link state database (LSDB). By synchronizing LSDBs between all neighboring routers, each router has each other router's LSA in its database. Therefore, every router has the same LSDB. From the LSDB, entries for the router's routing table are calculated using the Dijkstra algorithm to determine the least cost path, the path with the lowest accumulated cost, to each network in the internetwork.

OSPF has the following features:

Fast Convergence OSPF can detect and propagate topology changes faster than RIP. Count-to-infinity does not occur with OSPF.

Loop-Free Routes OSPF-calculated routes are always loop-free.

Scalability With OSPF, an AS can be subdivided into contiguous groups of networks called areas. Routes within areas can be summarized to minimize route table entries. Areas can be configured with a default route summarizing all routes outside the AS or outside the area. As a result, OSPF can scale to large and very large internetworks. In contrast, RIP for IP internetworks cannot be subdivided and no route summarization is done beyond the summarizing for all subnets of a network ID.

Subnet Mask Advertised with the Network OSPF was designed to advertise the subnet mask with the network. OSPF supports variable-length subnet masks (VLSM), disjointed subnets, and supernetting.

Support for Authentication Information exchanges between OSPF routes can be authenticated. Windows 2000 OSPF supports simple password authentication.

Support for External Routes Routes outside of the OSPF AS are advertised within the AS so that OSPF routers can calculate the least cost route to external networks.

Note Simple password authentication for OSPF is designed to prevent unauthorized OSPF routers from being placed on the network. The simple password is not secure, however, because it is sent on the network in clear text. Anyone with a protocol analyzer such as Microsoft Network Monitor can capture the OSPF messages and view the authentication password.

OSPF Operation

The main operation of the OSPF protocol occurs in the following consecutive stages and leads to the convergence of the internetwork:

1. Compiling the LSDB.
2. Calculating the Shortest Path First (SPF) Tree.
3. Creating the routing table entries.

Formation of the LSDB Using Link State Advertisements

The LSDB is a database of all OSPF router LSAs, summary LSAs, and external route LSAs. The LSDB is compiled by an ongoing exchange of LSAs between neighboring routers so that each router is synchronized with its neighbor. When the AS has converged, all routers have the appropriate entries in their LSDB.

To create the LSDB, each OSPF router must receive a valid LSA from each other router in the AS. This is performed through a procedure called flooding. Each router initially sends out an LSA which contains its own configuration. As it receives LSAs from other routers, it propagates those LSAs to its neighbor routers.

In this way, an LSA from a given router is flooded across the AS so that each other router contains that router's LSA. While it appears that the flooding of LSAs across the AS causes a large amount of network traffic, OSPF is very efficient in the propagation of LSA information. Figure 3.11 shows a simple OSPF AS, the flooding of LSAs between neighboring routers, and the LSDB.

The exact details of the synchronization of the LSDB between neighboring routers are discussed in the section on creating adjacencies.

Autonomous System (AS)

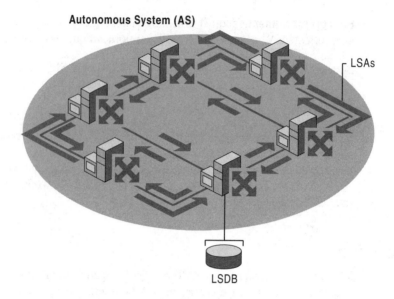

LSAs

LSDB

Figure 3.11   OSPF Link State Database (LSDB)

You can view the current OSPF link state database by right-clicking the **OSPF** routing protocol and clicking **Show Link State Database** in the **Routing and Remote Access** snap-in.

Router ID

To keep track of LSAs in the LSDB, each router is assigned a Router ID, a 32-bit dotted decimal number that is unique to the AS. The Router ID identifies the router in the AS, not the IP address of one of the router's interfaces. The Router ID is not used as a destination IP address for sending information to the router. It is a common industry convention to use the largest or smallest IP address assigned to the router as the Router ID. Because IP addresses are unique, this convention ensures that the OSPF Router IDs are also unique.

Calculating the SPF Tree Using Dijkstra's Algorithm

Once the LSDB is compiled, each OSPF router performs a least cost path calculation called the Dijkstra algorithm on the information in the LSDB and creates a tree of shortest paths to each other router and network with themselves as the root. This tree is known as the SPF Tree and contains a single, least cost path to each router and network in the AS. Because the least cost path calculation is performed by each router with itself as the root of the tree, the SPF tree is different for each router in the AS.

The Dijkstra algorithm is from a branch of mathematics called graph theory and is an efficient method of calculating a set of least cost paths relative to a source node.

To Calculate the SPF Tree Using the Dijkstra Algorithm

The result of the Dijkstra algorithm is the set SPF{}, a cost sorted list of least cost paths containing the path (the series of nodes and links) and its accumulated cost from the source node S.

1. Define the set E{} to be the set of nodes (routers) that have been evaluated.

2. Define the set R{} to be the set of nodes (routers) that are remaining (have not been evaluated).

3. Define the set O{} to be a cost-sorted list of ordered paths between nodes. An ordered path can consist of multiple nodes connected together in a multi-hop configuration (they do not have to be neighboring).

4. Define the set SPF{} to be a cost-sorted list of least cost paths containing the path and its accumulated cost.

5. Initialize the set E{} to contain the source node S and the set R{} to contain all other nodes. Initialize the set O{} to be the cost-sorted list of directly connected paths from S. Initialize the set SPF{} to be the empty set.

6. If O{} is empty or the first path in O{} has an infinite metric, mark all the nodes in R as unreachable and terminate the algorithm.

7. From the set O{}, examine P, the shortest ordered path in O{}. Remove P from O{}. Let V be the last node on the ordered path of P.

   If V is already a member of E{}, return to step 6.

   – Or –

   If P is the shortest path to V, move V from R{} to E{}. Add a member to the set SPF{} consisting of P and its accumulated cost from S.

8. Build a new set of paths by concatenating P and each of the links adjacent to V. The cost of these paths is the sum of the cost of P and the metric of the link appended to P. Insert the new links in the set O{} and sort by cost. Return to step 6.

Calculating the Routing Table Entries from the SPF Tree

The OSPF routing table entries are created from the SPF tree, and a single entry for each network in the AS is produced. The metric for the routing table entry is the OSPF-calculated cost, not a hop count.

To calculate the IP routing table entries from the SPF Tree, the resulting set SPF{} is analyzed. The result of the analysis is a series of OSPF routes containing the IP destination (the network ID) and its network mask (subnet mask), the forwarding IP address of the appropriate neighboring router, the interface over which the neighboring router is reachable, and the OSPF-calculated cost to the network. The OSPF routes are added to the IP routing table.

Example of OSPF Operation

The following examples illustrate how an OSPF internetwork compiles the LSDB, performs the least cost analysis, and creates routing table entries. This example is deliberately simplified to help you gain an understanding of the basic principles of OSPF convergence.

Compiling the LSDB

Consider the simple AS in Figure 3.12. At each router interface, a unitless cost metric is assigned as a reflection of the preference of using that interface. These cost values can be a reflection of bandwidth, delay, or reliability factors and are assigned by the network administrator.

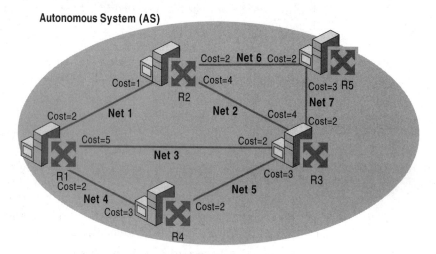

Figure 3.12   AS with Link State Database Information

After convergence, when each router has an LSA from each other router in the AS, they each contain the LSDB shown in Table 3.1.

Table 3.1   Link State Database

Router	Attached Networks and Costs
R1	Net 1-Cost 2, Net 3-Cost 5, Net 4-Cost 2
R2	Net 1-Cost 1, Net 2-Cost 4, Net 6-Cost 2
R3	Net 2-Cost 4, Net 3-Cost 2, Net 5-Cost 3, Net 7-Cost 2
R4	Net 4-Cost 3, Net 5-Cost 2
R5	Net 6-Cost 2, Net 7-Cost 3

Calculating the SPF Tree

The next step is to apply Dijkstra's algorithm to our sample OSPF AS. Figure 3.13 illustrates the resulting SPF Tree calculation as performed by router R4. With R4 as the root, the SPF Tree calculation determines the series of connected routers and networks that represent the least cost path to each router and to each network.

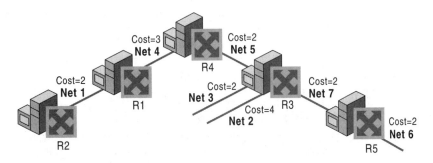

Figure 3.13   SPF Tree

Creating Routing Table Entries

The routing table is created from the results of the SPF Tree as shown in Figure 3.14.

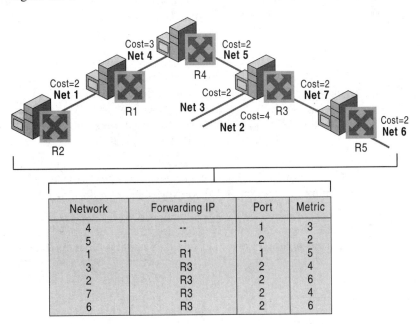

Network	Forwarding IP	Port	Metric
4	--	1	3
5	--	2	2
1	R1	1	5
3	R3	2	4
2	R3	2	6
7	R3	2	4
6	R3	2	6

Figure 3.14   Routing Table Entries

Note A large OSPF network might require a short but large burst of bandwidth as LSAs are exchanged. Once the LSAs are exchanged a large amount of memory is required to hold the LSDB before convergence. Running the SPF algorithm requires high CPU utilization. Networks with frequently appearing and disappearing links might cause performance issues on any router because of the three-step LSA generation, holding the LSDB, and running the SPF process. The overhead and performance issues of OSPF can be minimized by dividing the OSPF AS into areas. For more information, see "OSPF Areas" later in this chapter.

OSPF Network Types

OSPF message addresses are determined by the type of network to which the OSPF interface is connected. One of the following OSPF network types must be selected when configuring an interface on an OSPF router.

Broadcast A network that can connect more than two routers with a hardware broadcast facility where a single packet sent by a router is received by all routers attached to that network. Ethernet, Token Ring, and FDDI are broadcast networks. OSPF messages sent on broadcast networks use IP multicast addresses.

Point-to-Point A network that can connect only two routers. Leased-line WAN links such as Dataphone Digital Service (DDS) and T-Carrier are point-to-point networks. OSPF messages sent on point-to-point networks use IP multicast addresses.

Non-Broadcast Multiple Access A network that can connect more than two routers but has no hardware broadcast facility. X.25, Frame Relay, and ATM are Non-Broadcast Multiple Access (NBMA) networks. Because multicasted OSPF messages do not reach all the OSPF routers on the network, OSPF must be configured to unicast to the IP addresses of the routers on the NBMA network.

OSPF communication on these network types is discussed in "OSPF Communication on OSPF Networks" later in this chapter.

Note The use of OSPF over nonpermanent, non-persistent, dial-up WAN links such as analog phone lines or ISDN is not recommended.

Synchronizing the LSDB Through Adjacencies

Link-state routing algorithms rely on the synchronization of LSDB information between routers in the AS. Rather than each router verifying synchronization with every other router in the AS, each router is only required to synchronize with its neighboring routers. The relationship between neighboring routers for the purposes of synchronizing the LSDB is called an adjacency. Adjacencies are required to compile the proper entries in the LSDB before the calculation of the SPF Tree and the entries in the routing table. Failure to establish adjacencies is one of the main problems in converging OSPF internetworks. For information about troubleshooting OSPF adjacencies, see "Troubleshooting OSPF" later in this chapter.

Forming an Adjacency

When an OSPF router initializes, it sends out a periodic OSPF Hello packet. The OSPF Hello packet contains configuration information such as the router's Router ID and the list of neighboring routers for which the router has received a Hello packet. Initially, the neighbor list in the OSPF Hello packet does not contain any neighbors.

The initializing OSPF router also listens for neighboring routers' Hello packets. From the incoming Hello packets, the initializing router determines the specific router or routers with which an adjacency is to be established. Adjacencies are formed with the designated router (DR) and backup designated router (BDR) which are identified in the incoming Hello packets. Designated routers and backup designated routers are discussed in more detail later in this chapter.

To begin the adjacency, the routers forming the adjacency describe the contents of their LSDBs through a sequence of Database Description Packets. This is known as the Database Exchange Process during which the two neighboring routers form a master/slave relationship. The contents of each router's LSDB is acknowledged by its neighboring router.

Each router compares its LSAs with the LSAs of its neighbor and notes which LSAs need to be requested from the neighbor to synchronize the LSDB. The missing or more recent LSAs are then requested through Link State Request packets. Link State Update packets are sent in response to the Link State Request packets and their receipt is acknowledged. When all Link State Requests of both routers have been satisfied, the LSDBs of the neighboring routers are fully synchronized and an adjacency is formed.

After the adjacency has formed, each neighboring router sends a periodic Hello packet to inform its neighbor that the router is still active on the network. The lack of Hello packets from a neighbor is used to detect a downed router.

If an event occurs such as a downed link or router or the addition of new network which changes the LSDB of one router, the LSDB of adjacent routers are no longer synchronized. The router whose LSDB has changed sends Link State Update packets to its adjacent neighbor. The receipt of the Link State Update packets is acknowledged. After the exchange, the LSDBs of the adjacent routers are once again synchronized.

Neighbor States

The neighboring routers go through a series of states during the establishment of an adjacency. Table 3.2 lists these states in the adjacency relationship in progressive order.

Table 3.2   Neighbor States for Adjacent Routers

Neighbor State	Description
Down	The initial state. No information has been received from the neighbor router.
Attempt	No information has been received despite attempts to contact the neighbor (for NBMA networks only).
Init	A Hello packet has been received from the neighbor, but the router does not appear in the neighbor list of the neighboring router's Hello packet.
2-Way	A Hello packet has been received from the neighbor, and the router does appear in the neighbor list of the neighboring router's Hello packet.
ExStart	Master and slave roles for the Database Exchange Process are being negotiated. This is the first phase of the adjacency relationship.
Exchange	The router is sending Database Description packets to its neighbor.
Loading	Link State Request packets are being sent to the neighbor requesting missing or more recent LSAs.
Full	The neighboring routers' LSDBs are synchronized, and the two routers are fully adjacent.

▶ **To view the neighbor state of neighboring routers**

- In the **Routing and Remote Access** snap-in, in the **IP Routing** container, right-click **OSPF**, and then click **Show Neighbors**.

  The **OSPF Neighbors** window displays all neighboring routers.

Because of the election of designated routers (DRs) and backup designated routers (BDRs), each OSPF router might not form an adjacency with each other router.

For those neighbor routers where an adjacency is established, **Full** should appear in the State column. For those neighbor routers where an adjacency is not established nor will be established because the router is not a DR or BDR, **2-way** should appear in the State column. Designated routers and backup designated routers are discussed later in this chapter.

Adjacency Configuration Parameters

A common OSPF problem is that an adjacency which should form between two neighboring routers does not. The following parameters *must match* between the two routers in order for an adjacency to be established:

- If authentication is being used, the neighboring routers must be using the same authentication type.
- If simple password authentication is enabled, the neighboring routers must be using the same password.
- The Hello Interval (default of 10 seconds), the periodic interval at which Hello packets are sent, must be the same.
- The Dead Interval (default of 40 seconds), the amount of time after which an adjacent router is considered down after ceasing to hear that router's Hello packets, must be the same. The RFC-recommended value is four times the Hello Interval.
- The Area ID, which identifies the area of the AS to which the router is attached, must be the same. The Area ID is configured on each router interface. Areas are discussed in more detail later in this chapter.
- The two neighbor routers must agree as to whether they are in a stub area or not. Stub areas are discussed in more detail later in this chapter.

The Router ID of the two neighboring routers *must not match* in order for an adjacency to be established. Router IDs are designed to be globally unique to the AS. Duplicate Router IDs prevent an adjacency.

Adding a Router to a Converged OSPF Internetwork

When a new OSPF router initializes on an existing and converged OSPF internetwork, the LSA for the new OSPF router must be propagated to all the OSPF routers in the internetwork through flooding. After the new LSA is received, each router must perform Dijkstra's algorithm, recalculate the SPF Tree, and create new routing table entries. After all the routing tables on all the routers are updated, the internetwork has converged.

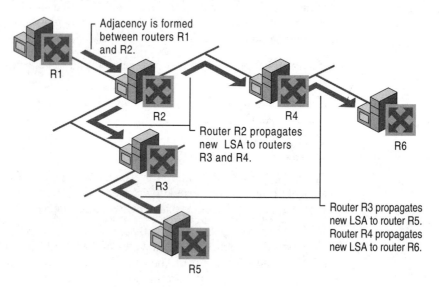

Figure 3.15   New Adjacency Propagation

Figure 3.15 illustrates the convergence process for a new router and new adjacency propagation in a sample OSPF internetwork.

1. Router R1 initializes and begins sending periodic Hello packets across the point-to-point WAN link. Router R2 also sends periodic Hello packets across the link. R1 and R2 decide to form an adjacency.

2. R1 and R2 exchange Database Description Packets. R1's Database Description Packet contains only information about itself. R2's Database Description Packet contains the latest LSAs of all the routers in the internetwork (except R1).

3. R1 sends a Link State Request packet to R2 requesting the LSAs of all the routers on the internetwork. R2 sends the requested LSAs to R1 as Link State Update packets.

4. R2 sends a Link State Request packet to R1 requesting its LSA. R1 sends its LSA to R2 as a Link State Update packet. R1 and R2 now have synchronized LSDBs. Upon receipt of the LSAs, R1 and R2 calculate their respective SPF trees and routing tables.

5. Once synchronized with R1, R2 sends a Link State Update packet to all other OSPF routers to which it is adjacent (routers R3 and R4). The Link State Update packet contains the LSA learned from R1. Upon receipt of the LSA from R2, R3 and R4 calculate their respective SPF trees and routing tables.

6. R3 and R4 flood the information in a separate Link State Update packet to their adjacent routers (routers R5 and R6). Upon receipt of the flooded LSA for R1, R5 and R6 calculate their respective SPF trees and routing tables.

The OSPF internetwork has reconverged after adding R1 and its associated network.

Designated Routers

On a point-to-point link (such as a dedicated WAN link), the adjacency must occur between the two routers on either side of the link. However, on multi-access networks (such as broadcast or NBMA networks) the adjacencies must be controlled. Consider a broadcast network with 6 OSPF routers. Without controlling the adjacency behavior, each router could establish an adjacency with each other router for a total of 15 adjacency relationships. On a broadcast network with n routers, a total of $n*(n-1)/2$ adjacencies would be formed. The number of adjacencies scales as $O(n^2)$. In addition, unneeded flooding traffic would occur as each router attempts to synchronize with all of its adjacent routers.

To solve this scaling problem, every multi-access network (broadcast and NBMA) elects a Designated Router (DR). The DR forms adjacencies with all other routers on the network. On a broadcast network with n routers, a total of $(n-1)$ adjacencies need to be formed. Because the DR is adjacent with all other routers, it acts as a hub for the distribution of link state information and the LSDB synchronization process.

The DR is elected through the exchange of OSPF Hello packets. Each Hello packet contains the current DR (if elected), the sending router's Router ID, and the sending router's Router Priority. The Router Priority is an interface-specific OSPF configuration parameter that is used to elect the DR. The router with the highest Router Priority is elected the DR. The default Router Priority is 1. A Router Priority of 0 means that the router does not become a DR. If multiple routers have the same highest Router Priority, the router with the highest Router ID is elected the DR.

Caution Router Priorities must be assigned so that at least one router on the multi-access network (broadcast or NBMA) is configured with a Router Priority of 1 or greater. If all routers on a multi-access network are configured with a Router Priority of 0, no router becomes the DR and no adjacencies are established. Without adjacencies, the LSDB cannot be synchronized and no transit traffic (traffic across that network) can be passed.

Note If a DR is already elected for a network, an initializing router on the network does not become the DR if it has a higher Router Priority than the current DR.

DRs on Broadcast Networks

Figure 3.16 illustrates the utility of the DR on a broadcast network. Without a DR, six separate adjacencies would be formed on a broadcast network containing four routers. The redundant adjacencies consume local and network resources maintaining the adjacencies and propagating changes to the LSDB.

With a DR, only three adjacencies are needed to maintain synchronization of the LSDB.

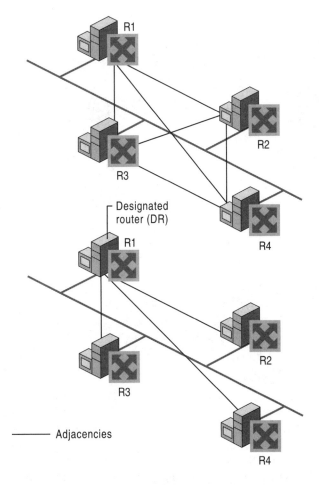

Figure 3.16   Designated Routers on Broadcast Networks

DRs on NBMA Nets

For NBMA networks, such as a Frame Relay network in a hub and spoke configuration, the DR must be the hub router because only the hub router can communicate with all the other routers. To ensure that the hub router is the DR, set its Router Priority to 1 (or greater). To ensure that no spoke router becomes a DR, set spoke router Router Priorities to 0.

Figure 3.17 illustrates a DR in a Frame Relay network.

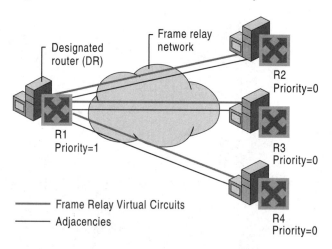

Figure 3.17   Designated Routers on a Frame Relay Network

Backup Designated Router

The DR acts as a central distribution point for topological changes on a multi-access network. If the DR becomes unavailable, all new adjacencies must be formed with a new DR. Until the adjacencies form and the internetwork converges, a temporary loss of connectivity for transit traffic might result.

To prevent the loss in connectivity associated with the loss of a DR, a Backup Designated Router (BDR) is also elected for each multi-access network. Like the DR, the BDR is adjacent to all routers on the network. When the DR fails, the BDR immediately becomes the DR by sending LSAs to all of its adjacent routers announcing its new role. There is a very short period of time where transit traffic could be impaired as the BDR takes over the role of the DR.

Like the DR, the BDR is elected by the exchange of Hello packets. Each Hello packet contains a field for the BDR of the network. If the BDR is not specified, the router with the highest Router Priority that is not already the DR becomes the BDR. If there are multiple routers with the highest Router Priority, the router with the highest Router ID is elected the BDR.

Interface States

Each OSPF interface can be in one of several states after forming adjacencies. Table 3.3 lists the possible interface states.

Table 3.3   Interface States for Adjacent Routers

Interface State	Description
Down	The initial interface state. No Hello packets have been sent or received.
Loopback	The interface to the network is looped back (internally configured so that no packets are sent) through hardware or software.
Waiting	The interface is sending and receiving Hello packets to determine the DR and BDR for the network.
Point-to-Point	The interface is adjacent to its neighbor on a point-to-point network or through a virtual link.
Other	The interface is on a multi-access network and is not the DR or BDR.
Designated Router	The interface is the DR for the attached network.
Backup Designated Router	The interface is the BDR for the attached network.

To view the interface state for an OSPF interface on a Windows 2000 OSPF router, in the **Routing and Remote Access** snap-in, in the **IP Routing** container, click **OSPF**. The contents pane displays the OSPF interfaces. The **State** column indicates the interface's current state. By viewing the interface state for each OSPF interface on a given network, you can determine the DR and the BDR for the network.

OSPF Communication on OSPF Networks

The way in which OSPF routers address OSPF packets varies with the OSPF network type.

Broadcast Networks For broadcast networks, OSPF routers use the following two reserved IP multicast addresses:

- 224.0.0.5 - AllSPFRouters: Used to send OSPF messages to all OSPF routers on the same network. The AllSPFRouters address is used for Hello packets. The DR and BDR use this address to send Link State Update and Link State Acknowledgment packets.

- 224.0.0.6 - AllDRouters: Used to send OSPF messages to all OSPF DRs (the DR and the BDR) on the same network. All OSPF routers except the DR use this address when sending Link State Update and Link State Acknowledgment packets to the DR.

Point-to-Point Networks Point-to-Point networks use the AllSPFRouters address (224.0.0.5) for all OSPF messages.

NBMA Networks NBMA networks have no multicasting capability. Therefore, the destination IP address of any Hello or Link State packets is the unicast IP address of a specific neighbor. The neighbor IP address is a required part of OSPF configuration for NBMA network links.

OSPF Areas

In a very large AS with a large number of networks, each OSPF router must keep the LSA of every other router in its LSDB. Each router in a large OSPF AS has a large LSDB. The SPF calculation of a large LSDB can require a substantial amount of processing. Also, the resulting routing table can be very large, containing a route to each network in the AS.

In an effort to reduce the size of the LSDB and the processing overhead for the SPF tree and routing table calculation, OSPF allows the AS to be divided up into contiguous groups of networks called areas. Areas are identified through a 32-bit Area ID expressed in dotted decimal notation.

An Area ID is an administrative identifier and has no relation to an IP address or IP network ID. Area IDs are not used to reflect routing data. However, if all of the networks within an area correspond to a single subnetted network ID, the area ID can be set to reflect the network ID for administrative convenience. For example, if an area contains all of the subnets of the IP network 10.1.0.0, the area ID can be set to 10.1.0.0.

Reducing the Size of the LSDB

To keep the size of the LSDB for each router to a minimum, LSAs for an area's networks and routers are flooded within the area but not to routers outside the area. Each area becomes its own link state domain with its own LSDB.

If a router is connected to multiple areas, it has multiple LSDBs and SPF Trees. The routing table is a combination of the routing table entries of all the SPF Trees for the router as well as static routes, SNMP configured routes, and routes learned from other routing protocols.

Reducing the Size of the Routing Table

To reduce the number of entries in the routing table of OSPF routers, the networks inside of the area can be advertised outside the area using summary route advertisements. In Figure 3.18, the router on the border of Area 0.0.0.1, known as an area border router (ABR), advertises a summary of all of the networks inside Area 0.0.0.1 in the form of [Destination, Network Mask] pairs to the ABRs of Area 0.0.0.2 and Area 0.0.0.3. Through route summarization, the topology (the networks and their path costs) of an area is hidden from the rest of the AS.

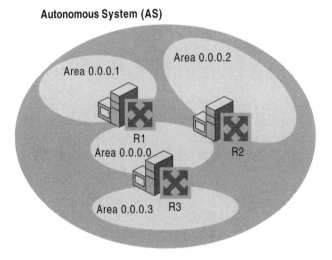

Figure 3.18   OSPF AS and Areas

When the topology of an area is hidden, the rest of the AS is protected from route flapping, events that cause networks to come up or go down. If a network comes up, the event is propagated as a Link State Update and flooded through adjacencies to routers within the area. However, because all the networks within the area are advertised outside the area using summary routes, the Link State Update is not flooded outside the area.

You can view the current OSPF areas by right-clicking the **OSPF** routing protocol and clicking **Show Areas** in the **Routing and Remote Access** snap-in.

Backbone Area

An OSPF internetwork, whether or not it is subdivided into areas, always has at least one area called the backbone. The backbone has the reserved area ID of 0.0.0.0. The OSPF backbone area is also known as area 0.

The backbone acts as a hub for inter-area transit traffic and the distribution of routing information between areas. Inter-area traffic is routed to the backbone, then routed to the destination area, and finally routed to the destination host within the destination area (for more information, see "Inter-Area Routing" later in this chapter). Routers on the backbone also advertise the summarized routes within their areas to the other routers on the backbone. These summary advertisements are flooded into area routers. Therefore, each router in an area has a routing table that reflects the routes available within its area and the routes corresponding to the summary advertisements of the ABRs of the other areas in the AS.

For example, in Figure 3.18, router R1 advertises all of the routes (the list of address ranges) in Area 0.0.0.1 to all backbone routers (routers R2 and R3) using a summary advertisement. R1 receives summary advertisements from R2 and R3. R1 is configured with summary advertisement information for Area 0.0.0.0. Through flooding, R1 propagates that summary routing information to all of the routers within Area 0.0.0.1. For each router within Area 0.0.0.1, the summary routing information from Areas 0.0.0.0, 0.0.0.2, and 0.0.0.3 is incorporated into the calculation of the routing table.

OSPF Router Types

When an OSPF AS is subdivided into areas, the routers are classified by one or more of the categories defined in Table 3.4.

Table 3.4   OSPF Router Types

Router Type	Description
Internal Router	A router with all interfaces connected to the same area. Internal routers each have a single LSDB.
Area Border Router (ABR)	A router with interfaces connected to different areas. ABRs have multiple LSDBs, one for each attached area.
Backbone Router	A router with an interface on the backbone area. This includes all ABRs and internal routers of the backbone area.
AS Boundary Router (ASBR)	A router that exchanges routes with sources outside of the OSPF AS. ASBRs advertise external routes throughout the OSPF AS.

Inter-Area Routing

Routing within an area is performed by OSPF routers using the least cost path to the destination network. Because routes within an area are not summarized, each router has a route to each network within its area or areas.

Routing between areas takes the following course:

1. Routers within the source area forward the packet along the least cost path to the nearest ABR.
2. Backbone routers forward the packet along the least cost path to the nearest ABR connected to the area containing the IP address of the destination host.
3. Routers within the area containing the IP address of the destination host forward the packet along the least cost path to the destination host.

In Figure 3.19, the packet is forwarded across the routers of Area 0.0.0.1 to router R1, a backbone area router. Then, the packet is forwarded across the routers of the backbone area (Area 0.0.0.0) to Router R2. And finally, the packet is forwarded across the routers of Area 0.0.0.2 to the destination host.

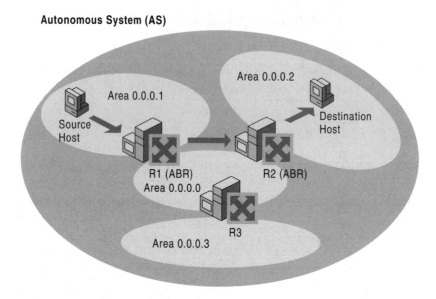

Figure 3.19   Inter-Area Routing in OSPF

Note OSPF routers do not make routing decisions based on area IDs. All routing decisions are based on the entries in the IP routing table. For example, in the inter-area routing shown in Figure 3.19, the backbone routers are not explicitly forwarding the packet to Area 0.0.0.2. They are forwarding it along the least cost path to the route that is the best match for the destination IP address in the packet.

Virtual Links

It is possible to define areas in such a way that they do not have an ABR physically connected to the backbone. Backbone connectivity for the area is still possible by configuring a virtual link between the non-backbone area and the backbone.

Virtual links can be configured between any two routers that have an interface to a single common non-backbone area. The common non-backbone area is known as the transit area. The transit area must have an ABR that is connected to the backbone. Virtual links cannot be configured across multiple transit areas.

A virtual link is not a physical link. It is a logical link using the least cost path between the ABR of the non-backbone connected area and the backbone ABR of the transit area. A virtual adjacency across the virtual link is formed, and routing information is exchanged. Just as in physical adjacencies, the settings of the two virtual link routers (such as the password, the Hello Interval, and Dead Interval) must match before an adjacency can be successfully established.

In Figure 3.20, Area 0.0.0.3 does not have a router physically connected to the backbone, Area 0.0.0.0. Therefore, a virtual link is configured across the transit area of Area 0.0.0.2 between routers R2 and R3. R2 and R3 are known as virtual link neighbors.

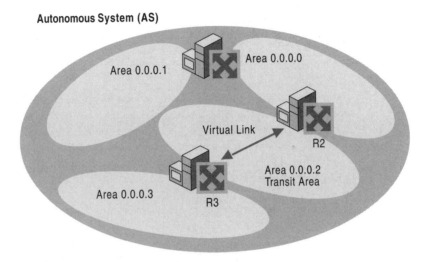

Figure 3.20   OSPF Virtual Link

Configuring Virtual Links

To configure a virtual link, configure a virtual interface in the **Routing and Remote Access** snap-in from the properties of the **OSPF** routing protocol on each virtual link neighbor with the following:

- The Area ID of the transit area for the virtual link.
- The OSPF Router ID of the virtual link neighbor.
- Adjacency settings such as the Retransmit Interval, Hello Interval, Dead Interval, and Password. The Hello Interval, Dead Interval, and Password must match between the two routers on each side of the virtual link in order for an adjacency to be established. The Retransmit Interval specifies how long the OSPF router waits before retransmitting Link State packets.

▶ **To view the virtual links**

- In the **Routing and Remote Access** snap-in, in the **IP Routing** container, right-click **OSPF**, and then click **Show Virtual Interfaces**.

    The **Virtual Interfaces** window displays all configured virtual interfaces and their state.

External Routes

An external route is defined as any route that is not within the OSPF AS. External routes can come from many sources:

- Other routing protocols such as RIP for IP (v1 and v2), EGP, or BGP.
- Static routes.
- Routes set on the router through SNMP.

External routes are learned and propagated throughout the OSPF AS through one or more ASBRs. The ASBR advertises the availability of external routes using a series of external route LSAs. The external route LSAs are flooded throughout the AS (except in stub areas) and become part of the SPF Tree and routing table calculation. Traffic to external networks is routed within the AS using the least cost path to the ASBR.

Figure 3.21 shows an AS with an ASBR and external routes.

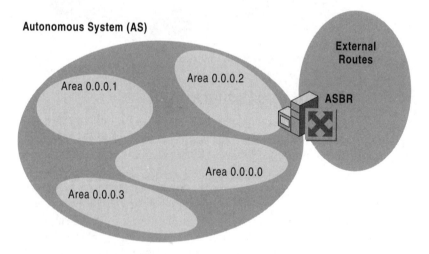

Figure 3.21   OSPF External Routes

External Route Filters

By default, OSPF routers acting as ASBRs import and advertise all external routes. You might want to filter out external routes to protect the AS from improper or malicious routing information.

For the Windows 2000 Router, external routes can be filtered on the ASBR by the external route source or by the individual route. You can configure the ASBR to accept or ignore the routes of certain external sources such as routing protocols (RIP v2) or other sources (static routes or SNMP). You can also configure the ASBR to accept or discard specific routes by configuring one or multiple [Destination, Network Mask] pairs.

A combination of these filters configured at the ASBR can ensure that the OSPF AS only receives the correct external routes from the proper sources.

ASBRs and Default Routes

When a router is configured to be an ASBR, it advertises by default all external routes including its own default static route. This default route needs to be valid for all OSPF routers in your AS. An example of an invalid default route is one that points to another router within the OSPF AS. The router used as the default gateway ends up with a default route with the next hop IP address of itself. If this occurs, the packets forwarded using the default route on that router are dropped.

If the default route is not valid for all OSPF routers, it should not be advertised. A valid default route would have the next hop gateway address external to your OSPF AS. This route would only be configured on the router that can directly reach the external network.

There are two ways to avoid this problem:

1. Do not configure a default gateway on the ASBR.
2. If the ASBR must have a default gateway, create an OSPF external route filter to filter out its own default route (destination of 0.0.0.0 with a network mask of 0.0.0.0).

Stub Areas

To further reduce the amount of routing information flooded into areas, OSPF allows the use of stub areas. A stub area can contain a single entry and exit point (a single ABR), or multiple ABRs when any of the ABRs can be used to reach external route destinations. For stub areas with multiple ABRs, the external routes are advertised by an ASBR that is outside of the area. AS external routes are not flooded into and throughout a stub area. Routing to all AS external networks in a stub area is done through a default route (destination 0.0.0.0 with the network mask of 0.0.0.0). Thus, a single entry in the routing tables of the routers in a stub area is used to route to all AS external locations.

To create the default route, the ABR of a stub area advertises a default route into the stub area. The default route is flooded to all the routers within the stub area, but not outside the stub area. The default route is used by the routers in a stub area for any destination IP address that is not reachable within the AS.

For example, Area 0.0.0.3 in Figure 3.22 is configured as a stub area because all external traffic must travel through its single ABR, router R3. R3 advertises a default route for distribution inside Area 0.0.0.3 instead of flooding the AS external networks into the area.

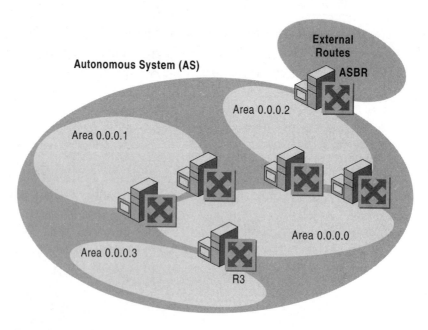

Figure 3.22   OSPF Stub Areas

All routers in a stub area must be configured so that they do not import or flood AS external routes within the stub area. Therefore, all area configurations for all router interfaces within a stub area must be configured for a stub area. Whether or not a router interface is in a stub area is indicated in a special option bit called the E-bit in the OSPF Hello packet. When the E-bit is set to 1, the router is allowed to accept and flood AS external routes. When the E-bit is set to 0, the router is not allowed to accept and flood AS external routes. Routers receiving Hello packets on interfaces verify that the E-bit of the received Hello packet matches their configuration before establishing an adjacency.

Stub areas have the following constraints:

- Virtual links cannot be configured using a stub area as a transit area.
- An ASBR cannot be placed inside a stub area.

Stub areas as defined in the OSPF RFC collapse all external routes into a single default route. Therefore, within a stub area, a router's routing table contains intra-area routes, inter-area routes, and a default route. The Windows 2000 Router also supports the collapsing of all non-intra-area routes into a single default route. This is known as a totally stubby area. A router's routing table within a totally stubby area contains intra-area routes and a default route. The default route summarizes all inter-area routes and all external routes.

To configure a stub area on a Windows 2000 Router, when configuring general properties for an area, select the **Stub area** check box and select the **Import summary advertisements** check box. To configure a totally stubby area on a Windows 2000 Router, select the **Stub area** check box but do not select the **Import summary advertisements** check box.

Troubleshooting OSPF

If an OSPF environment is properly configured, OSPF routers learn all the least cost routes from adjacent OSPF routers after convergence. The exact list of routes added by OSPF to the IP routing table depends, among other factors, on whether or not areas are configured to summarize their routes, whether or not stub areas or totally stubby areas are being used, and whether or not ASBRs and route filtering is being used.

Most OSPF problems are related to the formation of adjacencies, either physical or logical (through virtual links). If adjacencies cannot form, the LSDBs cannot be synchronized and the OSPF routes will not accurately reflect the topology of the internetwork. Other OSPF problems are related to the lack of routes or existence of improper routes in the IP routing table.

Adjacency Is Not Forming

- Before proceeding, verify that the two neighboring routers *should* form an adjacency. If the two routers are the only routers on the network, an adjacency should form. If there are more than two routers on the network, adjacencies only form with the DR and BDR. If the two routers have already formed adjacencies with the DR and the BDR, they will not form adjacencies with each other. In this case, their neighbor should appear as **2-way** under neighbor state.

- Ping the neighboring router to ensure basic IP and network connectivity. Use the **tracert** command to trace the route to the neighboring router. There should not be any routers between the neighboring routers.

- Use OSPF logging to log errors and warnings to record information about why the adjacency is not forming. To obtain additional information about OSPF processes, enable tracing for the OSPF component. For more information about tracing, see "Routing and Remote Access Service" in this book.

- Verify that the areas are enabled for authentication and the OSPF interfaces are using the same password. Windows 2000 OSPF routers have authentication enabled by default and the default password is "12345678". Change the authentication to match all neighboring OSPF routers on the same network. The password can vary per network.

- Verify that the routers are configured for the same Hello Interval and Dead Interval. By default the Hello Interval is 10 seconds and the Dead Interval is 40 seconds.

- Verify that the routers agree as to whether the area to which the common network belongs is a stub area or not.

- Verify that the interfaces of the neighboring routers are configured with the same Area ID.

- If the routers are on a Non-Broadcast Multiple Access (NBMA) network such as X.25 or Frame Relay and the connection to the NBMA network appears as a single adapter (rather than separate adapters for each virtual circuit), their neighbors must be manually configured using the unicast IP address of the neighbor or neighbors to which the link state information needs to be sent. Also verify that Router Priorities are configured so that one router can become the DR for the network.

- On broadcast networks (Ethernet, Token Ring, FDDI) or NBMA networks (X.25, Frame Relay), verify that all routers do not have a Router Priority of 0. At least one router must have a Router Priority of 1 or greater so that it can become the DR for the network.

- Verify that IP packet filtering is not preventing the receiving (through input filters) or sending (through output filters) of OSPF messages on the router interfaces enabled for OSPF. OSPF uses the IP protocol number 89.

- Verify that TCP/IP packet filtering is not preventing the receiving of OSPF messages on the interfaces enabled for OSPF.

Virtual Link Is Not Forming

- Verify that the virtual link neighbor routers are configured for the same password, Hello Interval, and Dead Interval.

- For each router, verify that the virtual link neighbor's Router ID is correctly configured.

- Verify that both virtual link neighbors are configured for the correct transit area ID.

- For large internetworks with substantial round-trip delays across the transit area, verify that the re-transmit interval is long enough.

Lack of OSPF Routes or Existence of Improper OSPF Routes

- If you are not receiving summarized OSPF routes for an area, verify that all the ABRs for the area are configured with the proper {Destination, Network Mask} pairs summarizing that area's routes.

- If you are receiving both individual and summarized OSPF routes for an area, verify that all the ABRs for the area are configured with the proper {Destination, Network Mask} pairs summarizing that area's routes.

- If you are not receiving external routes from the ASBR, verify that the source and route filtering configured on the ASBR is not too restrictive, preventing proper routes from being propagated to the OSPF AS. External source and route filtering is configured on the **External Routing** tab on the properties of the **OSPF** routing protocol in the **Routing and Remote Access** snap-in.

- Verify that all ABRs are either physically connected to the backbone or logically connected to the backbone using a virtual link. There should not be backdoor routers—routers connecting two areas without going through the backbone.

DHCP Relay Agent

The Windows 2000 Router is an RFC 1542–compliant Boot Protocol (BOOTP) relay agent relaying Dynamic Host Configuration Protocol (DHCP) messages between DHCP clients and DHCP servers on different IP networks. In this role, the Windows 2000 Router functions as the DHCP Relay Agent. Without a DHCP Relay Agent, a DHCP server is required on every subnet that contains DHCP clients. The DHCP Relay Agent takes broadcasted DHCP messages from DHCP clients and forwards them to the IP addresses of DHCP servers. The responses from the DHCP server are sent to the IP address of the DHCP Relay Agent, which then forwards them to the DHCP client.

For more information about DHCP and its implementation in Windows 2000, see "Dynamic Host Configuration Protocol" in the *Microsoft® Windows® 2000 Server Resource Kit TCP/IP Core Networking Guide*.

DHCP Across IP Routers

In a large IP internetwork, DHCP servers should be placed in strategic locations servicing DHCP clients of multiple networks. For this configuration to work effectively, DHCP messages must be able to cross IP routers using a DHCP Relay Agent.

In addition to propagating DHCP messages, a DHCP Relay Agent takes an active role in recording information necessary for DHCP configuration and helps direct DHCP messages between the DHCP server and the DHCP client.

Initial DHCP Configuration

Initial DHCP configuration is done by a DHCP client that has never leased an IP address, has released its IP address, or has received a DHCPNack in response to attempting to lease a previous IP address. The initial DHCP configuration process consists of four DHCP messages: DHCPDiscover, DHCPOffer, DHCPRequest, DHCPAck.

DHCPDiscover

The DHCP client sends the DHCPDiscover, containing the MAC address of the DHCP client, to the limited broadcast IP address (255.255.255.255) and the MAC-level broadcast address. The DHCP Relay Agent receives and processes the DHCPDiscover.

As established in RFC 1542, the DHCP Relay Agent can forward the packet to an IP broadcast, multicast, or unicast address. In practice, DHCP Relay Agents forward DHCPDiscover messages to unicast IP addresses which correspond to DHCP servers. Before forwarding the original DHCPDiscover message, the DHCP Relay Agent makes the following changes:

- Increments the Hop Count field in the DHCP header. The DHCP Hop Count field is separate from the Time to Live (TTL) field in the IP header and is used to indicate on how many networks this DHCPDiscover has existed as a broadcast. When the configured maximum Hop Count is exceeded, the DHCPDiscover is silently discarded. The default maximum hop count for the Windows 2000 DHCP Relay Agent is 4.

- If needed, updates the Relay IP Address field (also known as the Gateway IP Address field) in the DHCP header. When the DHCP client sends the DHCPDiscover message, the Relay IP Address field is set to 0.0.0.0. If the Relay IP Address is 0.0.0.0, the DHCP Relay Agent records the IP address of the interface on which the DHCPDiscover message was received. If the Relay IP Address is not 0.0.0.0, the DHCP Relay Agent does not modify it. The Relay IP Address field records the first router interface encountered by the DHCPDiscover message.

- Changes the source IP address of the DHCPDiscover message to the IP address of the interface on which the broadcasted DHCPDiscover was received.

- Changes the destination IP address of the DHCPDiscover message to the configured unicast address of the DHCP server.

The DHCP Relay Agent sends the DHCPDiscover message as a unicasted IP packet rather than as an IP and MAC-level broadcast. If the DHCP Relay Agent is configured with multiple DHCP servers, it sends each DHCP server a copy of the DHCPDiscover message.

DHCPOffer

When responding to the DHCP client's request for an IP address, the DHCP server uses the Relay IP Address field in the following ways:

- The Relay IP Address and the subnet masks of the server's configured scopes are compared through a logical **AND** comparison to find a scope whose network ID matches the network ID of the Relay IP Address. When a match is found, the DHCP server allocates an IP address from that scope.

- When sending the offer back to the client, the DHCP server sends the DHCPOffer message to the Relay IP Address as the destination IP address.

Once received by the DHCP Relay Agent, the Relay IP Address is used to determine which interface to which the DHCPOffer message is to be forwarded. It then forwards the DHCPOffer message to the client using the offered IP address as the destination IP address and the client's MAC address as the destination MAC address.

DHCPRequest

As it does with the DHCPDiscover message, the DHCP client sends the DHCPRequest message, containing the MAC address of the client, to the limited IP broadcast address 255.255.255.255 and to the MAC-level broadcast address. The DHCP Relay Agent receives this packet and forwards it as a directed IP packet to the configured DHCP server or servers.

DHCPAck

The DHCP server initially sends the DHCPAck message to the Relay IP Address, as it did with the DHCPOffer message. When the DHCP Relay Agent receives the DHCPAck message, it re-addresses it to the client's offered IP address and MAC address.

Rebooted Renewal

When a Microsoft-based DHCP client shuts down, it does not send a DHCPRELEASE message to the DHCP server. Instead, when the DHCP client restarts, it attempts to obtain the IP address it was last using through a DHCPRequest and DHCPAck exchange of messages.

DHCPRequest

When a Microsoft-based DHCP client reboots, it attempts to lease its previously allocated IP address through a broadcasted DHCPRequest message. The DHCPRequest, sent to the limited IP broadcast address 255.255.255.255 and to the MAC-level broadcast address, contains the MAC address and the previously allocated IP address of the client. The DHCP Relay Agent receives this packet and treats the message in much the same way as a DHCPDiscover message. Before forwarding, the DHCP Relay Agent:

- Increments the Hop Count field in the DHCP header.

- Records the IP address of the interface on which the DHCPRequest message was received in the Relay IP Address field.

- Changes the source IP address to the IP address of the interface on which the broadcasted DHCPDiscover message was received.

- Changes the destination IP address to the unicast address of the DHCP server recorded in the DHCPRequest and forwards it as a directed IP packet.

DHCPAck and DHCPNack

When the DHCP server receives the DHCPRequest, it compares the network ID of client's previously allocated IP address to the network ID of the Relay IP Address.

- If the two network IDs are the same and the IP address can be reallocated to the DHCP client, the DHCP server initially sends a DHCPAck to the IP address found in the Relay IP Address field. When the DHCP Relay Agent receives the DHCPAck, it re-addresses it to the client's offered IP address and MAC address.

- If the two network IDs are the same and the IP address cannot be reallocated to the DHCP client, the DHCP server initially sends a DHCPNack to the IP address found in the Relay IP Address field. When the DHCP Relay Agent receives the DHCPNack, it re-addresses it to the client's offered IP address and MAC address. At this point, the DHCP client must restart the IP address allocation process with a DHCPDiscover.

- If the two network IDs are not the same, the DHCP client has moved to a different subnet, and the DHCP server sends a DHCPNack to the IP address found in the Relay IP Address field. When the DHCP Relay Agent receives the DHCPNack, it re-addresses it to the client's offered IP address and MAC address. At this point, the DHCP client must restart the IP address allocation process with a DHCPDiscover.

Troubleshooting the DHCP Relay Agent

If the Windows 2000 DHCP Relay Agent is not providing relay services for DHCP clients on a network, check for the following:

- Verify that the interface on the Windows 2000 Router that connects to the network where the DHCP clients are located is added to the DHCP Relay Agent IP routing protocol.

- Verify that the **Relay DHCP packets** check box is selected for the DHCP Relay Agent interface connected to the network where the DHCP clients are located.

- Verify that the IP addresses of DHCP servers configured on the global properties of the DHCP Relay Agent are the correct IP addresses for DHCP servers on your internetwork.

- From the router with the DHCP Relay Agent enabled, use the PING utility to ping each of the DHCP servers configured in the global DHCP Relay Agent dialog. If you cannot ping the DHCP servers from the DHCP Relay Agent router, troubleshoot the lack of connectivity between the DHCP Relay Agent router and the DHCP server or servers.

- Verify that IP packet filtering is not preventing the receiving (through input filters) or sending (through output filters) of DHCP traffic. DHCP traffic uses the UDP ports of 67 and 68.

- Verify that TCP/IP filtering on the router interfaces is not preventing the receiving of DHCP traffic.

Network Address Translator

A Network Address Translator (NAT) is an IP router defined in RFC 1631 that can translate IP addresses and TCP/UDP port numbers of packets as they are being forwarded. Consider a small business network with multiple computers connecting to the Internet. A small business would normally have to obtain an Internet Service Provider (ISP)–allocated public IP address for each computer on their network. With the NAT, however, the small business can use private addressing (as described in RFC 1597) and have the NAT map its private addresses to a single or to multiple public IP addresses as allocated by its ISP.

For example, if a small business is using the 10.0.0.0 private network for its intranet and has been granted the public IP address of 198.200.200.1 by its ISP, the NAT maps (using static or dynamic mappings) all private IP addresses being used on network 10.0.0.0 to the public IP address of 198.200.200.1.

When a private user on the small business intranet connects to an Internet resource, the user's IP stack creates an IP packet with the following values set in the IP and TCP or UDP headers (bold text indicates the fields changed by the NAT):

- Destination IP Address: Internet resource IP address
- Source IP Address: **Private IP address**
- Destination Port: Internet resource TCP or UDP port
- Source Port: **Source application TCP or UDP port**

The source host or another router forwards this IP packet to the NAT, which translates the addresses of the outgoing packet as follows (bold text indicates the fields changed by the NAT):

- Destination IP Address: Internet resource IP address
- Source IP Address: **ISP-allocated public address**
- Destination Port: Internet resource TCP or UDP port
- Source Port: **Remapped source application TCP or UDP port**

The NAT sends the remapped IP packet over the Internet. The responding computer sends back the response to the NAT. When received by the NAT, the packet contains the following addressing information (bold text indicates the fields changed by the NAT):

- Destination IP Address: **ISP-allocated public address**
- Source IP Address: Internet resource IP address
- Destination Port: **Remapped source application TCP or UDP port**
- Source Port: Internet resource TCP or UDP port

When the NAT maps and translates the addresses and forwards the packet to the intranet client, it contains the following addressing information (bold text indicates the fields changed by the NAT):

- Destination IP Address: **Private IP address**
- Source IP Address: Internet resource IP address
- Destination Port: **Source application TCP or UDP port**
- Source Port: Internet resource TCP or UDP port

For outgoing packets, the source IP address and TCP/UDP port numbers are mapped to a public source IP address and a possibly changed TCP/UDP port number. For incoming packets, the destination IP address and TCP/UDP port numbers are mapped to the private IP address and original TCP/UDP port number.

Static and Dynamic Address Mapping

The NAT can use either static or dynamic mapping. A static mapping is configured so that traffic is always mapped a specific way. You could map all traffic to and from a specific private network location to a specific Internet location. For instance, to set up a Web server on a computer on your private network, you create a static mapping that maps [Public IP Address, TCP Port 80] to [Private IP Address, TCP Port 80].

Dynamic mappings are created when users on the private network initiate traffic with Internet locations. The NAT automatically adds these mappings to its mapping table and refreshes them with each use. Dynamic mappings that are not refreshed are removed from the NAT mapping table after a configurable amount of time. For TCP connections, the default time-out is 24 hours. For UDP traffic, the default time-out is one minute.

Proper Translation of Header Fields

By default, a NAT translates IP addresses and TCP/UDP ports. These modifications to the IP datagram require the modification and recalculation of the following fields in the IP, TCP, and UDP headers:

- Source IP Address (outbound from private network), Destination IP Address (inbound to private network)
- IP Checksum
- Source Port (outbound from private network), Destination Port (inbound to private network)
- TCP Checksum
- UDP Checksum

If the IP address and port information is only in the IP and TCP/UDP headers—for example, with HTTP (or World Wide Web) traffic, the application protocol can be translated transparently. There are applications and protocols, however, that carry IP or port addressing information within their headers. FTP, for example, stores the dotted decimal representation of IP addresses in the FTP header for the FTP **port** command. If the NAT does not properly translate the IP address, connectivity problems can occur. Additionally, in the case of FTP, because the IP address is stored in dotted decimal format, the translated IP address in the FTP header can be a different size. Therefore, the NAT must also modify TCP sequence numbers to ensure that no data is lost.

NAT Editors

In the case where the NAT component must additionally translate and adjust the payload beyond the IP, TCP, and UDP headers, a NAT editor is required. A NAT editor is an installable component that can properly modify otherwise nontranslatable payloads so that they can be forwarded across a NAT.

Windows 2000 includes built-in NAT editors for the following protocols:

- FTP
- ICMP
- PPTP
- NetBIOS over TCP/IP

Additionally, the NAT routing protocol includes proxy software for the following protocols:

- H.323
- Direct Play
- LDAP-based ILS registration
- RPC

Note IPSec traffic is not translatable.

NAT Processes in the Windows 2000 Router

For the Windows 2000 Routing and Remote Access service, the NAT component is a routing protocol known as Network Address Translation or NAT. The NAT component can either be enabled by adding Network Address Translation as a routing protocol in the Routing and Remote Access snap-in.

Note NAT services are also available with the Internet connection sharing feature available from the Network and Dial-up Connections folder. Internet connection sharing performs the same function as the NAT routing protocol in the Routing and Remote Access service but it allows very little configuration flexibility. For information about configuring Internet connection sharing and why you would choose Internet connection sharing over the NAT routing protocol of the Routing and Remote Access service, see Windows 2000 Server Help.

Installed with the NAT routing protocol are a series of NAT editors. NAT consults the editors when the payload of the packet being translated matches one of the installed editors. The editors modify the payload and return the result to the NAT component.

NAT interacts with the TCP/IP protocol in two important ways:

- To support dynamic port mappings, the NAT component requests unique TCP and UDP port numbers from the TCP/IP protocol stack when needed.
- With TCP/IP so that packets being sent between the private network and the Internet are first passed to the NAT component for translation.

Figure 3.23 shows the NAT components and their relation to TCP/IP and other router components.

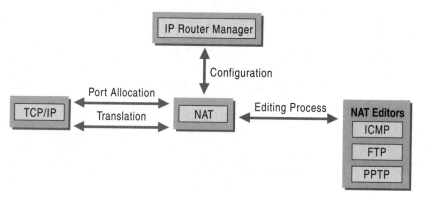

Figure 3.23   NAT Components

Outbound Internet Traffic

For traffic from the private network that is outbound on the Internet interface, the NAT first assesses whether or not an address/port mapping, static or dynamic, exists for the packet. If not, a dynamic mapping is created. The NAT creates a mapping depending on whether there are single or multiple public IP addresses available.

- If a single public IP address is available, the NAT requests a new unique TCP or UDP port for the public IP address and uses that as the mapped port.
- If multiple public IP addresses are available, the NAT performs private IP address to public IP address mapping. For these mappings, the ports are not translated. When the last public IP address is needed, the NAT switches to performing address and port mapping as it would in the case of the single public IP address.

After mapping, the NAT checks for editors and invokes one if necessary. After editing, the NAT modifies the TCP, UDP, and IP headers and forwards the frame using the Internet interface.

Figure 3.24 shows the NAT processing for outbound Internet traffic.

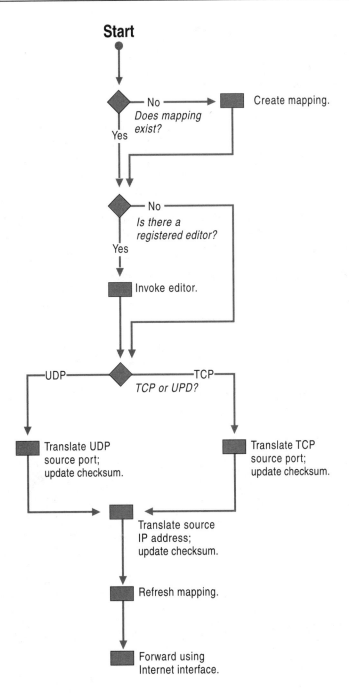

Figure 3.24   NAT Processing of Outbound Internet Traffic

Inbound Internet Traffic

For traffic from the private network that is inbound on the Internet interface, the NAT first assesses whether an address/port mapping, static or dynamic, exists for the packet. If a mapping does not exist for the packet, it is silently discarded by the NAT.

This behavior protects the private network from malicious users on the Internet. The only way that Internet traffic is forwarded to the private network is either in response to traffic initiated by a private network user that created a dynamic mapping or because a static mapping exists so that Internet users can access specific resources on the private network.

After mapping, the NAT checks for editors and invokes one if necessary. After editing, the NAT modifies the TCP, UDP, and IP headers and forwards the frame using the private network interface.

Figure 3.25 shows the NAT processing for inbound Internet traffic.

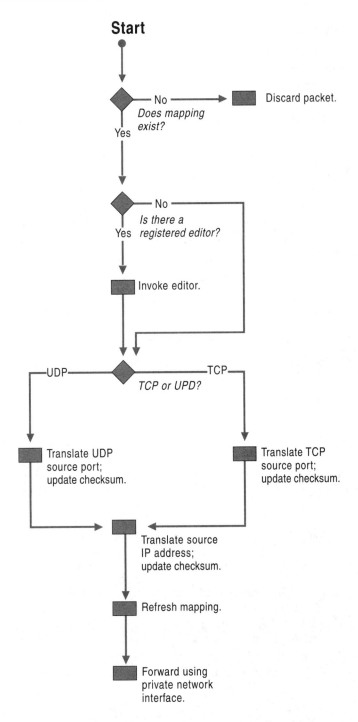

Figure 3.25   NAT Processing of Inbound Internet Traffic

Additional NAT Routing Protocol Components

To help simplify the configuration of small office/home office (SOHO) networks to the Internet, the NAT routing protocol for Windows 2000 also includes a DHCP allocator and a DNS proxy.

DHCP Allocator

The DHCP allocator component provides IP address configuration information to the other computers on the SOHO network. The DHCP allocator is a simplified DHCP server that allocates an IP address, a subnet mask, a default gateway, the IP address of a DNS server, and the IP address of a DNS server. You must configure computers on the DHCP network as DHCP clients in order to receive the IP configuration automatically. The default TCP/IP configuration for Windows 2000, Windows NT, Windows 95, and Windows 98 computers is as a DHCP client.

Table 3.5 lists the DHCP options in the DHCPOffer and DHCPAck messages issued by the DHCP allocator during the DHCP lease configuration process. You cannot modify these options or configure additional DHCP options.

Table 3.5   DHCP Allocator DHCP Options

Option Number	Option Value	Description
1	255.255.0.0	Subnet Mask
3	IP address of private interface	Router (default gateway)
6	IP address of private interface	DNS server (only issued if DNS proxy is enabled)
58 (0x3A)	5 minutes	Renewal time
59 (0x3B)	5 days	Rebinding time
51	7 days	IP address lease time
15 (0x0F)	primary domain name of NAT computer	DNS domain

The DHCP allocator only supports a single scope of IP addresses as configured from the **Address Assignment** tab on the properties of the **Network Address Translation (NAT)** routing protocol in the **Routing and Remote Access** snap-in. The DHCP allocator does not support multiple scopes, superscopes, or multicast scopes. If you need this functionality, you should install a DHCP server and disable the DHCP allocator component of the NAT routing protocol.

DNS Proxy

The DNS proxy component acts as a DNS server to the computers on the SOHO network. DNS queries sent by a SOHO computer to the NAT computer are re-sent by the NAT computer as DNS queries from the NAT computer to the NAT computer's configured DNS server. Responses to DNS queries corresponding to outstanding requests of SOHO computers received by the NAT computer are re-sent by the NAT computer to the original SOHO computer.

Troubleshooting NAT

Most NAT problems deal with the inability of the NAT to translate packets. Other problems are related to address allocation and name resolution.

The network address translation computer is not properly translating packets

- Verify that the interface on the Windows 2000 Router that connects to the Internet is added to the **Network Address Translation (NAT)** routing protocol.

- Verify that the **Public interface connected to the Internet** option on the **General** tab on the properties page of the Internet interface is selected.

- Verify that the **Private interface connected to private network** option on the **General** tab on the properties page of the private network interface is selected.

- If you only have a single public IP address, verify that the **Translate TCP/UDP headers** option on the **General** tab on the properties page of the Internet interface is selected.

- If you have multiple public IP addresses, verify that they are typed correctly in text boxes provided on the **Address Pool** tab on the properties page of the Internet interface. If your address pool includes an IP address that was not allocated to you by your ISP, inbound Internet traffic that is mapped to that IP address is routed by the ISP to another location.

- If you have some applications that do not seem to work through the NAT, try running them from the NAT computer. If they work from the NAT computer and not from a computer on the private network, the payload of the application might not be translatable. Check the protocol being used by the application against the list of supported NAT editors. If needed, contact the vendor of the application for information about how their application works in translated environments.

- Verify that IP packet filtering on the private network and Internet interfaces is not preventing the receiving (through input filters) or sending (through output filters) of Internet-based traffic.

- Verify that TCP/IP filtering on the private network and Internet interfaces is not preventing the receiving of traffic.

- For special ports, verify the configuration of the public address and port and the private address and port.

Private network hosts are not receiving IP address configuration

- Verify that the DHCP allocator is enabled from the **Address Assignment** tab of the properties of the **Network Address Translation (NAT)** routing protocol.

Name resolution for private network hosts is not working

- Verify that the DNS proxy is enabled from the **Address Assignment** tab of the properties of the **Network Address Translation (NAT)** routing protocol.

- Verify the name resolution configuration of the network address translation computer by using the ipconfig command. There are two ways that you can configure name resolution when dialing an ISP:

    - Statically assigned name servers

      You must manually configure the TCP/IP protocol with the IP address (or addresses) of the name servers provided by the ISP. If you have statically assigned name servers, you can use the ipconfig command at any time to get the IP addresses of your configured name servers.

    - Dynamically assigned name servers

      Manual configuration is not required. The IP addresses of the name servers provided by the ISP are dynamically assigned whenever you dial the ISP. If you have dynamically assigned name servers, you must run the ipconfig command after a connection to the ISP has been made.

IP Packet Filtering

To provide security, an IP router can allow or disallow the flow of very specific types of IP traffic. This capability, called IP packet filtering, provides a way for the network administrator to precisely define what IP traffic is received and sent by the router. IP packet filtering is an important element of connecting corporate intranets to public networks like the Internet.

IP packet filtering consists of creating a series of definitions called filters, which define for the router what types of traffic are allowed or disallowed on each interface. Filters can be set for incoming and outgoing traffic.

- Input filters define what inbound traffic on that interface the router is allowed to route or process.
- Output filters define what traffic the router is allowed to send from that interface.

Because you can configure both input and output filters for each interface, it is possible to create contradictory filters. For example, the input filter on one interface allows the inbound traffic but the output filter on the other interface does not allow the same traffic to be sent. The end result is that the traffic is not passed across the Windows 2000 Router.

Packet filtering can also be implemented on a non-router computer running Windows 2000 to filter incoming and outgoing traffic to a specific subset of traffic.

Packet filters should be implemented carefully to prevent the filters from being too restrictive, which would impair the functionality of other protocols that might be operating on the computer. For example, if a computer running Windows 2000 is also running Internet Information Services (IIS) as a Web server and packet filters are defined so that only Web-based traffic is allowed, you can not use PING (which uses ICMP Echo Requests and Echo Replies) to perform basic IP troubleshooting. If the Web server is a Silent RIP host, the filters prevent the Silent RIP process from receiving the RIP announcements.

Note When troubleshooting connectivity or IP-based network problems on a computer running Windows 2000 that is using packet filtering, first verify whether the packet filtering configured on that computer is preventing outgoing or incoming packets for the protocol having the problem.

Windows 2000 IP Packet Filtering

Windows 2000 IP packet filtering is based on exceptions. You can configure Windows 2000 to either pass all traffic except those disallowed by filters or to discard all traffic except those allowed by filters. For example, you might want to configure a filter to allow all traffic except Telnet traffic (TCP port 23). Or you might want to set up filters on a dedicated Web server to process only Web-based TCP traffic (TCP port 80).

Note The Windows 2000 Router does not allow the use of user-definable filters where a network administrator can create a filter based on any field of the IP, TCP, UDP or ICMP header. The Windows 2000 Router does not support filtering on any protocols other than IP, TCP, UDP, and ICMP.

Windows 2000 allows filtering on various fields in IP, TCP, UDP, and ICMP headers of incoming and outgoing packets.

IP Header

In the IP header, filters can be defined for the following fields:

IP Protocol An identifier used to demultiplex the payload of an IP packet to an upper layer protocol. For example, TCP uses a Protocol of 6, UDP uses a Protocol of 17, and ICMP uses a Protocol of 1. When you select a protocol such as TCP, UDP, or ICMP in the **IP Filters** dialog box, the default values for those protocols are assumed. Windows 2000 allows you to type any value in the **IP Protocol** text box.

Source IP Address The IP address of the source host, which can be configured with a subnet mask, allowing an entire range of IP addresses (corresponding to an IP network) to be specified with a single filter entry.

Destination IP Address The IP address of the destination host which can be configured with a subnet mask, allowing an entire range of IP addresses (corresponding to an IP network) to be specified with a single filter entry.

TCP Header

In the TCP header, filters can be defined for two fields: the TCP Source Port field, used to identify the source process which is sending the TCP segment; and for the TCP Destination Port, used to identify the destination process for the TCP segment.

Note The Windows 2000 Router does not support the configuration of a range of TCP ports. For a range of TCP ports, a separate filter for each port in the range must be configured.

UDP Header

In the UDP header, filters can be defined for two fields: the UDP Source Port field, used to identify the source process which is sending the UDP message; and for the UDP Destination Port, used to identify the destination process for the UDP message.

Note The Windows 2000 Router does not support the configuration of a range of UDP ports. For a range of UDP ports, a separate filter for each port in the range must be configured.

ICMP Header

In the ICMP header, filters can be defined for two fields: the ICMP Type field, indicating the type of ICMP packet (such as Echo Request or Echo Reply); and for the ICMP Code field, indicating one of the possible multiple functions within a specified type. If there is only one function within a type, the Code field is set to 0.

Table 3.6 lists commonly used ICMP types and codes.

Table 3.6   Common ICMP Types and Codes

ICMP Type	ICMP Code	Use
0	0	Echo Reply
8	0	Echo Request
3	0	Destination Unreachable - Network Unreachable
3	1	Destination Unreachable - Host Unreachable
3	2	Destination Unreachable - Protocol Unreachable
3	3	Destination Unreachable - Port Unreachable
3	4	Destination Unreachable - Fragmentation Needed and Don't Fragment Flag set
4	0	Source Quench
5	1	Redirect - Redirected datagrams for the host
9	0	Router Advertisement
10	0	Router Solicitation
11	0	Time Exceeded - TTL expiration
11	1	Time Exceeded - Fragmentation Reassembly expiration
12	0	Parameter Problem

Note For a complete list of ICMP types and codes, see the link at http://windows.microsoft.com/windows2000/reskit/webresources.

Input Filters

Input filters are configured on an exception basis. You can configure the filter action to either receive all traffic except that which is specified, or to drop all traffic except that which is specified.

When multiple filters are configured, the separate filters applied to the inbound packet are compared through a logical **OR**. If the packet matches at least one of the configured filters, it is received or dropped depending on the filter action setting.

Output Filters

Output filters are configured on an exception basis. You can configure the filter action to either transit all traffic except that which is specified, or to drop all traffic except that which is specified.

When multiple filters are configured, the separate filters applied to the outbound packet are compared through a logical **OR**. If the packet matches at least one of the configured filters, it is transmitted or dropped depending on the filter action setting.

Configuring a Filter

When adding or editing an input or an output filter, you configure the parameters of the filter in the **Add IP Filter** or **Edit IP Filter** dialog boxes. When multiple parameters are configured on a particular filter, as the filter is applied to the incoming packet, the parameters of the filter are compared through a logical **AND**. The fields in the packet must match all of the configured parameters of the filter to meet the criteria of the filter.

Note You cannot configure separate active filters for **Receive all packets except those that meet the criteria below** and **Drop all packets except those that meet the criteria below**.

You can configure the following fields in the **Add IP Filter** or **Edit IP Filter** dialog boxes:

Source Network

- IP Address: Type the source IP network ID or a source IP address.

- Subnet Mask: Type the subnet mask corresponding to the source network ID or type 255.255.255.255 for a source IP address. The subnet mask bits must encompass all of the bits being used in the IP Address field. The IP address cannot be more specific than the subnet mask.

Destination Network

- IP Address: Type the destination IP network ID or a destination IP address.

- Subnet Mask: Type the subnet mask corresponding to the destination network ID, or type 255.255.255.255 for a destination IP address. The subnet mask bits must encompass all of the bits being used in the IP Address field. The IP address cannot be more specific than the subnet mask.

Protocol

- TCP (Protocol = 6): Select this option to reach text boxes in which you type a source TCP port and a destination TCP port. One or both can be specified. If nothing is specified in these text boxes, they default to 0, meaning any port.

- TCP [established] (Protocol = 6): Select this option when you want to define TCP traffic (source TCP port and destination TCP port) for TCP connections established by or with the router.

- UDP (Protocol = 17): Select this option to reach text boxes in which you type a source UDP port and a destination UDP port. One or both can be specified. If nothing is specified in these text boxes, they default to 0, meaning any port.

- ICMP (Protocol = 1): Select this option to reach text boxes in which you type an ICMP code and an ICMP type. One or both can be specified. If nothing is specified in these text boxes, they default to 255, meaning any code or any type.

- Any: Select this option to make *any* IP protocol value assumed.

- Other: Select this option to reach the text box in which you type any IP protocol.

Filtering Scenarios

This section illustrates filter configurations for commonly implemented filtering scenarios.

Caution If you combine any of the sample sets of filters, make sure that the desired subset of traffic is allowed and the desired level of security is maintained. For example, if you combine the local host filtering and Web traffic filtering, due to the way that the filters are applied (**AND** is used within a filter; **OR** is used between filters), all traffic destined for the host is allowed. The Web traffic input filter is essentially ignored.

Local Host Filtering

Use local host filtering to ensure that only traffic destined for the host is allowed to be processed. This disables the forwarding of packets on the interface on which local host filtering is enabled. Local host filtering is used when an intranet is connected to the Internet and direct routing of packets between the intranet and the Internet is not desired. In this scenario, local host filtering is configured on the Internet interface.

Configure the following filters on the Internet interface. With these filters configured, only traffic destined for this host or for all hosts on the host's network, or multicast traffic is allowed on the interface.

Using the **Drop all packets except those that meet the criteria below** filter action, create a series of input filters with the following attributes:

Destination IP Address of Host IP Address

- In the **Add IP Filter** dialog box, select the **Destination network** check box, and then type the IP address of the host and the subnet mask of 255.255.255.255 in the appropriate text boxes.

Destination IP Address of Subnet Broadcast

1. In the **Add IP Filter** dialog box, select the **Destination network** check box, and then type the IP address of the host's subnet broadcast IP address and the subnet mask of 255.255.255.255 in the appropriate text boxes.

2. To define the Subnet broadcast, set all the host bits to 1. For example, if a host is configured with an IP address of 172.16.5.98 with a subnet mask of 255.255.255.0 (a subnet of the private IP network 172.16.0.0), this filter would be filtering on the Destination IP address of 172.16.5.255.

Destination IP Address of All Subnets-Directed Broadcast

- In the **Add IP Filter** dialog box, select the **Destination network** check box, and then type the IP address of the host's all subnets-directed broadcast address and the subnet mask of 255.255.255.255 in the appropriate text boxes.

The all subnets-directed broadcast is class-based broadcast address where the host bits before subnetting are set to all 1. For the example host, this filter would be filtering on the Destination IP address of 172.16.255.255. The filter for the all subnets-directed broadcast is only necessary when subnetting.

Destination IP Address of the IP Limited Broadcast

- In the **Add IP Filter** dialog box, select the **Destination network** check box, and then type the IP address of 255.255.255.255 and the subnet mask of 255.255.255.255 in the appropriate text boxes.

The Limited Broadcast is the destination IP address of 255.255.255.255.

Destination IP Address for All Possible Multicast Traffic

- In the **Add IP Filter** dialog box, select the **Destination network** check box, and then type the IP address of 224.0.0.0 and the subnet mask of 240.0.0.0 in the appropriate text boxes. All possible inbound multicast traffic is allowed on the interface.

Note Local host filtering on an interface effectively disables unicast routing on that interface because the only unicast traffic allowed through the interface is destined for the host. Transit traffic is dropped.

Web Traffic Filtering

Web traffic filtering is done on hosts that are Web servers so that only Web-based traffic to and from the Web server service on the host is allowed to be processed. This is done to secure the Web server from malicious attacks on other services running on the Web server. For a Web server connected to the Internet, Web traffic filtering is configured on the Internet interface.

Using the **Drop all packets except those that meet the criteria below** filter action, configure the following filters to confine the allowed traffic to packets to and from the Web server service:

- An input filter for the Destination IP Address of Web server and the TCP Destination Port 80.
- An output filter for the Source IP Address of Web server and the TCP Source Port 80.

If these filters are the only filters configured, the only traffic allowed through the interface is TCP traffic to and from the Web server service on the Windows 2000 Server–based computer.

Note The preceding example assumes the default port of the Web server is port 80. If you are using a port other than 80, substitute the appropriate port for port 80 in these filters.

FTP Traffic Filtering

FTP traffic filtering is done on hosts that are FTP servers so that only FTP-based traffic to and from the FTP server service on the host is allowed to be processed. This is done to secure the FTP server from malicious attacks on other services running on the FTP server. For a FTP server connected to the Internet, FTP traffic filtering is configured on the Internet interface.

Using the **Drop all packets except those that meet the criteria below** filter action, configure the following filters to confine the allowed traffic to packets to and from the FTP server service:

- Input filters for the Destination IP Address of FTP Server and the TCP Destination Port 21 (the FTP control port), and for the Destination IP Address of FTP Server and the TCP Destination Port 20 (the FTP data port).
- Output filters for the Source IP Address of FTP Server and the TCP Source Port 21 (the FTP control port), and for the Source IP Address of FTP Server and the TCP Source Port 20 (the FTP data port).

If these filters are the only filters configured, the only traffic allowed through the interface is TCP traffic to and from the FTP server service on the Windows 2000 Server–based computer.

Note The preceding example assumes the default ports, 20 and 21, of the FTP server. If you are using ports other than 20 and 21, substitute the appropriate ports for ports 20 and 21 in these filters.

PPTP Traffic Filtering

Point-to-Point Tunneling Protocol (PPTP) traffic filtering is done on hosts that are PPTP servers so that only PPTP-based traffic to and from the PPTP server service on the host is allowed to be processed. This is done to secure the PPTP server from malicious attacks on other services running on the PPTP server. For a PPTP server connected to the Internet, PPTP traffic filtering is configured on the Internet interface.

Using the **Drop all packets except those that meet the criteria below** filter action, configure the following filters to confine the allowed traffic to packets to and from the PPTP service running on the server:

- Input filters for the Destination IP Address of the PPTP server and TCP Destination Port 1723, and for the Destination IP Address of the PPTP server and IP Protocol 47 (Generic Routing Encapsulation [GRE]).

- Output filters for the Source IP Address of the PPTP server and the TCP Source Port 1723, and for the Source IP Address of the PPTP server and the IP Protocol 47 (GRE).

If the PPTP server is also to be used as a PPTP client to initiate tunneled connections to branch offices in a virtual private network (VPN) scenario, configure the following additional filters:

- An input filter for the Destination IP Address of the PPTP server and the TCP (established) Source Port 1723.

- An output filter for the Source IP Address of the PPTP server and the TCP (established) Destination Port 1723.

The TCP (established) filter is used to allow only traffic on the TCP connection that was established by the PPTP client. If TCP (established) is not used, a malicious Internet hacker can penetrate the PPTP server by sending packets from applications using TCP port 1723.

If these filters are the only filters configured, the only traffic allowed through the interface is TCP traffic and tunneled data (GRE traffic) to and from the PPTP server and PPTP client on the Windows 2000 Server–based computer.

For more information about PPTP, see "Virtual Private Networking" in this book.

L2TP Server Filtering

Layer Two Tunneling Protocol (L2TP) over IPSec traffic filtering is done on hosts that are L2TP servers so that only L2TP-based traffic to and from the L2TP server service on the host is allowed to be processed. This is done to secure the L2TP server from malicious attacks on other services running on the L2TP server. For a L2TP server connected to the Internet, L2TP traffic filtering is configured on the Internet interface.

Using the **Drop all packets except those that meet the criteria below** filter action, configure the following filters to confine the allowed traffic to packets to and from the server running L2TP:

- An input filter for the Destination IP Address of the L2TP server and UDP Destination Port 1701.

- An input filter for the Destination IP Address of the L2TP server and UDP Destination Port 500.

- An output filter for the Source IP Address of the L2TP server and the UDP Source Port 1701.

- An output filter for the Source IP Address of the L2TP server and the UDP Source Port 500.

The filters for UDP port 1701 are for the L2TP protocol. The filters for UDP port 500 are for the Internet Key Exchange (IKE) used to create the IPSec security association. Packet filters for the IPSec Encapsulating Security Payload (ESP) header using IP protocol 50 are not needed because the inbound and outbound packets are first processed by IPSec, which adds or removes the ESP header before the Routing and Remote Access service IP packet filters are applied.

If these filters are the only filters configured, the only traffic allowed through the interface is UDP traffic to and from the L2TP server and client on the Windows 2000 Server–based computer.

For more information about L2TP over IPSec, see "Virtual Private Networking" in this book.

Denying Spoofed Packets from Private IP Addresses

Another method of performing denial of service attacks is to flood servers with packets, such as TCP connection request packets, from addresses to which there can be no reply. In these cases, the malicious users spoof, or substitute, the source IP address of the packets with something other than the IP address of the interface on which the packets originated. An easy address to spoof is a private address because a response sent to a private address on the Internet results in an ICMP Destination Unreachable message.

To drop Internet traffic from spoofed private IP addresses, configure input filters on the Internet interface to accept all packets except the following:

- The Source IP Address of 10.0.0.0 with the subnet mask 255.0.0.0.
- The Source IP Address of 172.16.0.0 with the subnet mask 255.240.0.0.
- The Source IP Address of 192.168.0.0 with the subnet mask 255.255.0.0.

Fragmentation Filtering

The Routing and Remote Access service also supports the filtering of fragmented IP datagrams. A fragmented IP datagram is an IP datagram that contains a fragment of an IP payload. Source hosts or routers fragment IP payloads so that the resulting IP datagram is small enough to be sent on the network segment of the next hop. Routing and Remote Access service fragmentation filtering only applies to incoming traffic.

▶ **To enable fragmentation filtering**

1. In the **Routing and Remote Access** snap-in, open the **IP Routing** container for the desired server.

2. Open the **General** container, right-click the desired interface, and click **Properties**.

3. From the **General** tab, select the **Enable fragmentation checking** check box.

To prevent the router from forwarding fragmented IP packets for transit traffic on any interface, select this setting on all interfaces of the router. This does not prevent the forwarding of fragmented packets sent from the router.

Fragmentation filtering can be employed to prevent the Ping of Death, a denial of service attack where malicious users send one or multiple 64-KB ICMP Echo Request messages. The 64-KB messages are fragmented and must be reassembled at the destination host. For each separate 64-KB message, the TCP/IP protocol must allocate memory, tables, timers, and other resources. With enough fragmented messages, a Windows 2000 Server–based computer can become bogged down so that the servicing of valid information requests is impaired. By using fragmentation filtering, incoming fragmented IP datagrams are immediately discarded.

ICMP Router Discovery

The Windows 2000 Router includes support for the router advertisement and discovery scheme as documented in RFC 1256. To aid in the ease of configuring IP hosts with the IP addresses of local routers and to provide a way for hosts to sense downed routers, RFC 1256 describes the use of ICMP messages to send Router Advertisements and Router Solicitations.

Router Advertisements

A router sends out a periodic Router Advertisement using an ICMP message (Type 9, Code 0). The Router Advertisement can be sent to the all-hosts IP multicast address of 224.0.0.1, the local IP broadcast address, or the limited broadcast address (255.255.255.255). In practice, the Router Advertisement is sent to the multicast address. Router Advertisements are explicit notifications to the hosts on the network that the router is still available.

The Router Advertisement message contains an Advertisement Lifetime, the time after the last received Router Advertisement that the router can be considered down (default of 30 minutes), and a Preference Level, an indication of the router's preferred status as the default gateway for the network. The highest preference level router becomes the default gateway.

Router Solicitations

When a host that supports RFC 1256 needs to be configured with a default gateway (either upon initialization or because its default gateway is down), it sends out a Router Solicitation using an ICMP message (Type 10, Code 0). The Router Solicitation can be sent to the all-routers IP multicast address of 224.0.0.2, the local IP broadcast address, or the limited broadcast address (255.255.255.255). In practice, hosts send Router Solicitation messages to the multicast address. Routers on the host's network that support RFC 1256 immediately respond with a Router Advertisement, and the host chooses the router with the highest preference level as its default gateway.

Note ICMP router discovery is not a routing protocol. Routers only advertise their existence, not the best way to reach a given destination network. If a host uses a non-optimal route, ICMP Redirect messages redirect the host to the better route.

Table 3.7 describes the settings for ICMP Router Discovery.

Table 3.7   ICMP Router Discovery Settings

Router Discovery Setting	Description
Level of Preference	The preference level of this router to be the default gateway. The default value is 0.
Advertisement Lifetime (minutes)	The time, in minutes, after which a host considers a router down (after it has received its last Router Advertisement). The default time is 30 minutes.
Advertisement interval minimum time (minutes)	The minimum amount of time between Router Advertisements sent by this router. The default is 7 minutes.
Advertisement interval maximum (minutes)	The maximum amount of time between Router Advertisements sent by this router. The default is 10 minutes. Router Advertisements are sent at a random interval between the minimum and maximum times.

▶ **To enable router discovery advertisements**

1. In the **Routing and Remote Access** snap-in, open the **IP Routing** container for the desired server.

2. Open the **General** container, right-click the desired interface, and click **Properties**.

3. From the **General** tab, select the **Enable router discovery advertisements** check box.

Windows 2000, with the **Enable router discovery advertisements** option selected, sends Router Advertisements periodically and in response to Router Solicitations using the IP multicast address of 224.0.0.1. TCP/IP for Windows 2000 and Windows 98 supports the use of Router Solicitation messages to discover the default gateway. For information about how to disable router discovery for TCP/IP for Windows 2000, see "Windows 2000 TCP/IP" in the *TCP/IP Core Networking Guide*.

Additional Resources

For more information about IP routing, see:

- *Routing in the Internet* by Christian Huitema, 1995, Englewood Cliffs, NJ: Prentice Hall.

- *OSPF: Anatomy of an Internet Routing Protocol* by John T. Moy, 1998, Reading, MA: Addison-Wesley.

C H A P T E R   4

IP Multicast Support

Microsoft® Windows® 2000 provides support for the sending, receiving, and forwarding of IP multicast traffic. The IP multicast components of the Routing and Remote Access service allow you to send and receive IP multicast traffic from remote access clients and multicast-enabled portions of the Internet or a private intranet.

In This Chapter

Related Information in the Resource Kit

- For more information about IP multicast basics, see "Introduction to TCP/IP" in the *Microsoft® Windows® 2000 Server Resource Kit TCP/IP Core Networking Guide*.

- For more information about IP multicast support in TCP/IP for Windows 2000, see "Windows 2000 TCP/IP" in the *Windows 2000 TCP/IP Core Networking Guide*.

- For more information about remote access, see "Remote Access Server" in this book.

- For more information about the Windows 2000–based routers, see "Routing and Remote Access Service" in this book.

IP Multicasting Overview

In addition to unicast and broadcast support, IP also provides a mechanism to send and receive IP multicast traffic. IP multicast traffic is sent to a single destination IP address but is received and processed by multiple IP hosts, regardless of their location on an IP internetwork. A host listens for a specific IP multicast address and receives all packets to that IP address.

IP multicast is more efficient than IP unicast or broadcast for one-to-many delivery of data. Unlike unicast, only one copy of the data is sent. Unlike broadcast, the traffic is only received and processed by computers that are listening for it.

The additional elements of IP multicast include the following:

- The set of hosts listening on a specific IP multicast address is called a host group.
- Host group membership is dynamic, and hosts can join and leave the group at any time.
- There are no limitations to the size of a host group.
- A host group can span IP routers across multiple network segments. This configuration requires IP multicast support on IP routers and the ability for hosts to register themselves with the router. Host registration is accomplished using the Internet Group Management Protocol (IGMP).
- A host can send traffic to an IP multicast address without belonging to the corresponding host group.

IP multicast addresses, also known as group addresses, are in the class D range of 224.0.0.0 to 239.255.255.255 as defined by setting the first four high order bits to 1110. In network prefix or Classless Inter-Domain Routing (CIDR) notation, IP multicast addresses are summarized as 224.0.0.0/4. Multicast addresses in the range 224.0.0.0 to 224.0.0.255 (224.0.0.0/24) are reserved for the local subnet and are not forwarded by IP routers regardless of the Time to Live (TTL) in the IP header.

The IP multicast addresses from 224.0.1.0 to 238.255.255.255 are either reserved or assigned to a multicasting application. The addresses from 239.0.0.0 to 239.255.255.255 (239.0.0.0/8) are reserved for applications that can be administratively scoped. For more information about these addresses, see "Multicast Boundaries" later in this chapter.

The following are examples of reserved IP multicast addresses:

- 224.0.0.1 - all hosts on this subnet.
- 224.0.0.2 - all routers on this subnet.
- 224.0.0.5 - Open Shortest Path First (OSPF) Version 2, designed to reach all OSPF routers on a network.
- 224.0.0.6 - OSPF Version 2, designed to reach all OSPF designated routers on a network.
- 224.0.0.9 - Routing Information Protocol (RIP) Version 2.
- 224.0.1.1 - Network Time Protocol.

For the latest list of reserved multicast addresses, see the Information Sciences Institute link at http://windows.microsoft.com/windows2000/reskit/webresources.

For more information about IP multicast support, see Internet Engineering Task Force (IETF) Request for Comments (RFC) 1112.

Mapping IP Multicast to MAC-Layer Multicast

To support IP multicasting, the Internet authorities have reserved the multicast address range of 01-00-5E-00-00-00 to 01-00-5E-7F-FF-FF for Ethernet and Fiber Distributed Data Interface (FDDI) media access control (MAC) addresses. As shown in Figure 4.1, the high order 25 bits of the 48-bit MAC address are fixed and the low order 23 bits are variable.

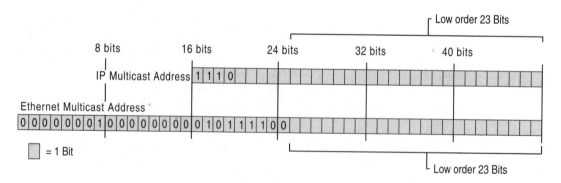

Figure 4.1   Mapping IP Multicast Addresses to Ethernet and FDDI MAC Addresses

To map an IP multicast address to a MAC-layer multicast address, the low order 23 bits of the IP multicast address are mapped directly to the low order 23 bits in the MAC-layer multicast address. Because the first 4 bits of an IP multicast address are fixed according to the class D convention, there are 5 bits in the IP multicast address that do not map to the MAC-layer multicast address. Therefore, it is possible for a host to receive MAC-layer multicast packets for groups to which it does not belong. However, these packets are dropped by IP once the destination IP address is determined.

For example, the multicast address 224.192.16.1 becomes 01-00-5E-40-10-01. To use the 23 low order bits, the first octet is not used, and only the last 7 bits of the second octet is used. The third and fourth octets are converted directly to hexadecimal numbers. The second octet, 192 in binary is 11000000. If you drop the high order bit, it becomes 1000000 or 64 (in decimal), or 0x40 (in hexadecimal). For the next octet, 16 in hexadecimal is 0x10. For the last octet, 1 in hexadecimal is 0x01. Therefore, the MAC address corresponding to 224.192.16.1 becomes 01-00-5E-40-10-01.

Token Ring uses this same method for MAC-layer multicast addressing. However, many Token Ring network adapters do not support it. Therefore, by default, the functional address 0xC0-00-00-04-00-00 is used for all IP multicast traffic sent over Token Ring networks. For more information about Token Ring support for IP multicasting, see RFC 1469.

Note Microsoft® Windows NT® version 4.0 and earlier do not support IP multicast on Token Ring network adapters.

IP Multicast–Enabled Intranet

In an IP multicast–enabled intranet, any host can send IP multicast traffic to any group address, and any host can receive IP multicast traffic from any group address regardless of their location. To facilitate this capability, IP multicast must be supported by the hosts and routers of the intranet.

Hosts

A host supports IP multicast at one of the following levels:

- Level 0 - No support to send or receive IP multicast traffic.
- Level 1 - Support exists to send but not receive IP multicast traffic.
- Level 2 - Support exists to both send and receive IP multicast traffic.

TCP/IP for Windows 2000 supports all levels of IP multicasting and by default is configured for level 2 support for IP multicast traffic. For information about changing the level of multicast support, see "Windows 2000 TCP/IP" in the *TCP/IP Core Networking Guide.*

For a host to send IP multicast packets, it must:

- Determine the IP multicast address to use.

  To determine the IP multicast address to use, the application must first determine whether to create a new host group or use an existing host group. To join an existing group, the application can use a service location protocol to determine the group address for a specific service.

  The multicast address for a new group can either be determined by the application or obtained through a mechanism that allocates a unique multicast address such as Multicast Address Dynamic Client Allocation Protocol (MADCAP). MADCAP is an extension to the Dynamic Host Configuration Protocol (DHCP) protocol standard that you can use to support dynamic assignment and configuration of IP multicast addresses on TCP/IP-based networks.

  Ordinarily, you use DHCP scopes to provide client configurations by allocating ranges of unicast IP addresses. MADCAP scopes can be used to allocate ranges of IP multicast addresses. For more information about MADCAP and its support in Windows 2000, see "Dynamic Host Configuration Protocol" in the *TCP/IP Core Networking Guide.*

- Place the IP multicast packet on the medium.

  The sending host must construct an IP packet containing the wanted destination IP multicast address and place it on the medium. In the case of shared access technologies such as Ethernet, FDDI, and Token Ring, the destination MAC address is created from the IP multicast address as previously described.

For a host to receive IP multicast packets, it must:

- Inform IP to receive multicast traffic.

  To determine the IP multicast address to use, the application must first determine whether to create a new host group or use an existing host group. To join an existing group, the application can use a service location protocol to determine the group address for a specific service.

  After the group address is determined, an application must inform IP to receive multicasts at a specified destination IP multicast address. If multiple applications are using the same IP multicast address, then IP must pass a copy of the multicast to each application. IP must track which applications are using which multicast addresses as applications join or leave a host group. Additionally, for a multihomed host, IP must track the application membership of host groups for each subnet.

- Register the multicast MAC address with the network adapter.

  If the network technology supports hardware-based multicasting, then the network adapter is told to pass up packets for a specific multicast address. In the case of shared access technologies such as Ethernet, FDDI, and Token Ring, the **NdisRequest** function is used to program the network adapter to respond to a multicast MAC address corresponding to the wanted IP multicast address.

- Inform local routers.

  The host must inform local subnet routers that it is listening for multicast traffic at a specific group address. The protocol that registers host group information is the Internet Group Management Protocol (IGMP).

  IGMP is required on all hosts that support level 2 IP multicasting. The IGMP Host Membership Report message is sent by a host to register membership in a specific host group. TCP/IP for Windows 2000 supports IGMP version 2. For more information about IGMP, see "IGMP v1" and "IGMP v2" later in this chapter.

Routers

To forward IP multicast packets to only those subnets for which there are group members, an IP multicast router must be able to:

- Receive all IP multicast traffic.
- Forward IP multicast traffic.
- Receive and process IGMP Host Membership Report messages.
- Query attached subnets for host membership status.
- Communicate group membership to other IP multicast routers.

Receive All IP Multicast Traffic

For shared access technologies, such as Ethernet and FDDI, the normal listening mode for network adapters is unicast listening mode. The listening mode is the way that the network adapter analyzes the destination MAC address of incoming frames to decide to process them further. In unicast listening mode, the only frames that are considered for further processing are in a table of interesting destination MAC addresses on the network adapter. Typically, the only interesting addresses are the broadcast address (0xFF-FF-FF-FF-FF-FF) and the unicast address, also known as the media access control (MAC) address, of the adapter.

However, for an IP multicast router to receive all IP multicast traffic, it must place the network adapter in a special listening mode called multicast promiscuous mode. Multicast promiscuous mode analyzes the Institute of Electrical and Electronics Engineers (IEEE)-defined multicast bit to determine whether the frame requires further processing. The multicast bit for Ethernet and FDDI addresses is the last bit of the first byte of the destination MAC address.

The values of the multicast bit are the following:

- If the multicast bit is set to 0, then the address is a unicast or individual address.
- If the multicast bit is set to 1, then the address is a multicast or group address. The multicast bit is also set for the broadcast address.

When the network adapter is placed in multicast promiscuous listening mode, any frames with the multicast bit set to 1 are passed up for further processing.

Multicast promiscuous mode is different than promiscuous mode. In promiscuous mode, all frames—regardless of the destination MAC address—are passed up for processing. Promiscuous mode is used by protocol analyzers, also known as network sniffers, such as the full version of Microsoft Network Monitor that is part of the Microsoft® Systems Management Server.

Multicast promiscuous mode is supported by most network adapters. A network adapter that supports promiscuous mode might not support multicast promiscuous mode. Consult your network adapter documentation or manufacturer for information about whether your network adapter supports multicast promiscuous mode.

Forward IP Multicast Traffic

The ability to forward IP multicast packets is a capability of the TCP/IP protocol, and the Windows 2000 implementation of TCP/IP includes this functionality. When multicast forwarding is enabled, non-local subnet IP multicast packets are analyzed to determine over which interfaces the packet is forwarded. The analysis is done by comparing the destination group address to entries in the IP multicast forwarding table. Upon receipt of a non-local IP multicast packet, the Time to Live (TTL) in the IP header is decremented by 1. If the TTL is greater than 0 after decrementing, then the multicast forwarding table is checked. If an entry in the multicast forwarding table is found that matches the destination IP multicast address, the IP multicast packet is forwarded with its new TTL over the appropriate interfaces.

The multicast forwarding process does not distinguish between hosts on locally attached subnets who are receiving multicast traffic or hosts on a network segment that are downstream from the locally attached subnet across another router on the subnet. In other words, a multicast router might forward a multicast packet on a subnet for which there are no hosts listening. The multicast packet is forwarded because another router on that subnet indicated that a host in its direction is receiving the multicast traffic.

The multicast forwarding table does not record each host group member or the number of host group members; only that there is at least one host group member for a specific group address.

For information about how to view the IP multicast forwarding table on a Microsoft® Windows® 2000 Server–based computer running the Routing and Remote Access service, see "IP Multicast Troubleshooting Tools" later in this chapter.

Multicast forwarding is enabled by setting the value of the **EnableMulticastForwarding** registry entry (HKEY_LOCAL_MACHINE\System\CurrentControlSet\Services\Tcpip) \Parameters to 1. This registry entry is created and set to 1 when you install the Routing and Remote Access service.

Caution   Do not use a registry editor to edit the registry directly unless you have no alternative. The registry editors bypass the standard safeguards provided by administrative tools. These safeguards prevent you from entering conflicting settings or settings that are likely to degrade performance or damage your system. Editing the registry directly can have serious, unexpected consequences that can prevent the system from starting and require that you reinstall Windows 2000. To configure or customize Windows 2000, use the programs in Control Panel or Microsoft Management Console (MMC) whenever possible.

Receive and Process IGMP Host Membership Report Messages

Multicast routers receive IGMP Host Membership Report messages from all hosts on all locally attached subnets. This information is used to track host group membership by placing entries in the multicast forwarding table. Because all multicast routers are listening in multicast promiscuous mode, they receive all IGMP Host Membership Report messages sent to any group address.

For the Windows 2000 Routing and Remote Access service, this functionality is provided by adding the IGMP routing protocol and enabling IGMP router mode on an interface. For more information, see "IGMP Protocol" later in this chapter.

Query Attached Subnets for Host Membership Status

On a specific subnet, there can be a mixture of IGMP v1 hosts and IGMP v2 hosts. When an IGMP v1 host stops receiving IP multicast traffic for a specific group address (the host leaves the group), it does not send a specific message to inform the local routers. Consequently, the host can leave the group; if it is the last member on the subnet, then the local routers continue to forward multicast traffic for that group to the subnet.

To improve the leave latency, the time between when the last host on a subnet has left the group and when no more multicast traffic for that group is forwarded to that subnet, multicast routers periodically send IGMP Host Membership Query messages to the local subnet for host membership information. A host that is still a member of a multicast group responds to the query with an IGMP Host Membership Report message. To keep multiple hosts on a particular subnet from sending IGMP Host Membership Report messages for the same group, a random response timer is used on the hosts to delay the transmission of the IGMP Host Membership Report message. If the message is sent by another host on that subnet before the response timer expires, a message is not sent.

To further improve leave latency, an IGMP v2 host that is the last host of a group on a subnet sends an IGMP Leave Group message. After sending group-specific queries to the group being left and receiving no response, the IGMP v2 router can determine that there are no more group members on that subnet.

Communicate Group Membership to Other IP Multicast Routers

To create multicast-enabled IP internetworks containing more than one router, multicast routers must communicate group membership information to each other so group members can receive IP multicast traffic regardless of their location on the IP internetwork.

Multicast routers exchange host membership information using a multicast routing protocol such as Distance Vector Multicast Routing Protocol (DVMRP), Multicast Open Shortest Path First (MOSPF), or Protocol Independent Multicast (PIM). Group membership is either communicated explicitly, by exchanging group address and subnet information, or implicitly, by informing upstream routers whether or not group members exist downstream from the source of the multicast traffic.

The goals of a multicast routing protocol include the following:

- Forward traffic away from the source to prevent loops.
- Minimize or eliminate multicast traffic to subnets that do not need the traffic.
- Minimize CPU and memory load on the router for scalability.
- Minimize the overhead of the routing protocol.
- Minimize the join latency, the time it takes for the first host member on a subnet to begin receiving group traffic.

Multicast routing is more complex than unicast routing. With unicast routing, unicast traffic is forwarded to a globally unique destination. Unicast routes summarize ranges of globally unique destinations. Unicast routes in the network are comparatively consistent and only need to be updated when the topology of the IP internetwork changes.

With multicast routing, multicast traffic is forwarded to an ambiguous group destination. Group addresses represent individual groups, and in general, cannot be summarized in the multicast forwarding table. The location of group members is not consistent, and the multicast forwarding tables of multicast routers might need to be updated whenever a host group member joins or leaves a host group.

Just as unicast routing protocols update the unicast IP routing table, multicast routing protocols update the IP multicast forwarding table. The Windows 2000 Routing and Remote Access service does not include any multicast routing protocols, although it provides a platform on which third-party protocols can run. The only component provided with Windows 2000 that can update entries in the multicast forwarding table is IGMP.

MBone

The Internet Multicast Backbone, or MBone, is the portion of the Internet that supports multicast routing and forwarding of Internet-based IP multicast traffic. The MBone structure consists of a series of multicast-enabled islands, collections of contiguous networks, connected together using tunnels. Multicast traffic is passed from one island to another by tunneling: encapsulating the IP multicast packet with an additional IP header addressed from one router in a multicast island to another router in another multicast island. Tunneling allows the multicast traffic to travel across portions of the Internet that do not support multicast forwarding.

The MBone is used for audio and video multicasts of Internet Engineering Task Force (IETF) meetings, the National Aeronautics and Space Administration, and the United States House of Representatives and Senate, among others. Support for the MBone might vary among Internet service providers (ISPs).

IGMP

Internet Group Management Protocol (IGMP) is used between hosts and their local multicast router. IGMP messages are encapsulated by IP and use the IP protocol number 0x02.

There are two versions of IGMP:

- IGMP version 1 is supported by TCP/IP for Windows NT version 4.0 Service Pack 3 and earlier and Microsoft® Windows® 95.
- IGMP version 2 is supported by TCP/IP for Microsoft Windows NT 4.0 Service Pack 4 and later, Microsoft® Windows® 98, and Windows 2000.

IGMP version 2 is backward compatible with IGMP version 1. The differences between the two versions are discussed in the following sections.

Note IGMP is only used to maintain host group membership on a local subnet. IP multicast traffic is not sent using an IGMP header. Typical IP multicast traffic uses a User Datagram Protocol (UDP) header.

IGMP v1

IGMP version 1 is a simple protocol consisting of two messages. The structure of IGMP version 1 messages is shown in Figure 4.2.

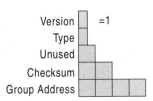

Figure 4.2   IGMP Version 1 Message Structure

Version   A 4-bit field set to the value of 0x1 for IGMP v1.

Type   A 4-bit field containing either 0x1 or 0x2. 0x1 indicates a Host Membership Query sent by an IP multicast router to query a subnet for current host membership. 0x2 indicates a Host Membership Report sent by IP multicast hosts when joining a group or in response to a Host Membership Query.

Unused   An unused 1-byte field set to the value of 0x00 by the sender and whose value is ignored by the receiver.

Checksum   A 2-byte field set to the value of the 16-bit checksum calculation on the IGMP message. The IGMP checksum does not include the IP header.

Group Address   A 4-byte field set to either 0.0.0.0 for a Host Membership Query, or the specific group address for a Host Membership Report.

Host Membership Report

When a host joins a multicast group, it sends an IGMP Host Membership Report message to the specific group address, regardless of whether there are already other hosts on its subnet that are host group members. Unlike a multicast router, a host does not keep track of the host group membership of other hosts on its subnet. Because a multicast router is listening in multicast promiscuous mode, it receives and processes IGMP Host Membership Report messages sent to any multicast address.

For a Windows 2000 Routing and Remote Access service configured with the IGMP routing protocol and an interface running in IGMP router mode, if this is the first host to join a host group on a particular subnet, the IGMP routing protocol creates an entry in the interface group table. If needed, an entry in the IP multicast forwarding table is created, containing the group address being registered and the interface on which the IGMP Host Membership Report message was received.

Host Membership Query

An IGMP v1 multicast router periodically sends an IGMP Host Membership Query message to 224.0.0.1 (the all hosts group) to refresh its knowledge of host members on the subnet. For each host group for which there are members on the subnet, one host group member responds with an IGMP Host Membership Report message. As previously discussed, a random response timer is used to stagger and randomly distribute the individual host group member who sends the IGMP Host Membership Report message for each group.

Upon receiving a response from a host group, the Windows 2000 Routing and Remote Access service updates the IGMP interface group table with a new expiry time, and the existing entry for the host group remains in the IP multicast forwarding table. If no hosts respond to the query for the host group and the expiry time for the entry in the IGMP interface group table becomes 0, then IGMP removes the host group entry from the multicast forwarding table.

Table 4.1 summarizes the values of the source and destination IP addresses and the TTL in the IP header and the value of the Group Address in the IGMP header for the two different types of IGMP v1 messages.

Table 4.1   Addresses and TTLs Used for IGMP v1 Messages

Address	IGMP Host Membership Query	IGMP Host Membership Report
Source IP Address	[Router interface IP address]	[Host interface IP address]
Destination IP Address	224.0.0.1	[Group address]
TTL	1	1
Group Address	0.0.0.0	[Group address]

For more information, see Appendix I of RFC 1112.

IGMP v2

IGMP version 2 extends the functionality of IGMP while maintaining backward compatibility with IGMP v1.

With IGMP v1, the router that sends the periodic queries is elected by the multicast routing protocols. IGMP v2 uses a simple election process to choose the multicast querier, the single router on each subnet that sends the periodic IGMP Host Membership Query messages. The router with the numerically lowest IP address is elected the multicast querier. The election process consists of listening for IGMP queries from other routers. If a query is received with a lower source IP address, the listening router remains a non-querier. If no query is received from other routers, the listening router becomes a querier.

IGMP v2 adds two new message types, an IGMP v2 Host Membership Report and a Leave Group message. It also adds a variation on the Host Membership Query called the Group-Specific Host Membership Query. The details of these new message types are discussed in the following sections.

The structure of IGMP version 2 messages is shown in Figure 4.3.

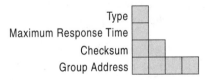

Type
Maximum Response Time
Checksum
Group Address

Figure 4.3   IGMP Version 2 Message Structure

Type Specifies the type of IGMP packet. IGMP v2 combines the two 4-bit IGMP v1 Version and Type fields into a single 8-bit Type field.

Table 4.2 lists the defined IGMP v2 message types.

Table 4.2   IGMP v2 Message Types

Hexadecimal Value	Decimal value	Message Type and Description
0x11 (The IGMP v1 Version field of 0x1 and IGMP v1 Type field 0x1 become the IGMP v2 Type field of 0x11.)	17	Host Membership Query For a general query, the Group Address field is set to 0.0.0.0. For a group-specific query, the Group Address field is set to the host group address.
0x12 (The IGMP v1 Version field of 0x1 and IGMP v1 Type field 0x2 become the IGMP v2 Type field of 0x12.)	18	Host Membership Report The Group Address field is set to the host group.
0x16	22	Version 2 Host Membership Report The Group Address field is set to the host group.
0x17	23	Leave Group The Group Address field is set to the host group.

Maximum Response Time   A 1-byte field that specifies the maximum time allowed in 1/10's of a second before sending a Host Membership Report after receiving a Host Membership Query. The Maximum Response Time field is only used in general or group-specific query messages. The Maximum Response Time is configured as the value for the Query response interval setting from:

- The **Router** tab on the properties of an IGMP interface in the Routing and Remote Access snap-in.
- The **netsh routing ip igmp set interface** command.

Checksum   A 2-byte field set to the value of the 16-bit checksum calculation on the IGMP message. The IGMP checksum does not include the IP header.

Group Address   A 4-byte field set to either 0.0.0.0 for a general Host Membership Query message or the specific group address for the Host Membership Report, Leave Group, and group-specific Host Membership Query messages.

IGMP v2 Host Membership Report

The IGMP v2 Host Membership Report has the same function as the IGMP v1 Host Membership Report except that it is intended to be received by IGMP v2 routers.

Leave Group Message

The Leave Group message is used to reduce the time it takes for the multicast router to stop forwarding multicast traffic when there are no longer any members in the host group. If a host responds to the last IGMP query, it might be the last or only member of the host group. When this host leaves the group it sends an IGMP Leave Group message to 224.0.0.2 (the all routers group). Upon receipt of the Leave Group message, the router sends a series of group-specific queries for the host group. If no host responds to the group-specific queries, the router determines that there are no more members of that host group on that particular subnet and removes the entry from the IGMP interface group table.

IGMP Group-Specific Query

An IGMP Host Membership Query is sent to 224.0.0.1 (the all hosts group) to query for the group membership of all hosts on the subnet. IGMP v2 routers can also send a group-specific query, a query for a specific multicast group sent to the group address.

Table 4.3 summarizes the values of the source and destination IP addresses and the TTL in the IP header and the value of the Group Address in the IGMP header for the two additional types of IGMP v2 messages.

Table 4.3   Addresses and TTLs Used for IGMP v2 Messages

Address	IGMP Group-Specific Query	IGMP Leave Group Message
Source IP Address	[Router interface IP address]	[Host interface IP address]
Destination IP Address	[Host group being queried]	224.0.0.2
TTL	1	1
Group Address	[Host group being queried]	[Host group being left]

For more information, see RFC 2236.

Routing and Remote Access Service IP Multicast Support

IP multicast support provided by the Windows 2000 Routing and Remote Access service consists of the following elements:

- The IGMP protocol
- Multicast boundaries
- Multicast heartbeat
- IP-in-IP tunnels
- Multicast static routes

IGMP Protocol

Because there are no multicast routing protocols provided with Windows 2000, the maintenance of entries in the IP multicast forwarding table is a function of IGMP, a component that is added as an IP routing protocol. After the IGMP routing protocol is added, router interfaces are added to IGMP. Each interface added to the IGMP routing protocol can be configured in one of two operating modes: IGMP router mode and IGMP proxy mode. The operating modes are discussed in more detail in the following sections.

While the IGMP protocol provides some limited ability to create or extend multicast-enabled IP internetworks, it is not the equivalent of a multicast routing protocol, such as DVMRP or PIM. Do not use the Windows 2000 IGMP routing protocol to create a multicast-enabled IP internetwork of an arbitrary size or topology. For more information about how Windows 2000 routers with the IGMP routing protocol component can be used, see "Supported Multicast Configurations" later in this chapter.

IGMP Router Mode

When an IGMP routing protocol interface is configured in IGMP router mode, it performs the following functions:

- Listens in multicast promiscuous mode.

  The IGMP router mode interface is enabled for multicast promiscuous mode. If multicast promiscuous mode is not supported by the network adapter, then IP Router Manager event number 20157 is logged.

- Listens for IGMP Host Membership Report messages and Leave Group messages.

  The IGMP router mode interface listens for IGMP Host Membership Report messages and Leave Group messages sent by hosts on the subnet.

- Sends IGMP Host Membership Queries.

  The IGMP router mode interface sends periodic general queries and group-specific queries after receiving a Leave Group message.

- Elects an IGMP querier.

  As an IGMP multicast router, the IGMP router mode interface elects an IGMP querier for the subnet.

- Maintains entries in IP multicast forwarding table.

  Based on the current group membership for hosts on the subnet, IGMP maintains the appropriate entries in the IP multicast forwarding table.

IGMP router mode can be enabled on multiple interfaces. For each interface, either version of IGMP can be configured. The default version is IGMP v2.

IGMP Router Mode Settings

The operation of IGMP v2 running in IGMP router mode is configurable for each interface. You can modify the operation of IGMP router mode using:

- The **Router** tab on the properties of an IGMP interface in the Routing and Remote Access snap-in.
- The **netsh routing ip igmp set interface** command.

Figure 4.4 shows the IGMP router mode settings for the **Local Area Connection** interface in the Routing and Remote Access snap-in.

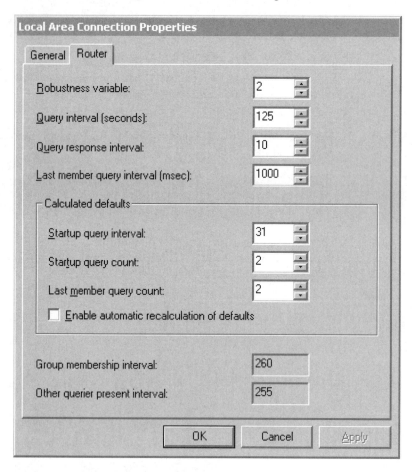

Figure 4.4   IGMP v2 Router Properties

Robustness Variable   The robustness variable is a way of indicating how susceptible the subnet is to lost packets. IGMP can recover from robustness variable minus 1 lost IGMP packets. You can also click the scroll arrows to select a new setting. The robustness variable should be set to a value of 2 or greater. The default robustness variable value is 2.

Query Interval   The query interval is the amount of time in seconds between IGMP General Query messages sent by the router (if the router is the querier on this subnet). You can also click the scroll arrows to select a new setting. The default query interval is 125 seconds.

Query Response Interval   The query response interval is the maximum amount of time in seconds that the IGMP router waits to receive a response to a General Query message. The query response interval is the Maximum Response Time field in the IGMP v2 Host Membership Query message header. You can also click the scroll arrows to select a new setting. The default query response interval is 10 seconds and must be less than the query interval.

Last Member Query Interval   The last member query interval is the amount of time in seconds that the IGMP router waits to receive a response to a Group-Specific Query message. The last member query interval is also the amount of time in seconds between successive Group-Specific Query messages. You can also click the scroll arrows to select a new setting. The default last member query interval is 1 second.

Calculated Defaults   IGMP variables can be manually configured or automatically calculated based on the values of the robustness variable and the query interval. For automatic calculation, select the **Enable automatic recalculation of defaults** check box.

Startup Query Interval   The startup query interval is the amount of time in seconds between successive General Query messages sent by a querier during startup. You can also click the scroll arrows to select a new setting. The default startup query interval is one-fourth of the value for the query interval.

Startup Query Count   The startup query count is the number of general query messages sent at startup. You can also click the scroll arrows to select a new setting. The default startup query count is 2.

Last Member Query Count   The last member query count is the number of Group-Specific Query messages sent before the router assumes that there are no members of the host group being queried on this interface. You can also click the scroll arrows to select a new setting. The default last member query count is 2.

Enable Automatic Recalculation of Defaults Specifies whether the values in startup query interval, startup query count, and last member query count are calculated automatically based on the following:

- The startup query interval is one-fourth of the value for the query interval.
- The startup query count is the same value as the robustness variable.
- The last member query count is the same value as the robustness variable.

Group Membership Interval The group membership interval is the number of seconds that must pass before a multicast router determines that there are no more members of a host group on a subnet. The group membership interval is calculated as the (robustness variable) * (query interval) + (query response interval). The group membership interval is a calculated value and is not configurable.

Other Querier Present Interval The other querier present interval is the number of seconds that must pass before a multicast router determines that there is no other multicast router that takes precedence as the querier. The other querier present interval is the robustness variable multiplied by the query interval plus the query response interval divided by two. The other querier present interval is a calculated value and is not configurable.

Note For more information about these settings and their relationship to each other, see RFC 2236.

IGMP Proxy Mode

While the purpose of IGMP router mode is to act as a multicast router, the purpose of IGMP proxy mode is to act as a multicast proxy for hosts on interfaces on which IGMP router mode is enabled. When an IGMP routing protocol interface is configured in IGMP router mode, it performs the following functions:

- Forwards IGMP Host Membership Reports

  All IGMP Host Membership Reports received on IGMP router mode interfaces are retransmitted on the IGMP proxy mode interface.

- Registers multicast MAC addresses

  For shared access technologies such as Ethernet, the network adapter is left in unicast listening mode. For each unique group registered by IGMP Host Membership Reports forwarded on the IGMP proxy mode interface, the network adapter is programmed to pass up frames with the corresponding multicast MAC address. Each additional multicast MAC address is an entry in the table of interesting destination MAC addresses on the network adapter. Each network adapter has a maximum number of entries it can store. If the maximum number of entries is used, then the IGMP routing protocol enables multicast promiscuous listening mode on the network adapter.

- Adds entries to the multicast forwarding table

  When non-local multicast traffic is received on an IGMP router mode interface, the IGMP routing protocol adds or updates an entry to the multicast forwarding table to forward the multicast traffic out the IGMP proxy mode interface. The end result of this process is that any non-local multicast traffic received on IGMP router mode interfaces is flooded, or copied, to the IGMP proxy mode interface.

- Receives multicast traffic received on IGMP proxy mode interfaces

  Multicast traffic received on the IGMP proxy mode interface corresponding to the groups registered by hosts on IGMP router mode interfaces are forwarded to the appropriate interfaces using the IP protocol and the multicast forwarding table.

The purpose of IGMP proxy mode is to connect a Windows 2000 router to a multicast-enabled IP internetwork, such as the MBone, or a private intranet that is using multicast routing protocols, such as DVMRP and PIM. The IGMP proxy mode interface acts like a host and joins host groups on behalf of hosts on its IGMP router mode interfaces. Multicast traffic sent to host members on IGMP router mode interfaces are received on the IGMP proxy mode interface and forwarded by the IP multicast forwarding process. Multicast traffic sent by hosts on IGMP router mode interfaces are flooded on the IGMP proxy mode interface where a downstream IP multicast-enabled router can either forward the traffic or ignore it.

IGMP proxy mode can only be enabled on a single IGMP routing protocol interface. The correct interface on which to enable IGMP proxy mode is the interface attached to a subnet containing a multicast router running multicast routing protocols. In other words, the IGMP proxy mode interface "points" to the multicast-enabled intranet.

Router Mode vs. Proxy Mode

Table 4.4 summarizes the features and behavior of IGMP router mode and IGMP proxy mode.

Table 4.4   IGMP Router Mode and IGMP Proxy Mode

Behavior	IGMP Router Mode	IGMP Proxy Mode
Listening mode	Multicast promiscuous mode.	Unicast listening mode.
IGMP router or host	Acts as an IGMP-based multicast router and listens for IGMP Host Membership Report messages.	Acts as an IGMP-based host by forwarding IGMP Host Membership Reports and responding to IGMP queries. Listens for IGMP Host Membership Report messages as a host, not as a router.
Updating of IP multicast forwarding table	Updates the IP multicast forwarding table based on IGMP traffic.	Updates the IP multicast forwarding table to flood non-local multicast traffic received on IGMP router mode interfaces.
Sends IGMP queries	Sends IGMP queries to maintain a current forwarding table.	Sends no IGMP queries.

Multicast Boundaries

Multicast boundaries are configurable administrative barriers that limit the extent of the IP internetwork over which multicast traffic can be forwarded. Without boundaries, an IP multicast router forwards all appropriate IP multicast traffic. With a Windows 2000–based router, you can define multicast boundaries by a range of IP addresses known as a multicast scope, by the value of the TTL field in the IP header, or by the rate of multicast traffic.

Multicast boundaries are configured per interface from the **Multicast Boundaries** tab from the properties of an interface in the **General** node under **IP Routing** in the Routing and Remote Access snap-in.

Scope-Based Boundaries

The 239.0.0.0/8 range of IP multicast addresses is defined as the administratively scoped IP multicast address space. Multicast addresses in this range can be prevented from propagating in either direction (send or receive) through the use of scope-based boundaries. A scope-based boundary defines the edge or boundary beyond which a multicast packet for a specified range is not forwarded.

To configure a scope (a range of IP multicast addresses) for address-based boundaries, you must first add the scope from:

- The **Multicast Scopes** tab of the properties of the **General** node under **IP Routing** in the Routing and Remote Access snap-in.
- The **netsh routing ip set scope** command.

You must enter the address range corresponding to the scope as an IP address and mask. However, the Local Scope of 239.255.0.0/16 is excluded. Therefore, configured scopes must be in the range of 239.0.0.0 to 239.254.255.255. For a range of IP multicast addresses, determine the appropriate IP address and mask that define the range. For a single group address, the IP address is the group address being scoped and the mask is 255.255.255.255.

Once the scopes are created, scope-based boundaries are configured per interface.

For more information about administrative scoping for IP multicast traffic, see RFC 2356.

TTL-Based Boundaries

TTL-based boundaries prevent the forwarding of IP multicast traffic with a TTL less than a specified value. TTL-based boundaries apply to all multicast packets regardless of the multicast group. Typically used TTL thresholds are listed in Table 4.5.

Table 4.5   TTL Thresholds and Their Scope

TTL Threshold	Scope
0	Restricted to the same host.
1	Restricted to the same subnet.
15	Restricted to the same site.
63	Restricted to the same region.
127	Worldwide.
191	Worldwide; limited bandwidth.
255	Unrestricted in scope.

Therefore, setting a TTL scope of 15 on an interface prevents the forwarding of IP multicast traffic that is intended to be restricted to the site. Only regional or beyond traffic is forwarded.

TTL-based boundaries are less effective than scope-based boundaries due to interactions with multicast routing protocols. For more information, see RFC 2365.

Multicast Rate Limiting

With multicast rate limiting, you can restrict multicast traffic forwarding for traffic beyond a specified rate in kilobytes per second.

Multicast Heartbeat

Multicast heartbeat is the ability of the Windows 2000–based router to listen for a regular multicast notification to a specified group address. Multicast heartbeat is used to verify that IP multicast connectivity is available on the network. If the heartbeat is not received within a configured amount of time, the multicast heartbeat status of the configured interface is set to inactive. To detect that the multicast heartbeat is missing, you must create a polling mechanism that periodically checks the multicast heartbeat status. If the status becomes inactive, then you can create a notification event. For more information, see the Microsoft Platform SDK link at http://windows.microsoft.com/windows2000/reskit/webresources.

For example, you could create a mechanism that sends a Simple Network Management Protocol (SNMP) trap to the configured SNMP management station when the multicast heartbeat status becomes inactive. This requires the creation of an SNMP sub-agent; the SNMP agent on the Windows 2000 router must be configured with the SNMP community name and the destination to send traps. For more information, see "Simple Network Management Protocol" in the *TCP/IP Core Networking Guide*.

A common protocol used for multicast heartbeat is Simple Network Time Protocol (SNTP). SNTP uses the reserved IP multicast address 224.0.1.1 and is used for time synchronization. If the source of the heartbeat traffic (the SNTP server) is strategically placed, the loss of the heartbeat indicates a problem with the IP multicast routing infrastructure. Windows 2000 includes an SNTP server called the Windows Time Synchronization service (W32Time) and an SNTP client. For more information about SNTP, see RFC 1769.

You can configure multicast heartbeat from the **Multicast Heartbeat** tab of the properties of the **General** node under **IP Routing** in the Routing and Remote Access snap-in.

IP-in-IP Tunnels

IP-in-IP tunnels are used to forward information between endpoints acting as a bridge between portions of an IP internetwork that have differing capabilities. A typical use for IP-in-IP tunnels is the forwarding of IP multicast traffic from one area of the intranet to another area of the intranet, across a portion of the intranet that does not support multicast forwarding or routing.

With IP-in-IP tunneling, an IP datagram is encapsulated with another IP header addressed to and from the endpoints of the IP-in-IP tunnel, as shown in Figure 4.5. An IP-in-IP tunnel is indicated by setting the IP Protocol field to 4 in the outer IP header. For more detailed information about IP-in-IP tunneling, see RFC 1853.

Figure 4.5   IP-in-IP Tunnel Packet Structure

IP-in-IP Interfaces

An IP-in-IP interface is a logical interface that sends IP packets in a tunneled mode. To create an IP-in-IP interface, in the Routing and Remote Access snap-in, right-click **Routing Interfaces,** click **New,** and then click **Tunnel (IP only)**. After the tunnel is created, add it as an IP routing interface by right-clicking the **General** node under **IP Routing**, and then clicking **New Interface**.

After IP-in-IP interfaces are created and added as an IP routing interface, you must configure the tunnel endpoints. Then, you can configure them the same as any other IP interface, including setting packet filters to confine the traffic that is allowed into and out of the interface, and multicast scopes and boundaries.

Multicast Static Routes

When an IP multicast packet is received on an interface of a Windows 2000 multicast-enabled router, the source and destination IP address of the IP multicast packet is compared to the entries in the IP multicast forwarding table. If an entry is found, the IP multicast packet is forwarded according to the found entry. If there are no downstream host group members, the packet is eventually discarded.

If an entry is not found, an entry must be created. An entry in the IP multicast forwarding table consists of the multicast group address, the source IP address, a list of interfaces to which the traffic is forwarded (next hop interfaces), and the single interface on which the traffic must be received in order to be forwarded (the previous hop interface). The multicast group and source IP addresses are obtained from the multicast packet. The next hop interfaces are determined by the registration of multicast group members using IGMP (and any multicast routing protocols, if present).

The previous hop interface is the interface that is closest—in terms of routing metrics—to the source of the IP traffic. To determine the previous hop interface, a multicast routing table is checked. Based on the entries in the multicast routing table, a single interface is chosen as the previous hop interface based on the best route back to the source of the IP multicast packet. The best route is the closest matching multicast route with the best metric.

The multicast routing table is logically separate from the unicast routing table. In the Routing and Remote Access service, the Route Table Manager (RTM) keeps a master list of routes. Each route is flagged as either a unicast route, a multicast route, or both. Therefore, the list of routes that you obtain depends on your view. The set of unicast routes in the RTM route table is called the unicast view. The set of multicast routes in the RTM route table is called the multicast view. The multicast view of the RTM routing table is used to determine the previous hop interface and the previous hop neighbor, which is needed for multicast diagnostic utilities, such as mtrace.

By default, all unicast routes obtained by the Routing Information Protocol (RIP) and the Open Shortest Path First (OSPF) routing protocols, and static routes manually configured with the Routing and Remote Access snap-in, are flagged as appearing in both views. If your unicast routers are also your multicast routers, no other modifications are necessary.

However, in some configurations, the unicast infrastructure and multicast infrastructure are different. For example, to balance the load between unicast and multicast traffic, a different set of routers is used. In these configurations, you might need to override the default behavior of adding all routes as both a unicast and multicast route by creating multicast static route using the **netsh routing ip add rtmroute** command.

An example is a Windows 2000 router with two interfaces; Interface 1 is connected to a unicast router, Interface 2 is connected to a multicast router. For simplicity, assume that a single static default route is used to forward all non-local unicast IP traffic to a downstream router using Interface 1. Because the static route was configured using the Routing and Remote Access snap-in, it is flagged as both a unicast and multicast route. Consider what happens when an IP multicast packet is received on Interface 2:

- To create the IP multicast forwarding table entry, the previous hop interface must be determined. Based on the multicast view of the RTM route table, the previous hop interface is determined to be Interface 1, not Interface 2 (Interface 1 is closest to the multicast source in terms of routing metrics). Because the previous hop interface is the only interface on which IP multicast packets for the group and source IP address can be received, subsequent IP multicast packets received on Interface 2 for the group and source IP address are silently discarded.

To fix this multicast forwarding problem, use the **netsh routing ip add rtmroute** command to create a multicast static default route that uses Interface 2 and has a lower metric. This new route overrides the manually configured static default route.

Supported Multicast Configurations

Because the IGMP router and IGMP proxy component of the Windows 2000 Routing and Remote Access service are not designed to be a substitute for a multicast routing protocol such as DVMRP or PIM, the following sections describe recommended and supported configurations of a Windows 2000 router using the IGMP routing protocol, IGMP router mode, and IGMP proxy mode.

Single Router Intranet

The Windows 2000 router can provide full multicast capabilities in a single router intranet. In this configuration, all interfaces are added to the IGMP routing protocol and each interface is configured for IGMP router mode. Any host on any subnet can both send and receive multicast traffic from any other host. All multicast traffic is forwarded to subnets where there are host members.

The single router intranet configuration is shown in Figure 4.6.

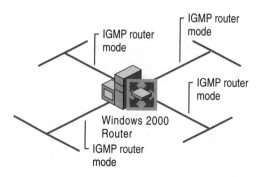

Figure 4.6   Single Router Intranet

Single Router Intranet Connected to the MBone

The Windows 2000 router can provide multicast capabilities in a single router intranet connected to the Internet MBone. In this configuration, all interfaces on are added to the IGMP routing protocol. All private subnet interfaces are configured for IGMP router mode and the Internet interface is configured for IGMP proxy mode.

Hosts joining multicast groups send IGMP Host Membership Reports, which are then copied on the Internet interface. Multicast traffic from the Internet is sent to the Internet interface. When received, the multicast traffic is forwarded to the host on the appropriate subnet. Multicast traffic sent by a host on an intranet subnet is copied to the Internet interface. The multicast router at the ISP either ignores or forwards the multicast traffic.

In this configuration, multicast traffic sent between two hosts on the private intranet is still copied to the Internet interface, resulting in inefficient use of the bandwidth of the link to the ISP. To prevent intranet multicast traffic from being copied to the Internet interface, configure the applications or the ranges of multicast addresses on your MADCAP servers on the intranet to use IP multicast addresses from the administratively scoped range of 239.0.0.0 to 239.254.255.255, and configure the appropriate scope-based boundary on the Internet interface.

The single router intranet connected to the MBone configuration is shown in Figure 4.7.

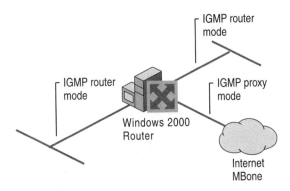

Figure 4.7   Single Router Intranet Connected to the MBone

Peripheral Router in a Multicast-Enabled Intranet

In a configuration very similar to the single router intranet connected to the MBone, a Windows 2000–based router can provide multicast capabilities as a peripheral router connected to a multicast-enabled private intranet. A peripheral router is a router attached to multiple subnets; however, only a single attached subnet contains another router. In this case, the other router is a multicast core router, a multicast router running routing protocols that is part of the multicast-enabled intranet.

In this configuration, all interfaces are added to the IGMP routing protocol. All interfaces not containing the multicast router are configured for IGMP router mode and the interface connected to the subnet containing the multicast core router is configured for IGMP proxy mode.

Hosts joining multicast groups send IGMP Host Membership Reports, which are copied on the interface attached to the subnet containing the multicast core router. Multicast traffic from the intranet is forwarded to the IGMP proxy mode interface subnet. When received, the multicast traffic is forwarded to the host on the appropriate subnet. Multicast traffic sent by a host on an attached subnet is copied to the IGMP proxy mode interface subnet. The multicast core router either ignores the multicast traffic or forwards it to downstream host group members.

The peripheral router in a multicast-enabled intranet configuration is shown in Figure 4.8.

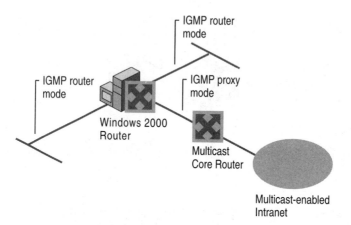

Figure 4.8   Peripheral Router in a Multicast-Enabled Intranet

Multicast Support for Remote Access Clients

A common use for the Windows 2000 IGMP routing protocol is to provide multicast services to dial-up or virtual private network (VPN) remote access clients. As in the previously discussed configurations, the remote access or VPN server is acting as a peripheral router to a multicast-enable IP internetwork.

There are two possible configurations, depending on the connectivity provided to the remote access clients:

- MBone access for dial-up clients by an ISP.
- Access to a private multicast-enabled intranet for dial-up or VPN clients.

MBone Access for ISP Dial-Up Clients

If you are using the Windows 2000 Routing and Remote Access service to provide Internet access to dial-up clients as an ISP:

1. Add the **Internal** interface, and the interface connecting to the rest of the Internet, to the IGMP routing protocol. The **Internal** interface represents all remote access clients.

2. Configure the **Internal** interface for IGMP router mode.

3. Configure the Internet interface for IGMP proxy mode.

Connected remote access clients joining multicast groups send IGMP Host Membership Reports, which are copied on the Internet interface. Multicast traffic from the Internet is sent to the Internet interface. When received, the multicast traffic is forwarded to the connected host. Multicast traffic sent by a connected host is forwarded to other connected host group members and copied to the Internet interface. The downstream multicast router in the Internet either ignores the multicast traffic or forwards it to downstream group members.

The MBone access configuration for ISP dial-up clients is shown in Figure 4.9.

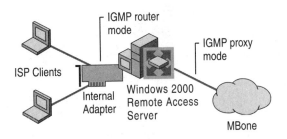

Figure 4.9   MBone Access for ISP Dial-Up Clients

Private Intranet Access for Dial-Up or VPN Clients

If you are using the Windows 2000 Routing and Remote Access service to provide intranet access for dial-up or VPN remote access clients, perform the following steps:

1. Add the **Internal** interface and the interface connecting to the private intranet to the IGMP routing protocol. The **Internal** interface represents all remote access clients. The private intranet interface must be attached to a subnet containing a multicast core router.

2. Configure the **Internal** interface for IGMP router mode.

3. Configure the private intranet interface for IGMP proxy mode.

Connected remote access clients joining multicast groups, send IGMP Host Membership Reports, which are copied on the intranet interface. Multicast traffic from the intranet is sent to the IGMP proxy mode interface subnet. When received, the multicast traffic is forwarded to connected group members. Multicast traffic sent by a connected host is forwarded to other connected host group members and copied to the IGMP proxy mode interface subnet. The multicast core router either ignores the multicast traffic or forwards it to downstream group members.

The private intranet access for dial-up or VPN clients configuration is shown in Figure 4.10.

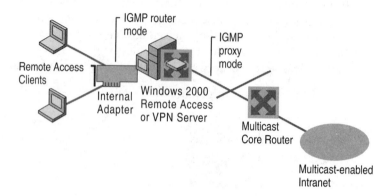

Figure 4.10   Private Intranet Access for Dial-Up or VPN Clients

For more information about multicast support for the remote access server, see "Remote Access Server" in this book.

Multicast Support for Branch Office Networks

The Windows 2000 router can provide full multicast capabilities for single router branch offices connected to a hub office with a multicast-enabled intranet. This configuration requires proper configuration of both the branch office and hub office router.

For the branch office router, all interfaces are added to the IGMP routing protocol and the interfaces for the branch office subnets are configured for IGMP router mode. The interface that connects to the hub office router is configured for IGMP proxy mode. The interface that connects to the hub office router can be a LAN interface (such as when using a T-Carrier or Frame Relay connection) or a demand-dial interface (such as when using dial-up analog phone lines, ISDN, or a router-to-router VPN connection). A demand-dial interface can be either on-demand or persistent. For more information about demand-dial interfaces and configuration, see "Demand-Dial Routing" in this book.

For the hub office router, all interfaces are added to the IGMP routing protocol and the interface connected to the branch office is configured for IGMP router mode. The interface that connects to the branch office router can be a LAN interface (such as when using a T-Carrier or Frame Relay connection) or a demand-dial interface (such as when using dial-up analog phone lines, ISDN, or a router-to-router VPN connection). The interface that connects the multicast core router subnet is configured for IGMP proxy mode.

IGMP Group Membership Report messages for group members are copied across the branch office link to the multicast core router subnet. Multicast traffic from branch office hosts is flooded from the branch office subnet across the branch office link to the multicast core router subnet.

In this configuration, multicast traffic sent between two hosts on the branch office intranet is copied to the branch office link, resulting in inefficient use of the bandwidth of the link to the hub office. To prevent intra-branch office multicast traffic from being copied to the branch office link, configure the applications or the ranges of multicast addresses on your MADCAP servers on the intranet to use IP multicast addresses from the administratively scoped range of 239.0.0.0 to 239.254.255.255, and configure the appropriate scope-based boundaries on the interface to the hub office.

The multicast support for branch office networks configuration is shown in Figure 4.11.

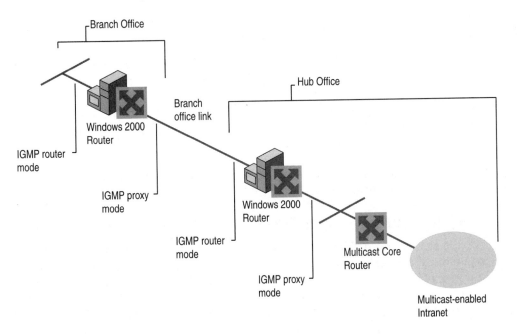

Figure 4.11   Multicast Support for Branch Office Networks

IP Multicast Troubleshooting Tools

To troubleshoot IP multicast problems, the Windows 2000 Routing and Remote Access service provides the following tools:

- Routing and Remote Access snap-in tables
- Mrinfo command
- Mtrace support
- Netsh commands
- IGMP event logging
- Tracing

For more information about general multicast troubleshooting, see the Internet Draft titled "Multicast Debugging Handbook."

Routing and Remote Access Snap-In Tables

There are three tables containing IP multicast information that can be viewed with the Routing and Remote Access snap-in:

- Multicast forwarding table
- Multicast statistics
- IGMP interface group table

Their location within the Routing and Remote Access snap-in depends on the component that maintains the table.

Multicast Forwarding Table

The multicast forwarding table is the table used by IP to forward IP multicast traffic. Each entry records a specific host group and the source of the traffic. The Type column is set to **Active** for the entry if packets for the host group are being forwarded and set to **Negative** if the traffic is seen on the network but the router is not forwarding because no hosts have registered for this group.

To view the multicast forwarding table, right-click the **General** node under **IP Routing**, and then click **Show Multicast forwarding table**.

Multicast Statistics

Multicast statistics are counters and other information compiled by IP for each multicast group being forwarded. An entry for multicast statistics records the group address, the IP address of the multicast source, the interface on which it was received, the number of packets received, and other information.

To view multicast statistics, right-click the **General** node under **IP Routing**, and then click **Show Multicast statistics**.

IGMP Group Table

The IGMP group table displays IGMP host group membership information for all host groups registered on all interfaces configured for IGMP router mode. Each entry records uptime (number of seconds since the group was first registered), expiry time (the number of seconds left before the group expires if no hosts send host membership reports for this address), and other information.

To view the IGMP Group Table, right-click the **IGMP** node under **IP Routing**, and then click **Show group table**.

IGMP Interface Group Table

The IGMP interface group table displays IGMP host group membership information for host groups registered on a specific interface configured for IGMP router mode. Each entry records uptime (number of seconds since the group was first registered), expiry time (the number of seconds left before the group expires if no hosts send host membership reports for this address), and other information.

To view the IGMP Interface Group Table, right-click the interface in the **IGMP** node under **IP Routing**, and then click **Show interface group table**.

Mrinfo Command

Windows 2000 includes the **mrinfo** tool, which you can use to display the configuration of a multicast router. The configuration information can be used to aid in the troubleshooting of multicast forwarding and routing problems.

mrinfo queries a specified multicast router with a special message. The response to the query contains a version number, the list of interfaces and the neighbors on each interface, metrics, Time-to-Live (TTL) thresholds, and flags. **mrinfo** syntax includes:

```
mrinfo [ -d debug_level ] [ -r retry_count ] [  -t timeout_count ]
multicast_router
```

Table 4.6   Mrinfo Command Options

Option	Description
-d	Specifies the debug level. The default value is 0. When debug level is set to 1, all packet warnings are displayed. When debug level is set to 2, downed network notifications and all level 1 messages are displayed. When debug level is set to 3, packet time-out notifications and all level 2 messages are displayed.
-r	Specifies the neighbor query retry limit. The default value is 3.
-t	Specifies how long in seconds **mrinfo** waits for a neighbor query reply. The default value is 4.

Example of using **mrinfo**:

```
C:\>mrinfo 10.1.0.1
10.1.0.1(test1.ntdev.microsoft.com) [version 20.50,mtrace,snmp]:
    10.1.0.1 -> 0.0.0.0 (local) [1/0/querier/leaf]
    10.2.0.1 -> 10.2.0.2 (test2.ntdev.microsoft.com) [1/0]
    10.2.0.1 -> 10.2.0.3 (test3.ntdev.microsoft.com) [1/0]
    10.3.0.1 -> 0.0.0.0 (local) [1/0/querier/leaf]
```

In the previous example, **mrinfo** is run against a multicast router at 10.1.0.1. The first line shows the multicast router configuration: version number (for Windows 2000 routers, the version number reflects the build number of Windows 2000) and flags (mtrace and SNMP supported).

Each additional line displays the interfaces on the multicast router and the neighbors on each interface. Interfaces 10.1.0.1 and 10.3.0.1 have no neighbors. Interface 10.2.0.1 has two neighbors, 10.2.0.2 and 10.2.0.3. For each line, **mrinfo** displays the interface and neighbor, the domain name for the neighbor, the multicast routing metric, the TTL threshold, and flags indicating its role on the network such as the IGMP querier of the network (querier) or whether it has no neighbors (leaf).

Mtrace Support

Although Windows 2000 does not provide a version of the multicasting tracing utility called mtrace, the Windows 2000 multicast router does respond to mtrace queries from third-party mtrace utilities.

Netsh Commands

To view multicast tables and gather information to aid in the troubleshooting of multicast routing and forwarding problems, use the following netsh command lines:

- **netsh routing ip show mfe**

  Displays the entries in the multicast forwarding table. This is equivalent to the multicast forwarding table available from the Routing and Remote Access snap-in.

- **netsh routing ip show mfestats**

  Displays packet statistics and input and output interface information for entries in the multicast forwarding table. This is equivalent to the multicast statistics window available from the Routing and Remote Access snap-in.

- **netsh routing ip igmp show grouptable**

  Displays IGMP host group membership information for all host groups registered on all interfaces configured for IGMP router mode. This is equivalent to the IGMP group table in the Routing and Remote Access snap-in.

- **netsh routing ip igmp show ifstats**

  Displays IGMP statistics for each interface.

- **netsh routing ip igmp show iftable**

  Displays host group membership information for host groups registered on a specific interface configured for IGMP router mode. This is equivalent to the IGMP interface group table in the Routing and Remote Access snap-in.

- **netsh routing ip igmp show rasgrouptable**

  Displays the group table for the Internal interface used by the remote access server.

- **netsh routing ip igmp show proxygrouptable**

  Displays the group table for the IGMP proxy mode interface.

IGMP Event Logging

The level of event logging for events recorded in the Windows 2000 system event log for the IGMP routing protocol is set:

- Through the properties of the IGMP routing protocol under **IP Routing** in the Routing and Remote Access snap-in.
- The **netsh routing ip igmp set global** command.

The logging levels are:

- Log errors only
- Log errors and warnings
- Log the maximum amount of information
- Disable event logging

The default level is **Log errors only**. When troubleshooting a problem with the IGMP routing protocol, set the logging level to **Log the maximum amount of information**. Once the appropriate information is obtained, set the logging level back to **Log errors only**.

Tracing

Tracing records the sequence of programming functions called during a process to a file. To record detailed information about IGMP routing protocol processes in the log file *SystemRoot*\tracing\IGMPv2.log, set the value of the **EnableFileTracing** registry entry (HKEY_LOCAL_MACHINE\Software\Microsoft\tracing\IGMPV2) to 1. After you are done viewing the traced information, set **EnableFileTracing** back to its original setting of 0.

The tracing information can be complex and very detailed. This information is predominantly useful only to Microsoft support professionals, or to network administrators who are very experienced with the Windows 2000 Routing and Remote Access service. The tracing information can be saved as files and sent to Microsoft support for analysis. For more information about the tracing facility, see "Routing and Remote Access Service" in this book.

Additional Resources

- For more information about IP multicast, see *Deploying IP Multicast in the Enterprise* by Thomas A. Maufer, 1998, Upper Saddle River, NJ: Prentice Hall PTR.

C H A P T E R   5

IPX Routing

The Microsoft® Windows® 2000 Server Router is a fully functional Internetwork Packet Exchange(IPX) router supporting Routing Information Protocol (RIP) for IPX, the primary routing protocol used in IPX internetworks; Novell NetWare Service Advertising Protocol (SAP) for IPX, a protocol for the collection and distribution of service names and addresses; and NetBIOS over IPX broadcast forwarding.

In This Chapter

Related Information in the Resource Kit

- For more information about unicast routing, see "Unicast Routing Overview" in this book.

- For more information about the Windows 2000 Router, see "Routing and Remote Access Service" in this book.

- For more information about demand-dial routing, see "Demand-Dial Routing" in this book.

- For more information about interoperability with NetWare, see "Interoperability with NetWare" in this book.

Windows 2000 and IPX Routing

An Internetwork Packet Exchange (IPX) router is a combination of an IPX routing agent and a Service Advertising Protocol (SAP) agent. The IPX routing agent routes IPX packets between IPX networks and maintains its routing table using Routing Information Protocol (RIP) for IPX. The SAP agent collects and distributes SAP information (a list of services available on the network and their corresponding IPX internetwork addresses) and responds to client SAP requests. For more information about the IPX router components in Microsoft® Windows® 2000, see "Routing and Remote Access Service" in this book.

Microsoft® Windows NT® Server version 4.0 and earlier provided a SAP agent service that allowed Windows NT applications and services, such as File and Print Services for NetWare or Microsoft® Exchange Server, to advertise their service names and addresses for NetWare clients. Microsoft® Windows NT® version 3.51 (Service Pack 2 and later) and Windows NT Server 4.0 provided an IPX routing agent using the RIP for IPX routing protocol. Windows 2000 Server provides an integrated IPX router with an IPX routing agent using the RIP for IPX routing protocol and a SAP agent.

Windows 2000 Router Features for the IPX Protocol Suite

The Windows 2000–based computer running the Routing and Remote Access service, known as the Windows 2000 Router, provides a rich set of features to support IPX internetworks:

IPX Packet Filtering Input and output filters for each interface, configured using key fields in the IPX header.

RIP for IPX Full support for Routing Information Protocol (RIP) for IPX, the primary routing protocol used in IPX internetworks.

IPX Route Filtering Filtering for incoming routes and for the announcement of routes.

Static IPX Routes Static IPX routes that are advertised using RIP for IPX.

SAP for IPX Full support for Service Advertising Protocol (SAP), the mechanism by which the names and addresses of services running on IPX nodes are collected and distributed for NetWare clients.

SAP Filtering The filtering of incoming service names and the announcement of service names.

Static SAP Services Static SAP service names that are advertised using SAP.

NetBIOS Broadcast Propagation The forwarding of NetBIOS over IPX broadcasts, flexibly configured over local area networks (LAN) and demand-dial interfaces.

Static NetBIOS Names Static NetBIOS names that can be configured so that NetBIOS over IPX name query broadcasts for specific NetBIOS names can be forwarded using specific interfaces.

Platform to Support Other IPX Routing Protocols A platform to support additional IPX routing protocols, such as NetWare Link Services Protocol (NLSP). (The Windows 2000 Router does not provide NLSP, but NLSP can be provided by third party independent software vendors.)

IPX Packet Filtering

In addition to routing IPX traffic, an IPX router can allow or disallow the flow of very specific types of IPX traffic. This capability, called IPX packet filtering, provides a way to precisely define the type of IPX traffic allowed to cross the router.

You can create a series of definitions called filters that indicate to the router the type of traffic allowed or disallowed on each interface. You can set these filters for incoming and outgoing traffic. Input filters define the incoming traffic on a specific interface that is allowed to be routed or processed by the router. Output filters define the traffic that is allowed to be sent from that interface.

Figure 5.1 illustrates IPX packet filtering.

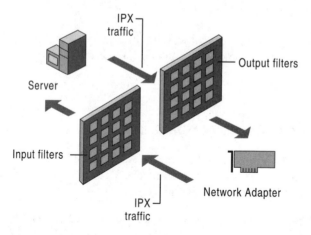

Figure 5.1   IPX Packet Filtering

Because both input and output filters can be defined for each interface, it is possible to create contradictory filters. For example, the input filter on one interface allows the inbound traffic, but the output filter on the other interface does not allow the outbound traffic. The result is that the desired traffic is not passed across the router.

The Windows 2000 Router has the capability to perform input and output filtering for each interface based on key fields in the IPX header. The next section explains the structure of an IPX header to help you gain an understanding of the types of IPX filtering that the Windows 2000 Router can perform.

IPX Header Structure

The IPX header, which comes immediately after media and Data Link Layer headers (such as Ethernet, Token Ring, or Point-to-Point Protocol [PPP]), is shown in Figure 5.2.

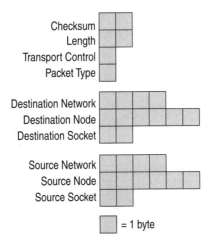

Figure 5.2   IPX Header

Checksum   A 16-bit checksum on the IPX header and its payload is typically unused. If unused, the Checksum field is set to **0xFF-FF**. If the Checksum is used, the IPX node cannot be configured to use the ETHERNET_802.3 frame type.

Length   The length field indicates the length of the IPX packet (IPX header and IPX payload) in bytes. To accommodate older routers and network adapters, sometimes an IPX node must be configured to ensure that the IPX packet is an even number of bytes. If the packet contains an odd number of bytes, an extra byte is used to fill out the packet to an even number of bytes. The extra byte is not included in the Length field.

Transport Control The Transport Control field indicates the number of IPX routers that have processed the IPX packet, known as the hop count. Sending nodes set this field to zero, and it is incremented by one by each IPX router in the path from the source to the destination. RIP for IPX routers limit the maximum number of routers in a network path to 16. At the 17th RIP for IPX router, the IPX packet is discarded by the router without notifying the sending node, known as a silent discard. NetWare Link Services Protocol (NLSP) for IPX routers can support a hop count of up to 127.

Packet Type The Packet Type field indicates the contents of the payload portion of the IPX packet. It allows a number of client protocols to use IPX and be identified by the IPX router. Table 5.1 lists some common defined values of the IPX Packet Type.

Table 5.1   IPX Packet Type Values

Client Protocol	Packet Type (Hexadecimal)
Unspecified	00
RIP	01
SAP/Normal IPX	04
SPX	05
IPX WAN Broadcast (used for NetBIOS over IPX Broadcasts)	14 (20 in decimal)

Routers can filter out IPX traffic based on the Packet Type field. For example, some routers by default do not propagate NetBIOS over IPX Broadcast traffic and must be manually configured to enable packets with a packet type value of 20.

Network (Destination and Source) The Destination Network and Source Network fields each identify the network (a segment of the IPX internetwork bounded by IPX routers) to which an IPX node is connected. IPX network numbers are a flat addressing space. No subnetting (the subdivision of network IDs) or summarization of groups of IPX networks is possible with RIP for IPX routing. RIP for IPX routers must have a route to each network number in their routing tables. All IPX networks must be given a unique IPX network number.

Node (Destination and Source) The Destination Node and Source Node fields each identify a node on an IPX network. The 6-byte fields can be used to store physical addresses — also known as Media Access Control (MAC) addresses.

Socket (Destination and Source) The Destination Socket and Source Socket fields identify the software process addresses of the destination and source applications respectively. With multiple processes communicating between the same two computers, the IPX Network and Node numbers are the same. The IPX Socket number is a software process identifier that is used to forward the IPX payload to the proper process.

Many socket numbers are well known. For example, the file server process running on Novell NetWare or compatible file servers uses the well-known socket address of 0x451. Any requests to socket 0x451 on the NetWare file server are forwarded to the NetWare file server process. NetWare file server clients and IPX applications that do not use a well-known socket number use dynamically allocated socket numbers. Table 5.2 lists some common, defined values for IPX socket numbers.

Table 5.2   IPX Socket Numbers

Process	Socket Number (Hexadecimal)
NCP Server	451
RIP	453
SAP	452
NetBIOS	455

Note The IPX socket is not the same as a socket in the Windows Sockets 2.*x* API (Winsock). A socket in Winsock is a generalized process endpoint. A TCP/IP-based Winsock socket is a combination of the IP Address and port number that identifies a process endpoint on an IP internetwork. An IPX-based Winsock socket is a combination of the IPX Network, IPX Node, and IPX Socket numbers that identifies a process endpoint on an IPX internetwork.

Demultiplexing an IPX Packet

When an IPX packet arrives at its destination and is handed to the IPX protocol, the application data must be demultiplexed, or forwarded to the proper process.

The demultiplexing of the IPX packet within the destination host is done in two stages. First, the IPX module checks the Destination Network and Node numbers to ensure that they correspond to a locally configured IPX interface. Second, the IPX module checks the Destination Socket number and based on its value, passes the IPX payload (the resulting packet minus the IPX header) to the appropriate process.

Figure 5.3 illustrates the IPX demultiplexing process.

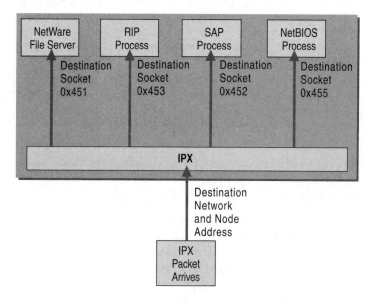

Figure 5.3   Demultiplexing an IPX Packet

For example, a NetWare client sends a file sharing request to a NetWare server. Upon arrival at the NetWare server's IPX module, the destination Network and Node numbers are checked to verify that it corresponds to a local IPX interface. The IPX module then notes the Destination Socket field value of 0x451 and passes the IPX payload to the NetWare file server process.

The Windows 2000 Router IPX Packet Filtering

The Windows 2000 Router IPX packet filtering is based on exceptions. You can either configure the Windows 2000 Router to pass all IPX traffic except those disallowed by filters or to discard all IPX traffic except those allowed by filters. For example, you might want to set up output filters to forward all traffic except for SAP advertisements. Or, you might want to set up an input filter on a dedicated SQL server to disregard all but SQL-based Sequenced Packet Exchange (SPX) traffic.

The Windows 2000 Router allows configuration of IPX filters based on the following fields:

- Packet Type
- Source Network
- Source Node
- Source Socket
- Destination Network
- Destination Node
- Destination Socket

Note Both the Source and Destination Network numbers can be configured with a network mask allowing a range of IPX network numbers to be specified with a single filter entry. To determine whether the network number of an IPX packet matches the filter, the Windows 2000 Router uses **AND** to combine the Network Mask and the network number in the IPX packet and compares the result to the filter network number. The digit **0** can be used as a wildcard for a hexadecimal digit and **F** for a specific hexadecimal digit.

Configuring an IPX Filter

You can configure IPX input or output filtering by selecting a filter action and adding a series of filters using the **IPX Packet Filters Configuration** dialog box, as shown in Figure 5.4.

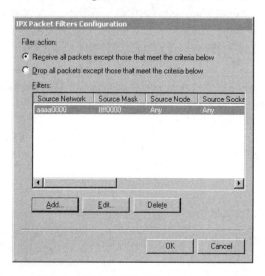

Figure 5.4   IPX Packet Filters Configuration Dialog Box

Note You cannot configure separate active filters for **Receive all packets except those that meet the criteria below** and **Drop all packets except those that meet the criteria below**.

You can specify the parameters of an input or output filter using the **Add IPX Filter** or **Edit IPX Filter** dialog box shown in Figure 5.5. If multiple parameters are configured, the logical operation, **AND**, combines the parameters of the filter during the filtering process. For example, if the Packet Type and Destination Socket are specified in the filter, the IPX packet passes the filter if both the IPX packet's Packet Type and its Destination Socket match those of the filter.

Note All numbers in the **Add IPX Filter** or **Edit IPX Filter** dialog box shown in Figure 5.5 are entered in hexadecimal.

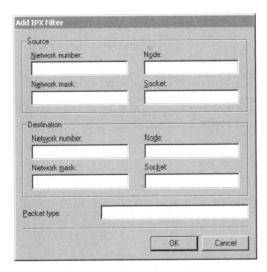

Figure 5.5   Add IPX Filter Dialog Box

The following two sample IPX filters provide examples of IPX filtering scenarios and the implementation of IPX filtering using the fields in the **Add IPX Filter** or **Edit IPX Filter** dialog box. These examples are provided to illustrate how IPX filters are configured, not as a recommendation of specific IPX filtering for your network.

▶ **To configure an IPX input filter using the network mask (Example)**

To allow only the processing of received IPX packets with the Destination Network number starting with the hexadecimal digits **AB**, configure the input filter as follows:

1. In the **IPX Packet Filters Configuration** dialog box, click **Add**.

2. In the **Add IPX Filter** dialog box in the **Network number** text box, under **Destination**, type **AB000000**.

3. In the **Network mask** text box, under **Destination**, type **FF000000**.

4. Click **OK**.

5. In the **IPX Packet Filters Configuration** dialog box, select the **Drop all packets except those that meet the criteria below** option.

6. Click **OK**.

This filter uses the network mask to express a range of IPX network numbers from AB000000 to ABFFFFFF.

▶ **To configure an IPX output filter using the network mask (Example)**

To prevent the transmission or forwarding of all IPX traffic from the Source Network number of CC000001, configure the output filter as follows:

1. In the **IPX Packet Filters Configuration** dialog box, click **Add**.

2. In the **Add IPX Filter** dialog box, in the **Network number** text box, under **Source**, type **CC000001**.

3. In the **Network mask** text box, under **Source**, type **FFFFFFFF**.

4. Click **OK**.

5. In the **IPX Packet Filters Configuration** dialog box, select the **Receive all packets except those that meet the criteria below** option.

6. Click **OK**.

This filter uses the network mask to express the single IPX network number CC000001.

Note The network mask in the **Add IPX Filter** or **Edit IPX Filter** dialog box is used only as an administrative convenience to express a range of IPX network IDs. This does not mean that the Windows 2000 Router is implementing a subnetting scheme for IPX internetworks. RIP for IPX internetworks use a flat network addressing space and do not support subnetting or route summarization.

RIP for IPX

RIP for IPX, a distance vector routing protocol, distributes routing information on an IPX internetwork. RIP for IPX was derived from the Xerox Network Systems (XNS) form of RIP but contains an additional field called the Tick Count. The Tick Count is an estimate of the amount of time it takes an IPX packet to reach the destination network. The Tick Count enables the RIP for IPX router to choose the route that has the lowest delivery delay.

To reduce convergence time, RIP for IPX uses split horizon and triggered updates. For information about split horizon and triggered updates, see "Unicast IP Routing" in this book.

RIP for IPX consists of the following types of messages:

- RIP clients, such as workstations, can locate the optimal route to an IPX network number by broadcasting a RIP GetLocalTarget route request.

- Routers can request routing information from other routers by broadcasting a RIP general route request.

- Routers can respond to RIP GetLocalTarget and RIP general route requests.

- Routers can periodically (every 60 seconds by default) broadcast their routing tables using split horizon.

- Routers can perform a triggered-update broadcast to inform adjacent routers of a change in the IPX internetwork configuration.

IPX Routing Tables

The IPX routing table is maintained by the RIP for IPX routing protocol. An entry in an IPX routing table contains the following fields:

Network Number The IPX Network Number that is matched to the destination network number in a packet's IPX header.

Forwarding MAC Address The destination MAC address of the IPX packet when it is forwarded to the next hop. For directly attached networks, the Forwarding MAC Address field is blank.

Tick Count The number of ticks it takes to reach the destination network where one tick is approximately 1/18 of a second. This estimate is based on ongoing RIP requests and replies and is determined by the transmission speed of network segments. LAN links are typically one tick, and WAN links, such as a T1 link, are usually six or seven ticks. The tick count is an estimated, not precise, measurement of delay.

Hop Count The number of routers that must be crossed to reach the IPX network number.

Interface (or Port) The interface (or network interface card) that is used when forwarding IPX traffic using this route. The router has one interface installed for each attached network segment.

Figure 5.6 shows the structure of the IPX routing table.

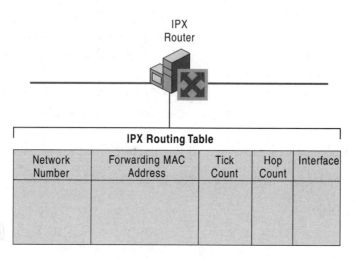

Figure 5.6   IPX Routing Table

If there are multiple routes to an IPX network number, IPX routers use the following process to select a route:

1. Select the route with the lowest number of ticks.
2. If there are multiple routes with the lowest number of ticks, select the route with the lowest number of hops.
3. If there are multiple routes with the lowest number of ticks and the lowest number of hops, the router is free to choose among the set of routes with the lowest number of ticks and the lowest number of hops.

RIP for IPX Operation

The RIP operation for an IPX router consists of the following processes:

Initialization   At startup, the IPX router broadcasts a RIP packet on each of its attached networks informing adjacent routers of the network numbers that are directly attached to the IPX router. Adjacent IPX routers process the broadcast and add appropriate entries to their routing tables. The initializing IPX router also broadcasts a RIP general request on all of its attached networks. The adjacent IPX routers respond to the RIP general request by sending their routing tables to the initializing IPX router, which uses them to build its own routing table.

Ongoing Maintenance   Every 60 seconds, the IPX router broadcasts its routing table (using split horizon) to all attached networks. Adjacent IPX routers receive the announced routes and update their routing tables accordingly.

Administrative Router Shutdown   If an IPX router is brought down through an administrative action, it sends a RIP broadcast on all locally attached networks. In this broadcast all routes available through the router have a hop count of 16, indicating that these routes are no longer available. (All IPX routes must have a hop count of less than 16 to be considered reachable.) Neighboring routers propagate this change throughout the IPX internetwork through a triggered update.

Downed Link   If a link corresponding to one of the router's interfaces goes down and this failure is detected by the interface hardware and indicated to the routing process, IPX routes learned through the interface are no longer reachable. The unreachable IPX network numbers are announced, with a hop count of 16, in a triggered update. Note that most LAN-based interface hardware does not detect media faults, and therefore, the downed link is not immediately sensed. Many WAN adapters, however, have the ability to sense that a link to the WAN service provider is down.

Downed Router   An IPX router that goes down due to a power outage or other hardware or software failure does not have the ability to inform neighboring routers that routes once available through it are now unavailable. To prevent the lingering existence of unavailable network numbers in routing tables, each learned entry in the IPX routing table has a time-out value of three minutes (default value). If the entry is not refreshed in three minutes, it is set to unreachable (it is given a hop count of 16) and eventually removed. Therefore, if an IPX router goes down, it takes up to three minutes for the neighboring routers to time out routing table entries for routes that had been available through the downed router. The adjacent routers then broadcast those changes through a triggered update.

RIP for IPX Packet Structure

The RIP for IPX header (shown in Figure 5.7) comes immediately after the IPX header. RIP for IPX packets have a Packet Type of 0x1 and Source and Destination Socket numbers of 0x453.

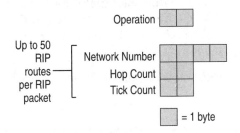

Figure 5.7   The RIP for IPX Packet Structure

Operation The 2-byte Operation field indicates the type of RIP for IPX message. Two values are defined:

- **0x00-01 - RIP Request** is set by a client attempting to find the best route to a destination network (a RIP GetLocalTarget request), or by a router to request all available routes from adjacent routers upon startup (a RIP general request).

- **0x00-02 - RIP Response** is set by a router replying to either a RIP GetLocalTarget or general request. Periodic announcements are also sent as RIP Response messages.

Following the Operation field is one or multiple RIP routes.

For RIP Requests, a single RIP route is included. For the RIP GetLocalTarget request, the single route includes the IPX network number of the desired destination network. For the RIP general request, the IPX network number is set to 0xFF-FF-FF-FF.

For RIP Responses, one or multiple RIP routes are included. For the response to the GetLocalTarget request, a single route is included. For the response to the RIP general request or a periodic announcement, up to 50 IPX routes can be sent in a single RIP for IPX packet. The maximum size for a RIP for IPX packet is 432 bytes. If more than 50 routes need to be sent, they are sent in multiple RIP for IPX packets.

Network Number The 4-byte Network Number field indicates the IPX Network Number.

Hop Count The 2-byte Hop Count field indicates the number of routers that are crossed when using this route.

Tick Count The 2-byte Tick Count field indicates the number of ticks it takes for an IPX packet to be sent using this route.

RIP for IPX Route Filters

RIP for IPX filters are available from the **Input Filters** and **Output Filters** options in the **RIP for IPX Configuration** dialog box. RIP route filtering allows input and output filtering on each interface and is based on exceptions. You can either configure the Windows 2000 Router to:

Accept or announce all RIP for IPX routes except those disallowed by filters.

– Or –

Discard or not announce all RIP for IPX routes except those allowed by filters.

Figure 5.8 shows the **Input Route Filters** and the **Route Filter** dialog boxes.

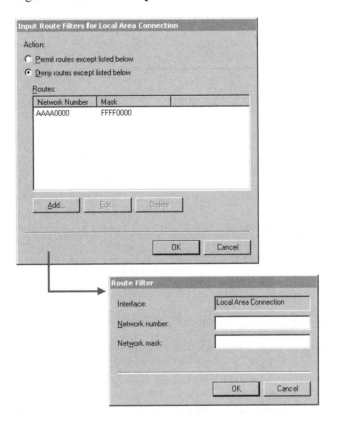

Figure 5.8   RIP for IPX Route Filter Dialog Boxes

The following two sample RIP route filters provide examples of route filtering scenarios and the implementation of route filtering using the fields in the **Route Filter** dialog box. These examples are provided to illustrate how route filters are configured, not as a recommendation of specific route filtering for your network.

▶ **To set a RIP for IPX route input filter (Example)**

Set the following input filter in order to discard all RIP for IPX routes except those starting with the hexadecimal digit **A**.

1. In the **Input Route Filters** dialog box, click **Add**.
2. In the **Network number** text box, type **A0000000**.
3. In the **Network mask** text box, type **F0000000**.
4. Click **OK**.
5. In the **Input Route Filters** dialog box, select the **Deny routes except listed below** option.
6. Click **OK**.

This filter uses the network mask to express a range of IPX network numbers from A0000000 to AFFFFFFF.

▶ **To set a RIP for IPX route output filter (Example)**

Set the following output filter in order to announce all RIP for IPX routes except the specific IPX Network Number of BB0000099.

1. In the **Output Route Filters** dialog box, click **Add**.
2. In the **Network number** text box, type **BB0000099**.
3. In the **Network mask** text box, type **FFFFFFFF**.
4. Click **OK**.
5. In the **Output Route Filters** dialog box, select the **Permit routes except listed below** option.
6. Click **OK**.

This filter uses the network mask to express the single IPX network number BB000009.

Note The network mask above is used only as an administrative convenience to express a range of IPX network numbers. This does not mean that the Windows 2000 Router is implementing a subnetting scheme for IPX internetworks. RIP for IPX internetworks use a flat network addressing space and do not support subnetting or route summarization.

Note You cannot configure separate active filters for **Permit routes except listed below** and **Deny routes except listed below**.

Static IPX Routes

The Windows 2000 Router allows the configuration of static IPX routes in the IPX routing table. Static IPX routes are typically used to define the IPX network numbers that are available across a dial-up connection. For more information about how static IPX routes are used over dial-up connections, see "Demand-Dial Routing" in this book.

Static IPX routes are announced over LAN interfaces using normal RIP for IPX processes.

▶ **To add a static route**

1. In the **Routing and Remote Access** snap-in console tree, click the plus sign (+) next to **IPX Routing,** right-click **Static Routes**, and then click **New Route**.

2. To define a static IPX route, in the **Static Route** dialog box, shown in Figure 5.9, type the following in the appropriate text boxes:

   - **Network number** (4-byte IPX Network Number in hexadecimal [8 hexadecimal digits]).

   - **Next hop MAC address** (6-byte MAC address of the next hop in hexadecimal [12 hexadecimal digits]).

   - **Tick count** (number of ticks to get to the Network Number).

   - **Hop count** (number of routers to be traversed to get to the Network Number).

   - **Interface** (Windows 2000 Router interface through which the Network Number can be reached. For dial-up connections, the name of the appropriate demand-dial interface is selected).

Figure 5.9 shows the IPX **Static Route** dialog box.

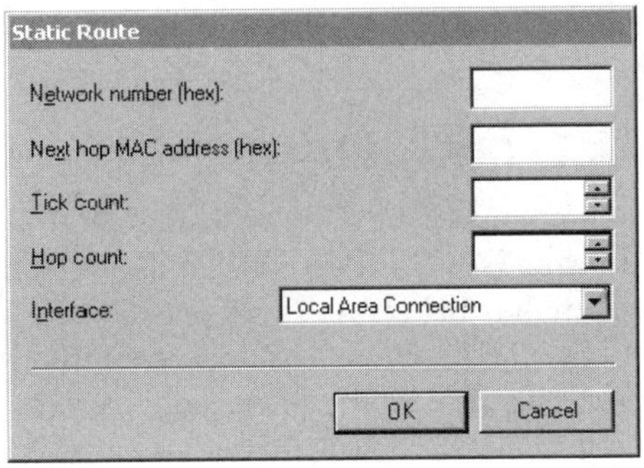

Figure 5.9   Static IPX Route Dialog Box

SAP for IPX

The Novell NetWare Service Advertising Protocol (SAP) for IPX provides a name resolution mechanism for clients to resolve the addresses of services on an IPX internetwork. Through SAP, service-providing hosts, such as file servers, print servers, and application servers advertise their service names, service types, and IPX internetwork addresses using broadcasts. The service and IPX internetwork address information is collected in a database called a SAP table by IPX routers and Novell NetWare servers.

The SAP table information is periodically advertised and propagated throughout the internetwork, in a way similar to that in which IPX routes are announced. Services are added and removed from the SAP table dynamically: they are added and maintained in the SAP table based on periodic announcements, and they are removed from the SAP table through a time-out mechanism when announcements are no longer received. To reduce convergence time, SAP uses split horizon and triggered updates. For information about split horizon and triggered updates, see "Unicast IP Routing" in this book.

SAP for IPX consists of the following types of messages:

- SAP clients such as workstations request the name and address of the nearest server of a specific type by broadcasting a SAP GetNearestServer request.

- Routers or SAP clients request the names and addresses of all services or of all services of a specific type by broadcasting a SAP general service request.

- Routers respond to SAP GetNearestServer or SAP general service requests.

- Routers periodically (every 60 seconds by default) broadcast their SAP tables using split horizon.

- Service-providing hosts that are not routers periodically (every 60 seconds by default) broadcast their services.

- Routers perform a triggered update broadcast to inform neighboring routers of a change in the SAP table.

IPX Routers and the Internal Network Number

To facilitate optimal communication to services running on IPX routers advertising themselves using Novell NetWare Service Advertising Protocol (SAP), IPX routers that are hosting services, such as Novell NetWare servers or Windows 2000 Server–based computers, require the configuration of an IPX internal network number. The IPX internal network is a virtual network inside the router. Attached to this virtual network is a virtual network interface card with the MAC address of 0x00-00-00-00-00-01. The IPX internal network is announced using RIP for IPX just as physical IPX networks are. When services running on the router are advertised with SAP, they are advertised with the IPX internetwork address of the internal network number and the virtual MAC address.

The IPX internal network allows for the optimal routing of packets to services running on the IPX router. The following analysis of the IPX traffic before and after the use of the IPX internal network clearly illustrate this optimization.

IPX Traffic Before the IPX Internal Network

Figure 5.10 depicts a simple IPX internetwork and a file server process where the IPX internal network is not being used.

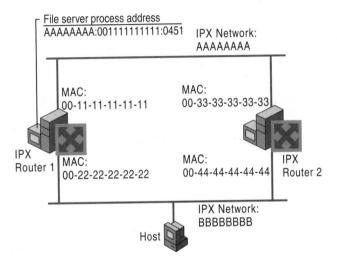

Figure 5.10   Prior to Defining an IPX Internal Network Number

1. The NetWare file server process running on IPX Router 1 advertises its location (using SAP) at the server address of AAAAAAAA:001111111111:0451 (IPX network:IPX Node:IPX Socket).

2. The Host resolves the file server address by querying its default NetWare server (not shown in Figure 5.10).

3. The Host broadcasts a RIP GetLocalTarget request on network BBBBBBBB requesting the best route to IPX network AAAAAAAA.

4. IPX Router 1 responds with a route that is one hop and two ticks away.

5. IPX Router 2 responds with a route that is one hop and two ticks away.

6. The Host chooses IPX Router 2's response (either because it was the first response received or through a random selection of multiple routers with the lowest tick count).

7. The Host sends a connection request packet to the file server process at AAAAAAAA:001111111111:0451 by forwarding it to IPX Router 2 at the MAC address of 00-44-44-44-44-44 on network BBBBBBBB.

8. IPX Router 2 forwards the connection request packet to Router 1 at its MAC address 00-11-11-11-11-11 on network AAAAAAAA.

9. The file server process on Router 1 responds to the connection request packet by forwarding it to the Host's MAC address (not shown in the figure) on network BBBBBBBB.

The end result of the RIP GetLocalTarget request sent by the Host is that packets sent from the Host to the file server process take a route that is not optimal. They are forwarded to IPX Router 2 when the optimal route is to IPX Router 1.

IPX Traffic After the IPX Internal Network

Figure 5.11 depicts the same simple IPX internetwork and file server process where the IPX internal network is being used.

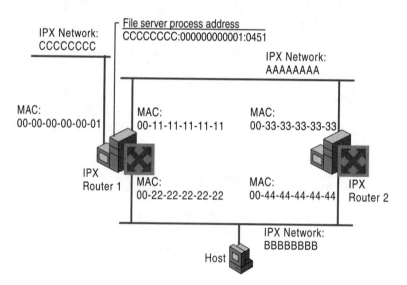

Figure 5.11   After Defining an IPX Internal Network Number

1. The NetWare file server process running on IPX Router 1 advertises its location (using SAP) on the internal network at the server address of CCCCCCCC:000000000001:0451 (IPX network:IPX Node:IPX Socket).

2. The Host resolves the file server address by querying its default NetWare server (not shown in Figure 5.11).

3. The Host broadcasts a RIP GetLocalTarget packet on network BBBBBBBB requesting the best route to IPX network CCCCCCCC.

4. IPX Router 1 responds with a route that is one hop and two ticks away.

5. IPX Router 2 responds with a route that is two hops and three ticks away.

6. The Host always chooses IPX Router 1's response because Router 1's route to network CCCCCCCC has the lowest tick count.

7. The Host sends a connection request packet to the file server process at CCCCCCCC:00000000001:0451 by forwarding it to IPX Router 1 at the MAC address of 00-22-22-22-22-22 on network BBBBBBBB.

8. The file server process on Router 1 responds to the connection request packet by forwarding it to the Host's MAC address (not shown in the figure) on network BBBBBBBB.

The end result of the RIP GetLocalTarget request by the Host is that packets sent from the Host to the file server process always take the optimal route.

Windows 2000 Router and the IPX Internal Network and Internal Adapter

A Windows 2000 Router supporting IPX routing can be configured with a unique IPX internal network number that is entered in the properties of the IPX/SPX/NetBIOS Compatible Transport. If the internal IPX network number is not configured, a unique IPX network number is automatically configured during the startup of the Windows 2000 Router.

The Windows 2000 Router automatic configuration process picks a random IPX network number and sends out a RIP GetLocalTarget packet requesting a route to the chosen IPX network number. If a RIP response is received, the chosen IPX network number cannot be used, and a new random IPX network number is chosen. If a RIP response is not received, the chosen IPX network number is automatically entered in the properties of the IPX/SPX/NetBIOS Compatible Transport.

To see the virtual network adapter corresponding to the IPX internal network, in the **Routing and Remote Access** snap-in, open your server, then **IPX Routing**, then **General**. The **Internal** interface appears in the details pane as an IPX routing interface and is the virtual network adapter for the IPX internal network of the server (see Figure 5.12).

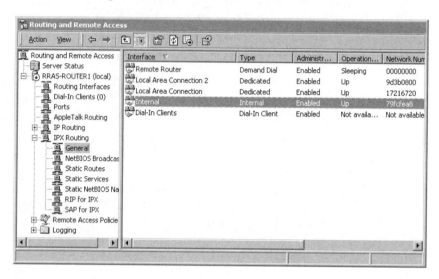

Figure 5.12   IPX Internal Adapter

SAP Tables

An entry in a SAP table contains the following fields:

Server Name   The name of the server hosting the service.

Server Type   The type of service (for example, file server, print server, or application server)

Server Address   The full Network:Node:Socket IPX address of the service. For example, the file and print sharing process on a NetWare server might have the Server Address of 000000AA:0000000000001:0451.

Hop Count   The number of routers to cross to reach the server hosting the service. The maximum hop count for services is 15. Services 16 hops away or greater are considered unreachable.

Interface (or Port)   The interface (network interface card) on which the SAP entry was learned.

Figure 5.13 illustrates the structure of the SAP table.

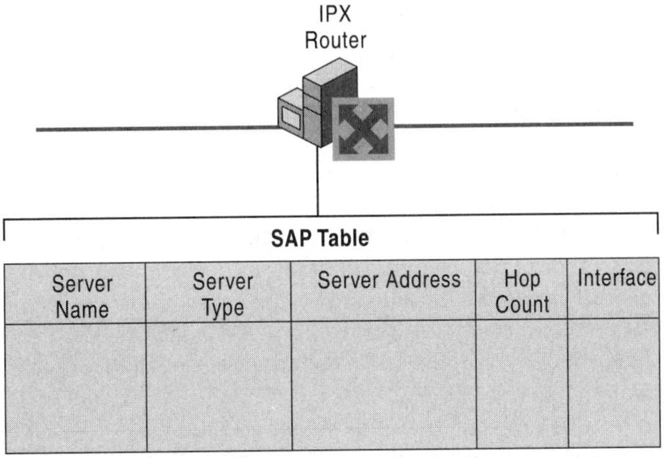

Figure 5.13   SAP Table

If there are multiple entries for the same Server Name and Server Type, IPX routers select the SAP table entry with the lowest number of hops. If multiple SAP table entries have equally low hop counts, the router chooses randomly from those.

SAP Operation for an IPX Router

SAP operation for an IPX router consists of the following processes:

Initialization If the IPX router is also a hosting service, such as a Novell NetWare server or Windows 2000 Server–based computer, it broadcasts a SAP packet onto each attached network informing adjacent routers of its own services. The IPX router then broadcasts a SAP general request for all services onto each attached network. The responses to the SAP general request are used to build the SAP table.

Ongoing Maintenance Every 60 seconds, the IPX router broadcasts its SAP Table using split horizon on all attached networks. Adjacent IPX routers receive the advertised services and update their SAP tables appropriately.

Administrative Router Shutdown If an IPX router is brought down properly through an administrative action, it sends a SAP broadcast on all attached networks indicating that the services previously available through the router are no longer available. The SAP Agent sets the hop count for the services to 16 to indicate that these services are unreachable. Adjacent routers propagate this change throughout the IPX internetwork with a triggered update.

Downed Link If a link corresponding to one of the router's interfaces goes down and this failure is detected by the interface hardware and indicated to the router, SAP services learned through the interface are unreachable. The unreachable SAP services are advertised with a hop count of 16 in a triggered update. Note that most LAN-based interface hardware does not currently detect media faults and therefore this change is not immediately sensed and propagated. Many WAN adapters, however, have the ability to sense that a link to the WAN service provider is down.

Downed Router If a router goes down due to a power outage or other hardware failure, it does not have the ability to inform the adjacent routers that the services available through the router are no longer available. To prevent the lingering existence of inaccessible services in SAP tables, each learned entry in the SAP table of each IPX router has a default time-out value of three minutes. If the entry is not refreshed in three minutes, it is given a hop count of 16 and eventually removed. Therefore, if an IPX router goes down, it takes up to three minutes for the adjacent routers to time out the entries in their SAP table for the services that were available through the downed router. The adjacent routers then broadcast those changes through a triggered update.

SAP Packet Structure

The SAP header, shown in Figure 5.14, immediately follows the IPX header. SAP packets have an IPX Packet Type of 0x04 or 0x00 and Source and Destination Socket numbers of 0x0452.

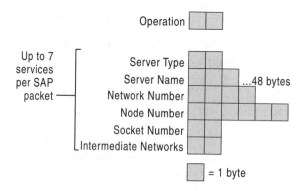

Figure 5.14   SAP for IPX Packet Structure

Note Figure 5.14 depicts the packet structure for the SAP Response and SAP GetNearestServer Response. The SAP Request and SAP GetNearestServer Requests packets only contain the Operation and Service Type fields and are 34-byte packets (30 bytes for the IPX header, 4 bytes for the SAP header).

Operation   The 2-byte Operation field indicates the type of SAP message. Table 5.3 defines the values for the Operation field.

Table 5.3   SAP Operations

Operation	Type of Message	Description
1	Request	Sent by a router or SAP client to request all services or all services of a specified type.
2	Response	A reply to a SAP Request. Periodic SAP advertisements are also sent as a SAP Response.
3	GetNearestServer Request	Sent by a workstation to request the IPX internetwork address of the nearest (quickest response) server of a specified service type.
4	GetNearestServer Response	Sent in response to the SAP GetNearestServer Request and contains a single name and IPX internetwork address of the nearest server of a requested service type.

Following the Operation field is a series of up to seven SAP services in the same SAP message for a maximum SAP packet size of 480 bytes. If more than seven services need to be sent, they are sent in multiple SAP packets.

Service Type   The 2-byte Service Type field indicates the type of service that the service provides. Service types are assigned uniquely by Novell, Inc. Some commonly defined SAP service types are listed in Table 5.4. For a complete list of SAP service types, see the SAP link at http://windows.microsoft.com/windows2000/reskit/webresources.

Table 5.4   SAP Service Types

Server	Service Type (hexadecimal)
Unknown	00-00
NetWare File Server	00-04
NetWare Print Server	00-07
Microsoft RPC Server	06-40
General SAP Request	FF-FF

Server Name   The 48-byte Server Name field stores the name of the server advertising the service. The combination of Server Name and Service Type uniquely identifies a service on an IPX internetwork. Server names under 48 bytes are terminated with the ASCII NULL character.

Network Number The 4-byte Network Number field indicates the IPX network number where the server hosting the service resides.

Node Number The 6-byte Node Number field indicates the IPX node number where the server hosting the service resides.

Socket Number The 2-byte Socket Number field indicates the socket number on which the service process is listening.

Intermediate Networks The 2-byte Intermediate Networks field indicates the number of routers to traverse to reach the server hosting the service.

SAP Filters

SAP filters are available from the **Input Filters** and **Output Filters** buttons in the **SAP for IPX Configuration** dialog box. You can configure input and output SAP filtering on each Windows 2000 Router interface to either permit or deny services based on exceptions, as shown in Figure 5.15.

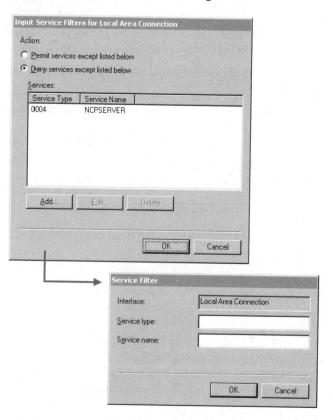

Figure 5.15   SAP for IPX Input Filter Dialog Boxes

Note You cannot configure separate active filters for **Permit services except listed below** and **Deny services except listed below**.

Note When applying the filter, the logical operator, **AND**, is used to combine specified parameters within each filter. **OR** is used to combine the specified parameters between filters.

Static Services

The Windows 2000 Router allows the creation of static services in the SAP table. Static services are advertised using normal SAP processes. Static SAP services are typically used to define the services that are available across a dial-up connection. For more information about how static SAP services are used over dial-up connections, see "Demand-Dial Routing" in this book.

To add static services, in the **Routing and Remote Access** snap-in console tree, click the plus sign (+) next to **IPX Routing,** right-click **Static Services**, and then click **New Service**. Figure 5.16 shows the resulting **Static Services** dialog box.

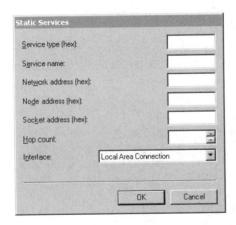

Figure 5.16   SAP Static Services Dialog Box

NetBIOS Broadcasts

To facilitate the operation of NetBIOS-based applications on an IPX internetwork, NetBIOS over IPX provides standard NetBIOS services such as datagrams (single packets sent without acknowledgement such as broadcasts), sessions (multiple packets sent with acknowledgements between two endpoints) and name management (registering, querying, and releasing NetBIOS names).

For more information about NetBIOS, see "Introduction to TCP/IP" in the *TCP/IP Core Networking Guide*.

NetBIOS over IPX is implemented with two different packet structures:

NetBIOS Over IPX Broadcasts Used to perform NetBIOS datagram and name management functions, such as Name Queries and Name Registrations. IPX routers might or might not forward NetBIOS over IPX broadcast packets.

NetBIOS Over IPX Sessions Used to provide connection-oriented, reliable data transfers between two NetBIOS applications on an IPX internetwork. NetBIOS over IPX session traffic is unicast to a specific IPX internetwork address, rather than broadcasted. NetBIOS over IPX sessions are characterized by an IPX packet type of 0x04 (Normal IPX), and an IPX Source or Destination Socket of 0x455.

Because all NetBIOS over IPX session traffic is forwarded by IPX routers, the following sections discuss only NetBIOS over IPX broadcasts and how the Windows 2000 Router supports them.

IPX WAN Broadcast

An IPX router must be able to propagate broadcast traffic in order for nonroutable protocols (such as NetBIOS), which rely on broadcast traffic, to function properly in an IPX internetwork. (NetBIOS relies on broadcast traffic to register and resolve NetBIOS names.) Support for the propagation of broadcast traffic across IPX routers is provided by a special IPX packet called the IPX WAN Broadcast or IPX Packet Type 20.

The IPX WAN Broadcast header is characterized by an IPX packet type of 0x14 (20 in decimal) and the IPX Destination Node address of 0xFF-FF-FF-FF-FF-FF. IPX routers can be configured to either propagate or silently discard IPX WAN Broadcasts.

NetBIOS over IPX Broadcasts contain the IPX WAN Broadcast header.

IPX WAN Broadcasts and Microsoft Networking

In Windows 2000, Windows NT 4.0 and earlier, Windows for Workgroups, or Windows 95 or Windows 98 networking, server, and workstation services using Server Message Blocks (SMBs) for file and print sharing communication can use NetBIOS over IPX or just IPX. The process of sending SMBs over IPX without NetBIOS is known as direct hosting.

IPX WAN Broadcasts are used for the following NetBIOS over IPX SMB–based networking processes:

- NetBIOS Name Registration
- NetBIOS Name Query
- Browser Host Announcement
- NetLogon

IPX WAN Broadcasts are used for the following direct hosting SMB-based networking processes:

- Locate Server Name Query
- Browser Host Announcement

When direct hosting, an IPX over NetBIOS header is not used. Instead, the SMBs are sent directly over IPX. The Locate Server Name Query and Browser Host Announcement direct hosting messages are sent using an IPX WAN Broadcast without the corresponding NetBIOS fields.

Disabling the propagation of IPX WAN Broadcasts can impair the ability of Microsoft SMB–based computers to propagate browsing information, resolve names, and establish connections on an IPX internetwork.

Note When you run the Routing and Remote Access Server Setup Wizard, the default settings for NetBIOS over IPX broadcast propagation are to accept and deliver broadcasts for the **Internal** interface and to accept but never deliver broadcasts for all LAN interfaces. In this default configuration, propagation of IPX broadcasts is disabled on the Windows 2000 router. To enable propagation, configure the appropriate LAN interfaces to always deliver NetBIOS over IPX broadcasts from the properties of the LAN interface in the **IPX Routing\NetBIOS Broadcasts** node in the Routing and Remote Access snap-in.

NetBIOS Over IPX Broadcast Packet Structure

The NetBIOS over IPX Broadcast header, shown in Figure 5.17, is a combination of the IPX WAN Broadcast header and a NetBIOS header, which is placed immediately after the IPX header. NetBIOS over IPX Broadcast packets have a Packet Type of 0x14, a Destination Node number of 0xFF-FF-FF-FF-FF-FF, and a Source and Destination Socket number of 0x455.

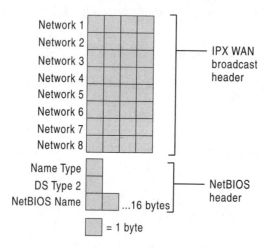

Figure 5.17   NetBIOS Over IPX Broadcast Packet Structure

Network 1–Network 8 (IPX WAN Broadcast Header)

The first eight fields (Network 1 through Network 8) are the IPX WAN Broadcast header. The series of IPX networks on which the IPX WAN Broadcast packet has traveled is recorded by IPX routers as the packet is propagated through an IPX internetwork. To prevent loops, this network path information is analyzed upon receipt at a router and the packet is forwarded to all networks except those on which it has already been.

After eight networks, the IPX WAN Broadcast packet is silently discarded by the last router in the path. However, recall that the maximum hop count for any IPX packet on a RIP for IPX–based internetwork is 16. The difference in the maximum number of hops between an IPX WAN Broadcast and a normal IPX packet can cause confusion in large IPX internetworks.

For example, a NetWare server 10 hops away is reachable from a NetWare client because its IPX internetwork address is discovered by querying the SAP table or directory tree of its default NetWare server. Connection requests sent to the NetWare server are unicast traffic that reach the NetWare server because it is within 16 hops.

On the other hand, a Windows 2000 Server–based computer 10 hops away is not reachable for a Microsoft SMB–based client because its IPX internetwork address is discovered using a NetBIOS Name Query sent using a NetBIOS over IPX Broadcast packet that is discarded after eight networks. Because there is no response to the Name Query, the IPX internetwork address of the Windows 2000 Server–based computer is not resolved and a connection cannot be established. To prevent this problem, design your IPX internetwork so that there are no more than seven IPX routers between any two Windows 2000 computers.

Name Type Flags (NetBIOS Header)

The 1-byte Name Type Flags field of the NetBIOS header contains a series of flags to indicate the state of the NetBIOS name. The individual bits are defined in Table 5.5.

Table 5.5   Name Type Flag Bits

Name Type Bit	Description
1	Group Name (1) or Unique Name (0)
2	Name in Use (1) or Name Unused (0)
3, 4, 5	Unused
6	Name Registered (1) or Name Not Registered (0)
7	Name Duplicated (1) or Name Not Duplicated (0)
8	Name Deregistered (1) or Name Not Deregistered (0)

Bits are numbered from the high-order bit (Bit 1) to the low-order bit (Bit 8).

Data Stream Type 2 (NetBIOS Header)

The 1-byte Data Stream Type 2 field of the NetBIOS header indicates the type of NetBIOS packet. Table 5.6 lists the defined values for the Data Stream Type 2 field.

Table 5.6   Data Stream Type 2 Values

Data Stream Type 2	Description
1	Find Name (for NetBIOS Name Queries)
2	Name Recognized
3	Add Name (for NetBIOS Name Registrations)

NetBIOS Name (NetBIOS Header)

The 16-byte NetBIOS Name field of the NetBIOS header stores the NetBIOS name.

Static NetBIOS Names

When the **Only for statically seeded names** NetBIOS broadcast delivery option is selected in the **NetBIOS Broadcast** dialog box for an interface, NetBIOS over IPX broadcasts are only propagated for a defined series of NetBIOS names and in a preferred direction. Static NetBIOS names can be used to confine NetBIOS over IPX broadcast traffic in environments where client-side NetBIOS applications need to access a small set of server-side NetBIOS applications.

For example, in a NetBIOS over IPX Lotus Notes environment, numerous Lotus Notes clients need to access a relatively small number of Lotus Notes servers and to resolve the IPX internetwork addresses of those servers. In this situation, the network administrator configures the routers to pass NetBIOS over IPX broadcasts for only those NetBIOS names that correspond with the names of the Lotus Notes servers.

To add statically configured NetBIOS names, in the **Routing and Remote Access** snap-in console tree, click the plus sign (+) next to **IPX Routing,** right-click **Static NetBIOS Names,** and then click **New NetBIOS Name**. Figure 5.18 shows the resulting **Static NetBIOS Name** dialog box.

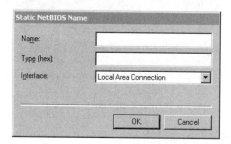

Figure 5.18   Static NetBIOS Name Dialog Box

Additional Resources

- For more information about IPX, see *Novell's Guide to LAN/WAN Analysis: IPX/SPX* by Laura A. Chappel, 1998, San Jose, CA: Novell Press.

CHAPTER 6

Demand-Dial Routing

Microsoft® Windows® 2000 provides extensive support for demand-dial routing, the routing of packets over point-to-point links such as analog phone lines and ISDN. Demand-dial routing allows you to connect to the Internet, to connect branch offices, or to implement router-to-router virtual private network (VPN) connections.

In This Chapter

Related Information in the Resource Kit

- For more information about unicast routing, see "Unicast Routing Overview" in this book.

- For more information about Windows 2000 and IP routing, see "Unicast IP Routing" in this book.

- For more information about Windows 2000 and IPX routing, see "IPX Routing" in this book.

- For more information about PPP connection establishment and the PPP protocol suite, see "Remote Access Server" in this book.

- For more information about virtual private networks, see "Virtual Private Networking" in this book.

- For more information about the Windows 2000 Router, see "Routing and Remote Access Service" in this book.

Introduction to Demand-Dial Routing

Demand-dial routing is the forwarding of packets across a Point-to-Point Protocol (PPP) link. The PPP link is represented inside the Windows 2000 router as a demand-dial interface. Demand-dial interfaces can be used to create on-demand connections across dial-up, non-permanent or persistent media.

With local area network (LAN) and permanent wide area network (WAN) links, the interface that is being used to forward the packet is always in an active or connected state. The packet can be forwarded without having to create the physical or logical connection. However, the demand-dial interface can either be in a connected state or a disconnected state. If in a disconnected state when the packet is being forwarded, the demand-dial interface must be changed to a connected state before the packet can be forwarded.

The connection establishment process, consisting of creating a physical connection or a logical connection and a PPP connection, introduces a delay in the forwarding of the packet called the connection establishment delay. The length of the connection establishment delay varies for the type of physical or logical connection being established. For example, the connection establishment delay for analog phone lines or X.25 dialing in to a packet assembler-disassembler (PAD) can be 10 to 20 seconds or more. For Integrated Services Digital Network (ISDN) lines, the connection establishment delay can be as small as 3 to 5 seconds.

The connection establishment delay is an important consideration for applications being used across a demand-dial connection. There are two behaviors of applications to consider:

- How long it takes for the application to abandon the attempt to establish network communications, also known as application time-out. If the application time-out is longer than the connection establishment delay, then the application fails to establish communications and presents an error message to the user.

- How many times it attempts to establish network communications. On the first attempt, network traffic is forwarded to the demand-dial router which begins the connection establishment process. Due to the size of a finite buffer in the router, additional packets to be forwarded across the demand-dial connection that arrive during the connection establishment process might overwrite the initial application connection attempt packet. If the application tries to establish communications multiple times, then there is a better chance of forwarding an application connection attempt packet once the connection is established.

Applications that have long time-outs or multiple retries might not fail while waiting for the link to become available. Interactive applications such as Web browsers and Telnet might fail when first connecting. However, when the user retries the connection attempt, it succeeds because the first connection attempt created the demand-dial connection.

Once the connection is established, packets are forwarded across the demand-dial connection. Because the costs of demand-dial connections are typically time sensitive, after a configured amount of idle time the demand-dial link is terminated. Demand-dial connections have the benefit of allowing the user to use cheaper dial-up WAN links and only pay for the link when it is being used.

Demand-Dial Routing and Remote Access

Demand-dial routing is not the same as remote access; remote access connects a single user to a network, and demand-dial routing connects networks together. However, both remote access and demand-dial routing use PPP as the protocol mechanism to negotiate and authenticate the connection and encapsulate data sent on the connection. As implemented in the Windows 2000 Routing and Remote Access service, both remote access and demand-dial connections can be enabled separately but share the same:

- Behavior of the dial-in properties of user accounts.
- Security, including authentication protocols and encryption.
- Use of remote access policies.
- Use of Windows or Remote Authentication Dial-In User Service (RADIUS) as authentication providers.
- IP and Internetwork Packet Exchange (IPX) address allocation configuration.
- Use of PPP features such as Microsoft Point-to-Point Compression (MPPC), Multilink, and Bandwidth Allocation Protocol (BAP).
- Troubleshooting facilities including event logging, Windows or RADIUS authentication and accounting logging, and tracing.

Types of Demand-Dial Connections

Demand-dial connections can be characterized in the following ways:

- On-demand or persistent
- Two-way initiated or one-way initiated

The decision to use one or the other impacts the configuration of the demand-dial interface.

On-Demand and Persistent Connections

On-demand connections are used when the cost of using the communications link is time-sensitive. For example, long distance analog phone calls are charged on a per-minute basis. With on-demand connections, the connection is made when traffic is forwarded, and the connection is terminated after a configured amount of idle time.

Idle disconnect behavior can be configured on the calling router and the answering router:

- To configure idle disconnect on the calling router, the router initiating the connection, set an idle disconnect time on the **General** tab of the properties of the demand-dial interface.

- To configure idle disconnect on the answering router, the router accepting the connection attempt, set an idle disconnect time on the **Dial-In Constraints** tab of the profile properties of remote access policy being used by the demand-dial connection.

Persistent demand-dial connections use a dial-up WAN technology when the cost of the link is fixed and the connection can be active 24 hours a day. Examples of WAN technologies for persistent demand-dial connections include local calls that use analog phone lines, leased analog lines, and flat-rate ISDN. If a persistent connection is lost, the calling router immediately attempts to reestablish the connection.

Persistent connection behavior must be configured on the calling router and the answering router.

▶ **To configure connection persistence on the calling router**

1. In the **Routing and Remote Access** snap-in, right-click the demand-dial interface under **Routing Interfaces**, and then click **Properties**.

2. On the **Options** tab, select **Persistent connection.**

▶ **To configure connection persistence on the answering router**

1. In the **Routing and Remote Access** snap-in, right-click the remote access policy being used by the demand-dial connection under **Remote Access Policies**, and then click **Properties**.

2. Click **Edit profile**.

3. On the **Dial-in Constraints** tab, clear the **Disconnect if idle for** check box.

Both the calling router and the answering router must be configured for connection persistence. If the calling router is configured for a persistent connection and the answering router is configured for an idle disconnect, then the answering router terminates the connection after the specified idle time. The calling router must then reestablish the demand-dial connection, causing a pause in the forwarding of packets equal to the connection establishment delay.

Two-Way and One-Way Initiated Connections

With two-way initiated connections, either router can be the answering router or the calling router depending on who is initiating the connection. Both routers must be configured to initiate and accept a demand-dial connection. You use two-way initiated connections when traffic from either router can create the demand-dial connection. Two-way initiated demand-dial connections require that:

- Both routers are configured as LAN and WAN routers.
- User accounts are added for both routers so that the authentication credentials of the calling router are accessed and validated by the answering router.
- Demand-dial interfaces, with the same name as the user account that is used by the calling router, are fully configured at both routers, including the phone number of the answering router and user account credentials to authenticate the calling router.
- Static routes are configured on both routers.

For two-way initiated demand-dial routing to work properly, the user name of the calling router must match the name of a demand-dial interface on both sides of the connection. Table 6.1 shows an example of this configuration.

Table 6.1   Example of Two-Way Initiated Connection Configuration

Router	Demand-Dial Interface Name	User Account Name
Corporate office router	NewYorkRouter	CorpHub
Branch office router	CorpHub	NewYorkRouter

With one-way initiated connections, one router is always the answering router and one router is always the calling router. In one-way initiated connections, the routing configuration is simplified because user accounts, demand-dial interfaces, and static IP routes do not need to be fully configured on both sides of the connection. Instead of configuring a demand-dial interface and static routes on the answering router, static routes are added to the dial-in properties of the user account of the calling router.

When the connection is made, the static routes on the user account of the calling router are added to the IP routing table of the answering router. If routing protocols are used to propagate the new static routes, then there is a delay between the time the connection is made and the time when all of the routers on the intranet of the answering router are aware of the new route. Therefore, hosts on the intranet of the calling router might experience a delay between the time that the connection is made and the time when they begin to receive traffic back from hosts on the intranet of the answering router.

If your answering router is in a Windows 2000 mixed-mode domain or in a Microsoft® Windows NT® version 4.0 domain, static routes on the user account are not available. In this case, one-way initiated connections require that:

- Both routers are configured as LAN and WAN routers.

- A user account is added for the authentication credentials of the calling router.

- A demand-dial interface is configured at the calling router with the user credentials of the user account. A demand-dial interface is configured at the answering router with the same name as the user account that is used by the calling router. The demand-dial interface of the answering router is not used to dial out, therefore it is not configured with the phone number of the calling router or with valid user credentials.

Components of Demand-Dial Routing

The main components of demand-dial routing are the calling router, the answering router, and the connection medium as illustrated in Figure 6.1.

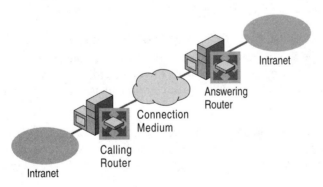

Figure 6.1   Components of Demand-Dial Routing

Calling Router

The calling router initiates the demand-dial connection. It contains the following components:

- **Routing and Remote Access service**

  The Routing and Remote Access service on the calling router must be configured as a LAN and WAN router and configured for IP address allocation (either using DHCP or a static pool) and authentication methods.

- **Port**

  A port is a logical or physical communications channel capable of supporting a single PPP connection. Physical ports are based on equipment installed in the calling router. Virtual private network (VPN) ports are logical ports.

- **Demand-dial interface**

  A demand-dial interface configured on the calling router represents the PPP connection and contains configuration information such as the port to use, the addressing used to create the connection (such as a phone number), authentication and encryption methods, and authentication credentials.

- **Route**

  An IP or IPX route in the routing tables of the calling router is configured to use a demand-dial interface to forward traffic.

Answering Router

The answering router, the router that accepts an initiated demand-dial connection from a calling router, contains the following components:

- **Routing and Remote Access service**

  The Routing and Remote Access service on the answering router must be configured as a LAN and WAN router and configured for IP address allocation (either using DHCP or a static pool) and user authentication.

- **Port**

  A port is a logical or physical communications channel capable of supporting a single PPP connection. Physical ports are based on equipment installed in the answering router. Virtual private network (VPN) ports are logical ports.

- **User account**

  To authenticate the calling router, the credentials of the calling router must be verified by the properties of a corresponding user account. A user account for the calling router must be either locally present or available through Windows 2000 security. If the answering router is configured for RADIUS authentication, then the RADIUS server must have access to the user account of the calling router.

  The user account must have the following settings:

  - On the **Dial-in** tab, remote access permission is set to either **Allow access** or **Control access through Remote Access Policy**.

  - On the **General** or **Account** tab, **User must change password at next logon** is disabled and **Password never expires** is enabled.

  For a one-way initiated connection, configure static IP routes that are added to the answering router's routing table when the demand-dial connection is made.

- **Demand-dial interface**

  For two-way initiated connections, a demand-dial interface configured on the answering router represents the PPP connection to the calling router. For a one-way initiated connection using static routes on the user account of the calling router, a demand-dial interface on the answering router does not need to be configured.

- **Route**

  For two-way initiated connections, an IP or IPX route in the routing tables of the calling router is configured to use a demand-dial interface to forward traffic.

  For one-way initiated connections, you can configure the user account of the calling router with static IP routes.

- **Remote access policy**

  To specify connection parameters that are specific to demand-dial connections, create a separate remote access policy that uses the **Windows-Groups** attribute set to the group, which has all of the user accounts for calling routers as members. A separate remote access policy for demand-dial connections is not required.

Connection Medium

The PPP link is established over either a physical medium or a tunnel medium. Physical mediums include analog phone lines and ISDN. Tunnel mediums include Point-to-Point Tunneling Protocol (PPTP) and Layer Two Tunneling Protocol (L2TP).

Demand-Dial Routing Process

The following sequence outlines the demand-dial routing process when both the calling router and the answering router are Windows 2000 routers:

1. Upon receipt of a packet, the calling router finds the best route to forward the packet.

2. If the interface on the best route is a demand-dial interface, the connection state of the interface is checked.

   If the connection state is "Connected," then the packet is forwarded across the interface subject to the packet filters configured on the interface.

   If the connection state is "Disconnected," then the IP or IPX forwarder component calls the Dynamic Interface Manager with instructions to bring up the demand-dial interface in the route.

3. The Dynamic Interface Manager checks the dial-out hours and demand-dial filters configured on the interface. If dial-out hours or demand-dial filters prohibit the initiation of the demand-dial connection, the connection attempt is terminated and the **Unreachability reason** on the interface is set. For more information about the unreachability reason, see "Troubleshooting Tools" later in this chapter.

4. If the demand-dial connection is allowed, the Dynamic Interface Manager retrieves the configuration of the indicated demand-dial interface from *SystemRoot*\system32\ras\router.pbk.

5. Based on the port of the demand-dial interface configuration, a physical or logical connection with the endpoint of the connection is made.

   For direct serial or direct parallel configurations, there is no phone number. A physical connection is made between the two computers using the serial or parallel port.

   For modem or ISDN ports, the configured phone number is dialed using the configured port. If the configured port is not available, another port of the same type is used. If no other ports of the same type are available, then the connection attempt is terminated and the unreachability reason is set.

   For VPN connections, the configured IP address or host name is used to establish either a PPTP tunnel (for PPTP connections) or an IPSec security association and an L2TP tunnel (for L2TP over IPSec connections).

6. Once the physical or logical connection is made, a PPP connection is negotiated with the endpoint. PPP connection behavior that is specific to demand-dial connections is as follows:

   - The calling router is allocated an IP address by the answering router and the answering router is allocated an IP address by the calling router. The allocated IP addresses should be on different subnets to prevent both routers from allocating the same IP address.

- If the calling router is configured with the IP addresses of Domain Name System (DNS) or Windows Internet Name Service(WINS) servers, then DNS and WINS server IP addresses are not requested. If the calling router is not configured with the IP addresses of DNS and WINS servers, then DNS and WINS servers are requested. The answering router never requests DNS and WINS server IP addresses from the calling router.

- Unlike Windows 2000 remote access clients, the calling router does not create a default route or send a DHCPINFORM message to the answering router. By default, the calling router does not register itself with the DNS or WINS servers of the answering router unless the **RegisterRoutersWithNameServers** registry value (HKEY_LOCAL_MACHINE\System\CurrentControlSet\Services\Rasman \PPP\ControlProtocols\BuiltIn) is set to 1.

7. The credentials of the calling router are sent during the PPP authentication phase based on the negotiated PPP authentication protocol.

   Based on the user credentials, the answering router either:

   - Checks the appropriate account database and local remote access policies to accept the connection.

   - Sends the connection attributes to a configured RADIUS server. If the RADIUS server is a Windows 2000 Internet Authentication Service (IAS) server, it checks the appropriate user account database and remote access policies to accept the connection.

8. If the user account of the calling router has static routes configured, those routes become static routes in the IP routing table of the answering router.

9. The answering router looks in *SystemRoot*\System32\ras\router.pbk for the name of a demand-dial interface that matches the user name of the user credential of the calling router.

   If a demand-dial interface name matching the calling router user name is found, the demand-dial interface is changed to a "Connected" connection state.

10. Once the PPP connection establishment is completed, the calling router forwards packets across the demand-dial connection subject to the packet filters configured on the demand-dial interface.

If the user name credential of the calling router does not match the name of a demand-dial interface, the calling router is interpreted as a remote access client. If there are no static routes configured on the user account, you might have routing problems.

For example, if the calling router uses a user name credential that does not correspond to a demand-dial interface on the answering router, then the calling router is identified as a remote access client rather than a router. Packets forwarded from the calling router's intranet are forwarded across the demand-dial connection and then forwarded by the answering router.

However, when response packets sent back to the calling router's intranet are received by the answering router, the routes for the calling router's intranet are configured to use a demand-dial interface. Because the demand-dial interface is in a "Disconnected" state, the answering router attempts a demand-dial connection to the calling router. If another port of the same type is available, a second demand-dial connection is made. If another port of the same type is not available, the packet is dropped and the unreachability reason is set. The end result is that either two demand-dial connections are created when only one is needed or the packet is dropped.

On-Demand Router-to-Router VPN

A router-to-router VPN connection is typically used to connect remote offices together when both routers are connected to the Internet through permanent WAN links, such as T1 or Frame Relay. In this configuration, the VPN connection is persistent and available 24 hours a day. However, when a permanent WAN link is not possible or practical, you can configure an on-demand router-to-router VPN connection.

Figure 6.2 shows an on-demand router-to-router VPN connection.

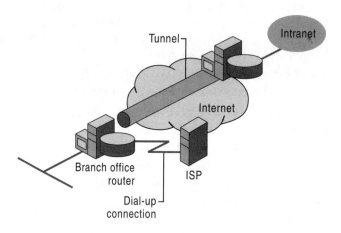

Figure 6.2   On-Demand Router-to-Router VPN Connection

An on-demand router-to-router VPN connection consists of two demand-dial interfaces that are configured on the VPN client (the calling router):

1. A demand-dial interface to dial-in to a local Internet service provider (ISP).

2. A demand-dial interface for the router-to-router VPN connection.

An on-demand router-to-router VPN connection is automatically established when you route traffic to a specific location. For example, in a branch office configuration, when a packet is received to be routed to the corporate office, the branch office router uses a dial-up link to connect to a local ISP and then creates a router-to-router VPN connection with the corporate office router located on the Internet.

Note This discussion assumes that the corporate office router (the answering router) is connected to the Internet using a permanent WAN link. It is possible to have both routers connected to the Internet by using a dial-up WAN link. However, this is only feasible if the Internet service provider (ISP) supports demand-dialing routing to customers; the ISP calls the customer router when an IP packet is to be delivered to the customer. Demand-dial routing to customers is not widely supported by ISPs.

To configure an on-demand router-to-router VPN connection at the branch office router, do the following:

- Create a demand-dial interface for the Internet connection that is configured for the appropriate equipment (a modem or ISDN device), the phone number of the local ISP, and the user name and password to gain Internet access.

- Create a demand-dial interface for the VPN connection with the corporate office router that is configured for a VPN port (a PPTP or L2TP port), the IP address of the interface on the Internet for the corporate office router, and a user name and password that can be verified by the VPN server. The user name must match the name of a demand-dial interface on the corporate office router.

- Create a static host route for the IP address of the corporate office router's Internet interface that uses the ISP demand-dial interface.

- Create a static route (or routes) for the IP network of the corporate intranet that uses the VPN demand-dial interface.

To configure the corporate office router, do the following:

- Create a demand-dial interface for the VPN connection with the branch office that is configured for a VPN port (a PPTP or L2TP port). The demand-dial interface must have the same name as the user name in the authentication credential that is used by the branch office router to create the VPN connection.

- Create a static route (or routes) for the IP network IDs of the branch office that uses the VPN demand-dial interface.

The router-to-router VPN connection is automatically initiated by the branch office router through the following process:

1. Packets sent to a corporate network location from a computer in the branch office are forwarded to the branch office router.

2. The branch office router checks its routing table and finds a route to the corporate intranet network, which uses the VPN demand-dial interface.

3. The branch office router checks the state of the VPN demand-dial interface and finds it is in a disconnected state.

4. The branch office router retrieves the configuration of the VPN demand-dial interface.

5. Based on the VPN demand-dial interface configuration, the branch office router attempts to initialize a router-to-router VPN connection at the IP address of the corporate office router on the Internet.

6. To establish a VPN, either a TCP (by using PPTP) or UDP (by using L2TP over IPSec) packet must be sent to the corporate office router that acts as the VPN server. The VPN establishment packet is created.

7. To forward the VPN establishment packet to the corporate office router, the branch office router checks its routing table and finds the host route that is using the ISP demand-dial interface.

8. The branch office router checks the state of the ISP demand-dial interface and finds it is in a disconnected state.

9. The branch office router retrieves the configuration of the ISP demand-dial interface.

10. Based on the ISP demand-dial interface configuration, the branch office router uses its modem or ISDN device to dial and establish a connection with its local ISP.

11. Once the ISP connection is made, the VPN establishment packet is sent to the corporate office router.

12. A router-to-router VPN connection is negotiated between the branch office router and the corporate office router. As part of the negotiation, the branch office router sends authentication credentials that are verified by the corporate office router.

13. The corporate office router checks its demand-dial interfaces and finds one that matches the user name sent during authentication and changes the interface to a connected state.

14. The branch office router forwards the routed packet across the VPN and the corporate office router forwards the packet to the appropriate intranet location.

15. When the intranet location responds to the packet sent to it by the user in the branch office, the packet is forwarded to the corporate office router.

16. The corporate office router checks its routing table and finds a route to the branch office network that uses the VPN demand-dial interface.

17. The corporate office router checks the state of the VPN demand-dial interface and finds it is in a connected state.

18. The response packet is forwarded across the Internet by using the VPN connection.

19. The response packet is received by the branch office router and is forwarded to the original user.

Testing Demand-Dial Connections

You can test whether a demand-dial connection works correctly either manually or automatically.

Manual Test

By manually testing a demand-dial connection, you are testing whether the PPP link can be established. Manual testing verifies that the configuration of the authentication methods, encryption, user credentials, and address for the demand-dial interface are valid.

▶ **To manually connect a demand-dial interface**

1. In the **Routing and Remote Access** snap-in, double-click **Routing Interfaces**.

2. Right-click the appropriate demand-dial interface.

3. Click **Connect**.

Once the demand-dial connection is made, the **Connection Status** column of the demand-dial interface changes from **Disconnected** to **Connected**.

If you cannot manually connect the demand-dial interface, see "Troubleshooting Demand-Dial Routing" later in this chapter.

Automatic

By automatically testing a demand-dial connection, you are testing whether the demand-dial connection is automatically initiated when traffic matching a configured route is sent to the demand-dial router. Before automatic testing, ensure that the appropriate static routes are configured on the calling router and answering router.

To test for an automatic connection, verify that the demand-dial interface being tested is in a disconnected state. Next, generate network traffic for a location that exists across the demand-dial connection. One easy way to generate IP traffic is to use the ping or tracert commands.

For ping and tracert, the first attempt might fail due to the connection establishment delay. However, the first packet being sent across the interface causes the demand-dial interface to be connected. Subsequent use of the testing utility is successful once the connection has been made. One way to see the connection process from an application viewpoint is to use the ping command with the "-t" command line option to continue sending Internet Control Message Protocol (ICMP) Echo Request messages until interrupted. You see "Request timed out" messages until the demand-dial connection is made, after which you see the replies.

If you cannot automatically connect the demand-dial interface, see "Troubleshooting Demand-Dial Routing" later in this chapter.

Monitoring Initiated Demand-Dial Connections with Rasmon

The connection status of a demand-dial interface can be seen from the Routing Interfaces node in the Routing and Remote Access snap-in. However, details of the demand-dial connection such as the line speed, device statistics, connection statistics, and device errors cannot be seen. To view this information for demand-dial connections initiated by the router, run the rasmon Resource Kit tool on the demand-dial router. Only demand-dial connections initiated by the router acting as a calling router will be present in rasmon. Demand-dial interfaces in a connected state due to the router acting as an answering router are not shown. The rasmon Resource Kit tool is equivalent to the rasmon tool present in Windows NT version 4.0.

Demand-Dial Routing Security

Security for demand-dial connections uses the same security features as remote access connections including:

- Remote access permission
- Authentication
- Encryption
- Callback
- Caller ID
- Remote access account lockout

For more information about callback, caller ID, and remote access account lockout, see "Remote Access Server" in this book and Windows 2000 Server Help.

Remote Access Permission

The user account of the calling router must be a valid account in the security database of the answering router or RADIUS server (if RADIUS authentication is being used) and it must either be granted remote access permission either explicitly in the user account (remote access permission of the dial-in properties of the user account is set to **Allow access**) or implicitly through the remote access permission setting on a remote access policy (the remote access permission of the dial-in properties of the user account is set to **Control access through Remote Access Policy** and a matching remote access policy remote access permission is set to **Grant remote access**).

Authentication

The calling router can be authenticated at the user level and the computer level.

User-Level Authentication

As part of the PPP connection establishment process, the calling router's credentials must be authenticated. User-level authentication occurs through one of the following PPP authentication methods:

- Password Authentication Protocol (PAP)
- Shiva Password Authentication Protocol (SPAP)
- Challenge Handshake Authentication Protocol (CHAP)
- Microsoft Challenge Handshake Authentication Protocol version 1 (MS-CHAP v1)
- Microsoft Challenge Handshake Authentication Protocol version 2 (MS-CHAP v2)
- Extensible Authentication Protocol-Message Digest 5 CHAP (EAP-MD5)
- Extensible Authentication Protocol-Transport Layer Security (EAP-TLS)

In all of the previously listed authentication methods except EAP-TLS, the calling router's credentials consist of a user name, a domain, and a password. In all of the previously listed authentication methods except PAP, the password is sent over the connection in an encrypted or hashed form.

In the case of EAP-TLS, the calling router's credentials consist of a user certificate that is validated by the answering router. EAP-TLS requires a public key infrastructure (PKI) to issue and validate certificates.

Computer-Level Authentication

Computer-level authentication occurs in two cases for demand-dial routing:

1. When IPSec is used for a L2TP over IPSec demand-dial connection, computer-level authentication is performed through the exchange of computer certificates (also known as machine certificates) during the establishment of the IPSec security association .

2. When EAP-TLS is used for user-level authentication, the answering router authenticates itself to the calling router by sending its computer certificate.

Computer certificates require a public key infrastructure (PKI) to issue and validate certificates.

One-Way and Mutual Authentication

Authentication of the demand-dial connection can be one-way or mutual.

One-Way Authentication

With one-way authentication, the calling router authenticates itself to the answering router. PAP, SPAP, CHAP, MS-CHAP v1, and EAP-MD5 authentication methods only provide for the passing of credentials from the calling router to the answering router. With one-way authentication, the calling router does not receive any verification that the answering router is the proper router. One-way authentication does not provide protection from unauthorized or masquerading answering routers.

Mutual Authentication

With mutual authentication, the calling router authenticates itself to the answering router and the answering router authenticates itself to the calling router. Both ends of the connection verify the identity of the other end of the connection. MS-CHAP v2 and EAP-TLS authentication methods provide mutual authentication.

With MS-CHAP v2, both sides of the connection send a hash of a challenge string and the user password. If successful, both ends of the connection are ensured that the other end of the connection has access to the user account's password.

With EAP-TLS, the calling router sends a user certificate that is validated by the answering router and the answering router sends a computer certificate that is validated by the calling router. EAP-TLS is the most secure form of mutual authentication, however it requires a PKI.

Note Windows NT 4.0 with the Routing and Remote Access Service (RRAS) supports a feature called two-way authentication. Two-way authentication uses one-way authentication methods to perform mutual authentication. When two-way authentication is enabled on a demand-dial interface, the calling router forces the answering router to authenticate itself after the calling router authenticates itself to the answering router. A Windows 2000 calling router never requests to authenticate a Windows NT 4.0 RRAS answering router. However, a Windows 2000 answering router authenticates itself when requested by a Windows NT 4.0 RRAS calling router.

Encryption

There are two forms of encryption available for demand-dial connections: Microsoft Point-to-Point Encryption (MPPE) and Internet Protocol Security (IPSec).

MPPE

All PPP connections, including PPTP but not including L2TP, can use Microsoft Point-to-Point Encryption (MPPE). MPPE uses the Rivest-Shamir-Adleman (RSA) RC4 stream cipher and is only used when either the EAP-TLS or MS-CHAP (version 1 or version 2) authentication methods are used.

MPPE can use 40-bit, 56-bit, or 128-bit encryption keys. The 40-bit key is designed for backward compatibility. By default, the highest key strength supported by the calling router and answering router is negotiated during the connection establishment process. If the answering router requires a higher key strength than is supported by the calling router, the connection attempt is rejected.

IPSec

For demand-dial connections using L2TP over IPSec, encryption is determined by the establishment of the IPSec security association (SA). The available encryption algorithms include:

- DES with a 56-bit key.
- Triple DES (3DES), which uses three 56-bit keys and is designed for high-security environments.

The initial encryption keys are derived from the IPSec authentication process. For more information about IPSec settings for L2TP over IPSec connections, see "Virtual Private Networking" in this book. For more information about IPSec, see "Internet Protocol Security" in the *Microsoft® Windows® 2000 Server Resource Kit TCP/IP Core Networking Guide.*

Demand-Dial Interface Packet Filtering

IP and IPX packet filters on the demand-dial interface can be used to restrict the types of traffic that are allowed in to (input filters) and out of (output filters) the interface. IP and IPX packet filtering only occurs when the demand-dial interface is in a connected state.

Packet filtering is especially useful for an extranet, a portion of your private intranet that is accessible to business partners over demand-dial connections. For example, when a business partner makes a demand-dial connection, packet filters on the demand-dial interface can restrict the TCP/IP traffic to only specific network segments or specific resources as identified by IP address and TCP or UDP port number.

Remote Access Policy Profile Packet Filtering

In addition to demand-dial interface packet filtering, TCP/IP packet filters can be configured on the profile of the remote access policy configured for calling routers. While primarily designed to restrict the traffic of remote access connections, remote access policy profile–based TCP/IP packet filters can be used for demand-dial routing. Rather than configure the same IP packet filters on many demand-dial interfaces, if all the demand-dial connections share the same IP packet filters and remote access policy, then remote access policy profile packet filters allow you to configure the IP packet filters once for all the demand-dial connections.

Creating User Accounts with the Demand-Dial Wizard

When a demand-dial interface is created with the Demand-Dial wizard in the Routing and Remote Access snap-in, the **Add a user account so a remote router can dial in** option on the **Protocols and Security** page of the wizard allows you to create a new user account that is used by the calling router. When this option is selected, a user account with the same name as the demand-dial interfaces is created in the security accounts database being used by the router on which the demand-dial interface is being created.

Table 6.2 lists where the user account is created.

Table 6.2   Location of User Accounts Created by the Demand-Dial Wizard

Router	Where the Account Is Created
Stand-alone	A local account as if created through the Local Users and Groups snap-in.
Domain controller	A domain account as if created through the Active Directory Users and Groups snap-in.
Member of a domain	A local account as if created through the Local Users and Groups snap-in.

In all cases, the remote access permission is set to **Allow access** even though for a new account in a Windows 2000 native mode domain or a stand-alone router, the default remote access permission for newly created accounts is set to **Control access through Remote Access Policy**. This behavior can cause some confusion if you are using the access by policy administrative model. In the access by policy administrative model, the remote access permission of all user accounts is set to **Control access through Remote Access Policy** and the remote access permission of individual policies are set to either **Grant remote access** or **Deny remote access**.

When the user account is created, it is created with the current default password settings and policies set for your domain. Verify that each user account used by calling routers have the following password settings on the **Account** tab on the properties sheet of the user account:

- **User must change password at next logon** is disabled.

  If enabled, then you must manually disable this setting for accounts created with the Demand-Dial Wizard. If you do not disable this setting, then a demand-dial router is unable to connect using this account. When the calling router sends its credentials, the calling router is prompted to change the password. Because the initiation of a demand-dial connection is not an interactive process involving a user, the calling router is unable to change the password and aborts the connection attempt.

- **Password never expires** is enabled.

  Because the demand-dial connection process is not interactive, if the password expires, the calling router is prompted to change the expired password and the connection attempt is aborted.

Preventing Demand-Dial Connections

While on-demand demand-dial routing provides a lower cost solution than a dedicated WAN link, each connection that a demand-dial router makes can incur a monetary cost. For example, the cost of dial-up analog lines are time and distance sensitive. For ISDN lines, you might be charged for each call that is made in addition to time and distance charges.

To prevent demand-dial connections from occurring, and therefore incurring the costs associated with each connection, Windows 2000 demand-dial routing allows the configuration of demand-dial filters and dial-out hours.

Demand-Dial Filters

Demand-dial filters are used to specify what types of TCP/IP traffic either creates the connection or ignores it for the purposes of creating the connection. For example, if you only want a demand-dial connection to be initiated for Web traffic, set the demand-dial filters so that only traffic to TCP destination port 80 can initiate the connection. Demand-dial filters are only relevant for a demand-dial interface that is in a disconnected state.

▶ **To set demand-dial filters on a demand-dial interface**

1. In the **Routing and Remote Access** snap-in, double-click **Routing Interfaces**, and then right-click the appropriate demand-dial interface.

2. Click **Set IP Demand-Dial filters**.

3. Click **Add**, configure the filter settings, and then click **OK**.

4. Click the appropriate filter action, either **Only for the following traffic** to initiate a demand-dial connection for traffic matching the configured filters or **For all traffic except** to not initiate a demand-dial connection for traffic matching the configured filters.

Note Demand-dial filters are different than IP packet filters. Demand-dial filters define what traffic initiates a demand-dial connection. IP packet filters define what traffic is allowed in and out of the demand-dial interface once it is connected. Because IP packet filters are applied after the connection is initiated, it is recommended that if you have configured IP output packet filters that prevent the flow of TCP/IP traffic on the demand-dial interface, then configure the same filters as demand-dial filters. If you do, then the demand-dial connection is never established for traffic that is discarded by the IP packet filters for the demand-dial interface.

Dial-Out Hours

Dial-out hours are used to specify when the demand-dial connection can be made. With dial-out hours, you can specify the time of day and day of the week that a demand-dial connection is either allowed or denied. For example, if a specific demand-dial interface is intended to be used for backing up data from 12:00 midnight to 4:00 A.M. during weekdays, then you can set the dial-out hours to only permit connections during those days and times.

▶ **To set dial-out hours on a demand-dial interface**

1. In the **Routing and Remote Access** snap-in, double-click **Routing Interfaces**, and then right-click the appropriate demand-dial interface.

2. Click **Dial-out Hours**.

3. In the **Dial-out Hours** dialog box, select days and times to either permit or deny a connection, and then click **OK**.

The day and time used for comparison with the configured dial-out hours is the current day and time of the Windows 2000 router on which the demand-dial interface resides. By default, all times on all days are permitted.

When the current time corresponds to a time that the demand-dial connection is denied with dial-out hours, a demand-dial interface that is in a connected state is not automatically disconnected. Dial-out hours only apply to demand-dial interfaces in a disconnected state.

Demand-Dial Routing and Routing Protocols

The method of updating the routing tables of demand-dial routers depends on the type of demand-dial connection.

- For on-demand connections, use static routing.
- For persistent connections, use dynamic routing with routing protocols.

On-Demand Connections

The recommendation of static routing for on-demand demand-dial connections is based on the fact that the routing protocols provided with the Windows 2000 Routing and Remote Access Service (Routing Information Protocol [RIP] for IP, Open Shortest Path First [OSPF], RIP for IPX, Service Advertising Protocol [SAP] for IPX) have a periodic advertising behavior that can cause the connection to be made for each advertisement or to keep the connection up permanently if the advertising interval is less than the idle time-out. Due to the time, distance, and cost-sensitive nature of typical dial-up WAN links, running routing protocols over on-demand connections is not recommended.

Static routes for demand-dial routing are either manually configured or automatically configured by using autostatic updates, discussed later in this section.

Manual Configuration of Static Routes

Manual configuration of static routes is the adding of static routes that are available across the demand-dial interface using the Routing and Remote Access snap-in. For TCP/IP traffic, static IP routes must be added.

▶ **To add a static IP route that uses a demand-dial interface**

1. In the **Routing and Remote Access** snap-in, double-click **IP Routing**, and then right-click **Static routes**.
2. Select **New**, and then click **Static route**.
3. In the **Interface** box, select the demand-dial interface.
4. Type the appropriate values for **Destination**, **Network mask**, and **Metric**.
5. If you do not want traffic for this static route to initiate the demand-dial connection, clear the **Use this route to initiate demand-dial connections** check box.

Note The Gateway field is not available when a demand-dial interface is selected. A demand-dial interface is a point-to-point connection and the forwarding IP address of the Gateway field is not needed to forward the IP traffic.

For IPX traffic, static IPX routes and static SAP services must be added.

Using a Default IP Route for an On-Demand Connection

Make sure to use the default IP route (0.0.0.0/0) carefully. While the default route can be used to simplify configuration of static routing over on-demand connections, you must consider its implications. The default IP route effectively summarizes all IP destinations and becomes the route used to forward IP packets when another more specific route is not found.

The use of the default route is an assumption that all other destinations is in the direction of the default route. When you are using a demand-dial interface to connect to the Internet, this is a valid assumption. However, when you are using a demand-dial interface to connect a branch office to a corporate office in a private intranet, the use of a default route needs to be carefully considered.

If a default IP route is configured to use a demand-dial interface, then the demand-dial connection can be initiated for IP traffic that is unreachable. For example, if an organization is using the private IP network 10.0.0.0/8 for its address space and a branch office uses 10.1.1.0/24 for the hosts of the branch office, then the static routing of the branch office router can be configured in the following ways:

- Configure a static route for 10.0.0.0/8 using the on-demand demand-dial interface.

  If someone in the branch office attempts to send traffic to the destination IP address of 192.168.0.1, the router at the branch office does not have a route in its routing table for the packet. The packet is discarded and an ICMP Destination Unreachable-Host Unreachable message is sent to the sending host.

- Configure a default route for 0.0.0.0/0 using the on-demand demand-dial interface.

  If someone in the branch office attempts to send traffic to the destination IP address of 192.168.0.1, the router at the branch office initiates the connection and forward the packet across the demand-dial connection to the corporate router. Neither the corporate router nor another router on the corporate intranet has a route in its routing table for the packet. The packet is discarded and an ICMP Destination Unreachable-Host Unreachable message is sent to the sending host.

Using a default route for branch office connectivity can produce undesirable results for unreachable traffic.

Autostatic Updates

While manually entering a small number of static routes might be a feasible solution, when the number of routes is large or routes change, manual configuration is no longer a viable administrative option. To automatically add routes and services to the routing tables of a Windows 2000 router, the Routing and Remote Access service supports autostatic updates across demand-dial interfaces.

An autostatic update requests all known routes or services from the router on the other side of the connection and adds them to the routing tables of the requesting router. An autostatic update is a one-time, one-way exchange of routing information. After the routes are sent, the two routers do not periodically advertise even though the connection remains in a connected state.

Note The "auto" in autostatic is the automatic adding of routes as static routes in a routing table. Autostatic updates do not occur automatically when the demand-dial connection is made.

To use autostatic updates for IP routes, the demand-dial interface must be added to the **RIP** routing protocol. The default operation mode for demand-dial interfaces for RIP is **Autostatic update mode**. The default outgoing packet protocol is **RIP version 2 multicast**. The default settings are correct when initiating a connection with another Windows 2000 router.

To use autostatic updates for IPX routes and SAP services, the demand-dial interface must be added to the **RIP for IPX** and **SAP for IPX** routing protocols. The default update mode for demand-dial interfaces for RIP for IPX is **No update**. You must change the update mode to **Autostatic**. The default update mode for demand-dial interfaces for SAP for IPX is **No update**. You must change the update mode to **Autostatic**.

▶ **To change the update mode**

1. In the **Routing and Remote Access** snap-in, double-click **IPX Routing**.

2. For RIP for IPX, click **RIP for IPX**, right-click the appropriate demand-dial interface, click **Autostatic** under **Update mode**, and then click **OK**.

3. For SAP for IPX, click **SAP for IPX**, right-click the appropriate demand-dial interface, click **Autostatic** under **Update mode**, and then click **OK**.

Note When an autostatic update is requested, the existing routes that were obtained through a previous autostatic update are deleted before the request for routes is sent. If there is no response to the request, then the router cannot replace the routes it has deleted. This might lead to a loss of connectivity to remote networks.

Autostatic updates can be made manually or on a scheduled basis.

Manual Autostatic Updates

To manually update static IP routes across a demand-dial interface, perform the following procedure.

▶ **To manually perform an IP autostatic update**

1. In the **Routing and Remote Access** snap-in, double-click **IP Routing,** and then double-click **General**.

2. Right-click the appropriate demand-dial interface, and then click **Update Routes**.

If the demand-dial interface is in a disconnected state, the connection is automatically made. After the link is in a connected state, the autostatic update begins. The autostatic update only transfers routing information from the answering router to the calling router. To transfer routing information from the calling router to the answering router, perform the preceding procedure on the answering router.

The transfer of IP routing information occurs through RIP for IP. The router on which the update was initiated sends a General RIP Request. The router on the other end of the connection responds with a RIP Response containing all of the appropriate routes in its IP routing table. The RIP routes received by the requesting router are automatically added as static routes to the requesting router's IP routing table. For more information about RIP messages, see "Unicast IP Routing" in this book.

To manually update static IPX routes and SAP services across a demand-dial interface, perform the following procedure.

▶ **To manually perform an IPX and SAP autostatic update**

1. In the **Routing and Remote Access** snap-in, double-click **IPX Routing** and then open **General**.

2. Right-click the appropriate demand-dial interface, and then click **Update Routes**.

Just as in the case of an IP autostatic update, if the demand-dial interface is in a disconnected state, the connection is automatically made. After the link is in a connected state, the auto static update begins. The autostatic update only transfers routing and service information from the answering router to the calling router. To transfer routing and service information from the calling router to the answering router, perform the preceding procedure on the answering router.

The transfer of IPX routing information occurs through RIP for IPX. The router on which the update was initiated sends a RIP General Request. The router on the other end of the connection responds with a RIP Response containing all of the appropriate routes in its IPX routing table. The RIP for IPX routes received by the requesting router are added as static routes to the requesting router's IPX routing table. For more information about RIP messages, see "IPX Routing" in this book.

The transfer of SAP service information occurs through SAP for IPX. The router on which the update was initiated sends a SAP General Request. The router on the other end of the connection responds with a SAP Response containing all of the appropriate services in its SAP service table. The SAP services received by the requesting router are added as static services to the requesting router's SAP service table. For more information about SAP messages, see "IPX Routing" in this book.

Scheduled Autostatic Updates

Autostatic updates can be scheduled to occur periodically through a combination of a batch file or **netsh** script and Windows 2000 Scheduled Tasks. To perform an autostatic update using RIP for IP and the netsh script, the following netsh commands are run:

```
netsh interface set interface name=<Demand-Dial interface name>
connect=CONNECTED
netsh routing ip rip update <Demand-Dial interface name>
netsh interface set interface name=<Demand-Dial interface name>
connect=DISCONNECTED
```

For example, to update IP routes using a demand-dial interface called CorpHub, the netsh commands are:

```
netsh interface set interface name=CorpHub connect=CONNECTED
netsh routing ip rip update CorpHub
netsh interface set interface name=CorpHub connect=DISCONNECTED
```

The netsh commands can be run from a Windows 2000 batch file or they can be placed in a netsh script file. For example, the following script file Corphub.scp is created to run the preceding commands:

```
interface set interface name=CorpHub connect=CONNECTED
routing ip rip update CorpHub
interface set interface name=CorpHub connect=DISCONNECTED
```

To run the preceding script file, run the following at the command line:

```
netsh -f corphub.scp
```

After the Windows 2000 batch file or netsh script file is created, you can configure it to run periodically through Windows 2000 Scheduled Tasks.

Persistent Connections

For persistent demand-dial connections, routing protocols can be enabled to operate in the same fashion as LAN interfaces to provide dynamic updates of routing tables. Special configuration of the routing protocol for a persistent demand-dial interface is outlined in Table 6.3.

Table 6.3   Changes to Default Routing Protocol Configuration for Demand-Dial Interfaces

Routing Protocol	Configuration Change
RIP for IP	Change the default operation mode to Periodic update mode and enable triggered updates.
OSPF	Select the Point-to-point network type on the General tab on the properties of an OSPF interface. This is the default network type for demand-dial interfaces. For a persistent router-to-router VPN connection, you might want to increase the values of the transit delay, the re-transmit interval, the hello interval, and the dead interval on the Advanced tab on the properties of an OSPF interface to account for the delay of forwarding OSPF packets across the Internet.
RIP for IPX	Change the update mode to **Standard**.
SAP for IPX	Change the update mode to **Standard**.

In all cases, including autostatic updates, routing protocols provided by the Windows 2000 Routing and Remote Access service must run over a numbered connection. A numbered connection is assigned an IP or IPX address during the PPP connection process. Unnumbered connections are supported by the Routing and Remote Access service, but routing protocols do not work over them. An unnumbered connection is typically used when dialing an Internet service provider who does not want to waste IP addresses for the point-to-point connection. The Internet connection can be unnumbered because you would typically configure a default static IP route, rather than run a routing protocol.

Using Multilink and BAP

Multilink and Bandwidth Allocation Protocol (BAP) can be used with demand-dial routing to automatically add physical connections to a Multilink PPP connection when network traffic increases and remove physical connections when the network traffic decreases.

▶ **To create a Multilink or BAP demand-dial connection**

1. In the **Routing and Remote Access** snap-in, double-click **Routing Interfaces**.

2. Right-click **Routing Interfaces**, point to **New**, and then click **Demand-dial interface**.

3. In the Demand-Dial Wizard, select the modem that you want to use for the first physical connection.

4. Right-click the demand-dial interface, and then click **Properties**.

5. On the **General** tab under **Connect using**, select the modems or ports that you want to use for the connection and the order in which you want to use them.

   If each of the separate physical connections calls a different number, then clear **All devices call the same numbers**. The number to call is negotiated by BAP at the time the connection is required.

6. On the **Options** tab under **Multiple devices**, click **Dial devices only as needed**.

7. Click **Configure** to specify when a new physical connection is made and when an existing physical connection is dropped. The **Automatic Dialing and Automatic Hanging Up** dialog box is shown in Figure 6.3.

   Under **Automatic dialing**, select the appropriate conditions under which a new line is dialed. The default setting is two minutes at 75 percent or more capacity of the exiting MP connection.

   Under **Automatic hangup**, select the appropriate conditions under which a line is hung up. The default setting is two minutes at 10 percent or less capacity of the line.

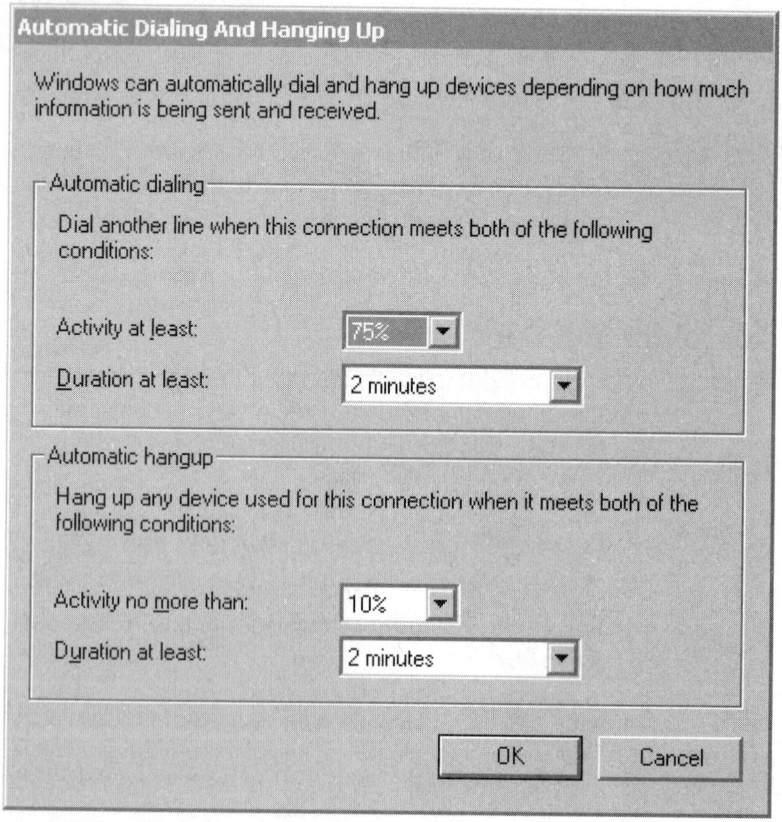

Figure 6.3   Automatic Dialing and Automatic Hanging Up Dialog Box

---

Note If a link within the multilink bundle is dropped when using multilink without BAP, then it does not automatically reconnect. To force a reconnection of dropped links in a multilink bundle, use BAP and configure your links for settings that always cause the links to be initialized when the demand-dial connection is created and always reinitialized when the line is dropped. For example, set automatic dialing conditions for **Activity at least** to 1% and **Duration at least** to 3 seconds.

IPX Demand-Dial Connections

IPX-based demand-dial connections have two different ways in which the IPX parameters of the connection are negotiated, corresponding to two different IPX control protocols:

- IPXCP

  IPX Control Protocol (IPXCP) is the Link Control Protocol (LCP) for IPX negotiation for PPP connections and is documented in RFC 1552. IPXCP is the default control protocol for IPX connections. For more information about IPXCP, see "Remote Access Server" in this book.

- IPX WAN

  IPX WAN is a control protocol used by Novell NetWare and compatible remote access servers and routers. Use IPX WAN when calling a Novell NetWare server or router or other router that supports the IPX WAN control protocol.

▶ **To change the IPX control protocol on a demand-dial interface**

1. Use the **Routing and Remote Access** snap-in and open **IPX Routing** and then click **General**.
2. Right-click the desired demand-dial interface.
3. Click either **IPX CP** or **IPX WAN** and click **OK**.

NCP Watchdog Spoofing

Novell NetWare clients communicate with Novell NetWare servers using a file sharing protocol called NetWare Core Protocol (NCP). NetWare Core Protocol is a connection-oriented, reliable protocol that provides file and printer sharing on NetWare networks. Once an NCP connection is made, the connection is maintained using the NCP Watchdog protocol. The NCP Watchdog protocol is a simple protocol that a NetWare server uses to poll a NetWare client to verify that the client is still present and operating over the open NCP connection.

The NCP Watchdog packet is a message sent by the internal adapter of the NetWare server to the NetWare client consisting of the NCP connection number and a signature character (0x3F). If the client is still active on the connection, the client returns the connection number and signature character back to the NetWare server.

By default, if a client has not sent any NCP connection data for 4 minutes and 56.6 seconds, the NetWare server sends a NCP Watchdog packet. If no response is received, then the NetWare server sends up to 10 more NCP Watchdog packets at intervals of 59.3 seconds. This behavior is configurable on the NetWare server. Consult your NetWare server documentation for more information.

The NCP Watchdog protocol keeps a demand-dial connection open even though the client or server are not sending data on the NCP connection. To keep the NCP Watchdog protocol from keeping time-sensitive on-demand connections open, the Windows 2000 Routing and Remote Access service spoofs, or answers on behalf of NetWare clients, the replies to NCP Watchdog packets across a demand-dial connection.

If the demand-dial router receives a NCP Watchdog packet sent from a NetWare server to a NetWare client that is reachable through a route that uses a demand-dial interface, it replies to the NCP Watchdog packet for the NetWare client. By spoofing the NCP Watchdog protocol, NCP Watchdog packets do not keep the demand-dial connection open, incurring additional costs. Spoofing the NCP Watchdog packets on behalf of the NetWare client does not cause the NetWare client to time out the NCP connection.

After the configured idle time, the demand-dial connection is terminated and the Windows 2000 Routing and Remote Access service continues to spoof NCP Watchdog packets. When either the NetWare server or the NetWare client sends data on the NCP connection, the on-demand connection is made and the data is forwarded.

Troubleshooting Demand-Dial Routing

Remote access problems typically include the following:

- On-demand connection not being made automatically.
- Unable to make demand-dial connection.
- Unable to reach locations beyond the calling router or answering router.
- Autostatic updates not working.

The following sections give troubleshooting tips to isolate the configuration or infrastructure problem causing the demand-dial routing problem.

On-demand connection not being made automatically

- Verify that the correct static routes exist and are configured with the appropriate demand-dial interface.

- For the static routes using a demand-dial interface, verify that the **Use this route to initiate demand-dial connections** check box is selected.

- Verify that the demand-dial interface is not in a disabled state. To enable, right-click the demand-dial interface and select **Enable**.

- Verify that the dial-out hours for the demand-dial interface on the calling router are not preventing the connection attempt.

- Verify that the demand-dial filters for the demand-dial interface on the calling router are not preventing the connection attempt.

Unable to make a demand-dial connection

- Verify that the Routing and Remote Access service is running on both the calling router and the answering router.

- Verify that routing is enabled with local and remote routing (LAN and WAN routers) on both the calling router and the answering router.

- Verify that the dial-up ports being used on both the calling router and answering router are configured to allow demand-dial routing (inbound and outbound).

- Verify that all of the dial-up ports on both the calling router and answering router are not already connected.

- Verify that the calling router and the answering router in conjunction with a remote access policy are enabled to use at least one common authentication method.

- Verify that the calling router and the answering router in conjunction with a remote access policy are enabled to use at least one common encryption method.

- Verify that the calling router's credentials consisting of user name, password, and domain name are correct and can be validated by the answering router.

- For demand-dial connections using MS-CHAP v1 and attempting to negotiate 40-bit MPPE encryption, verify that the user's password is not larger than 14 characters.

- Verify that the user account of the calling router has not been disabled or is not locked out on the properties of the user account. If the password on the account has expired, verify that the remote access client is using MS-CHAP v1 or MS-CHAP v2. MS-CHAP v1 and MS-CHAP v2 are the only authentication protocols provided with Windows 2000 that allow you to change an expired password during the connection process.

  For an administrator-level account whose password has expired, reset the password using another administrator-level account.

- Verify that the user account of the calling router has not been locked out due to remote access account lockout. For more information, see "Remote Access Server" in this book.

- Verify that account options on the **Account** tab on the properties sheet of the user account of the calling router are configured to not change the password at the next logon attempt, so that the password never expires.

- Verify that the parameters of the connection attempt are accepted by the currently configured dial-in properties of the user account of the calling router and remote access policies. If the answering router is configured to use Windows authentication, the remote access policies stored on the answering router are used. If the answering router is configured to use RADIUS authentication and the RADIUS server being used is a Windows 2000 Internet Authentication Service (IAS) server, then the remote access policies of the IAS server are used.

In order for the connection to be established, the parameters of the connection attempt must:

1. Match all of the conditions of at least one remote access policy.

2. Be granted remote access permission, either through the remote access permission of the user account (set to **Allow access**), or the user account is set to **Control access through Remote Access Policy** and the remote access permission of the matching remote access policy is set to **Grant remote access permission**.

3. Match all the settings of the profile.

4. Match all the settings of the dial-in properties of the user account.

- Verify that the settings of the remote access policy profile are not in conflict with properties of the answering router.

The properties of the remote access policy profile and the properties of the answering router both contain settings for:

- Multilink
- Bandwidth Allocation Protocol
- Authentication protocols

If the settings of the profile of the matching remote access policy are in conflict with the settings of the answering router, then the connection attempt is denied. For example, if the matching remote access policy profile specifies that the EAP-TLS authentication protocol must be used and EAP-TLS is not enabled through the properties of the answering router, then the answering router denies the connection attempt.

- If the answering router is configured with a static IP address pool, verify that there are enough addresses in the pool.

  If all of the addresses in the static pool have been allocated to connected demand-dial routers or remote access clients, then the answering router is unable to allocate an IP address. If the calling router is only configured to route IP packets, the connection attempt is aborted.

- Verify the configuration of the authentication provider of the answering router.

  The answering router can be configured to use either Windows authentication or RADIUS to authenticate the credentials of the calling router. If RADIUS is selected, verify the RADIUS configuration of the answering router.

- For an answering router that is a member server in mixed-mode or native-mode Windows 2000 domain that is configured for Windows 2000 authentication, verify that:

  - The **RAS and IAS Servers** security group exists in the Active Directory™ directory service. If not, then create the group and set the group type to **Security** and the group scope to **Domain local**.

  - The **RAS and IAS Servers** security group has Read permission to the **RAS and IAS Servers Access Check** object.

  - The computer account of the answering router computer is a member of the **RAS and IAS Servers** security group. You can use the **netsh ras show registeredserver** command at the Windows 2000 command prompt to view the current registration. You can use the **netsh ras add registeredserver** command to register the server in a specified domain.

    If you add the answering router computer to the **RAS and IAS Servers** security group, the answering router might not immediately authenticate the credentials of incoming connections (due to the way that Windows 2000 caches authentication information). For immediate authentication ability, you need to restart the answering router.

- For an answering router that is a member of a Windows 2000 native-mode domain, verify that the answering router has joined the domain.

- For a Windows NT version 4.0 Service Pack 4 and later answering router that is a member of a Windows 2000 mixed-mode domain or a Windows 2000 answering router that is a member of a Windows NT 4.0 domain that is accessing user account properties for a user account in a trusted Windows 2000 domain, verify that the Everyone group is added to the Pre-Windows 2000 Compatible Access group with the **net localgroup "Pre-Windows 2000 Compatible Access"** command. If not, issue the **net localgroup "Pre-Windows 2000 Compatible Access" everyone /add** command on a domain controller computer and then restart the domain controller computer.

- For a Windows NT version 4.0 Service Pack 3 and earlier answering router that is a member of a Windows 2000 mixed mode domain, verify that Everyone group has been granted list contents, read all properties, and read permissions to the root node of your domain and all sub-objects of the root domain.

- For RADIUS authentication, verify that the answering router computer can communicate with the RADIUS server.

- If the answering router is using **Windows authentication** and is a member of Windows 2000 mixed-mode domain, when the mixed-mode domain is upgraded to a native mode domain, you must restart the answering router computer before the answering router can successfully authenticate calling router and remote access credentials.

- Verify that if Windows 2000 Fax service and the Routing and Remote Access service are sharing the same modem, that the modem supports adaptive answer. If the modem does not support adaptive answer, you must disable fax on the modem to receive incoming demand-dial routing and remote access connections.

- For certificate-based demand-dial routing, verify the following on the calling router:

  - EAP is enabled as an authentication protocol.

  - The correct certificate for the root certificate authority certificate of the answering router is selected.

  - The correct router (offline request) certificate is selected when configuring the credentials of the demand-dial interface.

- For certificate-based demand-dial routing, verify the following on the answering router:

  - EAP is enabled as an authentication protocol.

  - The correct machine certificate for the root certificate authority of the answering router is selected.

Unable to reach locations beyond the calling router or answering router

- For a two-way initiated demand-dial connection, verify that the demand-dial connection is not being interpreted as a remote access connection. In order for the answering router to determine that the incoming call is a router rather than remote access client, the user name of the calling router's credentials must match the name of a demand-dial interface configured on the answering router.

  If the incoming caller is a router, the port on which the call was received shows a status of **Active**, and the corresponding demand-dial interface is in a **Connected** state. If the name of the calling router's user name credential appears under **Remote Access Clients**, then the calling router has been interpreted by the answering router as a remote access client.

For two-way initiated connections, either router can be the calling router or the called router. The user names and demand-dial interface names must be properly matched. For example, two-way initiated connections should work under the following configuration:

Router 1 has a demand-dial interface called NEW-YORK, which is configured to use SEATTLE as the user name when sending authentication credentials.

Router 2 has a demand-dial interface called SEATTLE, which is configured to use NEW-YORK as the user name when sending authentication credentials.

This example assumes that the SEATTLE user name can be validated by Router 2 and the NEW-YORK user name can be validated by Router 1.

- For a one-way initiated demand-dial connection, verify that the appropriate static routes are enabled on the user account of the calling router and that the answering router is configured with a routing protocol so that when a connection is made, the static routes of the user account of the calling router are advertised to neighboring routers.

- Verify that there are routes on both sides of the demand-dial connection that support the two-way exchange of traffic. Unlike a remote access client connection, a demand-dial connection does not automatically create a default IP route. Routes on both sides of the demand-dial connection have to be created so that traffic can be routed to and from the other side of the demand-dial connection.

- Verify that there are routes in the intranet routers on the calling router and answering router's intranet that support the forwarding of packets between hosts on the intranets. Routes can be added to the routers of each intranet through static routes or by enabling a routing protocol on the intranet interface of the calling and answering routers.

- Verify that there are no IP or IPX packet filters on the demand-dial interfaces that are preventing the flow of wanted traffic. Each demand-dial interface can be configured with IP and IPX input and output filters that allow you to control the exact nature of TCP/IP and IPX traffic allowed in to and out of the demand-dial interface.

- Verify that there are no configured TCP/IP packet filters on the profile properties of the remote access policies on the answering router (or the RADIUS server if IAS is used) that are preventing the sending or receiving of TCP/IP traffic.

Autostatic updates not working

- For IP autostatic updates, verify on both routers that the appropriate demand-dial interface is added to the RIP routing protocol, that its operation mode is set to **Autostatic update mode,** and that the outgoing packet protocol is **RIP version 2 multicast.**

- For IPX autostatic updates, verify that the desired demand-dial on both routers is added to the RIP for IPX and SAP for IPX routing protocols and that for each routing protocol, the update mode is set to **Autostatic.**

Troubleshooting Tools

The following tools, which enable you to gather additional information about the source of your problem, are included with Windows 2000.

Unreachability Reason

If a demand-dial connection attempt fails, the demand-dial interface is left in an unreachable state. A Windows 2000 router records the reason why the connection failed through the unreachability reason. You can troubleshoot further based on the information in the unreachability reason.

▶ **To check the unreachability reason**

1. In the **Routing and Remote Access** snap-in, right-click the appropriate demand-dial interface.

2. Click **Unreachability reason.**

3. From the **Routing and Remote Access** dialog box, read the text for the **Unreachability reason,** and then click **OK.**

The following are reasons why the demand-dial interface is left in an unreachable state:

- There are no more ports of the type being used by the demand-dial interface.

- The Routing and Remote Access service has paused.

- The demand-dial interface is disabled.

- Dial-out hours are preventing the connection.

When a demand-dial interface is configured, a port is selected. A port is a hardware or software channel that represents a single point-to-point connection. Ports are grouped by type such as analog phone ports, ISDN B-channel ports, and VPN ports such as PPTP and L2TP.

While you might configure a demand-dial interface to use a specific port, you are also configuring the demand-dial interface to use a port type. If the specific port is not available when the connection needs to be made, the Routing and Remote Access service attempts to use another port of the same type. For example, if you have two modems and you configure a demand-dial interface to use a specific modem and that modem is in use when the demand-dial connection needs to be made, the calling router uses the other modem automatically.

The Routing and Remote Access snap-in allows you to configure more demand-dial interfaces for a given port type than there are actual ports. For example, you can configure multiple demand-dial interfaces that are all configured to use the same modem port. If that modem port is in use when the demand-dial connection needs to be initiated and there are no other ports of that port type available, the connection attempt fails and the unreachability reason is recorded.

Event Logging

Event logging is the recording of events in the Windows 2000 system event log. Event logging is typically used for troubleshooting or for notifying network administrators of unusual events.

On the **Event logging** tab on the properties sheet of an answering router, there are four levels of logging. Select **Log the maximum amount of information** and try the connection again. After the connection fails, check the system event log for events logged during the connection process. After you are done viewing events, select the **Log errors and warnings** option on the **Event logging** tab.

Windows Accounting and Logging

The Routing and Remote Access service supports the logging of authentication and accounting information for demand-dial and remote access connections when Windows accounting is enabled. This logging is separate from the events recorded in the system event log. You can use the information that is logged to track demand-dial and remote access usage and authentication attempts. Logging is especially useful for troubleshooting remote access policy issues. For each authentication attempt, the name of the remote access policy that either accepted or rejected the connection attempt is recorded.

The authentication and accounting information is stored in a configurable log file or files stored in the *SystemRoot*\System32\LogFiles folder. The log files are saved in IAS 1.0 or IAS 2.0 format. IAS 2.0 format is database–compliant, meaning that any database program can read the log file directly for analysis.

You can configure the type of activity to log (accounting or authentication activity) and log file settings from the properties of the **Remote Access Logging** folder in the Routing and Remote Access snap-in.

Network Monitor

Network Monitor is a packet capture and analysis tool that you can use to view the traffic sent between demand-dial routers during the connection establishment process and during data transfer. Network Monitor does not interpret the compressed or encrypted portions of demand-dial traffic.

The proper interpretation of the PPP connection establishment traffic with Network Monitor requires an understanding of PPP protocols described in "Remote Access Server" in this book. Network Monitor captures can be saved as files and sent to Microsoft support for analysis.

Tracing

Tracing records the sequence of programming functions called during a process to a file. Enable tracing for remote access or demand-dial components and try the connection again. After you are done viewing the traced information, reset the tracing settings back to their default values.

The tracing information can be complex and very detailed. Most of the time, this information is useful only to Microsoft support professionals, or to network administrators who are very experienced with the Routing and Remote Access service. The tracing information can be saved as files and sent to Microsoft support for analysis.

For more information about PPP tracing, see "Remote Access Server" in this book.

PART 2

Remote Access

Dial-up remote access, virtual private networking, and centralized authentication, authorization, and accounting using RADIUS allow for secure and scalable remote access connectivity solutions. This section details the remote access technologies provided by the Microsoft® Windows® 2000 Routing and Remote Access and Internet Authentication Service.

In This Part

C H A P T E R   7

Remote Access Server

Microsoft® Windows® 2000 has extensive support for remote access technology to connect remote clients to corporate networks or the Internet. This chapter describes how remote access works and details how to troubleshoot remote access problems.

This chapter is intended for network engineers and support professionals who are already familiar with TCP/IP, IP routing, IPX routing, and wide area network technology, and assumes that you have read the section about remote access in Windows 2000 Server Help.

In This Chapter

Related Information in the Resource Kit

- For more information about TCP/IP routing, see "Introduction to TCP/IP" in the *Microsoft® Windows® 2000 Server Resource Kit TCP/IP Core Networking Guide*.

- For more information about unicast IP routing, see "Unicast IP Routing" in this book.

- For more information about IPX routing, see "IPX Routing" in this book.

- For more information about demand-dial routing, see "Demand-Dial Routing" in this book.

- For more information about virtual private networking, see "Virtual Private Networking" in this book.

Note This chapter mentions Windows 2000 registry entries. For more information about these registry entries, see the *Technical Reference to the Windows 2000 Registry* on the Windows 2000 Resource Kit CD-ROM.

Remote Access Overview

With Windows 2000 remote access, remote access clients connect to remote access servers and are transparently connected to the remote access server, known as point-to-point remote access connectivity, or transparently connected to the network to which the remote access server is attached, known as point-to-LAN remote access connectivity. This transparent connection allows remote access clients to dial-in from remote locations and access resources as if they were physically attached to the network.

Windows 2000 remote access provides two different types of remote access connectivity:

1. Dial-up remote access

   With dial-up remote access, a remote access client uses the telecommunications infrastructure to create a temporary physical circuit or a virtual circuit to a port on a remote access server. Once the physical or virtual circuit is created, the rest of the connection parameters can be negotiated.

2. Virtual private network (VPN) remote access

   With virtual private network remote access, a VPN client uses an IP internetwork to create a virtual point-to-point connection with a remote access server acting as the VPN server. Once the virtual point-to-point connection is created, the rest of the connection parameters can be negotiated.

Note This chapter is primarily devoted to the discussion of dial-up remote access; however, many topics also apply to VPN remote access. For a complete understanding of VPNs, read this chapter first and then read the chapter "Virtual Private Networking" in this book.

Remote Access Versus Remote Control

The distinctions between remote access and remote control solutions are the following:

- The remote access server is a software-based multi-protocol router; remote control solutions work by sharing screen, keyboard, and mouse over the remote link. In remote access, the applications are run on the remote access client computer.

- In a remote control solution, users share a CPU or multiple CPUs on the server. In remote control, the applications are run on the server. The remote access server's CPU is dedicated to facilitating communications between remote access clients and network resources, not to running applications.

Elements of a Dial-Up Remote Access Connection

A dial-up remote access connection consists of a remote access client, a remote access server and a wide area network (WAN) infrastructure as illustrated in Figure 7.1.

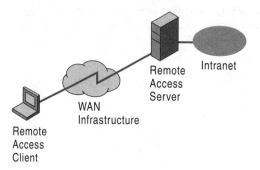

Figure 7.1   Elements of a Dial-Up Remote Access Connection

Remote Access Client

Windows 2000, Microsoft® Windows NT® 3.5 or later, Microsoft® Windows® 95, Microsoft® Windows® 98, Microsoft® Windows® for Workgroups, Microsoft® MS-DOS®, and Microsoft® LAN Manager remote access clients can all connect to a Windows 2000 remote access server. Almost any third-party Point-to-Point Protocol (PPP) remote access clients including UNIX and Apple Macintosh can also connect to a Windows 2000 remote access server.

Remote Access Server

The Windows 2000 remote access server accepts dial-up connections and forwards packets between remote access clients and the network to which the remote access server is attached.

Note The term remote access server as it is used in this chapter refers to a Windows 2000 Server computer running the Routing and Remote Access service and configured to provide remote access.

Dial-Up Equipment and WAN Infrastructure

The physical or logical connection between the remote access server and the remote access client is facilitated by dial-up equipment installed at the remote access client, the remote access server, and the telecommunications infrastructure. The nature of the dial-up equipment and telecommunications infrastructure varies depending on the type of connection being made.

PSTN

The Public Switched Telephone Network (PSTN), also known as Plain Old Telephone Service (POTS), is the analog phone system designed to carry the minimal frequencies to distinguish human voices. Because the PSTN was not designed for data transmissions, there are limits to the maximum bit rate of a PSTN connection. Dial-up equipment consists of an analog modem for the remote access client and the remote access server. For large organizations, the remote access server is attached to a modem bank containing up to hundreds of modems. With analog modems at both the remote access server and the remote access client, the maximum bit rate supported by PSTN connections is 33,600 bits per second, or 33.6 kilobits per second (Kbps).

Figure 7.2 illustrates a PSTN connection.

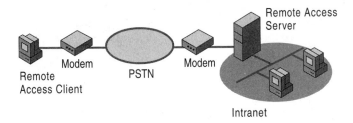

Figure 7.2   Dial-Up Equipment and WAN Infrastructure for PSTN Connections

Digital Links and V.90

The maximum bit rate of the PSTN is a function of the range of frequencies being passed by PSTN switches and the signal-to-noise ratio of the connection. The modern-day analog phone system is only analog on the local loop, the set of wires that connects the customer to the central office (CO) PSTN switch. Once the analog signal reaches the PSTN switch, it is converted to a digital signal. The analog-to-digital conversion introduces noise on the connection known as quantization noise.

When a remote access server is connected to a CO using a digital switch based on T-Carrier or ISDN rather than an analog PSTN switch, there is no analog-to-digital conversion when the remote access server sends information to the remote access client. There is no quantization noise in the downstream path to the remote access client, and therefore, there is a higher signal-to-noise ratio and a higher maximum bit rate.

With this new technology, called V.90, remote access clients can send data at 33.6 Kbps and receive data at 56 Kbps. In North America, the maximum receive bit rate is 53 Kbps due to Federal Communications Commission (FCC) power rules.

To obtain V.90 speeds, the following must be true:

- The remote access client must call using a V.90 modem.

- The remote access server must be using a V.90 digital switch and be connected to the PSTN using a digital link, such as T-Carrier or ISDN.

- There cannot be any analog-to-digital conversions in the path from the remote access server to the remote access client.

Figure 7.3 illustrates a V.90-based PSTN connection.

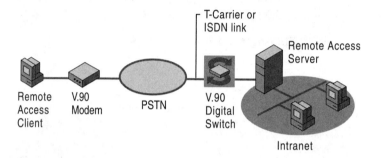

Figure 7.3   Dial-Up Equipment and WAN Infrastructure for V.90 Connections

ISDN

The Integrated Services Digital Network (ISDN) is a set of international specifications for a digital replacement of the PSTN providing a single digital network to handle voice, data, fax, and other services over existing local loop wiring. ISDN behaves like an analog phone line except that it is a digital technology at higher data rates with a much lower connection time. ISDN offers multiple channels; each channel operates at 64 Kbps and because the network is digital end-to-end, there are no analog to digital conversions.

Dial-up equipment consists of an ISDN adapter for the remote access client and the remote access server. Remote access clients typically use Basic Rate ISDN (BRI) with two 64-Kbps channels, and large organizations typically use Primary Rate ISDN (PRI) with 23 64-Kbps channels.

Figure 7.4 illustrates an ISDN connection.

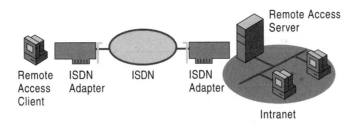

Remote Access
Server

Remote   ISDN   ISDN   ISDN
Access   Adapter   Adapter
Client

Intranet

Figure 7.4   Dial-Up Equipment and WAN Infrastructure for ISDN Connections

X.25

X.25 is an international standard for sending data across public packet switching networks. Windows 2000 remote access supports X.25 in two ways:

1. The remote access client supports the use of X.25 smart cards, which can connect directly to the X.25 data network and use the X.25 protocol to establish connections and send and receive data. The remote access client also supports dialing into a packet assembler/disassembler (PAD) of an X.25 carrier using an analog modem.

2. The remote access server only supports the use of X.25 smart cards.

For more information about the configuration of X.25 and PADs, see Windows 2000 Server Help.

Note X.25 smart cards are adapters that use the X.25 protocol and can directly connect to an X.25 public data network. X.25 smart cards are not related to smart cards used for authentication and secure communications.

Figure 7.5 illustrates an X.25 connection.

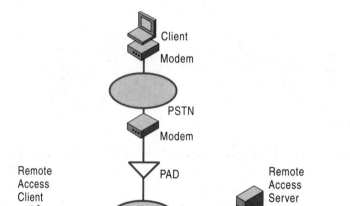

Figure 7.5   Dial-Up Equipment and WAN Infrastructure for X.25 Connections

ATM over ADSL

Asymmetric Digital Subscriber Line (ADSL) is a new local loop technology for small business and residential customers. Although ADSL provides higher bit rates than PSTN and ISDN connections, the bit rate is not the same in the upstream and downstream directions. Typical ADSL connections offer 64 Kbps from the customer and 1.544 megabits per second (Mbps) to the customer. The asymmetric nature of the connection fits well with typical Internet use. Most Internet users receive a lot more information than they send.

ADSL equipment can appear to Windows 2000 as either an Ethernet interface or a dial-up interface. When an ADSL adapter appears as an Ethernet interface, the ADSL connection operates in the same way as an Ethernet connection to the Internet.

When an ADSL adapter appears as a dial-up interface, ADSL provides a physical connection and the individual LAN protocol packets are sent using Asynchronous Transfer Mode (ATM). An ATM adapter with an ADSL port is installed in both the remote access client and remote access server.

Figure 7.6 illustrates an ATM over ADSL connection.

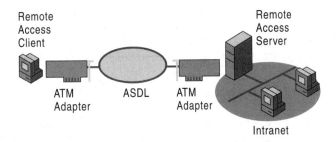

Figure 7.6   Dial-Up Equipment and WAN Infrastructure for ATM over ADSL Connections

Remote Access Protocols

Remote access protocols control the connection establishment and transmission of data over wide area network (WAN) links. The operating system and LAN protocols used on remote access clients and servers dictate which remote access protocol your clients can use.

There are three types of remote access protocols supported by Windows 2000 remote access:

1. Point-to-Point Protocol (PPP) is an industry-standard set of protocols providing the best security, multi-protocol support, and interoperability.

2. Serial Line Internet Protocol (SLIP) is used by older remote access servers.

3. Microsoft RAS protocol, also known as Asynchronous NetBEUI or AsyBEUI, is a remote access protocol used by legacy remote access clients running Microsoft operating systems, such as Microsoft® Windows NT® 3.1, Windows for Workgroups, MS-DOS, and LAN Manager.

Table 7.1 summarizes the remote access protocols and their use in Windows 2000.

Table 7.1   Remote Access Protocols and Their Use in Windows 2000

Remote Access Protocols	Remote Access Client	Remote Access Server
PPP	X	X
SLIP	X	
AsyBEUI	X	X

LAN Protocols

LAN protocols are the protocols used by the remote access client to access resources on the network connected to the remote access server. Windows 2000 remote access supports TCP/IP, IPX, AppleTalk, and NetBEUI. For more information, see "Remote Access and TCP/IP and IPX" later in this chapter.

Elements of Secure Remote Access

Because remote access is designed to transparently connect a remote access client to a network and its potentially sensitive data, security of remote access connections is an important consideration. Windows 2000 remote access offers a wide range of security features including secure user authentication, mutual authentication, data encryption, callback, and caller ID.

Secure User Authentication

Secure user authentication is obtained through the encrypted exchange of user credentials. This is possible with the PPP remote access protocol using either the Extensible Authentication Protocol (EAP), Microsoft Challenge Handshake Authentication Protocol (MS-CHAP) version 1 and version 2, Challenge Handshake Authentication Protocol (CHAP), or Shiva Password Authentication Protocol (SPAP) authentication protocols. The remote access server can be configured to require a secure authentication method. If the remote access client cannot perform the required secure authentication, the connection is denied.

Mutual Authentication

Mutual authentication is obtained by authenticating both ends of the connection through the encrypted exchange of user credentials. This is possible with the PPP remote access protocol using either the EAP-Transport Level Security (EAP-TLS) or MS-CHAP version 2 authentication protocols. During mutual authentication, the remote access client authenticates itself to the remote access server, and then the remote access server authenticates itself to the remote access client.

It is possible for a remote access server to not request authentication from the remote access client. However, in the case of a Windows 2000 remote access client configured for only MS-CHAP version 2 or only EAP-TLS, the remote access client will force the mutual authentication of the client and server. If the remote access server does not respond to the authentication request, the connection is terminated by the client.

Data Encryption

Data encryption encrypts the data sent between the remote access client and the remote access server. Remote access data encryption only provides data encryption on the communications link between the remote access client and the remote access server. If end-to-end encryption is needed, use IPSec to create an encrypted end-to-end connection after the remote access connection has been made.

Note IPSec can also be used for encrypting a Layer Two Tunneling Protocol (L2TP) virtual private network connection. For more information, see "Virtual Private Networking" in this book.

Data encryption on a remote access connection is based on a secret encryption key known to the remote access server and remote access client. This shared secret key is generated during the user authentication process.

Data encryption is possible over dial-up remote access links when using the PPP remote access protocol and the EAP-TLS or MS-CHAP authentication protocols. The remote access server can be configured to require data encryption. If the remote access client cannot perform the required encryption, the connection attempt is rejected.

Windows 2000, Microsoft® Windows NT® 4.0, Windows 98, and Windows 95 remote access clients and remote access servers support the Microsoft Point-to-Point Encryption Protocol (MPPE). MPPE uses the Rivest-Shamir-Adleman (RSA) RC4 stream cipher and either 40-bit, 56-bit, or 128-bit secret keys. MPPE keys are generated from the MS-CHAP and EAP-TLS user authentication process.

Callback

With callback, the remote access server calls the remote access client after the user credentials have been verified. Callback can be configured on the server to call the remote access client back at a number specified by the user of the remote access client during the time of the call. This allows a traveling user to dial-in and have the remote access server call them back at their current location, saving phone charges. Callback can also be configured to always call the remote access client back at a specific location, which is the secure form of callback.

Caller-ID

Caller-ID can be used to verify that the incoming call is coming from a specified phone number. Caller-ID is configured as part of the dial-in properties of the user account. If the Caller-ID number of the incoming connection for that user does not match the configured Caller-ID, the connection is denied.

Caller-ID requires that the caller's phone line, the phone system, the remote access server's phone line, and the Windows 2000 driver for the dial-up equipment all support Caller-ID. If a Caller-ID is configured for a user account and the Caller-ID is not being passed from the caller to the Routing and Remote Access service, then the connection is denied.

Caller-ID is a feature designed to provide a higher degree of security for network that support telecommuters. The disadvantage of configuring Caller-ID is that the user can only dial-in from a single phone line.

Remote Access Account Lockout

The remote access account lockout feature is used to specify how many times an remote access authentication fails against a valid user account before the user is denied remote access. Remote access account lockout is especially important for remote access virtual private network (VPN) connections over the Internet. Malicious users on the Internet can attempt to access an organization intranet by sending credentials (valid user name, guessed password) during the VPN connection authentication process. During a dictionary attack, the malicious user sends hundreds or thousands of credentials by using a list of passwords based on common words or phrases. With remote access account lockout enabled, a dictionary attack is thwarted after a specified number of failed attempts.

The remote access account lockout feature does not distinguish between malicious users who attempt to access your intranet and authentic users who attempt remote access but have forgotten their current passwords. Users who have forgotten their current password typically try the passwords that they remember and, depending on the number of attempts and the MaxDenials setting, may have their accounts locked out.

If you enable the remote access account lockout feature, a malicious user can deliberately force an account to be locked out by attempting multiple authentications with the user account until the account is locked out, thereby preventing the authentic user from being able to log on.

As the network administrator, you must decide on two remote access account lockout variables:

1. The number of failed attempts before future attempts are denied.

   After each failed attempt, a failed attempts counter for the user account is incremented. If the user account's failed attempts counter reaches the configured maximum, future attempts to connect are denied.

   A successful authentication resets the failed attempts counter when its value is less than the configured maximum. In other words, the failed attempts counter does not accumulate beyond a successful authentication.

2. How often the failed attempts counter is reset.

   You must periodically reset the failed attempts counter to prevent inadvertent lockouts due to normal mistakes by users when typing in their passwords.

Remote access account lockout feature is configured by changing settings in the Windows 2000 registry on the computer that provides the authentication. If the remote access server is configured for Windows authentication, modify the registry on the remote access server computer. If the remote access server is configured for RADIUS authentication and Windows 2000 Internet Authentication Service (IAS) is being used, modify the registry on the IAS server computer.

To enable account lockout, you must set the MaxDenials entry in the registry (HKEY_LOCAL_MACHINE\SYSTEM\CurrentControlSet\Services \RemoteAccess\Parameters\AccountLockout) to 1 or greater. MaxDenials is the maximum number of failed attempts before the account is locked out. By default, MaxDenials is set to 0, which means that account lockout is disabled.

To modify the amount of time before the failed attempts counter is reset, you must set the ResetTime (mins) entry in the registry (HKEY_LOCAL_MACHINE\SYSTEM\CurrentControlSet\Services \RemoteAccess\Parameters\AccountLockout) to the required number of minutes. By default, ResetTime (mins) is set to 0xb40, or 2,880 minutes (48 hours).

To manually reset a user account that has been locked out before the failed attempts counter is automatically reset, delete the following registry subkey that corresponds to the user's account name:

HKEY_LOCAL_MACHINE\SYSTEM\CurrentControlSet\Services\RemoteAcce ss\Parameters\AccountLockout\domain name:*user name*

Note The remote access account lockout feature is not related to the **Account locked out** setting on the **Account** tab on the properties of a user account and the administration of account lockout policies using Windows 2000 group policies.

Managing Remote Access

Remote access has the following management issues:

- Where is the user account data to be stored?
- How are addresses assigned to remote access clients?
- Who is allowed to create remote access connections?
- How does the remote access server verify the identity of the user attempting the remote access connection?
- How does the remote access server record the remote access activity?
- How can the remote access server be managed using industry-standard network management protocols and infrastructure?

Managing Users

Because it is administratively unsupportable to have separate user accounts for the same user on separate servers and to try to keep them all simultaneously current, most administrators set up a master account database at a domain controller (PDC) or on a Remote Authentication Dial-in User Service (RADIUS) server. This allows the remote access server to send the authentication credentials to a central authenticating device.

Managing Addresses

For PPP connections, IP, IPX, and AppleTalk addressing information must be allocated to remote access clients during the connection establishment process. The Windows 2000 remote access server must be configured to allocate IP addresses, IPX network and node addresses, and AppleTalk network and node addresses.

More information about address allocation for IP and IPX can be found later in this chapter.

Managing Access

In Windows NT versions 3.5x and 4.0, authorization was based on a simple **Grant dial-in permission to user** option in User Manager or the Remote Access Admin utility. Callback options were also configured on a per-user basis. In Windows 2000, authorization is granted based on the dial-in properties of a user account and remote access policies.

Remote access policies are a set of conditions and connection settings that give network administrators more flexibility in authorizing connection attempts. The Windows 2000 Routing and Remote Access service and Windows 2000 Internet Authentication Service (IAS) both use remote access policies to determine whether to accept or reject connection attempts. For more information about remote access policies, see "Internet Authentication Service" in this book.

With remote access policies, you can grant remote access by individual user account or through the configuration of specific remote access policies.

Access by User Account

Access by user account is the administrative model used in Windows NT version 3.5x and 4.0. In Windows 2000, if you wish to manage remote access on an individual per-user basis, set the remote access permission on those user accounts that are allowed to create remote access connections to **Allow access** and modify the profile properties of the default remote access policy called **Allow access if dial-in permission is enabled** for the needed connection parameters.

If the remote access server is only providing dial-up remote access connections and no VPN connections, then delete the default remote access policy called **Allow access if dial-in permission is enabled** and create a new remote access policy with a descriptive name, such as **Dial-up remote access if dial-in permission is enabled**.

As an example of typical settings to allow dial-up remote access connections, configure the remote access policy permission to **Deny remote access permission** and set the conditions and profile settings as listed in Tables 7.2 and 7.3. For detailed information about configuring these settings, see Windows 2000 Server Help.

Table 7.2   Remote Access Policy Conditions for Dial-Up Access by User Account

Conditions	Setting
NAS-Port-Type	Select all except **Virtual**.

Table 7.3   Remote Access Policy Profile Settings for Dial-Up Access by User Account

Profile Tab	Setting
Authentication tab	Enable **Microsoft encrypted authentication version 2 (MS-CHAP v2)** and **Microsoft encrypted authentication (MS-CHAP)**.

Access by Policy

The access by policy administrative model is intended for Windows 2000 remote access servers that are either standalone or a member of a Windows 2000 native mode domain. To manage remote access by policy, set the remote access permission on all user accounts to **Control access through Remote Access Policy**. Then define the new remote access policies that allow or deny access based on your needs. If the remote access server computer is a member of a Windows NT 4.0 domain or a Windows 2000 mixed domain and you want to manage access by policy, set the remote access permission on all user accounts to **Allow access**. Then, remove the default policy called **Allow access if dial-in permission is enabled** and create new policies that allow or deny access. A connection that does not match any configured remote access policy is denied, even if the remote access permission on the user account is set to **Allow access**.

A typical use of policy-based access is to allow access through group membership. For example, create a Windows 2000 group with a name, such as DialUpUsers, whose members are those users who are allowed to create dial-up remote access connections.

To create a remote access server that only allows dial-up remote access connections, delete the default remote access policy called **Allow access if dial-in permission is enabled** and then create a new remote access policy with a descriptive name, such as **Dial-up remote access if member of DialUpUsers group**.

As an example of typical settings to allow dial-up remote access for only members of a specific group, configure the remote access policy permission to **Grant remote access permission** and set the conditions and profile settings as listed in Tables 7.4 and 7.5. For detailed information about configuring these settings, see Windows 2000 Server Help.

Table 7.4   Remote Access Policy Conditions for Dial-Up Access by User Account

Conditions	Setting
NAS-Port-Type	Select all except **Virtual**.
Windows-Groups	DialUpUsers (example)

Table 7.5   Remote Access Policy Profile Settings for Dial-Up Access by User Account

Profile Tab	Setting
Authentication tab	Enable **Microsoft encrypted authentication version 2 (MS-CHAP v2)** and **Microsoft encrypted authentication (MS-CHAP)** (example)

Managing Authentication

The remote access server can be configured to use either Windows or RADIUS as an authentication provider.

Windows Authentication

If Windows is selected as the authentication provider, then the user credentials sent by users attempting remote access connections are authenticated using normal Windows authentication mechanisms.

If the remote access server is a member server in mixed or native Windows 2000 domain and is configured for Windows authentication, the computer account of the remote access server computer must be a member of the RAS and IAS Servers security group. This can be done by a domain administrator with the Active Directory User and Groups snap-in or with the **netsh ras add registeredserver** command before the installation of the Routing and Remote Access server. If the user installing the Routing and Remote Access service is a domain administrator, then the computer account is automatically added to the RAS and IAS Servers security group during the installation of the Routing and Remote Access service.

RADIUS Authentication

If RADIUS is selected and configured as the authentication provider on the remote access server, then user credentials and parameters of the connection request are sent as a series of RADIUS request messages to a RADIUS server such as a computer running Windows 2000 Server and the Internet Authentication Service (IAS).

The RADIUS server receives a user-connection request from the remote access server and authenticates the client against its authentication database. A RADIUS server can also maintain a central storage database of other relevant user properties. In addition to the simple yes or no response to an authentication request, RADIUS can inform the remote access server of other applicable connection parameters for this user — such as maximum session time, static IP address assignment, and so on.

RADIUS can respond to authentication requests based upon its own database, or it can be a front end to another database server such as a generic Open Database Connectivity (ODBC) server or a Windows 2000 PDC. The latter server could be located on the same machine as the RADIUS server, or could be centralized elsewhere. In addition, a RADIUS server can act as a proxy client to a remote RADIUS server.

The RADIUS protocol is described in RFCs 2138 and 2139. For more information about remote access server authentication scenarios and the remote access server as a RADIUS client, see Windows 2000 Server Help. For more information about IAS, see "Internet Authentication Service" in this book.

Note Both the Routing and Remote Access service when configured for Windows authentication and IAS use the same process to provide authentication and authorization of incoming connection requests. For more information on this process, see "Internet Authentication Service" in this book.

Managing Accounting

The remote access server can be configured to use either Windows or RADIUS as an accounting provider. If Windows is selected as the accounting provider, then the accounting information is accumulated in a log file on the remote access server. If RADIUS is selected as the accounting provider, RADIUS accounting messages are sent to the RADIUS server for accumulation and later analysis.

Most RADIUS servers can be configured to place authentication request records into an accounting file. There are also a set of messages (from the remote access server to the RADIUS server) that request accounting records at the start of a call, the end of a call, and at predetermined intervals during a call. A number of third parties have written billing and audit packages that read these RADIUS accounting records and produce various useful reports.

Network Management

The computer acting as the remote access server can participate in a Simple Network Management Protocol (SNMP) environment as an SNMP agent by installing the Windows 2000 SNMP Service. The remote access server records management information in various object identifiers of the Internet Management Information Base (MIB) II that is installed with the Windows 2000 SNMP service. Objects in the Internet MIB II are documented in RFC 1213.

Remote Access Server Architecture

The architecture of the remote access server consists of the following elements, as illustrated in Figure 7.7:

- The NDIS wrapper, Ndis.sys, providing the NDIS packet-level interface to protocols, such as TCP/IP, IPX, NetBEUI, and AppleTalk.

- The NDISWAN driver, Ndiswan.sys, is an intermediate NDIS driver that provides an IEEE 802.3 miniport interface to protocol drivers and a protocol interface to WAN miniport drivers. NDISWAN provides framing, compression, and encryption services for remote access connections.

- WAN miniport drivers are NDIS miniport drivers that contain the necessary code to operate the dial-up equipment. In order to use an adapter supporting WAN media, such as ISDN or ATM with Windows 2000 remote access, the adapter vendor must create a WAN miniport driver.

- Remote access components are a series of libraries that provide the Remote Access Service (RAS) programming interface for applications, PPP protocols (link control, authentication, and network control protocols), and so on. Remote access components can communicate directly with the NDISWAN driver or by accessing the Telephony API (TAPI).

- TAPI components are a series of libraries that provide a call control programming interface for all TAPI-aware applications. TAPI components communicate directly with the NDISWAN driver to manage connections. For more information about TAPI in Windows 2000, see "Telephony Conferencing and Integration" in this book.

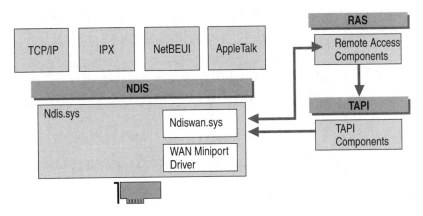

Figure 7.7   Remote Access Architecture in Windows 2000

Connections are established by remote access clients that call the RAS programming interface, which in turn uses TAPI to pass call connection information to the dial-up equipment. Once the physical connection is made, TAPI is no longer used and additional remote access components negotiate the connection with link, authentication, and network control protocols by communicating directly with NDISWAN.

Once a remote access connection is established, protocol drivers can communicate over that connection using standard NDIS calls like NdisSend(). NdisSend() calls for dial-up connections are forwarded to NDISWAN, which then determines the appropriate device and port, performs compression and encryption, provides PPP framing, and then forwards the completed frame to the WAN miniport driver. The WAN miniport driver then forwards the frame to the dial-up adapter.

All inbound remote access client connections, initiated by remote access clients to the remote access server, are represented as a single adapter called the RAS server interface. For each outbound remote access client connection, initiated by the remote access server, a separate interface is created.

To accept calls, the remote access server instructs each WAN miniport driver to indicate when it goes into a line-up state. When the call is placed, the WAN miniport driver passes the line-up state indicator up through NDISWAN to the TAPI components. TAPI returns a call handle to NDISWAN to be used to refer to the physical connection, and then NDISWAN and the remote access components negotiate the rest of the remote access connection.

IP, IPX, and AppleTalk Router

Once the remote access connection is established, the remote access client can begin sending LAN protocol traffic to the remote access server or to locations beyond the remote access server. When the remote access client sends LAN protocol traffic that is not destined for the remote access server, the remote access server must forward the LAN traffic to its appropriate destination. To accomplish this, the remote access server must have forwarding capabilities enabled on its routable protocols and act as an IP, IPX, and AppleTalk router.

When the Routing and Remote Access service is installed and enabled to provide point-to-LAN remote access connectivity, it enables forwarding between the installed LAN adapters and the WAN miniport interface.

Figure 7.8 illustrates the remote access server architecture as it appears when routing packets. (In an effort to simplify the illustration, only IP routing is shown.) However, IPX and AppleTalk routing work in the same fashion.

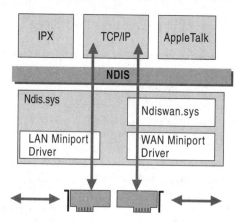

Figure 7.8   IP Routing on the Remote Access Server

Packets from Remote Access Clients

The following process describes how IP packets sent by the remote access client are forwarded by the remote access server.

1. Depending on the dial-up technology, either the entire PPP frame is received by the WAN hardware and passed up as a single frame to the appropriate WAN miniport driver or individual bits of the PPP frame are passed up to the appropriate WAN miniport driver.

2. The WAN miniport driver passes the PPP frame to Ndiswan.sys.

3. Ndiswan.sys verifies the PPP checksum and uses the PPP protocol ID to determine that it is an IP datagram. For more information about PPP, see "Point-to-Point Protocol" later in this chapter.

4. The IP datagram is passed to the TCP/IP protocol driver.

5. The TCP/IP protocol driver, which is enabled for IP forwarding, determines a forwarding interface and an IP address based on the destination IP address in the IP datagram and the contents of its routing table.

6. To forward the IP datagram using the LAN adapter, the TCP/IP protocol calls NDIS with an NdisSend(), along with instructions to send it using the LAN adapter.

7. NDIS forwards the IP datagram to the appropriate LAN miniport driver.

8. The LAN miniport forwards the IP datagram to the LAN adapter through NDIS.

The end result is that packets from the remote access client are forwarded using the same IP routing process used for all IP routing. The success of the IP forwarding process depends on whether the remote access server can find a suitable entry in the IP routing table. Therefore, either the remote access server is configured with a default gateway, or the remote access server has specific routes to all the locations on the intranet to which the remote access server is attached. Specific routes can be added through static routes, or by enabling a routing protocol on the remote access server.

Packets to Remote Access Clients

The following process describes how IP packets sent by intranet hosts to the remote access client are forwarded by the remote access server.

1. The LAN adapter passes a frame to its appropriate LAN miniport driver through NDIS. The details of how an IP datagram is forwarded to the MAC address of the remote access server can be found in the next section, "TCP/IP On-Subnet and Off-Subnet Addressing."

2. The LAN miniport driver passes the IP datagram to the TCP/IP protocol driver through NDIS.

3. The TCP/IP protocol driver, which is enabled for IP forwarding, determines a forwarding interface and IP address based on the destination IP address in the IP datagram and the contents of its routing table. When the remote access client connects, a host route is created in the IP routing table for the IP address allocated to the remote access client that points to the RAS server interface.

4. To forward the IP datagram using the WAN adapter, the TCP/IP protocol calls NDIS with an NdisSend() with instructions to send it using NDISWAN and a specific connection handle.

5. NDISWAN resolves the connection handle to a specific device and port, adds a PPP header and trailer, and forwards the IP datagram to the appropriate WAN miniport driver through NDIS.

6. The WAN miniport driver forwards the IP datagram to the WAN adapter through NDIS.

The end result is that packets from intranet hosts are forwarded using the same IP routing process used for all IP routing. The success of the IP forwarding process depends on whether the IP addresses of remote access clients are reachable from the hosts on the intranet.

TCP/IP On-Subnet and Off-Subnet Addressing

The exact mechanism of how an IP node on a subnet to which the remote access server is attached resolves the media access control (MAC) address of the LAN interface of the remote access server depends on whether the remote access server is configured for on-subnet or off-subnet addressing:

- On-subnet addressing is the allocation of IP addresses to remote access clients that are in a range defined by a subnet to which the remote access server is attached. On-subnet addressing uses a subset of addresses of an attached subnet.

- Off-subnet addressing is the allocation of IP addresses to remote access clients that are not in a range defined by a subnet to which the remote access server is attached. Off-subnet addressing uses a separate subnet address space that is unique to the intranet.

On-Subnet Addressing and Proxy ARP

With on-subnet addressing, remote access clients are logically on the same subnet as a subnet attached to the remote access server. Proxy ARP is used by the remote access server to receive IP datagrams being forwarded to remote access clients.

There are two cases where Proxy ARP is used:

1. When the remote access server is configured to use DHCP to obtain addresses for IP-based remote access clients

2. When the remote access server is configured with a static IP address pool consisting of address ranges that are a subset of the addresses for a subnet to which the remote access server is attached.

In either case, the remote access clients are logically on the same subnet as the remote access server. Therefore, IP nodes on that subnet forwarding IP datagrams to a remote access client perform a direct delivery by sending a broadcast Address Resolution Protocol (ARP) Request frame for the remote access client's IP address.

The remote access client cannot respond to the ARP Request because the remote access server does not forward the ARP Request frame to the remote access client, and the remote access client does not have a media access control (MAC) address corresponding to the remote access connection.

Therefore, the remote access server responds with an ARP Reply frame with its own MAC address. The node forwarding the packet then sends the IP datagram to the remote access server's MAC address. The remote access server then uses the IP routing process to forward the IP datagram across the dial-up connection to the remote access client.

Off-Subnet Addressing and IP Routing

With off-subnet addressing, remote access clients are logically on a separate subnet reachable across the remote access server. In this case, Proxy ARP is not used. The remote access server is acting as a router between the subnet of the remote access clients and the subnets to which the remote access server is attached. IP nodes on the LAN-based subnets attached to the remote access server forwarding IP datagrams to a remote access client perform an indirect delivery by sending a broadcast Address Resolution Protocol (ARP) Request frame for the remote access server's IP address.

In order for the remote access clients to be reachable from IP nodes on the intranet, routes representing the address ranges of the IP address pool and pointing to the LAN interface of the remote access server must be present in intranet routers.

When the first TCP/IP-based remote access client connects, routes corresponding to the off-subnet address ranges pointing to the RAS server interface are added to the IP routing table of the remote access server. If the remote access server is configured with an IP routing protocol, the new routes are advertised to neighboring routers using the normal advertising process of the configured routing protocol. If the remote access server is not configured with an IP routing protocol, routes corresponding to the off-subnet address ranges pointing to the remote access server's LAN interface must be added to the routers of the intranet.

NetBIOS Gateway

Windows 2000 includes the NetBIOS gateway for remote access clients that use either the NetBEUI protocol with the PPP remote access protocol or the AsyBEUI remote access protocol. With the NetBIOS gateway, a remote access client using NetBEUI can access any NetBIOS-based network resource that is reachable from the remote access server.

With the NetBIOS gateway, the remote access client can access any of the following resources:

- Network resources available from the remote access server using NetBEUI
- Network resources available from the remote access server using NetBIOS over TCP/IP
- Network resources available from the remote access server using NetBIOS over IPX

The NetBIOS gateway component is responsible for:

- Managing NetBIOS names.

  When the initial connection is made, the remote access client passes its NetBIOS name, which is then added to the NetBIOS name table at the remote access server.

- Passing NetBIOS packets from the remote access client to the LAN.

  When the remote access client sends NetBEUI packets across the phone line, those packets are submitted to the NetBIOS gateway and sent over the NetBIOS providing protocols.

- Passing NetBIOS packets from the LAN to the remote access client.

  NetBIOS packets from the LAN, from any of the NetBIOS-providing protocols, are inspected for the NetBIOS computer name of the remote access client and sent back to the remote access client using NetBEUI.

Note The NetBIOS gateway cannot be used to access non-NetBIOS resources, such as Web servers, FTP servers, and other types of Windows Sockets–based resources.

Figure 7.9 illustrates the NetBIOS gateway architecture of the remote access server.

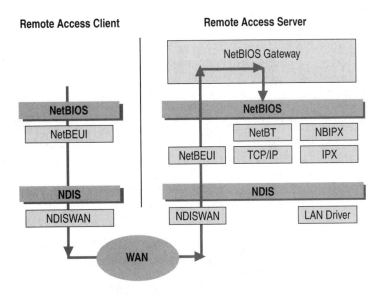

Figure 7.9   NetBIOS Gateway

Point-to-Point Protocol

The Point-to-Point Protocol (PPP) is an industry standard method of utilizing point-to-point links to transport multi-protocol datagrams. PPP is documented in RFC 1661. The Routing and Remote Access service stores PPP settings in the Windows 2000 registry under HKLM\System\CurrentControlSet\Services\RASMan\PPP.

PPP performs the following functions:

- Provides multi-protocol data-link layer encapsulation

  PPP creates frames that contain separate IP datagrams, IPX datagrams, or NetBEUI frames.

- Establishes, maintains, and ends the logical link

  The PPP protocol uses the Link Control Protocol (LCP) to establish and configure the parameters of the data-link connection. Part of the LCP negotiation is authenticating the credentials of the remote access client.

- Provides protocol configuration

  After the data-link connection has been negotiated, network layer protocols such as IP, IPX, and AppleTalk are configured. For example, for TCP/IP, an IP address is allocated to the remote access client by the remote access server. Compression and encryption are also negotiated.

PPP Encapsulation

PPP encapsulation uses a variant of the ISO High Level Data Link Control (HDLC) protocol to encapsulate multi-protocol datagrams as the payload of PPP frames. The PPP header and trailer is shown in Figure 7.10 and contains the following fields:

- **Flag** - Set to 0x7E (bit sequence 011111110) to signify the start and end of a PPP frame. In successive PPP frames only a single Flag character is used.

- **Address** - In HDLC environments, the Address field is used to address the frame to the destination node. On a point-to-point link, the destination node does not need to be addressed. Therefore, for PPP, the Address field is set to 0xFF, the broadcast address. If both PPP peers agree to perform address and control field compression during LCP negotiation, the Address field is not included.

- **Control** - In HDLC environments, the Control field is used for data-link layer sequencing and acknowledgments. PPP does not provided link-to-link reliable data transfer. Therefore, for all PPP frames, the Control field is set to 0x03 to indicate an unnumbered information (UI) frame. If both PPP peers agree to perform address and control field compression during LCP negotiation, the Control field is not included.

- **Protocol ID** - The 2-byte Protocol ID field identifies the protocol of the PPP payload. If both PPP peers agree to perform protocol field compression during LCP negotiation, the Protocol ID field is one byte for Protocol IDs in the range 0x00-00 to 0x00-FF.

- **Frame Check Sequence (FCS)** - A 16-bit checksum that is used to check for bit level errors in the PPP frame. If the receiver's calculation of the FCS does not match the FCS in the PPP frame, the PPP frame is silently discarded.

The maximum size of a PPP frame, known as the maximum receive unit (MRU), is determined during the negotiation of the logical link. The default MRU is 1,500 bytes. If negotiated lower, a PPP host must still have the ability to receive 1,500-byte frames in the event of link synchronization failure.

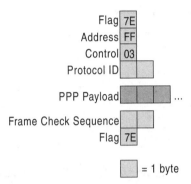

Figure 7.10   PPP Encapsulation

Typical values for the PPP protocol ID are listed in Table 7.6.

Table 7.6   PPP Protocol IDs

Protocol	Protocol ID/Compressed Value
Internet Protocol (IP)	0x00-21 / 0x21
AppleTalk	0x00-29 / 0x29
IPX	0x00-2B / 0x2B
Van Jacobsen Compressed TCP/IP	0x00-2D / 0x2D
Multilink	0x00-3D / 0x3D
NetBEUI	0x00-3F / 0x3F
Microsoft Point-to-Point Compression Protocol (MPPC)	0x00-FD / 0xFD
Microsoft Point-to-Point Encryption Protocol (MPPE)	0x00-FD / 0xFD

If MPPE or MPPC are negotiated, then the PPP protocol ID is set to 0x00-FD. With MPPE and MPPC both using the same PPP Protocol ID, each peer must know that the resulting PPP payload either is encrypted or compressed, or both.

- If only MPPC is negotiated, then the PPP Protocol ID is set to 0x00-FD and the PPP payload is compressed.

- If only MPPE is negotiated, then the PPP Protocol ID is set to 0x00-FD and the PPP payload is encrypted.

- If both MPPC and MPPE are negotiated, then compression always occurs before encryption. The compressed PPP frame, consisting of the PPP protocol ID field set to 0xFD and the compressed data, is then encrypted and encapsulated with another PPP header consisting of the protocol ID field set to 0xFD and a 2-byte MPPE header.

Preventing the Occurrence of the Flag Character

The use of the Flag character introduces a problem. What if the Flag character (0x7E) appears elsewhere in the PPP frame besides the beginning or end of the PPP frame? PPP employs two different methods to prevent the occurrence of the Flag character depending on whether PPP is being used on an asynchronous link or a synchronous link.

PPP on Asynchronous Links

On asynchronous links, such as analog phone lines, PPP uses a technique called character stuffing to prevent the occurrence of the Flag character within the PPP frame. If the Flag character (0x7E) occurs elsewhere in the PPP frame, the sender replaces it with the sequence 0x7D-5E. The 0x7D character is known as the PPP Escape character. If the PPP Escape character occurs, the sender replaces it with the sequence 0x7D-5D. The receiver translates 0x7D-5E sequences back to 0x7E and 0x7D-5D sequences back to 0x7D.

Additionally, character values less than 0x20 can be modified to prevent the serial drivers from interpreting them as control characters. If negotiated by LCP, characters below 0x20 are modified by sending the sequence: 0x7D-[Original character with the 6th bit complemented]. For example, the byte 0x01 would be transmitted as 0x7D-0x21.

PPP on Synchronous Links

With synchronous links, such as T-Carrier, ISDN, or other digital links, a technique called bit stuffing is used to prevent the occurrence of the Flag character within the PPP frame. Recall that the Flag character is the bit sequence 01111110. Bit stuffing ensures that six 1 bits in a row occur only when the Flag character is sent. To accomplish this, bit stuffing sends the Flag character unmodified and elsewhere inserts a 0 bit whenever a sequence of five 1 bits occurs. Therefore, the bit sequence 111111 is encoded on the medium as 1111101 and the bit sequence 111110 is encoded as 1111100 (the stuffed bits are underlined). Bit stuffing means that a byte can be encoded on the medium as more than eight bits, but the stuffed bits are added and removed by the synchronous link hardware.

PPP Link Negotiation with LCP

The PPP Link Control Protocol (LCP) is documented in RFC 1661. LPC negotiates link and PPP parameters to dynamically configure the data link layer of a PPP connection. Common LCP options include the PPP MRU, the authentication protocol, compression of PPP header fields, callback, and multilink options.

LCP Packet Structure

LCP uses the PPP Protocol ID of 0xC0-21. The packet structure of LCP is illustrated in Figure 7.11. Each LCP packet is a single LCP message consisting of an LCP Code field identifying the type of LCP packet, an Identifier field so that requests and replies can be matched, a Length field indicating the size of the LCP packet and LCP packet type–specific data.

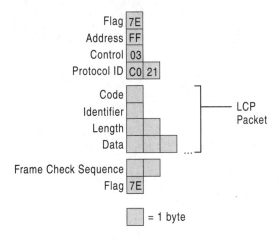

Figure 7.11   LCP Packet Structure

Table 7.7 lists the LCP packet types documented in RFC 1661.

Table 7.7   LCP Packet Types

LCP Code	LCP Packet Type	Description
1	Configure-Request	Sent to open or reset a PPP connection. Configure-Request contains a list of LCP options with changes to default option values.
2	Configure-Ack	Sent when all of the values of all of the LCP options in the last Configure-Request received are recognized and acceptable.
		When both PPP peers send and receive Configure-Acks, the LCP negotiation is complete.
3	Configure-Nack	Sent when all the LCP options are recognized, but the values of some options are not acceptable. Configure-Nack includes the offending options and their acceptable values.
4	Configure-Reject	Sent when LCP options are not recognized or not acceptable for negotiation. Configure-Reject includes the unrecognized or non-negotiable options.
5	Terminate-Request	Optionally sent to close the PPP connection.
6	Terminate-Ack	Sent in response to the Terminate-Request.
7	Code-Reject	Sent when the LCP code is unknown. The Code-Reject message includes the offending LCP packet.
8	Protocol-Reject	Sent when the PPP frame contains an unknown Protocol ID. The Protocol-Reject message includes the offending LCP packet.
		Protocol-Reject is typically sent by a PPP peer in response to a PPP NCP for a LAN protocol not enabled on the PPP peer.
9	Echo-Request	Optionally sent to test the PPP connection.
10	Echo-Reply	Sent in response to an Echo-Request.
		The PPP Echo-Request and Echo-Reply are not related to the ICMP Echo Request and Echo Reply messages.
11	Discard-Request	Optionally sent to exercise the link in the outbound direction.

LCP Options

When using the Configure-Request, Configure-Ack, Configure-Nack, and Configure-Reject LCP packet types, the LCP data portion of the LCP packet consists of one or more LCP options as illustrated in Figure 7.12. Each LCP option consists of an option Type field, a Length field indicating the total length in bytes of the option and the data associated with the option.

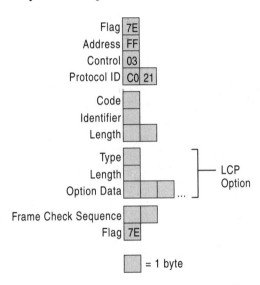

Figure 7.12   LCP Options

Table 7.8 lists common LCP options negotiated by Microsoft PPP peers. For information about other LCP options, see RFC 1661.

Table 7.8   LCP Options

Option Name	Option Type	Option Length	Description
Maximum Receive Unit (MRU)	1	4	The maximum size (up to 65,535) of the PPP frame. The default MRU is 1,500. If neither peer is changing the default, this option is not negotiated.
Asynchronous Control Character Map (ACCM)	2	6	A bit map that enables (bit set to 1) or disables (bit set to 0) the use of character escapes for asynchronous links for the 32 ASCII control characters from 0x00 to 0x20. By default, character escapes are used. The ACCM bit map is set to 0x00-00-00-00 for links with XON/XOFF software flow control.
Authentication Protocol	3	5 or 6	Indicates the authentication protocol used during the authentication phase of the connection.
			Values for this field for Microsoft PPP peers are 0xC2-27 for EAP, 0xC2-23-80 for MS-CHAP version 1, 0xC2-23-81 for MS-CHAP version 2, 0xC2-23-05 for MD5-CHAP, 0xC0-27 for SPAP, and 0xC0-23 for PAP.
Magic Number	5	6	A random number chosen to distinguish a peer and detect looped back lines.
Protocol Compression	7	2	A flag indicating that the PPP protocol ID be compressed to a single octet when the 2-byte protocol ID is in the range 0x00-00 to 0x00-FF.
Address and Control Field Compression	8	2	A flag indicating that the PPP Address field (always set to 0xFF) and the PPP Control field (always set to 0x03) be removed from the PPP header.
Callback	13 or 0x0D	3	A 1-octet indicator of how callback is to be determined. For remote access clients and server running Microsoft® Windows 32-bit operating systems, the callback option octet is set to 0x06, indicating that the callback is determined during Callback Control Protocol (CBCP) negotiation.

LCP Negotiation Process

The LCP negotiation is a series of LCP packets exchanged between PPP peers to negotiate a set of options and option values when sending data. The LCP negotiation is actually two separate dialogs between two PPP peers (Peer 1 and Peer 2):

1. Peer 1 asks, negotiates, and then receives confirmation of the LCP options that are used when sending data to Peer 2. This dialog starts with Peer 1 sending a Configure-Request message and ends when Peer 2 sends a Configure-Ack message.

2. Peer 2 asks, negotiates, and then receives confirmation of the LCP options that are used when sending data to peer 1. This dialog starts with Peer 2 sending a Configure-Request message and ends when Peer 1 sends a Configure-Ack message.

Peer 1 and Peer 2 do not have to use the same set of LCP options.

When a PPP peer sends its initial Configure-Request, the response is any of the following:

- A Configure-Nack message because one or more options have unacceptable values.

- A Configure-Reject message because one or more of the options are unknown or not negotiable.

- A Configure-Ack message because all of the options have acceptable values.

When a PPP peer receives a Configure-Nack message or Configure-Reject message in response to its Configure-Request message, it sends a new Configure-Request message with modified options or option values. When a Configure-Ack message is received, the PPP peer is ready to send data.

Figure 7.13 shows a hypothetical LCP negotiation process for Peer 1 using the fictional options W, X, Y, Z.

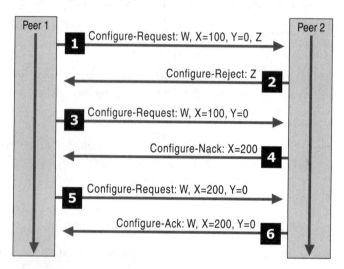

Figure 7.13   Sample LCP Negotiation

From the LCP messages in Figure 7.13:

1. Peer 1 sends a Configure-Request message requesting option W, option X set to 100, option Y set to 0, and option Z. Options W and Z are flag options.

2. Peer 2 does not understand option Z so it sends a Configure-Reject message containing option Z.

3. Peer 1 sends a new Configure-Request message requesting option W, option X set to 100, and option Y set to 0.

4. Peer 2 prefers that option X be set to 200 so it sends a Configure-Nack message containing option X and its preferred value.

5. Peer 1 sends a new Configure-Request message requesting option W, option X set to 200, and option Y set to 0.

6. Peer 2 sends a Configure-Ack message.

Each time Peer 1 sends a new Configure-Request message, it changes the Identifier value in the LCP header so that Configure-Request messages can be matched with their responses.

The previous process only configures how Peer 1 sends data to Peer 2. A separate LCP negotiation must be done so that Peer 2 can be configured to send data to Peer 1. Very often, the LCP packets for the two dialogs are intermixed during the connection process. Peer 1 is configuring the way it sends data at the same time as Peer 2.

Callback Negotiation with the Callback Control Protocol

Callback Control Protocol (CBCP) negotiates the use of callback where the remote access server, after authenticating the remote access client, terminates the physical connection, waits a specified amount of time, and then calls the remote access client back at either a static or dynamically configured phone number. Common CBCP options include the phone number being used by the remote access server to call the remote access client back. For more information about CBCP, see "Proposal for Callback Control Protocol (CBCP)" at the Internet Working Group link on the Web Resources pages at http://windows.microsoft.com/windows2000/reskit/webresources.

Packet Structure

CBCP uses the PPP Protocol ID of 0xC0-29. The packet structure of CBCP is exactly the same for LCP; however, only the Callback-Request (type 1), Callback-Response (type 2), and Callback-Ack (type 3) types are used. For all CBCP packet types, the CBCP data portion of the CBCP packet consists of one or more CBCP options. Each CBCP option consists of an option Type field, an option Length field indicating the total length in bytes of the option, and the data associated with the option.

Negotiated Options

Table 7.9 lists the CBCP options negotiated by Microsoft PPP peers.

Table 7.9   CBCP Options

Option Name	Option Type	Option Length	Description
No callback	1	2	Specifies that no callback is used for the connection.
Callback to a user-specified number	2	variable	The user of the remote access client computer determines the callback number.
Callback to an administrator-defined number	3	variable	Settings on the remote access server determine the callback number.
Callback to any of a list of numbers	4	variable	The remote access server callbacks to one of a list of phone numbers.

PPP Network Layer Negotiation with NCP

Once the link and PPP parameters have been negotiated with LCP, the PPP peers then use a series of Network Control Protocols (NCPs) to negotiate the parameters of individual LAN protocols. Microsoft PPP supports the following NCPs:

- Internet Protocol Control Protocol (IPCP) to negotiate the use of IP.
- Internetwork Packet Exchange Control Protocol (IPXCP) to negotiate the use of IPX.
- AppleTalk Control Protocol (ATCP) to negotiate the use of AppleTalk.
- NetBIOS Frames Control Protocol (NBFCP) to negotiate the use of NetBEUI.

IPCP

Internet Protocol Control Protocol (IPCP) as used by Microsoft PPP peers is documented in RFCs 1332 and 1877. IPCP negotiates IP-based parameters to dynamically configure a TCP/IP-based PPP peer across a point-to-point link. Common IPCP options include an IP address and the IP addresses of DNS and NetBIOS name servers.

Packet Structure

IPCP uses the PPP Protocol ID of 0x80-21. The packet structure of IPCP is exactly the same for LCP, except only packet types 1 through 7 are defined. For Configure-Request, Configure-Ack, Configure-Nack, and Configure-Reject IPCP packet types, the IPCP data portion of the IPCP packet consists of one or more IPCP options. Each IPCP option consists of an Option Type field, an Option Length field indicating the total length in bytes of the option, and the data associated with the option.

Negotiated Options

Table 7.10 lists the IPCP options negotiated by Microsoft PPP peers.

Table 7.10   IPCP Options

Option Name	Option Type	Option Length	Description
IP compression protocol	2	4	Van Jacobsen TCP compression protocol.
IP address	3	6	The IP address to be allocated to the remote access client.
Primary DNS server address	129 or 0x81	6	The primary DNS server for the remote access client.
Primary NBNS server address	130 or 0x82	6	The primary NBNS (WINS) server for the remote access client.
Secondary DNS server address	131 or 0x83	6	The secondary DNS server for the remote access client.
Secondary NBNS server address	132 or 0x84	6	The secondary NBNS (WINS) server for the remote access client.

Notice that there are no IPCP options for these common TCP/IP configuration items:

- Subnet mask

  The subnet mask is assumed by the remote access client to be the class-based subnet mask of the IP address that is allocated to the remote access client.

- Default gateway

  The default gateway IP address is not allocated by the remote access server. However, a default route is created on the remote access client, which points to the remote access connection. If a default route already exists in the routing table, then the metric of the existing default route is increased and a new default route is added with a lower metric. This is the default behavior for remote access clients running Windows 32-bit operating systems and can be modified by disabling the **Use Default Gateway on Remote Network** setting on the TCP/IP properties of a remote access client's phone book entry or dial-up connection object.

- DNS domain name

  The DNS domain name configured from the TCP/IP protocol properties on the remote access server is not negotiated during IPCP. For Windows 2000 remote access clients, the DNS domain name can be obtained through a DHCPInform message. For more information, see "Remote Access and TCP/IP and IPX" later in this chapter.

- NetBIOS Node Type

  If the IP addresses of primary or secondary NetBIOS name servers are negotiated, then the hybrid NetBIOS node type (H-node) is assumed.

IPXCP

Internetwork Packet Exchange Control Protocol (IPXCP) as used by Microsoft PPP peers is documented in RFC 1552. IPXCP negotiates IPX-based parameters to dynamically configure an IPX-based PPP peer across a point-to-point link. Common IPXCP options include IPX network and node addresses.

Packet Structure

IPXCP uses the PPP Protocol ID of 0x80-2B. The packet structure of IPXCP is exactly the same for LCP, except only packet types 1 through 7 are defined. For Configure-Request, Configure-Ack, Configure-Nack, and Configure-Reject IPXCP packet types, the IPXCP data portion of the IPXCP packet consists of one or more IPXCP options. Each IPXCP option consists of an option Type field, an option Length field indicating the total length in bytes of the option, and the data associated with the option.

Negotiated Options

Table 7.11 lists the IPXCP options negotiated by Microsoft PPP peers.

Table 7.11   IPXCP Options

Option Name	Option Type	Option Length	Description
IPX Network Number	1	6	The IPX network number for the remote access client.
IPX Node Number	2	6	The IPX node number for the remote access client.

ATCP

AppleTalk Control Protocol (ATCP) as used by Microsoft PPP peers is documented in RFC 1378. ATCP negotiates AppleTalk-based parameters to dynamically configure an AppleTalk-based PPP peer across a point-to-point link. Common ATCP options include an AppleTalk address and server information.

Packet Structure

ATCP uses the PPP Protocol ID of 0x80-29. The packet structure of ATCP is exactly the same as LCP, except that only packet types 1 through 7 are defined. For Configure-Request, Configure-Ack, Configure-Nack, and Configure-Reject ATCP packet types, the ATCP data portion of the ATCP packet consists of one or more ATCP options. Each ATCP option consists of an option Type field, an option Length field indicating the total length in bytes of the option, and the data associated with the option.

Negotiated Options

Table 7.12 lists the ATCP options negotiated by Microsoft PPP peers.

Table 7.12   ATCP Options

Option Name	Option Type	Option Length	Description
AppleTalk Address	1	6	Negotiates the AppleTalk network and node numbers
Server Information	3	16	Used to convey information about the remote access server

NBFCP

NetBIOS Frames Control Protocol (NBFCP) as used by Microsoft PPP peers is documented in RFC 2097. NBFCP negotiates NetBEUI-based parameters to dynamically configure a NetBEUI-based PPP peer across a point-to-point link. Common NBFCP options include multicast filtering options and peer information.

Packet Structure

NBFCP uses the PPP Protocol ID of 0x80-3F. The packet structure of NBFCP is exactly the same for LCP, except that only packet types 1 through 7 are defined. For Configure-Request, Configure-Ack, Configure-Nack, and Configure-Reject NBFCP packet types, the NBFCP data portion of the NBFCP packet consists of one or more NBFCP options. Each NBFCP option consists of an option Type field, an option Length field indicating the total length in bytes of the option, and the data associated with the option.

Negotiated Options

Table 7.13 lists the NBFCP options negotiated by Microsoft PPP peers.

Table 7.13   NBFCP Options

Option Name	Option Type	Option Length	Description
Multicast filtering	3	5	Negotiates the handling of multicast packets
Peer information	2	17	Used to convey NetBIOS configuration information

Compression Control Protocol

Compression Control Protocol (CCP) is documented in RFC 1962. CCP negotiates parameters to dynamically configure, enable, and disable data compression algorithms between PPP peers across a point-to-point link. Common CCP options include an organization identifier and the use of MPPC.

Packet Structure

CCP uses the PPP Protocol ID of 0x80-FD. The packet structure of CCP is exactly the same for LCP, except only packet types 1 through 7 are defined. For Configure-Request, Configure-Ack, Configure-Nack, and Configure-Reject CCP packet types, the CCP data portion of the CCP packet consists of one or more CCP options. Each CCP option consists of an option Type field, an option Length field indicating the total length in bytes of the option, and the data associated with the option.

Negotiated Options

Table 7.14 lists the CCP options negotiated by Microsoft PPP peers.

Table 7.14   CCP Options

Option Name	Option Type	Option Length	Description
Organization Unique Identifier	0	6 or larger	Used to negotiate an organization's proprietary compression protocol.
MPPC	18 or 0x12	6	Used to indicate the use of MPPC, MPPE, and the encryption strength.

MPPE and MPPC

With CCP option 18, Microsoft PPP peers negotiate both MPPC and MPPE at the same time. The option data field for CCP option 18 is 4 bytes (32 bits) long. Bits within this data field are used as flags to indicate:

- Whether compression is enabled (0x00-00-00-01).

- Whether 40-bit session keys are derived from the LAN Manager version of the user's password (0x00-00-00-10).

- Whether 40-bit session keys are derived from the Windows NT version of the user's password (0x00-00-02-00).

- Whether 56-bit session keys are derived from the Windows NT version of the user's password (0x00-00-00-80).

- Whether 128-bit session keys are derived from the Windows NT version of the user's password (0x00-00-00-40).

- Whether the encryption keys are refreshed with each PPP frame (0x01-00-00-00).

For multiple choices, the flag values are added together. For example, for compression (0x00-00-00-01) and 128-bit encryption keys (0x00-00-00-40), the resulting 32-bit option data field is set to 0x00-00-00-41.

For more information about MPPE, see the Internet draft, "Microsoft Point-To-Point Encryption (MPPE) Protocol."

ECP

The Encryption Control Protocol (ECP) is used to negotiate a specific encryption method and is documented in RFC 1968. However, for Microsoft PPP peers, the only encryption that is supported is MPPE that is negotiated during CCP with the negotiation of MPPC. Therefore, Microsoft PPP peers do not use ECP.

PPP Connection Process

There are four distinct phases of negotiation of a PPP connection. Each of these four phases must complete successfully before the PPP connection is ready to transfer user data. The four phases of a PPP connection are:

1. PPP configuration
2. Authentication
3. Callback
4. Protocol configuration

Phase 1: PPP Configuration

PPP configures PPP protocol parameters using LCP (Link Control Protocol). During the initial LCP phase, each peer negotiates communication options that are used to send data and include:

- PPP parameters, such as MRU, address and control field compression, and protocol ID compression.
- Which authentication protocols are used to authenticate the remote access client. An authentication protocol is selected but not implemented until the authentication phase.
- Multilink options.

Phase 2: Authentication

After LCP is complete, the authentication protocol agreed upon by the remote access server and the remote access client is implemented. The nature of this traffic is specific to the PPP authentication protocol. For more details, see "PPP Authentication Protocols" later in this chapter.

Phase 3: Callback

The Microsoft implementation of PPP includes an optional callback phase using the Callback Control Protocol (CBCP) immediately after authentication. In order for a remote access client user to get called back, the dial-in properties of the user account must be enabled for callback and either the remote access client can specify the callback number or the remote access server must specify the callback number.

If a connection is implementing callback, both PPP peers hang up and the remote access server calls the remote access client at the negotiated number.

Phase 4: Protocol Configuration

Once the PPP is configured and callback is complete (optional), network layer protocols can be configured. With remote access on Windows 32-bit operating systems, the remote access server sends the remote access client Configuration-Request messages for all of the LAN protocols enabled for remote access on the remote access server. The remote access client either continues the negotiation of the LAN protocols enabled at the remote access client or sends an LCP Protocol-Reject message containing the Configuration-Request message.

IPCP, IPXCP, ATCP, and NBFCP each go through a negotiation process very similar to LCP negotiation to configure their corresponding network layer protocol. CCP packets are exchanged to configure MPPC and MPPE.

A Sample PPP Connection

To actually see the PPP connection establishment process in Windows 2000, there are two tools available:

1. Network Monitor, a packet capture and analysis tool, is used to capture all PPP packets sent over a serial link including connection establishment and PPP-encapsulated user data.

2. PPP tracing is used to create a log of the PPP packets exchanged during the PPP connection establishment process.

Network Monitor

To capture PPP packets with Network Monitor, set the capture network to the network corresponding to the dial-up connection and begin capturing PPP frames as desired. You can use Network Monitor to:

- Troubleshoot the PPP connection establishment process.

- Ensure that PPP payloads are being encrypted.

- Ensure that PPP payloads are being compressed.

Note If compression or encryption is being used, then the PPP payload is not interpreted by Network Monitor. Compressed or encrypted payloads are indicated with the PPP protocol ID of 3D (assuming protocol ID compression). To see the structure of user data within PPP payloads, disable compression and encryption.

When using Network Monitor, keep the following in mind:

- Captured PPP frames do not contain a Flag character but do contain an Ethernet-like source address and destination address. This behavior is due to the fact that Network Monitor receives the packets from the Ndiswan.sys driver. Recall that Ndiswan.sys is an intermediate NDIS driver that looks like an Ethernet adapter to protocols.

  For each PPP frame, the Ethernet-like source and destination addresses are both set to either **SEND** or **RECV** to indicate that the PPP frame was either sent or received by the computer on which the capture was taken. The **SEND** and **RECV** addresses do not necessarily identify the traffic of a remote access server or remote access client. If the capture was taken on the remote access server, then **SEND** frames were sent by the remote access server and **RECV** frames were sent by the remote access client. If the capture was taken on the remote access client, then **SEND** frames were sent by the remote access client and **RECV** frames were sent by the remote access server.

- Captured PPP frames contain an Address or Control field regardless of whether address and control field compression are negotiated.

- Protocol ID compression is usually negotiated with Microsoft PPP peers, making the PPP Protocol ID a single byte when possible.

- Use Network Monitor display filtering to view only the traffic of desired protocols. For example, to view only the IPCP negotiation, set the display filters to disable the display of all protocols except IPCP.

The following printout is an example of a PPP connection establishment process captured with Network Monitor showing only the frame summaries. The entries are indented to improve readability.

```
1      8.726    SEND        SEND         LCP
                Config Req Packet, Ident = 0x00, Length = 36
2      8.796    RECV        RECV         LCP
                Config Req Packet, Ident = 0x00, Length = 25
3      8.796    SEND        SEND         LCP
                Config Ack Packet, Ident = 0x00, Length = 25
4      8.816    RECV        RECV         LCP
                Config Reject Packet, Ident = 0x00, Length = 17
5      8.816    SEND        SEND         LCP
                Config Req Packet, Ident = 0x01, Length = 23
6      8.886    RECV        RECV         LCP
                Config Ack Packet, Ident = 0x01, Length = 23
7      8.886    SEND        SEND         LCP
                Ident Packet, Ident = 0x02, Length = 18
8      8.886    SEND        SEND         LCP
                Ident Packet, Ident = 0x03, Length = 23
9      8.886    RECV        RECV         PPPCHAP
                Challenge, ID = 0x 1: Challenge
10     8.886    SEND        SEND         PPPCHAP
                Challenge, ID = 0x 1: Response, administrator
11     8.976    RECV        RECV         PPPCHAP
                Challenge, ID = 0x 1: Success
12     8.976    RECV        RECV         CBCP
                Callback Request, Ident = 0x01
13     8.976    SEND        SEND         CBCP
                Callback Response, Ident = 0x01
14     8.996    RECV        RECV         CBCP
                Callback Acknowledgement, Ident = 0x01
15     8.996    SEND        SEND         CCP
                Configuration Request, Ident = 0x04
16     8.997    SEND        SEND         IPCP
                Configuration Request, Ident = 0x05
17     8.997    RECV        RECV         CCP
                Configuration Request, Ident = 0x01
18     9.017    RECV        RECV         IPCP
                Configuration Request, Ident = 0x02
19     9.037    RECV        RECV         IPXCP
                Configuration Request, Ident = 0x03
20     9.037    RECV        RECV         NBFCP
                Configuration Request, Ident = 0x04
21     9.117    SEND        SEND         IPXCP
                Configuration Request, Ident = 0x06
22     9.147    SEND        SEND         CCP
                Configuration Acknowledgement, Ident = 0x01
23     9.147    SEND        SEND         IPCP
                Configuration Acknowledgement, Ident = 0x02
```

```
24      9.167   SEND        SEND        IPXCP
                Configuration Acknowledgement, Ident = 0x03
25      9.167   SEND        SEND        LCP
                Protocol Reject Packet, Ident = 0x07, Length = 32
26      9.237   RECV        RECV        CCP
                Configuration Reject, Ident = 0x04
27      9.237   RECV        RECV        IPCP
                Configuration Reject, Ident = 0x05
28      9.237   SEND        SEND        IPCP
                Configuration Request, Ident = 0x08
29      9.257   RECV        RECV        IPXCP
                Configuration No Acknowledgement, Ident = 0x06
30      9.257   SEND        SEND        IPXCP
                Configuration Request, Ident = 0x09
31      9.287   RECV        RECV        IPCP
                Configuration No Acknowledgement, Ident = 0x08
32      9.287   SEND        SEND        IPCP
                Configuration Request, Ident = 0x0A
33      9.287   RECV        RECV        IPXCP
                Configuration Acknowledgement, Ident = 0x09
34      9.327   RECV        RECV        IPCP
                Configuration Acknowledgement, Ident = 0x0A
35     10.729   SEND        SEND        CCP
                Configuration Request, Ident = 0x04
36     10.960   RECV        RECV        CCP
                Configuration Reject, Ident = 0x04
37     10.960   SEND        SEND        CCP
                Configuration Request, Ident = 0x0B
38     10.960   RECV        RECV        CCP
                Configuration Acknowledgement, Ident = 0x0B
```

The trace was captured on the remote access client. Therefore, the SEND frames were sent from the remote access client and the RECV frames were sent from the remote access server. In this trace, you can see the four phases of the PPP connection establishment:

- Phase 1: PPP configuration is done in frames 1 through 8 by using the exchange of LCP configuration packets.

- Phase 2: Authentication is done in frames 9 through 11 where the user's credentials are verified.

- Phase 3: Callback is done in frames 12 through 14.

- Phase 4: Protocol configuration is done in frames 15 through 38 where compression, encryption, IP, and IPX are configured.

In addition to the summary view, Network Monitor can also expand frames for detailed analysis. For example, frame 1 from this trace is displayed as:

```
FRAME: Base frame properties
      FRAME: Time of capture = Nov 18, 1998 15:23:6.967
      FRAME: Time delta from previous physical frame: 0 milliseconds
      FRAME: Frame number: 1
      FRAME: Total frame length: 50 bytes
      FRAME: Capture frame length: 50 bytes
      FRAME: Frame data: Number of data bytes remaining = 50 (0x0032)
PPP: Link Control Protocol Frame (0xC021)
      PPP: Destination Address =  SEND_
      PPP: Source Address =  SEND_
      PPP: Protocol = Link Control Protocol
LCP: Config Req Packet, Ident = 0x00, Length = 36
      LCP: Code = Configuration Request
      LCP: Identifier = 0 (0x0)
      LCP: Length = 36 (0x24)
      LCP: Options: ASYNC.MAP:00 00 00 00-MAGIC#:0x0C05-PROT.COMP-
ADR/CF.COMP-CALL.BACK:Unkn---
            LCP: ASYNC.MAP:00 00 00 00
                LCP: Option Type = Async Control Character Map
                LCP: Option Length = 6 (0x6)
                LCP: Async Control Character Map = 00 00 00 00
            LCP: MAGIC#:0x0C05
                LCP: Option Type = Majic Number
                LCP: Option Length = 6 (0x6)
                LCP: Magic Number = 3077 (0xC05)
            LCP: PROT.COMP
                LCP: Option Type = Protocol Field Compression
                LCP: Option Length = 2 (0x2)
            LCP: ADR/CF.COMP
                LCP: Option Type = Address and Control Field Compression
                LCP: Option Length = 2 (0x2)
            LCP: CALL.BACK:Unkn
                LCP: Option Type = Callback
                LCP: Option Length = 3 (0x3)
                LCP: CallBack = 0x06
            LCP: Multilink Maximum Receive Reconstructed Unit
                LCP: Option Type = 0x11
                LCP: Option Length = 4 (0x4)
            LCP: Multilink Endpoint Discriminator
                LCP: Option Type = 0x13
                LCP: Option Length = 9 (0x9)
```

Network Monitor captures can also be saved as files and sent to Microsoft support professionals for analysis.

PPP Tracing

Tracing is a facility of Windows 2000 remote access and routing components that allow you to optionally enable and disable the recording of programming code and network events to a file.

You enable PPP tracing by selecting **Enable Point-to-Point Protocol (PPP) Logging** from the **Event Logging** tab on the properties of a remote access server in the **Routing and Remote Access** snap-in.

The file Ppp.log is created in the *%Systemroot%*\tracing folder and contains information about the PPP connection establishment process. The PPP log generated by PPP tracing contain the programming calls and actual packet contents of PPP packets for PPP control protocols. PPP tracing cannot be used to view PPP user data sent across the connection.

The following printout is an excerpt from a PPP trace of a PPP connection establishment process. The entries are indented to improve readability.

```
[1472] 15:57:50:094: Line up event occurred on port 5
[1472] 15:57:50:104: Starting PPP on link with IfType=0x0,IPIf=0x0,
                     IPXIf=0x0
[1472] 15:57:50:104: RasGetBuffer returned ae70054 for SendBuf
[1472] 15:57:50:104: FsmInit called for protocol = c021, port = 5
[1472] 15:57:50:104: ConfigInfo = 273e
[1472] 15:57:50:104: APs available = 1
[1472] 15:57:50:104: FsmReset called for protocol = c021, port = 5
[1472] 15:57:50:104: Inserting port in bucket # 5
[1472] 15:57:50:104: Inserting bundle in bucket # 6
[1472] 15:57:50:104: FsmOpen event received for protocol c021 on port 5
[1472] 15:57:50:104: FsmThisLayerStarted called for protocol = c021,
                     port = 5
[1472] 15:57:50:104: FsmUp event received for protocol c021 on port 5
[1472] 15:57:50:104: <PPP packet sent at 11/04/1998 23:57:50:104
[1472] 15:57:50:104: <Protocol = LCP, Type = Configure-Req, Length =
                     0x2f, Id = 0x0, Port = 5
[1472] 15:57:50:104: <C0 21 01 00 00 2D 02 06 00 00 00 00 03 05 C2 23
                     |.!...-........#|
[1472] 15:57:50:104: <80 05 06 72 5F 50 9A 07 02 08 02 0D 03 06 11 04
                     |...r_P..........|
[1472] 15:57:50:104: <06 4E 13 09 03 00 60 08 3E 46 07 17 04 00 03 00
                     |.N....`.>F......|
[1472] 15:57:50:104: InsertInTimerQ called portid=6,Id=0,Protocol=c021,
                     EventType=0,fAuth=0
[1472] 15:57:50:104: InsertInTimerQ called portid=6,Id=0,Protocol=0,
                     EventType=3,fAuth=0
[1472] 15:57:50:104: >PPP packet received at 11/04/1998 23:57:50:104
[1472] 15:57:50:104: >Protocol = LCP, Type = Configure-Req, Length =
                     0x26, Id = 0x0, Port = 5
[1472] 15:57:50:104: >C0 21 01 00 00 24 02 06 00 00 00 00 05 06 00 00
```

```
                           | .!...$..........|
[1472] 15:57:50:104: >C0 05 07 02 08 02 0D 03 06 11 04 06 4E 13 09 03
                           | ._.........N...|
[1472] 15:57:50:104: >00 60 08 52 F9 D8 00 00 00 00 00 00 00 00 00 00
                           | .`.R...........|
```

The last three lines of this trace excerpt is a hexadecimal display of the same LCP
packet as frame 1 of the previous Network Monitor trace. To understand this
frame, you must manually parse this frame according to the PPP and LCP packet
structure. An example of the parsing of this PPP frame is listed in Table 7.15.

Table 7.15   Parsing of the LCP Configuration-Request

Bytes	Meaning
C0 21	PPP Protocol ID for LCP.
01	LCP Code for a Configure-Request.
00	LCP Identifier for this Configure-Request.
00 24	Length in bytes of the LCP packet (36 bytes long).
02	LCP option for Asynchronous Control Character Map (ACCM).
06	Length in bytes of the ACCM option.
00 00 00 00	Data for the ACCM option.
05	LCP option for the magic number.
06	Length in bytes of the magic number option.
00 00 C0 05	Data for the magic number option.
07	LCP option for protocol compression.
02	Length in bytes of the protocol compression option.
08	LCP option for address and control field compression.
02	Length in bytes of the address and control field compression option.
0D	LCP option for callback.
03	Length in bytes of the callback option.
06	Callback option data.
11	LCP option for the Multilink Maximum Receive Reconstructed Unit. Multilink LCP options are discussed in the "Multilink and Bandwidth Allocation Protocol" section of this chapter.
04	Length in bytes of the Multilink Maximum Receive Reconstructed Unit option.
06 4E	Multilink Maximum Receive Reconstructed Unit option data.
13	LCP option for the Multilink Endpoint Discriminator option.
09	Length in bytes of the Multilink Endpoint Discriminator option.
03 00 60 08 52 F9 D8	Multilink Endpoint Discriminator option data.

As you can see, Network Monitor is the easier tool for the interpretation of PPP traffic. However, the PPP trace contains valuable internal component interaction information that can be useful to troubleshoot connection problems and behavior. When in doubt, obtain both a Network Monitor capture and a PPP trace.

Note PPP tracing in Windows 2000 is the same as the PPP log feature found in Windows NT 4.0 and earlier.

PPP Connection Termination

PPP can terminate the link at any time. Termination generally occurs due to carrier loss, authentication failure, link quality failure, time-out, or link closure by the dial-up client or system administrator. When the link is closing, PPP informs the network layer protocols so that they can take appropriate action.

PPP Authentication Protocols

Phase 2 of the PPP connection establishment process is the authentication of the remote access client. Authentication for PPP is accomplished through a PPP authentication protocol. During Phase 1, both PPP peers agree on a single, specific PPP authentication protocol.

Windows 2000 remote access supports Extensible Authentication Protocol (EAP), Challenge Handshake Authentication Protocol (CHAP), Microsoft Challenge Handshake Authentication Protocol (MS-CHAP) version 1 and version 2, Shiva Password Authentication Protocol (SPAP), and Password Authentication Protocol (PAP).

A secure authentication scheme provides protection against replay attacks, remote access client impersonation, and remote access server impersonation.

- A replay attack occurs when a person captures the packets of a successful connection attempt and then replays those packets in an attempt to obtain an authenticated connection.

- Remote access client impersonation occurs when a person takes over an existing authenticated connection. The intruder waits until the connection is authenticated and then obtains the connection parameters, disconnects the user, and takes control of the authenticated connection.

- Remote server impersonation occurs when a computer appears as the remote access server to the remote access client. The impersonator appears to verify the remote access client credentials and then captures all of the traffic from the remote access client.

PAP

Password Authentication Protocol (PAP) is a simple, plaintext authentication scheme. The user name and password are requested by the remote access server and returned by the remote access client in plaintext. PAP, however, is not a secure authentication protocol. A person capturing the PAP packets between the remote access server and remote access client can easily determine the remote access client's password. PAP offers no protection against replay attacks, remote client impersonation, or remote server impersonation.

The use of PAP is negotiated during LCP negotiation by specifying the authentication protocol LCP option (type 3) and the authentication protocol 0xC0-23. Once LCP negotiation is complete, PAP messages use the PPP protocol ID of 0xC0-23.

PAP is a simple exchange of messages:

1. The remote access client sends a PAP Authenticate-Request message to the remote access server containing the remote access client's user name and clear text password.

2. The remote access server checks the user name and password and sends back either a PAP Authenticate-Ack message when the user's credentials are correct, or a PAP Authenticate-Nak message when the user's credentials are not correct.

PAP is included in Windows 2000 so that remote access clients running Windows 32-bit operating systems can connect to older remote access servers that do not support a secure authentication protocol, and remote access clients not running Microsoft operating systems that do not support a secure remote access protocol can connect to a remote access server running Windows 32-bit operating systems.

Note To make your remote access server more secure, ensure that PAP is disabled. However, older remote access clients not running Microsoft operating systems that do not support secure authentication protocols are unable to connect.

SPAP

The Shiva Password Authentication Protocol (SPAP) is a reversible encryption mechanism employed by Shiva remote access servers. A Windows 2000 remote access client can use SPAP to authenticate itself to a Shiva remote access server. A remote access client running Windows 32-bit operating systems can use SPAP to authenticate itself to a Windows 2000 remote access server. SPAP is more secure than PAP but less secure than CHAP or MS-CHAP. SPAP offers no protection against remote server impersonation.

The use of SPAP is negotiated during LCP negotiation by specifying the authentication protocol LCP option (type 3) and the authentication protocol 0xC0-27. Once LCP negotiation is complete, SPAP messages use the PPP protocol ID of 0xC0-27.

Like PAP, SPAP is a simple exchange of messages:

1. The remote access client sends an SPAP Authenticate-Request message to the remote access server containing the remote access client's user name and encrypted password.

2. The remote access server decrypts the password, checks the user name and password, and sends back either an SPAP Authenticate-Ack message when the user's credentials are correct, or an SPAP Authenticate-Nak message with a reason why the user's credentials were not correct.

CHAP

The Challenge Handshake Authentication Protocol (CHAP) is a challenge-response authentication protocol documented in RFC 1994 that uses the industry-standard Message Digest 5 (MD5) one-way encryption scheme to hash the response to a challenge issued by the remote access server.

CHAP is used by various vendors of dial-in servers and clients. CHAP is supported by both the Windows 2000 remote access server and remote access client.

CHAP is an improvement over PAP and SPAP in that the password is never sent over the link. Instead, the password is used to create a one-way hash from a challenge string. The server, knowing the client's password, can duplicate the operation and compare the result with that sent in the client's response.

The use of CHAP is negotiated during Phase 1 by specifying the authentication protocol LCP option (type 3), the authentication protocol 0xC2-23, and the algorithm 0x05. Once LCP negotiation is complete, CHAP messages use the PPP Protocol ID of 0xC2-23.

CHAP authentication is an exchange of three messages:

1. The remote access server sends a CHAP Challenge message containing a session ID and an arbitrary challenge string.

2. The remote access client returns a CHAP Response message containing the user name in cleartext and a hash of the challenge string, session ID, and the client's password using the MD5 one-way hashing algorithm.

3. The remote access server duplicates the hash and compares it to the hash in the CHAP Response. If the hashes are the same, the remote access server sends back a CHAP Success message. If the hashes are different, a CHAP Failure message is sent.

CHAP protects against replay attacks by using an arbitrary challenge string per authentication attempt. However, CHAP does not protect against remote server impersonation.

CHAP requires that local or domain passwords be stored in a reversibly encrypted form. For more information, see Windows 2000 Server Help.

MS-CHAP v1

The Microsoft Challenge Handshake Authentication Protocol version 1 (MS-CHAP v1) is an encrypted authentication mechanism very similar to CHAP. As in CHAP, the remote access server sends a challenge to the remote client that consists of a session ID and an arbitrary challenge string. The remote client must return the user name and a Message Digest 4 (MD4) hash of the challenge string, the session ID, and the MD4-hashed password.

One difference between CHAP and MS-CHAP v1 is that, in CHAP, the plaintext version of the password must be available to validate the challenge response. With MS-CHAP v1, the remote access server only requires the MD4 hash of the password to validate the challenge response. In Windows 2000, the user's password is stored as an MD4 hash and in a reversibly encrypted form. When CHAP is used, the remote access server decrypts the reversibly encrypted password to validate the remote access client's response.

MS-CHAP v1 authentication is an exchange of three messages:

1. The remote access server sends an MS-CHAP Challenge message containing a session ID and an arbitrary challenge string.

2. The remote access client returns an MS-CHAP Response message containing the user name in cleartext and a hash of the challenge string, session ID, and the MD4 hash of the client's password using the MD4 one-way hashing algorithm.

3. The remote access server duplicates the hash and compares it to the hash in the MS-CHAP Response. If the hashes are the same, the remote access server sends back an MS-CHAP Success message. If the hashes are different, an MS-CHAP Failure message is sent.

The use of MS-CHAP v1 is negotiated during LCP negotiation by specifying the authentication protocol LCP option (type 3), the authentication protocol 0xC2-23, and the algorithm 0x80. Once LCP negotiation is complete, MS-CHAP v1 messages use the PPP protocol ID of 0xC2-23.

MS-CHAP v1 also allows for error codes including a "password expired" code and password changes. MS-CHAP v1 protects against replay attacks by using an arbitrary challenge string per authentication attempt. MS-CHAP v1 does not provide protection against remote server impersonation.

If MS-CHAP v1 is used as the authentication protocol and MPPE is negotiated, then shared secret encryption keys are generated by each PPP peer. MS-CHAP v1 also provides a set of messages that allows a user to change their password during the user authentication process.

MS-CHAP v2

Windows 2000 includes support for Microsoft Challenge Handshake Authentication Protocol version 2 (MS-CHAP v2) that provides stronger security for remote access connections. MS-CHAP v2 offers the additional security features:

- LAN Manager encoding of responses and password changes is no longer supported.

- Two-way authentication verifies the identity of both sides of the connection. The remote access client authenticates against the remote access server and the remote access server authenticates against the remote access client. Two-way authentication, also known as mutual authentication, ensures that the remote access client is dialing into a remote access server that has access to the user's password. Mutual authentication provides protection against remote server impersonation.

- Separate cryptographic keys are generated for transmitted and received data.

- The cryptographic keys are based on the user's password and the arbitrary challenge string. Each time the user connects with the same password, a different cryptographic key is used.

The use of MS-CHAP v2 is negotiated during LCP negotiation by specifying the authentication protocol LCP option (type 3), the authentication protocol 0xC2-23, and the algorithm 0x81. Once LCP negotiation is complete, MS-CHAP messages use the PPP protocol ID of 0xC2-23.

MS-CHAP v2 authentication is an exchange of three messages:

1. The remote access server sends an MS-CHAP v2 Challenge message to the remote access client that consists of a session identifier and an arbitrary challenge string.

2. The remote access client sends an MS-CHAP v2 Response message that contains:

   - The user name.

   - An arbitrary peer challenge string.

   - An Secure Hash Algorithim (SHA) hash of the received challenge string, the peer challenge string, the session identifier, and the MD4-hashed version of the user's password.

3. The remote access server checks the MS-CHAP v2 Response message from the client and sends back an MS-CHAP v2 Response message containing:

   - An indication of the success or failure of the connection attempt.

   - An authenticated response based on the sent challenge string, the peer challenge string, the client's encrypted response, and the user's password.

4. The remote access client verifies the authentication response and if it is correct, uses the connection. If the authentication response is not correct, the remote access client terminates the connection.

EAP

The Extensible Authentication Protocol (EAP) is an extension to PPP that allows for arbitrary authentication mechanisms to be employed for the validation of a PPP connection. With PPP authentication protocols such as MS-CHAP and SPAP, a specific authentication mechanism is chosen during the link establishment phase. Then, during the connection authentication phase, the negotiated authentication protocol is used to validate the connection. The authentication protocol itself is a fixed series of messages sent in a specific order.

With EAP, the specific authentication mechanism is not chosen during the link establishment phase. Instead, each PPP peer negotiates to perform EAP during the connection authentication phase. Once the connection authentication phase is reached, the PPP peers must first negotiate the use of a specific EAP authentication scheme known as an EAP type. Once the EAP type is agreed upon, EAP allows for an open-ended conversation between the remote access client and the remote access server that can vary based on the parameters of the connection. The conversation consists of requests for authentication information and the responses. The length and detail of the authentication conversation is dependent upon the EAP type.

For example, when EAP is used with security token cards, the remote access server could separately query the remote access client for a name, PIN, and card token value. As each query is asked and answered, the user passes through another level of authentication. When all questions have been answered satisfactorily, the user is authenticated and permitted access to the network.

The use of EAP is negotiated during LCP negotiation by specifying the authentication protocol LCP option (type 3) and the authentication protocol 0xC2-27. Once LCP negotiation is complete, EAP messages use the PPP Protocol ID of 0xC2-27. Windows 2000 includes support for the EAP-MD5 and EAP-TLS EAP types.

Architecturally, EAP is designed to allow authentication plug-in modules at both the client and server ends of a connection. By installing an EAP type library file on both the remote access client and the remote access server, a new EAP type can be supported. This presents vendors with the opportunity to supply a new authentication scheme at any time. EAP provides the highest flexibility in authentication uniqueness and variations.

EAP-MD5

EAP-MD5 is the CHAP authentication mechanism used within the EAP framework. Rather than negotiating to perform MD5 authentication during the link establishment phase, the authenticator and peer negotiate to do EAP during the connection authentication phase.

Once the connection authentication phase is reached, the following process verifies the client:

1. The authenticator sends an EAP-Request message requesting the identity of the client.
2. The client sends its user ID to the authenticator as an EAP-Response message.
3. The authenticator sends an EAP-Request message containing the MD5 challenge string.
4. The client sends the MD5 hash of its user ID and password to the authenticator as an EAP-Response message.
5. If the response is proper, the authenticator sends a Success message to the client.

EAP-MD5 is a required EAP type and can be used to test EAP interoperability. Like, CHAP, EAP-MD5 requires that local or domain passwords be stored in a reversibly encrypted form. For more information, see Windows 2000 Server Help.

EAP-TLS

The Transport Layer Security (TLS) protocol, based on the Secure Sockets Layer, allows applications to communicate securely. TLS provides authentication (user and data), data integrity, and data confidentiality services. To achieve these services, TLS specifies a framework that allows the following:

- Client and two-way authentication using symmetric or asymmetric encryption.
- Negotiation of the specific encryption algorithm (the cipher-suite).
- Secured exchange of encryption keys to be used for encrypting messages.
- Message integrity and user authentication using a message authentication code.

For more information about the details of TLS, see RFC 2246. For more information about EAP-TLS, see RFC 2716.

EAP-TLS is the use of TLS during the establishment of a PPP connection. With EAP-TLS, mutual authentication between the PPP client and the authenticator is done through the exchange and verification of certificates. The client attempting the connection sends a user certificate, and the authenticator sends a machine certificate.

EAP-TLS is only supported on Windows 2000 Server remote access server computers that are a member of a Windows 2000 mixed or native domain. Stand-alone Windows 2000 remote access servers do not support EAP-TLS.

EAP-RADIUS

EAP-RADIUS is not an EAP type, but the passing of EAP messages of any EAP type by the remote access server to a RADIUS server for authentication. The EAP messages sent between the remote access client and remote access server are encapsulated and formatted as RADIUS messages between the remote access server and the RADIUS server. The remote access server becomes a pass-through device passing EAP messages between the remote access client and the RADIUS server. All processing of EAP messages occurs at the remote access client and the RADIUS server.

EAP-RADIUS is used in environments where RADIUS is used as the authentication provider. An advantage of using EAP-RADIUS is that EAP types do not need to be installed at each remote access server, only at the RADIUS server.

In a typical use of EAP-RADIUS, the remote access server is configured to use EAP and to use RADIUS as its authentication provider. When a connection attempt is made, the remote access client negotiates the use of EAP with the remote access server. When the client sends an EAP message to the remote access server, the remote access server encapsulates the EAP message as a RADIUS message and sends it to its configured RADIUS server. The RADIUS server processes the EAP message and sends a RADIUS-encapsulated EAP message back to the remote access server. The remote access server then forwards the EAP message to the remote access client.

Unauthenticated Connections

Windows 2000 also supports unauthenticated PPP connections. In an unauthenticated PPP connection, the authentication phase of the PPP connection establishment is skipped. Neither the remote access client or the remote access server exchange credentials. The use of unauthenticated PPP connections must be carefully considered, as connections are allowed without verifying the identity of the remote access client.

There are two common cases where unauthenticated connections are desired:

1. When using Automatic Number Identification/Calling Line Identification (ANI/CLI) authentication, the authentication of a connection attempt is based on the phone number of the caller. ANI/CLI service returns the number of the caller to the receiver of the call and is provided by most standard telephone companies.

   ANI/CLI authentication is different from caller ID authorization. In caller ID authorization, the caller sends a valid user name and password. The caller ID that is configured for the dial-in property on the user account must match the connection attempt; otherwise, the connection attempt is rejected. In ANI/CLI authentication, a user name and password are not sent.

2. When using guest authentication, the Guest account is used as the identity of the caller.

For information about procedures to implement these common unauthenticated connection scenarios, see Windows 2000 Server Help.

Remote Access and TCP/IP and IPX

The following sections describe how the Windows 2000 remote access server allocates network configuration parameters for TCP/IP and IPX-based remote access clients.

TCP/IP

To configure a TCP/IP-based remote access client with IPCP, the remote access server allocates an IP address and assigns the IP addresses of DNS and WINS servers.

IP Address Allocation

To allocate an IP address to a remote access client, the remote access server is either configured to use Dynamic Host Configuration Protocol (DHCP) to obtain IP addresses, or with a static IP address pool.

DHCP and Automatic Private IP Addressing

When the remote access server is configured to use DHCP to obtain IP addresses, the Routing and Remote Access service instructs the DHCP client component to obtain 10 IP addresses from a DHCP server. The remote access server uses the first IP address obtained from DHCP for the RAS server interface, and subsequent addresses are allocated to TCP/IP-based remote access clients as they connect. IP addresses freed due to remote access clients disconnecting are reused.

When all 10 IP addresses are used, the remote access server uses the DHCP client component to obtain 10 more. You can modify the number of IP addresses obtained at a time by changing the value of the **InitialAddressPoolSize** registry entry:

HKEY_LOCAL_MACHINE\System\CurrentControlSet\Services\RemoteAccess \Parameters\Ip

With the Windows NT 4.0 remote access server, the DHCP allocated addresses are recorded and reused when the remote access service is restarted. The Windows 2000 remote access server now releases all DHCP allocated IP addresses using DHCPRELEASE messages each time the service is stopped.

If the remote access server initially starts using DHCP-allocated addresses and the DHCP server becomes unavailable, then an IP address cannot be allocated to additional TCP/IP-based remote access clients.

If a DHCP server is not available when the Routing and Remote Access service is started, then the DHCP client returns 10 addresses in the range 169.254.0.1 to 169.254.255.254 to allocate to remote access clients. The address range 169.254.0.0/16 is used for Automatic Private IP Addressing (APIPA). APIPA addresses for point-to-LAN remote access connectivity work only if the network to which the remote access server computer is attached is also using APIPA addresses. If the local network is not using APIPA addresses, remote access clients are only able to obtain point-to-point remote access connectivity.

If a DHCP server does become available, the next time IP addresses are needed by the Routing and Remote Access service, DHCP-obtained addresses are then allocated to remote access clients that connect after the DHCP addresses were obtained.

The remote access server uses a specific LAN interface to obtain DHCP-allocated IP addresses for remote access clients. You can select which LAN interface to use from the **IP** tab on the properties of a remote access router in the **Routing and Remote Access** snap-in. By default, **Allow RAS to select adapter** is selected, which means that the Routing and Remote Access service randomly picks a LAN interface to use.

Static IP Address Pool

When a static IP address pool is configured, the remote access server uses the first IP address in the first address range for the RAS server interface, and subsequent addresses are allocated to TCP/IP-based remote access clients as they connect. IP addresses freed due to remote access clients disconnecting are reused.

If an address range in the static IP address pool is for off-subnet addresses, either enable an appropriate routing protocol on the remote access server or add the routes corresponding to the IP address ranges to the routers of your intranet. For more information, see "TCP/IP On-Subnet and Off-Subnet Addressing" earlier in this chapter.

DNS and WINS Address Assignment

As part of the IPCP negotiation, the remote access server assigns the IP addresses of DNS and WINS servers. Exactly which set of DNS and WINS server IP addresses are assigned to the remote access client depends on the following factors:

- Whether DNS and WINS server IP address assignment is prohibited.
- Whether DNS and WINS server IP addresses for remote access clients are globally configured by using data stored in the registry.
- Whether the remote access server has more than one LAN interface.
- Whether the DNS and WINS server IP addresses for the remote access server are configured statically or are obtained through DHCP.

Prohibiting DNS and WINS IP Address Assignment

If you do not want the remote access server to assign DNS and WINS IP addresses, set the values of **SuppressDNSNameServers** and **SuppressWINSNameServers** in:

HKEY_LOCAL_MACHINE\System\CurrentControlSet\Services\RemoteAccess\Parameters\Ip to 1

Configuring Global DNS and WINS IP Address Assignment

To globally configure DNS and WINS server IP addresses for remote access clients, enter the IP addresses in the values of **DNSNameServers** and **WINSNameServer** in:

HKEY_LOCAL_MACHINE\System\CurrentControlSet\Services\RemoteAccess\Parameters\Ip

Multiple LAN Interfaces

If the DNS and WINS server IP address assignment is not prohibited or globally configured, then the remote access server allocates the DNS and WINS server IP addresses of a LAN interface on the remote access server to remote access clients. If there is only one LAN interface, which is the typical configuration of a dial-up remote access server, the remote access server allocates the DNS and WINS server IP addresses of the single LAN interface to remote access clients. If there is more than one LAN interface, the DNS and WINS server IP addresses of a specific LAN interface must be determined.

With multiple LAN interfaces, which is the typical configuration of a VPN remote access server, the remote access server by default picks one LAN interface randomly during startup and uses the DNS and WINS server IP addresses of the chosen LAN interface to allocate to remote access clients. To override this behavior, you can select the desired LAN interface through the **IP** tab on the properties of a remote access router in the **Routing and Remote Access** snap-in. By default, **Allow RAS to select adapter** is selected.

Static Configuration or DHCP

Once the LAN adapter for DNS and WINS server IP address assignment has been determined:

- If the LAN adapter has a static IP configuration, then the IP addresses of the statically configured DNS and WINS servers are allocated to remote access clients.

- If the LAN adapter obtained its IP configuration using DHCP, then the IP addresses of the DHCP-obtained DNS and WINS servers are allocated to remote access clients.

The way that the remote access server determines the set of DNS and WINS server IP addresses to assign to remote access clients during IPCP negotiation is illustrated in Figure 7.14.

Start

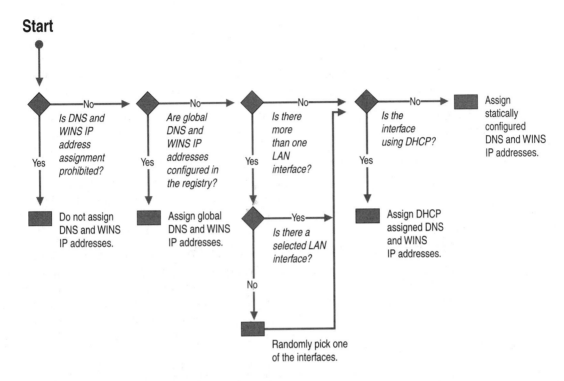

Figure 7.14   DNS and WINS Server IP Address Determination

Overriding IPCP-Allocated DNS and WINS Server IP Addresses with DHCPInform

After IPCP is completed, Windows 2000 and Windows 98 remote access clients send their remote access servers a DHCPInform message. DHCPInform is a DHCP message used by DHCP clients to obtain DHCP options. While PPP remote access clients do not use DHCP to obtain IP addresses for the remote access connection, Windows 2000 and Windows 98 remote access clients use the DHCPInform message to obtain DNS server IP addresses, WINS server IP addresses, and a DNS domain name. The DHCPInform message is sent after the IPCP negotiation is concluded.

The DHCPInform message received by the remote access server is then forwarded to a DHCP server. The remote access server forwards DHCPInform messages only if it has been configured with the DHCP Relay Agent as discussed in the following section. The response to the DHCPInform message is forwarded back to the requesting remote access client.

If the DHCPInform response contains DNS and WINS server IP address options, then these new values override what was allocated during IPCP. When the remote access client is a Windows 2000 remote access client and the DHCPInform response contains a DNS domain name, the DNS domain name is used as the per-adapter DNS suffix for the remote access connection of the remote access client. For more information on per-adapter DNS suffixes, see "Windows 2000 DNS" in the *TCP/IP Core Networking Guide*.

Remote Access Server and the DHCP Relay Agent

To facilitate the forwarding of DHCPInform messages between remote access clients and DHCP servers, the remote access server uses the DHCP Relay Agent, a component of the Windows 2000 remote access router. To configure the remote access server to use the DHCP Relay Agent, add the **Internal** interface to the DHCP Relay Agent IP routing protocol with the **Routing and Remote Access** snap-in.

If the remote access server is using DHCP to obtain IP addresses for remote access clients, then the remote access server uses the DHCP Relay Agent to forward DHCPInform messages to the DHCP server of the selected LAN interface, on the **IP** tab on the properties of a remote access router in the **Routing and Remote Access** snap-in.

If the remote access server is using a static IP address pool to obtain IP addresses for remote access clients, then the DHCP Relay Agent must be configured with the IP address of at least one DHCP server. Otherwise, DHCPInform messages sent by remote access clients are silently discarded by the remote access server.

IPX

To configure an IPX-based remote access client with IPXCP, the remote access server allocates an IPX network number and an IPX node number. The network number allocation behavior is configured from the **IPX** tab on the properties of a remote access router in the **Routing and Remote Access** snap-in. The main capabilities of IPX configuration are:

- IPX network numbers for remote access clients can be automatically allocated or specified as a range by the network administrator. For automatically allocated IPX network numbers, the remote access server ensures that the IPX network number is not being used on the IPX internetwork by sending a RIP GetLocalTarget packet on its LAN interfaces. If there is a response to the RIP GetLocalTarget, then the IPX network number is in use and another IPX network number is chosen.

- The same IPX network number can be assigned to all remote access clients.

- Specific IPX node numbers can be requested by remote access clients.

You can set the first IPX node number as a 12-digit hexadecimal number to be allocated to IPX remote access clients.To do so, add the **FirstWanNode** (REG_SZ) registry entry to:

HKEY_LOCAL_MACHINE\System\CurrentControlSet\Services\RemoteAccess \Parameters\Ipx

And enter the desired IPX node number in the value of the entry.

Subsequent IPX clients are assigned incrementally increasing node numbers. If this registry entry does not appear in the registry, a random IPX node number, in the form 0x2E-xx-xx-xx-xx (where you specify each x digit), is assigned when the remote access client does not request a specific IPX node number.

Remote Access Policies

In Windows 2000, remote access connections are accepted based on the dial-in properties of a user account and remote access policies. A remote access policy is a set of conditions and connection parameters that define the characteristics of the incoming connection and the set of constraints imposed on it. Remote access policies can be used to specify allowed connections conditioned by the time of day and day of the week, the Windows 2000 group to which the dial-in user belongs, the type of remote access client (dial-up or VPN), and so on. Remote access policies can be used to impose connection parameters such as maximum session time, idle disconnect time, required secure authentication methods, required encryption, and so on.

With multiple remote access policies, different sets of conditions can be applied to different remote access clients or different requirements can be applied to the same remote access client based on the parameters of the connection attempt. For example, multiple remote access policies can be used to:

- Allow or deny connections if the user account belongs to a specific group.
- Define different days and times for different user accounts based on group membership.
- Configure different authentication methods for dial-up and VPN remote access clients.
- Configure different authentication or encryption settings for Point-to-Point Tunneling Protocol (PPTP) or Layer Two Tunneling Protocol (L2TP) connections.
- Configure different maximum session times for different user accounts based on group membership.
- Send network access server–specific RADIUS attributes to a RADIUS client.

When you have multiple Windows 2000 remote access or VPN server and you want all of the servers to use a centralized set of remote access policies to authorize incoming connections, you must configure a computer to run Windows 2000 and Internet Authentication Service (IAS) and then configure each remote access or VPN server as a RADIUS client to the IAS server computer.

For more information about remote access policies, including common remote access policy scenarios and their configuration, see Windows 2000 Server Help.

Connection Attempt Processing

To process a connection attempt, the parameters of the connection attempt are compared to the user name, password, and dial-in properties of the user account and the configured remote access policies.

Some general characteristics of remote access connection attempt processing are:

- If a connection attempt does not use a valid user name and password, then the connection attempt is denied.
- If there are no configured policies, then all connection attempts are denied.
- If the connection attempt does not match any of the remote access policies, then the connection attempt is denied.
- If the remote access permission of the user account for the remote access user is set to **Deny Access**, the connection attempt is always denied for that remote access user.
- The only time that a connection attempt is allowed is when it matches the conditions of a remote access policy, and remote access permission is enabled either through the dial-in properties of the user account or through the remote access permission of the remote access policy (assuming the user's remote access permission is set to control access through remote access policies), and the parameters of the connection attempt match or conform to the parameters and conditions of the dial-in properties of the user account and the remote access policy profile properties.

Figure 7.15 depicts the specific processing of remote access connection attempts using the dial-in properties of the user account and remote access policies. Figure 7.15 assumes that the user name and password sent during the authentication process match a valid user account.

Start

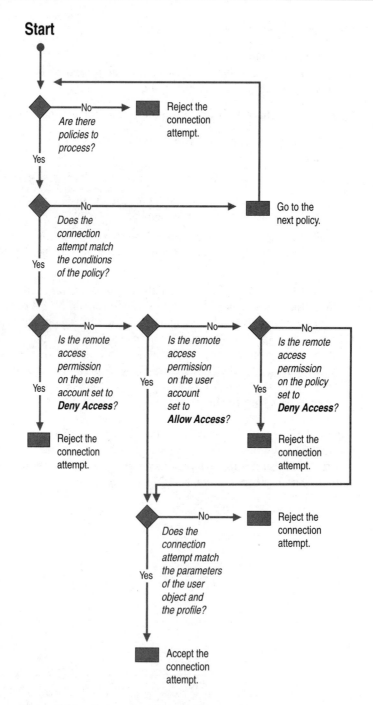

Figure 7.15   Connection Attempt Processing

Troubleshooting Remote Access Policies

A common problem with remote access policies is that a connection attempt is denied when it should be allowed. When in doubt, apply the logic of Figure 7.7 to the parameters of the connection attempt, the dial-in properties of the user account, and the remote access policies. However, troubleshooting the denial of the connection attempt can be very time consuming when there are multiple remote access policies in place.

When multiple remote access policies are configured and you want to determine which remote access policy is denying the connection attempt, then enable the logging of authentication requests for local files from **Remote Access Logging** in the **Routing and Remote Access** snap-in. Logged authentication requests contain the name of the remote access policy used in either accepting or rejecting the connection attempt.

Multilink and Bandwidth Allocation Protocol

Windows 2000 remote access supports the PPP Multilink Protocol (MP), the Bandwidth Allocation Protocol (BAP), and the Bandwidth Allocation Control Protocol (BACP):

- MP allows multiple physical links to appear as a single logical link over which data can be sent and received.
- BAP is a PPP control protocol that is used to dynamically add or remove additional links to an MP connection.
- BACP is a PPP NCP that elects a favored peer in case both PPP peers request to add or remove a connection at the same time.

Each of these protocols is discussed in greater detail in the following sections.

PPP Multilink Protocol

The PPP Multilink Protocol (MP) protocol is defined in RFC 1990 and used to aggregate multiple physical links into a single logical link. A good example is the aggregation of both B-channels of an ISDN Basic Rate Interface (BRI) connection. MP fragments, sequences, and re-orders alternating packets sent across multiple physical connections so that the end result is a single logical link with the combined bandwidth of all of the aggregated physical links. MP is the recommended method of combining multiple B-channels of a BRI connection because the support for bonding—the combining of ISDN B-channels through hardware support—can be specific to the ISDN adapter. MP can be done for any ISDN adapter. MP must be supported on both sides of the connection.

Figure 7.16 illustrates the structure of an MP frame. The payload of a Multilink PPP packet is either a fragment of a PPP frame or the entire PPP frame. Multilink PPP fragmentation need not occur if the Multilink PPP packet fits within the MRU of the link. To prevent improper ordering of the datagrams or fragments across multiple links, additional fields are used between the PPP Protocol field and the IP datagram. Multilink PPP uses the PPP Protocol ID of 0x00-3D.

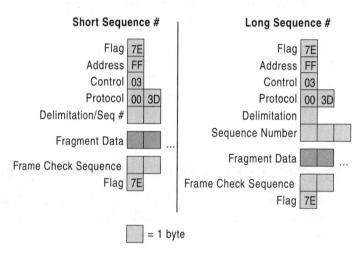

Figure 7.16   Multilink PPP

RFC 1717 defines two different packet formats for short sequence numbers and long sequence numbers. When using either short or long sequence numbers, the sequence number is used to prevent misordering of frames that are sent across multiple links, not to sequence fragments.

For short sequence numbers, a two byte Delimitation/Sequence # field consists of four bits used for delimitation and 12 bits used for the sequence number. Within the delimitation field are two flags. The first bit (the Beginning bit) is an indicator that this fragment begins a sequence of fragments corresponding to a packet. The second bit (the Ending bit) is an indicator that this fragment ends a sequence of fragments corresponding to a packet. The other bits in the first four bits of the short sequence number header are set to 0.

For a PPP frame that is sent without fragmentation, both the Beginning and Ending bits are set. For a PPP frame that is larger than the MRU of the physical link, the PPP frame is fragmented, and each fragment is sent as a separate PPP packet. MP performs a data-link layer fragmentation that is not related to IP fragmentation.

For long sequence numbers, a four byte Delimitation/Sequence # field consists of eight bits (one byte) used for delimitation, and 24 bits (3 bytes) used for the sequence number. Within the delimitation field, the same bits as the short sequence number header define the Beginning bit and the Ending bit. The other bits in the first byte of the long sequence number header are set to 0. The long sequence number header is used by default, unless the short sequence number is chosen during LCP negotiation.

Table 7.16 lists Multilink LCP options negotiated by Microsoft PPP peers. For information about other Multilink options, see RFC 1990.

Table 7.16   Multilink LCP Options

Option Name	Option Type	Option Length	Description
Multilink Maximum Receive Reconstructed Unit	17 or 0x11	4	Specifies the number of octets that a peer can reconstruct when performing reassembly of fragmented MP frames.
Short Sequence Number Header Format	18 or 0x12	2	Specifies the use of the short sequence number in the MP header.
Multilink Endpoint Discriminator	19 or 0x13	9	A unique system identifier to differentiate links from two PPP peers with the same authenticated name.

Bandwidth Allocation Protocol (BAP)

While MP allows for multiple physical links to be aggregated, MP does not provide a mechanism to adapt to changing conditions by adding extra links when needed or terminating extra links when unneeded. This additional capability is provided by the Bandwidth Allocation Protocol (BAP) and the Bandwidth Allocation Control Protocol (BACP) defined in RFC 2125. BAP is a PPP control protocol that is used on an MP connection to dynamically manage links. BAP uses the PPP Protocol of ID 0xC0-2D.

For example, an MP and BAP-enabled remote access client and remote access server create an MP connection consisting of a single physical link. As the utilization of the single link rises to a configured level, the remote access client uses a BAP Call-Request message to request an additional link. The BAP Call-Request message specifies the type of link desired, such as analog phone, ISDN, or X.25. The remote access server then sends a BAP Call-Response message containing the phone number of an available port on the remote access server of the same type specified by the remote access client in the BAP Call-Request.

When the utilization on the second link drops to a specific level, either the remote access client or the remote access server can send a BAP Link-Drop-Query-Request message to drop the link.

BAP also supports a Callback-Request message where the requesting peer specifies the link type and the number to call back to. For more information about BAP messages, see RFC 2125.

Table 7.17 lists BAP LCP options negotiated by Microsoft PPP peers.

Table 7.17   BAP LCP Options

Option Name	Option Type	Option Length	Description
BAP Link Discriminator	23 or 0x17	4	A unique number used to identify a particular link in a Multilink PPP connection.

Multilink PPP and BAP are enabled on the remote access server through the **PPP** tab on the properties of the remote access router in the **Routing and Remote Access** snap-in. Properties of Multilink and BAP are configured from the **Multilink** tab on the properties of a remote access policy profile.

▶ **To set the phone number of a port that is sent in the BAP Call-Response message**

1. Use the **Routing and Remote Access** snap-in to obtain properties on the **Ports** object.

2. Select the desired port, and click **Configure**.

3. Type the phone number in the **Phone number of this device** text box.

Bandwidth Allocation Control Protocol (BACP)

The Bandwidth Allocation Control Protocol (BACP) is a PPP NCP that negotiates a single option: the election of a favored peer. If both peers of an MP and BAP-enabled connection send BAP Call-Request or BAP Link-Drop-Query-Request messages at the same time, the favored peer is the peer whose requests are implemented.

BACP uses the PPP Protocol ID of 0xC0-2B. The packet structure of BACP is exactly the same for LCP, except that only packet types 1 through 7 are defined. For Configure-Request, Configure-Ack, Configure-Nack, and Configure-Reject BACP packet types, the BACP data portion of the BACP packet consists of the single BACP Favored-Peer option listed in Table 7.18.

Table 7.18   BACP Favored Peer Option

Option Name	Option Type	Option Length	Description
Favored-Peer	1	6	A randomly allocated 4-byte magic number used to elect a favored BAP peer. The favored peer is the peer with the lowest magic number.

Remote Access Server and IP Multicast Support

The Windows 2000 remote access server also supports the forwarding of IP multicast traffic between remote access clients and the networks to which the remote access server is attached.

IP multicast support for remote access clients requires the following three elements, as illustrated in Figure 7.17.

1. Internet Group Management Protocol (IGMP) router mode is enabled on the interface connected to all of the remote access clients. In the **Routing and Remote Access** snap-in, this is the **Internal** interface.

2. IGMP proxy mode is enabled on a single interface.

3. The network corresponding to the interface on which IGMP proxy mode is enabled is part of an IP multicast–enabled network. An IP multicast–enabled network uses multicast routing protocols to propagate IP multicast traffic from multicast sources located on any network, to hosts located on any network. For example, the IP multicast-enabled portion of the Internet is called the Multicast Backbone or *MBone*.

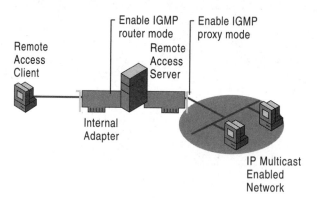

Figure 7.17   Multicast Support for Remote Access

For more information about IP multicasting and its support in Windows 2000 Server, see "IP Multicast Support" in this book.

Note Depending on your choices when running the Routing and Remote Access Server Setup Wizard, IGMP router mode and IGMP proxy mode may already be enabled on the appropriate interfaces.

Multicast Traffic to Remote Access Clients

To facilitate the forwarding of IP multicast traffic from multicast sources on the IP multicast–enabled network to remote access clients:

1. The multicast groups being listened to by remote access clients must be registered with the IP multicast routers of the IP multicast-enabled network.
2. IP multicast traffic from multicast sources must be forwarded to the remote access clients.

Remote Access Client Group Registration

Remote access clients register the IP multicast addresses from which they want to receive traffic by sending IGMP Membership Report messages across the remote access connection. The remote access server records the multicast groups registered by each remote access client and then forwards the IGMP Membership Report message using the interface on which IGMP proxy mode is enabled.

The forwarded IGMP Membership Report message is received by the IP multicast routers attached to the remote access server's network segment. The IP multicast routers of the IP multicast–enabled network use multicast routing protocols to create entries in their multicast forwarding tables, so that multicast traffic sent to the multicast groups — registered by the remote access clients –– are forwarded to the network segment of the remote access server.

Forwarding Multicast Traffic

When the multicast source sends multicast traffic to the multicast group registered by the remote access clients, IP multicast routers forward the multicast traffic to the network segment of the remote access server for the interface on which IGMP proxy mode is enabled.

When the remote access server receives multicast traffic on the interface on which IGMP proxy mode is enabled, the multicast traffic is checked to determine whether any connected remote access client has registered an IGMP Membership Report for that multicast group. If the multicast traffic corresponds to a multicast group registered by a remote access client, the multicast traffic is forwarded to the remote access client.

Multicast Traffic from Remote Access Clients

To facilitate the forwarding of IP multicast traffic from remote access clients that are multicast sources:

1. The multicast groups being listened to by hosts must be registered with the IP multicast routers of the IP multicast–enabled network.

2. IP multicast traffic from the remote access clients must be forwarded to the group members.

Host Group Registration

Hosts on the IP multicast–enabled network register the IP multicast addresses for which they want to receive traffic from by sending IGMP Membership Report messages on their local network segments. The IP multicast routers of the IP multicast–enabled network use multicast routing protocols to create entries in their multicast forwarding tables. Therefore, multicast traffic sent to the multicast groups registered by the hosts are forwarded to the host's network segment.

Forwarding Multicast Traffic

When the remote access client sends multicast traffic across the remote access connection, the multicast traffic is forwarded to the network segment of the interface on the remote access server enabled for IGMP proxy mode. IP multicast routers on that network segment receive the forwarded multicast traffic and forward it to the network segments of the group members.

Additionally, the remote access server forwards the IP multicast traffic to other remote access clients that are listening for the IP multicast traffic of the remote access client that is the multicast source.

Internet-Based IP Multicast Traffic

If the remote access server is being used to provide Internet access to dial-up clients, then the following configuration allows IP multicast traffic to and from connected remote access clients:

1. The remote access server has a direct connection to the Internet's MBone or an indirect connection to the MBone through a logical tunnel.

2. The interface corresponding to the direct or indirect connection to the MBone is added to the IGMP routing protocol and enabled for IGMP proxy mode.

3. The **Internal** interface is added to the IGMP routing protocol and enabled for IGMP router mode.

Organization-Based IP Multicast Traffic

If the remote access server is being used to provide a connection to an organization's intranet to dial-up or VPN clients, then the following configuration allows IP multicast traffic to and from connected remote access clients:

1. The remote access server has a LAN interface on the organization's intranet, which is a network segment on the organization's IP multicast-enabled network.

2. The LAN interface connection to the organization intranet is added to the IGMP routing protocol and enabled for IGMP proxy mode.

3. The **Internal** interface is added to the IGMP routing protocol and enabled for IGMP router mode.

Troubleshooting the Remote Access Server

Troubleshooting remote access is a combination of troubleshooting IP connectivity, addressing, routing, and dial-up hardware. A firm understanding of all of these topics is required. The following sections outline common remote access problems and the troubleshooting tools provided with Windows 2000.

To troubleshoot VPN connections, see "Virtual Private Networking" in this book. To troubleshoot demand-dial routing connections, see "Demand-Dial Routing" in this book.

Common Remote Access Problems

Remote access problems typically include the following:

- Connection attempt is rejected when it should be accepted.
- Connection attempt is accepted when it should be rejected.
- Unable to reach locations beyond the remote access server.
- Miscellaneous remote access problems.

The following sections give troubleshooting tips to isolate the configuration or infrastructure problem causing the remote access problem.

Connection Attempt Is Rejected When It Should Be Accepted

- Verify that the Routing and Remote Access Service is running on the remote access server.

- Verify that remote access is enabled on the remote access server.

- Verify that the dial-up ports on the remote access server are configured to allow inbound remote access connections.

- Verify that the remote access client and the remote access server in conjunction with a remote access policy are enabled to use at least one common authentication method.

- Verify that the remote access client and the remote access server in conjunction with a remote access policy are enabled to use at least one common encryption method.

- Verify that the parameters of the connection attempt are accepted by the currently configured dial-in properties of the user account and remote access policies.

In order for the connection to be established, the parameters of the connection attempt must:

1. Match all of the conditions of at least one remote access policy.

2. Be granted remote access permission, either through the remote access permission of the user account (set to **Allow access**), or the user account is set to **Control access through Remote Access Policy** and the remote access permission of the matching remote access policy is set to **Grant remote access permission**.

3. Match all the settings of the profile.

4. Match all the settings of the dial-in properties of the user account.

- Verify that the settings of the remote access policy profile are not in conflict with properties of the remote access router.

The properties of the remote access policy profile and the properties of the remote access router both contain settings for:

- Multilink

- Bandwidth allocation protocol

- Authentication protocols

If the settings of the profile of the matching remote access policy are in conflict with the settings of the remote access router, then the connection attempt is denied. For example, if the matching remote access policy profile specifies that the EAP-TLS authentication protocol must be used and EAP-TLS is not enabled through the properties of the remote access router, then the remote access server denies the connection attempt.

- For a remote access server that is a member server in a mixed-mode or native-mode Windows 2000 domain that is configured for Windows 2000 authentication, verify that:

  - The **RAS and IAS Servers** security group exists. If not, then create the group and set the group type to **Security** and the group scope to **Domain local**.

  - The **RAS and IAS Servers** security group has **Read** permission to the **RAS and IAS Servers Access Check** object.

  - The computer account of the remote access server computer is a member of the **RAS and IAS Servers** security group. You can use the **netsh ras show registeredserver** command at the Windows 2000 command prompt to view the current registration. You can use the **netsh ras add registeredserver** command to register the server in a specified domain.

- If you add or remove the remote access server computer to the **RAS and IAS Servers** security group, the change does not take effect immediately (due to the way that Windows 2000 caches Active Directory™ directory service information). For the change to take effect immediately, you need to restart the remote access server computer.

- Verify that your dial-up equipment is working properly.

- Verify that all of the dial-up ports on the remote access server are not already connected.

- Verify that the LAN protocols being used by the remote access clients are either enabled for routing or remote access.

- Verify that the remote access client's credentials consisting of user name, password, and domain name are correct and can be validated by the remote access server.

- For connections using MS-CHAP v1 and attampting to negotiate 40-bit MPPE encryption, verify that the user's password is not larger than 14 characters.

- Verify that the user account has not been disabled or is not locked out on the properties of the user account. If the password on the account has expired, verify that the remote access client is using MS-CHAP v1 or MS-CHAP v2. MS-CHAP v1 and MS-CHAP v2 are the only authentication protocols provided with Windows 2000 that allow you to change an expired password during the connection process.

  For an administrator-level account whose password has expired, reset the password using another administrator-level account.

- Verify that the user account has not been locked out due to remote access account lockout.

- If the remote access server is configured with a static IP address pool, verify that there are enough addresses in the pool.

  If all of the addresses in the static pool have been allocated to connected remote access clients, then the remote access server is unable to allocate an IP address. If the remote access client is only configured to use TCP/IP as a LAN protocol, the connection attempt is denied.

- If the remote access client is configured to request its own IPX node number, verify that the server is configured to allow IPX clients to request their own IPX node number.

- If the remote access server is configured with a range of IPX network numbers, verify that the IPX network numbers in the range are not being used elsewhere on your IPX internetwork.

- Verify the configuration of the authentication provider.

  The remote access server can be configured to use either Windows 2000 or RADIUS to authenticate the credentials of the remote access client.

- For a remote access server that is a member of a Windows 2000 native-mode domain, verify that the remote access server has joined the domain.

- For a Windows NT version 4.0 Service Pack 4 and later remote access server that is a member of a Windows 2000 mixed mode domain or a Windows 2000 remote access server that is a member of a Windows NT 4.0 domain that is accessing user account properties for a user account in a trusted Windows 2000 domain, verify that the Everyone group is added to the Pre-Windows 2000 Compatible Access group with the **net localgroup "Pre-Windows 2000 Compatible Access"** command. If not, issue the **net localgroup "Pre-Windows 2000 Compatible Access" everyone /add** command on a domain controller computer and then restart the domain controller computer.

- For a Windows NT version 4.0 Service Pack 3 and earlier remote access server that is a member of a Windows 2000 mixed mode domain, verify that Everyone group has been granted list contents, read all properties, and read permissions to the root node of your domain and all sub-objects of the root domain.

- For RADIUS authentication, verify that the remote access server computer can communicate with the RADIUS server.

- If you are using MS-CHAP v1, verify that you are not using a user password over 14 characters long. If so, either use a different authentication protocol or change the password so that it is 14 characters or less in length.

- Verify that if the Windows 2000 Fax service and the Routing and Remote Access service are sharing the same modem, that the modem supports adaptive answer. If the modem does not support adaptive answer, you must disable fax on the modem to receive incoming remote access connections.

Connection Attempt Is Accepted When It Should Be Rejected

- Verify that the parameters of the connection does not have permission through remote access policies.

  In order for the connection to be rejected, the parameters of the connection attempt must be denied remote access permission one of two ways. Either set the remote access permission of the user account to **Deny access** or set the user account to **Control access through Remote Access Policy,** and then set the remote access permission of the first remote access policy that matches the parameters of the connection attempt to **Deny remote access permission**.

Unable to Reach Locations Beyond the Remote Access Server

- Verify that the LAN protocols being used by the remote access clients are either enabled for routing or enabled to allow access to the network to which the remote access server is attached.

- Verify the IP address allocation settings of the remote access server.

  If the remote access server is configured to use a static IP address pool, verify that the destinations of the address ranges of the static IP address pool are reachable by the hosts and routers of the intranet. If not, then routes corresponding to the address ranges, as defined by the IP address and mask of the range, must be added to the routers of the intranet or enable the routing protocol of your routed infrastructure on the remote access server. If the routes to the remote access client address ranges are not present, remote access clients cannot receive traffic from locations on the intranet. Routes for the address ranges are implemented either through static routing entries or through a routing protocol, such as Open Shortest Path First (OSPF) or Routing Information Protocol (RIP).

  If the remote access server is configured to use DHCP for IP address allocation and no DHCP server is available, the remote access server allocates addresses from the Automatic Private IP Addressing (APIPA) address range from 169.254.0.1 through 169.254.255.254. Allocating APIPA addresses for remote access clients works only if the network to which the remote access server is attached is also using APIPA addresses.

  If the remote access server is using APIPA addresses when a DHCP server is available, verify that the proper adapter is selected from which to obtain DHCP-allocated IP addresses. By default, the remote access server randomly chooses the adapter to use to obtain IP addresses through DHCP. If there is more than one LAN adapter, then the Routing and Remote Access service may choose a LAN adapter for which there is no DHCP server available. You can manually choose a LAN adapter from the **IP** tab on the properties of a remote access server in the **Routing and Remote Access** snap-in.

- If the address ranges of the static IP address pool are a subset of the range of IP addresses for the network to which the remote access server is attached, verify that the address ranges of the static IP address pool are not assigned to other TCP/IP nodes, either through static configuration or through DHCP.

- Verify that packet filters on the remote access policy profile are not preventing the flow of needed IP traffic. TCP/IP packet filters can be configured on the profile properties of the remote access policies on the remote access server (or the RADIUS server if Internet Authentication Service is used) that are used to define traffic that is allowed on the remote access connection.

- If Microsoft remote access clients using only the IPX protocol are unable to create file and print sharing connections to servers that are beyond the remote access server, then NetBIOS over IPX broadcast forwarding must be enabled on the **Internal** interface and the appropriate LAN interfaces. For more information on NetBIOS over IPX broadcasts, see "IPX Routing" in this book.

Callback Problems

- Verify that callback is enabled on the dial-in properties of the user account.

- Verify that **Link Control Protocol (LCP) Extensions** is enabled on the **PPP** tab on the properties of a remote access server in the **Routing and Remote Access** snap-in.

- Verify that the callback numbers are not too long. Callback numbers may be truncated when a remote access server running Windows NT 4.0 requests dial-in properties of a user account in a Windows 2000 native-mode domain.

Troubleshooting Tools

The following tools, which enable you to gather additional information about the source of your problem, are included with Windows 2000.

Authentication and Accounting Logging

A remote access server running Windows 2000 supports the logging of authentication and accounting information for remote access connections in local logging files when Windows authentication or Windows accounting is enabled. This logging is separate from the events recorded in the system event log. You can use the information that is logged to track remote access usage and authentication attempts. Authentication and accounting logging is especially useful for troubleshooting remote access policy issues. For each authentication attempt, the name of the remote access policy that either accepted or rejected the connection attempt is recorded.

The authentication and accounting information is stored in a configurable log file or files stored in the *%SystemRoot%*\System32\LogFiles folder. The log files are saved in Internet Authentication Service (IAS) 1.0 or database format, meaning that any database program can read the log file directly for analysis.

If the remote access server is configured for RADIUS authentication and accounting and the RADIUS server is a Windows 2000 computer running IAS, then the authentication and accounting logs are stored in the *%SystemRoot%*\System32\LogFiles folder on the IAS server computer.

Event Logging

On the **Event logging** tab on the properties of a remote access server, there are four levels of logging. Select **Log the maximum amount of information** and try the connection again. After the connection fails, check the system event log for events logged during the connection process. After you are done viewing remote access events, select the **Log errors and warnings** option on the **Event logging** tab.

Tracing

Tracing records the sequence of programming functions called during a process to a file. Enable tracing for remote access components and try the connection again. After you are done viewing the traced information, reset the tracing settings back to their default values. You can enable PPP tracing from the **Event logging** tab on the properties of a remote access server.

The tracing information can be complex and very detailed. Most of the time this information is useful only to Microsoft support professionals, or to network administrators who are very experienced with the Routing and Remote Access service. The tracing information can be sent to Microsoft support for analysis.

Network Monitor

Network Monitor is a packet capture and analysis tool that you can use to view the traffic sent between a remote access server and remote access client during the remote access connection process and during data transfer. Network Monitor does not interpret the compressed or encrypted portions of remote access traffic.

The proper interpretation of the remote access traffic with Network Monitor requires an understanding of PPP protocols described in this chapter and the referenced RFCs. Network Monitor captures can be saved as files and sent to Microsoft support for analysis.

CHAPTER 8

Internet Authentication Service

The Internet Authentication Service (IAS) in Microsoft® Windows® 2000 is the Microsoft implementation of a Remote Authentication Dial-in User Service (RADIUS) server. IAS performs centralized authentication, authorization, auditing, and accounting (AAAA) of connections for dial-up and virtual private network (VPN) remote access and demand-dial connections, and it can be used in conjunction with the Windows 2000 Routing and Remote Access service. IAS enables the use of a single or multiple vendor network of remote access or VPN equipment.

In This Chapter

Related Information in the Resource Kit

- For more information about remote access, see "Remote Access Server" in this book.

- For more information about virtual private networks, see "Virtual Private Networking" in this book.

- For more information about security policies, see "Security Policies" in the *Microsoft® Windows® 2000 Server Resource Kit Distributed Systems Guide.*

IAS Overview

Internet service providers (ISPs) and corporations maintaining remote access service for their employees are faced with the increasing challenge of managing all remote access from a single point of administration— regardless of the type of remote access equipment employed. The RADIUS standard supports this functionality in a homogeneous, as well as heterogeneous environment. RADIUS is a client-server protocol, which enables remote access equipment acting as RADIUS clients to submit authentication and accounting requests to a RADIUS server.

The RADIUS server has access to user account information and can check remote access authentication credentials. If the user's credentials are authentic and the connection attempt is authorized, the RADIUS server authorizes the user's access based on specified conditions and logs the remote access connections as accounting events.

The use of RADIUS allows the remote access user authentication and authorization and accounting data to be maintained in a central location, rather than on each network access server (NAS). Users connect to RADIUS-compliant NASs, such as a Windows 2000–based computer that is running the Routing and Remote Access service, which in turn, forward authentication requests to the centralized IAS server.

For more information about the RADIUS protocol, see RFCs 2138 and 2139.

IAS also allows companies to outsource remote access infrastructure to ISPs while retaining control over user authentication and authorization, as well as accounting.

Different types of IAS configurations can be created for using Internet technology, such as:

- Dial-up access to your network.
- Extranet access for business partners.
- Internet access.
- Outsourced corporate access through service providers.

Note A company might need to make certain resources on its network available to other companies with which it has partnership agreements. IAS can be used to limit partner access to the corporate network resources, based on restrictions defined for each partner.

IAS Features

The IAS features include the following:

Centralized User Authentication

The authentication of users attempting connections is an important security concern. IAS supports a variety of authentication protocols and allows you to use arbitrary authentication methods to meet your authentication requirements.

The following section describes the authentication methods supported in Windows 2000.

- Point-to-Point Protocol (PPP) is a set of industry-standard framing and authentication protocols that enables remote access solutions to be interoperable in a multivendor network. IAS supports the authentication protocols within PPP, such as Password Authentication Protocol (PAP), Challenge Handshake Authentication Protocol (CHAP), Microsoft Challenge Handshake Authentication Protocol (MS-CHAP) versions 1 and 2, and Extensible Authentication Protocol (EAP).

- Extensible Authentication Protocol (EAP) is an infrastructure that allows the addition of arbitrary authentication methods such as Smart Cards, certificates, one-time passwords, and Token Cards.

- Dialed Number Identification Service (DNIS) is an authorization method based on the number called by the user.

- Automatic Number Identification/Calling Line Identification (ANI/CLI) is an authorization method based on the number the user called from. ANI is also known as Caller ID.

- Guest authentication is an authorization method where the caller does not send a user name or password during the authentication process. If unauthenticated access is enabled, the Guest account is used as the identity of the caller by default.

Outsourced Dialing and Worldwide Remote Access

Outsourced dialing (also referred to as wholesale dialing) involves a contract between an organization or private company (the customer) and an ISP in which the ISP allows the company's employees to connect to the ISP's network before establishing the VPN tunnel to the company's private network. When an employee connects to the ISP's remote access server, the authentication and usage records are forwarded to the IAS server at the company. The IAS server allows the company to control user authentication, track usage, and manage which employees are allowed to gain access the ISP's network.

The advantage of outsourcing is the potential savings. For example, by using an ISP's routers, network access servers, and T1 lines (instead of buying your own), you can save a great deal on hardware (infrastructure) costs. You can also significantly decrease your long-distance phone bill costs by dialing into the ISP's with worldwide connections or roaming consortium's scattered Point of Presence (POPs) belonging to other ISPs. Thus, by handing off support to the provider, you can eliminate a large amount of your administrative budget.

Centralized User Authorization

To grant the connecting user-appropriate access to the network, IAS authenticates users in Microsoft® Windows NT® version 4.0 domains and Windows 2000 Local Security Accounts Manager (SAM). IAS also supports new features in Active Directory directory service, such as user principal names and Universal Groups.

Remote access policies are a set of conditions that network administrators can use to get more flexibility in granting remote access. They provide flexibility in controlling who is allowed to connect to your network. Although it is simple to manage remote access permission for each user account, this approach can become unwieldy as your organization grows. Remote access policies provide a more powerful and flexible way to manage remote access permission.

You can use remote access policies to control remote access based on a variety of conditions, such as:

- User membership in a Windows 2000 security group.
- The time of day, or day of the week of the connection.
- The type of media through which the user is connecting (for example, ISDN, modem, or a VPN tunnel).
- The type of VPN tunneling protocol used (Point-to-Point Tunneling Protocol or Layer Two Tunneling Protocol).
- The phone number the user calls.
- The phone number the user calls from.

Each remote access policy contains a profile of a setting from which you can control connection parameters. For example, you can:

- Permit or deny the use of certain authentication methods.
- Control the amount of time the connection can be idle.
- Control the maximum time of a single session.
- Control the number of links in a multilink session.
- Control encryption settings.
- Add packet filters to control what the user can access when connected to the network. For example, you can use filters to control which IP addresses, hosts, and ports the user is allowed to send or receive packets.
- Create a mandatory tunnel that forces all packets from that connection to be securely tunneled through the Internet and terminated in a private network.
- Allow users to request a specific IP address, or specify that the remote access server must assign an IP address.

Centralized Administration of Remote Access Servers

Support for the RADIUS standard allows IAS to control connection parameters for any network access server that implements that standard. The RADIUS standard also allows individual remote access vendors to create proprietary extensions called vendor-specific attributes. IAS has incorporated the extensions from a number of vendors in its multivendor dictionary.

Centralized Auditing and Usage Accounting

Support for the RADIUS standard allows IAS to collect the usage (accounting) records sent by a NAS at a single point. IAS logs audit information (for example, authentication Accepts and Rejects) and usage information (for example, logon and logoff records) to log files. IAS supports a log-file format that can be directly imported into a database. The data in the database can be analyzed by using third-party data-analysis software.

Integration with Routing and Remote Access Service

The Windows 2000 Routing and Remote Access service is configured to use Windows authentication and accounting, or to use RADIUS authentication and accounting. When RADIUS authentication or accounting is selected, any RFC-compliant RADIUS server can be used. However, using an IAS server is recommended to achieve the optimum level of integration in Windows 2000 environments and take advantage of centralized remote access policies.

For example, in a small network environment or branch offices with a small number of remote access servers and no requirements for centralized management of remote access, the Routing and Remote Access service can be configured to use Windows authentication and accounting.

In a global enterprise with large numbers or remote access servers deployed worldwide, centralized authentication and accounting using IAS can be beneficial. However, if a small branch office is experiencing a low bandwidth connection to the global enterprise with the centralized IAS server, the Windows authentication and accounting configuration can be copied from a central location to the remote access servers of the branch office.

IAS and the Routing and Remote Access service share the same remote access policies and authentication and accounting logging capabilities. When the Routing and Remote Access service is configured for Windows authentication, local policies, and logging are used. When the Routing and Remote Access service is configured as a RADIUS client to an IAS server, the policies and logging of the IAS server are used.

This integration provides consistent implementation across IAS and the Routing and Remote Access service. It allows you to deploy the Routing and Remote Access service in small sites without the need for a separate, centralized IAS server; it also provides the capability to scale up to a centralized remote access management model when you have multiple remote access servers in your organization. In this case, IAS in conjunction with remote access servers implements a single point of administration for remote access to your network for outsourced-dial, demand-dial, and VPN access. The policies within IAS at a central large site can be exported to the independent remote access server in a small site.

Graphical User Interface

IAS provides a graphical user interface (snap-in) that enables you to configure local or remote IAS servers.

Remote Monitoring

You can monitor IAS by using Windows 2000–based tools, such as Event Viewer or System Monitor, or by using Simple Network Management Protocol (SNMP).

Scalability

You can use IAS in a variety of network configurations of varying size, from stand-alone servers for small networks to large corporate and ISP networks.

IAS Software Development Kit

The IAS Software Development Kit (SDK) can be used to:

- Control the number of end-user network sessions.
- Extend the remote access authorizations currently provided by IAS.
- Export usage/audit data to a database.
- Create custom authentication methods for IAS (non-EAP).

EAP Software Development Kit

Provides the capability to implement arbitrary authentication methods using EAP.

Import/Export of Configuration to Manage Multiple IAS Servers

IAS configuration can be imported/exported by running **netsh** from the command prompt.

RADIUS Protocol

Remote Authentication Dial-In User Service (RADIUS) is an industry standard for providing authorization, identification, authentication, and accounting services for distributed dial-up/remote access networking. A RADIUS client, typically a dial-up server used by an ISP, sends user information to a RADIUS server. The RADIUS server validates the RADIUS client request.

For more information about the RADIUS protocol, see RFCs 2138 and 2139.

RADIUS Authentication Operation

The RADIUS authentication process begins when a remote access user presents authentication information to the RADIUS client. After the RADIUS client has obtained such information, it might authenticate by using RADIUS.

For example, when the remote access user sends their credentials using the Challenge Handshake Authentication Protocol (CHAP), the RADIUS client creates a RADIUS Access-Request packet containing such attributes as the user's name, the user's password, the ID of the client and the Port ID the user is accessing. When a password is present, CHAP encrypts the password using a method based on Rivest-Shamir-Adleman (RSA) Message Digest 5 (MD5).

The RADIUS Access-Request packet is sent to the RADIUS server. If no response is returned within a length of time, the request can be re-sent a number of times. The RADIUS client can also forward requests to an alternate server or servers in the event that the primary server is down or unreachable. An alternate server can be used either after a number of tries to the primary server fail, or in a round-robin fashion.

In the case of Routing and Remote Access service, multiple RADIUS servers can be added and prioritized as authentication providers. If a primary RADIUS server does not respond within a three-second time period, the Routing and Remote Access service automatically switches to the RADIUS server with the next highest score.

After the RADIUS server receives the request, it validates the sending RADIUS client. Validation occurs by verifying that the RADIUS Access-Request packet is sent from a configured RADIUS client. If the Access-Request packet was sent by a valid RADIUS client, and if digital signatures are enabled for the RADIUS client, the digital signature in the packet is checked using the shared secret.

A request from a RADIUS client for which the RADIUS server does not have a shared secret is silently discarded. If the RADIUS client is valid, the RADIUS server consults a database of users to find the user whose name matches the request. The user account contains a list of requirements that must be met to allow access for the user. This can include verification of the password, but can also specify whether the user is allowed access.

If any condition where the authentication or authorization is not met, the RADIUS server sends a RADIUS Access-Reject packet in response, indicating that this user request is invalid.

If all conditions are met, the list of configuration values for the user are placed into a RADIUS Access-Accept packet that is sent back to the RADIUS client. These values include a list of RADIUS attributes and all necessary values to deliver the desired service. For SLIP and PPP service types, this can include values such as IP address, subnet mask, MTU, desired compression, and desired packet filter identifiers.

RADIUS Packet Format

The following section provides information that might be useful for the following:

- Debugging a Network Monitor trace.
- Understanding the different packet formats for analyzing the accounting log.
- Entering vendor-specific attribute numbers.

RADIUS packets sent to the RADIUS server are sent as User Datagram Protocol (UDP) messages using UDP port 1812 for RADIUS authentication messages and UDP port 1813 for RADIUS accounting messages. Some older network access servers use UDP port 1645 for RADIUS authentication messages and UDP port 1646 for RADIUS accounting messages. IAS supports the receiving of RADIUS messages on both sets of UDP ports. Exactly one RADIUS packet is encapsulated in the UDP payload.

General Packet Structure

Figure 8.1 shows the general structure of a RADIUS packet.

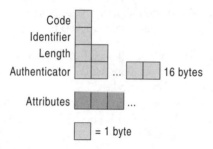

Figure 8.1   General Structure of RADIUS Packet

Code

The Code field is 1 byte long and indicates the type of RADIUS packet. A packet with an invalid Code field is silently discarded. The defined values for the RADIUS Code field are listed in Table 8.1.

Table 8.1   Values for the RADIUS Code Field

Codes (Decimal)	Packets
1	Access-Request
2	Access-Accept
3	Access-Reject
4	Accounting-Request
5	Accounting-Response
11	Access-Challenge
12	Status-Server (experimental)
13	Status-Client (experimental)
255	Reserved

Identifier

The Identifier field is 1 byte long and is used to match a request with its corresponding response.

Length

The Length field is two octets long and indicates the entire length of the packet and RADIUS message, including the Code, Identifier, Length, and Authenticator fields, and the RADIUS Attributes. The Length field can vary from 20 to 4,096 bytes.

Authenticator

The Authenticator field is sixteen octets long and contains the information that the RADIUS client and server use to authenticate each other.

Attributes

The Attributes section of the RADIUS packet contains one or more RADIUS attributes, which carry the specific authentication, authorization, information, and configuration details for RADIUS packets. For attributes that have multiple instances, the order of the attributes must be preserved. Otherwise, attribute types do not have to have their order preserved.

RADIUS Attributes

Figure 8.2 shows the structure of each RADIUS attribute. RADIUS attributes use the common Type-Length-Value format used by other protocols.

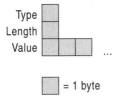

Figure 8.2   RADIUS Attribute Structure

Type

The Type field is 1 byte long and indicates the specific type of RADIUS attribute. For information about the most recent RADIUS attributes, see the Radius Types link on the Web Resources page at http://windows.microsoft.com/windows2000/reskit/webresources.

Some of the attributes are listed in Table 8.2. For information about other RADIUS attributes and their use, see RFCs 2138 and 2139.

Table 8.2   RADIUS Attribute Types

Type Values	Description
1	User-Name
2	User-Password
3	CHAP-Password
4	NAS-IP-Address
5	NAS-Port
6	Service-Type
7	Framed-Protocol
8	Framed-IP-Address
9	Framed-IP-Netmask
10	Framed-Routing
11	Filter-ID
12	Framed-MTU
13	Framed-Compression
19	Reply-Message
24	State
25	Class
26	Vendor-Specific
27	Session-Timeout
28	Idle-Timeout
29	Termination-Action
32	NAS-Identifier
61	NAS-Port-Type
62	Port-Limit

Type values 192 through 223 are reserved for experimental use, values 224 through 240 are reserved for implementation-specific use, and values 241 through 255 are reserved and must not be used. Value 26 is reserved for vendor-specific attributes (VSAs).

Length

The Length field indicates the length of the attribute, including the Type, Length, and Value fields.

Value

The Value field is zero or more octets and contains information specific to the Attribute. The format and length of the Value field is based on the type of RADIUS attribute.

Vendor-Specific Attributes

VSAs are available to allow vendors to support their own proprietary attributes that are not covered by RFC 2138. IAS includes VSAs from a number of vendors in its multivendor dictionary. However, this list evolves over time and new attributes and vendors are always being added.

To accommodate for attributes that are not in the IAS multivendor dictionary, IAS allows you to add them as Vendor-Specific (attribute type 26) in the **Advanced** tab of a remote access policy profile. To use attribute type 26, an administrator needs to know the VSA format, as well as the exact information to enter. The VSA formats are documented in the following section. For information about what to enter, see your NAS documentation.

The structure of the vendor-specific attribute is shown in Figure 8.3.

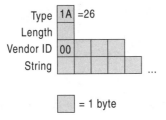

Figure 8.3   Vendor-Specific Attribute Structure

Type
The Type value is set to 26 (0x1A) to indicate a VSA.

Length
The Length value is set to the number of bytes in the VSA.

Vendor-ID
The high-order octet is 0 (0x00) and 4 octets long, and the low-order 3 octets are the Structure and Identification of Management Information (SMI) Network Management Private Enterprise Code of the vendor.

String

The String field is the VSA consisting of one or more octets. To conform with the recommendation of RFC 2138, the String field should consist of the fields as shown in Figure 8.4.

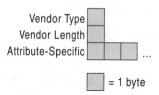

Vendor Type
Vendor Length
Attribute-Specific

 ...

 = 1 byte

Figure 8.4   Structure of the String Field

Vendor Type

The Type value is used to indicate a specific VSA for the vendor.

Vendor Length

The Type value is set to the number of bytes in the string.

Attribute-Specific

The Attribute-Specific field contains the data for the specific vendor attribute.

Vendors that do not conform to RFC 2138 use the attribute type 26 to identify a vendor-specific attribute but do not use the Vendor Type, Vendor Length, and Attribute-Specific fields within the String field. In this case, the vendor-specific attribute format appears as shown in Figure 8.4.

When adding a VSA for a particular NAS as type 26, you need to know whether the attribute conforms to RFC 2138. For information about whether your NAS uses the VSA format documented in Figure 8.4, see your NAS documentation.

VSAs are configured from the **Vendor-Specific Attribute Information** dialog box when adding a Vendor-Specific Attribute from the **Advanced** tab of a remote access policy profile. If the VSA format conforms to RFC 2138, select the **Yes. It conforms.** option and configure the attribute with the vendor-assigned attribute number, attribute format, and attribute value as defined in NAS documentation. If the VSA format does not conform to RFC 2138, choose **No. It does not conform.**, and configure the attribute with the hexadecimal attribute value, which includes the string of the VSA format (everything after Vendor-ID) as defined in NAS documentation. For more information about configuring vendor-specific attributes, see "IAS Authorization" later in this chapter.

RADIUS Packet Example

A Windows 2000 PPTP client attempts a remote access connection to a Windows 2000 VPN server. The VPN server is at the IP address 10.10.210.13, and the IAS server is at the IP address 10.10.210.12.

Access-Request Packet

The following Network Monitor trace shows the Access-Request packet sent by the VPN server to the IAS server.

```
+ IP: ID = 0x850; Proto = UDP; Len: 248
+ UDP: Src Port: Unknown, (1327); Dst Port: Unknown (1812); Length = 228
(0xE4)
  RADIUS: Message Type: Access Request(1)
      RADIUS: Message Type = Access Request
      RADIUS: Identifier = 2 (0x2)
      RADIUS: Length = 220 (0xDC)
      RADIUS: Authenticator = 8A 6F DC 03 23 5F 4B 62 CA 40 92 38 DC 75
                              CB 74
      RADIUS: Attribute Type: NAS IP Address(4)
          RADIUS: Attribute type = NAS IP Address
          RADIUS: Attribute length = 6 (0x6)
          RADIUS: NAS IP address = 10.10.210.13
      RADIUS: Attribute Type: Service Type(6)
          RADIUS: Attribute type = Service Type
          RADIUS: Attribute length = 6 (0x6)
          RADIUS: Service type = Framed
      RADIUS: Attribute Type: Framed Protocol(7)
          RADIUS: Attribute type = Framed Protocol
          RADIUS: Attribute length = 6 (0x6)
          RADIUS: Framed protocol = PPP
      RADIUS: Attribute Type: NAS Port(5)
          RADIUS: Attribute type = NAS Port
          RADIUS: Attribute length = 6 (0x6)
          RADIUS: NAS port = 32 (0x20)
      RADIUS: Attribute Type: Vendor Specific(26)
          RADIUS: Attribute type = Vendor Specific
          RADIUS: Attribute length = 12 (0xC)
          RADIUS: Vendor ID = 311 (0x137)
          RADIUS: Vendor string =      □
      RADIUS: Attribute Type: Vendor Specific(26)
          RADIUS: Attribute type = Vendor Specific
          RADIUS: Attribute length = 18 (0x12)
          RADIUS: Vendor ID = 311 (0x137)
          RADIUS: Vendor string = MSRASV5.00
      RADIUS: Attribute Type: NAS Port Type(61)
          RADIUS: Attribute type = NAS Port Type
          RADIUS: Attribute length = 6 (0x6)
          RADIUS: NAS port type = Virtual
```

```
RADIUS: Attribute Type: Tunnel Type(64)
    RADIUS: Attribute type = Tunnel Type
    RADIUS: Attribute length = 6 (0x6)
    RADIUS: Tag = 0 (0x0)
    RADIUS: Tunnel type = Point-to-Point Tunneling Protocol(PPTP)
RADIUS: Attribute Type: Tunnel Media Type(65)
    RADIUS: Attribute type = Tunnel Media Type
    RADIUS: Attribute length = 6 (0x6)
    RADIUS: Tag = 0 (0x0)
    RADIUS: Tunnel media type = IP (IP version 4)
RADIUS: Attribute Type: Calling Station ID(31)
    RADIUS: Attribute type = Calling Station ID
    RADIUS: Attribute length = 14 (0xE)
    RADIUS: Calling station ID = 10.10.14.226
RADIUS: Attribute Type: Tunnel Client Endpoint(66)
    RADIUS: Attribute type = Tunnel Client Endpoint
    RADIUS: Attribute length = 14 (0xE)
    RADIUS: Tunnel client endpoint = 10.10.14.226
RADIUS: Attribute Type: User Name(1)
    RADIUS: Attribute type = User Name
    RADIUS: Attribute length = 18 (0x12)
    RADIUS: User name = NTRESKIT\johndoe
RADIUS: Attribute Type: Vendor Specific(26)
    RADIUS: Attribute type = Vendor Specific
    RADIUS: Attribute length = 24 (0x18)
    RADIUS: Vendor ID = 311 (0x137)
    RADIUS: Vendor string = □¦ì½+-_¦e□$+fN<àN
RADIUS: Attribute Type: Vendor Specific(26)
    RADIUS: Attribute type = Vendor Specific
    RADIUS: Attribute length = 58 (0x3A)
    RADIUS: Vendor ID = 311 (0x137)
    RADIUS: Vendor string = □4
```

The RADIUS attributes sent by the VPN server include the user name, the service types, the framed protocol, various tunnel attributes for the PPTP connection, and a series of vendor-specific attributes for MS-CHAP authentication. For more information about Microsoft VSAs, see RFC 2548.

Access-Accept Packet

The following Network Monitor trace shows the Access-Accept packet sent by the IAS server to the VPN server.

```
+ IP: ID = 0xB18; Proto = UDP; Len: 248
+ UDP: Src Port: Unknown, (1812); Dst Port: Unknown (1327); Length = 228
(0xE4)
  RADIUS: Message Type: Access Accept(2)
      RADIUS: Message Type = Access Accept
      RADIUS: Identifier = 2 (0x2)
      RADIUS: Length = 220 (0xDC)
      RADIUS: Authenticator = 52 E2 19 98 2E F8 E2 D3 B7 3B E1 24 5B 72
                              55 9E
      RADIUS: Attribute Type: Framed Protocol(7)
          RADIUS: Attribute type = Framed Protocol
          RADIUS: Attribute length = 6 (0x6)
          RADIUS: Framed protocol = PPP
      RADIUS: Attribute Type: Service Type(6)
          RADIUS: Attribute type = Service Type
          RADIUS: Attribute length = 6 (0x6)
          RADIUS: Service type = Framed
      RADIUS: Attribute Type: Class(25)
          RADIUS: Attribute type = Class
          RADIUS: Attribute length = 32 (0x20)
          RADIUS: Class = <$□@
      RADIUS: Attribute Type: Vendor Specific(26)
          RADIUS: Attribute type = Vendor Specific
          RADIUS: Attribute length = 42 (0x2A)
          RADIUS: Vendor ID = 311 (0x137)
          RADIUS: Vendor string = □$Ç□DZ¦,S‾c7□_æ:+□RW_tÖ-qxF¦
(-+¦%p6
      RADIUS: Attribute Type: Vendor Specific(26)
          RADIUS: Attribute type = Vendor Specific
          RADIUS: Attribute length = 42 (0x2A)
          RADIUS: Vendor ID = 311 (0x137)
          RADIUS: Vendor string = □$Ç□
      RADIUS: Attribute Type: Vendor Specific(26)
          RADIUS: Attribute type = Vendor Specific
          RADIUS: Attribute length = 51 (0x33)
          RADIUS: Vendor ID = 311 (0x137)
          RADIUS: Vendor string = □-
      RADIUS: Attribute Type: Vendor Specific(26)
          RADIUS: Attribute type = Vendor Specific
          RADIUS: Attribute length = 21 (0x15)
          RADIUS: Vendor ID = 311 (0x137)
          RADIUS: Vendor string =
```

The RADIUS attributes sent by the IAS server include the user name, the service type, the framed protocol, the service class, and a series of vendor-specific attributes for MS-CHAP authentication.

IAS Authentication

In the process of identifying dial-up users and admitting them to a secure network or site, different servers handle different aspects of the task.

A network access server (NAS) operates as a client of an IAS server. The client is responsible for passing user information to designated IAS servers, and then acting on the response.

IAS is responsible for receiving user connection requests, authenticating the user, authorizing the connection attempt, and then returning all configuration information necessary for the RADIUS client to deliver service to the user. Figure 8.5 illustrates the general IAS authentication process.

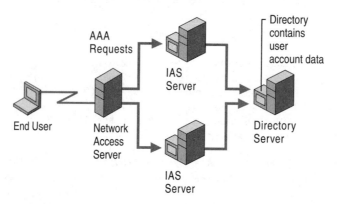

Figure 8.5   IAS Authentication Process

When a user attempts to connect to a network through a dial-up connection or virtual private network, the authentication request is processed as follows:

1. The NAS tries to negotiate a connection with the remote access client by using the most secure protocol first, then the next least secure protocol, and so on, down to the least secure protocol (for example, NAS tries to negotiate a connection by using EAP, MS-CHAP, then CHAP, and finally PAP).

2. The NAS forwards the authentication request to an IAS server in the form of a RADIUS Access-Request packet.

3. The IAS server first verifies that the RADIUS Access-Request packet is sent from a configured RADIUS client by checking the source IP address. If the Access-Request packet was sent by a valid RADIUS client, and if digital signatures are enabled for the RADIUS client, the digital signature in the packet is checked using the shared secret. A shared secret is a text string that serves as a special password between RADIUS server and the RADIUS clients connected to it. Each IAS server must have a shared secret for each NAS or other IAS server that forwards RADIUS requests to it.

There are a few rules you must follow to successfully set up a shared secret:

- The shared secret must be exactly the same at both servers.

- Secrets are case-sensitive.

- Secrets can use any standard alphanumeric characters or any special characters.

4. If digital signatures are enabled and the verification of the digital signature fails, IAS server silently discards the packet. When the NAS does not get a response within its time-out period, it retries and then disconnects the user. If IAS server cannot connect to the domain controller or cannot find the domain controller the user belongs to, it silently discards the packet. This allows a RADIUS proxy to retransmit the request to the backup IAS server, which would then attempt to authenticate the user against the domain's database.

5. If digital signatures are enabled and the verification of the digital signature is successful, the IAS server queries the Windows 2000–based domain controller, which validates the user credentials.

6. If the user credentials are authentic, the IAS server evaluates the connection attempt against the configured remote access policies and the dial-in properties of the user's account to decide whether to authorize the request. If the connection attempt matches the conditions of at least one policy and the user account dial-in properties, remote access policy properties and the remote access policy profile properties authorize the connection, IAS sends a RADIUS Access-Accept message to the NAS that sent the Access-Request message. The Access-Accept message authorizes the connection but also contains connection parameters based on the remote access policy profile settings and the dial-in properties of the user account. The NAS interprets this authorization data to determine the connection parameters that the server has authorized.

If the user is not authentic or the user's attempt to connect does not match conditions in at least one policy, or matches conditions in a policy that denies access, IAS sends a RADIUS Access-Reject message to the NAS, and the NAS disconnects the user.

IAS Step-by-Step Authentication and Authorization

The diagram shown in Figure 8.6a and Figure 8.6b demonstrates the step-by-step IAS authentication and authorization process.

Note The authentication and authorization process for the Routing and Remote Access service, when configured for Windows authentication, uses steps 4 through 14 of this process. In all steps, no RADIUS packets are sent. The authentication and authorization success and failure are the return values of functions called by the Routing and Remote Access service. Local event or authentication logging depends on the configured logging settings of the Routing and Remote Access service. For more information, see "Routing and Remote Access Service" in this book.

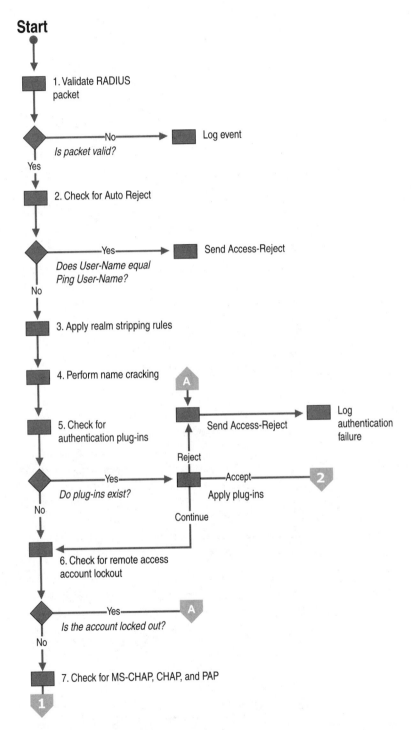

Figure 8.6a   IAS Authentication and Authorization Process

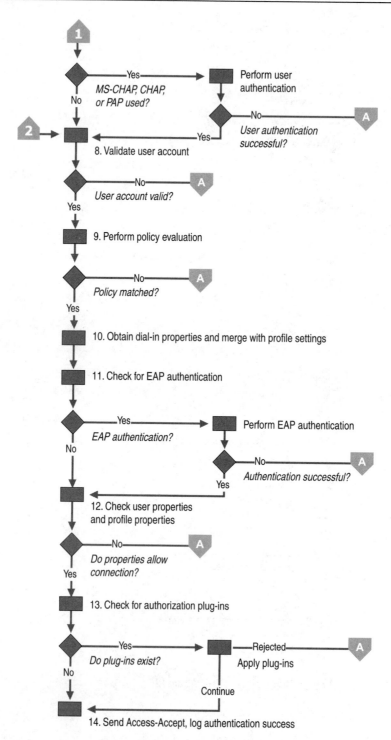

Figure 8.6b   IAS Authentication and Authorization Process

1. Validate RADIUS packet

   The incoming Access-Request packet is validated for source IP address, the digital signature, valid attributes, and so on.

   If the RADIUS packet is not valid, an event is logged in the system event log and the RADIUS Access-Request packet is discarded. An Access-Reject message is not sent.

2. Check for Auto Reject

   Auto Reject is used to send an immediate Access-Reject packet when the User-Name attribute in the Access-Request packet matches a specific value. The periodic sending of an Access-Request packet and reception of an Access-Reject packet assures the RADIUS client that the RADIUS server is still present on the network. An Auto Reject Access-Request message requires special handling because it does not need to be evaluated for authentication and authorization. No authentication log entry is created for Auto Reject requests. This is done to prevent Auto Reject messages from filling up the authentication log file.

   To configure IAS for Auto Reject, configure the **Ping User-Name** registry setting (HKEY_LOCAL_MACHINE\SYSTEM\CurrentControlSet\Services\IAS \Parameters) with the user name for Auto Reject packets. If the User-Name attribute of the Access-Request packet matches the Ping User-Name registry setting, an Access-Reject message is sent.

3. Apply realm stripping rules

   If the User-Name attribute in the Access-Request packet is not the Auto Reject name, then the user identity is determined. User identity is how IAS identifies the user for the purposes of authentication and authorization. Normally, the user identity is the string value of the User-Name RADIUS attribute. If the User-Name attribute is not present, the user identity is set to the Guest account or the account specified by the **Default User Identity** registry value (HKEY_LOCAL_MACHINE\SYSTEM\CurrentControlSet\Services \RemoteAccess\Policy).

   However, IAS can use any RADIUS attribute to identify the user. The RADIUS attribute that IAS uses to identify the user is configurable by setting the **User Identity Attribute** registry setting (HKEY_LOCAL_MACHINE\SYSTEM\CurrentControlSet\Services\RemoteA ccess\Policy) to the number of the RADIUS attribute that is used for the user identity. By default, **User Identity Attribute** is set to 1, the RADIUS type value for the User-Name RADIUS attribute. For more information about the use of the **User Identity Attribute** registry setting, see "Unauthenticated Access" later in this chapter.

Realm stripping rules are then applied and define how the user identity is manipulated before the name is checked for existence. The realm stripping rules consist of an ordered set of <Original string to match>, <Replacement String>. IAS applies the realm stripping rules to the user identity in the configured order. For information about how to configure realm stripping and examples of using pattern matching syntax to create realm stripping rules, see Windows 2000 Server Help.

4. Perform name cracking

   Name cracking is the resolution of the user identity to a user account using user principal names, Lightweight Directory Access Protocol (LDAP), distinguished names (DNA), Canonical Names, and so on. If a user principal name is encountered by IAS, IAS performs a query to the Active Directory Global Catalog in an attempt to resolve the name. To speed up this process, a copy of the Global Catalog must be located on a domain controller within the same site as the IAS server.

   When the user identity does not contain a domain name, IAS supplies a domain name. By default, the IAS-supplied domain name is the domain for which the IAS server is a member. You can specify the IAS-supplied domain through the DefaultDomain registry setting (HKEY_LOCAL_MACHINE\SYSTEM\CurrentControlSet\Services\RasMan\ PPP\ControlProtocols \BuiltIn).

5. Check for authentication plug-ins

   The existence of authentication plug-ins is checked. Authentication plug-ins are optional components created using the IAS SDK. Each plug-in can return either Accept, Reject, or Continue. If an authentication plug-in returns an Accept, the user is considered to be authenticated and the account is then validated. If the authentication plug-in returns a Reject, an Access-Reject packet is sent and the authentication failure event is logged in the system event log or the IAS authentication log, depending on the configured logging settings. If the authentication plug-in returns a Continue, the next plug-in is checked. If there are no more plug-ins, the user still needs to be authenticated.

   The authentication plug-in can also return RADIUS attributes to be included in the Access-Accept packet.

6. Check for remote access account lockout

   After the authentication plug-ins are checked, the registry on the IAS server is read for the remote access account lockout entry for the user account. If the account is locked out through remote access account lockout, IAS sends an Access-Reject message back to the NAS and logs an authentication event.

Note Remote access account lockout is a security feature that is enabled through the Windows 2000 registry. Remote access account lockout is used to prevent dictionary attacks against user accounts. For more information about remote access account lockout, see "Remote Access Server" in this book. Remote access account lockout is not related to account lockout on the Windows 2000 user account and the implementation of account lockout policies by using Windows 2000 Group Policy.

7. Check for MS-CHAP, CHAP, and PAP

   If the Microsoft Challenge Handshake Authentication Protocol (MS-CHAP) version 1 or version 2, CHAP, or Password Authentication Protocol (PAP) are used to authenticate the remote access client, IAS consults an authentication submodule based on the authentication protocol to perform the authentication. The user's credentials, the user name and password, are authenticated against the user name and password of the accounts database (a domain or the local accounts database) and the group membership of the user account is determined. The exact method of authentication varies depending on the authentication protocol.

   If the authentication of the credentials is not successful, an Access-Reject packet is sent and the authentication failure event is logged in the system event log or the IAS authentication log depending on the configured logging settings.

   If either EAP or unauthenticated access is being used, then the user authentication process is bypassed. EAP authentication takes place later in this process. For unauthenticated access, no user authentication is performed.

8. Validate user account

   Based on the user account determined through name cracking, the user account is validated to check whether the account is locked out (which is not the same as remote access account lockout), whether the account is disabled, and whether the user account's password has expired. If the user account is not valid, an Access-Reject packet is sent and the authentication failure event is logged in the system event log or the IAS authentication log depending, on the configured logging settings.

9. Perform policy evaluation

   Remote access policies configured on the IAS server are evaluated to find a policy that matches the parameters of the connection. If a matching policy is not found, an Access-Reject packet is sent and an event is logged. For more information about remote access policies and policy evaluation logic, see "Remote Access Policies" later in this chapter.

10. Obtain dial-in properties and merge with profile settings

    The dial-in properties for the user account associated with the connection and the profile properties from the matching policy are merged into a set of properties for the connection.

11. Check for EAP authentication

    If EAP is the authentication protocol used for the connection attempt, EAP authentication takes place. The initial negotiation for EAP consists of selecting EAP as the PPP authentication protocol and negotiating an EAP type. Based on the EAP type, the profile settings for the matching policy are checked to ensure that the EAP type is allowed. If the EAP type is not allowed with the profile settings, an Access-Reject packet is sent and the authentication failure event is logged in the system event log or the IAS authentication log, depending on the configured logging settings.

    If the EAP type is allowed with the profile settings, EAP authentication for the EAP type occurs. IAS sends an EAP challenge to NAS asking it to start EAP negotiation. Communications between EAP dynamic-link libraries (DLLs) on a client and server side are tunneled between the client and the IAS server using the RADIUS protocol. After complete, an EAP provider can return attributes that are sent back to the NAS in the Access-Accept packet. If EAP authentication fails, an Access-Reject packet is sent and the authentication failure event is logged in the system event log or the IAS authentication log, depending on the configured logging settings.

12. Check user properties and profile properties

    The dial-in properties of the user account and the profile properties of the matching remote access policy are evaluated against the parameters of the connection attempt to ensure that the connection attempt is allowed. If the connection attempt is not allowed, an Access-Reject packet is sent and the authentication failure event is logged in the system event log or the IAS authentication log, depending on the configured logging settings.

13. Check for authorization plug-ins

    The existence of authorization plug-ins is checked. Authorization plug-ins are optional components created using the IAS SDK. Each plug-in can return either Reject or Continue. If the authorization plug-in returns a Reject, an Access-Reject packet is sent and the authentication failure event is logged in the system event log or the IAS authentication log, depending on the configured logging settings. If the authorization plug-in returns Continue, the next plug-in is checked. If there are no more plug-ins, the user is considered to be authorized.

    The authorization plug-in can also return RADIUS attributes to be included in the Access-Accept packet.

14. Send Access-Accept

   If the dial-in properties of the user account, the profile properties of the matching remote access policy, and the conditions imposed by authorization plug-ins allow the connection attempt, an Access-Accept packet is sent back to the NAS with the set of RADIUS attributes for the restrictions on the connection and an authentication success event is logged in the system event log or the IAS authentication log, depending on the configured logging settings.

Compulsory Tunneling with IAS

The benefit of using IAS with tunnels is that IAS can be configured to direct the traffic from the client through a tunnel to a particular location. Depending on the category of authenticating user, a tunnel can be created to different parts of the corporate network.

Note For information about tunneling and the use of tunneling in Windows 2000, see "Virtual Private Networking" in this book.

Tunnels can be created in different ways. The following sections describe the two main tunnel types: voluntary tunneling and compulsory tunneling.

Voluntary Tunneling

A user or client computer can issue a VPN request to configure and create a voluntary tunnel. In this case, the user's computer is a tunnel endpoint and acts as the tunnel client. Voluntary tunneling occurs when a workstation or router uses tunneling client software to create a VPN connection to the target tunnel server. In order to accomplish this, the appropriate tunneling protocol must be installed on the client computer.

In a dial-up situation, the client must establish a dial-up connection to the internetwork before the client can set up a tunnel. This is the most common case. The best example of this is the dial-up Internet user, who must dial an ISP and obtain an Internet connection before a tunnel over the Internet can be created. Figure 8.7 shows a voluntary tunnel created between a dial-up user and a tunnel server.

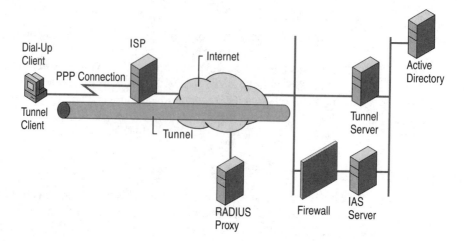

Figure 8.7   Voluntary Tunnel Created by a Dial-Up User

Figure 8.7 shows IAS as it is used in an outsourced bulk dial scenario for voluntary tunneling. A dial-up client establishes a dial-up connection to an ISP. In the outsourced bulk, dial scenario, the dial-up client calls an ISP that is providing Internet access for all the employees of an organization. Based on the dial-up connection parameters, the NAS dialed by the dial-up client sends an Access-Request packet to a configured RADIUS proxy computer. The RADIUS proxy, based on the realm name in the User-Name attribute, forwards the Access-Request packet to the IAS server of the organization that is reachable on the Internet through a firewall. The organization IAS server authenticates and authorizes the connection attempt of the dial-up client and sends an Access-Accept packet back to the RADIUS proxy. The RADIUS proxy forwards the Access-Accept packet to the ISP NAS and the ISP NAS connects the dial-up client to the Internet.

After on the Internet, the dial-up client initiates a tunnel connection with the organization tunnel server on the Internet. Based on the tunnel connection parameters, the tunnel server sends an Access-Request packet to the organization IAS server. The organization IAS server authenticates and authorizes the connection attempt of the tunnel client and sends an Access-Accept packet back to the tunnel server. The tunnel server completes the tunnel creation and the tunnel client can now send packets to the organization intranet through the tunnel.

Note The authentication type and level of encryption might be different for the dial-up connection and the tunnel. For example, the dial-up connection to the ISP might use CHAP, but the tunnel might choose a more secure authentication type such as MS-CHAP v2 or EAP-TLS.

Compulsory Tunneling

Compulsory tunneling is the creation of a secure tunnel by another computer or network device on the client computer's behalf. Compulsory tunnels are configured and created automatically for the user without their knowledge or intervention. With a compulsory tunnel, the user's computer is not a tunnel endpoint. Another device between the user's computer and the tunnel server is the tunnel endpoint, acting as the tunnel client. The dial-up access server dialed by the client computer is the tunnel endpoint, acting as the tunnel client.

A number of vendors that sell dial-up access servers have implemented the ability to create a tunnel on behalf of a dial-up client. The computer or network device providing the tunnel for the client computer is known as a Front End Processor (FEP) in PPTP, an L2TP Access Concentrator (LAC) in L2TP, or an IP Security Gateway in IPSec. For the purposes of this chapter, the term FEP is used to describe this functionality, regardless of the tunneling protocol. To carry out its function, the FEP must have the appropriate tunneling protocol installed and must be capable of establishing the tunnel when the client computer attempts a connection.

A corporation can contract with an ISP to deploy a nationwide set of FEPs. These FEPs can establish tunnels across the Internet to a tunnel server connected to the corporation's private network, thereby consolidating calls from geographically diverse locations into a single Internet connection at the corporate network.

Figure 8.8 shows the client computer placing a dial-up call to a tunneling-enabled NAS at the ISP, in order to authenticate against an IAS server on the other side of the tunnel.

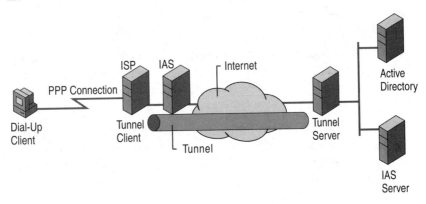

Figure 8.8   Compulsory Tunnel Created by a Tunneling-Enabled NAS

Figure 8.8 shows IAS as it is used in an outsourced bulk dial scenario for compulsory tunneling.

A dial-up client establishes a dial-up connection to an ISP. In the outsourced bulk dial scenario, the dial-up client calls an ISP that is providing tunneled access across the Internet for all the employees of an organization. Based on the dial-up connection parameters, the NAS dialed by the dial-up client sends an Access-Request packet to a configured IAS server. The ISP IAS server authorizes the tunnel connection and sends back an Access-Accept packet with a series of tunnel attributes. If needed, the IAS NAS creates a tunnel to the organization tunnel server on the Internet.

Note Normally IAS provides both authentication and authorization. In this case, however, it is common for the ISP IAS server to provide authorization only. Because the dial-in client is performing authentication against the organization tunnel server, authentication against the ISP NAS is not necessary.

The ISP NAS then sends a PPP message to the dial-up client to restart the authentication process so that the dial-up user can be authenticated against the organization tunnel server. The dial-up client sends its authentication information to the IAS NAS, which encapsulates it and sends it through the tunnel to the tunnel server.

After the authentication credentials are received by the tunnel server, the tunnel server sends an Access-Request packet to the organization IAS server. The organization IAS server authenticates and authorizes the connection of the dial-up client to the tunnel server and sends an Access-Accept packet to the tunnel server. The tunnel server then completes the connection to the dial-up client.

All data that is sent by the dial-up client is automatically sent through the tunnel to the tunnel server by the ISP NAS.

This configuration is known as compulsory tunneling because the client is compelled to use the tunnel created by the FEP. After the initial connection is made, all network traffic to and from the client is automatically sent through the tunnel. IAS can be configured to instruct a FEP to tunnel different dial-up clients to different tunnel servers.

Unlike the separate tunnels created for each voluntary client, a compulsory tunnel between the FEP and tunnel server can be shared by multiple dial-up clients. When a second client dials into the access server (the FEP) to reach a destination for which a tunnel already exists, the data traffic for the new client is carried over the existing tunnel.

Note Using a RADIUS proxy in compulsory tunnels is not recommended. A proxy can decrypt a tunnel's password because it uses the shared secret between the proxy and IAS to encrypt the password.

The following RADIUS Attributes are used to carry the tunneling information from the IAS server to the NAS.

Used in authorization only:

- Tunnel-Private-Group-ID
- Tunnel-Assignment-ID
- Tunnel-Preference
- Tunnel-Password (not for use with proxies)

Used in authorization and accounting:

- Tunnel-Type (PPTP, L2TP, and so on)
- Tunnel-Medium-Type (X.25, ATM, Frame Relay, IP, and so on)
- Tunnel-Client-Endpoint
- Tunnel-Server-Endpoint

Used for accounting only:

- Acct-Tunnel-Connection

The Windows 2000 Routing and Remote Access service cannot be used as a FEP for compulsory tunneling.

Authentication Methods

There are a number of PPP authentication protocols that are supported by the RADIUS protocol. Each protocol has advantages and disadvantages in terms of security, usability, and breadth of support. The protocol used is determined by the configuration of the NAS device. See your NAS documentation if you are configuring a dial-up network, or consult your ISP if you are using an ISP for dial-up access to your LAN.

The following sections focus on the advantages and disadvantages of the authentication protocols currently supported by IAS. The information is also useful in configuring a particular authentication method for remote access.

Password Authentication Protocol

Password Authentication Protocol (PAP) passes a password as a string from the user's computer to the NAS device. When the NAS forwards the password, it is encrypted using the RADIUS shared secret as an encryption key. PAP is the most flexible protocol because passing a plaintext password to the authentication server enables that server to compare the password with nearly any storage format. For example, UNIX passwords are stored as one-way encrypted strings that cannot be decrypted. PAP passwords can be compared to these strings by reproducing the encryption method.

Because it uses a plaintext version of the password, PAP has a number of security vulnerabilities. Although the RADIUS protocol encrypts the password, it is transmitted as plaintext across the dial-up connection.

Enabling PAP

To enable PAP-based authentication, you must do the following:

1. Enable PAP as an authentication protocol on the remote access server. For information about a default setting on a particular NAS, see your NAS documentation. On the Routing and Remote Access service, PAP is disabled by default.

2. Enable PAP on the appropriate remote access policy. PAP is disabled by default.

3. Enable PAP on a remote access client.

Note Enabling PAP as an authentication protocol means that user passwords are sent from a client to a NAS in plaintext form. The NAS encrypts the password using the shared secret and sends it in an Access-Request packet. Because a RADIUS proxy must encrypt the PAP password using the shared secret of its forwarding RADIUS server, a RADIUS proxy must decrypt the PAP password using the shared secret between the RADIUS proxy and the NAS. A malicious user at a RADIUS proxy can record user names and passwords for PAP connections. For this reason, the use of PAP is highly discouraged, especially for virtual private network connections.

Challenge Handshake Authentication Protocol

Challenge Handshake Authentication Protocol (CHAP) is designed to address the concern of passing passwords in plaintext. By using CHAP, the NAS sends a random number challenge to the user's computer. The challenge and the user's password are then hashed by using MD5. The client computer then sends the hash as a response to the NAS challenge and the NAS forwards both the challenge and response in the RADIUS Access-Request packet.

When the authenticating server receives the RADIUS packet, it uses the challenge and the user's password to create its own version of the response. If the version of the server matches the response supplied by the user's computer, the access request is accepted.

CHAP responses cannot be reused because NAS devices send a unique challenge each time a client computer connects to them. Because the algorithm for calculating CHAP responses is well known, it is very important that passwords be carefully chosen and sufficiently long. CHAP passwords that are common words or names are vulnerable to dictionary attacks if they can be discovered by comparing responses to the CHAP challenge with every entry in a dictionary. Passwords that are not sufficiently long can be discovered by brute force by comparing the CHAP response to sequential trials until a match to the user's response is found.

Historically, CHAP is the most common dial-up authentication protocol used. When the server does not store the same password that was used to calculate the CHAP response, it cannot calculate an equivalent response. Because standard CHAP clients use the plaintext version of the password to create the CHAP challenge response, passwords must be stored in plaintext on the server to calculate an equivalent response.

Although the IAS server supports CHAP, a Windows NT 4.0–based domain controller cannot validate CHAP requests without support for storing reversibly encrypted passwords. This support is available in Windows 2000; in Windows NT 4.0, this support is available through an update to the Windows NT 4.0–based domain controller.

Enabling CHAP

To enable CHAP-based authentication, you must do the following:

1. Enable CHAP as an authentication protocol on the remote access server. For information about a default setting on a particular NAS, see your NAS documentation. For the Routing and Remote Access service, CHAP is enabled by default.

2. Enable CHAP on the appropriate remote access policy. CHAP is enabled by default.

3. Enable storage of a reversibly encrypted form of the user's password. For a Windows 2000–based stand-alone server, use machine Group Policy to enable storage of reversibly encrypted passwords for all users of the computer. For Windows 2000 domains, Group Policy at the domain or Organizational Unit (OU) level can be used. For information about enabling reversibly encrypted passwords in a Windows 2000 domain, see Windows 2000 Server Help.

4. Force a reset of user's passwords so that the new password is in a reversibly encrypted form. When you enable passwords to be stored in a reversibly encrypted form, the current passwords are in a nonreversibly encrypted form and are not automatically changed. You must either reset user passwords or set user passwords to be changed the next time you log on. After the password is changed, it is stored in a reversibly encrypted form.

   If you set user passwords to be changed at the next attempt to log on, the user must log on using a LAN connection and change their password before they attempt to log on with a remote access connection using CHAP. CHAP does not support the changing of passwords during the authentication process and the logon attempt fails. One workaround for the remote access user is to temporarily log on using MS-CHAP to change their password.

5. Enable CHAP on the remote access client.

Microsoft Challenge Handshake Authentication Protocol

Microsoft Challenge Handshake Authentication Protocol (MS-CHAP) is a variant of CHAP that does not require a plaintext version of the password on the authenticating server. In MS-CHAP the challenge response is calculated with an MD4 hashed version of the password and the NAS challenge. This enables authentication over the Internet to a Windows 2000 domain controller (or a Windows NT 4.0 domain controller on which the update has not been installed).

MS-CHAP passwords are stored more securely at the server but have the same vulnerabilities to dictionary and brute force attacks as CHAP. When using MS-CHAP, it is important to ensure that passwords are well chosen (not found in a standard dictionary) and long enough that they cannot be calculated readily. Many large customers require passwords to be at least six characters long with upper and lower case characters and at least one numeral.

See your NAS documentation, or consult your ISP to see whether the ISP currently supports MS-CHAP.

Note By default, MS-CHAP v1 for Windows 2000 supports LAN Manager authentication. If you want to prohibit the use of LAN Manager authentication with MS-CHAP v1 for older Microsoft operating systems such as Windows NT 3.5x and Windows 95, you must set Allow LM Authentication (HKEY_LOCAL_MACHINE\SYSTEM\CurrentControlSet\Services \RemoteAccess\Policy) to 0 on the authenticating server.

If a user attempt authenticates using MS-CHAP using an expired password, MS-CHAP prompts the user to change the password while connecting to the server. Other authentication protocols do not support this feature effectively locking out the user who used the expired password.

Enabling MS-CHAP

To enable MS-CHAP-based authentication, you must do the following:

1. Enable MS-CHAP as an authentication protocol on the remote access server. MS-CHAP is enabled by default on the Routing and Remote Access service. For information about default settings on other NASs, see your NAS documentation.

2. Enable MS-CHAP on the appropriate remote access policy. MS-CHAP is enabled by default.

3. Enable MS-CHAP on a remote access client.

Microsoft Challenge Handshake Authentication Protocol Version 2

Microsoft Challenge Handshake Authentication Protocol version 2 (MS-CHAP v2) provides mutual authentication, stronger initial data encryption keys, and different encryption keys for sending and receiving. For VPN connections, Windows 2000 servers offer MS-CHAP v2 before offering the legacy MS-CHAP. Updated Windows clients accept MS-CHAP v2 when it is offered.

MS-CHAP v2 is a one-way encrypted password, mutual authentication process that works as follows:

1. The remote access server sends a challenge to the remote access client that consists of a session identifier and an arbitrary challenge string.

2. The remote access client sends a response that contains:
   - The user name.
   - An arbitrary peer challenge string.
   - A one-way encryption of the received challenge string, the peer challenge string, the session identifier, and the user's password.

3. The remote access server checks the response from the client and sends back a response containing:
   - An indication of the success or failure of the connection attempt.
   - An authenticated response based on the sent challenge string, the peer challenge string, the encrypted response of the client, and the user's password.

4. The remote access client verifies the authentication response and, if correct, uses the connection. If the authentication response is not correct, the remote access client terminates the connection.

If a user authenticates by using MS-CHAP v2 and attempts to use an expired password, MS-CHAP prompts the user to change the password while connecting to the server. Other authentication protocols do not support this feature effectively locking out the user who used the expired password.

Enabling MS-CHAP v2

To enable MS-CHAP v2–based authentication, you must do the following:

1. Enable MS-CHAP v2 as an authentication protocol on the remote access server. MS-CHAP v2 is enabled by default on the Routing and Remote Access service. For information about default settings on other NASs, see your NAS documentation.

2. Enable MS-CHAP v2 on the appropriate remote access policy. MS-CHAP v2 is enabled by default.

3. Enable MS-CHAP v2 on the Windows 2000 remote access client.

Note Windows 95 and Windows 98 support MS-CHAP v2 only for virtual private network (VPN) connections. Windows 95 and Windows 98 do not support MS-CHAP v2 for dial-up connections.

Extensible Authentication Protocol

Extensible Authentication Protocol (EAP) is an extension to the Point-to-Point protocol (PPP) that works with dial-up, PPTP, and L2TP clients. EAP allows the addition of new authentication methods known as EAP types. Both the dial-in client and the remote access server must support the same EAP type for successful authentication to occur.

Windows 2000 includes an EAP infrastructure and two EAP types, EAP-MD5 CHAP and EAP-TLS. The IAS implementation in Windows 2000 has the ability to pass EAP messages to a RADIUS server (EAP-RADIUS).

EAP-MD5 CHAP

Message Digest 5 Challenge Handshake Authentication Protocol (EAP-MD5 CHAP) is a required EAP type that uses the same challenge-handshake protocol as PPP-based CHAP, but the challenges and responses are sent as EAP messages. A typical use for EAP-MD5 CHAP is to authenticate the credentials of remote access clients by using user name and password security systems. You can use EAP-MD5 CHAP to test EAP interoperability.

EAP-TLS

EAP-Transport Level Security (EAP-TLS) is an EAP type that is used in certificate-based security environments. If you are using smart cards for remote access authentication, you must use the EAP-TLS authentication method. The EAP-TLS exchange of messages provides mutual authentication, negotiation of the encryption method, and secured private key exchange between the remote access client and the authenticating server. EAP-TLS provides the strongest authentication and key exchange method. EAP-TLS is supported only on a remote access server that is running Windows 2000 and is a member of a Windows 2000 mixed or native domain.

EAP-RADIUS

EAP-RADIUS is not an EAP type, but the passing of EAP messages of any EAP type by a remote access server to a RADIUS server for authentication. The EAP messages sent between the remote access client and remote access server are encapsulated and formatted as RADIUS messages between the remote access server and the RADIUS server.

EAP-RADIUS is used in environments where RADIUS is used as the authentication provider. An advantage of using EAP-RADIUS is that EAP types do not need to be installed at each remote access server, only at the RADIUS server. In a typical use of EAP-RADIUS, a remote access server is configured to use EAP and to use RADIUS as its authentication provider. When a connection is made, the remote access client negotiates the use of EAP with the remote access server. When the client sends an EAP message to the remote access server, the remote access server encapsulates the EAP message as a RADIUS message and sends it to its configured RADIUS server. The RADIUS server processes the message and sends a RADIUS-encapsulated EAP message back to the remote access server. The remote access server then forwards the EAP message to the remote access client. In this configuration, the remote access server is only a pass-through device. All processing of EAP messages occurs at the remote access client and the RADIUS server.

Enabling EAP

To enable EAP-based authentication, you must do the following:

1. Enable EAP as an authentication protocol on the remote access server.

2. Enable EAP; if needed, configure the EAP type on the appropriate remote access policy.

3. Enable and configure EAP on a remote access client.

In addition to the EAP types defined and supported in Windows 2000, new EAP authentication methods can be included through the use of EAP Software Development Kit.

Unauthenticated Access

The unauthenticated access method allows remote access users to log on without checking their credentials. For example, IAS does not verify the user's name and password. The only user validation performed in the unauthenticated access method is authorization. Enabling unauthenticated access presents security risks that must be carefully considered when deciding whether to enable this authentication method.

This section discusses three scenarios of unauthenticated access:

- Guest Access
- Dialed Number Identification Service (DNIS) authorization
- Automatic Number Identification/Calling Line Identification (ANI/CLI) authorization

Guest Access for PPP Users

Guest access is the ability to log on to a domain without a user name and/or a password. Both Routing and Remote Access service and IAS must be configured to support unauthenticated access.

When a remote access server receives a connection attempt, it negotiates with the user different authentication types enabled at the server. If the client accepts one of them, it sends the appropriate credentials for the accepted authentication type. It the user refuses authentication, Routing and Remote Access service checks its properties to verify if unauthenticated access is enabled and, if enabled, forwards the Access-Request packet to IAS. This Access-Request packet does not contain a User-Name attribute or any other credentials.

When IAS receives the packet without a User-Name attribute, it assumes that the user wants to dial in using guest access. In this case, IAS uses the name of the guest account in a domain as the user identity. It proceeds to evaluate policies in order to determine the right profile. If a match is found, and unauthenticated access is enabled in the profile, other authorizations are validated, and an Access-Accept packet is returned. The accounting log file logs the user identity and authentication type, which can be used to determine whether the user was logged on with guest access.

Enabling Guest Access

To enable Guest access, perform the following steps:

1. Enable unauthenticated access on the remote access server.
2. Enable unauthenticated access on the appropriate remote access policy.
3. Enable the Guest account.
4. Set the remote access permission on the Guest account to either **Allow access** or **Control access through Remote Access Policy** depending on your remote access policy administrative model.

If you do not want to enable the Guest account, create a user account and set the remote access permission to either **Allow access** or **Control access through Remote Access Policy**. Then set the **Default User Identity** registry value (HKEY_LOCAL_MACHINE\SYSTEM\CurrentControlSet\Services\RemoteAccess\Policy) on the authenticating server (either the remote access server or the IAS server) to the name of the account.

For more information about enabling authentication protocols, configuring authentication, and enabling a disabled user account, see Windows 2000 Server Help.

Guest Access Example

1. During PPP negotiation, the dial-in client rejects all of the PPP authentication protocols of the NAS.

2. If the NAS is configured to allowed unauthenticated access, the NAS sends an Access-Request packet without the User-Name attribute and without a password. For the Windows 2000 Routing and Remote Access service, unauthenticated access is enabled from the **Authentication** tab on the properties of a server in the Routing and Remote Access snap-in.

3. Because the User-Name attribute is not included in the Access-Request packet and by default the IAS user identity is using the User-Name attribute, the user identity is set to Guest (or the value of Default User Identity).

4. With the user identity of Guest and an unauthenticated connection attempt, the authentication and authorization process as discussed earlier in the chapter is performed. If the connection attempt matches a policy whose profile settings have unauthenticated access enabled and the Guest account is enabled and has the appropriate remote access permission, IAS sends an Access-Accept packet to the NAS.

DNIS Authorization

Dialed Number Identification Service (DNIS) authorization is the authorization of a connection attempt based on the number called. This attribute is referred to as Called Station ID. DNIS is used by standard telecommunication companies. This service returns the number called to the called party. Based on the Called Station ID attribute, IAS can deliver different services to dial-up/remote access users.

Enabling DNIS Authorization

The following steps are required in order to enable DNIS authorization:

1. Enable unauthenticated access on the remote access server.

2. Create a remote access policy on the authenticating server (remote access server or IAS server) for DNIS-based authorization with the Called-Station-ID condition set to the phone number.

3. Enable unauthenticated access on the remote access policy for DNIS-based authorization.

ANI Authorization

ANI authorization is based on the number the user called from. This attribute is referred to as Calling Station ID, or Caller ID. Based on the Calling-Station-ID attribute, IAS can deliver different services to dial-up/remote access users.

Using ANI authorization is different from using the Caller ID dial-in property of a user account. ANI authorization is performed when the user does not type in any user name or password, and refuses to use any valid authentication method. In this case, IAS receives Calling-Station-ID, and no user name and password. To support ANI authorization, the Active Directory must have user accounts with Caller IDs as user names. This kind of authentication is used with the cellular phone authentication and by ISPs in Germany and Japan.

When using the Caller ID property on a user account, the user types in his credentials, such as a user name and password, and uses a valid authentication method to log on. IAS uses the user name and password to authenticate the user, and then compares the Calling-Station-ID attribute in the Access-Request to the Caller ID property of the user account as a way of authorizing the connection attempt.

Enabling ANI Authorization

1. Enable unauthenticated access on the remote access server.

2. Enable unauthenticated access on the appropriate remote access policy for ANI/CLI-based authentication.

3. Create a user account for each number calling, for which you want to provide ANI/CLI authorization. The name of the user account must match the number that the user is dialing from. For example, if a user is dialing in from 555-0100, create a "5550100" user account.

4. Set the **User Identity Attribute** registry value (HKEY_LOCAL_MACHINE\SYSTEM\CurrentControlSet\Services\ RemoteAccess\Policy) to 31 on the authenticating server.

   This registry setting tells the authenticating server to use the calling number (RADIUS attribute 31, Calling-Station-ID) as the identity of the calling user. The user identity is set to the calling number only when there is no user name being supplied in the connection attempt.

   To always use the calling number as the user identity, set the **Override User-Name** registry value:

   HKEY_LOCAL_MACHINE\SYSTEM\CurrentControlSet\Services\ RemoteAccess\Policy

   to 1 on the authenticating server.

However, if you set Override User-Name to 1 and the User Identity Attribute to 31, the authenticating server can perform only ANI/CLI-based authentication. Normal authentication by using authentication protocols such as MS-CHAP, CHAP, and EAP is disabled.

ANI Example

The following example explains how ANI/CLI authorization works for an dial-up client dialing in from the phone number 555-0100 and a user account called 5550100 exists.

1. During PPP negotiation, the dial-in client rejects all of the PPP authentication protocols of the NAS.

2. If the NAS is configured to allowed unauthenticated access, the NAS sends an Access-Request packet without the User-Name attribute and without a password. For the Windows 2000 Routing and Remote Access service, unauthenticated access is enabled from the **Authentication** tab on the properties of a server in the Routing and Remote Access snap-in.

3. Because the User-Name attribute is not included in the Access-Request packet and the IAS user identity is set to use the Calling-Station-ID attribute, the user identity is set to 5550100.

4. With the user identity of 5550100 and an unauthenticated connection attempt, the authentication and authorization process as discussed earlier in the chapter is performed. If the connection attempt matches a policy whose profile settings have unauthenticated access enabled and the 550100 account has the appropriate remote access permission, IAS sends an Access-Accept packet to the NAS.

IAS Authorization

An administrator can use the authorization feature of IAS to allow or deny connection attempts that are based on the connection parameters. The following sections include in-depth information about configuring remote access policies and vendor-specific attributes.

Remote Access Policies

In Windows NT 4.0, remote access privileges were granted based solely on a dial-in permission assigned to a user. In Windows 2000, remote access connections are granted based on the dial-in properties of a user object and remote access policies. Remote access policies are a set of conditions and connection parameters that administrators can use to get more flexibility in granting remote access permissions and usage. Remote access policies are stored on the local computer and are shared between the Routing and Remote Access service and IAS.

By using remote access policies, an administrator can specify remote access permissions by the time of day and day of the week, by the Windows 2000 group to which the remote access user belongs, by the type of connection being requested (dial-in or virtual private network connection), and so on. You can configure settings that limit the maximum session time, specify the authentication and encryption methods, set Bandwidth Allocation Protocol (BAP) policies, and so on.

It is important to remember that a remote connection is accepted only if the settings of the connection attempt match at least one of remote access policies (subject to the conditions of the dial-in properties of the user object and the profile properties of the remote access policy). If the settings of the connection attempt do not match at least one of the remote access policies, the connection attempt is rejected regardless of the dial-in properties of the user account.

For Windows 2000 IAS servers, remote access policies are administered from the Routing and Remote Access administrative tool (when configured for Windows authentication) or the Internet Authentication Service administrative tool.

Note Windows 2000 supports customized authorization through the use of the Software Development Kit.

Local vs. Centralized Policy Management

Because remote access policies are stored locally on either a remote access server or an IAS server, for centralized management of a single set of remote access policies for multiple remote access or VPN servers, you must do the following steps:

1. Install the Windows 2000 Internet Authentication Service (IAS) as a Remote Authentication Dial-In User Service (RADIUS) server on a computer.

2. Configure IAS with RADIUS clients that correspond to each of the Windows 2000 remote access or VPN servers.

3. On the IAS server, create the central set of policies that all Windows 2000 remote access servers are using.

4. Configure each of the Windows 2000 remote access servers as a RADIUS client to the IAS server.

After you configure a Windows 2000 remote access server as a RADIUS client to an IAS server, the local remote access policies stored on the remote access server are no longer used.

Centralized management of remote access policies are also used when you have remote access servers that are running Windows NT 4.0 with the Routing and Remote Access Service (RRAS). You can configure the server that is running Windows NT 4.0 with RRAS as a RADIUS client to an IAS server. You cannot configure a remote access server that is running Windows NT 4.0 without RRAS to take advantage of centralized remote access policies.

Dial-in Properties of a User Object

In Windows 2000, the user object for a stand-alone or Active Directory–based server contains a set of dial-in properties that are used when allowing or denying a connection attempt made by a user. For a stand-alone server, the dial-in properties are available on the **Dial-in** tab of the user object in the local User Manager. For an Active Directory–based server, the dial-in properties are available on the **Dial-in** tab of the user object in Active Directory Users and Computers snap-in. The Windows NT 4.0 User Manager for Domains administrative tool cannot be used for Active Directory–based servers.

The dial-in properties for a user object are the following:

- Remote Access Permission (Dial-in or VPN)

  Use this property to set whether remote access is explicitly allowed, denied, or determined through remote access policies. If access is explicitly allowed, remote access policy conditions or user object or profile properties can override the setting. The **Control access through Remote Access Policy** option is available only on user objects for stand-alone Windows 2000 Routing and Remote Access service servers or members of a native Windows 2000 domain.

  By default, the Administrator and Guest accounts on a stand-alone remote access server or in a Windows 2000 native-mode domain are set to **Control access through Remote Access Policy** and for a Windows 2000 mixed-mode domain are set to **Deny access**. New accounts created on a stand-alone remote access server or in a Windows 2000 native-mode domain are set to **Control access through Remote Access Policy**. New accounts created in a Windows 2000 mixed-mode domain are set to **Deny access**.

- Verify Caller ID

  If this property is enabled, the server verifies the caller's phone number. If the caller's phone number does not match the configured phone number, the connection attempt is denied.

Caller ID must be supported by the caller, the phone system between the caller and the Routing and Remote Access service server, as well as by the Routing and Remote Access service server. Caller ID on the Routing and Remote Access service server consists of call answering equipment that supports the passing of Caller ID information and appropriate driver inside Windows 2000 that support the passing of Caller ID information to the Routing and Remote Access service.

If you configure a Caller ID phone number for a user and you do not have support for the passing of Caller ID information all the way from the caller to the Routing and Remote Access service, the connection attempt is denied.

- Callback Options

  If this property is enabled, the server calls the caller back during the connection establishment at a phone number set by the caller or a specific phone number set by the administrator.

- Assign a Static IP Address

  If this property is enabled, the administrator assigns a specific IP address to the user when the connection is made.

- Apply Static Routes

  If this property enabled, the administrator defines a series of static IP routes that are added to the routing table of the remote access server when a connection is made. This setting is designed for user accounts that Windows 2000 routers use for demand-dial routing.

If a Windows 2000 Routing and Remote Access service server is a member of a Windows NT 4.0 domain or a Windows 2000 mixed domain, then:

- Only the Remote Access Permission (Allow access and Deny access options) and Callback Options dial-in properties are available.

- The User Manager for Domains administrative tool can be used to grant or deny dial-in access and set callback options.

If the Windows 2000 Routing and Remote Access service server is a stand-alone server or a member of a Windows 2000 native domain, the callback number can be of unlimited size. If a Windows 2000 Routing and Remote Access service server is a member of a Windows NT 4.0 domain or a Windows 2000 mixed domain, the callback number can only be 128 characters long. Callback numbers that are long than 128 characters are truncated during a callback connection attempt, which results in a failed callback connection.

When a Windows NT 4.0 RAS server uses a native 2000 domain to obtain the dial-in properties of a user account, the **Control access through Remote Access Policy** option is interpreted as **Deny access**. Callback settings are interpreted correctly.

User accounts upgraded to Windows 2000 that were configured with dial-in permission enabled are set to **Allow access**. User accounts upgraded to Windows 2000 that were configured with dial-in permission disabled are set to **Control access through Remote Access Policy**.

A Windows NT 4.0 RAS server does not use remote access policies. It is recommended that you upgrade Windows NT 4.0 RAS servers to take advantage of remote access policies.

Elements of a Remote Access Policy

A remote access policy is a named rule that consists of the following elements:

Conditions

Remote access policy conditions are one or more attributes that are compared to the settings of the connection attempt. If there are multiple conditions, all of the conditions must match the settings of the connection attempt in order for the connection attempt to match the policy.

Table 8.3 shows the condition attributes that you can set for a remote access policy.

Table 8.3   Condition Attributes for a Remote Access Policy

Attribute Name	Description
NAS IP Address	The IP address of the network access server (NAS). This attribute is a character string. You can use pattern matching syntax to specify IP networks. This attribute is designed for the IAS server.
Service Type	The type of service being requested. Examples include framed (such as PPP connections) and login (such as Telnet connections). For more information about RADIUS service types, see RFC 2138. This attribute is designed for the IAS server.
Framed Protocol	The type of framing for incoming packets. Examples are PPP, AppleTalk, SLIP, Frame Relay, and X.25. This attribute is designed for the IAS server.
Called Station ID	The phone number of the NAS. This attribute is a character string. You can use pattern matching syntax to specify area codes. In order to receive called station ID information during a call, the phone line, the hardware, and the Windows 2000 driver for the hardware must support the passing of the called ID. Otherwise, the called station ID is manually set for each port.
Calling Station ID	The phone number used by the caller. This attribute is a character string. You can use pattern matching syntax to specify area codes.
NAS Port Type	The type of media used by the caller. Examples are analog phone lines (also known as "asynch"), ISDN, and tunnels or virtual private networks (known as virtual).

continued

Table 8.3   Condition Attributes for a Remote Access Policy *(continued)*

Attribute Name	Description
Day and Time Restrictions	The day of the week and the time of day of the connection attempt of the server.
Client IP Address	The IP address of the network access server (the RADIUS client). This attribute is a character string. You can use pattern matching syntax to specify IP networks. This Attribute is designed for the IAS server.
NAS Manufacturer	The vendor of NAS requesting authentication. The Windows 2000 remote access server is the Microsoft RAS NAS manufacturer. You can use this Attribute to configure separate policies for different NAS manufacturers who are RADIUS clients to an IAS server. This Attribute is designed for the IAS server.
Client Friendly Name	The name of the RADIUS client computer that is requesting authentication. This Attribute is a character string. You can use pattern matching syntax to specify client names. This Attribute is designed for the IAS server.
Windows Groups	The names of the Windows groups to which the user attempting the connection belongs. There is no condition attribute for a specific user name. It is not necessary to have a separate remote access policy for each group. Instead, you can use nested groups to consolidate group membership and delegate administration of group membership. For a Windows 2000 native mode domain-based remote access or IAS server, it is recommended that you use universal groups.
Tunnel Type	The type of tunnel being created by the requesting client. Tunnel types include the Point-to-Point Tunneling Protocol (PPTP) and the Layer Two Tunneling Protocol (L2TP) used by Windows 2000 remote access clients and demand-dial routers. You can use this condition to specify profile settings such as authentication methods or encryption strengths for a specific type of tunneling technology.

Note If conditions that use an Attribute designed for the IAS server are evaluated against a remote access server connection attempt, the result is no match and the policy is not applied.

Not all network access servers send all of the IAS server-specific attributes.

You cannot use the built-in local groups of a stand-alone remote access server that is running Windows 2000 for the Windows Groups attribute.

Remote Access Permission

If all the conditions of a remote access policy are met, remote access permission is either granted or denied. Use the **Grant remote access permission** option or the **Deny remote access permission** option to set remote access permission for a policy.

Remote access permission is also granted or denied for each user account. The user remote access permission overrides the policy remote access permission. When remote access permission on a user account is set to the **Control access through Remote Access Policy** option, the policy remote access permission determines whether the user is granted access.

Granting access through the user account permission setting or the policy permission setting is only the first step in accepting a connection. The connection attempt is then subjected to the settings of the user account properties and the policy profile properties. If the connection attempt does not match the settings of the user account properties or the profile properties, the connection attempt is rejected.

By default, the **Deny remote access permission policy** permission is selected.

Profile

A remote access policy profile is a set of properties that are applied to a connection when the connection is granted remote access permission, either through the user account permission setting or the policy permission setting. A profile consists of the following groups of properties:

- Dial-in constraints
- IP
- Multilink
- Authentication
- Encryption
- Advanced

Dial-In Constraints

You can set the following dial-in constraints:

- Idle disconnect time

  The time after which a connection is disconnected when there is no activity. By default, this property is not set and the remote access server does not disconnect an idle connection.

- Maximum session length

  The maximum amount of time that a connection is connected. The connection is disconnected by the remote access server after the maximum session length. By default, this property is not set and the remote access server has no maximum session limit.

- Day and time limits

  The days of the week and hours of each day that a connection is allowed. If the day and time of the connection attempt do not match the configured day and time limits, the connection attempt is rejected. By default, this property is not set and the remote access server has no day or time limits. The remote access server does not disconnect active connections that are connected at a time when connection attempts are not allowed.

- Dial-in number

  The specific phone number that a caller must call for a connection to be allowed. If the dial-in number of the connection attempt does not match the configured dial-in number, the connection attempt is rejected. By default, this property is not set and the remote access server allows all dial-in numbers.

- Dial-in media

  The specific types of media, such as modem (known as asynch), ISDN, or virtual private network (known as virtual) that a caller must use for a connection to be allowed. If the dial-in medium of the connection attempt does not match the configured dial-in media, the connection attempt is rejected. By default, this property is not set and the remote access server allows all dial-in media types.

IP

You can set IP properties to specify whether a particular IP address for a connection can be requested by the client. By default, the remote access server automatically allocates an IP address and the client is not allowed to request a specific IP address.

You can also use the IP properties to define remote access policy profile filtering. To define the allowed traffic across the connection after the connection had been made, you can configure IP packet filters for remote access policy profiles. You can use profile packet filters to configure IP traffic that is allowed out of the connection (to client) or into the connection (from client) on an exception basis: either all traffic except traffic specified by filters or no traffic except traffic specified by filters. Remote access policy profile filtering applies to all connections that match the remote access policy.

Multilink

You can set Multilink properties that enable Multilink and determine the maximum number of ports that a Multilink connection can use. Additionally, you can set Bandwidth Allocation Protocol (BAP) policies that determine BAP usage and when extra BAP lines are dropped. The Multilink and BAP properties are specific to Microsoft Windows 2000 remote access. By default, Multilink and BAP are disabled.

The remote access server must have Multilink and BAP enabled in order for the Multilink properties of the profile to be enforced.

Authentication

You can set authentication properties to enable the types of authentication that are allowed for a connection and specify the EAP type that must be used. Additionally, you can configure the EAP type. By default, **Microsoft Encrypted Authentication (MS-CHAP)** and **Microsoft Encrypted Authentication version 2 (MS-CHAPv2)** are enabled.

The remote access server must have the corresponding authentication types enabled in order for the authentication properties of the profile to be enforced.

Encryption

You can set encryption properties for the following encryption strengths:

- No Encryption

  When selected, this option allows an unencrypted connection. To require encryption, clear the **No Encryption** option.

- Basic

  For dial-up and PPTP-based VPN connections, Microsoft Point-to-Point Encryption (MPPE) with a 40-bit key is used. For L2TP over IPSec-based VPN connections, 40-bit DES encryption is used.

- Strong

  For dial-up and PPTP-based VPN connections, MPPE with a 56-bit key is used. For L2TP over IPSec-based VPN connections, 56-bit DES encryption is used.

- Strongest

  For dial-up and PPTP-based VPN connections, MPPE with a 128-bit key is used. For L2TP over IPSec-based VPN connections, triple DES (3DES) encryption is used.

Advanced

You can set advanced properties to specify the series of RADIUS Attributes that are sent back to the RADIUS client by the IAS server. RADIUS Attributes are specific to performing RADIUS authentication and are ignored by the remote access server. By default, Framed-Protocol is set to PPP and Service-Type is set to Framed.

The only attributes that are used by the remote access server are **Account-Interim-Interval**, **Framed-Protocol**, **Framed-MTU**, **Reply-Message**, and **Service-Type**.

Default Remote Access Policy

A default remote access policy named **Allow access if dial-in permission is enabled** is created. The default policy has the following configuration:

- The Day-and-Time-Restrictions condition is set to all times and all days.
- Permission is set to Deny remote access permission.
- All profile properties are set to default values.

Note Elements of a remote access policy correspond to RADIUS attributes that are used during RADIUS-based authentication. For an IAS server, verify that the network access servers that you use are sending the RADIUS attributes that correspond to the configured remote access policy conditions and profile settings. If a NAS does not send a RADIUS attribute that corresponds to a remote access policy condition or profile setting, all RADIUS authentications from that NAS are denied.

Vendor Profiles

Some vendors use vendor-specific attributes (VSAs) to provide functionality that is not supported in standard attributes. IAS enables you to create or modify vendor-specific attributes to take advantage of the proprietary functionality that is supported by some NAS vendors.

If you need to configure more than one VSA for a specific profile, you must arrange them in the appropriate order. If you are using filters and the order of the filters is important, use the arrow buttons to rearrange the attributes.

Example 1

The following example demonstrates the procedure of adding a Cisco VSA to a profile. The example illustrates only the mechanism of adding a standard-conforming VSA to a profile. Cisco VSAs are readily available through the IAS multi-vendor dictionary.

Cisco vendor-specific attributes conform to the RADIUS RFC for Vendor-Specific Attributes (type 26). The following information is for a Cisco attribute to specify a primary DNS server:

- Vendor ID: 9. This is the unique ID for Cisco. When you specify that vendor, this is automatically supplied.
- Vendor Type: 1. This is the vendor-type number for vendor-specific attributes that take the attribute-value pair form, referred to in Cisco documentation as "cisco-avpair."
- Data Type: String.
- Format: If the attribute is mandatory, the format is: <protocol>: attribute=value

If the attribute is optional, the attribute-value pair is separated by an asterisk (*) instead of an equal sign (=). In this example, <protocol> is a value of the Cisco "protocol" attribute for a particular type of authorization. "Attribute" and "value" represent an appropriate attribute/value (AV) pair defined in the Cisco TACACS+ specification. This allows the full set of features available for TACACS+ authorization to also be used for RADIUS.

The Cisco attribute used to specify a primary DNS server appears as follows:

```
ip:dns-servers=10.10.10.10
```

▶ **To add the vendor-specific attribute to a dial-in profile**

1. In IAS, click **Remote Access Policies**.

2. Right-click the policy for which you want to configure a vendor-specific attribute, and then click **Properties**.

3. Click **Edit Profile**, click the **Advanced** tab, and then click **Add**.

4. In the list of available RADIUS attributes, double-click **Vendor-Specific**.

5. Click **Add**.

6. In **Network access server vendor**, click **Cisco**.

7. Click **Yes, It conforms**, and then click **Configure Attribute**. In **Vendor-assigned attribute number**, type **1**.

8. In **Attribute format**, click **String**.

9. In **Attribute value**, type the following:

   ip:dns-servers=10.10.10.10

Example 2

The following example demonstrates how to add a 3Com/U.S. Robotics VSA to a profile.

Note Example 2 is included only to illustrate the mechanism of adding a standard nonconforming VSA to a profile. 3Com/U.S. Robotics VSAs are readily available through the IAS multivendor dictionary.

U.S. Robotics vendor-specific attributes do not conform to the recommended format for Vendor-Specific Attributes (type 26) in RADIUS RFC 2138. Therefore, all U.S. Robotics VSAs must be entered in hexadecimal format.

The following information is for a U.S. Robotics attribute to specify a primary DNS/NBNS server:

- Vendor ID: 429. This is the unique ID for U.S. Robotics. When you specify that vendor, this ID is automatically supplied.

- Indicator: 0x900F

- Data Type: String

- Format: The VSA must be entered in hexadecimal format.

▶ **To specify an IP address of 10.10.10.10 for a primary DNS/NBNS server**

1. In IAS, click **Remote Access Policies**.

2. Right-click the policy for which you want to configure a vendor-specific attribute, and then click **Properties**.

3. Click **Edit Profile**, click the **Advanced** tab, and then click **Add**.

4. In the list of available RADIUS attributes, double-click **Vendor-Specific**, and then click **Add**.

5. Click **Select** from the list, and then click **US Robotics**.

6. Click **No**. It does not conform, and then click **Configure Attribute**.

7. In Hexadecimal attribute value, type the following:

   0x900f31302e31302e31302e31302e

For more information about the proprietary attributes of U.S. Robotics, see your U.S. Robotics documentation.

Accepting a Connection Attempt

When a user attempts a connection, the connection attempt is accepted or rejected based on the following:

1. The first policy in the ordered list of remote access policies is checked. If there are no policies, reject the connection attempt.

2. If all the conditions of the policy do not match the connection attempt, go to next policy. If there are no more policies, reject the connection attempt.

3. If all the conditions of the policy match the connection attempt, check the remote access permission setting for the user attempting the connection. For example:

   - If **Deny access** is selected, reject the connection attempt.

   - If **Allow access** is selected, apply the user account properties and profile properties.

   - If the connection attempt does not match the settings of the user account properties and profile properties, reject the connection attempt.

   - If the connection attempt matches the settings of the user account properties and profile properties, accept the connection attempt.

- If the remote access permission is not set to **Allow access** or **Deny access**, the remote access permission must be set to **Control access through Remote Access Policy**. Therefore, check the remote access permission setting of the policy.

- If **Deny remote access permission** is selected, reject the connection attempt.

- If **Grant remote access permission** is selected, apply the user account properties and profile properties.

- If the connection attempt does not match the settings of the user account properties and profile properties, reject the connection attempt.

- If the connection attempt matches the settings of the user account properties and profile properties, accept the connection attempt.

Remote Access Policy Administrative Models

In Windows 2000, there are three primary models for administering remote access permissions and connection settings:

- Access by user.
- Access by policy in a Windows 2000 native-mode domain.
- Access by policy in a Windows 2000 mixed-mode domain.

Access by User

In the access-by-user administrative model, remote access permissions are determined by the remote access permission on the **Dial-in** tab of the user account. You enable or disable remote access permission on a per-user basis by setting the remote access permission to either **Allow access** or **Deny access**.

The remote access permission setting on the remote access policy is effectively overridden if the user account's remote access permission is set to either **Allow access** or **Deny access**. However, you can modify remote access policy conditions and profile properties to enforce connection settings, such as encryption requirements and idle time-outs.

You can administer access-by-user remote access with multiple remote access policies. Each remote access policy has its own profile settings. You must configure these settings carefully because a connection attempt might be rejected even when the remote access permission on the user account is set to **Allow access**. If a connection attempt matches the conditions of a policy but does not match the profile settings or does not match any of the remote access policies, the connection attempt is rejected.

In the access-by-user administrative model, you can control three behaviors:

- Explicit allow

  The remote access permission for the user account is set to Allow access and the connection attempt matches the conditions of a policy subject to the settings of the profile and the dial-in properties of the user account.

- Explicit deny

  The remote access permission for the user account is set to Deny access.

- Implicit deny

  The connection attempt does not match the conditions of any remote access policies.

In Windows 2000, the access-by-user administrative model is equivalent to administering remote access on a Windows NT 4.0 RAS server.

You can use the access-by-user administrative model on a stand-alone remote access server, a remote access server that is a member of a Windows 2000 native-mode domain, a remote access server that is a member of a Windows 2000 mixed-mode domain, or a remote access server that is a member of a Windows NT 4.0 domain. You can also use the access-by-user administrative model if you have Windows NT 4.0 RAS or IAS servers.

Access by Policy in a Windows 2000 Native-Mode Domain

In the access-by-policy administrative model for a Windows 2000 native-mode domain, the remote access permission on every user account is set to **Control access through Remote Access Policy** and remote access permissions are determined by the remote access permission setting on the remote access policy. Therefore, the remote access permission setting on the remote access policy determines whether remote access permission is allowed or denied.

In the access-by-policy administrative model for a Windows 2000 native-mode domain, you can control three behaviors:

- Explicit allow

  The remote access permission on the remote access policy is set to **Grant remote access permission** and the connection attempt matches the conditions of the policy subject to the settings of the profile and the dial-in properties of the user account.

- Explicit deny

  The remote access permission on the remote access policy is set to **Deny remote access permission** and the connection attempt matches the conditions of the policy.

- Implicit deny

  The connection attempt does not match the conditions of any remote access policies.

If you use this administrative model and do not add any remote access policies and do not change the default remote access policy (named **Allow access if dial-in permission is enabled**), no users are allowed remote access. By default, the remote access permission on the default remote access policy is set to **Deny remote access permission**. If you change the setting to **Grant remote access permission**, all users are allowed remote access.

The access-by-policy administrative model for a Windows 2000 native-mode domain also applies to stand-alone remote access servers that are not a member of a domain.

You cannot use the access-by-policy administrative model for a Windows 2000 native-mode domain if you have Windows NT 4.0 RAS or IAS servers.

If you use the access-by-policy administrative model for a Windows 2000 native-mode domain and do not use groups to specify which users get access, verify that the Guest account is disabled and its remote access permission is set to **Deny access**.

Access by Policy in a Windows 2000 Mixed-Mode Domain

In the access-by-policy administrative model for a Windows 2000 mixed-mode domain, the remote access permission on every user account is set to **Allow access**, the default remote access policy is deleted, and separate remote access policies are created to define the types of connections that are allowed. On a remote access server that is running Windows 2000 that is a member of a Windows 2000 mixed-mode domain, the **Control access through Remote Access Policy** option is not available for remote access permission on the user account. If a connection attempt matches the conditions of a policy subject to the profile and user account dial-in settings, the connection is accepted.

This administrative model also applies to a remote access server that is running Windows 2000 that is a member of a Windows NT 4.0 domain.

In the access-by-policy administrative model for a Windows 2000 mixed-mode domain, you can control three behaviors:

- Explicit allow

  The connection attempt matches the conditions of a policy subject to the settings of the profile and the dial-in properties of the user account.

- Explicit deny

  The connection attempt matches the conditions of a policy but not the settings of the profile. You can do an explicit deny in this administrative model by enabling the **Restrict Dial-in to this number only** dial-in constraint and typing a number that does not correspond to any dial-in number being used by the remote access server.

- Implicit deny

  The connection attempt does not match the conditions of any remote access policies.

If you do not delete the default remote access policy named **Allow access if dial-in permission is enabled**, all users can obtain a remote access connection.

If you have Windows NT 4.0 Routing and Remote Access service (RRAS) servers, you can use the access-by-policy only in a Windows 2000 mixed-mode domain administrative model if the RRAS servers are configured as RADIUS clients to a Windows 2000 IAS server. You cannot use the access-by-policy in a Windows 2000 mixed-mode domain administrative model for Windows NT 4.0 RAS servers.

Note The administrative models described here are recommended ways of controlling remote access. You can administer remote access through a mixture of these models. However, you must do so carefully to produce the intended results. Improper configuration might lead to connection attempts that are rejected when they must be accepted and connection attempts that are accepted when they must be rejected. To troubleshoot these complex configurations, you can apply the logic the remote access server uses when processing connection attempts or enable authentication logging and check the authentication log.

For more information about remote access policies and scenarios using remote access policies, see Windows 2000 Server Help.

IAS Accounting

The following section describes IAS accounting features, as well as different formats of the IAS log file.

RADIUS Accounting

IAS supports RADIUS Accounting, which an administrator can use to track network usage for auditing and billing purposes. RADIUS Accounting provides the following benefits:

- Real-time data collection.
- Accounting data can be collected at the centralized place.
- Third-party products can be used to analyze RADIUS accounting data to provide charge-back, performance, and exception reports.

When a client is configured to use RADIUS Accounting, at the start of service delivery it generates an Accounting Start packet describing the type of service being delivered and the user it is being delivered to. The packet is then sent to the RADIUS Accounting server, which sends back an acknowledgment that the packet has been received. At the end of service delivery, the client generates an Accounting Stop packet describing the type of service that was delivered and statistics (optional), such as elapsed time, input and output octets, or input and output packets. It then sends that data to the RADIUS Accounting server, which sends back an acknowledgment that the packet has been received.

The Accounting-Request packet (whether for the Start or Stop packet) is submitted to the RADIUS accounting server through the network. If no response is returned within a length of time, the request is re-sent a number of times. The client can also forward requests to an alternate server or servers in the event that the primary server is down or unreachable. An alternate server can be used either after a number of tries to the primary server fail, or in a round-robin fashion. If the RADIUS accounting server is unable to successfully record the accounting packet, it does not send an Accounting-Response acknowledgment to the client. For example, when the log file gets filled up, IAS starts discarding accounting packets. This prompts the NAS to switch to the backup IAS server.

IAS Log File

IAS can create a log file based on the data returned by the network access servers. This information is useful for keeping track of usage and correlating authentication information with accounting records (for example, to discover missing records or instances of over-billing).

IAS supports two formats of the log file: IAS format and database.

Database format allows you to keep track of a predetermined set of attributes, and IAS format is more detailed and can contain information about all attributes.

Use database format if you want to import the data directly into a database. The IAS format can be used if you need to record more detailed information than the database log format allows.

Note   The IAS log file contains all the IAS user-related events. IAS service and system-related events are recorded in the Event log files.

IAS Authentication and Windows Domain Modes

This section concentrates on IAS authentication features and behavior in different Windows domain modes. The information is useful when making decision about a particular domain mode in which IAS is deployed.

IAS is capable of authenticating access requests received through the RADIUS protocol against Windows 2000 native mode domains, Windows 2000 mixed-mode domains, Windows NT 4.0 domains, or Windows 2000 local accounts database for a stand-alone IAS server. The IAS authentication features and capabilities available to administrators depends on a mode of a particular domain against which the users authenticate.

Windows 2000 Native-Mode Domains

Windows 2000 native mode provides the most flexibility in managing remote access through groups. From the remote access management perspective, the following benefits are available in the native mode domain:

- Full ability to manage remote access permissions through groups. An administrator can use the universal group feature to create a single policy for users in different domains. Nested groups can be used to organize extremely large numbers of users into smaller groups for better management.
- An ability to connect remote network to office network. You can specify routes for the remote network through Static Routes.
- Support for User Principal Names (UPNs).
- End users can have the same UPN regardless of what domain the user belongs to. This indirection provides scalability that might be required in organizations that have large number of domains.

The following is a detailed list of authentication and remote management features available for an IAS server that is a member of a Windows 2000 native domain.

- Dial-in User Account Properties
  - All Remote Access Permissions, including Allow access, Deny access, and Control access through Remote Access Policy
  - Caller-ID
  - Callback Options
  - Static IP Address
  - Static Routes
- Support for UPNs and Universal Groups
- Support for EAP-TLS

In order for the IAS server to access user account dial-in properties stored in Active Directory, IAS must run in the security context of a computer account that is a member of the **RAS and IAS Servers** security group. This assignment can be implemented through the Active Directory Users and Computers snap-in or by registering the IAS server in the Internet Authentication Service snap-in. You can also use the **netsh ras add registeredserver** command.

Windows 2000 Mixed-Mode Domains or Windows NT 4.0 Domains

Windows 2000 mixed-mode domains are mainly used for migration from Windows NT 4.0 to Windows 2000. For IAS, a mixed-mode domain acts exactly like a Windows NT 4.0 domain.

For an IAS server that is a member in a Windows 2000 mixed-mode domain, the following authentication and remote access management features are available:

- Dial-in User Account Properties
  - Remote Access Permissions include only Allow access and Deny access

    Missing the "Control access through Remote Access Policy" option makes it more difficult to use groups with Policy-based management because the user's remote access permission overrides remote access policy permissions. For more information about managing through policy in a mixed-mode domain, see "Remote Access Policies" earlier in this chapter.
  - Callback options

Just as in Windows 2000 native mode domains, in order for the IAS server to access user account dial-in properties stored in Active Directory, the Internet Authentication service must run in the security context of a computer account that is a member of the **RAS and IAS Servers** security group. This assignment can be implemented through the Active Directory Users and Computers or by registering the IAS server in the Internet Authentication Service snap-in. You can also use the **netsh ras add registeredserver** command.

If IAS is a member of Windows NT 4.0 domain but has to authenticate users against a trusted Active Directory domain, it is not able to gain access to Active Directory because its computer account cannot become a member of the RAS and IAS Servers security group. In this case, verify that the Everyone group is added to the Pre-Windows 2000 Compatible Access group with the **net localgroup "Pre-Windows 2000 Compatible Access"** command. If not, issue the **net localgroup "Pre-Windows 2000 Compatible Access" everyone /add** command on a domain controller computer and then restart the domain controller computer.

Windows 2000 Stand-Alone Servers

Windows 2000 stand-alone servers can be used in very small networks with no domains. All the users need to be defined in the local accounts database of a stand-alone server.

The following authentication features are available for granting remote access permissions to an IAS server on a Windows 2000 stand-alone server:

- Dial-in User Account Properties
    - Remote Access Permission (includes Allow access, Deny access, and Control access through Remote Access Policy)
    - Caller-ID
    - Callback Options
    - Static IP Address
    - Static Routes

Support for UPNs, Universal Groups, and EAP-TLS is not available in IAS running on a stand-alone Windows 2000 server.

User account dial-in properties can be administered through the Network and Dial-Up Connections folder or through Local Users and Groups.

Behavior Differences Between Windows 2000 and Windows NT 4.0 IAS

A previous version of IAS was released with the Windows NT 4.0 Option Pack. The following section describes the differences in behavior between the two versions.

Windows NT 4.0 IAS Behavior

- If no domain name is specified during authentication, the IAS server authenticates the user against only the local SAM database.
- IAS does not use the callback permissions for all user objects.
- IAS log files are written in ASCII.

Windows 2000 IAS Behavior

- IAS resolves a user name with no domain specified by using the following sequence:
    1. IAS determines a default domain from the registry, if one is specified there.
    2. If the IAS server is a member of a domain, IAS authenticates the user against that domain.
    3. If the IAS server is not a member of a domain, IAS authenticates the user against the local SAM database.
- IAS uses the callback permissions for all user objects.
- IAS log files are multi-language and are written in UTF-8.

Security Considerations

This section covers possible IAS security-related issues and recommendations on how to overcome them.

RADIUS Proxy Security Issues

It is not anticipated that a particular named user would be authenticated by multiple methods. This would make the user vulnerable to attacks that negotiate the least secure method from among a set. Instead, for each named user, there must be an indication of exactly one method used to authenticate that user name. If a user needs to make use of different authentication methods under different circumstances, distinct user names must be employed, each of which identifies exactly one authentication method. Passwords and other secrets must be stored at the respective ends, such that access to them is as limited as possible.

Ideally, the secrets must be accessible only to the process requiring access, in order to perform the authentication. The secrets must be distributed with a mechanism that limits the number of entities that handle (and gain knowledge of) the secret. Ideally, no unauthorized person must ever gain knowledge of the secrets.

Firewall Protection

A firewall provides additional security and protection to the services that are running on any operating system. The firewall might be a Windows NT–based or Windows 2000–based computer with the Proxy Server, or a third-party firewall package. The firewall can run on the same computer as the IAS server.

One option is to use the Proxy Server to hide the IP address of the server. In this way, the proxy IP address is exposed as the IAS address. You can also use a third-party firewall and enable the UDP traffic for the IAS server only for those ports used by the RADIUS server. For more security, allow traffic to come in only from specific IP Addresses, of NAS or RADIUS proxy, to the RADIUS server.

Remote Access Account Lockout

You can use the remote access account lockout feature to specify how many times an remote access authentication fails against a valid user account before future connection attempts using the user account name are denied. For more information about remote access account lockout, see "Remote Access Server" in this book.

Performance Tuning and Optimization

This section contains recommendations on IAS performance fine-tuning and monitoring. It also includes sample performance information that can be helpful in determining your IAS server performance and health conditions.

Consider the following points when fine-tuning the performance of an IAS server.

- If IAS authenticates users against a Windows 2000–based domain controller that is running in native mode, the domain controller should also contain the Global Catalog.
- High latency connections between the NAS and IAS server, or IAS server and the domain controller, can negatively impact authentication times, and cause retries and time-outs.

In very large ISP environments (millions of remote access users) with extremely heavy load conditions, where a large number of authentication requests, as well as accounting packets are being handled within seconds, the following items must be considered:

- As a general rule of thumb, number of authentications/second you get would depend on the hardware used for the domain controller. A faster domain controller should yield a better throughput.

- Consider using separate IAS servers for authentication and accounting.

- Consider running the IAS server on a domain controller with a Global Catalog. This would minimize network latency and would improve throughput.

- To achieve better throughput, use a registry entry to tune the number of concurrent authentication calls in progress at one time, between the IAS server and the domain controller. For information about registry entry details, see Windows 2000 Server Help.

- An administrator can deploy multiple IAS servers and use Windows Load Balance Service to point NASs to a single IP address representing a pool of IAS servers.

Monitoring Performance and Health of the IAS Server

The RADIUS authentication protocol distinguishes between the client function and the server function. In RADIUS authentication, clients send Access-Request packets, and servers reply with Access-Accept, Access-Reject, and Access-Challenge packets. Typically, NAS devices perform the client function and implement the RADIUS authentication client MIB, and RADIUS authentication servers perform the server function and implement the RADIUS authentication server MIB.

The two most commonly used counters for IAS performance monitoring are:

- Access Requests/sec
- Accounting Requests/sec

The most common counters used for health monitoring are described in the following section.

For more information about SNMP MIBs supported by IAS, see "Simple Network Management Protocol Service" in the *TCP/IP Core Networking Guide*.

Troubleshooting

The following sections provide information about troubleshooting for IAS installation and configuration problems, including common IAS problems reported from the field, and about advanced troubleshooting with Network Monitor traces.

Troubleshooting IAS Installation

The most common problems with IAS installation and their solutions are outlined here. In all cases, a valid user cannot log on and a Windows 2000 Event Viewer error message appears.

The error messages appear in bold type, and the possible solutions are described in the following paragraphs.

"Unknown user name or bad password."

"The specified user does not exist."

"The specified domain does not exist."

The user might have entered the wrong user name or password. Check the user's Windows 2000 user name and account password to make sure they are typed correctly and that the account is valid for the domain IAS is authenticating the user against.

Realm replacement might be set up incorrectly, or in the wrong order, so that the domain controller cannot recognize the user name. Adjust the realm replacement rules. For more information about realm names or configuring realm replacement, see your Windows 2000 Server information.

If the remote access server is a member of domain and the user response does not contain a domain name, the domain name of the remote access server is used. To use a domain name that is different from that of the IAS server, on the computer that is running IAS, set the following registry value to the name of the domain that you want to use:

HKEY_LOCAL_MACHINE\SYSTEM\CurrentControlSet\Services\RasMan \PPP\ControlProtocols\BuiltIn\DefaultDomain

---

Caution Do not use a registry editor to edit the registry directly unless you have no alternative. The registry editors bypass the standard safeguards provided by administrative tools. These safeguards prevent you from entering conflicting settings or settings that are likely to degrade performance or damage your system. Editing the registry directly can have serious, unexpected consequences that can prevent the system from starting and require that you reinstall Windows 2000. To configure or customize Windows 2000, use the programs in Control Panel or Microsoft Management Console (MMC) whenever possible.

Some NASs automatically strip the domain name from the user name before forwarding the user name to a RADIUS server. Turn off the feature that strips the domain name from the user name. For more information, see your NAS documentation.

"The authentication type is not supported on this system."

The user is trying to authenticate by using an authentication method that is not supported on this computer. For example, the user might be using an EAP type that has not been installed. Modify the dial-in profile to allow the protocol in question.

If a remote access policy denies access to the user, the following error messages might appear:

"The user's information did not match a remote access policy."

"The user is not allowed dial-in access to the network."

"User attempted an unauthorized authentication method."

"User tried to connect from an unauthorized calling station."

"User tried to dial-in outside of permitted hours."

"User tried to connect by calling an unauthorized NAS phone number."

"User tried to connect using an invalid port type."

"A constraint defined in the remote access policy failed."

A remote access policy might be denying access to the user. Check the policy list to make sure that you have not excluded users who must be granted access. Check the event log to see if the user is trying to connect with parameters not permitted by a remote access policy (for example, during an unauthorized time period, using an unauthorized wrong port type, calling from an unauthorized wrong phone number, or calling an unauthorized NAS phone number). You might have to revise the remote access policies accordingly to grant the user access.

Remote access policies might be in the wrong order. Authorization is granted or denied by the first policy whose conditions match the connection attempt. Use the **Move Up** button to move the policy that grants access to the users who are having trouble so that it is higher in the list.

"The user has exceeded the dial-in lockout count."

If remote access account lockout is enabled, previous failed access attempts might have caused the user account to be locked out. If so, increase the dial-in lockout count.

"The user's account is currently locked out and might not be logged on to."

The user's account is locked out and cannot be validated.

"The user is not allowed dial-in access to the network."

The user might be denied dial-in access. Check the user's information about the domain controller (or in Local Users and Groups) to see that dial-in access is granted for the user. If dial-in access is denied, this overrides any remote access policy that grants access.

"The current configuration supports only local user accounts."

IAS is set up to authenticate against the local SAM, and the user is not a member of the local user database. In this case, add the IAS server to Active Directory.

"The user's account domain is unreachable."

"The server is unavailable."

"The specified domain did not exist."

"IAS could not access the Global Catalog."

There might be a communication problem between the NAS and IAS, or between IAS and the domain controller or Global Catalog server. Use the **ping** command to check the communication with the domain controller or Global Catalog server. If **ping** works, try to connect to the server by using the command **net use \\servername\share**. If no packet information appears in the IAS log, check the Windows 2000 event log to see whether the attempt times out.

The user might be using CHAP, but Active Directory might not be configured to use plaintext passwords. To use CHAP authentication with IAS, configure the dial-in profile for a user or group to use CHAP. The NAS and the user's dialing program (such as Connection Manager) must also be configured to use CHAP authentication. You also need to enable CHAP on the domain controller.

Certain NASs do not recognize all the characters that IAS accepts for the shared secret. Try to change the shared secret to one with only alphanumeric characters.

The NAS might be sending packets that do not correspond to the format expected by IAS.

Right-click **Internet Authentication Service** and then click **Properties**. Make sure **Log rejected or discarded authentication requests** is selected, and then display the command to see if unexpected or malformed packets are being sent. If this is the case, you might need to set some vendor-specific attributes in IAS to solve communication problems with your NAS.

IAS cannot connect to the domain. Make sure IAS is authenticating against the correct domain name. If the domain name is correct, make sure that the IAS server is a member of that domain, or that there is a trust relationship between that domain and the domain to which the IAS server belongs.

IAS does not have permission to view user objects in Active Directory. Add the IAS server to Active Directory.

The user account is in an Active Directory forest that is different from the forest of which the IAS server is a member. Use a RADIUS proxy to route the authentication request to an IAS server that is a member of the other Active Directory forest.

The user is trying to use 128-bit encryption enabled, IAS has it enabled in a remote access policy, but Routing and Remote Access does not. Enable the Strongest security setting on the Routing and Remote Access server. (If you have not enabled it on this server before, you might need to install the Microsoft Encryption Pack.)

Your NAS might require framed routing; but on IAS, framed routing is not set by default. Enable framed routing.

▶ **To enable framed routing**

1. In IAS, click **Remote Access Policies**, and then double-click the policy that applies to the users who cannot log on.
2. Click **Edit Profile**, click the **Advanced** tab, and then click **Add**.
3. In the list of available RADIUS attributes, double-click **Framed-Routing**.
4. In **Attribute value**, click **None**.

Your NAS might require Van Jacobsen TCP/IP compression. Configure IAS to work with Van Jacobsen TCP/IP compression.

▶ **To configure IAS to work with Van Jacobsen TCP/IP header compression**

1. In IAS, click **Remote Access Policies**, and then double-click the policy that applies to the users who cannot log on.
2. Click **Edit Profile**, click the **Advanced** tab, and then click **Add**.
3. In the list of available RADIUS attributes, double-click **Framed-Compression**.
4. In **Attribute value**, click **Van Jacobsen TCP/IP header compression**.

If framed MTU is set on the NAS and not on IAS, users are not able to log on. Check your framed MTU settings on IAS, and make sure that they match the settings on your NAS.

▶ **To change framed MTU settings**

1. In IAS, click **Remote Access Policies**, and then double-click the policy that applies to the users who cannot log on.

2. Click **Edit Profile**, click the **Advanced** tab, and then click **Add**.

3. In the list of available RADIUS attributes, double-click **Framed-MTU**.

4. Click **Attribute value**, and then type the value that matches the settings for your NAS.

If IAS is returning the Access-Accept packet by using a different network adapter than the one by which the Access-Request packet was received, the NAS does not recognize the packet. In this event, check your IAS settings.

If the request is returned through a RADIUS proxy, the proxy might not support certain extensions that are necessary to support some features. For example:

- If you want your users to use EAP authentication, the RADIUS proxy must support digital signatures (according to RADIUS extensions).

- If you want your users to connect using compulsory tunnels, the RADIUS proxy must support encryption of the tunnel password.

- If you want connections to use Microsoft Encryption, the RADIUS proxy must support encryption of MPPE keys.

See your RADIUS proxy documentation to make sure that it supports the extensions necessary for the features that you want to use.

A remote access policy might be granting access to the user. Check the policy list to make sure that you have not included users who must be denied access.

Dial-in properties for the user object might be set to override the remote access policy. Check the dial-in properties for the user object.

Remote access policies might be in the wrong order. Authorization is granted or denied by the first policy whose conditions apply to the user who is trying to connect. Use the **Move Up** button to move the policy that denies access to the users so that it is higher in the list.

IAS is not set up to log rejected or discarded authentication requests. Set up IAS to log rejected or discarded authentication requests in the and see if any malformed packets are being logged. The NAS might require a different shared secret for RADIUS accounting. Make sure the shared secret for accounting is the same as the one used for authentication.

The dial-in profile for the remote access policy might not be set up to permit CHAP encryption. Check dial-in profile settings to be sure that IAS is set up for CHAP authentication. Check to see whether your NAS is set up for CHAP. For more information, see your NAS documentation. Also check to make sure the domain controller is configured to store reversibly encrypted passwords.

Passwords are not stored in a reversibly encrypted form until they are reset. Perform the following:

- After you enable passwords to be stored in a reversibly encrypted form, the current passwords are not in a reversibly encrypted form and are not automatically changed. You must either reset user passwords or set user passwords to be changed the next time each user logs on.

- After you switch a domain controller from mixed mode to native mode, every domain controller in the domain must be restarted so that the change replicates.

- Restart the domain controllers so that the servers can regain access to the domain controller.

  When a Routing and Remote Access server is set to use RADIUS authentication, Remote Access Policies are accessible only from Internet Authentication Service. This is intentional behavior.

For more information on troubleshooting IAS, see Windows 2000 Server Help.

Troubleshooting by Using Network Monitor

If a problem still exists after checking basic IAS configuration, the Network Monitor (NetMon) tool can be used to record a trace of the problem for further analysis.

When you use Network Monitor for IAS troubleshooting, consider the following:

- NetMon must be installed on a computer that is running IAS server.

- If you use NetMon in a switched network environment, you see only the traffic addressed to the computer that is running NetMon.

  For more information about setting up and using Network Monitor, see "Monitoring Network Performance" in the *Microsoft® Windows® 2000 Server Resource Kit Server Operations Guide*.

Set up Network Monitor for RADIUS troubleshooting by filtering NetMon on RADIUS packets in a trace.

Perform the following steps:

▶ **To filter NetMon on RADIUS packets in a trace**

1. Capture trace of a problem.
2. In the **Display** menu, select **Filter**.
3. Select **Protocol = Any** and then click **Edit Expression**. Click **Disable All** to disable all of the protocols. In the right pane, select **RADIUS protocol** and then click **Enable**.
4. Click **OK**.

C H A P T E R   9

Virtual Private Networking

Microsoft® Windows® 2000 includes extensive support for virtual private networking technology, which leverages the IP connectivity of the Internet to connect remote clients and remote offices. As a network professional, you should understand the important uses of virtual private networking for your organization and the underlying technologies that make it work: Point-to-Point Tunneling Protocol (PPTP), Layer Two Tunneling Protocol (L2TP), virtual private networks and security, virtual private networks and routing and translation, virtual private networks and firewalls, and the troubleshooting of virtual private network connections. You should already be familiar with TCP/IP, IP routing, IP Security (IPSec), and the Windows 2000 remote access server.

In This Chapter

Related Information in the Resource Kit

- For more information about TCP/IP, see "Introduction to TCP/IP" in the *Microsoft® Windows® 2000 Server Resource Kit TCP/IP Core Networking Guide*.

- For more information about IPSec, see "Internet Protocol Security" in the *TCP/IP Core Networking Guide*.

- For more information about unicast IP routing, see "Unicast IP Routing" in this book.

- For more information about demand-dial routing, see "Demand-Dial Routing" in this book.

- For more information about the Windows 2000 remote access server, see "Remote Access Server" in this book.

Virtual Private Networking Overview

A virtual private network (VPN) is the extension of a private network that encompasses links across shared or public networks like the Internet. A VPN enables you to send data between two computers across a shared or public internetwork in a manner that emulates the properties of a point-to-point private link. The act of configuring and creating a virtual private network is known as virtual private networking.

To emulate a point-to-point link, data is encapsulated, or wrapped, with a header that provides routing information allowing it to traverse the shared or public internetwork to reach its endpoint. To emulate a private link, the data being sent is encrypted for confidentiality. Packets that are intercepted on the shared or public network are indecipherable without the encryption keys. The link in which the private data is encapsulated and encrypted is known as a virtual private network (VPN) connection.

Figure 9.1 illustrates the logical concept of a VPN.

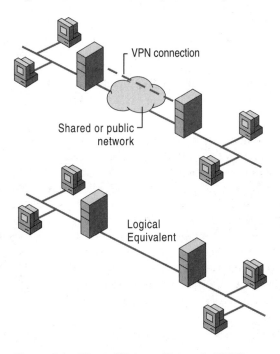

Figure 9.1   Virtual Private Network (VPN)

VPN connections allow users working at home or on the road to obtain a remote access connection to an organization server using the infrastructure provided by a public internetwork such as the Internet. From the user's perspective, the VPN is a point-to-point connection between the computer, the VPN client, and an organization server, the VPN server. The exact infrastructure of the shared or public network is irrelevant because it appears logically as if the data is sent over a dedicated private link.

VPN connections also allow organizations to have routed connections with geographically separate offices or with other organizations over a public internetwork such as the Internet while maintaining secure communications. A routed VPN connection across the Internet logically operates as a dedicated WAN link.

With both the remote access connection and with the routed connection, VPN connections allow an organization to trade in long distance dial-up or leased lines for local dial-up or leased lines to an Internet service provider (ISP).

Elements of a VPN Connection

A Microsoft® Windows® 2000 VPN connection includes the following components as illustrated in Figure 9.2:

VPN server. A computer that accepts VPN connections from VPN clients. A VPN server can provide a remote access VPN connection or a router-to-router VPN connection. For more information, see "VPN Connections" later in this chapter.

VPN client. A computer that initiates a VPN connection to a VPN server. A VPN client can be an individual computer that obtains a remote access VPN connection or a router that obtains a router-to-router VPN connection. Microsoft® Windows NT® version 4.0, Windows 2000, Microsoft® Windows® 95, and Microsoft® Windows® 98–based computers can create remote access VPN connections to a Windows 2000–based VPN server. Microsoft® Windows® 2000 Server and Microsoft® Windows NT® Server 4.0–based computers running the Routing and Remote Access service (RRAS) can create router-to-router VPN connections to a Windows 2000–based VPN server. VPN clients can also be any non-Microsoft Point-to-Point Tunneling Protocol (PPTP) client or Layer Two Tunneling Protocol (L2TP) client using IPSec.

Tunnel. The portion of the connection in which your data is encapsulated.

VPN connection. The portion of the connection in which your data is encrypted. For secure VPN connections, the data is encrypted and encapsulated along the same portion of the connection.

Note It is possible to create a tunnel and send the data through the tunnel without encryption. This is not a VPN connection because the private data is sent across a shared or public network in an unencrypted and easily readable form.

Tunneling protocols. Communication standards used to manage tunnels and encapsulate private data. (Data that is tunneled must also be encrypted to be a VPN connection.) Windows 2000 includes the PPTP and L2TP tunneling protocols. For detailed information about these protocols, see "Point-to-Point Tunneling Protocol" and "Layer Two Tunneling Protocol and Internet Protocol Security" later in this chapter.

Tunneled data. Data that is usually sent across a private point-to-point link.

Transit internetwork. The shared or public internetwork crossed by the encapsulated data. For Windows 2000, the transit internetwork is always an IP internetwork. The transit internetwork can be the Internet or a private IP-based intranet.

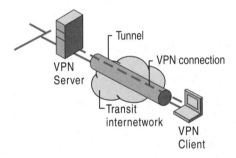

Figure 9.2   Components of a VPN Connection

VPN Connections

Creating the VPN is very similar to establishing a point-to-point connection using dial-up networking and demand-dial routing procedures. There are two types of VPN connections: the remote access VPN connection and the router-to-router VPN connection.

Remote Access VPN Connection

A remote access VPN connection is made by a remote access client, or a single user computer, that connects to a private network. The VPN server provides access to the resources of the VPN server or to the entire network to which the VPN server is attached. The packets sent across the VPN connection originate at the remote access client.

The remote access client (the VPN client) authenticates itself to the remote access server (the VPN server) and, for mutual authentication, the server authenticates itself to the client.

Router-to-Router VPN Connection

A router-to-router VPN connection is made by a router and connects two portions of a private network. The VPN server provides a routed connection to the network to which the VPN server is attached. On a router-to-router VPN connection, the packets sent from either router across the VPN connection typically do not originate at the routers.

The calling router (the VPN client) authenticates itself to the answering router (the VPN server), and, for mutual authentication, the answering router authenticates itself to the calling router.

Properties of VPN Connections

VPN connections that use PPTP and L2TP over IPSec have the following properties:

- Encapsulation
- Authentication
- Data encryption
- Address and name server assignment

Encapsulation

VPN technology provides a way of encapsulating private data with a header that allows the data to traverse the transit internetwork.

Authentication

Authentication for VPN connections takes two forms:

- User authentication

  For the VPN connection to be established, the VPN server authenticates the VPN client attempting the connection and verifies that the VPN client has the appropriate permissions. If mutual authentication is being used, the VPN client also authenticates the VPN server, providing protection against masquerading VPN servers.

- Data authentication and integrity

  To verify that the data being sent on the VPN connection originated at the other end of the connection and was not modified in transit, the data can contain a cryptographic checksum based on an encryption key known only to the sender and the receiver.

Data Encryption

To ensure confidentiality of the data as it traverses the shared or public transit internetwork, it is encrypted by the sender and decrypted by the receiver. The encryption and decryption processes depend on both the sender and the receiver having knowledge of a common encryption key.

Intercepted packets sent along the VPN connection in the transit internetwork are unintelligible to anyone who does not have the common encryption key. The length of the encryption key is an important security parameter. Computational techniques can be used to determine the encryption key. Such techniques require more computing power and computational time as the encryption key gets larger. Therefore, it is important to use the largest possible key size.

In addition, the more information that is encrypted with the same key, the easier it is to decipher the encrypted data. With some encryption technologies, you are given the option to configure how often the encryption keys are changed during a connection.

For more information about how encryption keys are managed for the VPN technologies in Windows 2000, see "VPN Security" later in this chapter.

Address and Name Server Allocation

When a VPN server is configured, it creates a virtual interface that represents the interface on which all VPN connections are made. When a VPN client establishes a VPN connection, a virtual interface is created on the VPN client that represents the interface connected to the VPN server. The virtual interface on VPN client is connected to the virtual interface on the VPN server creating the point-to-point VPN connection.

The virtual interfaces of the VPN client and the VPN server must be assigned IP addresses. The assignment of these addresses is done by the VPN server. By default, the VPN server obtains IP addresses for itself and VPN clients using the Dynamic Host Configuration Protocol (DHCP). You can also configure a static pool of IP addresses defined by an IP network ID and a subnet mask.

Name server assignment, the assignment of domain name system (DNS) and Windows Internet Name Service (WINS) servers, also occurs during the VPN connection establishment process. The VPN client obtains the IP addresses of the DNS and WINS servers from the VPN server for the intranet to which the VPN server is attached.

Internet and Intranet-Based VPN Connections

VPN connections can be used whenever a secure point-to-point connection is needed to connect users or networks. Typical VPN connections are either Internet-based or intranet-based.

Internet-Based VPN Connections

Using an Internet-based VPN connection, you can avoid long-distance and 1-800 telephone charges while taking advantage of the global availability of the Internet.

Remote Access over the Internet

Rather than a remote access client having to make a long distance or 1-800 call to a corporate or outsourced network access server (NAS), the client can call a local ISP. By using the established physical connection to the local ISP, the remote access client initiates a VPN connection across the Internet to the organization's VPN server. When the VPN connection is created, the remote access client can access the resources of the private intranet.

Figure 9.3 illustrates remote access over the Internet.

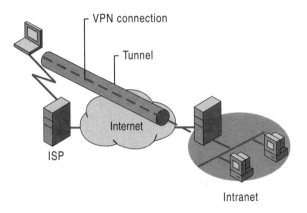

Figure 9.3   VPN Connection Connecting a Remote Client to a Private Intranet

Connecting Networks over the Internet

When networks are connected over the Internet (illustrated in Figure 9.4), a router forwards packets to another router across a VPN connection. To the routers, the VPN operates as a data-link layer link.

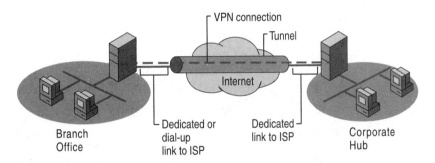

Figure 9.4   VPN Connecting Two Remote Sites Across the Internet

Connecting Networks Using Dedicated WAN Links   Rather than using an expensive long-distance dedicated WAN link between offices, the office routers are connected to the Internet using local dedicated wide area network (WAN) links to a local ISP. A router-to-router VPN connection is then initiated by either router across the Internet. When connected, routers can forward directed or routing protocol traffic to each other using the VPN connection.

Connecting Networks Using Dial-Up WAN Links Rather than having a branch office router make a long distance or 1-800 call to a corporate or outsourced NAS, the branch office router calls a local ISP. Using the established connection to the local ISP, a router-to-router VPN connection is initiated by the branch office router to the corporate hub router across the Internet. The corporate hub router acting as a VPN server must be connected to a local ISP using a dedicated WAN link.

For more information about configuring VPN connections using a dial-up connection to a local ISP, see "Addressing and Routing for VPNs" later in this chapter.

It is possible to have both offices connected to the Internet using a dial-up WAN link. However, this is only feasible if the ISP supports demand-dial routing to customers; the ISP calls the customer router when an IP datagram is to be delivered to the customer. Demand-dial routing to customers is not widely supported by ISPs.

Intranet-Based VPN Connections

The intranet-based VPN connection takes advantage of IP connectivity in an organization intranet.

Remote Access over an Intranet

In some organization intranets, the data of a department, such as a human resources department, is so sensitive that the department's network segment is physically disconnected from the rest of the organization's intranet. While this protects the department's data, it creates information accessibility problems for those users not physically connected to the separate network segment.

VPN connections allow the sensitive department's network segment to be physically connected to the organization intranet but separated by a VPN server. The VPN server does not provide a direct routed connection between the corporate intranet and the separate network segment. Users on the corporate intranet with the appropriate permissions can establish a remote access VPN connection with the VPN server and can gain access to the protected resources of the sensitive department's network. Additionally, all communication across the VPN connection is encrypted for data confidentiality. For those users who do not have permissions to establish a VPN connection, the separate network segment is hidden from view.

Figure 9.5 illustrates remote access over an intranet.

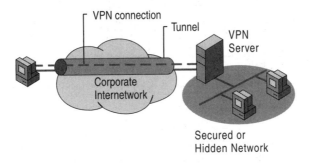

Figure 9.5   VPN Connection Allowing Remote Access to a Secured Network over an Intranet

Connecting Networks over an Intranet

You can also connect two networks over an intranet using a router-to-router VPN connection. This type of VPN connection might be necessary, for example, for two departments in separate locations, whose data is highly sensitive, to communicate with each other. For instance, the finance department might need to communicate with the human resources department to exchange payroll information.

The finance department and the human resources department are connected to the common intranet with computers that can act as VPN clients or VPN servers. When the VPN connection is established, users on computers on either network can exchange sensitive data across the corporate intranet.

Figure 9.6 illustrates networks connected over an intranet.

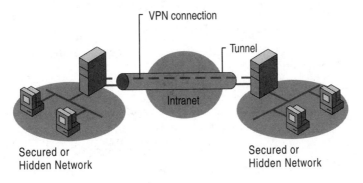

Figure 9.6   VPN Connection Connecting Two Networks over an Intranet

Combined Internet and Intranet VPN Connections

A VPN connection is a networking tool that can provide secured point-to-point connections in whatever manner you see fit. A less common combined Internet and intranet VPN connection, called a pass-through VPN connection, illustrated in Figure 9.7, allows a remote access client connected to one company's intranet to access the resources of another company's intranet using the Internet. In this scenario, a remote access VPN connection passes through one intranet and the Internet to access a second intranet.

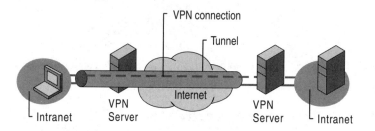

Figure 9.7   Pass-Through VPN Connection

For more information about pass-through VPNs, see "Pass-Through VPN Scenario" later in this chapter.

Managing Virtual Private Networking

Virtual private networking must be managed just like any other network resource, and VPN security issues, particularly with Internet VPN connections, must be addressed carefully. Consider the following questions:

- Where is the user account data to be stored?
- How are addresses assigned to VPN clients?
- Who is allowed to create VPN connections?
- How does the VPN server verify the identity of the user attempting the VPN connection?
- How does the VPN server record the VPN activity?
- How can the VPN server be managed using industry-standard network management protocols and infrastructure?

Managing Users

Because it is administratively unsupportable to have separate user accounts on separate servers for the same user and try to keep them all simultaneously current, most administrators set up a master account database at a domain controller (PDC) or on a Remote Authentication Dial-in User Service (RADIUS) server. This allows the VPN server to send the authentication credentials to a central authenticating device. The same user account is used for both dial-in remote access and VPN-based remote access.

Managing Addresses and Name Servers

The VPN server must have IP addresses available in order to assign them to the VPN server's virtual interface and to VPN clients during the IP Control Protocol (IPCP) negotiation phase of the connection establishment process. The IP address assigned to the VPN client is assigned to the virtual interface of the VPN client.

For Windows 2000–based VPN servers, the IP addresses assigned to VPN clients are obtained through DHCP by default. You can also configure a static IP address pool.

The VPN server must also be configured with DNS and WINS server addresses to assign to the VPN client during IPCP negotiation. For more information about how the VPN server assigns the IP addresses of DNS and WINS servers, see "Remote Access Server" in this book.

Managing Access

For Windows 2000, configure the dial-in properties on user accounts and remote access policies to manage access for dial-up networking and VPN connections.

Access by User Account

If you are managing remote access on a user basis, set the remote access permission on those user accounts that are allowed to create VPN connections to **Allow access**. If the VPN server is only allowing VPN connections, delete the default remote access policy called **Allow access if dial-in permission is enabled**. Then create a new remote access policy with a descriptive name such as **VPN access if allowed by user account**.

If the VPN server is also allowing dial-up remote access services, do not delete the default policy, but move it so that it is the last policy to be evaluated.

As an example of typical settings, configure the remote access policy permission to **Deny remote access permission** and set the conditions and profile settings as listed in Tables 9.1 and 9.2. For detailed information about configuring these settings, see Windows 2000 Server Help.

Table 9.1   Remote Access Policy Conditions for VPN Access by User Account

Conditions	Setting
NAS-Port-Type	**Virtual**

Table 9.2   Remote Access Policy Profile Settings for VPN Access by User Account

Profile settings	Setting
Authentication tab	Enable **Microsoft encrypted authentication version 2 (MS-CHAP v2)** and **Microsoft encrypted authentication (MS-CHAP)**.
Encryption tab	Select **Basic, Strong,** or **Strongest**. Clear **No Encryption**.

If you want to define different authentication, encryption, or other settings for PPTP or L2TP connections, create separate remote access policies using the **Tunnel-Type** remote access policy condition set to either the **Point-to-Point Tunneling Protocol** or the **Layer Two Tunneling Protocol**.

Access by Group Membership

If you are managing remote access on a group basis, set the remote access permission on all user accounts to **Control access through Remote Access Policy**. Create a Windows 2000 group with members who are allowed to create VPN connections. If the VPN server only allows VPN connections, delete the default remote access policy called **Allow access if dial-in permission is enabled**. Then create a new remote access policy with a descriptive name such as **VPN access if member of VPN-allowed group**.

If the VPN server also allows dial-up networking remote access services, do not delete the default policy but move it so that it is the last policy to be evaluated.

As an example of typical settings, configure the remote access policy permission to **Grant remote access permission** and set the conditions and profile settings as listed in Tables 9.3 and 9.4. For detailed information about configuring these settings, see Windows 2000 Server Help.

Table 9.3   Remote Access Policy Conditions for VPN Access by Windows 2000 Group

Conditions	Setting
NAS-Port-Type	**Virtual**
Windows-Groups	Windows 2000 group whose members are allowed to create VPN connections.

Table 9.4   Remote Access Policy Profile Settings for VPN Access by Windows 2000 Group

Profile Settings	Setting
Authentication tab	Enable **Microsoft encrypted authentication version 2 (MS-CHAP v2)** and **Microsoft encrypted authentication (MS-CHAP)**.
Encryption tab	Select **Basic**, **Strong**, or **Strongest**. Clear **No Encryption**.

Managing Authentication

The VPN server can be configured to use either Windows or RADIUS as an authentication provider. If Windows is selected as the authentication provider, the user credentials sent by users attempting VPN connections are authenticated using typical Windows authentication mechanisms.

If RADIUS is selected and configured as the authentication provider on the VPN server, user credentials and parameters of the connection request are sent as a series of RADIUS request messages to a RADIUS server.

The RADIUS server receives a user-connection request from the VPN server and authenticates the user using its authentication database. A RADIUS server can also maintain a central storage database of other relevant user properties. In addition to a yes or no response to an authentication request, RADIUS can inform the VPN server of other applicable connection parameters for this user — such as maximum session time, static IP address assignment, and so on.

RADIUS can respond to authentication requests based on its own database, or it can be a front end to another database server, such as a generic Open Database Connectivity (ODBC) server or a Windows 2000 PDC. The latter example can be located on the same computer as the RADIUS server, or elsewhere. In addition, a RADIUS server can act as a proxy client to a remote RADIUS server.

The RADIUS protocol is described in RFC 2138 and RFC 2139. For more information about the RADIUS protocol and the Windows 2000–based RADIUS server known as Internet Authentication Service, see "Internet Authentication Service" in this book.

Managing Accounting

You can configure the VPN server to use either Windows or RADIUS as an accounting provider. If you select Windows as the accounting provider, the accounting information accumulates on the VPN server for later analysis. If you select RADIUS, RADIUS accounting messages are sent to the RADIUS server for accumulation and later analysis.

You can configure most RADIUS servers to place authentication request records into an accounting file. A number of third parties have written billing and audit packages that read RADIUS accounting records and produce various useful reports. For more information about RADIUS accounting, see RFC 2139.

Network Management

The computer acting as the VPN server can participate in a Simple Network Management Protocol (SNMP) environment as an SNMP agent if the Windows 2000 SNMP Service is installed. The VPN server records management information in various object identifiers of the Internet Management Information Base (MIB) II, which is installed with the Windows 2000 SNMP service. Objects in the Internet MIB II are documented in RFC 1213.

Point-to-Point Tunneling Protocol

The Point-to-Point Tunneling Protocol (PPTP) encapsulates Point-to-Point Protocol (PPP) frames into IP datagrams for transmission over an IP-based internetwork, such as the Internet or a private intranet. PPTP is documented in RFC 2637.

The PPTP uses a TCP connection known as the PPTP control connection to create, maintain, and terminate the tunnel and a modified version of Generic Routing Encapsulation (GRE) to encapsulate PPP frames as tunneled data. The payloads of the encapsulated PPP frames can be encrypted or compressed or both.

PPTP assumes the availability of an IP internetwork between a PPTP client (a VPN client using the PPTP tunneling protocol) and a PPTP server (a VPN server using the PPTP tunneling protocol). The PPTP client might already be attached to an IP internetwork that can reach the PPTP server, or the PPTP client might have to dial into a network access server (NAS) to establish IP connectivity as in the case of dial-up Internet users.

Authentication that occurs during the creation of a PPTP-based VPN connection uses the same authentication mechanisms as PPP connections, such as Extensible Authentication Protocol (EAP), Microsoft Challenge-Handshake Authentication Protocol (MS-CHAP), CHAP, Shiva Password Authentication Protocol (SPAP), and Password Authentication Protocol (PAP). PPTP inherits encryption or compression, or both, of PPP payloads from PPP. For Windows 2000, either EAP-Transport Level Security (EAP-TLS) or MS-CHAP must be used in order for the PPP payloads to be encrypted using Microsoft Point-to-Point Encryption (MPPE).

MPPE provides only link encryption, not end-to-end encryption. End-to-end encryption is data encryption between the client application and the server hosting the resource or service being accessed by the client application. If end-to-end encryption is required, IPSec can be used to encrypt IP traffic from end-to-end after the PPTP tunnel is established.

For Internet-based PPTP servers, the PPTP server is a PPTP-enabled VPN server with one interface on the Internet and a second interface on the intranet.

Tunnel Maintenance with the PPTP Control Connection

The PPTP control connection is between the IP address of the PPTP client using a dynamically allocated TCP port and the IP address of the PPTP server using the reserved TCP port 1723. The PPTP control connection carries the PPTP call control and management messages that are used to maintain the PPTP tunnel. This includes the transmission of periodic PPTP Echo-Request and PPTP Echo-Reply messages to detect a connectivity failure between the PPTP client and PPTP server. PPTP control connection packets consist of an IP header, a TCP header, and a PPTP control message as illustrated in Figure 9.8. The PPTP control connection packet in Figure 9.8 also includes a data-link layer header and trailer.

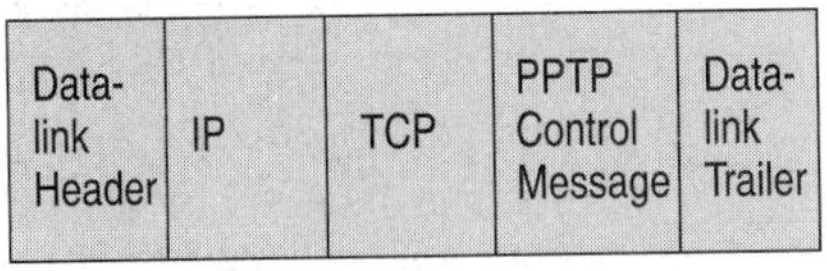

Data-link Header	IP	TCP	PPTP Control Message	Data-link Trailer

Figure 9.8   PPTP Control Connection Packet

Table 9.5 lists the primary PPTP control messages that are sent over the PPTP control connection. For all of the PPTP control messages, the specific PPTP tunnel is identified by the TCP connection.

Table 9.5   PPTP Call Control and Connection Management Messages

Message Type	Purpose
Start-Control-Connection-Request	Sent by the PPTP client to establish the control connection. Each PPTP tunnel requires a control connection to be established before any other PPTP messages can be issued.
Start-Control-Connection-Reply	Sent by the PPTP server to reply to the Start-Control-Connection-Request message.
Outgoing-Call-Request	Sent by the PPTP client to create a PPTP tunnel. Included in the Outgoing-Call-Request message is a Call ID that is used in the GRE header to identify the tunneled traffic of a specific tunnel.
Outgoing-Call-Reply	Sent by the PPTP server in response to the Outgoing-Call-Request message.
Echo-Request	Sent by either the PPTP client or PPTP server as a keep-alive mechanism. If the Echo-Request is not answered, the PPTP tunnel is eventually terminated.
Echo-Reply	The reply to an Echo-Request. **Note:** The PPTP Echo-Request and Echo-Reply messages are not related to the ICMP Echo Request and Echo Reply messages.
WAN-Error-Notify	Sent by the PPTP server to all VPN clients to indicate error conditions on the PPP interface of the PPTP server.
Set-Link-Info	Sent by the PPTP client or PPTP server to set PPP-negotiated options.
Call-Clear-Request	Sent by the PPTP client indicating that a tunnel is to be terminated.
Call-Disconnect-Notify	Sent by the PPTP server in response to a Call-Clear-Request or for other reasons to indicate that a tunnel is to be terminated. If the PPTP server terminates the tunnel, a Call-Disconnect-Notify is sent.
Stop-Control-Connection-Request	Sent by the PPTP client or the PPTP server to inform the other that the control connection is being terminated.
Stop-Control-Connection-Reply	Used to reply to the Stop-Control-Connection-Request message.

For information about the exact structure of PPTP control connection messages, see RFC 2637.

PPTP Data Tunneling

PPTP data tunneling is performed through multiple levels of encapsulation.

Figure 9.9 shows the resulting structure of PPTP tunneled data.

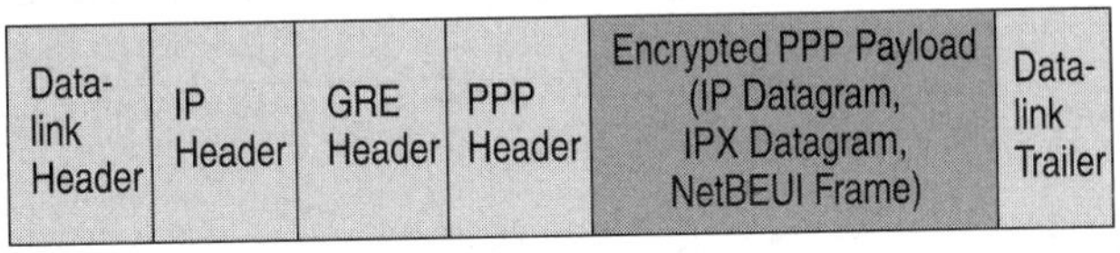

Data-link Header	IP Header	GRE Header	PPP Header	Encrypted PPP Payload (IP Datagram, IPX Datagram, NetBEUI Frame)	Data-link Trailer

Figure 9.9   PPTP Tunneled Data

Encapsulation of PPP Frame

The initial PPP payload is encrypted and encapsulated with a PPP header to create a PPP frame. The PPP frame is then encapsulated with a modified GRE header. GRE is documented in RFC 1701 and RFC 1702 and was designed to provide a simple, lightweight, general purpose mechanism for encapsulating data sent over IP internetworks. GRE is a client protocol of IP using IP protocol 47.

For PPTP, the GRE header is modified in the following ways:

- An acknowledgement bit is used to indicate that a 32-bit acknowledgement field is present and significant.
- The Key field is replaced with a 16-bit Payload Length field and a 16-bit Call ID field. The Call ID field is set by the PPTP client during the creation of the PPTP tunnel.
- A 32-bit Acknowledgement field is added.

Within the GRE header, the Protocol Type is set to 0x880B, the EtherType value for a PPP frame.

Note   GRE is sometimes used by ISPs to forward routing information within an ISP's network. To prevent the routing information from being forwarded to Internet backbone routers, ISPs filter out GRE traffic on the interfaces connected to the Internet backbone. As a result of this filtering, PPTP tunnels can be created using PPTP control messages, but PPTP tunneled data is not forwarded. If you suspect that this is a problem, contact your ISP.

Encapsulation of GRE Packet

The resulting GRE and PPP-encapsulated payload is then encapsulated with an IP header containing the appropriate source and destination IP addresses for the PPTP client and PPTP server.

Data-Link Layer Encapsulation

To be sent on a local area network (LAN) or WAN link, the IP datagram is finally encapsulated with a header and trailer for the data-link layer technology of the outgoing physical interface. For example, when IP datagrams are sent on an Ethernet interface, the IP datagram is encapsulated with an Ethernet header and trailer. When IP datagrams are sent over a point-to-point WAN link, such as an analog phone line or ISDN, the IP datagram is encapsulated with a PPP header and trailer.

Processing of the PPTP Tunneled Data

Upon receipt of the PPTP tunneled data, the PPTP client or PPTP server:

1. Processes and removes the data-link header and trailer.
2. Processes and removes the IP header.
3. Processes and removes the GRE and PPP headers.
4. Decrypts or decompresses, or both, the PPP payload (if needed).
5. Processes the payload for receipt or forwarding.

PPTP Packets and Windows 2000 Networking Architecture

Figure 9.10 illustrates the path that tunneled data takes through the Windows 2000 networking architecture from a VPN client over a remote access VPN connection using an analog modem. The following steps outline this process:

1. An IP datagram, IPX datagram, or NetBEUI frame is submitted by its appropriate protocol to the virtual interface that represents the VPN connection using Network Driver Interface Specification (NDIS).
2. NDIS submits the packet to NDISWAN, which encrypts or compresses the data, or both, and provides a PPP header consisting of only the PPP Protocol ID field. No Flags or Frame Check Sequence (FCS) fields are added. This assumes that address and control field compression were negotiated during the Link Control Protocol (LCP) phase of the PPP connection process. For more information about PPP and LCP, see "Remote Access Server" in this book.
3. NDISWAN submits the data to the PPTP protocol driver, which encapsulates the PPP frame with a GRE header. In the GRE header, the Call ID field is set to the appropriate value to identify the tunnel.
4. The PPTP protocol driver then submits the resulting packet to the TCP/IP protocol driver.
5. The TCP/IP protocol driver encapsulates the PPTP tunneled data with an IP header and submits the resulting packet to the interface that represents the dial-up connection to the local ISP using NDIS.
6. NDIS submits the packet to NDISWAN, which provides PPP headers and trailers.

7. NDISWAN submits the resulting PPP frame to the appropriate WAN miniport driver representing the dial-up hardware (for example, the asynchronous port for a modem connection).

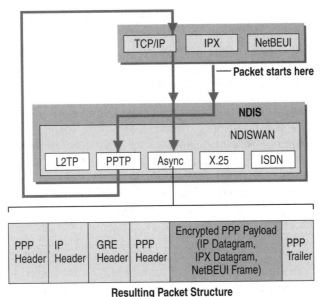

Resulting Packet Structure

Figure 9.10   PPTP Packet Development

Note It is possible to negotiate an encrypted PPP connection for the dial-up connection with the ISP. This is unnecessary and not recommended because the private data being sent, the tunneled PPP frame, is already encrypted. The additional level of encryption is not needed and can impact performance.

Using Network Load Balancing with PPTP

Windows 2000 Network Load Balancing allows you to build a cluster of PPTP servers to enhance the availability of PPTP servers for VPN connections. To create a load-balanced cluster of PPTP servers:

1. Configure each member of the cluster as a Windows 2000 PPTP server. For more information about configuring a Windows 2000 Server computer as PPTP a server, see Windows 2000 Server Help.

2. Configure the collection of PPTP server computers as a Network Load Balancing cluster. For more information about configuring Network Load Balancing, see Windows 2000 Advanced Server Help. When configuring Network Load Balancing on each PPTP server, enable Network Load Balancing on the interface that is receiving PPTP connection requests.

3. In configuring Network Load Balancing on each PPTP server, both a cluster IP address and a dedicated IP address are configured as multiple IP addresses on the interface that is receiving PPTP connection requests. To prevent problems creating PPTP connections with Windows 95, Windows NT 4.0, and Windows 98 PPTP clients, remove the dedicated IP address from the interface that is receiving PPTP connection requests using the properties of the TCP/IP protocol in Network and Dial-up Connections for each PPTP server in the cluster.

4. Removing the dedicated IP address will prevent individual servers from being remotely administered using the dedicated IP address. To allow remote administration of individual PPTP servers in the cluster, ensure that you have an additional LAN interface on each server in the cluster that is connected to a different network segment as the interface receiving PPTP connection requests. For Internet-connected PPTP servers, there is usually an additional interface connected to the intranet that is connected to a different network segment. After removing the dedicated IP address from the Internet interface, you can remotely administer the individual PPTP server from the intranet, but not from the Internet.

Note Windows 95, Windows NT 4.0, and Windows 98 PPTP clients may not be able to connect to the PPTP cluster unless the dedicated IP address is removed because these clients send their PPTP connection requests to the cluster IP address. An individual PPTP server may reply to the PPTP connection request from the dedicated IP address rather than the cluster IP address. If so, the PPTP client notices the change in IP address between the request and the reply, assumes the behavior is a violation of the security of the PPTP connection, and drops the connection.

Layer Two Tunneling Protocol and Internet Protocol Security

Layer Two Tunneling Protocol (L2TP) is a combination of PPTP and Layer 2 Forwarding (L2F), a technology proposed by Cisco® Systems, Inc. Rather than having two incompatible tunneling protocols competing in the marketplace and causing customer confusion, the IETF mandated that the two technologies be combined into a single tunneling protocol that represents the best features of PPTP and L2F. L2TP is documented in RFC 2661.

L2TP encapsulates PPP frames to be sent over IP, X.25, Frame Relay, or ATM networks. Currently, only L2TP over IP networks is defined. When sent over an IP internetwork, L2TP frames are encapsulated as User Datagram Protocol (UDP) messages. L2TP can be used as a tunneling protocol over the Internet or over private intranets.

L2TP uses UDP messages over IP internetworks for both tunnel maintenance and tunneled data. The payloads of encapsulated PPP frames can be encrypted or compressed, or both; however, Windows 2000 L2TP clients do not negotiate the use of MPPE for L2TP connections. Encryption for L2TP connections is provided by IPSec ESP.

It is possible to create L2TP connections in Windows 2000 that are not encrypted by IPSec. However, this is not a VPN connection because the private data being encapsulated by L2TP is not encrypted. Non-encrypted L2TP connections can be used temporarily to troubleshoot an L2TP over IPSec connection by eliminating the IPSec authentication and negotiation process.

L2TP assumes the availability of an IP internetwork between a L2TP client (a VPN client using the L2TP tunneling protocol and IPSec) and a L2TP server (a VPN server using the L2TP tunneling protocol and IPSec). The L2TP client might already be attached to an IP internetwork that can reach the L2TP server, or the L2TP client might have to dial into a NAS to establish IP connectivity as in the case of dial-up Internet users.

Authentication that occurs during the creation of L2TP tunnels must use the same authentication mechanisms as PPP connections such as EAP, MS-CHAP, CHAP, SPAP, and PAP.

For Internet-based L2TP servers, the L2TP server is an L2TP-enabled dial-up server with one interface on the external network, the Internet, and a second interface on the target private network.

L2TP tunnel maintenance and tunneled data have the same packet structure.

Tunnel Maintenance with L2TP Control Messages

Unlike PPTP, L2TP tunnel maintenance is not performed over a separate TCP connection. L2TP call control and management traffic is sent as UDP messages between the L2TP client and the L2TP server. In Windows 2000, the L2TP client and the L2TP server both use UDP port 1701.

Note The L2TP client and L2TP server in Windows 2000 always use UDP port 1701. The Windows 2000 L2TP server supports L2TP clients that use a UDP port other than 1701.

L2TP control messages over IP are sent as UDP datagrams. In the Windows 2000 implementation, L2TP control messages sent as UDP datagrams are sent as the encrypted payload of IPSec ESP as illustrated in Figure 9.11.

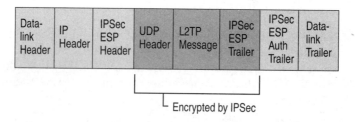

Figure 9.11   L2TP Control Message

Because a TCP connection is not used, L2TP uses message sequencing to ensure delivery of L2TP messages. Within the L2TP control message, the Next-Received field (similar to the TCP Acknowledgment field) and the Next-Sent field (similar to the TCP Sequence Number field) are used to maintain the sequence of control messages. Out-of-sequence packets are dropped. The Next-Sent and Next-Received fields can also be used for sequenced delivery and flow control for tunneled data.

L2TP supports multiple calls for each tunnel. In the L2TP control message and the L2TP header for tunneled data is a Tunnel ID that identifies the tunnel and a Call ID that identifies a call within the tunnel.

Table 9.6 lists the primary L2TP control messages.

Table 9.6   L2TP Control Messages

Message Type	Purpose
Start-Control-Connection-Request	Sent by the L2TP client to establish the control connection. Each L2TP tunnel requires a control connection to be established before any other L2TP messages can be issued. It includes an Assigned Tunnel-ID that is used to identify the tunnel.
Start-Control-Connection-Reply	Sent by the L2TP server to reply to the Start-Control-Connection-Request message.
Start-Control-Connection-Connected	Sent in reply to a Start-Control-Connection-Reply message to indicate that the tunnel establishment was successful.
Outgoing-Call-Request	Sent by the L2TP client to create an L2TP tunnel. Included in the Outgoing-Call-Request message is an Assigned Call ID that is used to identify a call within a specific tunnel.
Outgoing-Call-Reply	Sent by the L2TP server in response to the Outgoing-Call-Request message.
Start-Control-Connection-Connected	Sent in reply to a received Outgoing-Call-Reply message to indicate that the call was successful.
Hello	Sent by either the L2TP client or L2TP server as a keep-alive mechanism. If the Hello is not acknowledged, the L2TP tunnel is eventually terminated.
WAN-Error-Notify	Sent by the L2TP server to all VPN clients to indicate error conditions on the PPP interface of the L2TP server.
Set-Link-Info	Sent by the L2TP client or L2TP server to set PPP-negotiated options.
Call-Disconnect-Notify	Sent by either the L2TP server or L2TP client to indicate that a call within a tunnel is to be terminated.
Stop-Control-Connection-Notification	Sent by either the L2TP server or L2TP client to indicate that a tunnel is to be terminated.

For the exact structure of L2TP control messages, please see the L2TP Internet draft.

L2TP Data Tunneling

L2TP data tunneling is performed through multiple levels of encapsulation.

Figure 9.12 shows the resulting structure of L2TP over IPSec tunneled data.

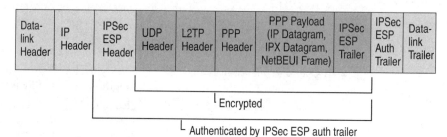

Figure 9.12   L2TP Packet Encapsulation

L2TP Encapsulation

The initial PPP payload is encapsulated with a PPP header and an L2TP header.

UDP Encapsulation

The L2TP encapsulated packet is then encapsulated with a UDP header with the source and destination ports set to 1701.

IPSec Encapsulation

Based on IPSec policy, the UDP message is encrypted and encapsulated with an IPSec Encapsulating Security Payload (ESP) header and trailer and an IPSec Authentication (Auth) trailer.

IP Encapsulation

The IPSec packet is encapsulated with a final IP header containing the source and destination IP addresses of the VPN client and VPN server.

Data-Link Layer Encapsulation

To be sent on a LAN or WAN link, the IP datagram is finally encapsulated with a header and trailer for the data-link layer technology of the outgoing physical interface. For example, when IP datagrams are sent on an Ethernet interface, the IP datagram is encapsulated with an Ethernet header and trailer. When IP datagrams are sent over a point-to-point WAN link such as an analog phone line or ISDN, the IP datagram is encapsulated with a PPP header and trailer.

De-encapsulation of L2TP over IPSec Tunneled Data

Upon receipt of the L2TP over IPSec tunneled data, the L2TP client or L2TP server:

1. Processes and removes the data-link header and trailer.

2. Processes and removes the IP header.

3. Uses the IPSec ESP Auth trailer to authenticate the IP payload and the IPSec ESP header.

4. Uses the IPSec ESP header to decrypt the encrypted portion of the packet.

5. Processes the UDP header and sends the L2TP packet to L2TP.

6. L2TP uses the Tunnel ID and Call ID in the L2TP header to identify the specific L2TP tunnel.

7. Uses the PPP header to identify the PPP payload and forward it to the proper protocol driver for processing.

L2TP over IPSec Packets and Windows 2000 Networking Architecture

Figure 9.13 illustrates the path that tunneled data takes through the Windows 2000 networking architecture from a VPN client over a remote access VPN connection using an analog modem. The following steps outline the process:

1. An IP datagram, IPX datagram, or NetBEUI frame is submitted by the appropriate protocol to the virtual interface that represents the VPN connection using NDIS.

2. NDIS submits a packet to NDISWAN, which optionally compresses and provides a PPP header consisting of only the PPP Protocol ID field. No Flags or FCS fields are added.

3. NDISWAN submits the PPP frame to the L2TP protocol driver, which encapsulates the PPP frame with a L2TP header. In the L2TP header, the Tunnel ID and the Call ID are set to the appropriate value identifying the tunnel.

4. The L2TP protocol driver then submits the resulting packet to the TCP/IP protocol driver with information to send the L2TP packet as a UDP message from UDP port 1701 to UDP port 1701 with the IP addresses of the VPN client and the VPN server.

5. The TCP/IP protocol driver constructs an IP packet with the appropriate IP header and UDP header. IPSec then analyzes the IP packet and matches it with a current IPSec policy. Based on the settings in the policy, IPSec encapsulates and encrypts the UDP message portion of the IP packet using the appropriate ESP headers and trailers.

    The original IP header with the Protocol field set to 50 is added to the front of the ESP packet.

    The TCP/IP protocol driver then submits the resulting packet to the interface that represents the dial-up connection to the local ISP using NDIS.

6. NDIS submits the packet to NDISWAN.

7. NSIDWAN provides PPP headers and trailers and submits the resulting PPP frame to the appropriate WAN miniport driver representing the dial-up hardware.

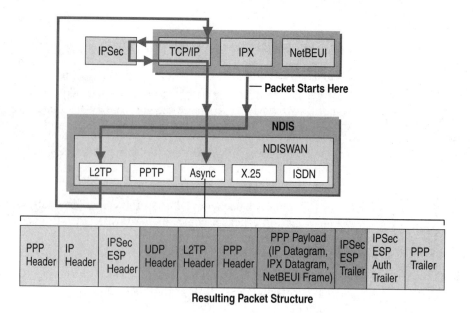

Resulting Packet Structure

Figure 9.13   L2TP Packet Development

Note It is possible to negotiate an encrypted PPP connection for the dial-up connection with an ISP. This is not necessary and not recommended because the private data being sent, the tunneled PPP frame, is already encrypted with IPSec. The additional level of encryption is not needed and can impact performance.

VPN Security

Security is a vital part of a VPN. Described in the following sections are the security facilities of PPTP and L2TP over IPSec VPN connections.

PPTP Connections

PPTP offers user authentication and encryption.

User Authentication with PPP

The user attempting the PPTP connection is authenticated using PPP-based user authentication protocols such as EAP, MS-CHAP, CHAP, SPAP, and PAP. For PPTP connections, EAP-TLS using smart cards or MS-CHAP version 2 is highly recommended as they provide mutual authentication and are the most secure methods of exchanging credentials.

Encryption with MPPE

PPTP inherits MPPE encryption, which uses the Rivest-Shamir-Adleman (RSA) RC4 stream cipher. MPPE is only available when either the EAP-TLS or MS-CHAP (version 1 or version 2) authentication protocols are used.

MPPE can use 40-bit, 56-bit, or 128-bit encryption keys. The 40-bit key provides backward compatibility with non-Windows 2000 clients. By default, the highest key strength supported by the VPN client and VPN server is negotiated during the connection establishment process. If the VPN server requires a higher key strength than is supported by the VPN client, the connection attempt is rejected.

MPPE was originally designed for encryption across a point-to-point link where packets arrive in the same order in which they were sent with little packet loss. For this environment, the decryption of each packet depends on the decryption of the previous packet.

For VPNs, however, IP datagrams sent across the Internet can arrive in a different order from the one in which they were sent, and a higher proportion of packets can be lost. Therefore, MPPE for VPN connections changes the encryption key for each packet. The decryption of each packet is independent of the previous packet. MPPE includes a sequence number in the MPPE header. If packets are lost or arrive out of order, the encryption keys are changed relative to the sequence number.

PPTP Packet Filtering

A PPTP-based VPN server typically has two physical interfaces: one interface on the shared or public network like the Internet, and another on the private intranet. It also has a virtual interface connecting to all VPN clients. For the VPN server to forward traffic between VPN clients, IP forwarding must be enabled on all interfaces. However, enabling forwarding between the two physical interfaces causes the VPN server to route all IP traffic from the shared or public network to the intranet. To protect the intranet from all traffic not sent by a VPN client, PPTP packet filtering must be configured so that the VPN server only performs routing between VPN clients and the intranet and not between potentially malicious users on the shared or public network and the intranet.

PPTP packet filtering can be configured on either the VPN server or on an intermediate firewall. For more information, see "VPNs and Firewalls" later in this chapter.

L2TP over IPSec Connections

L2TP over IPSec offers user authentication, mutual computer authentication, encryption, data authentication, and data integrity.

User Authentication with L2TP over IPSec

Authentication of the VPN client occurs at two different levels: the computer is authenticated, and then the user is authenticated.

IPSec Computer Authentication

Mutual computer authentication of the VPN client and the VPN server is performed when you establish an IPSec ESP security association (SA) through the exchange of computer certificates. IPSec Phase I and Phase II negotiation occurs, and an IPSec SA is established with an agreed encryption algorithm, hash algorithm, and encryption keys.

To use L2TP over IPSec, a computer certificate must be installed on both the VPN client and the VPN server. You can obtain computer certificates automatically by configuring an auto-enrollment Windows 2000 Group Policy or manually using the Certificates snap-in. For more information, see Windows 2000 Server Help.

L2TP User-Level Authentication

The user attempting the L2TP connection is authenticated using PPP-based user authentication protocols such as EAP, MS-CHAP, CHAP, SPAP, and PAP. Because the PPP connection establishment process is encrypted by IPSec, any PPP authentication method can be used. Mutual user-level authentication occurs if you use MS-CHAP v2 or EAP-TLS.

L2TP Tunnel Authentication

L2TP also provides a way to authenticate the endpoints of an L2TP tunnel during the tunnel establishment process known as L2TP tunnel authentication. By default, Windows 2000 does not perform L2TP tunnel authentication. For more information about configuring Windows 2000 for L2TP tunnel authentication, see the Microsoft Knowledge Base link on the Web Resources page at http://windows.microsoft.com/windows2000/reskit/webresources.

Encryption with L2TP over IPSec

Encryption is determined by the establishment of the IPSec SA. The available encryption algorithms include:

- DES with a 56-bit key.
- Triple DES (3DES), which uses three 56-bit keys and is designed for high-security environments.

Because IPSec was designed for IP internetworks where packets could be lost and arrive out of order, each IPSec packet is decrypted independent of other IPSec packets.

The initial encryption keys are derived from the IPSec authentication process. For DES-encrypted connections, new encryption keys are generated after every 5 minutes or 250 megabytes of data transferred. For 3DES-encrypted connections, new encryption keys are generated after every hour or 2 gigabytes of data transferred. For AH-protected connections, new hash keys are generated after every hour or 2 gigabytes of data transferred. For more information about IPSec, see "Internet Protocol Security" in the *TCP/IP Core Networking Guide*.

Data Authentication and Integrity with L2TP over IPSec

Data authentication and integrity is provided by one of the following:

- The hash message authentication code (HMAC) Message Digest 5 (MD5), a hash algorithm producing a 128-bit hash of the authenticated payload.
- The HMAC Secure Hash Algorithm (SHA), a hash algorithm producing a 160-bit hash of the authenticated payload.

L2TP over IPSec Packet Filtering

Just as in PPTP-based VPN connections, the enabling of forwarding between the interfaces on the public or shared network and the intranet causes the VPN server to route all IP traffic from the shared or public network to the intranet. To protect the intranet from all traffic not sent by a VPN client, you must configure L2TP over IPSec packet filtering so that the VPN server only performs routing between VPN clients and the intranet and not between potentially malicious users on the shared or public network and the intranet.

L2TP over IPSec packet filtering can be configured on either the VPN server or on an intermediate firewall. For more information, see "VPNs and Firewalls" later in this chapter.

Addressing and Routing for VPNs

To understand how VPNs work, you must understand how addressing and routing is affected by the creation of remote access VPNs and router-to-router VPNs. A VPN connection creates a virtual interface that must be assigned a proper IP address, and routes must be changed or added to ensure that the proper traffic is sent across the secure VPN connection instead of the shared or public transit internetwork.

Remote Access VPN Connections

For remote access VPN connections, a computer creates a remote access connection to a VPN server. During the connection process the VPN server assigns an IP address for the remote access VPN client and changes the default route on the remote client so that default route traffic is sent over the virtual interface.

IP Addresses and the Dial-Up VPN Client

For dial-up VPN clients who connect to the Internet before creating a VPN connection with a VPN server on the Internet, two IP addresses are allocated:

- When creating the PPP connection, IPCP negotiation with the ISP NAS assigns a public IP address.
- When creating the VPN connection, IPCP negotiation with the VPN server assigns an intranet IP address. The IP address allocated by the VPN server can be a public IP address or private IP address, depending on whether your organization is implementing public or private addressing on its intranet.

In either case, the IP address allocated to the VPN client must be reachable by hosts on the intranet and vice versa. The VPN server must have appropriate entries in its routing table to reach all the hosts on the intranet and the routers of the intranet must have the appropriate entries in their routing tables to reach the VPN clients.

The tunneled data sent through the VPN is addressed from the VPN client's VPN server-allocated address to an intranet address. The outer IP header is addressed between the ISP-allocated IP address of the VPN client and the public address of the VPN server. Because the routers on the Internet only process the outer IP header, the Internet routers forward the tunneled data to the VPN server's public IP address.

An example of dial-up client addressing is shown in Figure 9.14 where the organization uses private addresses on the intranet, and the tunneled data is an IP datagram.

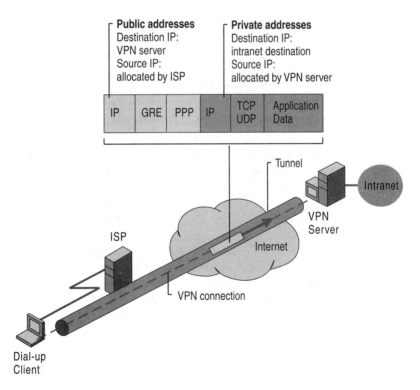

Figure 9.14   Public and Private Addresses in PPTP Tunneled Data

Default Routes and Dial-Up Clients

When a typical dial-up client dials the ISP, it receives a public IP address from the ISP NAS. A default gateway address is not allocated as part of the IPCP negotiation process. Therefore, in order to reach all Internet addresses, the dial-up client adds a default route to its routing table using the dial-up interface connected to the ISP. As a result, the client can forward the IP datagrams to the ISP NAS from where they are routed to its Internet location.

For dial-up clients with no other TCP/IP interfaces, this is the wanted behavior. However, this behavior can cause confusion for dial-up clients that have an existing LAN-based connection to an intranet. In this scenario, a default route already exists pointing to the local intranet router. When the dial-up client creates a connection with their ISP, the original default route remains in the routing table but is changed to have a higher metric. A new default route is added with a lower metric using the ISP connection.

As a result, the intranet locations that are not on the dial-up client's directly attached network are not reachable for the duration of the connection to the ISP. If the new default route is not created, all intranet locations are reachable, but Internet locations are not.

A Windows 2000–based dial-up client creates the default route by default.

▶ **To prevent the default route from being created**

   ▪ In the properties of the TCP/IP protocol of the dial-up connection object, in the **Advanced TCP/IP Settings** dialog box, click the **General** tab, and then clear the **Use default gateway on remote network** check box.

To achieve connectivity to both intranet and Internet locations while the ISP connection is active, leave the **Use default gateway on remote network** option selected and add the routes of the intranet to the routing table of the dial-up client. The intranet routes can be added through static persistent routes using the route utility, or, if Routing Information Protocol (RIP) version 1 is being used as the intranet routing protocol, you can use the Route Listening Service to listen to RIP version 1 routing protocol traffic and dynamically add intranet routes. When connected to the ISP, all intranet locations are reachable using the intranet routes and all Internet locations are reachable using the default route.

Default Routes and VPNs over the Internet

When the dial-up client calls the ISP, it adds a default route using the connection to the ISP as shown in Figure 9.15. At this point, it can reach all Internet addresses through the router at the ISP NAS.

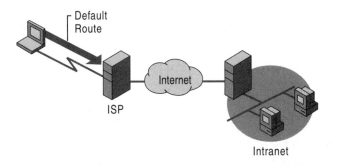

Figure 9.15   Default Route Created When Dialing an ISP

When the VPN client creates the VPN connection, another default route and a host route to the IP address of the tunnel server are added, as illustrated in Figure 9.16. The previous default route is saved but now has a higher metric. Adding the new default route means that all Internet locations except the IP address of the tunnel server are not reachable for the duration of the VPN connection.

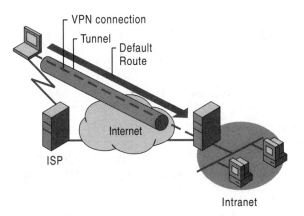

Figure 9.16   Default Route Created When Initiating the VPN

Just as in the case of a dial-up client connecting to the Internet, when a dial-up VPN client using voluntary tunneling creates a VPN connection to a private intranet across the Internet, one of the following occurs:

- Internet locations are reachable and intranet locations are not reachable when the VPN connection is not active.

- Intranet locations are reachable and Internet locations are not reachable when the VPN connection is active.

For most Internet-connected VPN clients, this behavior does not represent a problem because they are typically engaged in either intranet or Internet communication, not both.

For VPN clients who want concurrent access to intranet and Internet resources when the VPN is connected, the solution depends on the nature of the IP addressing in the intranet. In all cases, configure the VPN connection object so that it does not add a default gateway. When the VPN connection is created, the default route remains pointed to the ISP NAS, allowing access to all Internet addresses.

Based on the type of intranet addressing you use, enable concurrent access to intranet and Internet resources as follows:

Public Addresses Add static persistent routes for the public network IDs of the intranet using the IP address of the VPN server's virtual interface as the gateway IP address.

Private Addresses Add static persistent routes for the private network IDs of the intranet using the IP address of the VPN server's virtual interface as the gateway IP address.

Overlapping or Illegal Addresses If the intranet is using overlapping or illegal addresses (IP network IDs that are not private and have not been registered by Internet Network Information Center [InterNIC] or obtained from an ISP), those IP addresses might be duplicated by public addresses on the Internet. If static persistent routes are added on the VPN client for the overlapping network IDs of the intranet, the locations on the Internet for the overlapping addresses are not reachable.

In each of these cases, static persistent routes for the network IDs of the intranet need to be added to the VPN client. When the persistent routes are added, they are saved in the registry. With Windows NT 4.0 Service Pack 3 and later and with Windows 2000, the persistent routes are not actually added to the IP routing table (and are not visible with the **route print** command at the Windows 2000 command prompt) until the IP address of the gateway is reachable. The IP address of the gateway becomes reachable when the VPN connection is made.

For each route, type the following route utility syntax at a Windows 2000 command prompt:

```
ROUTE ADD <Intranet Network ID> MASK <NetMask> <IP address of VPN
server's virtual interface> -p
```

The gateway IP address in the route commands for each intranet route is the IP address assigned to the VPN server's virtual interface, not the IP address of the VPN server's Internet interface.

You can determine the IP address of the VPN server's virtual interface from the IP address of the **Internal** interface under **IP Routing** - **General** in the Routing and Remote Access snap-in. If you use DHCP to obtain IP addresses for dial-up networking and VPN clients, the IP address of the VPN server's virtual interface is the first IP address obtained when requesting DHCP addresses. If you have configured a static IP address pool, the IP address of the VPN server's virtual interface is the first IP address in the static IP address pool. You can also determine the IP address of the VPN server's virtual interface by double-clicking the virtual private networking connection object when the VPN connection is active. In the resulting **Status** dialog box, click the **Details** tab.

Caution   For all of these cases, you must add the routes very carefully to ensure that the private traffic to the intranet is forwarded using the VPN connection and not the PPP connection to the ISP. If the wrong routes are added, the traffic that you intend to forward across the VPN in an encrypted form is instead sent unencrypted across the Internet. For example, if your intranet is using the public network ID 207.46.130.0/24 (subnet mask 255.255.255.0), and you mistakenly add a persistent static route for 207.46.131.0/24, all traffic to the intranet network 207.46.130.0/24 is forwarded across the Internet in plaintext, rather than being encrypted and sent across the VPN connection.

Router-to-Router VPN Connections

For router-to-router VPNs, the routing interface used to forward packets is a demand-dial interface configured as follows:

- On the **General** tab, type the host name or IP address of the VPN server.
- On the **Security** tab, select either **Secure my password and data** or **Custom**. If you select **Custom**, you must also select the appropriate encryption and authentication options.
- On the **Networking** tab, select the appropriate server type and protocols to be routed. If you set the server type as **Automatic**, an L2TP over IPSec connection is attempted first, and then a PPTP connection.
- Under **Interface** credentials, type the user name, password, and domain name used to verify the calling router.

The creation of demand-dial interfaces is automated with the Demand-Dial Interface Wizard.

The names of the demand-dial interfaces and the calling router credentials may need to be properly matched to ensure a router-to-router VPN connection. For more information, see "Demand-Dial Routing" in this book.

Temporary vs. Persistent Router-to-Router VPNs

Router-to-router VPN connections can be either temporary or persistent.

- Temporary router-to-router VPN connections are made when there are packets to be routed across the VPN demand-dial interface and terminated after a specified amount of idle time. Idle time is configured on both the VPN client (the calling router) and the VPN server (the called router). The default idle time for demand-dial interfaces on the VPN client is unlimited. The default idle time for VPN connections on the VPN server is 20 minutes. Both idle times are configurable. Use temporary router-to-router VPN connections for branch offices who use dial-up connections to their local ISPs.

- Persistent router-to-router VPN connections are made when the router is started and remain connected regardless of the traffic being sent. If the VPN connection is terminated, it is automatically attempted again. Use persistent router-to-router VPN connections to connect offices that have permanent connections to the Internet.

▶ **To configure either a persistent or temporary connection**

1. In the Routing and Remote Access snap-in, select **Routing Interfaces**.

2. Right-click the demand-dial interface object, and then select **Properties**.

3. On the **Options** tab, under **Connection Type**, select either **Demand dial** or **Persistent**.

VPNs Using Dial-Up ISP Connections

When both the VPN server and the VPN client are directly connected to the Internet using a permanent WAN link such as T1 or Frame Relay, the VPN connection can be persistent and available 24 hours a day. However, when a permanent WAN link is not possible or practical, you can configure an on-demand router-to-router VPN connection using a dial-up ISP.

An on-demand router-to-router VPN connection using a dial-up ISP connection consists of two demand-dial interfaces:

- A demand-dial interface to dial-in to a local ISP.

- A demand-dial interface for the router-to-router VPN connection.

An on-demand router-to-router VPN connection is automatically established when traffic to be forwarded across the VPN connection is received by the branch office router. For example, when receiving a packet to be routed to the corporate office, the branch office router first uses a dial-up link to connect to a local ISP. When the Internet connection is made, the branch office router, the VPN client, creates a router-to-router VPN connection with the corporate office router, the VPN server.

▶ **To configure an on-demand VPN connection at the branch office router**

1. Create a demand-dial interface for the Internet connection configured for the appropriate equipment (a modem or ISDN device), the phone number of the local ISP, and the user name and password used to gain Internet access.

2. Create a demand-dial interface for the router-to-router VPN connection with the corporate office router configured for PPTP or L2TP, the IP address or host name of the corporate office VPN server's interface on the Internet, and a user name and password that can be verified by the VPN server. The user name must match the name of a demand-dial interface on the corporate office VPN server.

3. Create a static host route for the IP address of the VPN server's Internet interface that uses the demand-dial interface used to dial the local ISP.

4. Create a static route or routes for the IP network IDs of the corporate intranet that uses the VPN demand-dial interface.

▶ **To configure the corporate office router**

1. Create a demand-dial interface for the VPN connection with the branch office configured for a VPN device (a PPTP or L2TP port). The demand-dial interface must have the same name as the user name in the authentication credential that is used by the branch office router to create the VPN connection.

2. Create a static route or routes for the IP network IDs of the branch office that uses the VPN demand-dial interface.

The router-to-router VPN connection is automatically initiated by the branch office router through the following process:

1. Packets sent to a corporate hub network location from a user in the branch office are forwarded by the user to the branch office router.

2. The branch office router checks its routing table and finds a route to the corporate intranet network ID, which uses the VPN demand-dial interface.

3. The branch office router checks the state of the VPN demand-dial interface and finds it is in a disconnected state.

4. The branch office router retrieves the configuration of the VPN demand-dial interface.

5. Based on the VPN demand-dial interface configuration, the branch office router attempts to initialize a router-to-router VPN connection at the IP address of the VPN server on the Internet.

6. To establish a VPN, either a TCP connection (by using PPTP) or an IPSec negotiation must be established with the VPN server. The VPN establishment packet is created.

7. To forward the VPN establishment packet to the corporate office router, the branch office router checks its routing table and finds the host route using the ISP demand-dial interface.

8. The branch office router checks the state of the ISP demand-dial interface and finds it is in a disconnected state.

9. The branch office router retrieves the configuration of the ISP demand-dial interface.

10. Based on the ISP demand-dial interface configuration, the branch office router uses its modem or ISDN adapter to dial and establish a connection with its local ISP.

11. When the ISP connection is made, the VPN establishment packet is sent by the branch office router to the corporate office router.

12. A VPN is negotiated between the branch office router and the corporate office router. As part of the negotiation, the branch office router sends authentication credentials that are verified by the corporate office router.

13. The corporate office router checks its demand-dial interfaces and finds one that matches the user name sent during authentication and changes the interface to a connected state.

14. The branch office router forwards the packet across the VPN and the VPN server forwards the packet to the appropriate intranet location.

Static vs. Dynamic Routing

When the demand-dial interfaces are created and the choice has been made between temporary and persistent connections, you must choose one of the following methods for adding routing information to the routing table:

1. For temporary connections, you can manually add the appropriate static routes to reach network IDs in the other offices. Manual configuration of static routes is appropriate for small implementations with a small number of routes.

2. For temporary connections, you can use auto-static updates to periodically update the static routes that are available across the router-to-router VPN connection. Auto-static routes work well for larger implementations with a large amount of routing information. For more information about auto-static updates, see "Demand-Dial Routing" in this book.

3. For persistent connections, run the appropriate routing protocols over the router-to-router VPN connection treating the VPN connection as a point-to-point link.

Note Unlike demand-dial routing using direct physical connections, you cannot use a default IP route configured for the VPN demand-dial interface to summarize all the intranet routes available across the VPN. Because the router is connected to the Internet, you must use the default route to summarize all the routes of the Internet and configure it to use the Internet interface.

Pre-shared Key Authentication for L2TP over IPSec Router-to-Router VPN Connections

By default, both the L2TP client and L2TP server for Windows 2000 are pre-configured for certificate-based IPSec authentication. When you make an L2TP over IPSec connection, an IPSec policy is automatically created to specify that the Internet Key Exchange (IKE) will use certificate-based authentication during the negotiation of security settings for L2TP. This means that both the L2TP client and L2TP server must have a computer certificate (also known as a machine certificate) installed before a successful L2TP over IPSec connection can be established. Both computer certificates must either be from the same certificate authority (CA), or the root certificate of each computer's CA must be installed as a trusted root certificate authority in each other's trusted root certificate store. For more information about IPSec, see "Internet Protocol Security" in the *TCP/IP Core Networking Guide*.

In some cases, a certificate-based IPSec authentication method is not desired for L2TP-based router-to-router VPN connections. For example, if you have a small organization and do not want to deploy a certificate infrastructure, or you are connecting to routers that do not support certificate-based IPSec authentication. In these cases, you can manually configure IPSec policy to use pre-shared keys when creating router-to-router VPN connections. This pre-shared authentication key acts like a simple password in the IKE negotiation, if both sides can prove they know the same password, then they trust each other and will continue to negotiate private, symmetric encryption keys, and specific security settings for L2TP traffic.

Using an IKE pre-shared key is generally considered not as secure as using certificates because the IKE authentication (and implicit trust) is dependent on the key value only, which is stored in plain text format in the IPSec policy. Anyone who views the policy can see the pre-shared key value. If a malicious user views the pre-shared key, then they could configure their system to successfully establish IPSec security with your system. However, the L2TP connection requires user level authentication using a PPP authentication protocol. Therefore, a malicious user would have to know both the pre-shared key and the proper user credentials to successfully establish the L2TP over IPSec connection.

To perform pre-shared key authentication for L2TP over IPSec router-to-router VPN connections, you must change a registry setting and then configure IPSec policy settings.

To prevent the Routing and Remote Access service from automatically creating an IPSec policy for L2TP traffic, set the value of ProhibitIpSec to 1 (HKEY_LOCAL_MACHINE\SYSTEM\CurrentControlSet\Services\RasMan \Parameters). By default, ProhibitIpSec is set to 0. When ProhibitIpSec is set to 1, the encryption settings on the demand-dial interface configured on the calling router are ignored in favor of the encryption settings of the manually configured IPSec policy. The computer must be restarted for the changes to this registry setting to take effect.

Where you configure the IPSec settings depends on the following:

- If the VPN server is a stand-alone server or a member of a Windows NT 4.0 domain, then you must configure local machine IPSec policy.

- If the VPN server is a member of Windows 2000 domain, local IPSec policies are overwritten by assigned domain IPSec policies. In order to create IPSec policy that is only applied to the VPN server, create an organizational unit (OU) in the Active Directory™ directory service, place the VPN server computer account in the OU, and use the Group Policy to create and assign IPSec policies for the VPN server OU. The IPSec policies created for the VPN server OU will be propagated to the VPN server.

Before creating IPSec policy, you must decide whether all sites being connected will use the same pre-shared key or whether each connection will use a separate pre-shared key. This decision impacts how IPSec filter lists and policy are configured.

The same pre-shared key may be used when one administrator or company controls both L2TP tunnel endpoints.

Different pre-shared keys may be used when configuring L2TP tunnels between systems that are not under the same administrative or corporate security control. For example, one Windows 2000 VPN server may be configured to communicate to six different business partners, each of which need a different IKE pre-shared key for L2TP connections.

For example purposes, the following sections discuss the IPSec configuration required for a router that is using L2TP over IPSec pre-shared key authentication for router-to-router VPN connections between a corporate hub office in New York and two branch offices; one in Boston and one in London.

Note If you have a Windows 2000 VPN server that is communicating to other L2TP clients or servers using the default certificate-based IPSec authentication, and you want to use IPSec pre-shared key authentication for one L2TP/IPSec tunnel, then you must include rules to use certificate authentication for those systems already using it, as well as a rule for pre-shared key authentication in the same IPSec policy.

Same Pre-shared Key for All Connections

To use the same pre-shared key for all L2TP over IPSec router-to-router VPN connections, configure the following:

1. Using the Routing and Remote Access snap-in, create the appropriate demand-dial interfaces. In our example, create a demand-dial interface for the connection to the Boston branch office and a demand-dial interface to the London branch office.

2. Using the IP Security Policies snap-in, create an IPSec filter action that does not allow unsecured L2TP communication.

3. Create one IPSec filter list that contains filters for all the L2TP over IPSec connections using the same IKE pre-shared authentication key value. Each filter within the filter list is for a specific location. Using our example, you would configure a filter list with two filters, one filter defining the L2TP traffic to the Boston router and one filter defining the L2TP traffic to the London router.

4. Create a new IPSec policy that uses a single active rule; a rule that uses the filter action that does not allow unsecured L2TP communication, the filter list for all the L2TP over IPSec connections, and a pre-shared key as the authentication method.

Creating the Filter Action

To create a filter action that does not permit unsecured L2TP communication, create a filter action with the following properties:

- On the **General** tab:

  - Name: Secure L2TP (example)

  - Description: Requires inbound negotiation. Discards clear text inbound. Forces negotiation outbound. (example)

- On the Security Methods tab:

  - Select **Negotiate security** and add at least the **High** type to the list. Add additional types as needed.

  - Clear the Accept unsecured communication, but always respond using IPSec and Allow unsecured with non IPSec-aware computer check boxes. Select the Session key Perfect Forward Secrecy check box if needed.

The example discussed here use the same encryption strength for all destinations. However, you may need to create filter actions specific to a destination, depending on the IPSec security capabilities of the remote system. For example, a filter action for Boston may require only 3DES encryption, whereas a filter action for London may require only DES due to cryptography export restrictions. To handle both 3DES and DES in the same filter action, include them both in the filter action security method list, putting 3DES first to make sure it is selected first when possible.

Creating the Filter List for the Same Pre-shared Key for all Connections

To configure a filter list that contains all L2TP-based router-to-router VPN connections, create a filter list with the following properties:

- Name: L2TP connections (example)
- Description: Destinations for L2TP pre-shared key connections. (example)

Then, for each destination, create a filter within the filter list with the following configuration:

- On the **Addressing** tab:
  - Under **Source Address**, select **A specific IP Address** and type the IP address of an Internet interface of the local router. In our example, type the IP address of the New York router's Internet interface.
  - Under **Destination Address**, select **A specific IP Address** and type the IP address of an Internet interface of the router on the other end of this router-to-router VPN connection. In our example, for the Boston connection, type the IP address of the Boston router's Internet interface.
  - Select **Mirrored**.
- On the **Protocol** tab:
  - Under **Select a protocol type**, select **UDP**.
  - Under **Set the IP protocol port**, select **From this port** and type **1701**, and then select **To any port**.
- On the **Description** tab:
  - Under **Description**, type a description of this filter that describes its connection endpoint. For example, for the demand-dial connection to Boston, type the description: L2TP to Boston. This description appears in the IPSec monitor utility.

Configuring an IPSec Policy for the Same Pre-shared Key

To configure an IPSec policy that uses the same pre-shared key for all L2TP-based router-to-router VPN connections, create an IPSec policy with the following properties:

- On the **General** tab:

  - Name: Pre-shared key L2TP Connections (example)

  - Description: IPSec pre-shared key authentication for L2TP over IPSec router-to-router VPN connections. (example)

  - Change **Check for policy changes every** and **Advanced** settings as needed.

- On the **Rules** tab:

  - Clear the **Default Response** rule.

Add a rule with the following properties:

- On the IP Filter List tab:

  - Select the IP filter list that corresponds to all L2TP connections to all branch offices. Using our example, select the IP filter list called **L2TP connections**.

- On the **Filter Action** tab:

  - Select the filter action that does not allow unsecured L2TP communication. Using our example, select the filter action called **Secure L2TP**.

- On the **Authentication Methods** tab:

  - Under **Authentication Method preference order**, configure a single method that uses the pre-shared key. Type the pre-shared key that is common between all routers to which this router is making a pre-shared key L2TP over IPSec connection. When configuring a pre-shared key, choose a key that is at least 20 characters long and is a random mixture of upper and lower case letters, numbers and punctuation characters.

- On the **Tunnel Setting** tab:

  - Select **This rule does not specify an IPSec tunnel**.

- On the **Connection Type** tab:

  - Select **All network connections**.

Because the filter list contains all of the destinations for L2TP-based router-to-router VPN connections, only a single rule within the IPSec policy is required.

Different Pre-shared Keys for Different Connections

To use different pre-shared keys for all L2TP over IPSec router-to-router VPN connections, configure the following:

1. Create the appropriate demand-dial interfaces. In our example, create a demand-dial interface for the connection to the Boston branch office and a demand-dial interface to the London branch office.

2. Create a filter action that does not allow unsecured L2TP communication.

3. Create an IPSec filter list that contains a single filter for the L2TP over IPSec connection to a specific location. Using our example, configure a filter list with one filter defining the L2TP traffic to the Boston router. Then, configure another filter list with one filter defining the L2TP traffic to the London router.

4. Create a new IPSec policy that uses a series of rules; each rule uses the filter action that does not allow unsecured L2TP communication, the filter list for a specific L2TP over IPSec connection, and the pre-shared key for the specific connection as the authentication method.

Creating the Filter Action

The configuration of the filter action for the different pre-shared key for different connections is the same as the filter action for the same pre-shared key for all connections.

Creating the Filter List for a Different Pre-shared Key for all Connections

To configure a filter list for a specific router-to-router VPN connection, create a filter list with the following properties (using the connection to Boston as an example):

- Name: L2TP pre-shared key connection to Boston (example)

- Description: Boston destination for L2TP pre-shared key connection. (example)

Then, create a single filter with the following configuration:

- On the **Addressing** tab:
    - Under **Source Address**, select **A specific IP Address** and type the IP address of an Internet interface of the router. In our example, type the IP address of the New York router's Internet interface.
    - Under **Destination Address**, select **A specific IP Address** and type the IP address of an Internet interface of the router on the other end of this router-to-router VPN connection. For example, type the IP address of the Boston router's Internet interface.
    - Select **Mirrored**.

- On the **Protocol** tab:
    - Select a protocol type: Select **UDP**.
    - Set the IP protocol port: Select **From this port** and type **1701**, and then select **To this port**.
- On the **Description** tab:
    - Under **Description**, type a description of this filter that describes the connection endpoint. For example, for the demand-dial connection to Boston, type the description: L2TP to Boston. This description appears in the IPSec monitor utility.

Repeat this procedure for each L2TP over IPSec router-to-router VPN connection. Using our example, configure another IPSec filter list for the connection to the London router.

Configuring an IPSec Policy for a Different Pre-shared Key for Each Connection

To configure an IPSec policy that uses a different pre-shared key for each L2TP router-to-router VPN connection, create an IPSec policy with the following properties:

- On the **General** tab:
    - Name: Pre-shared key L2TP Connections (example)
    - Description: IPSec pre-shared key authentication for L2TP over IPSec router-to-router VPN connections. (example)
    - Change **Check for policy changes every** and **Advanced** settings as needed.
- On the **Rules** tab:
    - Clear the **Default Response** rule.

For each L2TP router-to-router VPN connection, add a rule with the following properties (using the connection to Boston as an example):

- On the **IP Filter List** tab:
    - Select the IP filter list that corresponds to an L2TP over IPSec connection. In our example, you would select the IP filter list called **L2TP pre-shared key connection to Boston**.
- On the **Filter Action** tab:
    - Select the filter action that does not allow unsecured L2TP communication. In our example, you would select the filter action called **Secure L2TP**.

- On the **Authentication Methods** tab:
  - Under **Authentication Method preference order**, configure a single method that uses pre-shared key. Type the pre-shared key that is common between the two routers on this router-to-router VPN connection. Using our example, type the pre-shared key used by the New York and Boston routers for the New York to Boston VPN connection. When configuring a pre-shared key, choose a key that is at least 20 characters long and is a random mixture of upper and lower case letters, numbers and punctuation characters.
- On the **Tunnel Setting** tab:
  - Select **This rule does not specify an IPSec tunnel**.
- On the **Connection Type** tab:
  - Select **All network connections**.

Add a separate rule for each L2TP over IPSec router-to-router VPN connection. Using our example, add another rule for the connection to the London router.

Note For an incoming L2TP over IPSec connection, the Routing and Remote Access service queries IPSec to discover the type of encryption that was negotiated. The query is for the encryption used for an IPSec security association (SA) for IP traffic to UDP port 1701. If an IPSec SA exists for IP traffic to UDP port 1701, the type of encryption used for the IPSec SA is returned. When ProhibitIpSec is set to 0, an IPSec SA is always found for this type of traffic because L2TP traffic filters are automatically created by the Routing and Remote Access service. The encryption type is then compared to the types of encryption allowed by the profile settings of the matching remote access policy for the L2TP connection. If the encryption type returned from the IPSec query does not match the allowed encryption strengths in the remote access policy profile, the connection attempt is rejected. If ProhibitIpSec is set to 1 and a specific filter for UDP port 1701 is not configured, the query fails to find an SA for IP traffic to UDP port 1701 and no encryption is assumed. This can cause the connection attempt to be rejected if the encryption setting on the matching remote access policy profile has the **No encryption** setting disabled. Therefore, the disconnection of encrypted L2TP over IPSec connections can occur when an IPSec filter exists that uses pre-shared key for all IP traffic and a specific filter for UDP port 1701 is not configured.

Using IPSecPol to Create the IPSec Policy

IPSec policy for pre-shared key L2TP over IPSec connections can also be configured using the IPSecPol Resource Kit tool. For more information, see the Windows 2000 Resource Kit Tools Help.

VPNs and Firewalls

A firewall employs packet filtering to allow or disallow the flow of very specific types of network traffic. IP packet filtering provides a way for you to define precisely what IP traffic is allowed to cross the firewall. IP packet filtering is important when you connect private intranets to public networks like the Internet.

VPN Server and Firewall Configurations

There are two approaches to using a firewall with a VPN server:

- The VPN server is attached to the Internet and the firewall is between the VPN server and the intranet.

- The firewall is attached to the Internet and the VPN server is between the firewall and the intranet.

VPN Server in Front of the Firewall

With the VPN server in front of the firewall attached to the Internet, as shown in Figure 9.17, you need to add packet filters to the Internet interface that only allow VPN traffic to and from the IP address of the VPN server's interface on the Internet.

For inbound traffic, when the tunneled data is decrypted by the VPN server it is forwarded to the firewall, which employs its filters to allow the traffic to be forwarded to intranet resources. Because the only traffic that is crossing the VPN server is traffic generated by authenticated VPN clients, firewall filtering in this scenario can be used to prevent VPN users from accessing specific intranet resources.

Because the only Internet traffic allowed on the intranet must go through the VPN server, this approach also prevents the sharing of File Transfer Protocol (FTP) or Web intranet resources with non-VPN Internet users.

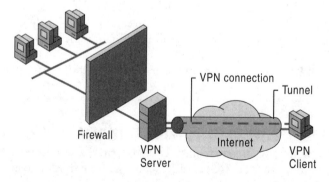

Figure 9.17   VPN Server on the Internet in Front of the Firewall

For the Internet interface on the VPN server, configure the following input and output filters using the Routing and Remote Access snap-in.

Packet Filters for PPTP

Configure the following input filters with the filter action set to **Drop all packets except those that meet the criteria below**:

- Destination IP address of the VPN server's Internet interface, subnet mask of 255.255.255.255, and TCP destination port of 1723 (0x06BB).

  This filter allows PPTP tunnel maintenance traffic from the PPTP client to the PPTP server.

- Destination IP address of the VPN server's Internet interface, subnet mask of 255.255.255.255, and IP Protocol ID of 47 (0x2F).

  This filter allows PPTP tunneled data from the PPTP client to the PPTP server.

- Destination IP address of the VPN server's Internet interface, subnet mask of 255.255.255.255, and TCP [established] source port of 1723 (0x06BB).

  This filter is required only if the VPN server is acting as a VPN client (a calling router) in a router-to-router VPN connection. When you select **TCP [established]**, traffic is accepted only if the VPN server initiated the TCP connection.

Configure the following output filters with the filter action set to **Drop all packets except those that meet the criteria below**:

- Source IP address of the VPN server's Internet interface, subnet mask of 255.255.255.255, and TCP source port of 1723 (0x06BB).

  This filter allows PPTP tunnel maintenance traffic from the VPN server to the VPN client.

- Source IP address of the VPN server's Internet interface, subnet mask of 255.255.255.255, and IP Protocol ID of 47 (0x2F).

  This filter allows PPTP tunneled data from the VPN server to the VPN client.

- Source IP address of the VPN server's Internet interface, subnet mask of 255.255.255.255, and TCP [established] destination port of 1723 (0x06BB).

  This filter is required only if the VPN server is acting as a VPN client (a calling router) in a router-to-router VPN connection. When you select **TCP [established]**, traffic is sent only if the VPN server initiated the TCP connection.

Packet Filters for L2TP over IPSec

Configure the following input filters with the filter action set to **Drop all packets except those that meet the criteria below**:

- Destination IP address of the VPN server's Internet interface, subnet mask of 255.255.255.255, and UDP destination port of 500 (0x01F4).

  This filter allows Internet Key Exchange (IKE) traffic to the VPN server.

- Destination IP address of the VPN server's Internet interface, subnet mask of 255.255.255.255, and UDP destination port of 1701 (0x6A5).

  This filter allows L2TP traffic from the VPN client to the VPN server.

Configure the following output filters with the filter action set to **Drop all packets except those that meet the criteria below**:

- Source IP address of the VPN server's Internet interface, subnet mask of 255.255.255.255, and UDP source port of 500 (0x01F4).

  This filter allows IKE traffic from the VPN server.

- Source IP address of the VPN server's Internet interface, subnet mask of 255.255.255.255, and UDP source port of 1701 (0x6A5).

  This filter allows L2TP traffic from the VPN server to the VPN client.

There are no filters required for IPSec ESP traffic for the IP protocol of 50. The Routing and Remote Access service filters are applied after the IPSec module of TCP/IP removes the ESP header.

VPN Server Behind the Firewall

In a more common configuration, illustrated in Figure 9.18, the firewall is connected to the Internet and the VPN server is another intranet resource connected to a demilitarized zone (DMZ). The DMZ is an IP network segment that typically contains resources available to Internet users such as Web servers and FTP servers. The VPN server has an interface on the DMZ and an interface on the intranet.

In this approach, the firewall must be configured with input and output filters on its Internet interface to allow the passing of tunnel maintenance traffic and tunneled data to the VPN server. Additional filters can allow the passing of traffic to Web servers, FTP servers, and other types of servers on the DMZ.

Because the firewall does not have the encryption keys for each VPN connection, it can only filter on the plaintext headers of the tunneled data, meaning that all tunneled data passes through the firewall. However, this is not a security concern because the VPN connection requires an authentication process that prevents unauthorized access beyond the VPN server.

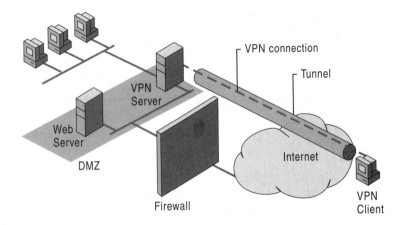

Figure 9.18   VPN Server Behind the Firewall on the Internet

For the Internet interface on the firewall, the following input and output filters need to be configured using the firewall's configuration software.

Packet Filters for PPTP

Configure the following input filters with the filter action set to **Drop all packets except those that meet the criteria below**:

- Destination IP address of the VPN server's DMZ interface and TCP destination port of 1723 (0x06BB).

  This filter allows PPTP tunnel maintenance traffic from the PPTP client to the PPTP server.

- Destination IP address of the VPN server's DMZ interface and IP Protocol ID of 47 (0x2F).

  This filter allows PPTP tunneled data from the PPTP client to the PPTP server.

- Destination IP address of the VPN server's DMZ interface and TCP [established] source port of 1723 (0x06BB).

  This filter is required only if the VPN server is acting as a VPN client (a calling router) in a router-to-router VPN connection. When you select **TCP [established]**, traffic is accepted only if the VPN server initiated the TCP connection.

Configure the following output filters with the filter action set to **Drop all packets except those that meet the criteria below**.

- Source IP address of the VPN server's DMZ interface and TCP source port of 1723 (0x06BB).

  This filter allows PPTP tunnel maintenance traffic from the VPN server to the VPN client.

- Source IP address of the VPN server's DMZ interface and IP Protocol ID of 47 (0x2F).

  This filter allows PPTP tunneled data from the VPN server to the VPN client.

- Source IP address of the VPN server's DMZ interface and TCP [established] destination port of 1723 (0x06BB).

  This filter is required only if the VPN server is acting as a VPN client (a calling router) in a router-to-router VPN connection. When you select **TCP [established]**, traffic is sent only if the VPN server initiated the TCP connection.

Packet Filters for L2TP over IPSec

Configure the following input filters with the filter action set to **Drop all packets except those that meet the criteria below**.

- Destination IP address of the VPN server's DMZ interface and UDP destination port of 500 (0x01F4).

  This filter allows IKE traffic to the VPN server.

- Destination IP address of the VPN server's DMZ interface and IP Protocol ID of 50 (0x32).

  This filter allows IPSec ESP traffic from the VPN client to the VPN server.

Configure the following output filters with the filter action set to **Drop all packets except those that meet the criteria below**.

- Source IP address of the VPN server's DMZ interface and UDP source port of 500 (0x01F4).

  This filter allows IKE traffic from the VPN server.

- Source IP address of the VPN server's DMZ interface and IP Protocol ID of 50 (0x32).

  This filter allows IPSec ESP traffic from the VPN server to the VPN client.

There are no filters required for L2TP traffic at the UDP port of 1701. At the firewall, all L2TP traffic including tunnel maintenance and tunneled data is encrypted as an IPSec ESP payload.

VPNs and Network Address Translators

A network address translator (NAT) is an IP router with the ability to translate the IP address and TCP/UDP port numbers of packets as they are forwarded. Consider the small business wanting to connect multiple computers to the Internet. It normally has to obtain a public address for each computer on the small business network. With a NAT, however, the small business does not need multiple public addresses. It can use private addresses (as documented in RFC 1597) on the small business network segment and use the NAT to map the private addresses to one or more public IP addresses as allocated by an ISP. NAT functionality is documented in RFC 1631.

For example, if a small business is using the 10.0.0.0/8 network for its private network, and has been granted the public IP address of *w.x.y.z* by the ISP, the NAT statically or dynamically maps all private IP addresses used on network 10.0.0.0/8 to the IP address of *w.x.y.z*.

For outgoing packets, the source IP address and TCP/UDP port numbers are mapped to *w.x.y.z* and a possibly changed TCP/UDP port number. For incoming packets, the destination IP address and TCP/UDP port numbers are mapped to the private IP address and original TCP/UDP port number.

By default, a NAT translates IP addresses and TCP/UDP ports. If the IP address and port information is only in the IP and TCP/UDP headers, the application protocol can be translated transparently, such as with HyperText Transfer Protocol (HTTP) traffic on the World Wide Web.

However, some applications and protocols store IP address or TCP/UDP port information within their own headers. FTP, for example, stores the dotted decimal representation of IP addresses in the FTP header for the FTP PORT command. If the NAT does not properly translate the IP address within the FTP header, connectivity problems can occur. In addition, some protocols do not use TCP or UDP headers but use fields in other headers to identify data streams.

When the NAT component must additionally translate and adjust the payload beyond the IP, TCP, and UDP headers, a NAT editor is required. A NAT editor properly modifies otherwise non-translatable payloads so that they can be forwarded across a NAT.

Address and Port Mapping for VPN Traffic

In order for PPTP and L2TP over IPSec tunnels to work over a NAT, the NAT must be able to map multiple data streams to and from a single IP address.

PPTP Traffic

PPTP traffic consists of a TCP connection for tunnel maintenance and GRE encapsulation for tunneled data. The TCP connection is NAT-translatable because the source TCP port numbers can be transparently translated. However, the GRE-encapsulated data is not NAT-translatable without an editor.

With tunneled data, the tunnel is identified by the source IP address and the Call ID field in the GRE header. When there are multiple PPTP clients on the private side of a NAT tunneling to the same PPTP server, all the tunneled traffic has the same source IP address. Also, because the PPTP clients are unaware that they are being translated, they might pick the same Call ID when establishing the PPTP tunnel. Therefore, it is possible for tunneled data from multiple PPTP clients on the private side of the NAT to have the same source IP address and same Call ID when translated.

To prevent this problem, a NAT editor for PPTP must monitor the PPTP tunnel creation and create separate mappings between a private IP address and Call ID as used by the PPTP client to a public IP address and unique Call ID received by the PPTP server on the Internet.

The NAT routing protocol of the Routing and Remote Access service, contains a PPTP editor that translates the GRE Call ID in order to distinguish between multiple PPTP tunnels on the private side of the NAT.

L2TP over IPSec Traffic

L2TP over IPSec traffic is not translatable by a NAT because the UDP port number is encrypted, and its value is protected with a cryptographic checksum. L2TP over IPSec is not translatable even with an editor for the following additional reasons:

Inability to distinguish multiple IPSec ESP data streams

The ESP header contains a field called the Security Parameters Index (SPI). The SPI is used in conjunction with the destination IP address in the plaintext IP header and IPSec security protocol (ESP or Authenticating Header [AH]) to identify an IPSec security association (SA).

For outbound traffic from the NAT, the destination IP address is not changed. For inbound traffic to the NAT, the destination IP address must be mapped to a private IP address. Just as in the case of multiple PPTP clients on the private side of a NAT, the destination IP address of inbound traffic for multiple IPSec ESP data streams is the same address. To distinguish one IPSec ESP data stream from another, the destination IP address and SPI can be mapped to a private destination IP address and SPI. However, because the ESP Auth trailer contains a cryptographic checksum that verifies the ESP header and its payload, the SPI cannot be changed without invalidating the cryptographic checksum.

Inability to change TCP and UDP checksums

In L2TP over IPSec packets, UDP and TCP headers contain a checksum that includes the source and destination IP address of the plaintext IP header. The addresses in the plaintext IP header cannot be changed without invalidating the checksum in the TCP and UDP headers. The TCP and UDP checksums cannot be updated because they are within the encrypted portion of the ESP payload.

Pass-Through VPN Scenario

As described in "Internet and Intranet-Based VPN Connections" earlier in this chapter, a pass-through VPN allows a remote access client connected to one company's intranet to access the resources of another company's intranet across the Internet. A remote access VPN connection is passed to one intranet through another intranet and the Internet.

In a typical case, company A and company B are business partners, and an employee of company A visits company B. When the employee of company A attends a meeting and connects a laptop computer to the company B intranet, a company B intranet IP address configuration is obtained. If the employee of company A needs to connect to the company A intranet, it can be done in one of two ways:

- Using a phone line in the conference room, the employee of company A can directly dial a company A remote access server to make a dial-up connection to the company A intranet or can dial a local ISP and make a VPN connection to the company A intranet.

- As illustrated in Figure 9.19, using VPN technology and the appropriate infrastructure, the employee of company A can create a tunnel across the company B intranet to the Internet and then create another tunnel across the company B intranet and the Internet to the company A intranet.

With the latter method, the VPN connection to the company A intranet is created by activating two connection objects in the Connections folder using the existing local physical network connection. Note that Tunnel 2 is inside Tunnel 1 on the company B intranet.

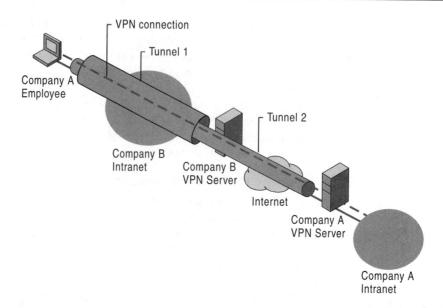

Figure 9.19   Pass-Through VPN Scenario

Configuration of the Company A VPN Server

Configure the company A VPN server to accept remote access VPN connections from remote clients on the Internet with the appropriate remote access policies to require strong authentication and encryption.

For more information, see Windows 2000 Server Help.

Configuration of the Company B VPN Server

Configure the company B VPN server as follows:

1. Configure the company B VPN server to accept remote access VPN connections. For more information, see Windows 2000 Server Help.

2. Manually configure the IP address pool that contains a range of public IP addresses.

3. Create a Windows 2000 group to contain the user accounts for visiting employees of other companies that are making pass-through VPN connections. For example, create the group VPN_PassThrough.

4. Create the user account that is used by the visiting employee of company A.

Assuming that this VPN server is only to be used for pass-through VPNs for the visiting employees of business partners, delete the default remote access policy called **Allow access if dial-in permission is enabled** and create a remote access policy called **VPN Pass-Through for Business Partners** with the remote access policy permission setting, **Grant remote access permission**, selected. Then set the conditions and profile settings as listed in Tables 9.7 and 9.8. For detailed information about configuring these settings, see Windows 2000 Server Help.

Table 9.7   Remote Access Policy Conditions for Company B VPN Server

Conditions	Setting
NAS-Port-Type	**Virtual**
Called-Station-ID	IP address of the VPN server interface accepting VPN connections
Windows-Groups	For example, VPN_PassThrough

Table 9.8   Remote Access Policy Profile Settings for Company B VPN Server

Profile settings	Setting
Authentication tab	Enable **Microsoft Encrypted Authentication (MS-CHAP)**.
Encryption tab	Select **Basic**, **Strong**, or **No encryption**.

The remote access policy settings outlined in Tables 9.7 and 9.8 assume that you are managing remote access on a group basis by setting the remote access permission on all user accounts to **Control access through Remote Access Policy**.

Note   The remote access policy profile settings do not require encryption. The tunnel from the employee of company A to the company B VPN server does not need to be encrypted because the tunnel from the employee of company A to the company A VPN server on the Internet is encrypted. Forcing the encryption of the first tunnel causes encryption to occur twice when it is not necessary and can impact performance.

Filtering Configuration

To ensure that the company B VPN server connected to the Internet is confined to accepting and forwarding pass-through VPN traffic, configure the following filters using the Routing and Remote Access snap-in.

▶ **To configure PPTP filtering**

1. On the intranet interface, configure the following input IP filters with the filter action set to **Drop all packets except those that meet the criteria below**:

   - Destination IP address of the VPN server intranet interface, subnet mask of 255.255.255.255, and TCP destination port of 1723.

   - Destination IP address of the VPN server intranet interface, subnet mask of 255.255.255.255, and IP protocol of 47.

2. On the intranet interface, configure the following output IP filters with the filter action set to **Drop all packets except those that meet the criteria below**:

   - Source IP address of the VPN server intranet interface, subnet mask of 255.255.255.255, and TCP source port of 1723.

   - Source IP address of the VPN server intranet interface, subnet mask of 255.255.255.255, and IP protocol 47.

3. On the Internet interface, configure the following input IP filters with the filter action set to **Drop all packets except those that meet the criteria below**:

   - Destination IP address and subnet mask of the public IP address pool and TCP source port of 1723.

   - Destination IP address and subnet mask of the public IP address pool and IP protocol of 47.

4. On the Internet interface, configure the following output IP filters with the filter action set to **Drop all packets except those that meet the criteria below**:

   - Source IP address and subnet mask of the public IP address pool and TCP destination port of 1723.

   - Source IP address and subnet mask of the public IP address pool and IP protocol of 47.

▶ **To configure L2TP over IPSec filtering**

1. On the intranet interface, configure the following input IP filters with the filter action set to **Drop all packets except those that meet the criteria below**:

   - Destination IP address of the VPN server intranet interface, subnet mask of 255.255.255.255, and destination UDP port of 1701.

   - Destination IP address of the VPN server intranet interface, subnet mask of 255.255.255.255, and destination UDP port of 500.

2. On the intranet interface, configure the following output IP filters with the filter action set to **Drop all packets except those that meet the criteria below**:

   - Source IP address of VPN server intranet interface, subnet mask of 255.255.255.255, and source UDP port of 1701.

   - Source IP address of VPN server intranet interface, subnet mask of 255.255.255.255, and source UDP port of 500.

3. On the Internet interface, configure the following input IP filters with the filter action set to **Drop all packets except those that meet the criteria below**:

   - Destination IP address and subnet mask of the public IP address pool and IP protocol of 50.

   - Destination IP address and subnet mask of the public IP address pool and source UDP port of 500.

4. On the Internet interface configure the following output IP filters with the filter action set to **Drop all packets except those that meet the criteria below**:

   - Source IP address and subnet mask of the public IP address pool and IP protocol of 50.

   - Source IP address and subnet mask of the public IP address pool and destination UDP port of 500.

Configuration of the VPN Client Computer for a Pass-Through VPN

The following sections detail the configuration of a Windows 2000–based VPN client for PPTP and L2TP over IPSec for a pass-through VPN.

▶ **To configure a PPTP connection**

1. Create a VPN connection object that connects the employee of company A with the VPN server of company B as follows:

   - On the **General** tab, type the host name or IP address of the intranet interface of the company B VPN server.

   - On the **Security** tab, select **Secure my password but not my data**.

   - On the **Networking** tab, select **Point-to-Point Tunneling Protocol (PPTP)** as the type of server into which you are dialing.

2. Create a VPN connection object that connects the employee of company A with the Internet VPN server of company A as follows:

   - On the **General** tab, type the host name or IP address of the Internet interface of the company A VPN server.

   - On the **Security** tab, select either **Secure my password and data** or **Custom**. If you select **Custom**, you must also select the appropriate encryption and authentication options.

   - On the **Networking** tab, select **Point-to-Point Tunneling Protocol (PPTP)** as the type of server into which you are dialing.

▶ **To configure an L2TP over IPSec connection**

1. Create a VPN connection object that connects the employee of company A with the VPN server of company B as follows:

   - On the **General** tab, type the host name or IP address of the intranet interface of the company B VPN server.

   - On the **Security** tab, select **Secure my password but not my data**.

   - On the **Networking** tab, select **Layer-2 Tunneling Protocol (L2TP)** as the type of server into which you are dialing.

2. Create a VPN connection object that connects the employee of company A with the Internet VPN server of company A as follows:

   - On the **General** tab, type the host name or IP address of the Internet interface of the company A VPN server.

   - On the **Security** tab, select either **Secure my password and data** or **Custom**. If you select **Custom**, you must also select the appropriate encryption and authentication options.

   - On the **Networking** tab, select **Layer-2 Tunneling Protocol (L2TP)** as the type of server into which you are dialing.

Creating the Pass-Through VPN Connection

After the following pass-through VPN connection is made, the employee of company A can access any company A intranet resource for the duration of the VPN connection with the company A VPN server.

▶ **To create a pass-through connection**

The employee of company A creates a pass-through VPN connection to the company A VPN server on the Internet using the following process:

1. In the **Connections** folder, double-click the connection object that creates the tunnel to the company B VPN server on the company B intranet.

2. When prompted for user credentials, type the credentials corresponding to the company B user account.

3. In the **Connections** folder, double-click the connection object that creates the VPN to the company A VPN server on the Internet.

4. When prompted for user credentials, type the credentials corresponding to the company A corporate account.

Troubleshooting VPNs

To troubleshoot VPNs, you must troubleshoot IP connectivity, remote access and demand-dial connection establishment, routing, and IPSec.

Common VPN Problems

VPN problems typically fall into the following categories:

- Connection attempt is rejected when it should be accepted.
- Connection attempt is accepted when it should be rejected.
- Unable to reach locations beyond the VPN server.
- Unable to establish a tunnel.

Use the following troubleshooting tips to isolate the configuration or infrastructure problem causing the stated VPN problem.

Connection attempt is rejected when it should be accepted

- Using the Ping command, verify that the host name or IP address of the VPN server is reachable. If a host name is being used, verify that the host name is resolved to its correct IP address. If the ping is not successful, packet filtering might be preventing the delivery of ICMP messages to or from the VPN server.

- Verify that the Routing and Remote Access service is running on the VPN server.

- For remote access VPN connections, verify that the VPN server is enabled for remote access. For router-to-router VPN connections, verify that the VPN server is enabled for demand-dial routing.

- For remote access VPN connections, verify that the PPTP and L2TP ports are enabled for inbound remote access. For router-to-router VPN connections, verify that the PPTP and L2TP ports are enabled for inbound and outbound demand-dial connections.

- Verify that the VPN client and the VPN server in conjunction with a remote access policy are configured to use at least one common authentication method.

- Verify that the VPN client and the VPN server in conjunction with a remote access policy are configured to use at least one common encryption method.

- Verify that the parameters of the connection have permission through remote access policies.

  In order for the connection to be established, the parameters of the connection attempt must:

  - Match all of the conditions of at least one remote access policy.

  - Be granted remote access permission through the user account (set to **Allow access**), or if the user account has the **Control access through Remote Access Policy** option selected, the remote access permission of the matching remote access policy must have the **Grant remote access permission** option selected.

  - Match all the settings of the profile.

  - Match all the settings of the dial-in properties of the user account.

  For more information about remote access policies, see Windows 2000 Server Help and "Remote Access Server" in this book.

- Verify that the settings of the remote access policy profile are not in conflict with properties of the remote access router.

  The properties of the remote access policy profile and the properties of the RAS server both contain settings for:

  - Multilink
  - Bandwidth allocation protocol
  - Authentication protocols

  If the settings of the profile of the matching remote access policy are in conflict with the settings of the VPN server, the connection attempt is rejected. For example, if the matching remote access policy profile specifies that the EAP-TLS authentication protocol must be used and EAP-TLS is not enabled on the VPN server, the VPN server rejects the connection attempt.

- For a VPN server that is a member server in a mixed-mode or native-mode Windows 2000 domain that is configured for Windows 2000 authentication, verify that:

  - The **RAS and IAS Servers** security group exists. If not, then create the group and set the group type to **Security** and the group scope to **Domain local**.

  - The **RAS and IAS Servers** security group has **Read** permission to the **RAS and IAS Servers Access Check** object.

  - The computer account of the VPN server computer is a member of the RAS and IAS Servers security group. You can use the netsh ras show registeredserver command to view the current registration. You can use the netsh ras add registeredserver command to register the server in a specified domain.

  - If you add or remove the VPN server computer to the **RAS and IAS Servers** security group, the change does not take effect immediately (due to the way that Windows 2000 caches Active Directory information). For the change to take effect immediately, you need to restart the VPN server computer.

- For remote access VPN connections, verify that the LAN protocols used by the VPN client are enabled for remote access on the VPN server.

- Verify that all of the PPTP or L2TP ports on the VPN server are not already being used. If necessary, change the number of PPTP to L2TP ports to allow more concurrent connections.

- Verify that the tunneling protocol of the VPN client is supported by the VPN server.

  By default, Windows 2000 remote access VPN clients have the **Automatic** server type option selected, which means that they try to establish a L2TP over IPSec-based VPN connection first, then they try a PPTP-based VPN connection. If either the **Point-to-Point Tunneling Protocol (PPTP)** or **Layer-2 Tunneling Protocol (L2TP)** server type option is selected, verify that the selected tunneling protocol is supported by the VPN server.

  By default, a Windows 2000 Server–based computer running the Routing and Remote Access service is a PPTP and L2TP server with five L2TP ports and five PPTP ports. To create a PPTP-only server, set the number of L2TP ports to zero. To create an L2TP-only server, set the number of PPTP ports to zero.

- For remote access L2TP over IPSec connections, verify that computer certificates, also known as machine certificates, are installed on the VPN client and the VPN server. For more information on troubleshooting IPSec connections, see "Internet Protocol Security" in the *TCP/IP Core Networking Guide*.

- Verify that the VPN client's credentials, consisting of user name, password, and domain name, are correct and can be validated by the VPN server.

- If the VPN server is configured with static IP address pools, verify that there are enough addresses.

  If all of the addresses in the static pools have been allocated to connected VPN clients, the VPN server is unable to allocate an IP address for TCP/IP-based connections, and the connection attempt is rejected.

- If the VPN client is configured to request its own IPX node number, verify that the VPN server is configured to allow IPX clients to request their own IPX node number.

- If the VPN server is configured with a range of IPX network numbers, verify that the IPX network numbers in the range are not being used elsewhere on your IPX internetwork.

- Verify the configuration of the authentication provider.

  The VPN server can be configured to use either Windows 2000 or RADIUS to authenticate the credentials of the VPN client.

- For a VPN server that is a member of a Windows 2000 native-mode domain, verify that the VPN server has joined the domain.

- For a Windows NT version 4.0 Service Pack 4 and later VPN server that is a member of a Windows 2000 mixed mode domain or a Windows 2000 VPN server that is a member of a Windows NT 4.0 domain that is accessing user account properties for a user account in a trusted Windows 2000 domain, verify that the Everyone group is added to the Pre-Windows 2000 Compatible Access group with the **net localgroup "Pre-Windows 2000 Compatible Access"** command. If not, issue the **net localgroup "Pre-Windows 2000 Compatible Access" everyone /add** command on a domain controller computer and then restart the domain controller computer.

- For a Windows NT version 4.0 Service Pack 3 and earlier VPN server that is a member of a Windows 2000 mixed mode domain, verify that Everyone group has been granted list contents, read all properties, and read permissions to the root node of your domain and all sub-objects of the root domain.

- For RADIUS authentication, verify that the VPN server computer can communicate with the RADIUS server.

- For PPTP connections using MS-CHAP v1 and attempting to negotiate 40-bit MPPE encryption, verify that the user's password is not larger than 14 characters.

Connection attempt is accepted when it should be rejected

- Verify that the parameters of the connection do not have permission through remote access policies.

  A connection can be rejected for the following reasons:

  The parameters of the connection attempt must be denied remote access permission through the remote access permission of the user account (with **Deny access** selected)

  The user account has the **Control access through Remote Access Policy** option selected, and the remote access permission of the first remote access policy that matches the parameters of the connection attempt has the **Deny remote access permission** selected.

  For more information about remote access policies, see Windows 2000 Server Help.

Unable to reach locations beyond the VPN server

- For remote access VPNs, verify that either the protocol is enabled for routing or the **Entire network** option is selected for LAN protocols being used by the VPN clients.

- For remote access VPNs, verify the IP address pools of the VPN server.

  If the VPN server is configured to use a static IP address pool, verify that the routes to the range of addresses defined by the static IP address pools are reachable by the hosts and routers of the intranet. If not, then IP route consisting of the VPN server static IP address pools, as defined by the IP address and mask of the range, must be added to the routers of the intranet or enable the routing protocol of your routed infrastructure on the VPN server. If the routes to the remote access VPN client subnets are not present, remote access VPN clients cannot receive traffic from locations on the intranet. Routes for the subnets are implemented either through static routing entries or through a routing protocol, such as Open Shortest Path First (OSPF) or Routing Information Protocol (RIP).

  If the VPN server is configured to use DHCP for IP address allocation and no DHCP server is available, the VPN server assigns addresses from the Automatic Private IP Addressing (APIPA) address range from 169.254.0.1 through 169.254.255.254. Allocating APIPA addresses for remote access clients works only if the network to which the VPN server is attached is also using APIPA addresses.

  If the VPN server is using APIPA addresses when a DHCP server is available, verify that the proper adapter is selected from which to obtain DHCP-allocated IP addresses. By default, the VPN server randomly chooses the adapter to use to obtain IP addresses through DHCP. If there is more than one LAN adapter, then the Routing and Remote Access service may choose a LAN adapter for which there is no DHCP server available. You can manually choose a LAN adapter from the **IP** tab on the properties of a remote access server in the Routing and Remote Access snap-in.

  If the static IP address pools are a range of IP addresses that are a subset of the range of IP addresses for the network to which the VPN server is attached, verify that the range of IP addresses in the static IP address pool are not assigned to other TCP/IP nodes, either through static configuration or through DHCP.

- For router-to router VPN connections, verify that there are routes on both sides of the router-to-router VPN connection that support the two-way exchange of traffic.

  Unlike a remote access VPN connection, a router-to-router VPN connection does not automatically create a default route. You need to create routes on both sides of the router-to-router VPN connection so that traffic can be routed to and from the other side of the router-to-router VPN connection.

You can manually add static routes to the routing table, or you can add static routes through routing protocols. For persistent VPN connections, you can enable Open Shortest Path First (OSPF) or Routing Information Protocol (RIP) across the VPN connection. For on-demand VPN connections, you can automatically update routes through an auto-static RIP update.

- For two-way initiated router-to-router VPN connections, verify that the router-to-router VPN connection is not interpreted by the VPN server as a remote access connection.

  If the user name of the calling router's credentials appears under **Remote Access Clients** in the Routing and Remote Access snap-in, the VPN server has interpreted the calling router as a remote access client. Verify that the user name in the calling router's credentials matches the name of a demand-dial interface on the VPN server.

- For one-way initiated router-to-router VPN connections, verify that the routes of the calling router's intranet are configured as static routes on the dial-in properties of the user account used by the calling router.

- Verify that there are no TCP/IP packet filters on the profile properties of the remote access policy being used by the VPN connection configured on the VPN server (or the RADIUS server if Internet Authentication Service is used) that are preventing the sending or receiving of TCP/IP traffic.

- For demand-dial VPN connections, verify that there are no packet filters on the demand-dial interfaces of the calling router and answering router that prevent the sending or receiving of traffic.

Unable to establish tunnel

- Verify that packet filtering on a router interface between the VPN client and the VPN server is not preventing the forwarding of tunneling protocol traffic.

  On a Windows 2000–based VPN server, IP packet filtering can be configured from the advanced TCP/IP properties and from the Routing and Remote Access snap-in. Check both places for filters that might be excluding VPN connection traffic.

  For more information about VPN connection traffic and packet filtering, see "VPNs and Firewalls" earlier in this chapter.

- Verify that the Winsock Proxy client is not currently running on the VPN client.

  When the Winsock Proxy client is active, Winsock API calls such as those used to create tunnels and send tunneled data are intercepted and forwarded to a configured proxy server.

  A proxy server–based computer allows an organization to access specific types of Internet resources (typically Web and FTP) without directly connecting that organization to the Internet. The organization can instead use InterNIC-allocated private IP network IDs (such as 10.0.0.0/8).

Proxy servers are typically used so that private users in an organization can have access to public Internet resources as if they were directly attached to the Internet. VPN connections are typically used so that authorized public Internet users can gain access to private organization resources as if they were directly attached to the private network. A single computer can act as a proxy server (for private users) and a VPN server (for authorized Internet users) to facilitate both exchanges of information.

For more information about troubleshooting remote access VPN connections, see "Remote Access Server" in this book. For more information about troubleshooting router-to-router VPN connections, see "Demand-Dial Routing" in this book.

Troubleshooting Tools

The following tools, which enable you to gather additional information about the source of your VPN problem, are included with Windows 2000.

Unreachability Reason

When a demand-dial interface fails to make a connection, the interface is left in an unreachable state. Right-click in the interface, and then select **Unreachability reason** to obtain more information about why the interface was unable to connect.

Event Logging

On the **Event Logging** tab in the properties of a VPN server, there are four levels of logging. Select **Log the maximum amount of information**, and then try the connection again. After the connection fails, check the system event log for events logged during the connection process. After you are done viewing remote access events, select the **Log errors and warnings** option on the **Event logging** tab to conserve system resources.

Tracing

Tracing records the sequence of programming functions called during a process to a file. Enable tracing for remote access and VPN components as described in "Routing and Remote Access Service" in this book, and then try the connection again. After you have viewed the traced information, reset the tracing settings back to their default values to conserve system resources.

Tracing information can be complex and very detailed. Most of the time this information is useful only to Microsoft support professionals or to network administrators who are very experienced with the Routing and Remote Access service. Tracing information can be saved as files and sent to Microsoft support for analysis.

Network Monitor

Use Network Monitor, a packet capture and analysis tool, to view the traffic sent between a VPN server and VPN client during the VPN connection process and during data transfer. You cannot interpret the encrypted portions of VPN traffic with Network Monitor.

The proper interpretation of the remote access and VPN traffic with Network Monitor requires an in-depth understanding of PPP, PPTP, IPSec, and other protocols. For more information about PPP, see "Remote Access Server" in this book. Network Monitor captures can be saved as files and sent to Microsoft support for analysis.

Additional Resources

- For more information about RFCs (Request For Comment Proposals), see the Internet Engineering Task Force link on the Web Resources page at http://windows.microsoft.com/windows2000/reskit/webresources.

P A R T   3

Interoperability

Interoperability with non-Windows operating systems continues to be an important issue for network managers. Part 3 examines Microsoft® Windows® 2000 features and add-on products that support interoperability between Windows 2000 and non-Windows operating systems.

In This Part

CHAPTER 10

Interoperability with IBM Host Systems

Microsoft® SNA Server is the Microsoft solution for integrating personal computer–based clients and servers with IBM host systems. Using SNA Server, you can provide Microsoft and non-Microsoft-based clients with secure access to IBM host data, applications, and network services. You can integrate SNA Server into your existing IBM host environment, and you can develop solutions that allow users to gain transparent access to host resources from their desktop operating system or Web browser interface.

In This Chapter

Note The interoperability solutions in this chapter are based on Microsoft® Windows NT® version 4.0–based applications and technologies. Future versions of these applications and technologies might change. Therefore, the material included in this chapter is also subject to change.

Related Information in the Resource Kit

- For more information about IBM host systems and SNA networks, see "IBM SNA Interoperability Concepts" in this book.

- For information about configuring and managing SNA Server, see SNA Server Help and the *Microsoft® BackOffice® Resource Kit.*

Overview of Microsoft SNA Server

SNA Server provides you with a comprehensive solution to integrate heterogeneous networks and intranets with IBM mainframe, midrange, and AS/400 host systems, as illustrated in Figure 10.1. SNA Server is a Microsoft® BackOffice® application that runs on the Microsoft® Windows® 2000 Server operating system, providing advanced network, data, and application integration services.

SNA Server provides interoperability between host systems that run SNA or TCP/IP protocols. If your IBM host system runs SNA protocols, SNA Server provides network connectivity by acting as a secure, high performance gateway between heterogeneous clients and IBM host systems. Because SNA Server runs on Windows 2000, heterogeneous clients can connect to SNA Server through standard networking protocols such as TCP/IP, IPX/SPX, NetBEUI, Banyan VINES IP, AppleTalk, and Windows 2000 Routing and Remote Access service. SNA Server then completes the network connection to the mainframe or AS/400 system using standard IBM SNA protocols.

Once SNA or TCP/IP-based network connectivity is established, clients can use SNA Server's advanced host integration features to gain secure access to IBM host data, applications, and network services without leaving their familiar desktop or Web browser interface.

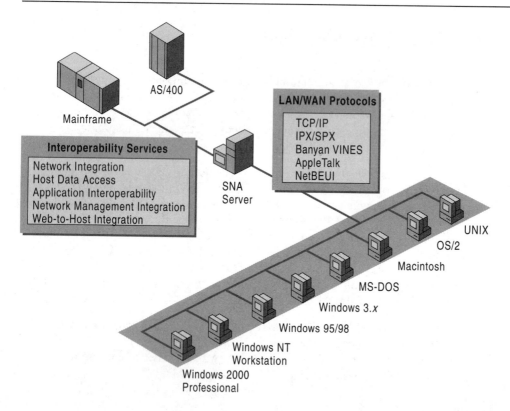

Figure 10.1   SNA Server Integrates Heterogeneous Networks with IBM Host Systems

The core of SNA Server's power is its ability to provide a wide range of host integration services. As such, SNA Server supports interoperability at each layer of the Windows 2000 interoperability model:

Network interoperability   Cross-platform network connectivity and protocols, security integration, and single sign-on. (Single sign-on allows users to log on once to access multiple servers, systems, or applications.)

Data access and integration   Transparent file transfer services, Universal Data Access technologies such as OLE DB and Open Database Connectivity (ODBC), and host data replication.

Application access and integration   Terminal access, integrated transaction services, Web-to-host integration, and messaging.

Network management integration   Integration between Windows 2000 network management services and IBM NetView–based management services.

Network Integration Services

When implementing cross-platform interoperability solutions, the first step is to establish secure and reliable connectivity between network platforms. SNA Server integrates heterogeneous networks with IBM mainframe, midrange, and AS/400 host systems using two types of connections, server-to-host and client-to-server.

The server-to-host connections are the physical units (PUs) and logical units (LUs) that connect the SNA Server to the host system.

The client-to-server connections enable network clients and application programs to connect to SNA Server over the local area network (LAN) or wide area network (WAN).

Because SNA Server operates on Windows 2000 Server, it can support a wide range of clients and protocols and can scale to support the needs of large enterprise networks. Table 10.1 introduces the services that SNA Server provides on the network integration level.

Table 10.1   Network Integration Services

Network Integration Services	Description
Supported Host Systems	IBM Mainframe Systems; AS/400 Systems; Advanced System 36; System/36; System/38; and IBM compatible mainframe systems from Amdahl, Fujitsu, Hitachi, Tandem, and Unisys.
Server Capacity	Up to 3,000 users operating up to 30,000 concurrent sessions on each server.
Hot Backup and Load Balancing	Up to 15 computers running SNA Server can be configured to provide failover for each other. LU pools can be shared across up to 15 servers to provide load-balancing.
Host Connection Methods	Supports standard connection methods including Channel (ESCON and Bus and Tag), Twinax, Open Systems Adapter (Token Ring, Ethernet, FDDI), SDLC, X.25, and DFT.
SNA Remote Access Service (SNA remote access server)	Integrates the LU 6.2 transport with Windows 2000 remote access server.
Heterogeneous Client Support	Microsoft® Windows® 2000 Professional, Microsoft® Windows® 95, Microsoft® Windows® 98, Microsoft® Windows® 3.x, Microsoft® MS-DOS®, Macintosh, OS/2, and UNIX.
Protocol Support	SNA, TCP/IP, IPX/SPX, Named Pipes, Banyan VINES IP, and AppleTalk.

continued

Table 10.1   Network Integration Services *(continued)*

Network Integration Services	Description
Distributed Link Service	SNA Server computers can share host connections with other SNA Server computers. Allows efficient tunneling of SNA data between SNA Server computers over standard WAN infrastructures such as TCP/IP-based networks.
Downstream Connections	Supports communications to PU type 2.0 devices using only SNA protocols. To downstream devices, SNA appears to be the actual host system, reducing host PU configuration requirements.
PU Pass-through Service	Full SNA-capable products can connect to the host by passing PU 2.1 or PU 2.0 data through SNA Server. SNA Server behaves like an IBM 3174 cluster controller.
Integrated Single Sign-on	Administrators can configure SNA Server to provide User ID and password information to the host based on Windows 2000 domain authentication credentials, eliminating the need to manage multiple sign-on combinations.
Password Synchronization	Supports third-party bi-directional password synchronization for ACF2, Resource Access Control Facility (RACF), and Top Secret security.
Data Encryption	Encrypts data streams between clients and SNA Server computers, isolating the transmission of cleartext data (required by many host applications) to the secure network environment in the data center.
LU Level Security	Administrators can give users access to LU pools or can restrict users to specific LUs.
Bulk Migration Tool for Host Security	Creates Windows 2000 domain accounts, enrolls users in the Host Security Domain, and synchronizes critical account information.

Data Access

The purpose of integrating heterogeneous networks is to provide users with cross-platform access to data and applications. Table 10.2 summarizes the advanced services SNA Server uses to provide users with access to host data and the associated host files and printing resources.

Table 10.2   Host Data Access and Integrated File and Printing Services

Database and File Transfer Services	Description
OLE DB Provider for AS/400 and VSAM	Provides read/write record-level access to mainframe VSAM files and OS/400 files. Supports the development of multiple-tier applications that give users transparent access to non-relational host data.
ODBC/DRDA Driver for DB2	Applications designed to use the ODBC interface and SQL can dynamically interact with host database systems (such as DB2) using the DRDA protocol. Can also be used with OLE DB–based applications.
Shared Folders Gateway	Allows users to gain access to AS/400 shared folders–based files as if they were local drives on a computer running Windows 2000 Server. Allows you to use Windows 2000 security permissions and access rights on host shared folders.
Advanced Program-to-Program Communications (APPC) File Transfer Protocol (AFTP) Service	Provides access to AFTP file transfer (the SNA APPC equivalent to TCP/IP File Transfer Protocol [FTP]).
FTP-AFTP Gateway Service	Allows standard FTP clients to access host AFTP files.
VSAM File Transfer Service	Allows authorized users to copy mainframe VSAM files to Windows 2000 Server.
Host Data Replicator Support	Acts as a gateway for the replication of host data to Microsoft® SQL Server™.
Host Print Services	Allows mainframe and AS/400 print jobs to be printed on LAN-attached printers.

Application Integration

Organizations often use IBM host systems for online transaction processing (OLTP) that supports real-time, line of business applications. Traditionally, users have relied on terminal emulation programs to gain access to these host applications. However, information technology departments are increasingly deploying solutions that provide a more seamless level of integration between modern intranet services and IBM host data and applications.

Table 10.3 summarizes the services SNA Server supports to integrate desktop clients with host applications and transaction services.

Table 10.3   Integration with Host Applications and Transaction Services

Application and Transaction Integration Services	Description
Supports 3270, TN3270, TN3270E, TN3287 Terminal Emulation	SNA Server includes a 3270 emulator for access to mainframe applications. SNA Server also supports third-party terminal emulation products for native access or TCP/IP-based access to mainframe applications.
Supports 5250 and TN5250 Terminal Emulation	SNA Server includes a 5250 emulator for access to AS/400 applications. SNA Server also supports third-party terminal emulation products for native access or TCP/IP-based access to AS/400 applications.
COM Transaction Integrator (COMTI) for CICS and IMS	Allows integration of Component Services with host CICS and IMS transactions, including distributed two-phase commit between Component Services and CICS.
Common Programming Interface for Communications (CPI-C)	Communicates with applications on any platform that supports APPC and CPI-C including mainframes, AS/400s, Windows 2000, and UNIX.
Web-to-Host Integration Technologies	Supports integration between host data and applications and Windows 2000–based applications such as Microsoft® Internet Information Services (IIS), SQL Server and Windows-based desktop applications.

Network Management Integration

Providing users with the ability to communicate, share data, and run applications across platforms allows organizations to develop more efficient and productive business processes. However, the integration process is not complete until network managers can monitor and control the integrated environment.

Table 10.4 summarizes the services SNA Server uses to integrate Windows 2000 Server–based management systems with IBM host management systems.

Table 10.4   Network Management Integration Services

Network Management Integration Services	Description
SNA Server Manager	Single console for adding, configuring, monitoring, and controlling all SNA Server components. Allows simultaneous, remote management of subdomains, servers, services, connection, LUs, sessions, users, and groups.
Integration with Windows 2000 Server management services	Full integration with Microsoft Management Console (MMC) and Windows 2000 event monitoring, security, and performance monitoring.
Integration with IBM NetView network management system	Automatic reporting of host link alerts to NetView; supports Response Time Monitor (if supported by the 3270 emulator). Also supports Windows 2000 NVAlert Services and NVRunCmd for remote management of SNA Server from the host NetView console.

Network Integration Methods

Using the SNA Server features described in the preceding tables, you can connect Windows 2000–based networks to hierarchical SNA networks and Advanced Peer-to-Peer Networking (APPN) networks, and provide network integration services for your users. To accomplish this goal, you must first choose a deployment model, organize your SNA Server computers within your Windows 2000 domains, and select your LAN-to-host connection methods.

Deployment Models

Consider the following when deciding how to deploy SNA Server throughout your enterprise:

- The type of host systems with which your users need to connect.
- The location of the users who require host access.
- Your existing network infrastructure.
- The level of performance and host availability your organization requires.
- The costs of deploying and managing the systems.

To accommodate different host connectivity requirements, SNA Server offers three deployment models.

Branch Deployment Model Consists of computers running SNA Server placed away from the host system and near your users.

Centralized Deployment Model Consists of SNA gateways placed close to the host system.

Distributed Deployment Model Consists of SNA gateways placed near the host system and close to your users.

These three models can also be combined to achieve the best configuration for your enterprise. The following sections explore the advantages and disadvantages of each SNA Server deployment model and assist you in making deployment decisions based on your current network model and your interoperability goals.

Branch Deployment Model

Traditionally, enterprises deploy SNA gateways using the branch-based deployment model. Clients use LAN protocols, such as TCP/IP, to communicate with a computer running SNA Server located on the LAN in the branch office.

The computer running SNA Server, in turn, communicates with the host using SNA protocols. With the branch approach, computers running SNA Server are connected to a host through 802.2 (using routers), SDLC, or X.25 connections, as shown in Figure 10.2. Each computer running SNA Server can be administered locally or remotely using Windows 2000 Routing and Remote Access service or IBM NetView.

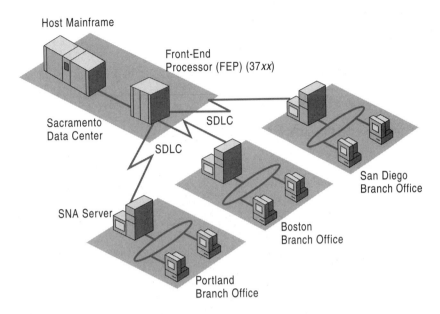

Figure 10.2   Branch-based SNA Server Deployment Model Using SDLC Connections

Advantages of the Branch Model

The branch deployment model offers four primary advantages:

Isolates SNA Traffic

A branch-based deployment model is ideal when a limited amount of bandwidth is available over the SNA Server-to-host connection. In general, network traffic is greater between the client and the computer running SNA Server. If your organization has implemented TCP/IP or another routable WAN protocol, isolating the SNA traffic over specific connections that require host connections—in this case between the SNA Server and the host—prevents unnecessary network traffic from being propagated over non-SNA WAN connections.

Leverages Existing SNA Infrastructure

The branch model is also ideal for organizations that are migrating toward a single, routable WAN protocol solution because it leverages existing investments in SNA data links. As you migrate toward an SNA-free WAN, you can tunnel SNA protocols (such as 802.2 and SDLC) from the branch office LANs to the central site LAN by deploying routers or Frame Relay Access Devices (FRADs) that support Data Link Switching (DLSw), frame relay, or Asynchronous Transfer Mode (ATM) connections.

For more information about frame relay, see RFC 1490.

Provides Flexible Support Options

Because computers running SNA Server are located physically near the clients that request host access services, local SNA Server administrators can usually manage users for their branch, responding more quickly to their needs. If necessary, however, computers running SNA Server can be configured and managed remotely across your WAN links.

Can Use Local Multi-Purpose Servers

By deploying SNA Server in branch offices, you can take advantage of other applications designed to run on Windows 2000 Server. The branch-based server can assume a number of roles in addition to performing SNA Server functions, such as messaging server, database server, and Web server. Components in the BackOffice suite of server applications can work together to provide integrated groupware solutions for your users.

Disadvantages of the Branch Model

The branch deployment model has two primary disadvantages:

Does Not Use High-Speed Mainframe Connections

In a branch-based network, you cannot implement high-speed mainframe connections such as channel attachment, Token Ring, or Ethernet. Local high-speed connections often face physical limitations or difficulty in implementing SNA protocols over a WAN connection. Traditionally, branch-based SNA gateways employ an SDLC-type solution that supports only one physical unit (PU) for each host adapter and only 254 logical units (LUs) over the connection.

Requires Sophisticated Routing

If you decide to use routers rather than dedicated SNA links to pass WAN traffic between the branch and SNA host systems, the routers must be sophisticated enough to prioritize interactive communications over the WAN, as multiple protocols in addition to SNA might be operating over the connection.

Centralized Deployment Model

In a centralized model, computers running SNA Server are deployed physically near the host to which they provide connectivity. The centralized computers running SNA Server provide 3270 and 5250 access for local and remote desktops that connect to the gateways using a routable protocol such as TCP/IP. Other desktop or server-based LU 0, LU 6.2 (APPC), or Telnet applications can connect through these gateways from anywhere on the WAN. Figure 10.3 illustrates the centralized deployment model.

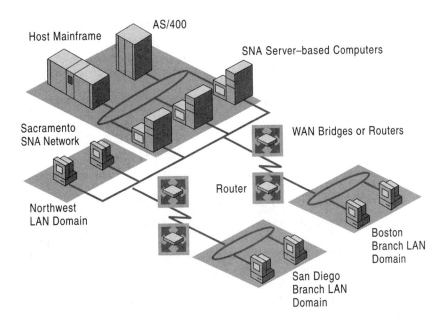

Figure 10.3   Centralized SNA Server Deployment Model Using Routers or Bridges

Advantages of the Centralized Model

The centralized model offers three primary advantages:

Supports Efficient Load Balancing and Fault Tolerance

Using the centralized model, LU pools and APPC session pairs can be configured across multiple computers running SNA Server in a logical organization called a subdomain to provide load balancing and fault tolerance services. Load balancing distributes server loads across all configured servers and prevents one server from being overworked. Fault tolerance or hot backup, ensures that other computers running SNA Server in a subdomain can automatically take over for a failed server. To your users, the switch to a backup computer is transparent. For more information about subdomains, see "Grouping Servers" later in this chapter.

Centralizes Administration

A centralized deployment model is also easier to administer and to secure than a branch-based model because all computers running SNA Server are located close to one another (in the branch-based model, SNA expertise is usually required in each branch office to maintain the servers). Also, changes to mainframe definitions can be coordinated between host and SNA Server administrators more readily if all personnel are located near one another.

Supports High-Speed Mainframe Connections

When computers running SNA Server are physically close to the SNA host, they can be linked by high-speed connections. The channel attachment method provides the highest throughput between SNA Server and a mainframe. In many cases, a channel-attached computer running SNA Server can bypass the front-end processor (FEP), thereby minimizing transaction response time. For AS/400 hosts, you can implement high-speed Token Ring or Ethernet connections.

Disadvantages of the Centralized Model

The centralized model has two primary disadvantages:

Requires an Efficient WAN Infrastructure

A centralized deployment model presupposes the existence of an efficient WAN environment. If a suitable WAN infrastructure is not in place, you must account for the cost in equipment, installation, and possible downtime while you deploy the required hardware. Because client/server transactions generate more network traffic than server/host transactions, this deployment model might yield less responsive client/server connections than a branch model.

Cannot Use Local Multipurpose Servers

With no computers running SNA Server in the branch offices, you cannot use the Windows 2000 Server–based computers, upon which SNA Server runs, as multipurpose servers. If other server applications need to be implemented at the branch locations, you need to install additional computers and hardware.

Distributed Deployment Model

The distributed deployment model combines the best elements of the branch and centralized deployment models. As shown in Figure 10.4, computers running SNA Server are deployed both in a central location near the SNA host and in the branch LANs near the clients.

Typically, the computers located near the host are linked by a high-performance connection, such as channel-attachment. These link services are then made available for distribution to the branch computers running SNA Server using Distributed Link Services, a feature that allows an SNA Server–based computer to share configured link services with other SNA Server–based computers. When implemented, the branch-based servers communicate with the SNA host through a virtual link service over a routable WAN protocol, such as TCP/IP.

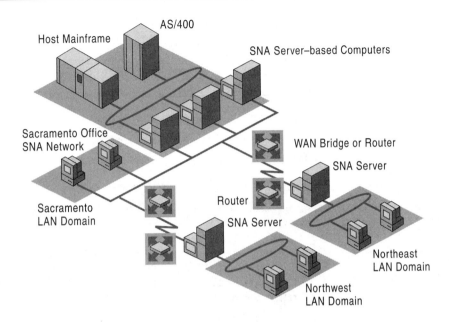

Figure 10.4   Distributed SNA Server Deployment Model

Advantages of the Distributed Model

The distributed model has the advantages of the two previous models while minimizing the disadvantages of each.

Combines the Benefits of the Branch and Centralized Models

The distributed model combines the high-capacity, server-to-host communication benefits of the centralized model with the branch model's ability to contain heavy client/server traffic to a localized WAN segment, such as a branch office LAN.

Supports Optimal Fault Tolerance and Load Balancing

The distributed model provides even greater flexibility than the branch or centralized plans when fault tolerance and load balancing are implemented. For example, multiple computers running SNA Server at a branch location can be configured to provide hot backup and load balancing for each other. These servers in turn can be connected to the SNA host using distributed link services shared by the centralized computers running SNA Server. If any of the servers fails, the other servers at the same location can take over for the failed unit.

Uses Standard WAN Protocols

The use of Distributed Link Services can also simplify your routing and network protocol choices. For your branch offices, you can use any of the LAN protocols supported by SNA Server, including IPX/SPX. You can implement a more efficient, routable protocol like TCP/IP between the branch and central SNA Server–based computers. SNA traffic is isolated to the connection between the high-speed SNA Server–based computers and the host system. SNA protocols do not need to be routed or bridged across the WAN, thereby simplifying network management.

Disadvantage of the Distributed Model

The one possible disadvantage of the distributed model is that it might require more servers.

Depending on your requirements, deploying SNA Server–based computers both in the central location and in your branch offices could require that you deploy more servers than you would use in a centralized or branch model. However, the additional reliability and performance offered by this model, combined with the ability to eliminate multiprotocol WAN infrastructures can more than offset any requirements for additional servers.

In general, the distributed deployment model provides the most flexible and robust SNA Server solution. This strategy is recommended for medium to large network environments that require the best performance and reliability. The distributed model is also easily scalable to meet your future needs.

SNA Server Integration with Windows 2000–Based Networks

After you choose an appropriate deployment model, you need to determine how to logically group your computers running SNA Server to provide fault tolerance, hot backup, and load-balancing services. How you organize your servers affects your ability to provide secure and robust host connectivity services to your users.

Windows 2000 Domains

The Active Directory™ directory service feature of Windows 2000 Server stores information about all objects on a local or global network and makes this information easy for users and administrators to find and use.

To accommodate the needs of diverse organizations, Active Directory can be partitioned into domains, and, in larger networks, hierarchies of domain trees. A Windows 2000 domain is a group of computers and resources that shares a common user account database and security policy. Windows 2000 domains contain domain controllers which manage user accounts and control access to network resources. The remaining computers in the domain are either user workstations or servers, such as computers running SNA Server, that provide resources to domain users.

For more information about Active Directory and domains, see the *Microsoft® Windows® 2000 Server Resource Kit Distributed Systems Guide.*

SNA Server Subdomains

Every computer running SNA Server is a member of a Windows 2000 domain and is also a member of an SNA Server subdomain. An SNA Server subdomain is a logical grouping of SNA Server–based computers that share common configuration information. These subdomains allow clients running SNA Server Client software to use any of the SNA Server–based computers in the same subdomain to connect to the host system or systems. To the clients running SNA Server Client software, these computers appear to function as a unit, providing a single set of SNA resources.

Although SNA Server runs on the Windows 2000 Server operating system, SNA Server subdomains play no role in Windows 2000 user authentication. Rather, SNA Server relies on Windows 2000 Server to authenticate users.

Note SNA Server can be configured to use Windows 2000 domain authentication to provide secure, single sign-on to designated host system resources. For more information, see "LAN-to-Host Security" later in this chapter.

Organizing SNA Server–Based Subdomains

Each SNA Server subdomain can contain up to 15 computers running SNA Server, and a Windows 2000 domain can contain an unlimited number of SNA Server subdomains. Because they rely on Windows 2000 domain security to control access to the network, all computers running SNA Server in a particular subdomain must belong to the same Windows 2000 domain.

When you are planning the scope of an SNA Server subdomain and the location of its members, you should consider the capacity of the network link that connects the subdomain members. Whenever the subdomain configuration is changed (by adding a new user or LU, for example), the changed configuration file is propagated to all SNA Server–based computers in a subdomain whose role is set to backup. (SNA Server roles are discussed in the following section.)

To minimize unnecessary replication traffic across slow WAN connections, a subdomain should usually be contained within an Active Directory site. An Active Directory site is one or more TCP/IP subnets that are connected by high-speed links. Windows 2000 allows administrators to control and optimize inter-site replications.

In the distributed deployment model presented earlier in this chapter, you could organize all computers running SNA Server at a branch office site into one subdomain and organize the computers running SNA Server at the central site (near the host) into a separate subdomain.

SNA Server offers additional mechanisms to specifically control SNA Server replication traffic. For example, using the SNA Server Manager, you can control replication traffic by configuring a parameter called Mean Time Between Server Broadcasts. For more information about fine-tuning SNA Server replications, see the SNA Server version 4.0 documentation.

Determining SNA Server Roles

After you have established your Windows 2000 domains and your subdomains, you must assign a role to each computer running SNA Server within each subdomain.

The designation of one of the following three roles identifies which computers running SNA Server have a copy of the SNA Server configuration for the SNA Server subdomain. SNA Server Client–based computers can connect to any computer running SNA Server in the subdomain regardless of its configuration role.

Primary. Provides host connectivity services to your users and contains the master copy of the configuration file. Only one computer can be designated as the primary SNA Server in a subdomain.

Backup. Contains a read-only copy of the configuration file maintained by the primary server. Backup servers can be promoted to a primary role if the primary server fails. An SNA Server subdomain can contain up to 14 backup servers.

Member. Does not contain a copy of the configuration file. Members rely on primary and backup servers to maintain configuration information. An SNA Server subdomain can contain up to 14 member servers.

Note The concept of a backup SNA Server is different from the concept of hot backup. Hot backup is the ability of computers running SNA Server to work together to provide session support even when a server or a connection is not working. When computers running SNA Server provide hot backup, it means that LUs and other resources are configured so that they can fill in and support sessions required by other servers in the subdomain, even if another, similar resource is not available.

The primary computer running SNA Server should be the first server you install in an SNA Server subdomain. If possible, you should have one or more backup servers in the subdomain, as well, to maintain copies of the SNA Server configuration file in case the primary computer running SNA Server fails. If security is an issue, the backup servers should be kept physically secure because each one contains a copy of the SNA Server configuration file.

After you have designated one primary server and its backup servers, the remaining servers can be designated as member servers (computers running SNA Server without a configuration file).

As long as the primary server is running, you can administer SNA Server from a member server just as you would from any other server. You can also manage SNA Server from a computer running Windows 2000 Professional that has SNA Server Manager installed. You can limit the ability of users or groups to administer SNA Server by setting up SNA Server permissions.

Connection Methods

Once you have determined a suitable deployment model and subdomain configuration, you must determine:

- How to connect computers running SNA Server to the IBM host systems.
- Which network protocols to use for communications between clients and SNA Server–based computers.
- Which network protocols to use for communications between different computers running SNA Server.

Connecting SNA Server–Based Computers to IBM Host Systems

This section explores how to connect computers running SNA Server to IBM mainframe and AS/400 host systems.

Understanding SNA Server-to-Host Connections

In SNA Server terms, a host connection is the data communications path between SNA Server and a host system. For a mainframe, this connection corresponds to a physical unit definition in the Virtual Telecommunications Access Method (VTAM). A physical unit (PU) is a combination of hardware and software that provides the services needed to use and manage a particular device. On the AS/400, this connection corresponds to an Advanced Program-to-Program Communications (APPC) controller definition. For more information about IBM host connection methods and other background information about SNA networking, see "IBM SNA Interoperability Concepts" in this book.

For each physical adapter or connection, an appropriate link service is installed and configured within SNA Server. The link service is a Windows 2000 service or device driver that is used to control server-to-host communication adapters supported by SNA Server. Once configured, the link service is available for use not only on the configured SNA Server, but on any SNA Server in the subdomain using the Distributed Link Service feature of SNA Server.

Once you configure your link services, you create connections over a defined link service. As mentioned previously, a connection is the data communication path between a computer running SNA Server and the IBM host. Using a host connection, a client computer on a LAN can communicate with the mainframe system. For some link services, it is possible to define multiple connections over a single host link.

In SNA terms, the combination of a connection and the link service it uses is equivalent to a PU. In SNA networks, SNA Server provides PU 2 or PU 2.1 functionality similar to a cluster controller. For more information about cluster controller functions, see "IBM SNA Interoperability Concepts" in this book.

Understanding Server-to-Host Connection Methods

To understand the connectivity options, you should first examine the different physical connections and network protocols that SNA Server supports. Table 10.5 summarizes all common connection methods that can be used with SNA Server.

Table 10.5   SNA Server-to-Host Connection Methods

Method	Throughput	Characteristics
Token Ring 802.2 Data Link Control (DLC)	4 or 16 Megabits per second (Mbps)	Mainframe or AS/400.
		Midrange performance using DLC protocol.
		Supports multiple host connections using a single adapter.
		Easy and inexpensive to implement.
		Suitable for a wide range of purposes.
Standard Ethernet 802.2 DLC	10 Mbps	Mainframe or AS/400.
		Midrange performance using DLC protocol.
		Supports multiple host connections using a single adapter.
		Easy and inexpensive to implement.
		Suitable for light to medium network traffic conditions.
		Ethernet contention can degrade performance under heavy loads.
Fast Ethernet 802.2 DLC	100 Mbps	Mainframe or AS/400.
		High performance using DLC protocol.
		Supports multiple host connections using a single adapter.
		Easy and inexpensive to implement.
		Suitable for higher performance connections.
		Ethernet contention can degrade performance under heavy loads.
Fiber Distributed Data Interface (FDDI) 802.2 DLC	100 Mbps	Mainframe or AS/400.
		High performance using DLC protocol.
		Supports multiple host connections using a single adapter.
		Relatively expensive to implement.
		Suitable for higher performance connections.
Synchronous Data Link Control (SDLC)	9,600 - 19,200 bps	Mainframe or AS/400.
		Generally low performance using SDLC protocol.
		Supports 256 sessions over a single host connection.
		Easy and inexpensive to implement.
		Suitable for low-traffic WAN connections.

continued

Table 10.5   SNA Server-to-Host Connection Methods *(continued)*

Method	Throughput	Characteristics
X.25	9,600 - 19,200 bps	Mainframes and AS/400.
		Generally low performance using Qualified Logical Link Control (QLLC) protocol.
		Supports 256 sessions over a single host connection.
		Easy and inexpensive to implement.
		Suitable for low-traffic WAN connections.
Distributed Function Terminal (DFT)	2.35 Mbps	Mainframes only.
		Low to midrange performance.
		Supports only five sessions over a single host connection.
		Inexpensive.
		Suitable for test environments or small networks with an existing DFT-based infrastructure.
Twinax	1 Mbps	AS/400 systems only.
		Low performance.
		Supports five sessions over a single host connection.
		Inexpensive.
		Suitable for AS/400 host environments with an existing Twinax infrastructure.
Channel - Bus & Tag	4.5 megabytes per second	Mainframes only.
		High performance.
		Supports a high number of host connections..
		Expensive.
		Suitable for high-performance connections.
Channel - ESCON	17 megabytes per second	Mainframes only.
		Highest performance.
		Supports a high number of host connections.
		Expensive.
		Suitable for conditions where maximum throughput is required.

When you choose a connection method, you should keep in mind several factors:

- The host systems to which you are connecting.
- The deployment model you are implementing.
- The host networking infrastructure that is in place.
- The expected usage level of host resources.
- The level of performance and response expected by your users.
- Cost.

In general, a high-speed Token Ring connection is a good choice when the same connection is used to connect a LAN to an SNA network that includes both a mainframe and AS/400 system. For greater performance in a dedicated mainframe environment, channel-type connections are generally recommended.

For some link services, multiple host connections are possible using a single adapter, most notably DLC and channel-type link services. Each instance of SNA Server supports up to 250 host connections, and up to four instances of SNA Server are supported on a single computer.

Connecting SNA Server to a Mainframe System

The hierarchical SNA network model provides access to a centralized processing resource from elements throughout the network. This model is most frequently associated with mainframe environments in which centralized applications are accessed from remote terminals across a network.

Devices in a hierarchical SNA network, such as terminals or cluster controllers, are called physical units (PUs). Each class of device is designated by a number. For example, the mainframe itself is known as a PU 5 device. For background information about hierarchical SNA networks, see "IBM SNA Interoperability Concepts" in this book.

SNA Server participates in a hierarchical SNA network by emulating a standard IBM PU 2, or cluster controller, and multiple LUs, which are protocols that provide a standardized format for delivery of data for specific applications, of type LU 0, LU 1, LU 2, and LU 3. This allows client computers that emulate IBM terminals and applications to communicate with the IBM host (PU 5).

SNA Server can connect to a mainframe computer in one of two ways: either directly to the PU 5, the host; or through a PU 4, a front-end processor (FEP).

Direct and Indirect Physical Connections to a Mainframe

You can make a direct physical connection (a connection that does not involve an FEP) between computers running SNA Server and a mainframe system using any of the following physical connection methods:

- Open Systems Interconnection, supporting Token Ring, Ethernet, and FDDI connections
- Bus & Tag channel connection
- ESCON channel connection

Indirect physical connections between SNA Server–based computers and a mainframe system (connections through an FEP) are also supported. These connections might be easier to implement depending on your existing infrastructure and the physical proximity of the computers running SNA Server to the mainframe. For this type of connection, one of the following methods can be used:

- Token Ring
- Ethernet
- FDDI
- SDLC
- X.25

Figure 10.5 illustrates both direct and indirect physical connections to a mainframe.

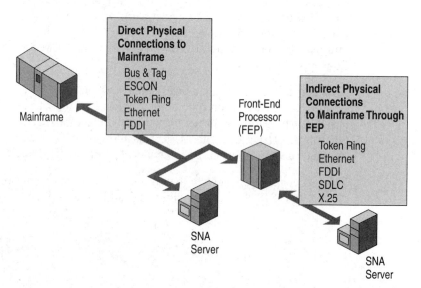

Figure 10.5   Direct and Indirect Physical Connections to a Mainframe

Logical Connections to a Mainframe

In a hierarchical SNA network, SNA Server emulates a cluster controller and supports all standard protocols:

- LU 2 for 3270 terminal sessions.
- LU 1 or 3 for SCS or 3270 printer sessions.
- LU 6.2 for APPC and Common Programming Interface for Communications (CPI-C) applications.
- LU 0, 1, 2, or 3 for LU application (LUA) Request User Interface (RUI) general-purpose, customized applications.

Any combination of these protocols can be used over a given physical connection, as illustrated in Figure 10.6.

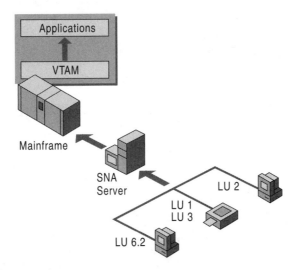

Figure 10.6   Logical Connections to a Mainframe

Connecting SNA Server to an AS/400 System

In the peer-oriented SNA network model, all computers on the network can communicate directly with each other. Advanced Peer-to-Peer Networking (APPN) is the architecture developed by IBM that enables distributed data processing. APPN defines how components communicate with each other, and the level of network-related services, like routing sessions, that are supplied by each computer in the network. For background information about SNA APPN, see "IBM SNA Interoperability Concepts" in this book.

In an APPN network, SNA Server emulates a type 2.1 physical unit device (PU 2.1). SNA Server operates as an APPN low entry network (LEN) node and communicates with other APPN nodes using the Advanced Program-to-Program Communications (APPC) or LU 6.2 protocol.

Computers running SNA Server can connect directly to an AS/400 using several connection methods, as shown in Figure 10.7:

- SDLC
- 802.2/DLC (Token Ring, Ethernet, FDDI)
- X.25
- Twinax
- Frame Relay

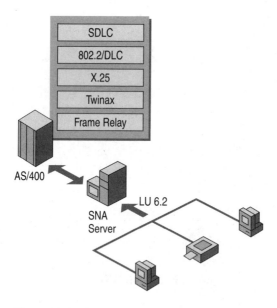

Figure 10.7   SNA Server Connections in a Peer-Oriented Network

Choosing Network Protocols

After your SNA Server–based computer-to-host connection is determined, you must choose the protocol or protocols to use for two additional SNA Server communication paths: between clients and SNA Server–based computers, and between different SNA Server–based computers. You can use one protocol for both, or you can use a combination of different protocols, provided that all servers share at least one client/server protocol and use it for server-to-server communication.

Deploying a single protocol across your WAN is the easiest way to manage your network communications.

However, you might decide to gradually implement SNA Server throughout your enterprise. In this case, you need to use existing protocols for certain connections. For example, you could use TCP/IP for server-to-server communications and use IPX/SPX for client-to-server communications. Similarly, other combinations of supported protocols can be used, provided that all the SNA Server–based computers share one protocol and use that protocol for server-to-server and client-to-server communication.

Choosing Client/Server Network Protocols

Computers running SNA Server Client software can communicate through a number of LAN protocols:

- TCP/IP
- IPX/SPX
- Named Pipes
- Banyan VINES IP
- AppleTalk

TCP/IP is quickly becoming the standard network protocol for client/server applications. Its high performance and support for sophisticated routing features make it suitable for many WAN environments. In many cases, TCP/IP is the best protocol choice for your network, especially if TCP/IP is already deployed to some degree in the LAN segment on which servers and clients running SNA Server reside.

If you deploy TCP/IP, it is recommended that you assign static IP addresses to SNA Server–based computers because it is easier to administer workstations that have a fixed SNA Server address. For computers that run SNA Server Client software, you can use the Dynamic Host Configuration Protocol (DHCP) to dynamically allocate client IP addresses without difficulty.

For more information about TCP/IP and DHCP, see the *Microsoft® Windows® 2000 Server Resource Kit TCP/IP Core Networking Guide.*

SNA Server Client Software

SNA Server Client software allows workstations to support SNA Server advanced host integration features. SNA Server Client software also provides application programming interfaces (APIs) that are used by third-party vendors to gain access to IBM host systems and applications. Third-party vendors provide 3270 and 5250 terminal emulators and additional host integration utilities.

SNA Server Client software creates network transport independence, allowing clients and applications to communicate using any of SNA Server's programmatic interfaces.

At this time, client software is available for the following platforms:

- Windows NT
- Windows 95
- Windows 3.*x*
- MS-DOS
- IBM OS/2
- Macintosh (third-party)
- UNIX (third-party)

Note SNA Server Client software is not required for clients that use TCP/IP for services such as TN3270, TN5250, and AFTP. Applications, such as TN3270 emulators, communicate directly with these services rather than using the SNA Server client/server interface.

For information about the host communication services and SNA application programming interfaces that SNA Server can support for each client platform, see "Heterogeneous Clients Services" later in this chapter.

Choosing Server-to-Server Network Protocols

Computers running SNA Server can communicate with each other using any of the following methods:

- TCP/IP
- IPX/SPX
- Named Pipes
- Banyan VINES IP

For more information about configuring protocols and optimizing server-to-server network traffic, see the SNA Server version 4.0 documentation.

Communications with Hierarchical SNA Networks

In traditional hierarchical SNA networks, remote terminals access centralized mainframe applications across a network.

This model uses the information display protocol for IBM mainframe computers known as 3270. This protocol facilitates conversations between the mainframe and devices such as terminals, printers, and controllers. SNA Server can provide access to these mainframe resources through the definition and assignment of 3270 LUs.

Once you have established the physical connection from SNA Server to the mainframe, you need to determine the types of 3270 connectivity that your users need.

3270 Access

SNA Server provides 3270 connectivity through dependent 3270 LUs. 3270 LUs are dependent because they require a mainframe to function. Each 3270 LU defined within SNA Server is configured to use an existing connection to the mainframe system and corresponds to a matching LU resource allocated on the host computer, usually specified within VTAM. The 3270 LU definition in SNA Server is identified by a number and a user-specified name. The number matches the number of the corresponding LU resource on the mainframe.

The 3270 LU is further classified by the type of service provided over the connection. Like PUs, LU types are designated by numbers. For example, 3270 display data streams are known as LU 2. A 3270 LU , as shown in Figure 10.8, can be configured as one of the following:

- Display (LU 2)
- Printer (LU 1 or LU 3)
- Application (LUA)
- Downstream

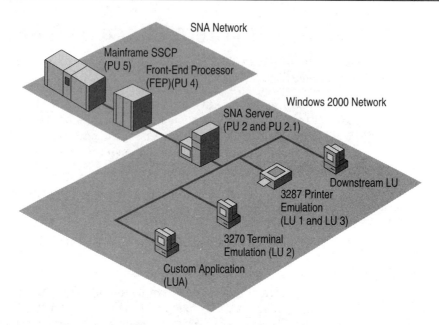

Figure 10.8   3270 Connectivity Using SNA Server

SNA Server Client software must be installed on each client that uses SNA Server LU services. The client software manages communications between a 3270 application and the server running SNA Server. Applications designed to use the SNA Server Client API use the LUs defined within SNA Server to establish a communications link from the client to the mainframe through SNA Server.

The link between the LU definition in SNA Server and the host LU resource is called a session. Sessions can be permanent and automatically started during initialization, or established on an as-needed basis. Concurrent sessions can share the same physical devices and communications links.

Using LU Pools

Although you can create individual LUs and assign them to users and groups, using LU pools to manage and deploy a large number of LUs is a more efficient method of administering these resources. LU pools are groupings of LUs that allow you to maximize access to these LUs, as shown in Figure 10.9. A user, an application, or a downstream system can access the LUs as long as any LU assigned to the pool is free. If any one of the pooled LUs ceases to function, another free LU in the pool is used.

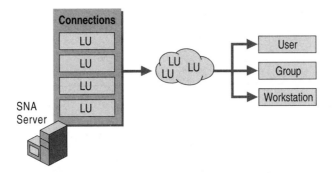

Figure 10.9   Creating and Assigning LU Pools

LU pools also allow groups of intermittent users to use a limited number of host resources more efficiently. Dedicating LUs to specific users who occasionally require host access wastes host resources. Using a pool, you can assign a smaller number of LUs to a group of users who require sporadic access. For example, if a group of 100 users requires host access 25 percent of the time, assigning a pool of 25 LUs to the group might fulfill their needs.

Assigning LUs to Workstations

LUs (and LU pools) can also be assigned to workstations rather than users, effectively locking LUs to a specific computer. This configuration makes it easier for users to find and access different resources.

For example, suppose you have 150 employees who share 50 workstations, each of which has a printer attached. Instead of assigning 50 printer LUs to a pool and making the pool available to each user, you can add each of the workstations to SNA Server and assign a printer LU to each workstation. Doing so allows users to log on to any of the 50 workstations, and the printer that is attached to the workstation is available in the list of LUs.

Providing Fault Tolerance

LU pools can also provide fault-tolerant connections to users. When a particular resource such as a host connection fails, hot backup allows for a similarly configured resource to automatically fill in and support the needed functions, as shown in Figure 10.10. Hot backup can be implemented across host connections on the same server or across several servers in a domain. Hot backup is a recommended strategy for any size enterprise and helps to provide reliable host access to your users.

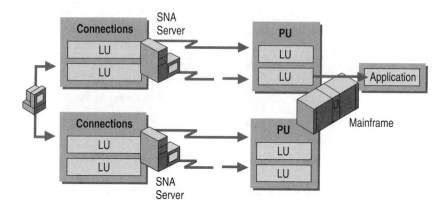

Figure 10.10   Hot Backup Across Connections and Servers

Providing Load Balancing

Load balancing is closely related to hot backup. Load balancing evenly distributes sessions across multiple host connections and multiple servers using 3270 LU pooling. For example, if you have two connections that each support ten 3270 display LUs, load balancing ensures that free LUs are allocated evenly from the two connections to users. Load balancing is implemented when a pool is configured with LUs from multiple servers or connections.

TN3270 Access

TN3270 is a type of Telnet service that allows access to mainframe computers over a TCP/IP network. Users can connect to mainframes using a TN3270 client and the TN3270 service provided with SNA Server, as shown in Figure 10.11.

The TN3270 service supports the following protocols:

- TN3270 for display sessions
- TN3287 for printer sessions
- TN3270E for extended display and print sessions

The TN3270 service uses SNA Server features to provide mainframe access and to address issues such as security and redundancy when the data communications path between the client and server contains one or more unsecured segments.

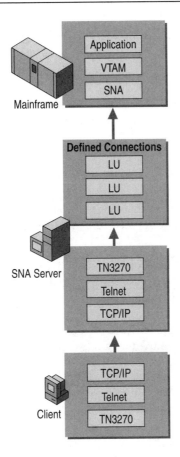

Figure 10.11   TN3270 Communications Through SNA Server

Because the TN3270 service communicates with SNA Server using the LUA API, LUA-type connections and LUs must be configured on the server. Once configured, LUAs and LU pools can be assigned to the TN3270 service and made available for use by TN3270 clients requesting mainframe access.

As with all TCP/IP services, TN3270 requires a free TCP port in which clients can locate the TN3270 service. The TN3270 service defaults to port 23, the same port as standard Telnet services. Because no two services can share the same TCP port, it is recommended that you change the TN3270 service to use TCP port 24 or some other unused TCP port. When attempting to connect to the TN3270 service from a client application, you must also specify the new TCP port within the application's connection settings.

Providing Hot Backup and Load Balancing

As described in "SNA Server Integration with Windows 2000–based Networks" earlier in this chapter, a Windows 2000 domain can contain one or more SNA Server subdomains. Like 3270 LUs, LUA LUs from multiple servers in different subdomains can be assigned to the TN3270 service. This allows you to distribute client sessions among the participating servers in the subdomain, thereby balancing the load.

Creating redundant connections to the mainframe and assigning them to a TN3270 service increases service availability. If one server fails, a client can still access LUA LUs on a different server. If no other SNA Server–based computers are used in a particular site, you can increase fault tolerance and available bandwidth by configuring a single server with redundant host links.

Assigning LUs to IP Addresses

Just as you can assign 3270 LUs to a user or workstation, you can restrict access to LUA LUs or pools by specifying an IP address or subnet mask for clients that must access the resource. If a workstation has a name that can be resolved using name resolution services like DHCP, DNS, or WINS, the name can be associated with the resource instead of the individual workstation. For information about TCP/IP addressing and services, see the *TCP/IP Core Networking Guide*.

Restricting access to clients with specific IP addresses or workstation names increases the security of the LUA resources. For more information about host security issues, see "LAN-to-Host Security" later in this chapter.

Downstream Connections

In hierarchical SNA environments, you configure 3270 communications between SNA nodes using SNA protocols. Usually those nodes are SNA Server–based computers and mainframes. A downstream system, however, is an SNA node that uses SNA Server as a PU gateway, as shown in Figure 10.12. To the downstream system, the SNA Server–based computer appears to be the actual mainframe providing the PUs and 3270 LUs.

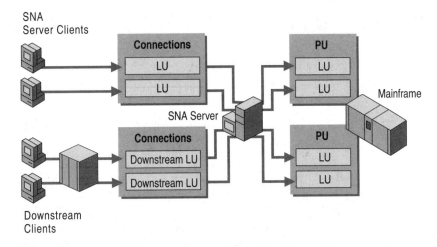

Figure 10.12   Downstream Connections Using SNA Server

A downstream system in this type of environment must be a PU 2 device. For example, an IBM 3745 cluster controller can be a downstream device. A client running a terminal emulator that emulates a PU 2 and acquires LU sessions from the SNA Server–based computer can also be a downstream device.

On the computer running SNA Server, two connections are required to support downstream systems:

- A host connection between the server and the mainframe. This can be any standard physical connection method supported by the mainframe.

- A downstream connection between the server and the downstream system. This physical connection can be an 802.2/DLC, SDLC, or X.25 connection.

Once configured, SNA Server can manage the downstream LUs in a manner similar to how it manages other LUs, including assigning them to LU pools.

This type of configuration is useful in environments where the downstream system is unable to communicate directly with the mainframe because of hardware or network incompatibilities that the intermediate SNA Server–based computer can resolve.

Using SNA Server as a PU concentrator can also help reduce host configuration requirements. LUs from one or more PUs can be shared with multiple downstream devices, alleviating the need to configure each downstream device in VTAM on the mainframe system. The result is a more efficient use of host resources.

For more information about communications with hierarchical SNA networks, see the SNA Server version 4.0 documentation.

Communications with Peer-to-Peer SNA Networks

Devices in peer-oriented SNA networks participate in Advanced Peer-to-Peer Networking (APPN). Each APPN device, known as a type 2.1 physical unit (PU 2.1) can communicate directly with other PU 2.1 devices using Advanced Program-to-Program Communications (APPC) sessions.

Each PU 2.1 device relies on its own intelligence and does not require constant access to a centrally located host system.

Note Although networks that use APPC are usually associated with AS/400 host systems, mainframe systems can also use APPC-based networking.

In an AS/400 environment, APPC is used for a variety of applications including 5250 access and file transfers. Programs that use APPC to communicate are called transaction programs (TPs). APPC TPs use LU 6.2 names to gain access to other systems and other transaction programs.

For background information about APPN networking, see "IBM SNA Interoperability Concepts" in this book.

APPC Using SNA Server

With SNA Server, a TP such as a 5250 terminal emulator might use an APPC LU alias to communicate with another TP. In this case, the LU alias maps to an LU name that is actually used to communicate with the TP on the other system.

When a client/server network TP requests a conversation with a TP on the AS/400 (the remote system), SNA Server (the local system) acts on behalf of the client request and negotiates an LU 6.2 to LU 6.2 session to the AS/400. The data sent or received from the AS/400 TP is handled by the server and sent to the client TP over the selected client/server protocol. Figure 10.13 shows an APPC conversation using SNA Server.

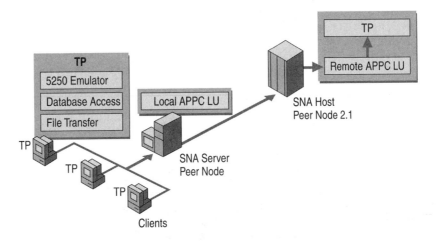

Figure 10.13   APPC Conversation Using SNA Server

Note In Figure 10.13, the perception of local and remote LUs depends on the system you are configuring. When configuring SNA Server, the local APPC LU corresponds to SNA Server and the remote LU corresponds to the AS/400. If you view the configuration from the AS/400 perspective, the AS/400 is the local APPC LU and SNA Server is the remote LU.

Common Programming Interface for Communications

Common Programming Interface for Communications (CPI-C) is an application programming interface (API) that uses the LU 6.2 communications architecture. Many organizations implement CPI-C because several platforms that support APPC can use CPI-C, including AS/400 and mainframe systems, Windows 2000, and several UNIX-based operating systems. CPI-C comprises a set of C programming language routines that allow applications on computers to communicate with one another to accomplish a processing task, such as copying a file or accessing a remote database.

CPI-C programming provides a mechanism called client-side information that associates a set of parameters with a specified CPI-C symbolic destination name. The CPI-C program uses the symbolic destination name to initialize a conversation using APPC LUs that are associated with the CPI-C symbolic name.

SNA Server supports the CPI-C API and provides for configuration of CPI-C parameters. For more information about programming using the CPI-C API, see the SNA Server version 4.0 documentation.

APPC Applications

APPC can be used to support a wide range of applications including:

- 5250 terminal access.
- TN5250 terminal access.
- APPC file transfers, including Shared Folders access.

5250 Access

AS/400 display sessions are provided through APPC using the 5250 data stream. Computers running SNA Server provide APPC access to AS/400s using 5250 emulation clients. Clients can only communicate with AS/400s using APPC.

To support 5250 services, the local APPC LU acts as an identifier for local SNA Server–based clients; the remote APPC LU identifies the AS/400 system. Figure 10.14 shows the local and remote LUs used for this configuration.

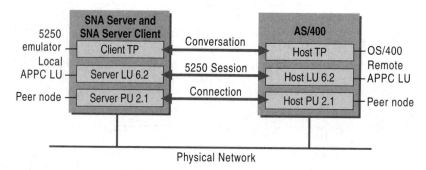

Figure 10.14   Components of 5250 Access Through SNA Server

TN5250 Access

TN5250 is a Telnet service that allows users to access AS/400 systems over a TCP/IP network using an appropriate TN5250 client terminal emulator. The TN5250 service provided with SNA Server enables any TN5250 client to connect to the AS/400 system by means of SNA Server, without installing or configuring TCP/IP on the AS/400 system, as illustrated in Figure 10.15. Full 5250 terminal emulation functions are supported by the service, as well as fault tolerance and security features similar to those provided with the TN3270 service.

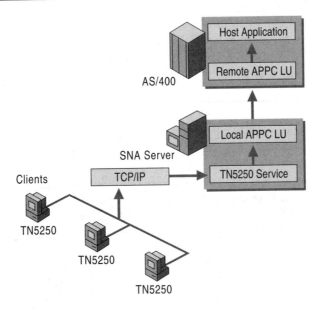

Figure 10.15   TN5250 Access Through SNA Server

APPC File Transfers

Although it is possible to perform file transfers between the client and the host system using $INDFILE or other mechanisms, APPC file transfers offer a robust and high performance alternative to emulator-based solutions.

SNA Server supports three host file transfer mechanisms based on APPC connectivity:

- APPC File Transfer Protocol (AFTP)
- FTP to AFTP Gateway
- Shared Folders

The file transfer method that you choose to deploy depends on the type of host system in your enterprise (mainframe or AS/400) and on the type of file transfer capabilities you wish to provide to your users.

APPC File Transfer Protocol

The APPC File Transfer Protocol (AFTP) is a client/server application that provides file transfer capabilities using APPC and LU 6.2 (FTP protocol is used on TCP/IP networks in a similar way). AFTP supports functions similar to standard FTP, including the ability to send, receive, and rename files, as well as to manipulate directories on a remote system.

The AFTP service is installed and configured on the computer running SNA
Server (or an SNA Server–based client) to allow AFTP client software (provided
with SNA Server) to access specific directories on the server.

For more information about configuring and using AFTP, see the SNA Server
version 4.0 documentation.

FTP-AFTP Gateway Service

The FTP-AFTP gateway service gives TCP/IP users the ability to access and
manipulate files on a mainframe or an AS/400 using a conventional FTP client
without installing TCP/IP on the host, as shown in Figure 10.16. The service
transparently converts incoming client FTP requests into AFTP commands and
manages the communications and data between the two services. This capability
can be used interactively by FTP users, or through applications that need access to
SNA host data.

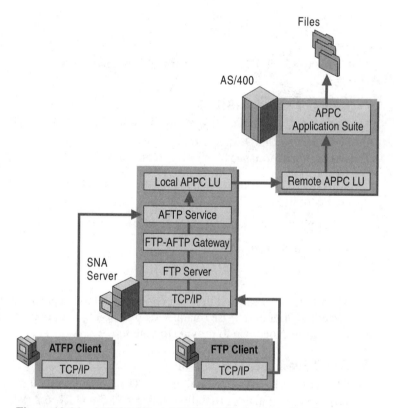

Figure 10.16   APPC FTP and FTP-AFTP Gateway Services

To run the FTP-AFTP Gateway Service, you must first install the FTP or AFTP
client software as well as the AFTP service on the SNA Server–based computer.

Shared Folders

Users on workstations that do not have the SNA Server Client software installed, but who still require file transfer capabilities with an AS/400 host, can use the Shared Folders Gateway Service provided by SNA Server. With this service, network users can share or store files on the AS/400 system as though it were another volume on the SNA Server–based computer, as shown in Figure 10.17.

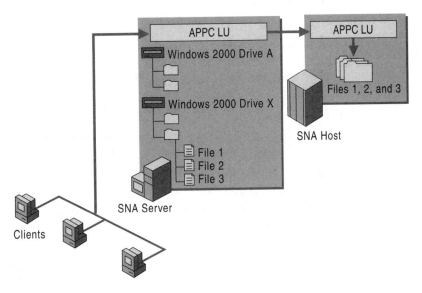

Figure 10.17   Using the Shared Folders Gateway Service

APPC Deployment Strategies

In most cases, deployment strategies are effective for APPC LUs regardless of the application that the LUs support. When deploying APPC connections with SNA Server, you should consider how to use the following types of LUs and LU configurations:

- Independent LUs
- Dependent LUs
- LU pools

Using Independent APPC LUs

An independent LU can communicate directly with a peer system and does not need the support of a host computer. Independent APPC LUs, as used in AS/400 APPN networks, provide the ability to run multiple, concurrent, parallel sessions between a local and remote LU pair.

When configuring independent APPC LUs, you should note that when SNA Server is used to communicate with a TP on a mainframe over an independent APPC LU, the host system must be running VTAM V3R2 or later. The version of Advanced Communication Function/Network Control Function (ACF/NCP) required on the mainframe is dependent on the type of FEP used. For 3725 systems, ACF/NCP V4R3 or later is required. For 3745 systems, ACF/NCP V5R2 or later is required.

For information about configuring independent APPC LUs, see the SNA Server version 4.0 documentation.

Using Dependent APPC LUs

A dependent local APPC LU requires the support of a mainframe to communicate with a remote TP. Dependent APPC LUs cannot be used to communicate with AS/400s. Unlike independent APPC LUs, dependent APPC LU only allow one session per LU.

Dependent APPC LUs are useful when configuring SNA Server to communicate with a mainframe using a version of VTAM earlier than V3R2 because independent LUs are not supported in earlier VTAM versions. SNA Server provides support for dependent APPC LUs. However, use independent LUs whenever possible.

When configuring APPC dependent LUs, you should specify the network name and LU name, even though they are not required. They are used by software running on the SNA Server–based computer, such as the Windows 2000 event log. For example, if a remote APPC LU is partnered with a dependent local APPC LU, naming the remote APPC LU helps to identify any events associated with it in the Windows 2000 event log.

For more information about configuring dependent APPC LUs, see the SNA Server version 4.0 documentation.

Using APPC LU Pools

Although you can create individual LUs and assign them to users and groups, using LU pools to manage and deploy a large number of LUs lets you administer these resources more efficiently.

LU pools also allow groups of intermittent users to use a limited number of host resources more efficiently. Dedicating LUs to specific users who occasionally require host access wastes host resources. Using a pool, you can assign a smaller number of LUs to a group of users who require sporadic access. For example, if a group of 100 users require host access 25 percent of the time, assigning a pool of 25 LUs to the group might meet their requirements.

For information about configuring LUs, see the SNA Server version 4.0 documentation and the *Microsoft® BackOffice® Resource Kit*.

Providing Fault Tolerance

In the AS/400 environment, SNA Server uses a combination of LU names and LU aliases over one or more servers to achieve transparent fault-tolerant connections to an AS/400 host, as shown in Figure 10.18.

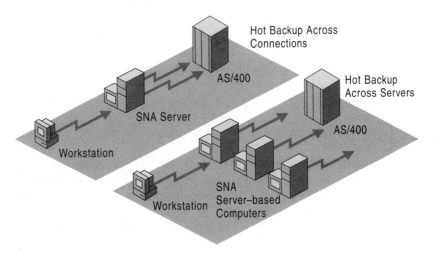

Figure 10.18   Hot Backup Across Connections and Servers

A single computer running SNA Server can use multiple connections to provide fault tolerance. To use this method, two or more APPC connections to the same AS/400 are configured as hot backups for one another. If one of the connections fails, the clients are reconfigured to select a working configuration.

SNA Server can also use multiple SNA Server–based computers as backups for one another. If one of the servers fails, the clients are shifted from the failed server to a working server.

Using a combination of hot backup methods across both connections and servers is recommended to maintain a high level of host availability in your enterprise.

For more information about configuring hot backup for APPC connections, see the SNA Server version 4.0 documentation.

TN5250 IP Settings

IP settings assigned to the TN5250 definitions allow TN5250 clients to connect to the AS/400. By default, the TN5250 definition is not assigned an IP address or a subnet mask. This allows any TN5250 client to connect to the AS/400.

You can restrict access to the TN5250 service by specifying the IP address or subnet mask of a client workstation. When these values are specified, only clients whose IP or subnet mask match those specified in the TN5250 configuration are allowed access to the AS/400 through the TN5250 service. You can also specify the workstation name in place of the IP, and use a WINS, DHCP, or other name resolution service to resolve a friendly name to an IP address.

SNA Remote Access Service

SNA Remote Access Service (SNA remote access server) integrates the LU 6.2 transport of SNA Server with Windows 2000 Routing and Remote Access service, allowing administrators to create virtual LAN connections between Windows 2000 systems across an existing SNA network. Figure 10.19 shows how, using SNA remote access server, the SNA network acts as a network backbone, passing network traffic between the Windows 2000 systems bridged with the host system.

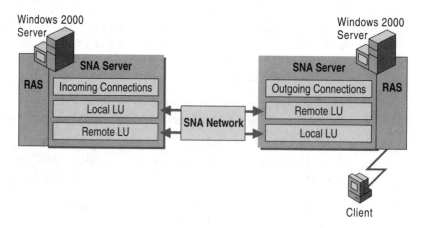

Figure 10.19   SNA Remote Access Service (SNA Remote Access Server)

The functions available with SNA remote access server are the same as those for remote access server over ISDN or X.25 except for the dial-back connection feature, which is not supported by SNA remote access server. SNA remote access server supports either the Windows 2000 Server Routing and Remote Access service or Windows 2000 Routing and Remote Access service client, depending on whether the computer on which SNA remote access server is installed, is an SNA Server–based server or client. In addition, a computer running Windows 2000 Professional, SNA Server Client software, and SNA remote access server can dial out through the SNA Server–based computer that is running SNA remote access server.

Because legacy SNA networks might include smaller bandwidth links like SDLC, and because LAN traffic typically generates more network traffic than can be effectively handled by slower connections, care should be taken to resolve bandwidth needs before deploying SNA remote access server in your enterprise.

For information about configuring SNA remote access server, see the SNA Server version 4.0 documentation.

Heterogeneous Client Services

SNA Server supports the LU types (and equivalent Telnet-based applications) and application programming interfaces (APIs) that support the most commonly used configurations for many desktop operating systems, including:

- Microsoft® Windows NT®
- Windows 95
- Windows 3.x
- MS-DOS
- IBM OS/2
- Macintosh
- UNIX-based operating systems

Integrating Heterogeneous Clients with Mainframes

Table 10.6 summarizes SNA Server client-to-mainframe services supported on each desktop platform.

Table 10.6   Heterogeneous Client to Mainframe Integration

Desktop Platform	LU Types/Telnet Services	SNA APIs
MS-DOS	LU0, LU1, LU2, LU3, and LU6.2. TN3270, TN3287, and TN3270E.	APPC, CPI-C, Common Service Verb (CSV), and LUA Request User Interface (RUI).
Windows 3.*x*, Windows for Workgroups	LU0, LU1, LU2, LU3, and LU6.2. TN3270, TN3287, and TN3270E.	APPC, CPI-C, CSV, LUI RUI, LUA Session Level Interface (SLI), and ODBC/DRDA.
OS/2	LU0, LU1, LU2, LU3, and LU6.2. TN3270, TN3287, and TN3270E.	APPC, CPI-C, CSV, LUA RUI, and LUA SLI.
Macintosh	TN3270, TN3287, and TN3270E.	(Uses Telnet-based services.)
UNIX[1]	LU0 and LU6.2. TN3270, TN3287, and TN3270E.	APPC, CPI-C, CSV, and LUA RUI.
Windows 95 and Windows 98	LU0, LU1, LU2, LU3, and LU6.2. TN3270, TN3287, and TN3270E.	APPC, CPI-C, CSV, LUA RUI, LUA SLI, ODBC/DRDA, and AFTP.
Microsoft® Windows NT® Workstation 4.0 and Windows 2000 Professional	LU0, LU1, LU2, LU3, and LU6.2. TN3270, TN3287, and TN3270E.	APPC, CPI-C, CSV, LUA RUI, LUA SLI, ODBC/DRDA, and AFTP.

[1] The UNIX client can use services beyond the Telnet-based services by using a third-party UNIX client for SNA Server developed by Parker Software in cooperation with Microsoft. For more information about the UNIX client for SNA Server, see http://www.microsoft.com/.

Session Types with Mainframes

SNA Server supports standard terminal and printer sessions with LU types 0 through 3. LU 0 is a device-independent LU used mainly in the financial industry to support teller terminals and automatic teller machines. LU types 1 and 3 are used to support printer emulation programs on client and server computers, including SNA Server's Host Print Service. LU type 2 provides terminal emulation support for a broad range of client 3270 emulator programs.

LU 6.2 supports Application Program-to-Program Communications (APPC), Common Programming Interface for Communications (CPI-C) and Common Service Verb (CSV). These APIs allow client- and server-based transaction programs and other processes to communicate with host systems, such as those running under IBM Customer Information Control System (CICS) and Information Management System (IMS). An example of a transaction-based process is a magnetic credit card reader at a point-of-sale terminal, such as a computer-based cash register that communicates from a branch store location to the home office through an SNA Server connection. The process to validate the cardholder's credit status uses APPC as the API supporting the transaction.

Host Utilities with Mainframes

As shown in Table 10.6, SNA Server offers a number of utilities that complement standard terminal and printer emulation sessions. One such utility is APPC File Transfer Protocol (AFTP). AFTP is part of a group of applications supported by the IBM APPC applications suite running on OS/390, MVS, VM, or OS/400.

As a server-based solution, AFTP works with SNA Server's FTP-to-AFTP gateway to provide a seamless means for clients to send and receive flat files to and from host systems. SNA Server converts the FTP commands to AFTP and uses APPC between the SNA Server–based computer and the host system. This allows the client to use an open TCP/IP protocol, while the host runs only its native SNA protocols. The result is greater efficiency and simplified management at the client and the host system.

Application Programming Interfaces with Mainframes

SNA Server includes a Software Development Kit (SDK), with online documentation and source code examples. This SDK provides the means to build complete AFTP, APPC, CPI-C, CSV, and LUA solutions, as well as add-on products to SNA Server core functionality. LUA is a customizable API that allows you to develop either at a low level in the SNA protocol stack, at the Request User Interface (RUI), or at a higher level, at the Session Level Interface. These APIs are commonly used by large institutional organizations building upon their legacy of banking and insurance applications, many of which had previously relied upon specialized control unit devices, such as the IBM 4147 financial series controller.

One series of APIs not directly supported by the SNA Server SDK are, High Level Language API (HLLAPI), Extended HLLAPI (EHLLAPI), and Windows HLLAPI (WinHLLAPI).

SNA Server APIs comply with the Windows Open Service Architecture (WOSA) guidelines. This means that on all Windows operating systems, the SNA Server APIs are WOSA versions: WinAPPC, WinCPI-C, and WinCSV.

Several independent software vendors (ISVs) contributed to the WOSA SNA API standards, among them IBM and Novell. Most major Windows SNA ISVs support WOSA APIs directly in their products, including Andrew, Attachmate, Eicon, NetManage, NetSoft, Wall Data, and WRQ. SNA Server's APIs comply with the standards published for other common operating systems as well. For example, on MS-DOS and OS/2, SNA Server APIs are binary compatible with IBM's Communications Manager/2 standards.

SNA client emulation vendors also support host connectivity through SNA Server by adapting their products to support the SNA Server Function Management Interface (FMI)—also called the Emulator Interface Specification (EIS). The FMI or 3270 EIS API is encapsulated in the SNA Server Client software. The emulator communicates with this SNA Server Client software, which in turn communicates with SNA Server through an SNA Server client/server connection. When you use a full-featured 3270 emulator with SNA Server, you are connecting to the SNA Server through the FMI. FMI supports LU types 1 through 3.

Integrating Heterogeneous Clients with AS/400 Systems

SNA Server supports the LU types (and equivalent Telnet-based applications) and application programming interfaces (APIs) that support the most commonly used configurations for all popular desktop operating systems. Table 10.7 describes in detail SNA Server client-to-AS/400 services.

Table 10.7   Heterogeneous Client-to-AS/400 Integration

Desktop Platform	LU Types/Telnet Services	SNA APIs
MS-DOS	LU 6.2 (terminal and printer emulation) and TN5250.	APPC and CPI-C.
Windows 3.x, Windows for Workgroups	LU 6.2 and TN5250.	APPC, CPI-C, CSV, EHNAPPC, and ODBC/DRDA.
OS/2	LU 6.2 and TN5250.	APPC, CPI-C, and CSV.
Macintosh	TN5250.	(Uses Telnet-based services.)
UNIX[1]	TN5250.	APPC, CPI-C, and CSV.
Windows 95 and Windows 98	LU 6.2 and TN5250.	APPC, CPI-C, CSV, EHNAPPC, ODBC/DRDA, and AFTP.
Windows NT Workstation 4.0 and Windows 2000 Professional	LU 6.2 and TN5250.	APPC, CPI-C, CSV, EHNAPPC, ODBC/DRDA, and AFTP.

[1] The UNIX client can use services beyond the Telnet-based services by using a third-party UNIX client for SNA Server developed by Parker Software in cooperation with Microsoft. For more information about the UNIX client for SNA Server, see http://www.microsoft.com/sna.

Session Types with AS/400 Systems

SNA Server supports all AS/400 session types on most popular desktop operating systems using LU type 6.2. Some older client emulators use LU type 4 for printer emulation and LU type 7 for terminal emulation. However, SNA Server and most modern client emulators support standard 5250 terminal and printer emulation through LU type 6.2 and APPC.

SNA Server supports Macintosh and UNIX clients through the TN5250 Service, which provides basic terminal emulation. However, teamed with the Host Print Service, Shared Folders Service, and FTP-to-AFTP Gateway, SNA Server can satisfy all Macintosh and UNIX client needs.

Host Utilities with AS/400 Systems

Utilities based on a computer running SNA Server offer administrative control of client-to-AS/400 connectivity. For example, SNA Server offers an optional Shared Folders Service that allows any Windows 2000 Server–based client to access AS/400 files without any special SNA software or protocols being installed on the client computer. Another example is the Host Print Service, which places printer emulation on the computer running SNA Server. Both of these utilities concentrate administration at the server and alleviate the need for configuration of advanced features on the clients.

Application Programming Interfaces with AS/400 Systems

AS/400 connectivity through SNA Server is fully compatible with EHNAPPC and supports the full range of Client Access/400 functions, including shared folders, virtual print, and file transfer. EHNAPPC is the standard Windows-based API supported by IBM's PC Support and Client Access/400 (CA/400) products. IBM has presented EHNAPPC to its ISV community as the way to write Windows-based applications that integrate with the AS/400.

The SNA Server Client software for Windows 32-bit operating systems can also support 16-bit Windows-based APPC and CPI-C applications that map the 16-bit APPC and CPI-C APIs to the native 32-bit SNA APIs. This allows users to run many of the 16-bit Windows-based applications that work with SNA Server in Windows 32-bit environments.

For more information about configuring and managing SNA Server Client software, see the SNA Server version 4.0 documentation.

Host Print Services

SNA Server supports three methods of printing host information to local or network-accessible printer resources.

Screen printing   Allows any 3270 or 5250 emulator to print what is on the display using the print screen features of the client operating system. The printer output can be directed to a printer attached to the client or to a network-accessible resource.

Client-based redirected printing   Delivers an SNA host printer data stream (such as 3287) to the appropriate emulation application running on an SNA Server-based client. The client software converts the data stream into data that can be output to a locally attached or network-accessible printer resource.

Server-based redirected printing   Uses a server process to convert SNA host printer data streams into data that can be redirected to a locally attached or network-accessible printer resource defined with the Windows 2000 Server Printer Manager.

The first two methods are provided using third-party products. The third method is supported by the SNA Server Host Print Service and third-party products.

SNA Server Host Print Service

The Host Print Service provides server-based 3270 and 5250 printer emulation, allowing host applications to print to a LAN printer supported by Windows 2000 Server or Novell NetWare. You can administer all Host Print Service functions using SNA Server Manager and control print characteristics, such as margin control and fonts. Printer output can also be redirected to files that are saved with incremental file names.

Each host printer definition also allows printing filters to be associated with print sessions. Filters are provided through third-party applications that allow the Host Print Service to participate in APF and other specialized print environments.

Mainframe Printing

For mainframe environments, shown in Figure 10.20, the Host Print Service supports both LU 1 and LU 3 print data streams, including transparent print jobs sent by host-based print preprocessors.

- Make host resources easier to access for authenticated users, yet maintain a secure and easy-to-administer host environment.

The following sections address each of these issues and describe how to implement SNA Server security features and Windows 2000 security features to create a secure LAN-to-host environment.

For more information about Windows 2000 security, see the *Distributed Systems Guide*.

Authentication

When SNA Server receives a request for access to a host resource, such as an LU for a terminal session, the server must have some way to verify the request. User validation is a fundamental security issue that is addressed using one of two methods depending on the type of service being requested: domain authentication or workstation authentication.

Domain Authentication

A Windows 2000 Active Directory domain is a group of computers that share a common user account database and have a common security policy. An Active Directory domain contains domain controllers that store security information and replicate that information to other domain controllers.

Within a Windows 2000 domain, computers running SNA Server are logically grouped into entities called subdomains, as shown in Figure 10.22. Each SNA Server subdomain can contain up to 15 SNA Server–based computers. A Windows 2000 domain can contain an unlimited number of these subdomains.

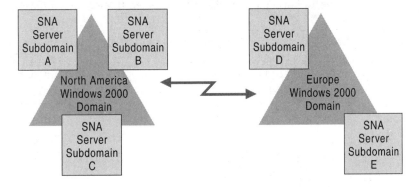

Figure 10.22   SNA Server Subdomains Located in Windows 2000 Domains

SNA Server relies on the Windows 2000 domain to provide authentication services to users requesting access to host resources, as shown in Figure 10.23.

Only users who have been validated by Windows 2000 security can gain access to resources provided by servers in the SNA Server subdomain.

Domain authentication is used to verify the identity of users who request resources provided by the following services:

- 3270 or 5250 terminal access from workstations using SNA Server Client software.
- AS/400 Shared Folders Gateway Service.
- Host Print Services.
- APPC, CPI-C, or LUA that use SNA Server APIs.

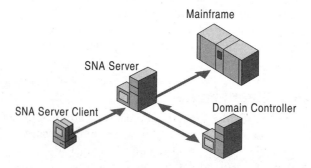

Figure 10.23   Domain Authentication Process for 3270 Terminal Access

Each user who needs access to SNA Server resources must have a Windows 2000 domain account. Once enrolled as a Windows 2000 domain user, the user's account is added to the SNA Server subdomain. After a user is added to the SNA Server subdomain, you can allocate specific SNA resources to that user.

Note Each computer running SNA Server also needs its own Windows 2000 domain account through which SNA Server services are run. SNA Server uses this account to log on to the domain to perform such functions as host printing and data encryption using the Distributed Link Services.

Resource Allocation

In most cases, you need to control who can access SNA Server resources in your environment. The method you use to secure those resources depends on your host environment and the types of services you wish to offer your users.

3270 Terminal Access

Users or groups who require access to 3270 sessions from workstations using SNA Server Client applications must be members of the SNA Server subdomain. By virtue of their subdomain membership, users and groups are also members of the Windows 2000 domain of which the subdomain is a part. Once enrolled in the SNA Server subdomain, you can assign specific 3270 (LU type 2) resources to the appropriate accounts. Users can access only the specific resources you allocate to them.

To maintain security in your environment, it is recommended that you use domain security to authenticate users, and then limit their access by assigning them only specified resources.

5250 Terminal Access and APPC Access

Users who want Advanced Peer-to-Peer Communications (APPC) access need not be defined in the SNA Server subdomain, but they must be members of the Windows 2000 domain. For 5250 terminal access using a computer running SNA Server Client software within the network, the AS/400 supplies the required logon security for access to the AS/400. For APPC access programmed into specific applications, security is maintained through the actual programmatic conversation, if required.

TN3270 and TN5250 Services

TN3270 and TN5250 services are secured by specifying client workstation IP addresses that have permission to use the resources provided. In the case of TN3270E clients, a workstation name can be specified in place of the client IP address. The method used to verify workstations can also be used to allow only specified IPs to request resources allocated to them.

Shared Folder Services

Access to AS/400 shared folders that are made available to Windows 2000 domain users using the Shared Folders Gateway Service can be controlled by specifying permissions for the resulting shared volumes and files. Permissions are set using the standard Windows 2000 method for local shares.

In some cases, you might want to provide open-ended access to LUs provided by SNA Server. To allow unrestricted access through Windows 2000 domain–authenticated services, you can use the Guest account or the Everyone group account.

To provide access using the Guest account, enable the account in the Windows 2000 domain as described in Windows 2000 Server Help. Add the Guest account to the SNA Server subdomain, and assign LUs to the account.

To provide access using the Everyone account, add the Everyone account to the SNA Server subdomain and assign LUs to the account.

To allow unrestricted access to TN3270 or TN5250 services, you can create LUs without specifying an IP or workstation name for each.

Data Encryption

SNA Server allows you to encrypt data for client-to-server and server-to-server communications, as shown in Figure 10.24.

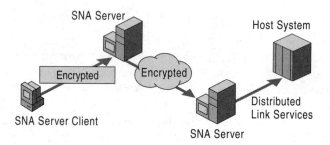

Figure 10.24   Model of Client-to-Server and Server-to-Server Data Encryption

Client-to-server encryption prevents information from being sent in plaintext between computers running SNA Server Client software and computers running SNA Server. Data encryption enhances network security on the client-to-server communications path for all applications using SNA Server Client connections, including 3270/5250 emulators and APPC logon IDs and passwords. Data encryption can be enabled on a user-by-user basis using the SNA Server Manager.

Server-to-server encryption can be used to provide secure communications across your network, the Internet, or any other wide area network (WAN). If a user enables data encryption, information transferred through the Distributed Link Services is secure.

Firewall Support

A firewall is a network security device that restricts access to network resources by allowing traffic only through specified port numbers. In many instances, the services of a firewall are provided in conjunction with a network route that bridges two network segments together.

If the SNA Server address is known, the client workstation configures the appropriate port and destination IP of the computer running SNA Server in the client software (1477 and 128.124.1.2, respectively, in Figure 10.25 below). Alternatively, the SNA Server–based computer's service port numbers can be changed to the port number requested by the client.

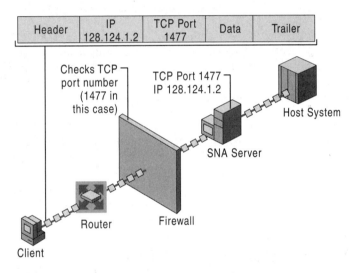

Figure 10.25   Using SNA Server with a Firewall

If the SNA Server address is not known, the SNA Server IP transport replaces the real destination IP address with the address of a firewall. The firewall then maps the connection request to the actual computer running SNA Server. This takes place when the transport opens a connection to an SNA Server–based computer for application sessions or a sponsor connection.

SNA Server supports firewalls primarily on TCP/IP networks. It is also possible to implement firewalls on IPX/SPX or Banyan VINES networks. Consult your network documentation for information about configuring a firewall in your specific installation.

Host Security Integration

In an enterprise-wide computing environment, users are likely to access different networking environments as they go about their day-to-day routines. A user might begin the day by turning on a computer running Windows 2000 Professional, logging on to a Windows 2000–based network, and then accessing an AS/400 database application through a terminal emulator.

Each system with which the user comes into contact enforces its own security requirements and logon procedures. For example, a Windows 2000 domain account might require a six-character user name and an eight-character, mixed-case password, whereas a mainframe environment might require a seven-character user name and seven-character alphanumeric password.

Frequently, users have to remember several different combinations of user names and passwords to gain access to various resources on the network. Despite policies to the contrary, users who must maintain multiple passwords often resort to writing their passwords down and keeping them in a convenient location near their computer, compromising network security.

One of SNA Server's most powerful security features is its ability to integrate the Windows 2000 domain security environment with your host security system. The Host Security Integration feature is a combination of tools and services that automate the process of synchronizing passwords and logging on to the different systems. Using these tools can help your users uphold corporate security standards and ease the administration required to maintain user accounts on your network and your host system.

Host Security Integration Components

Host Security Integration uses a host security domain concept to manage user accounts on your network and your host system. Your host security domain defines the different security domains that share a common user accounts database. A simple security domain can consist of a host domain, a Windows 2000 domain, and an SNA Server subdomain, as shown in Figure 10.26.

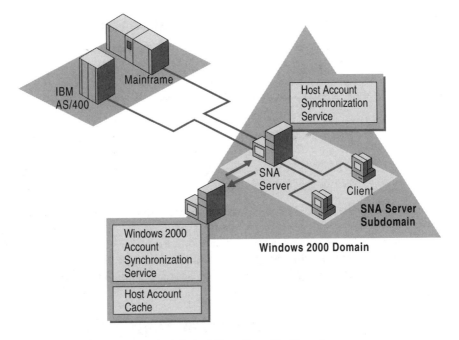

Figure 10.26   Elements of a Typical Host Security Domain

Host Security Integration is composed of three separately installable components:

- Host Account Cache
- Host Account Synchronization Service
- Windows 2000 Account Synchronization Service

Host Account Cache

The Host Account Cache maintains an encrypted database that maps host user accounts to Windows 2000 domain user accounts. The Host Account Cache is a Windows 2000 service that is installed on Windows 2000 domain controllers. For smaller networks, SNA Server itself might be installed on a Windows 2000 domain controller and, therefore, can be used to store the Host Account Cache.

Optionally, a backup Host Account Cache can be installed on any other Windows 2000 domain controller. The backup cache maintains a local copy of the user database for recovery purposes, or to eliminate network traffic for single sign-on lookups when installed on the same computer as SNA Server.

Host Account Synchronization Service

Host Security Integration is an SNA Server installation option that contains the Host Account Synchronization Service. This service can be installed on primary, backup, or member computers running SNA Server within the SNA Server subdomain. For more information about SNA Server roles, see "Determining SNA Server Roles" earlier in this chapter.

You can also install the service on non-SNA Server-based computers. The Host Account Synchronization Service supports third-party interfaces to various host security databases, allowing you coordinate password changes between the Windows 2000 security domain and the host security domain.

The Host Account Synchronization Service is not necessary if you use the single sign-on feature with manual password updates in which the administrator or users store host account information in the Host Account Cache through the Host Account Manager application (UDConfig). For more information about using the UDConfig tool, see the SNA Server version 4.0 documentation and the *Microsoft® BackOffice® Resource Kit*.

Windows 2000 Account Synchronization Service

The Account Synchronization component can automatically synchronize the passwords for your host accounts and Windows 2000 domain accounts. This component includes the Windows 2000 Password Synchronization Service and must be installed even if automatic password synchronization is not used because it coordinates the internal operation of other services.

The Windows 2000 Account Synchronization Service is installed on a Windows 2000 domain controller. Only one instance of the Windows 2000 Account Synchronization Service can be designated as primary; all others must be backup servers.

The ability to synchronize passwords from the Windows 2000 domain to an AS/400 security domain is built into SNA Server. Third-party products can provide enhanced synchronization services, such as two-way and automatic synchronization, to other host systems.

Password Synchronization Options

When you define your host security domain, a Windows 2000 group account is automatically created with the same name. User accounts are then added to the group to specify them as members of the host security domain. Once a host security domain is defined, two types of password synchronization options are available to you:

The **Replicated** option assumes that you would like to have the same user name or password on each security domain defined in the host security domain.

The **Mapped** option allows you to have different account names and passwords in each security domain. A database controlled by the Host Account Cache Service maintains the associations between the various accounts and passwords.

You can specify either of these options for the user name and either of them for the password of a user account. For example, you can choose to map the user names but replicate passwords across the different security domains. This allows you to have the same password but different user names on the different systems in the host security domain.

Once defined, host connections are assigned to the domain. SNA Server uses the assignment to look up the host mapping for a Windows 2000 user based on the session he or she is trying to open. A defined host connection can only be assigned to one security domain at a time.

After the connections are assigned to a host security domain, you can add users to the security domain by adding user accounts to the Windows 2000 group account created earlier. For each account associated with the host security domain, you can enable password synchronization options and automated logon features commonly referred to as single sign-on services. Single sign-on allows users to log on to their host account automatically if they are already logged on to their Windows 2000 domain account.

If you are planning to map user names, perform and store the initial mapping of host user names to Windows 2000 domain user names in the Host Account Cache.

Automating Password Synchronization

Within the SNA Server network, automated one-way LAN-to-AS/400 password synchronization is supported without any additional tools or products. In this scenario, the Host Account Synchronization Service, the Windows 2000 Account Synchronization Service, and the AS/400's host security system are interoperable and provide password synchronization for SNA Server users.

In other corporate network environments, third-party tools are required when implementing automated, two-way password synchronization or mainframe support. On a network, the Host Account Synchronization Service, the Windows 2000 Account Synchronization Service, and third-party security integration dynamic-link libraries (DLLs) cooperate with each other to support password synchronization. On the host, third-party products are usually required to facilitate password synchronization.

These components collectively allow two-way password synchronization between Windows 2000 and AS/400 or mainframe host computers. Changes made on one host can be replicated to other Windows 2000 or host computers. Similarly, changes to your Windows 2000 security domain can be automatically sent to all host computers.

Host-Initiated Changes

For host-initiated changes, third-party software must be installed on the host system to trap password changes initiated by users logged on to the host computer, and on the SNA Server–based computer to receive changes from the host.

When a change is made on the host system, the host computer sends notification of changes to a third-party product's security integration DLL, which is installed on the computer running SNA Server. The DLL then forwards the host-initiated changes to the Host Account Synchronization Service. This service then locates the network address of the primary Windows 2000 Account Synchronization Service using the resource location of the master Host Account Cache.

After the Host Account Cache is located, the Host Account Synchronization Service sends password changes to the Host Account Cache service using encrypted remote procedure call (RPC) messages. Once the changes are received by the service, it propagates the appropriate changes in all security domains defined in the host security domain.

Windows 2000–Initiated Changes

Windows 2000–initiated password synchronization works in a similar manner to host-initiated changes.

The Windows 2000 Account Synchronization Service is installed on a domain controller in one or more Windows 2000 domains. An associated DLL, installed in the same location, receives notice of any password changes that arise in the Windows 2000 domain, regardless of how the change was initiated. The DLL sends Windows 2000–initiated changes to the Windows 2000 Account Synchronization Service using encrypted RPC messages. Once the change is received, the service propagates the appropriate changes in all affected security domains.

Automating Logons

SNA Server can also automate the process of logging on to your host system as shown in Figure 10.27. This feature, commonly called single sign-on support, automatically logs users on to all security systems in a host security subdomain once they have been validated by any system within the subdomain. For example, if a user is logged on to the Windows 2000 domain, single sign-on can automate logon processes to host systems that are encompassed by the defined host security domain.

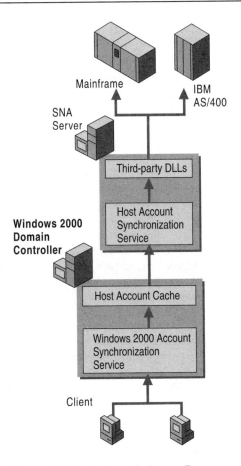

Figure 10.27   Automatic Logon Process

The following steps describe the automatic logon process, as illustrated in Figure 10.27:

Step 1

When a user starts a terminal emulator or other SNA application on a client workstation, the application works with the SNA Server subdomain to perform a resource location operation to determine which SNA Server–based computer and connection to use to open the session.

The SNA application provides a replacement keyword as a placeholder for security information during the session initialization phase. The exact format of this keyword is dependent on the type of LU session being established. For example, the string "MS$SAME" is used for APPC or CPI-C applications.

SNA Server detects the replacement keyword and determines the Windows 2000 user name under which the client is logged on. Because this step requires the support of Windows 2000 domain authentication, the ability to be logged on automatically is only supported for users running native client/server sessions (for example, sessions using a computer running SNA Server Client).

Note   TN3270 users are not supported because the TN3270 service cannot determine the client's Windows 2000 user name.

Step 2

Once the user name is determined, the computer running SNA Server uses the resource location to locate the Host Account Cache in the SNA Server subdomain. The cache might be located on either the actual computer running SNA Server or on a Windows 2000 domain controller in the SNA Server subdomain depending on your installation. SNA Server then sends a lookup message to the Host Account Cache that contains the Windows 2000 user name and password, and requests the corresponding host user name and password.

The Host Account Cache service verifies that the Windows 2000 account exists in the database, and that the account is a member of the Windows 2000 group in the host security domain. If either check fails, the user record is purged from the Host Account Cache.

Step 3

If all checks pass, the service replies to the computer running SNA Server with a message containing the appropriate host account user name and password in an encrypted RPC network message.

Step 4

SNA Server inserts the host account name and password into the SNA data stream, and sends a regular session initialization request to the host computer.

Step 5

The host computer receives the regular session initialization request containing the correct host account information and authenticates the user.

SNA Server natively supports single sign-on to an AS/400 host system. Single sign-on features are also available for APPC and CPI-C applications on both mainframes and AS/400 systems using third-party products. For a list of supported third-party vendors, see the SNA Server Web site at http://www.microsoft.com/.

For more information about SNA Server security and security integration, see the SNA Server version 4.0 documentation and the *Microsoft® BackOffice® Resource Kit*.

Host Data Access

One of the primary purposes of integrating Windows 2000 networks with IBM host systems is to provide users with access to host data. Host systems have long excelled at providing database-related services. In many mid- to large-sized companies, host databases are used to store and process large amounts of information needed by users across an enterprise network. Because of their availability and performance, host systems continue to play a large role in data warehousing strategies for many organizations.

As companies adopt LAN-based desktop computers, many organizations are looking for ways to integrate host database systems to develop new client/server applications accessible from a user's workstation. Using SNA Server, you can access host data sources through one of the following features:

- Open Database Connectivity (ODBC) Driver for DB2, for access to Distributed Relational Database Architecture (DRDA) database systems using ODBC interfaces.

- OLE DB Provider for AS/400 and VSAM, for record-level access of host data using OLE DB data access interfaces.

The following section describes how each feature is used and which data access method best suits a particular scenario.

Host Data Access Using ODBC

SNA Server lets applications designed to use the Open Database Connectivity (ODBC) interface and Structured Query Language (SQL) commands access host databases. Using the ODBC Driver for DB2, ODBC-enabled applications can be used to access and manipulate databases on a host system that uses the Distributed Relational Database Architecture (DRDA) protocol to manage distributed data without requiring a host-based database gateway. Drivers are provided for Windows NT, Windows 2000, Windows 95, Windows 98, and Windows 3.*x*. SNA Server–based clients are installed during the client setup process.

Figure 10.28 depicts host data access using the ODBC Driver for DB2.

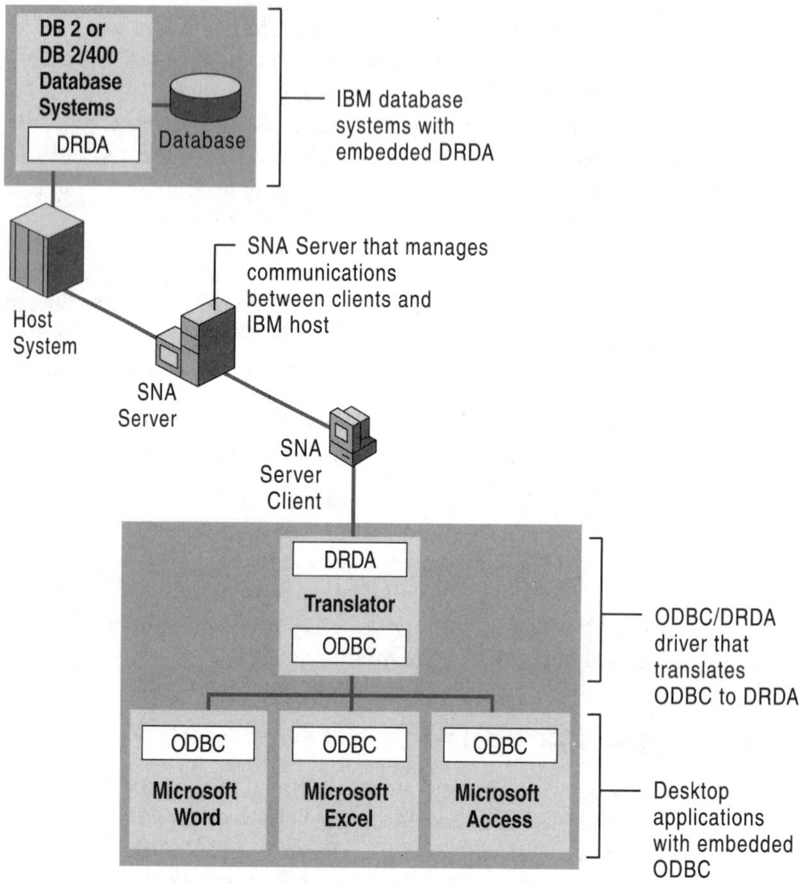

Figure 10.28   Host Data Access Using the ODBC Driver for DB2

The ODBC Driver operates by translating commands between the SQL and DRDA systems as shown in Figure 10.28. Each driver accepts SQL requests from a client application through ODBC, translates them to DRDA commands, and then sends them to the host system. The host processes the DRDA commands and returns the results to the driver on the client computer through SNA Server. The driver then converts the DRDA information to SQL data and passes the data back to the client application using the ODBC interface.

The ODBC Driver supports the following features:

- Transaction commit and rollback
- Asynchronous processing
- Canceled queries
- Primary and foreign keys
- Four levels of transaction isolation

The driver also supports the ability to pass SQL strings directly to the host database with translation. Supported database systems include:

- DB2 for MVS
- SQ/DS for VM and VSE
- DB2/400 for OS/400

For information about specific ODBC functions and data types supported by the ODBC Driver, see the SNA Server version 4.0 online documentation.

Host Data Access Using OLE DB

SNA Server provides record-level access to mainframe and AS/400 files using the OLE DB Provider for AS/400 and VSAM feature.

Leveraging the advantages of OLE DB as a common interface to dissimilar data sources, as shown in Figure 10.29, OLE DB Provider for AS/400 and VSAM lets you:

- Customize solutions for reading from and writing to AS/400 and mainframe file systems without first migrating the information to the client/server platform.
- Integrate nonstructured data with desktop and server-based databases and tools.
- Develop applications using high-level interfaces, such as Microsoft® ActiveX® Data Objects (ADO), which support Microsoft® Visual Basic® (VB), Microsoft® Visual C++® (VC++), Microsoft® Visual J++™ (VJ++), Microsoft® Visual Basic® for Applications (VBA), and Microsoft Scripting.

By providing applications with the ability to access and manipulate host files at the record level, you can leverage investments in host-based storage, management, backup, and security systems.

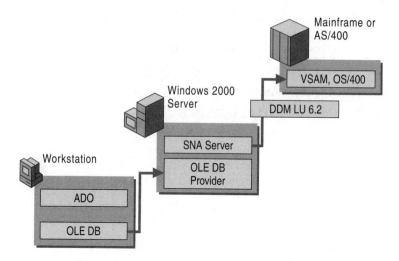

Figure 10.29   Host Data Access Using OLE DB Provider for AS/400 and VSAM

OLE DB Provider uses the record-level input/output (RLIO) protocol of the IBM Distributed Data Management (DDM) architecture (level 2 and higher). This feature is implemented as a source DDM requester and is interoperable with target DDM server implementations on most popular host environments, including MVS/ESA, OS/390, and OS/400.

Client applications communicate with a host database through an APPC (LU 6.2) connection to the host system established between the SNA Server Client software and SNA Server.

OLE DB Provider supports the following features:

- File and record locking
- File and record attribute preservation
- Indexed and sequential record access
- Fixed and variable logical record length

OLE DB Provider supports a variety of data file types for mainframe and AS/400 systems. For mainframe systems, OLE DB Provider supports SAM data sets, including BSAM and QSAM; VSAM data sets, including ESDS, KSDS, RRDS, VRRDS; alternate index for ESDS and KSDS data sets; and PDS/PDSE members. For AS/400, OLE DB Provider supports keyed and non-keyed physical files and logical files.

Complete information about using the OLE DB Provider for VSAM and AS/400 is provided in the SNA Server Software Development Kit, included with SNA Server.

Choosing a Host Data Access Method

The method with which you choose to integrate host databases depends on how you want to provide access to the database systems.

Enterprises that want to use ODBC-aware applications and SQL commands to access and manipulate tables on the host can use the ODBC/DRDA Driver. The widespread support of ODBC in many desktop applications, such as Microsoft® Excel and Microsoft® Access, makes it easy to create host-driven client/server solutions based on existing desktop applications.

In many environments, the OLE DB Provider for AS/400 and VSAM feature can be configured to perform the same functionality as the ODBC/DRDA Driver. In enterprises where little or no SQL expertise is present, however, OLE DB Provider is the better choice because no SQL understanding is required to access and manipulate host tables.

OLE DB support for the ADO interface in a wide variety of development environments, such as VB and VC++, also makes OLE DB Provider a good choice for highly customized client/server applications.

Host Application Integration Using COMTI

As SNA networks are integrated with client/server-based networks, many organizations are investigating ways to leverage the power of host systems to run new client/server applications accessible from the personal computer. One method is by using SNA Server's COM Transaction Integrator (COMTI) feature for IBM's Customer Information Control System (CICS) and IBM's Information Management System (IMS).

COMTI simplifies the process of creating applications that consist of Automation clients running on the desktop or server with COBOL servers running under CICS or IMS. Any application or development platforms that support Distributed COM (DCOM) and Automation can use COMTI components. For example, an application written in VB, VBA, or VBScript, can provide access to host data from within Excel. This feature can also be used through Web browsers that connect to Microsoft® Internet Information Services (IIS).

COMTI provides an interface between Automation components and mainframe-based applications. Running on Windows 2000 Server, components appear as simple Automation servers that developers can easily add to their application. Behind the scenes, however, COMTI functions as a proxy that communicates with an application running on IBM's Multiple Virtual Storage (MVS) operating system.

Applications that run in part on Windows platforms and in part on the mainframe are distributed applications. COMTI supports all distributed applications that adhere to Automation and DCOM specifications, although not all parts of the application have to adhere to these standards.

COMTI is composed of three parts:

- The Component Builder, which is used to create Automation components.
- Microsoft Management Console (MMC), which is used to manage components created with the Component Builder.
- The COM Transaction Integrator Runtime, which provides the Automation server interface for each component created with the Component Builder and which communicates with the mainframe programs. The run time operates within Component Services.

COMTI directly supports any transaction program (TP) that executes in CICS and is structured to use either distributed program linking or Advanced Program-to-Program Communications (APPC) verbs. It also directly supports IMS applications that are structured to use the IMS Message Queue. Because COMTI can access CICS programs, developers can extend the client application calls even further by using CICS to access any other program on an MVS mainframe, such as DB2.

Figure 10.30 shows how SNA Server can be integrated with a host application. A client application uses the COMTI feature hosted by Component Services to access a TP running on the mainframe. The specific TPs supported by the feature are IBM's CICS and IBM's IMS. An example of this type of distributed application is one that reads a mainframe-based DB2 database to update data in a SQL Server database on a Windows 2000–based server.

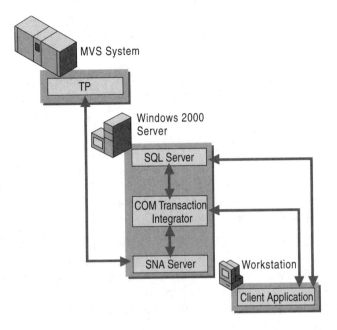

Figure 10.30   Integration with a Host Application

The client components can run on any platform that supports DCOM, including:

- Microsoft® Windows NT® Server
- Microsoft® Windows NT® Workstation
- Windows 95 and Windows 98

Because DCOM is language-independent, developers can build their client applications using the languages and tools with which they are most familiar. Common client/server application development environments include:

- Visual Basic (VB)
- Visual Basic for Applications (VBA)
- Visual C++ (VC++)
- Visual J++ (VJ++)
- Borland Delphi
- Sybase Powerbuilder
- Microfocus Object COBOL

Once created, the client components can make calls to the COMTI Automation object (or any other Automation object) registered on the computer running Windows 2000 Server.

Complete information about using COMTI, including sample applications, can be found in SNA Server COM Transaction Integrator Help.

Host Transaction Integration

Many organizations use host computer systems to support real-time transaction processing applications, such as IBM's CICS. These applications are accessed through interactive sessions with the host system, such as a 3270 or 5250 session supported by a terminal emulator.

We have already described how the SNA Server's COMTI feature can be used to access simple mainframe applications at the program level. This feature becomes an even more powerful tool when used to extend applications that use Windows 2000 Server Component Services. Windows-based applications that use Component Services can coordinate transactions with mainframe-based CICS applications.

When coupled with Component Services, COMTI can be used for a variety of purposes:

- Windows developers can describe, execute, and administer special Component Services objects that access CICS or IMS transaction programs (TPs).
- Mainframe developers can make mainframe TPs available to Windows-based Internet and intranet applications.
- Component Services component designers can include mainframe applications within the scope of Component Services two-phase commit transactions.

Developers using Component Services in their applications can decide which parts of the application require a transaction and which parts do not. COMTI extends this choice to the mainframe, as well, by handling both calls that require transactions and calls that do not.

For applications that require full integration between Windows-based two-phase commit and mainframe-based Sync Level 2 transactions, COMTI provides all the necessary functionality without requiring you to change the client application. Also, no executable code needs to be placed on the mainframe, and little or no changes to the mainframe TPs are required. The client application does not need to distinguish between the COMTI component and any other Component Services component reference.

Figure 10.31 illustrates how a Windows-based client application implicitly uses the Distributed Transaction Coordinator (DTC) to coordinate a distributed transaction involving SQL Server and a CICS transaction program. The DTC is the part of Component Services that coordinates two-phase commit transactions.

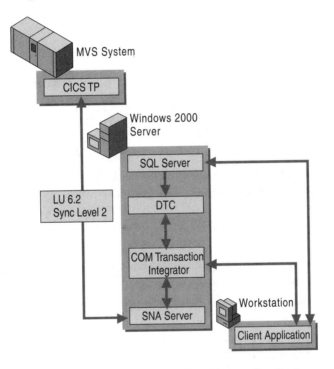

Figure 10.31   Integration with Host Transaction System

Complete information about using COMTI, including sample applications, can be found in the SNA Server version 4.0 documentation.

Transaction and Data Access Scenarios

COMTI should be considered for the following scenarios:

- Application-level database integration.
- COM integration with CICS and IMS.
- ADO access to legacy data.
- Integration of mainframe applications that own and control the host data. Transaction programs (TPs) often contain logic and data structures that define the rules for accessing host data. In some cases, these applications also contain integrity checks and consistency constraints. In these cases, accessing the host data through these TPs is the only safe option.

- Positioning of mid-tier applications to take advantage of the scalability benefits Component Services provides in addition to providing mainframe application access.

- Deployment of high-integrity, distributed transaction systems that span Windows 2000, MVS/CICS, and other Extended Architecture (XA)–compliant environments that are Component Services-enabled.

- Mainframe connectivity only.

OLE DB Provider should be considered for these scenarios:

- Record-level or file-level database integration.

- OLE DB and ADO access to legacy data.

- Rewriting of business rules, such as "Year 2000" solutions.

- Direct access to host data without going through the host SQL processor.

- Mainframe and AS/400 connectivity.

In some cases, you might choose to use both COMTI and OLE DB Provider to develop a complete host-connectivity solution.

Sample applications that use COMTI are installed when the COMTI component is selected during SNA Server setup. For more information about using the samples, see the samples folder on the SNA Server CD.

Web-to-Host Integration

The growth of the Internet and its related technologies has given corporate information technology departments new ways to extend client/server computing applications to both internal and external users. Information and resources that exist on internal, proprietary systems can now be accessed from a broader user base, giving corporations more ways to utilize their current investments in technology.

Enterprise networking is also experiencing a resurgence in popularity; the size of corporate databases that store mission-critical data continues to grow. As companies continue to use mainframe and AS/400 host systems for database hosting, transaction processing, and other applications, many organizations are investigating methods of integrating host networks with the Web.

SNA Server and Web Technology

The Microsoft Web-to-host model uses SNA Server to provide Web-to-host connectivity between an IBM host system and a Web server, such as IIS. In this model, as shown in Figure 10.32, Web browsers and servers communicate using the HTTP and TCP/IP protocols over the network. The Web server, in turn, communicates with SNA Server using a defined server interface, such as the Internet Server Application Programming Interface (ISAPI). The SNA Server–based computer then communicates with the host system using the SNA protocol over a defined connection.

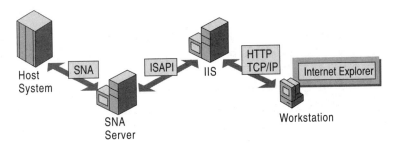

Figure 10.32   Web-to-Host Communications

The components illustrated in Figure 10.32 might be deployed on one or more computers across your enterprise. For example, smaller enterprises might be able to deploy a Web server and SNA Server on the same Windows 2000 Server–based computer and still maintain the desired server response levels. As the number of server and connection requests increases, it is recommended that the Web server and SNA Server applications be installed on separate Windows 2000 Server–based computers.

IIS is the recommended Web server for Windows 2000 Server–based systems because of its tight integration with the management and administrative features of the operating system. Integration with Windows 2000 Server also lets you easily couple IIS with other BackOffice applications, such as SQL Server or Microsoft® Exchange Server, in order to Web-enable enterprise applications such as database access and e-mail.

Web-to-Host Access Methods

SNA Server provides host-connectivity services for Web-based users in several ways. The following Web-to-host solutions are commonly adopted by enterprises:

- Browser-based terminal access solutions, which display 3270 and 5250 data streams in a Web browser window.
- Web-to-host data access solutions, which provide access to relational or non-relational host data through a Web browser.
- Web-to-host application access solutions, which provide access to transaction systems through a Web browser.

The following sections detail options for deploying SNA Server in each of these scenarios and describe the environments in which each is best deployed.

Browser-Based Terminal Access

Using a Web browser to provide access to host applications through a traditional 3270 or 5250 terminal interface is a simple and effective way of providing terminal access to your users. This Web-to-host solution is ideal if your user base is already familiar with the character-based terminal interface and is adept at using existing host applications. In most environments where this solution is deployed, existing host access technology is already in place, either through dumb terminals or software-based emulators.

SNA Server can provide browser-based terminal emulation through the deployment of SNA Server Web Client, as shown in Figure 10.33. SNA Server Web Client provides terminal emulation features through an ActiveX control that is part of a package downloaded to a user's browser from a Web server such as IIS. Once downloaded and invoked, the control establishes a connection with the sponsor SNA Server computer that provides a connection to the host system.

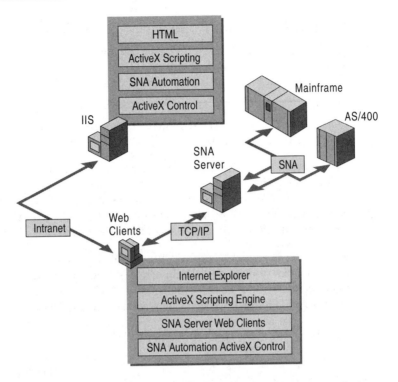

Figure 10.33   SNA Server Web Client Terminal Access Installation

Using this method, no configuration is required on the client workstation because all connection information is specified by the administrator before SNA Server Web Client is downloaded into the browser. When a user downloads the ActiveX package, the connection information is contained in the download, allowing SNA Server Web Client to automatically establish a connection to the host system.

Once SNA Server Web Client software is downloaded to the client workstation, it does not need to be downloaded again unless the browser detects a newer version of the software on the Web server; this can speed up the client startup time and minimizes the load on your server. Because SNA Server Web Client software is distributed from a central location, updates and changes to host configurations are easily propagated to your users the next time they start the SNA Server Web Client application.

SNA Server Web Client is currently available for Windows NT, Windows 2000, Windows 95, and Windows 98–based clients running Internet Explorer 3.02 or later. Both 3270 and 5250 terminal emulation clients are provided.

Complete information about configuring and installing SNA Server Web Client is provided in the SNA Server version 4.0 documentation.

Web-to-Host Data Access

As mentioned earlier, host systems are ideal platforms on which to provide large-scale database services for enterprises. Using SNA Server, Web technology can extend host database access to a broader range of users.

A common way to integrate Web technology with host databases is to use the rich-text capabilities of HTML to create visually appealing, user-friendly interfaces for character-based host database systems.

For example, a Web browser could be used to collect database queries on an HTML form. The queries could then be transferred, using ISAPI or some other common gateway interface, from the Web server to a service that can communicate with the host database system. The results of the query could then be formatted into HTML and viewed through the user's browser.

SNA Server is an ideal tool for deploying Web-to-host data access solutions because it can provide host database access without the need for host code or a modified database system. Using a feature such as OLE DB Provider, you can extend a wide range of services to Web users. Figure 10.34 illustrates how different data access components integrate with SNA Server and other services to provide access to host data files from a Web browser.

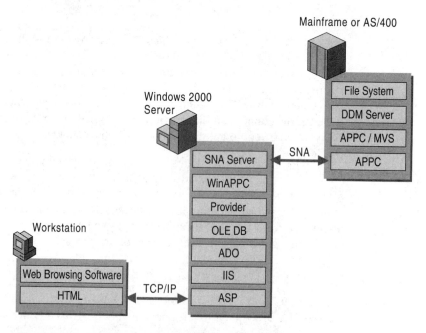

Figure 10.34   Web Access to Host Data File System

In the browser, the user loads and inputs data into an Active Server Page (ASP) hosted by the Web server (IIS). The ASP then sends the data through the ActiveX Data Objects (ADO) interface to the OLE DB Provider feature of SNA Server.

In this scenario, the OLE DB Provider uses the APPC record-level input/output (RLIO) protocol of the IBM Distributed Data Management (DDM) architecture (level 2 and higher) to communicate with the host database. This entire process is transparent to the host system and to the user.

The SNA Server OLE DB Provider is implemented as a source DDM requester and is interoperable with target DDM server implementations on most popular host environments, including MVS/ESA, OS/390, and OS/400.

Web-to-Host Application Access

A Web browser can also be used to access TPs that operate on a mainframe, such as CICS or IMS applications. Using SNA Server's COMTI feature, you can develop client/server applications that use Web browsers to interact with mainframe transaction systems. Because CICS programs can access DB2 databases, COMTI can also provide programmatic access to DB2 on a mainframe.

You can use any technique for accessing COM objects from the browser because COMTI creates a standard COM Automation server component that acts as a proxy for the mainframe CICS or IMS TPs. Figure 10.35 illustrates the components that could be involved in creating a Web application that uses server-side scripting to dynamically create objects and invoke methods.

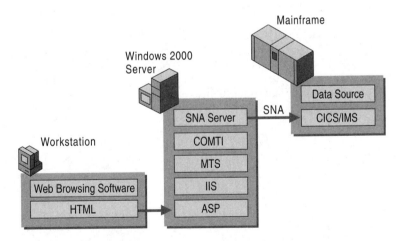

Figure 10.35   Web Access to Host Transaction System

Other applications that use technologies such as Remote Data Services (RDS) and client-side scripting can also be developed. In these scenarios, object creation and method invocation are launched from a client script executed on the server and the RDS control directs records back to the client over HTTP. Retrieved records can then be bound to an HTML grid control for display purposes.

For more information about sample applications that use these Web-to-host technologies, see the samples folder on the SNA Server CD.

Network Management Integration

Your LAN-to-host integration project is not complete until you can manage the integrated network environment. SNA Server provides integrated management services that enable you, or your IBM host system administrators, to manage SNA Server from:

- Windows 2000 Professional–based computers.
- Remote computers, using SNA Server Remote Access Service (SNA remote access server).
- IBM NetView applications running on an IBM host system.

SNA Server Management Services

You can configure and manage SNA Server using a graphical user interface application, SNA Server Manager, or from the command-line interface.

SNA Server Manager is a graphical Microsoft Management Console (MMC) snap-in that supports simultaneous monitoring, diagnosis, and management of SNA Server resources and services, including:

- SNA Server subdomains
- Computers
- Configurations
- Link services
- Connections
- LUs
- Sessions
- Services
- Users

SNA Server Manager integrates the administration of all services provided by SNA Server including TN3270 Service, TN5250 Service, Host Print Service, Shared Folders Gateway Service, and Host Security Integration.

With SNA Server Manager, you can view all computers running SNA Server in an SNA Server subdomain, and manage multiple subdomains at the same time, allowing for central configuration and administration of all SNA Server resources throughout an enterprise network.

You can remotely configure and manage computers running SNA Server across all common protocols, including:

- TCP/IP
- IPX/SPX
- Banyan VINES IP
- Named Pipes
- Windows 2000 Routing and Remote Access service

SNA Server Manager runs on any computer running Windows 2000 Professional that is configured with SNA Server Client. In addition, SNA Server Manager allows more than one administrator to simultaneously view and manage the same SNA Server subdomain.

Note SNA Server also provides a command-line management interface that allows you to store and use configuration commands in command files. For more information about command-line management functions, see the SNA Server version 4.0 documentation. and the *Microsoft® BackOffice® Resource Kit.*

Integration with Windows 2000 Management Services

Because SNA Server is a BackOffice application, SNA Server Manager is tightly integrated with the Windows 2000–based MMC snap-ins, including:

- User Manager
- System Monitor
- Event Viewer

Integration with User Manager provides a common user account database and security system for Windows 2000 users, SNA Server Client–based computers, and users of other BackOffice applications. Integration with System Monitor allows you to configure performance counters that monitor the SNA traffic volumes of your SNA Server–based computers. With Event Viewer you can quickly identify the type and sequence of events leading up to problems on any SNA Server subdomain.

For more information about managing SNA Server resources and services from the Windows 2000 MMC, see the SNA Server version 4.0 documentation and the *Microsoft® BackOffice® Resource Kit.*

Integration with IBM NetView Management Services

SNA Server can also support integrated management services with IBM NetView network management systems that run on IBM mainframes, as shown in Figure 10.36.

The NetView reporting system sends alerts and other information between a host system and the computers that connect to it. NetView functionality can be extended to encompass the Windows 2000/SNA Server environment through the following services:

- NVAlert service
- NVRunCmd service
- Response Time Monitor
- Link Alerts for SDLC and Token Ring

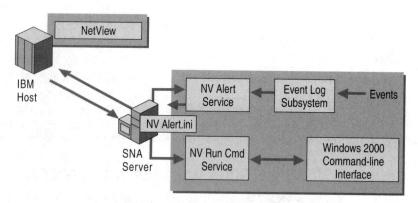

Figure 10.36   SNA Server Communication with IBM NetView

NVAlert Service

As shown in Figure 10.36, the NVAlert service sends events from the Windows 2000 event logs to IBM NetView system on the host computer. The events are sent as standard NetView alerts. NVAlert can send two categories of events: events generated by the Windows 2000 operating system and events generated by Windows 2000–based applications.

The events can be forwarded to the NetView console display on the host system or to a host system log file. NVAlert determines which events to forward to the NetView console by reading the NVAlert.ini file.

NVRunCmd Service

The NVRunCmd service allows commands issued from a host system NetView console to be carried out on the computer running Windows 2000 and SNA Server. The NVRunCmd service also returns the command results to the host NetView console in standard character or number formats.

Response Time Monitor

The Response Time Monitor (RTM) is an IBM host function that works in conjunction with NetView and 3270 sessions to measure the length of time it takes for a host to respond during a 3270 session. The SNA Server Response Time Monitoring tool allows you to specify when RTM should send data and to define the triggers that cause RTM to register that the host has responded.

Link Alerts for SDLC and Token Ring

When a Synchronous Data Link Control (SDLC) or Token Ring connection fails, SNA Server logs diagnostic information, called link alerts, about the connection failure. The alerts are logged in a log file that can be viewed using the Windows 2000 Event Viewer.

The link alerts are also used to build a network management vector transport (NMVT) alert, which includes probable causes and suggested actions for the alert. If a connection on the server running SNA Server has been designated for NetView, and the connection is active, the NMVT alert is sent on that connection.

For more information about SNA Server management services, including integration with Windows 2000 and IBM host management services, see the SNA Server version 4.0 documentation.

Additional Resources

- For more information about updated versions of SNA Server, evaluation disks, and white papers, see the SNA Server link on the Web Resources page http://windows.microsoft.com/windows2000/reskit/webresources.

C H A P T E R   1 1

Services for UNIX

Interoperability is essential in today's increasingly heterogeneous computing environment. By providing core interoperability components, Microsoft® Windows® Services for UNIX offers the means to integrate Windows into an existing UNIX environment and migrate existing UNIX scripts into the Windows environment, simplifying administrative tasks.

This chapter assumes an understanding of the information in "UNIX Interoperability Concepts" in this book.

Important At this printing, prior to the release of Microsoft® Windows® 2000, the current version of Services for UNIX is Version 1.0 for Microsoft® Windows NT® version 4.0. For updated information on new features, see the Microsoft Web site at http://www.microsoft.com.

In This Chapter

Related Information in the Resource Kit

- For more information about Windows file permissions, NTFS, and FAT, see "File Systems" in the *Microsoft® Windows® 2000 Server Resource Kit Server Operations Guide*.

- For more information about TCP/IP, see "Introduction to TCP/IP" in the *Microsoft® Windows® 2000 Server Resource Kit TCP/IP Core Networking Guide*.

- For more information about authentication, see "Authentication" in the *Microsoft® Windows® 2000 Server Resource Kit Distributed Systems Guide*.

- For more information about security, see "Planning Distributed Security" in the *Microsoft® Windows® 2000 Server Resource Kit Deployment Planning Guide*.

- For more information about printing, see "Network Printing" in the *Microsoft® Windows® 2000 Server Resource Kit Server Operations Guide*.

Overview

Services for Unix supports the following UNIX platforms:

- Digital® UNIX
- Hewlett-Packard HP-UX® 10.1+
- Sun Solaris® SPARC 2.5.1+

Services for UNIX provides the following features:

Network File System NFS server and client software enables users of Microsoft® Windows NT®–based computers to access files on UNIX computers and users of UNIX to access files on Windows NT-based computers.

Note Services for UNIX does not provide print services. Windows 2000 includes native line printer remote (LPR) and line printer daemon (LPD) UNIX print services. For more information, see "Network Printing" in the *Microsoft® Windows® 2000 Server Resource Kit Server Operations Guide*.

Telnet Client and Server Telnet Client and Server give users the ability to remotely log into and run commands on Windows NT-based and UNIX-based computers.

Password Synchronization Services for UNIX synchronizes passwords for users of Windows NT-based and UNIX-based computers. Changes to Windows passwords are automatically propagated to the UNIX-based computer.

UNIX Utilities and Scripting Services for Unix provides UNIX commands and Korn shell, which you can use to automate common processes and administrative tasks across Windows and UNIX platforms.

File Sharing with NFS

Network File System, defined in RFCs 1094 and 1813 of the Internet Engineering Task Force (IETF), is a set of protocols for file access across a network. For example, clients use NFS to access files located on remote servers. NFS uses a client/server model and is based on the remote procedure call (RPC) protocol, a method of message exchange between client and server (defined in RFCs 1831, 1050, and 1057), and the *external data representation* (XDR) protocol, a method for translation of data between heterogeneous systems (defined in RFCs 1832 and 1014). Remote file systems located on the server are mounted locally on the client, and to the client system, the file systems appear to reside locally and can be accessed using normal resources, such as system calls and programs. Through a system of distributed file sharing, NFS permits interoperability across heterogeneous networks.

NFS provides files services. These features allow hosts to share files with each other.

NFS is a protocol. This minimizes the risks associated with recovering from a system crash, but it can impact performance. After a crash, the computer can be rebooted without the necessity of recovering the previous state. Most NFS requests are idempotent, so that routines complete actions only once, with the exception of such requests as deletes.

Supported Versions of NFS

Two versions of NFS are available: version 2 (described in RFC 1094) and version 3 (described in RFC 1813).

Version 2 includes the following features and limitations:

- 4 GB. File size indicator limited to 32-bits.
- Network transport using User Datagram Protocol (UDP) or Transmission Control Protocol (TCP).
- NFS packet size limited to a maximum of 8 kilobytes (KB).
- A file-write packet must be committed to disk before the server sends an acknowledgement.

Version 3 includes the following features and limitations:

- File size indicator limited to 64-bits.
- Network transport using TCP or UDP.
- Maximum packet size is 64 KB with UDP.
- Packet size determines the number and frequency of client/server exchanges and acknowledgements.
- Server can cache client write requests unless the client requests that the write request be written to disk.

NFS version 3 uses TCP as its network transport, if TCP is supported by both the client and the server. TCP has the advantage of being more reliable than UDP, but it must maintain state, so it may provide less performance in certain circumstances

Server for NFS

Microsoft Server for NFS (Services for UNIX Version 1.0) is a 32-bit, Windows-based, multithreaded kernel program that is integrated into Windows NT. It enables users to share files in a mixed environment of computers, operating systems, and networks. Server for NFS enables a computer running the Microsoft Windows operating system to act as an NFS server. File access and administrative tasks are performed through the Windows NT interface. Administrative tasks for NFS are performed through a configuration utility.

Server for NFS uses the NFS protocol, which is based on the Open Network Computing Remote Procedure Call (ONC-RPC). Remote calls from clients appear to run locally, but run on the server. The Open Network Computing External Data Representation (ONC-XDR) protocol ensures portable data transmission betweeen NFS clients and the NFS server.

Sun Microsystems developed NFS and its associated protocols. Its architecture is shown in Figure 11.1.

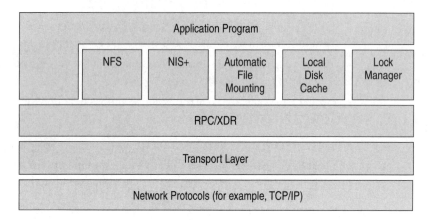

Figure 11.1   NFS Architecture

Server for NFS supports the following features:

Remote File Access   After Services for UNIX is installed on a Windows NT server, that server can make Windows directories and files accessible to NFS clients. Access control provides read, read-write, root and "no access" permissions to clients. Individual file permissions are controlled by Windows NT file permissions.

Global Permissions   NFS clients can be grouped. NFS share access can be controlled by either using names of clients or names of groups. This is a convenient way of controlling access for a group of computers. The available permissions include no access, read-only, read/write, and root access.

Security Permissions   Server for NFS is configurable for NTFS security permissions, including permissions mapping between UNIX and Windows.

User and Group Mapping   In order to provide security on Windows NT files that are accessed from UNIX, Server for NFS requires the system administrator to map UNIX user or group accounts to Windows NT user or group accounts. Users are then given the same access rights under UNIX that they have under Windows NT. Alternately, sites with less stringent security needs can bypass the mapping procedure and treat all UNIX users as anonymous users.

Read and Write Buffer Size   The buffer size can be managed to improve performance.

NFS Threads   The number of threads can be set so that a reasonable number of NFS service requests can be handled. The maximum number of threads permitted is 512.

Caching of Inode and Directory Information   The caching of the inode, which contains file attribute information, and of the directory name lookup information, which contains the paths of recently accessed directories, on the NFS server can reduce the number of system calls to the server. This can improve performance. The size of these caches can be configured by using Server for NFS.

Symbolic Links   Server for NFS can be configured to support symbolic links.

File Locking   File locking can be enabled either for NFS clients only (advisory locking) or for both NFS clients and Windows NT users (mandatory locking).

File Name Case Resolution   Server for NFS can be configured to resolve conflicts that arise between NFS file names and NTFS, file allocation table (FAT), or CD-ROM file system (CDFS) file names as a result of case-sensitivity issues. File names can be converted to uppercase or lowercase, or case can be ignored. A translation file can be used to translate valid UNIX characters into a different character sequence. For example, Windows 2000-based computers do not permit file names to contain colons, but you can use a translation file to select a sequence of valid character to be used as a replacement for any colons that appear in a file name from a UNIX-based computer.

NFS Version 2 and Version 3   Server for NFS can be configured to use either NFS version.

Data Transport Using TCP or UDP   Services for UNIX uses UDP for data transport by default. Server for NFS can be configured to use TCP, which is more reliable and has greater overhead.

Troubleshooting Tools   Services for UNIX provides the **showmount** and **rpcinfo** commands for use in troubleshooting NFS problems.

Client for NFS

Microsoft Client for NFS (Services for UNIX Version 1.0) allows a computer running Windows NT to act as an NFS client and access directories and files located on a server running NFS. The NFS client mounts a directory on the NFS server. The remote access is transparent to the user.

Client for NFS supports the following features:

Access to Remote Files   Exported directories and files from an NFS server can be mounted locally by an NFS client. A user's access to a directory or file is determined by that file system's export options and by the permissions applicable to the file itself.

Mount Options   Under UNIX, the user or system administrator connects to a remote file system by issuing the **mount** command. This command supports various options, depending on the implementation of UNIX. Services for UNIX supports mount options that determine the following:

- Buffer size, which determines the number of packets sent in a read or write request.
- Type of mount, hard or soft. Hard mounts retry system calls indefinitely when a server stops responding or fails; soft mounts do not. File systems that are exported with read/write access or that contain executable files need to be hard-mounted to guarantee data integrity.
- Time an RPC call waits for a response from the server before timing out.
- Number of times an RPC call is resent if the NFS server does not respond (soft mount only).
- File locking, which allows a user to have exclusive access to a file. NFS's file locking works best if all NFS clients have file locking enabled.
- Caching of read data on the NFS client, which reduces the number of calls to the NFS server.
- Caching of write data on the NFS server, to reduce the overhead of small write operations.

NFS Authentication Options   Three methods of authentication are supported:

- *Anonymous UID.* Identifier for users without a valid login and password on the NFS server.
- *Standard UNIX Authentication using an NIS server.* Authentication method for users with a valid login and password stored on an NIS server.
- *PCNFSD Authentication.* Authentication method that uses the pcnfsd daemon to authenticate the login and password for NFS client computers.

Resolution of Symbolic Links Services for UNIX permits the renaming and deletion of a symbolic link. For Client for NFS to find the target of a symbolic link that is located on a file system different from the file system that is currently mounted, an entry must exist in a special configuration file that maps the remote file system to that file system's server name or share name. If no entry is found in the configuration file, Client for NFS assumes that the target file is on the same computer.

Mapping of NFS Directories to Local Drives Mounted NFS directories can be mapped to a local Windows drive, enabling a user to browse the directory by using Windows Explorer.

Setting of File Access Permissions Client for NFS supports changes to UNIX permissions on remote files.

Resolution of File Name Case Since file naming in UNIX is case sensitive and Windows preserves case but ignores it, Services for UNIX provides options to resolve file naming conflicts.

Troubleshooting Tools Services for UNIX provides the **showmount** and **rpcinfo** commands for use in diagnosing NFS conflicts. These commands are discussed in this chapter.

NFS Architecture and Protocols

NFS consists of seven layers of protocols that correspond to the layers of the Open System Interconnection (OSI) model.

Table 11.1   OSI Layers and NFS Protocols

OSI Layers	NFS Layers
Application	NFS and NIS
Presentation	XDR
Session	RPC
Transport	TCP, UDP
Network	IP
Data Link	Ethernet
Physical	Ethernet

The Physical layer controls how data is physically transmitted across the network. The Data Link layer provides transfer of data that is combined into frames. Ethernet is the standard implementation of these two layers.

The Network layer is concerned with getting the data from one host to another on the network. The Internet Protocol (IP) is an implementation of this layer.

IP must get the packets to the correct destination. It is not concerned with data reliability or with data order. It can fragment packets that are too large. The Internet Protocol uses unique IP addresses to identify hosts

The Transport Layer, which is responsible for data flow and data reliability, is implemented by using UDP or TCP.

Transmission Control Protocol (TCP) provides reliable, ordered delivery of data packets and is stateful. TCP keeps track of the order of information and resends missing data. This protocol is best for long network connections, such as file transfer.

User Datagram Protocol (UDP) is a simple, connectionless protocol that does not ensure the order or the completeness of the datagrams. It is stateless and is best for short connections such as remote procedure calls.

The Session Layer is concerned with the exchange of messages between devices. NFS uses the Remote Procedure Call (RPC) protocol.

The Presentation Layer is concerned with the exchange of data types between heterogeneous systems. NFS uses the External Data Representation (XDR) protocol. This protocol specifies the format to which the data must be converted before being sent. Once received, the data is then reconverted.

For more information about the OSI model of networking, see "OSI Model" in the *TCP/IP Core Networking Guide*.

Remote Procedure Call Protocol

The Remote Procedure Call (RPC) protocol enables a computer to make a call that is executed on another computer on the network. The Remote Procedure Call protocol is based on a client/server model. The client makes a procedure call that appears to be local but is actually run on a remote computer. During this process, the procedure call arguments are bundled and passed through the network to the server. The arguments are unpacked and run on the server. The result is bundled and passed back to the client, where it is converted to a return value for the client's procedure call.

RPC can use either UDP or TCP; since RPC calls are short, UDP is preferred. Because of this, an RPC call must contain enough information to be run independently, since UDP does not deliver packets in order. In addition, the client can specify a time limit, after which, if the call is not completed successfully, it can be resent or sent to another server.

Four values define an RPC service: the program number, the version number of the RPC protocol, the procedure number (usually assigned sequentially), and whether UDP or TCP is the transport protocol. Each RPC service is assigned a program number.

RPC provides a collection of procedures called programs. Each program is identified by a program number. For example, NFS is a program with a program number of 100003.

When an RPC service starts under UNIX, it registers its service with the portmapper daemon. It registers the RPC program number and version and provides a TCP or UDP port number to which it listens for incoming requests. The portmapper itself is an RPC service that listens on TCP and UDP port 111.

The **rpcinfo** command is used to show all the RPC programs that are registered on a specified computer. Any RPC programs and their IP port numbers are listed in files by using either portmapper or rpcbind.

Table 11.2 lists some of the options you can use with **rpcinfo**.

Table 11.2   Command Line Options for rpcinfo

Option	Description
-p [*host*]	Lists all registered RPC programs on the specified host.
-u <*host program*> [*ver*] <*received*>	Sends the **null** command to the target host and RPC program using UDP and reports whether a response was received.
-t <*host program*> [*ver*] <*received*>	Sends the **null** command to the target host and RPC program using TCP and reports whether a response was received.
-b <*program version*>	Makes an RPC broadcast for a specific program and version using UDP and lists all responding hosts.

Rpcinfo is useful for diagnosing RPC problems, such as whether or not a server is active, problems with the portmapper daemon, or broadcast-related issues.

Table 11.3 lists the RPC calls that a NFS client can make to a server.

Table 11.3   NFS Version 2 RPC Calls

RPC Call Name	Description
create	Create file
getattr	Get file attributes
link	Create link to file
lookup	Look up file name
mkdir	Create directory
read	Read from file
readdir	Read from directory
readlink	Read from symbolic link
remove	Remove file
rename	Rename file
rmdir	Remove directory
setattr	Set file attributes
statfs	Get file system attributes
symlink	Create symbolic link
write	Write to file

Table 11.4   NFS Version 3 RPC Calls

RPC Call Name	Description
access	Check user access permission
create	Create file
commit	Commit cached data to stable storage
fsstat	Get file system attributes
fsinfo	Get file system information
getattr	Get file attributes
link	Create link to file
lookup	Look up file name
mkdir	Create directory
mknod	Create special device node
pathconf	Retrieve POSIX information
read	Read from file
readdir	Read from directory
readdirplus	Extended read from directory
readlink	Read from symbolic link
remove	Remove file
rename	Rename file
rmdir	Remove directory
setattr	Set file attributes
symlink	Create symbolic link
write	Write to file

NFS Threads

When a request is made for an NFS service, the Services for UNIX NFS server generates a thread to handle the request. Each thread can process one NFS request. A large pool of threads can allow a server to handle more NFS requests in parallel. The number of threads you make available needs to be determined by your performance needs as well as by their impact on other applications running on the system.

To determine the number of threads to make available, use the following formula:

$$16 + (4 \times processors)$$

where *processors* is the number of additional processors on the NFS server. Using this formula, a dual-processor server typically uses 20 threads. The maximum number of threads is 512.

PCNFSD Authentication

NFS can use PC/NFS daemon (PCNFSD), a user authentication daemon, for authentication. After authentication by PCNFSD, the user is assigned a user ID (UID) and a group ID (GID). If the UIDs and GIDs are the same on each UNIX NFS server, then only one server needs to be designated as the PCNFSD server. PCNFSD compares the user name and password provided with the contents of the /etc/passwd file. If a match is found, the PCNFSD server returns the corresponding UID and GID. If authentication is not implemented (that is, if you use neither PCNFSD nor NIS), Client for NFS assigns an anonymous UID of "-2" and an anonymous GID of "-1" to the user. If the NFS server is configured for anonymous access, the user can mount and access files, but only gains read-only access.

Using Showmount

The **showmount** command queries the mount daemon on a specified remote host for information about which clients are mounting from that host. The mount daemon is responsible for receiving a mount request from an NFS client, validating the request by comparing it to the list of exported file systems in /etc/exports, and if the request is valid, creating a file handle for the requested directory, and adding an entry to /etc/rmtab on the UNIX-based computer.

Table 11.5 lists some of the options you can use with showmount

Table 11.5   The Showmount Options

Option	Description
-a [*host*]	Lists both the client host name and the mounted directory (host: directory)
-d [*host*]	Lists the directories mounted by a client
-e [*host*]	Shows the NFS server's export list

Since the **showmount** command depends on the mount daemon for its information, the list of mounted directories might not be complete at any particular time. In addition, **showmount** sorts and processes its output to remove any repeated information, so a directory can be mounted more than once but only be listed once. For more information, see the Services for UNIX online help for **showmount**.

NFS Design Features

Understanding certain NFS features, discussed in this section, can help you optimize NFS performance.

Inodes

UNIX uses an inode, which has a unique ID number, to record information about a file. Every file and every directory has an inode. A file can have more than one file name (depending on the number of links), but only one inode. An inode contains the following items:

- Inode number.
- File name.
- File size and type.
- Date and time of file creation, modification, and access.
- Date and time of inode modification.
- File security information (owner, group, permissions).
- Number of links.
- Block map, with pointers to the data blocks that make up the file.

File Naming

The NFS server applies the following file naming rules to NFS client requests:

- File names can be no longer than 255 characters.
- The following special characters are not permitted: < > : " / \ |.
- The server recognizes "." (current working directory) and ".." (parent of current working directory).

File Permissions

Every file has a set of permissions associated with it that determine who can access the file and what they can do with the file. (Someone with superuser or root permissions can override the permissions assigned to a file.)

Windows NT and UNIX use different mechanisms to assign permissions to files. Windows NT uses a *d*iscretionary access-control list (DACL) to assign permissions to files, and UNIX uses the concept of access mode. The access mode can be changed using the **chmod** command provided with Services for UNIX.

UNIX file access permissions permit a user to read, write, or execute a file based on the type of user attempting to perform the action, *user, group,* or *other.* Permission given to *user* applies to the owner of the file, *group* applies to members of a group of users to which the file belongs (the file is owned by the primary group of the person creating the file), and *other* applies to users other than the owner and members of the group of the file.

Table 11.6   File Permission Capabilities

Permission	Description
Read	Permits reading a file or viewing a directory.
Write	Permits creating, changing, or deleting a file or directory.
Execute	Permits execution of an executable file or browsing a directory.

UNIX identifies users and groups by user ID (UID) and group ID (GID). Users have a single UID and one or more GIDs, which are stored in the file /etc/passwd.

Windows NT assigns permissions to a file by adding an access control entry (ACE) to the DACL. An ACE consists of a right granted to a specific user or group. Services for UNIX maps a Windows NT DACL into a UNIX access mode based on the owner of the file and the associated ACEs. To accomplish this, the UNIX users and groups must be properly mapped to the appropriate Windows NT users and groups using the Server for NFS User Manager.

On the Windows NT–based computer, the user, *johndo,* is created and added to the *Users* group. On the UNIX computer, the user, *johndo*, is created and added to the *Staff* group. In Server for NFS, the Windows NT user, *johndo*, is mapped to the UNIX user, *johndo*; the group, Users, is mapped to the UNIX group, Staff. The user, johndo, takes ownership of the file, letter.doc, on an exported NFS file system on the computer running Services for UNIX, grants Full Control permissions for himself and for the group, Users, and grants List permissions for Everyone. When the user, *johndo*, accesses the NFS file system on the computer running Services for UNIX from a UNIX-based NFS client and runs the **ls -l** command on the file, letter.doc, he sees the following file listing:

```
rwxrwxr-x   1 johndo staff    2116 Jul 1 14:54 letter.doc
```

The first nine characters—in groups of three—indicate the read, write, and execute permissions for the owner (rwx), the group (rwx), and other (r-x); a hyphen indicates the absence of permission. The permissions are followed in the listing by the number of hard links (1), the user name (johndo), the group name (staff), the file size (2116), the date and time the file was last modified (Jul 1 14:54), and the file name.

Note A special situation arises when the owner of the file is the Windows NT group Administrators. If the owner of the file is Administrators, then Server for NFS automatically maps the owner to UID 0 (root) on the UNIX-based computer.

If the owner of the file is not granted explicit permissions to the file by an ACE, the file listing shows that the owner has no access rights to the file (access mode of 0). The Server for NFS administrator can change this behavior by using the **Implicit Permissions** check box on the **Security Permissions** tab of the **Server for NFS Configuration** dialog box. If **Implicit Permissions** is selected, then Server for NFS combines the permissions for any groups in which the owner is a member and that are granted permissions to a file with the permissions for Everyone to determine the access permissions for the owner.

When a file is created in Windows NT, the file inherits the permissions of its parent directory. If either the **chgrp** or **chmod** command is run from an NFS client on an Services for UNIX server, then the default behavior for Server for NFS is to remove any existing DACL entries and write the entries for the three NFS entities (owner, group, and other) to everyone. As a result, the file loses its inherited permissions. The Server for NFS administrator can change this behavior by selecting **Augment DACL** in the **Security Permissions** tab. If Augment DACL is selected, Server for NFS also writes the inherited permissions of the parent directory.

Symbolic Links

A symbolic link is a file that points (that is, contains the path) to another file or directory. A symbolic link can point to a file or a directory on any UNIX file system accessible on the network. The system finds the linked file by reading the symbolic link and then accessing the indicated file or directory. Symbolic links are useful, for example, when a file must be accessible from more than one directory.

Symbolic links can point to an absolute path or a relative path. Since a symbolic link is resolved in terms of the link's location on the client's file system, it is possible for a symbolic link to point to a nonexistent file or directory on the client system or to files that reside in a directory that is not mounted. Such files are not accessible.

An RPC call to a server to determine the location of a symbolic link returns a path that is interpreted on the client but might point to a file system that has not been mounted by the client. If a client mounts a directory containing a symbolic link, the target must also be mounted by the client for the file to be accessible.

Client for NFS can optionally check a local, manually populated configuration file for the correct locations of the targets of symbolic links.

For example, the system administrator of a UNIX-based NFS server, *server1*, creates a symbolic link named "public" that points to a fictitious directory, */server2*. The **ls -l** command shows the following:

```
lrwxrwxrwx 2  root  other   8  Jul 1 16:25 public->/server2
```

Then, on the computer running Client for NFS, or on a network file system that is accessible to it, the system administrator creates a text file listing anticipated symbolic links with entries like the following:

```
server2      \server2\sharename
```

When the computer running Client for NFS connects to the exported file system on server1, it resolves the symbolic link, public, and initiates an NFS connection to \server2:\sharename. This allows the client to view files stored on the remote server, server2.

File Locking

File locking allows a process to have exclusive access to a file or part of a file. File locking is implemented on the server and the client. A server restarted after a crash attempts to restore the lock status to the previous condition. If the client crashes, the server releases the lock. However, after the client restarts, it has a short period of time to reclaim the lock. When a file is locked, the buffer cache is not used for that file. Each write request is immediately sent to the server.

File locking is implemented differently under BSD UNIX compared to System V UNIX, which are the two versions of UNIX from which most current UNIX operating systems descend. BSD has a locking mechanism only for local files; System V locks are handled separately from the NFS protocol by an RPC lock daemon, **lockd**, and a status monitoring daemon, **statd**, which monitors status and provides crash and recovery functions for NFS locking. The lock daemon runs on both the client and the server to process lock requests and lock releases. The Network Lock Manager (NLM) protocol defines the communication between remote lock daemons.

File Caching

File caching involves storing frequently used information in quickly accessed memory. The UNIX buffer cache is a portion of the system's memory that is allocated for file blocks that have been recently referenced. In NFS, file caching is used on the client to eliminate some RPC requests over the network and used on the server to improve data throughput. NFS maintains data integrity despite the existence of client-side and server-side caches.

The NFS redirector uses the Windows NT system cache when it opens a file for read or read/write access. When data is written to the file, it is also written to the cache. The data is flushed to the redirector later. If an unrecoverable network error occurs while the data is being transferred to the remote server, the write request might fail. In this case, the user sees a system message.

The Windows NT cache manager also does read-ahead, in which the next file block is read in advance and stored in the buffer cache. As a result, a one-to-one mapping between an application read/write request and an NFS call does not exist.

The NFS redirector supports file locking, using the Network Lock Manager (NLM) protocol, to ensure data consistency. If file locking is disabled, data caching is enabled.

File caching is not provided on Server for NFS.

Telnet Server and Client

Note Microsoft Windows 2000 provides a Telnet server that allows two client connection and a Telnet client, Telnetc.exe. For more information, see Windows 2000 Server Help.

Telnet client software allows a computer to connect to a remote computer. Telnet server software allows telnet clients to connect to a server, log in to that server, and run applications.

Services for UNIX Version 1.0 Telnet Server and Client can accept connections from and can connect to each other, as well as accept connections from and connect to UNIX-based telnet clients and servers. UNIX users can access Windows servers and run character-based applications; a UNIX shell, such as Korn shell, can be run on a Services for UNIX Telnet server. System administrators can use Services for UNIX Telnet to remotely administer Windows and UNIX servers.

Services for UNIX Telnet supports the following features:

- Remote administration from Windows to UNIX, from UNIX to Windows, and from Windows to Windows.
- Character-based Telnet server administration tool.
- Command line Telnet emulation interface to Telnet server.
- VTNT terminal type for connections between Services for UNIX Telnet client and Services for UNIX Telnet server.
- VT100, VT52, VTNT, and ANSI terminal emulation.
- NTLM authentication for Telnet sessions between Windows computers using Microsoft Telnet Server and Client.
- Well-known Telnet options and commands.

Telnet Protocol

Telnet uses the TELNET protocol, specified in RFC 854, to connect to a remote computer that is running telnet server software over the network. It provides a two-way communication facility that allows terminal devices and terminal-oriented processes to communicate with each other. Telnet uses TCP to transmit data and telnet control information. The default port for telnet is TCP port 23.

RFC 854 states: "The Telnet Protocol is built upon three main ideas: first, the concept of a 'Network Virtual Terminal;' second, the principle of negotiated options; and third, a symmetric view of terminals and processes."

Network Virtual Terminal

The Network Virtual Terminal (NVT) is a representation of a basic terminal and provides a standard that the computers on either end of a Telnet connection are assumed to follow. It defines how data and commands are sent across the network. Thus, NVT allows interoperability between Telnet and a variety of heterogeneous computers and operating systems. It consists of a virtual keyboard that generates user-specified characters and a printer that displays specific characters. Clients and servers can map their local devices to the characteristics and handling conventions of an NVT and can assume that other servers and clients are doing the same.

Telnet Session

The **telnet** command can be used with or without a computer name. If no computer name is used, Telnet provides command mode and provides a prompt to the user. The activation of Telnet results in a TCP connection to the server and to the Telnet daemon, tlntsvr. After a connection is established, Telnet enters input mode. Depending on the remote computer, typed text is sent from the client either a character at a time or a line at a time.

Users can access the Telnet command mode at any time by using an escape sequence. Terminal emulators provide an escape sequence for this purpose. (The Services for UNIX Telnet escape sequence is CTRL+A.) At the command line, users can set telnet options to change the behavior of telnet. After entering commands, users can return to input mode by pressing ENTER at the **Microsoft Telnet>** prompt.

Telnet Options

Clients and servers can negotiate additional options, beyond the default functionality provided by NVT. The telnet options are described in a number of extensions to the Telnet RFC, and RFC 855 describes the mechanism for specifying telnet options. Each telnet option is assigned a number.

Options are usually negotiated at the beginning of a Telnet session, but can also be requested during the session. Options are negotiated by exchanging option code sequences. One partner can request an option; the other can agree to the request or not. The negotiation syntax involves the use of four protocol verbs: WILL and DO, to request or offer to provide an option, and WON'T and DON'T, to do the opposite. The negotiation of options can potentially result in a nonterminating loop of acknowledgments.

Services for UNIX supports the following telnet options:

- NTLM authentication, which uses a randomization algorithm and an encrypted password to authenticate users.

- Terminal emulation, in which a program allows a computer to act like a specified terminal. Supported terminal types include VTNT, VT100, VT52, and ANSI.

Telnet Security

Services for UNIX provides two security options:

- UNIX authentication, which uses the UNIX login and password. The password is sent as plaintext. This may be a security hazard as other network users may be able to snoop this transmission.

- NTLM for authentication between a Services for UNIX Telnet Client and a Services for UNIX Telnet Server. NTLM uses pass-through authentication, in which the security credentials—domain name, user name, and hashed password—are passed through domain controllers for connections between trusted domains. The user is not prompted for login and password. This method is integrated with Windows security.

  Using NTLM, a user can use telnet to connect to a remote computer and access resources on that computer; however, the user cannot access other resources on the network without being authenticated again.

For more information about NTLM, see "Planning Distributed Security" in the *Deployment Planning Guide*.

Password Synchronization

Services for UNIX Version 1.0 Password Synchronization synchronizes passwords between computers running Windows and UNIX, enhancing the interoperability of the two systems. The password synchronization software maintains a common password on both the Windows-based and the UNIX-based computers.

The Password Synchronization component of Services for UNIX permits a system administrator to configure a network of Windows-based and UNIX-based computers so that a change made to a Windows password is automatically propagated to the matching user name in the password files in a group of UNIX-based computers. Services for UNIX can be configured so that the password changes are sent from the Windows NT–based computer to the UNIX-based computer as either plaintext or encrypted text. All user passwords must comply with the Windows password rules that are in effect as well as UNIX password rules. Consequently, users should use the stricter of the two sets of rules when selecting a password.

Services for UNIX Password Synchronization supports the following features:

- One-way password synchronization from Windows to UNIX.
- Plaintext password synchronization using **rlogin** (the unsecured method).
- Triple DES-encrypted password synchronization using a daemon provided by Services for UNIX, an encryption key for changing password in the file /etc/passwd, and Network Information Service (NIS) or NIS+ (the secured method).
- Administrative tools to manage all password synchronization processes, including configuration.

Using Password Synchronization

Consider the following when implementing Services for UNIX Password Synchronization:

User Name and Password   The user name and password must be exactly the same on the Windows-based and UNIX-based computers that are configured together for password synchronization. Both the user name and the password are case-sensitive.

Domain Controllers   If Services for UNIX Version 1.0 for Windows NT 4.0 is installed, all Windows NT domain controllers need to have Services for UNIX installed with Password Synchronization. If Services for UNIX is installed only on the primary domain controller (PDC) and it goes down, then a backup domain controller (BDC) will be promoted to a PDC. If this domain controller does not have Services for UNIX with Password Synchronization installed, then the password database can get out of synchronization.

Password Changes   After password synchronization is implemented, the UNIX system password need not be changed. If a UNIX password is changed, it is overwritten by the next change to the Windows password.

Synchronization Method   All computers within a UNIX pod must use the same password synchronization method, secured or unsecured. A UNIX pod is a group of UNIX-based computers, one of which successfully receives an updated password from Windows NT.

NIS/NIS+ and Password Synchronization   Services for UNIX does not support password updates to NIS or NIS+ using **rlogin**, so use the secured password synchronization method with UNIX computers that use NIS or NIS+ for managing system-independent information such as login names and passwords.

NIS and Password Change Propagation If an NIS domain is used as a password synchronization mode, Services for UNIX updates the NIS/NIS+ domain master, which propagates the changes to the NIS/NIS+ slave servers.

Installing the ssod Daemon If secured password synchronization is being used, the **ssod** daemon included with the Services for UNIX product CD must be installed on every UNIX-based computer in the pod.

Unsecured Password Synchronization If unsecured password synchronization is being used, the files /etc/hosts and .rhosts on the UNIX-based computers in the pod must be correctly configured so that rlogin can access the **passwd** command as a root logon. In addition, the file /etc/default/login on Sun Sparcstations must be modified and the console-only root logon must be disabled.

Security

Services for UNIX Password Synchronization sends password updates over the network as either plaintext or encrypted text. The plaintext method should only be used when security is not a concern. The encrypted method uses Triple DES encryption, described later in the chapter.

If the plaintext option is chosen, **rlogin** is used to change the password on the UNIX computer. The Password Synchronization service uses a login with root privileges to access the **passwd** command and update a user's UNIX password. The .rhosts file must contain the necessary computer names, the full host names (not the alias) of the Windows NT computer, and root. The /etc/hosts file must contain the necessary host name to IP address mappings. If you are using a Sun Sparcstation, you must modify the /etc/default/login file and disable the console-only **root** login.

Note NIS and NIS+ are not supported by **rlogin**. If your network uses NIS or NIS+, you must use the encrypted password synchronization scheme.

If the encrypted text option is chosen, the UNIX system administrator must copy the **ssod** program available on the Services for UNIX product CD onto the UNIX-based computer. The program must be installed as a daemon and must be configured to start when the computer is started. This daemon is responsible for opening a port and waiting for the password notification from the Windows NT–based computer. The system administrator must choose the encryption key and add it to the **ssod.config** file on the UNIX-based computer, as well as to the Windows NT-based computer using the Windows NT–to–UNIX Password Synchronization Service Administrator.

Services for UNIX includes versions of the binary files of **ssod** for Solaris, Digital UNIX, and HP-UX.

Each UNIX host in a pod must use the same encryption key. The encryption key must meet the following requirements:

- It must be at least 12 characters long.
- It must contain characters from at least three of the following groups:
    - Uppercase English letters.
    - Lowercase English letters.
    - Arabic numerals.
    - Special characters: (' ' ! @ # $ % ^ & * _ - + = | \ { } [ ] : ; / " < > , . /).

Example Files

This section provides some examples of UNIX files used by Services for UNIX Password Synchronization.

The file /etc/passwd contains user information. Each user entry contains seven colon-separated fields:

```
login-id: password:UID:GID:user_information:home-directory:shell
```

The *login-id* field contains the name the user enters at the login prompt. The *password* field can either contain the encrypted password or a special marker if the password is stored in /etc/shadow (which is only accessible to root users). The *UID* field contains the user's ID number. The *GID* field contains the ID number of the group of which the user is a member. The *user_information* field is used for additional information about the user which may be necessary. The *home-directory* field contains the absolute path for the user's home directory. The *shell* field indicates the program that runs when the user logs in. If desired, a specific shell can be indicated in this field (for example, /usr/bin/ksh for Korn shell or /usr/bin/sh for Bourne shell).

The file /etc/shadow contains information about the user's password and is only accessible by the superuser. It has nine colon-separated fields:

```
login-id:password:lastchg:min:max:warn:inactive:expire:flag
```

The *login-id* field is the name the user enters at the login prompt. The *password* field contains the encrypted password. The *lastchg* field contains the number of days from January 1, 1970 to the date of the last password change. The *min* field contains the minimum number of days required between password changes. The *max* field contains the maximum number of days that the password is valid. The *warn* field contains the number of days that the user receives a warning message about password expiration. The *inactive* field contains the number of days that a user is allowed to be inactive. The *expire* field contains the last day that the login can be used. The *flag* field is not currently used.

The file /etc/group contains group information. Each entry contains four colon-separated fields:

```
group-name:password:group-ID:list-of-names
```

The *group-name* field identifies the group. The password field can contain an optional, encrypted *password*. The *group-ID* field contains the numerical ID for the group. The *list-of-names* field contains the names (comma-separated) of all the members of the group.

The file /etc/hosts lists all the hosts, including the local host, that share the network. It is used to map between host names and IP addresses. Each line in the file, which describes a single host, consists of three fields separated by spaces:

```
IP-address host-name alias
```

The file /etc/hosts.equiv lists the hosts and users that can invoke remote commands on a local host without supplying a password (a trust relationship). The .rhosts file lists remote users who can use a local user account on a network without supplying a password. The file .rhosts is a hidden file that is located in a user's home directory and must be owned by the user. Both /etc/hosts.equiv and.rhosts have the same format:

```
host-name user-name
```

Both files support the use of a plus sign (+) as a wildcard. A plus sign after a host-name or user-name grants trust to all users from a particular host or from all hosts that a specific user has an account on. Trust can be granted to every user on every host in the network by placing a plus sign at the beginning of the file. This option should be used cautiously. Hosts or users whose names are omitted from a file are denied trust.

Triple DES

Triple DES, used for encryption by Services for UNIX Password Synchronization, is a variation on the Data Encryption Standard (DES). DES is an encryption method in which the sender and the receiver use the same secret key to encrypt and decrypt data. DES uses a 56-bit key. Triple DES encrypts data three times using the DES encryption algorithm. Three variations on this triple encryption are possible:

- Three encryptions using three different keys
- Encryption-decryption-encryption using three different keys
- Encryption-decryption-encryption using the same key for both encryptions

UNIX Utilities and Korn Shell

You can use UNIX utilities and Korn shell to automate common processes across Windows NT and UNIX platforms.

UNIX Shell

Services for UNIX Version 1.0 includes a Korn shell. The shell is a command language interpreter that acts as the interface to the UNIX operating system. The shell interprets commands, calls the appropriate program, and returns standard output. Many shells also provide a high-level programming language that can be used to achieve complex tasks by combining basic utilities and functions provided by the operating system.

Korn shell, developed by David Korn at AT&T, combines many of the desirable features of the C and Bourne shells. Bourne shell, developed at AT&T by Steven Bourne, was the first UNIX shell. Bourne shell provides a powerful programming language. C shell, another UNIX shell, provides a number of features not available with the Bourne shell, such as command aliases, a command history mechanism, and job control of command processing.

Table 11.7   Shell Feature Summary

	Bourne	C	Korn
Command Alias		X	X
Command History		X	X
Command-line Editing			X
Job Control		X	X
Shell Scripting	X	X	X

Other shells are available for the UNIX operating system. Bash (Bourne Again shell) is an extension of Bourne shell that incorporates features of both the Korn and C shells and is generally used with Linux. Tcsh is an extended version of C shell that includes command completion, a command-line editor, and enhanced history manipulation.

Using the Korn Shell

The implementation of the Korn shell included with Services for UNIX differs from the standard UNIX Korn shell in the following ways:

- Semicolons used instead of colons to separate entries in the PATH variable.

- Current directory in PATH is referred to as ;; or ;.; instead of period (.).

- Startup file is called profile.ksh instead of .profile.

- Startup file for system-wide environment variables is called /etc/profile.ksh instead of /etc/profile.

- History file, which stores the command history of a user, is called sh_histo file instead of sh_history.

- Partial job control enables running of jobs in the background using the ampersand on the command line.

If your system administrator sets up the Korn shell as your default shell in Telnet Server, it is the shell you log into when accessing a Services for UNIX server via Telnet. If you want to use Korn shell without logging into it, you can access it using the **sh** command (**ksh** in the standard UNIX Korn shell).

Environment Variables

A variable consists of a name and its assigned value. You can define variables and use them in shell scripts. Other variables, called *shell variables*, are set by the shell. A variable name can contain letters, numbers (but not as the first character), and the underscore. The equal sign with no spaces on either side is used to assign a value to the variable. Once a variable is defined, you must use the **export** command to make the value of the variable available to other processes.

The Korn shell runs the profile.ksh file when you login. The profile.ksh file is used to set user-specific environment variables and terminal modes. (The system administrator can also use /etc/profile.ksh to set variables system-wide for all user accounts on the system.) Some of the variables used in .profile include PATH, HOME, VISUAL, EDITOR, SHELL, HISTSIZE, HISTFILE, PS1, PS2, CDPATH.

Table 11.8 lists many of the environment variables used by the Services for UNIX Korn shell. For a complete list of the shell variables supported by the Services for UNIX Korn shell, consult the Services for UNIX online help for **sh**.

Table 11.8   Korn Shell Environment Variables

Variable Name	Description
–	Expands to the argument of the previously executed command.
CDPATH	The search path used by the cd command.
COLUMNS	Defines the width of the output display for programs that read the value, like vi.
EDITOR	Specifies a default editor for the system to call when no editor is otherwise specified.
ENV	If ENV is set, parameter substitution is performed on the value. When the shell is invoked, the named file is run first.
ERRNO	Value set by most recently failed subroutine.
FIGNORE	Contains a pattern that defines which files are ignored during file expansion.
FCEDIT	The editor for the fc command.
HISTFILE	The absolute path of the file (default sh_histo) containing the command history.
HISTSIZE	The number of commands in the history file.
HOME	The absolute path of your home directory, which becomes your current directory when you log on.
IFS	Characters used as internal field separators.
LINENO	The number of the line from standard input currently being executed by the shell script.
LINES	The number of output lines used by the **select** statement when printing its menu. Select writes specific words to standard error.
MAIL	The absolute path of the file where your mail is stored.
MAILCHECK	The number of seconds the shell waits before checking for new mail.
MAILPATH	The mailbox files where new mail notification is sent.
OLDPWD	The path of the previous working directory.
PATH	The absolute paths of the directories that the shell searches for executable files.
PPID	The process ID of the parent of the shell.
PS1	The prompt displayed by the shell. The default Korn shell prompt is $. Other options exist.
PS2	The secondary shell prompt

continued

Table 11.8   Korn Shell Environment Variables *(continued)*

Variable Name	Description
PWD	The path of the current working directory.
RANDOM	Generates a random number.
REPLY	Contains user input from the select statement.
SHELL	The absolute path of the current shell and is used by commands to invoke the shell.
TMOUT	The number of seconds the shell remains inactive before it terminates.
VISUAL	Specifies a default editor, overriding the EDITOR variable.

Metacharacters

Korn shell recognizes a special meaning for certain characters. When a regular expression contains a metacharacter, the Korn shell interprets the character as shown in Table 11.9.

Table 11.9   Korn Shell Metacharacters

Character	Meaning
\	Escape character. When immediately preceding another character, it removes the special meaning from the character it precedes.
*	Wildcard match for zero or more characters.
?	Wildcard match for one character.
[ ]	Wildcard match for the characters specified within the brackets.
<	Redirects standard input so that it comes from a specified file instead of the terminal.
>	Redirects standard output so that it goes to a specified file instead of the terminal.
>>	Appends standard output to the end of a specified file.
|	Pipe. Connects the standard output of one command to the standard input of another command.
&	Causes a process to run in the background when appended to a command line.
~	Represents the path of a user's home directory.
.	Current directory
..	Parent to the current directory.
$1 - $9	Represents the first nine arguments to a command.
/	Root directory.

continued

Table 11.9   Korn Shell Metacharacters *(continued)*

Character	Meaning
'	Takes a string literally. Variable substitution allowed.
"	Takes a string literally. Variable substitution allowed.
`	Back quotes around a command string tells the shell to run the command and use the output in place of the string.
( )	Groups commands together for execution.
;	Separates commands on a command line.
newline (ENTER)	Starts command execution.

Shell Commands

When you enter a command at the shell prompt, the shell evaluates the command, makes substitutions for variables and aliases, and then runs the command.

The basic structure of a command:

command-name argument1 argument2 >file-name

Commands can take options, which modify the action of a command. For example, **ls** lists the contents of a directory, but does not include the hidden (.) files. Use **ls -a** to also see the hidden files.

The shell processes the command after you press ENTER. Commands can also be separated by semicolons and entered on a single line; the commands on the line are not processed, however, until after you press ENTER.

When the shell runs a command, it starts a process. Each process has a process ID (PID), which is used to access the process. Processes can be run in the foreground or the background and can also be suspended or cancelled. Parent processes forked child processes, which are assigned their own PIDs.

A command receives standard input from the terminal and sends standard output and standard error to the terminal.

It is possible to redirect the standard input from the terminal to a file:

command-name < file-name

You can also redirect the standard output from the terminal to a file:

command-name > file-name

You can append it to an existing file:

command-name >> file-name

In addition, you can redirect the standard error to a file:

command-name 1>file-name1 2>file-name2

The standard output is sent to *file-name1* and the standard error is sent to *file-name2*.

Pipes can be used to connect the standard output of one command to the standard input of another command:

command-name | command-name >file-name

The Services for UNIX Korn shell is a programmable shell that supports the following structured commands. For a complete list of supported shell commands, see the Services for UNIX online help for **sh**.

Table 11.10   Shell Programming Services for UNIX Korn Shell

Command	Use
case	Runs commands based on a particular setting of another variable.
for	Runs a specific list of commands.
if	Specifies conditions in a script.
select	Writes specified words to standard error.
until	Runs a list of commands until a zero value is returned.
while	Runs a list of commands while a certain condition is true.

The Services for UNIX Korn shell has *built-in commands*. Built-in commands are run by the shell's own process. The built-in commands available with the Services for UNIX Korn shell are listed below. For details about each command, consult Services for UNIX online help.

Table 11.11   Services for UNIX Korn Shell Built-In Commands

Command	Description
.	Runs a shell file in the current environment.
:	Expands arguments. Returns an exit status of 0 (success).
alias	Assigns a new name to a command.
break	Exits from a for, while, or until loop.
cd	Changes the current working directory.
continue	Resumes with the next iteration of a for, while, or until loop.
echo	Displays its arguments to standard output.
environ	Standard environmental variables.
eval	Scans and runs the specified command.

continued

Table 11.11   **Services for UNIX Korn Shell Built-In Commands** (*continued*)

Command	Description
exec	Runs the specified without creating a new process.
exit	Exits the shell.
export	Makes the value of the variable available to child processes.
false	Returns an exit status of 1 (failure).
fc	Selects specified commands from command history.
getopts	Parses command line options.
jobs	Displays current jobs.
kill	Ends the specified job.
let	Evaluates the expression.
print	Displays arguments from the shell.
pwd	Displays current working directory.
read	Reads one line from standard output.
readonly	Makes the value of the variable read-only so it cannot be changed.
return	Exits a function.
set	Sets shell flags or command line argument variables.
shedit	Interactive command and history editing in the shell.
shift	Promotes each command line argument (for example, $3 to $2)
shpc	Features of Korn shell specific to Windows NT.
test	Checks for the properties of files, strings, and integers, and returns the results of the test as an exit value.
time	Displays run-time and CPU time.
times	Displays user program and system times accumulated by the shell.
trap	Specifies commands to run at a signal.
true	Returns exit status of 0 (success).
type	Identifies a name as interpreted by the shell.
typeset	Sets attributes and values for shell parameters.
umask	Changes access permissions.
unalias	Removes an alias.
unset	Removes a variable definition from the environment.
wait	Waits for a child process to terminate.
whence	Describes how the shell interprets a command name (as a function, shell keyword, command, alias, or executable file).

Command Aliases

You can assign an *alias*, which is a name, usually easy to remember, that the shell translates to another name or string, for a command, including command-line options. The shell substitutes the command and options for the alias you enter. Creating an alias at the command line makes the alias available in the current shell environment. To make the alias part of the work environment, add a line to the shell start-up file (.kshrc) that defines the alias and exports it:

alias *newname='command -option'*; **export** *newname*

The command **alias -x** exports the alias to the child process only.

To remove an alias, use **unalias** followed by the alias name:

unalias *newname*

The Services for UNIX Korn shell provides a set of predefined aliases. For more information, see the Services for UNIX online help for **alias**.

Command History

The Services for UNIX Korn shell features a history file, which contains a list of a defined number of executed commands. These commands can be accessed for editing and persist in the file between login sessions.

You can set the number of commands saved in the history file using the HISTSIZE variable:

HISTSIZE=*number*; **export HISTSIZE**

If you do not define this variable, UNIX saves a system-defined number of commands.

You can define the name and location of the history file using the HISTFILE variable:

HISTFILE=*file-name*; **export HISTFILE**

If you do not define this variable, your history file is named **.sh_histo** and stored in your home directory.

Command Line Editing

You can edit the commands in the history file, using built-in Korn shell editors such as vi or emacs, or the built-in **fc** command, or the complete vi editor. You can use this feature to correct mistakes or to reuse work you have completed.

To define vi as your default editor:

set -o vi

–Or–

VISUAL=/sfu/shell/vi; export VISUAL

The built-in editor provided with the Korn shell provide a subset of the full functionality available with the UNIX vi editor. You can access the vi editor to edit a command by entering the command, pressing ENTER, and then typing **vi**. This will allow you to edit a multiline command.

Arithmetic Evaluation

The Services for UNIX Korn shell has a built-in arithmetic expression feature. It supports logical and arithmetic operators. The syntax for arithmetic operators is $((<arithmetic expression>))$ or $(<arithmetic expression>)$. The Korn shell replaces the arithmetic expression with its value, beginning with the innermost nested expression. Table 11.12 lists the operators.

Table 11.12   Arithmetic and Logical Operators

Operator	Description
+	Plus
-	Minus
*	Multiply
/	Divide (with truncation)
%	Remainder
<<	Bit-shift left
>>	Bit-shift right
&	Bitwise and
&&	Logical and
|	Bitwise or
||	Logical or
^	Bitwise exclusive or
!	Logical not
~	Bitwise not
<	Less than
>	Greater than
<=	Less than or equal to
>=	Greater than or equal to
!=	Not equal to
=	Equal to

Shell Scripts

A shell script is a file containing a series of commands that together perform a function. You can access a Korn shell script from the command line if you are running the Korn shell and have permission to execute the script by typing the file name. You can also run the shell script if Korn shell is not running by entering the following command:

sh *file-name*

Windows NT does not support execution of a script invoked from the command line only by file name; under UNIX, scripts may be executed in this manner if the path and file name of the shell are specified on the first line of the script, like the following:

#!/bin/sh

Each file or file name extension must be associated with a program. In particular, **.sh** or **.ksh** can be associated with Korn shell.

Job Control

You can use job control to run a command in the foreground or the background or temporarily suspend it. In addition, you can see a list of the commands currently running.

When you enter a command, if it is not a built-in command, the shell forks a new process in which to run the command. The kernel schedules the process and gives it a process ID (PID). The shell keeps track of the process and gives it a job number.

Some processes are run in the foreground: they might be interactive or take only a very short time to run. Other processes are better run in the background, especially commands that take a long time to run, such as a large sort. You can move a process to the foreground or the background and get a list of the current jobs. You can also temporarily suspend a process or terminate it.

Table 11.13 lists the job control commands supported by Services for UNIX.

Table 11.13   Job Control Commands

Command	Description
jobs –l	Lists the current jobs. Each job is numbered. The -l option displays the PID.
command **&**	Runs the command in the background. For example, **sort** *file-name newfile* **&**
kill *job-number*	Kills the job specified by *job-number*. The job number is displayed when a job is started with **&** or by using the **jobs** command.

UNIX Utilities

The following UNIX utilities are available as part of Services for UNIX. For more information on these commands, see Services for UNIX Help.

Table 11.14   UNIX Utilities

UNIX Command	Description
sh	Invokes Korn shell.
basename	Removes the path, leaving only the file name. Deletes any prefix ending in / and any suffix from *string* and prints the result to standard output.
cat	Concatenates and displays file.
chmod	Changes or assigns the permissions mode of a file.
chown	Changes the owner of a file.
cp	Copies files.
dirname	Delivers all but the last level of the path in string. See *basename*.
find	Recursively searches directory hierarchy looking for files that match a specified Boolean expression.
grep	Searches files for a pattern and prints all line containing that pattern.
head	Copies first *n* lines of specified file names to standard output.
ln	Creates hard link to file. Links a file name to a target by creating a directory entry that refers to the target.
ls	Lists contents of a directory.
mkdir	Creates named directory with read, write, and execute permission for every type of user.
more	A filter that displays the contents of a text file on the terminal, one screen at a time.
mv	Moves file name to target.
rm	Removes entry for file from a directory.
rmdir	Removes directory.
sed	Stream editor. Copies named file name to standard output, edited according to a script of commands.
sort	Sorts lines of all named files together and writes result to standard output.
tail	Copies named file to standard output, beginning at the designated place.
tee	Transcribes standard input to standard output and makes copies in file name.
touch	Updates access time or modification time of a file.

continued

Table 11.14   UNIX Utilities *(continued)*

UNIX Command	Description
uniq	Reports repeated lines in a file.
wc	Displays a count of lines, words, or characters in a file.
vi	Screen-oriented visual display editor based on ex.
perl	An interpreted language used for scanning text files, extracting information from those files, and printing reports based on that information.

Using vi

The vi editor is an interactive text editor for creating and editing ASCII files. The vi editor requires you to enter a command to perform an action, such as entering text, deleting text, or moving the cursor. You can be in one of two modes when using vi: command mode or input mode. In command mode, you can enter commands to perform such actions as deleting text or moving the cursor in the file. In input mode, you can enter and change text. You enter input mode by entering a specific vi command. You leave input mode by pressing ESC. This section provides some basic information to get you started using vi. Once you understand the basic mechanics of using vi, you can explore its functionality. (The mechanics are simple; the details can seem obscure at first.) For further details on the complete functionality of vi, consult any of the available print or online sources. In addition, consult the Services for UNIX online help for **vi**.

To edit a file using vi, at the system prompt type:

vi *file-name*

and press ENTER.

If the file already exists, it appears on the screen. If the file does not exist, vi creates it.

Note You can take advantage of a file recovery feature that is provided with vi. If the system saves a copy of the last saved version of your file in a buffer, you can access that copy of the file, by typing **vi -r** *file-name* and pressing ENTER.

What you see on the screen is the text of the file (if it exists), a blinking cursor in the left-hand corner of the screen, a column of tildes along the left margin of the file representing blank lines (if there are any in view), and the name of the file in the last line of the screen. (The bottom of the screen is also used to display messages, to show commands you enter that begin with /, ?, !, and :, and the indication of input mode if showmode option is set.)

To begin entering text, press **i** (to insert text). You can then begin typing. The text you enter appears, beginning at the position of the cursor. When you are done entering text, press ESC.

To save the file and exit vi, type:

:wq

and press ENTER.

Use the *colon* to escape to the shell so that you can enter a command at the bottom of the screen. Press **w** to write the file to disk. Press **q** to quit the vi editor.

Table 11.15   Starting and Quitting vi

Command	Description
vi *file-name*	Edits *file-name* (this creates a new file or edits an existing one)
vi -r *file-name*	Recovers a file after a system crash and edit it
:q	Quits vi if no changes have been made
:q!	Quits vi without saving changes
:wq	Writes (save changes) and quit vi

After you have created a file using vi, you can move throughout the file. As the size of the size of the file increases, the ability to move at will to any place in the file becomes increasingly useful using the following commands in command mode.

Table 11.16   Moving the Cursor in Command Mode

Command	Description
Spacebar	Moves the cursor forward one character
Backspace	Moves the cursor back one character
l	Moves the cursor one character to the right
h	Moves the cursor one character to the left
j	Moves the cursor down one line
k	Moves the cursor up one line
Ctrl-d	Scrolls down half a screen
Ctrl-u	Scrolls up half a screen
Ctrl-f	Scrolls down one screen
Ctrl-b	Scrolls up one screen
*n***G**	Moves the cursor to line *n*
G	Moves the cursor to the end of the file

Many ways are provided for inserting and changing text that allow for detailed control.

Table 11.17   Input Mode

Command	Description
a	Insert text after the cursor
A	Insert text at end of the current line
i	Insert text before the cursor
I	Insert text before the current line
o	Open a line in the text below the cursor
O	Open a line in the text above the cursor

Table 11.18   Changing Text

Command	Description
r	Replace the current character with the next character typed; return to Command mode.
R	Replace text beginning with the current character, until ESC invoked.
cc	Changes the entire current line to the new text entered.
cw	Changes the current word, beginning at the cursor position, to the new text entered.
s	Substitutes the character at the cursor position with the new text entered.
S	Substitutes the entire current line with the new text entered.

Table 11.19 shows the possible ways to delete text in vi.

Table 11.19   Deleting Text

Command	Description
D	Delete from cursor to the end of the line
x	Delete the current character
dd	Delete the current line

You can *yank* and *put* — that is, copy and paste — text within a file and between files. The yank commands copies specified text and places it in a buffer. The put commands copy the text from the buffer to a specified place in the file. Named buffers and numbered buffers are available but are beyond the scope of this discussion.

Table 11.20   Yank and Put Commands

Command	Description
yy or Y	Yanks (copies) the current line.
5yy	Yanks five lines.
p	Puts (pastes) the text in the buffer in the line after the current one.
P	Puts (pastes) the text in the buffer in the line before the current one.

You can search for a character string within the file. Remember that the search tools are case-sensitive. If the pattern is not found, vi displays a message at the bottom of the screen telling you that it is unable to find the pattern.

Table 11.21   Search Commands

Command	Description
/pattern	Moves forward to the first character in the next occurrence of the character string *pattern*.
/	Repeats the previous forward search.
?pattern	Moves backward to the first character in the next occurrence of the character string *pattern*.
?	Repeats the previous backward search.

Global pattern substitution, a powerful tool, is available from the command line.

The command takes the form:

:s/*string***/***replacement***/g**

and press ENTER. In this command, *string* represents any regular expression that you want to search for, *replacement* represents the text that will replace *string*, and **g** specifies global replacement of all occurrences of *string*. If the trailing **g** is omitted, only the first occurrence of the string in each line is replaced. If you want to be prompted to confirm each substitution, type a **c** after the **g** in the command, as follows:

:s/*string***/***replacement***/gc**

Here are a few of the many other tools available in vi.

Table 11.22   Other Useful Commands

Command	Description
:sh	Escape to the shell to run a command
:!*command*	Run one command
u	Undo last change
U	Restore the last deleted line
~	Toggle the case of the current character
xp	Transpose the character in the current cursor position with the next character
.	Repeat last change

Scripting

Services for UNIX includes two tools that you can use for scripting: Perl and sh.

Perl is a scripting language that is useful for automated tasks, such as processing text files by using pattern matching techniques. Perl is "open source" software. Not all Perl functions are implemented in Services for UNIX. For more information, consult the Services for UNIX online help for **perl**.

The Korn shell provided with Services for UNIX can be used as a shell script processor. For more information on using the Korn shell for scripting, consult the Services for UNIX online help for **sh**.

Additional Resources

- For more information about NFS, see *Managing NFS and NIS* by Hal Stern, 1991, Sebastopol: O'Reilly & Associates, Inc.

- For more information about Windows NT and UNIX, see *Windows NT & UNIX Administration, Coexistence, Integration, & Migration* by G. Robert Williams and Ellen Beck Gardner, 1998, Reading, Massachusetts: Addison-Wesley Longman, Inc.

- For more information about UNIX, see *UNIX System V: A Practical Guide Third Edition* by Mark G. Sobell, 1995, Menlo Park, California: Addison-Wesley Publishing Company.

- For more information about TCP/IP and ONC/NFS, see *TCP/IP and ONC/NFS Internetworking in a UNIX Environment Second Edition* by Michael Santifaller, 1994, Wokingham, England: Addison-Wesley Publishing Company.

- For more information about Requests for Comments (RFCs) and Internet drafts, see the link to the IETF on the Web Resources page http://windows.microsoft.com/windows2000/reskit/webresources.

C H A P T E R   1 2

Interoperability with NetWare

Microsoft® Windows® 2000 provides protocols and services that allow you to integrate Windows 2000 networks with Novell NetWare networks. The following sections discuss the IPX/SPX/NetBIOS Compatible Transport Protocol (NWLink), Windows 2000 Gateway Service for NetWare, and Windows 2000 Client Service for NetWare.

With these features and other Microsoft interoperability products, your organization can support a heterogeneous environment composed of both Windows 2000 and NetWare servers. You can also migrate from NetWare to Windows 2000 using the Directory Services Migration Tool (DSMigrate) for NetWare, provided with Windows 2000.

In This Chapter

Related Information in the Resource Kit

- For information about Windows 2000 IPX routing services, see "IPX Routing" in this book.

- For information about network monitoring, see "Monitoring Network Performance" in the *Microsoft® Windows® 2000 Server Resource Kit Server Operations Guide*.

Windows 2000 Services for NetWare

Microsoft provides several tools for integrating computers running Windows 2000 with computers running Novell Directory Services (NDS) versions 4.*x*, 5.*x*, and 8.*x*, or NetWare 2.*x* and 3.*x* bindery-based servers. Some of these tools are included with Windows 2000 Server or with Windows 2000 Professional, and other tools are available as separate Microsoft products.

IPX/SPX/NetBIOS Compatible Transport Protocol (NWLink)

NWLink is the Windows 2000 implementation of the Internetwork Packet Exchange/Sequenced Packet Exchange (IPX/SPX) protocol, which can be used for connectivity between computers running Windows 2000 and computers running NetWare. NWLink also provides the functionality of NetBIOS and Routing Information Protocol (RIP).

NWLink can also function as either a protocol that connects computers running Windows 2000, Microsoft® Windows NT®, Microsoft® Windows® for Workgroups 3.11, Microsoft® Windows® 95, and Microsoft® Windows® 98, or as a protocol that connects computers running Microsoft® MS-DOS®, when used in combination with a redirector. Additionally, NWLink functions as an alternative transport protocol for servers running Microsoft® Exchange Server, Microsoft® SQL Server™, and Microsoft® SNA Server.

NWLink is included with both Windows 2000 Server and Windows 2000 Professional and installs automatically during Client Service for NetWare or Gateway Service for NetWare installation. Both Gateway Service for NetWare and Client Service for NetWare depend on the NWLink protocol.

Gateway Service for NetWare

Gateway Service for NetWare works with NWLink to provide access to NetWare file, print, and directory services by acting as a gateway through which multiple CIFS clients can access NetWare resources. With Gateway Service for NetWare, you can connect a computer running Windows 2000 Server to NetWare bindery-based servers and NetWare NDS servers through IPX. (If you want to use native IP to connect to a NetWare server, you must use a NetWare client instead.) Multiple Windows-based clients can then use Gateway Service for NetWare as a common gateway to access NetWare file, print, and directory services, without requiring an NCP-compatible.

Gateway Service for NetWare also supports direct access to NetWare services from the computer running Windows 2000 Server, in the same way that Client Service for NetWare supports direct access from the client computer. Additionally, Gateway Service for NetWare supports NetWare login scripts.

Gateway Service for NetWare is included only with Microsoft® Windows® 2000 Server and Microsoft® Windows® 2000 Advanced Server.

Client Service for NetWare

Like Gateway Service for NetWare, Client Service for NetWare works with NWLink to provide access to NetWare file, print, and directory services. However, rather than acting as a gateway for clients, Client Service for NetWare enables clients to connect directly to file and printer services on NetWare bindery-based servers and NetWare servers running NDS through IPX. Client Service for NetWare also supports NetWare login scripts.

Client Service for NetWare is included only with Windows 2000 Professional.

Note Instead of using Client Service for NetWare, you can use Novell Client for Windows 2000.

Directory Services Migration Tool

Directory Services Migration Tool (DSMigrate) enables you to migrate user accounts, groups, files, and permissions from either an NDS or a bindery-based NetWare server to Windows 2000 Active Directory™ directory service. The tool also supports trial migrations, allowing you to model and test the migration before committing it to Active Directory.

Windows NT version 4.0 supports two additional NetWare connectivity tools. At this writing, the tools run only on servers running Windows NT 4.0. For updates, see the ResourceLink link on the Web Resources page http://windows.microsoft.com/windows2000/reskit/webresources.

File and Print Services for NetWare

File and Print Services for NetWare enables a computer running Windows NT 4.0 to emulate a NetWare 3.1x server, directly providing file and print services to IPX-based client computers, such as NetWare computers. The Windows NT 4.0 server appears as any other NetWare server to the NetWare clients, and the clients can access volumes, files, and printers through the server. No changes or additions to the NetWare client software are necessary.

Directory Service Manager for NetWare

Directory Service Manager for NetWare extends Windows NT 4.0 Server directory service features to NetWare servers. With it, you can add NetWare servers to Windows NT domains and manage a single set of user and group accounts that are valid at multiple servers running either Windows NT Server or NetWare. Users need only one user account, with one password, to gain access to these servers.

NWLink

The IPX/SPX/NetBIOS Compatible Transport Protocol (NWLink) is the Microsoft 32-bit implementation of Internetwork Packet Exchange/Sequenced Packet Exchange (IPX/SPX). You must use this protocol if you want to use Gateway Service for NetWare or Client Service for NetWare to connect to NetWare servers.

NWLink provides only the transport protocol to support communications with NetWare file servers. To log on to a NetWare network from a Windows 2000 Professional–based computer, you must use Client Service for NetWare or a NetWare client such as Novell Client for Windows 2000. Alternately, you could use a gateway-based solution by installing Gateway Service for NetWare on a Windows 2000 Server–based computer. Client Service for NetWare and Gateway Service for NetWare are discussed later in this chapter.

Because NWLink is NDIS-compliant, the Windows 2000–based computer can simultaneously run other protocol stacks, such as TCP/IP, through which it can communicate with TCP/IP-based Windows computers. NWLink can bind to multiple network adapters with multiple frame types.

Note Like Windows 2000, NetWare 5.0 uses TCP/IP as the native protocol, and IPX is not installed by default. Neither Client Service for NetWare nor Gateway Service for NetWare support connecting to NetWare resources over IP. Therefore, when you use NWLink to connect to NetWare 5.0 servers you must enable IPX on NetWare 5.0 servers.

NWLink supports two networking application programming interfaces (APIs): NetBIOS and Windows Sockets. These APIs allow communication among computers running Windows 2000 and between computers running Windows 2000 and NetWare servers.

In addition to using NWLink to connect computers running Windows 2000 and computers running NetWare, you can use NWLink whenever you need IPX/SPX. For example, you can use NWLink to connect proxy servers or servers running Microsoft® Systems Management Server (SMS), SNA Servers, SQL Servers, or Exchange Servers, when an IPX/SPX-based protocol is used.

NWLink requires little or no initial client configuration on small non-routed networks.

NWLink Architecture

NWLink provides a comprehensive set of transport and network layer protocols that allow for integration with the NetWare environment. Table 12.1 lists the subprotocols and components and shows their function and associated drivers.

Table 12.1   NWLink Protocols

Protocol	Function	Driver
IPX	Provides connectionless datagram transfer services.	Nwlnkipx.sys
SPX and SPXII	Provide connection-oriented transfer services.	Nwlnkspx.sys
RIP	Provides route and router discovery services.	Nwlnkipx.sys
SAP	Collects and distributes service names and addresses.	Nwlnkipx.sys
NetBIOS	Provides compatible support with NetBIOS for IPX/SPX run on NetWare servers.	Nwlnknb.sys
Forwarder	Provides IPX router support.	Nwlnkfwd.sys

Figure 12.1 illustrates NWLink in the Windows 2000 architecture and the files in which each protocol is implemented.

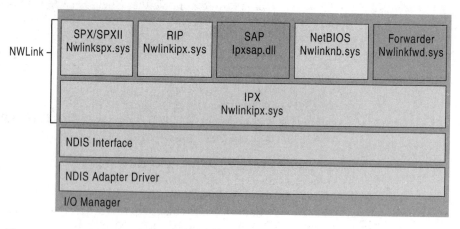

Figure 12.1   NWLink in Windows 2000 Architecture

IPX

IPX is a peer-to-peer networking protocol that provides connectionless datagram transfer services and controls addressing and routing of packets of data within and between network segments. With connectionless transmission, a session does not need to be set up each time packets are transmitted; packets are simply sent out on the wire. This requires less overhead than connection-oriented transmission, in which a session must be established each time packets are transmitted. Therefore, connectionless transmission is best when data is generated in intermittent short bursts.

Because IPX is a connectionless protocol, it does not provide for flow control or acknowledgment that the receiving station has received the datagram packet. Instead, individual datagram packets travel independently to their destination. There is no guarantee that packets arrive at their destination or that they arrive in sequence. However, because transmission on local area networks (LANs) is relatively error-free, IPX is efficient in delivering short burst data on LANs.

NWLink enables application programming for Windows Sockets and remote procedure calls (RPCs) over Windows Sockets. IPX supports Windows Socket IDs for use by Windows Sockets applications. IPX enables NetBIOS, Named Pipes, Mailslot, Network Dynamic Data Exchange (NetDDE), RPC over NetBIOS; and RPC over Named Pipes programming over NBIPX. NWLink also supports other applications that use IPX, through direct hosting. Direct hosting is a feature that allows computers to communicate over IPX, bypassing the NetBIOS layer. Direct hosting can lower overhead and increase throughput.

IPX Packet Structure

The IPX packet is encapsulated within the data field of an IEEE frame and immediately follows the media and data link layer headers (such as Ethernet, Token Ring, or FDDI). The first 30 bytes of an IPX packet contain the header information, shown in Figure 12.2. The remaining bytes contain the packet's data. For example, the data might be a client's request for service, a response from a server, or text information.

Figure 12.2 shows the basic IPX header structure.

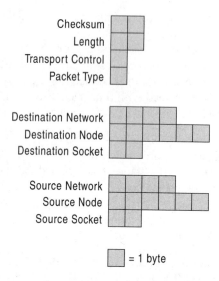

Checksum
Length
Transport Control
Packet Type

Destination Network
Destination Node
Destination Socket

Source Network
Source Node
Source Socket

☐ = 1 byte

Figure 12.2   IPX Header Structure

For more detailed information about IPX or the IPX header structure, see "IPX Routing" in this book.

For more information about IEEE frame types, see "NWLink and Supported IPX Frame Types" later in this chapter.

SPX

SPX is a transport protocol that offers connection-oriented services over IPX. Although connection-oriented service requires overhead for session setup, once a session is established, connection-oriented service requires less overhead for data transmission than connectionless service. Therefore, it works best for utilities that require a continuous connection. SPX provides reliable delivery through sequencing and acknowledgments and verifies successful packet delivery to any network destination by requesting a verification from the destination upon receipt of the data. SPX can track data transmissions consisting of a series of separate packets. If an acknowledgment request brings no response within a specified time, SPX retransmits the request for a total of eight times. If no response is received, SPX assumes the connection has failed.

SPXII

SPXII improves upon SPX in the following ways:

- SPXII allows for more outstanding unacknowledged packets than SPX.

  In SPX, there cannot be more than one outstanding unacknowledged packet at any time, while in SPXII, there can be as many outstanding packets as negotiated by the networked peers at connection setup time.

- SPXII allows for larger packets.

  SPX has a maximum packet size of 576 bytes, while SPXII can use the maximum packet size of the underlying LAN. For example, on an Ethernet network SPXII can use 1518 bytes.

- SPXII provides a packet burst mechanism.

  Packet burst, also known as burst mode, allows the transfer of multiple data packets without requiring that each packet be sequenced and acknowledged individually. By allowing multiple packets to be acknowledged once, burst mode can reduce network traffic on most IPX networks. Additionally, the packet burst mechanism monitors for dropped packets and retransmits only the missing packets.

  In Windows 2000, burst mode is enabled by default.

RIP

NWLink uses RIP over IPX (RIPX) to implement route and router discovery services used by SPX and NBIPX. Clients use RIP to determine the forwarding MAC address for outbound traffic. RIP runs on a layer equivalent to the OSI application layer. The RIP code is implemented within the Nwlnkipx.sys file.

NWLink includes the RIP protocol for Windows-based clients and for computers running Windows 2000 Server that do not have Routing and Remote Access service installed. These computers do not forward packets as routers do, but they use a RIP table to determine where to send packets. RIP clients, such as workstations, can locate the optimal route to an IPX network number by broadcasting a RIP GetLocalTarget route request. Each router that can reach the destination, responds to the GetLocalTarget route request with a single route. Based on the RIP responses from the local routers, the sending station chooses the best router to forward the IPX packet. However, clients using the RIP protocol without Routing and Remote Access service do not forward packets.

The RIP for IPX (RIPX) packet header comes immediately after the IPX packet header. Figure 12.3 shows the packet header.

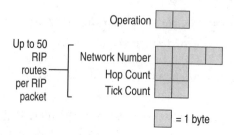

Figure 12.3   Packet Header for RIPX

SAP

Service Advertising Protocol (SAP) is the protocol routers use to distribute the names and addresses of services running on IPX nodes.

SAP clients use SAP broadcasts only when bindery-based or NDS queries fail. SAP clients send the following types of messages:

- SAP clients request the name and address of the nearest server of a specific type by broadcasting a SAP GetNearestServer request.
- SAP clients request the names and addresses of all services, or of all services of a specific type, by broadcasting a SAP general service request.

NWLink includes a subset of the SAP protocol for Windows-based clients and for computers running Windows 2000 Server that do not have IPX router installed.

For information about IPX routing, see "IPX Routing" in this book.

The SAP header immediately follows the IPX header. Figure 12.4 shows the SAP header.

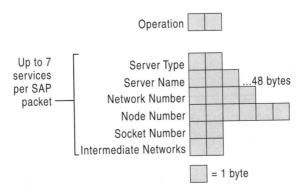

Figure 12.4   SAP Header

NetBIOS Over IPX

To facilitate the operation of NetBIOS-based applications on an IPX internetwork, NetBIOS over IPX (NWLnkNB.sys) provides standard NetBIOS services such as the following:

- Datagrams - single packets sent without acknowledgment. One example of a datagram is a broadcast.
- Sessions - multiple packets sent with acknowledgments between two endpoints.
- Name management - registering, querying, and releasing NetBIOS names.

Figure 12.5 shows the packet structure for NetBIOS over IPX.

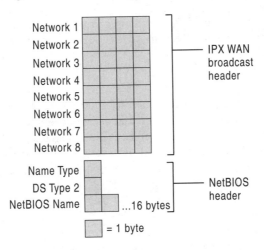

Figure 12.5   Packet Structure for NetBIOS over IPX

NWLnkNB is responsible for formatting NetBIOS-level requests and passing them to NWLink for transmission on the network. NWLnkNB includes the following performance enhancements:

- PiggyBackAck, which is an acknowledgment of previous frames within the response frames.

- A sliding window acknowledgment mechanism, which is a dynamic window–sizing algorithm that allows burst mode to adjust the number of frames that it can send.

Alternatively, computers can communicate directly over IPX, through direct hosting. For information about direct hosting, see "IPX," earlier in this chapter.

Forwarder

The Forwarder component is installed with NWLink but is used only when the Windows 2000–based server is used as an IPX router running Routing and Remote Access service. It operates in kernel mode.

When the IPX router software is activated, the Forwarder component works with the IPX Router Manager and the filtering component to forward packets. The Forwarder component obtains configuration information from the IPX Router Manager and stores a table of the best routes. When the Forwarder component receives an incoming packet, it passes it to the filtering driver so the filtering driver can check for input filters. When it receives an outgoing packet, it first passes it to the filtering driver. Assuming no outgoing filters prevent the packet from being transmitted, the filtering component passes the packet back, and then the Forwarder component forwards the packet over the appropriate interface.

For more information about the Forwarder in Windows 2000 IPX routing services, see "Routing and Remote Access Service" in this book.

Tuning NWLink

When multiple transport protocols are installed, Windows 2000 negotiates network connections in the order that the protocols are prioritized in the network services binding list. For example, if TCP/IP is ranked at the top of the services binding list, Windows 2000 attempts to make network connections with TCP/IP before it attempts to use other transport protocols. If users make the most of their network connections to servers using TCP/IP, this protocol priority would provide the best overall performance. However, if users make the most of their connections to NetWare servers using IPX/SPX, you can improve the overall performance for those users by changing the protocol priorities in their network services binding list, so that Windows 2000 attempts to make network connections with IPX/SPX before it uses the other installed protocols. To check or modify your protocol rankings, see Windows 2000 Help.

Frame Types and Network Numbers

NWLink uses frame types and network numbers to communicate with other computers on the same segment and to provide correct packet routing.

NWLink Auto Detect

In order for a computer running Windows 2000 to connect to computers running IPX/SPX, a frame type and network number must be configured for each computer. This frame type and network number must be identical to that used on the local network segment. The NWLink Auto Detect feature detects the frame type and external network number (also known as the network number) and is the recommended option for configuring these fields.

The Auto Detect feature works as follows:

1. When the NWLink protocol is initialized, it sends a RIPX request using a specific frame type. The RIPX request is a broadcast request for the local network. If a response is not received, NWLink sends additional requests.

2. When a response is received, the frame type for NWLink is set to the frame type of the response, and the IPX network number is set to the value of the Source Network number in the IPX header of the RIP response.

3. If the computer has multiple network adapters attached to different networks, such as Token Ring, FDDI, and Ethernet, you can run Auto Detect for each adapter.

4. If there are multiple RIPX responses, containing multiple network numbers, Auto Detect uses a counting algorithm to determine the most likely network number.

5. If there is no RIPX response to any request, NWLink sets the frame type to Ethernet 802.2 (for Ethernet network adapters) and the network number to 0.

Occasionally, a misconfigured host causes Auto Detect to select an inappropriate frame type and network number combination for the adapter. This is usually caused by an incorrect manual setting on a computer on the network. Because Auto Detect uses the response of the RIPX request, if a computer replies with an incorrect frame type and network number, Auto Detect detects this incorrect configuration and uses it. Auto Detect might also select an incorrect network number if multiple computers responded. It uses a heuristic algorithm to determine the most likely network number but does not validate the packet information it receives.

If the Auto Detect feature selects an inappropriate frame type for a particular adapter, you can manually reset an NWLink frame type or network number for that given adapter. To manually determine the frame type and external network number set on a computer running Windows 2000, execute the IPXROUTE CONFIG command at the command prompt. This is the only way to view IPX information on Windows 2000 servers. Figure 12.6 illustrates the resulting screen.

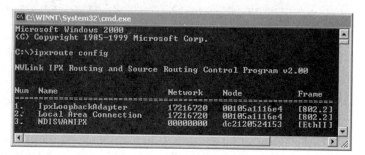

Figure 12.6   Frame Type Displayed in the Command-Line Interface

To manually determine the frame type, internal network number, and external network number set on a server running NetWare, type **CONFIG** on the NetWare server console or inspect the Autoexec.ncf file. Figure 12.7 shows the Autoexec.ncf file.

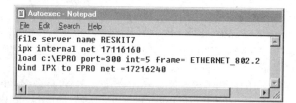

Figure 12.7   Frame Type Displayed in the NetWare Autoexec.ncf File

You can change the frame type and network number on a Windows 2000 computer. You must be a member of the Administrator group to do so.

Caution In most cases, you do not need to change the frame type and network number because Auto Detect should correctly detect them. If you choose an incorrect setting, your client cannot connect to resources using IPX.

▶ **To change the internal network number**

1. In Control Panel, double-click **Network and Dial-up Connections**.

2. Right-click a connection, and then click **Properties**.

3. On the **General** tab, click **NWLink IPX/SPX/NetBIOS Compatible Transport Protocol**, and then click **Properties**.

4. Type a unique value in the **Internal network number** box, and then click **OK**.

▶ **To change the frame type and external network number**

1. In Control Panel, double-click **Network and Dial-up Connections**.

2. Right-click a connection, and then click **Properties**.

3. On the **General** tab, click **NWLink IPX/SPX/NetBIOS Compatible Transport Protocol**, and then click **Properties**.

4. Select **Manual frame type detection**, and then click **Add**.

5. In the **Manual Frame Detection** dialog box, in **Frame type**, click a frame type.

6. In **Network number**, type the appropriate network number, and then click **Add**.

7. Repeat steps 4-6 for each frame type you want to include, and then click **OK**.

NWLink and Supported IPX Frame Types

Both Windows 2000 and NetWare support frame types for Ethernet, Token Ring, and Fiber Distributed Data Interface (FDDI) topologies.

Table 12.2 lists the frame types that Windows 2000 supports.

Table 12.2   Supported Frame Types

Network Type	Supported Frame Types
Ethernet	Ethernet II, 802.2, 802.3, 802.2 Subnet Access Protocol (SNAP)
Token Ring	802.5 and 802.5 SNAP
FDDI	802.2, 802.3, and SNAP

Frame types are based upon the Institute of Electrical and Electronics Engineers, Inc., (IEEE) standards and define packet formats used by various topologies.

Figure 12.8 shows the IEEE defined frame type packet structure.

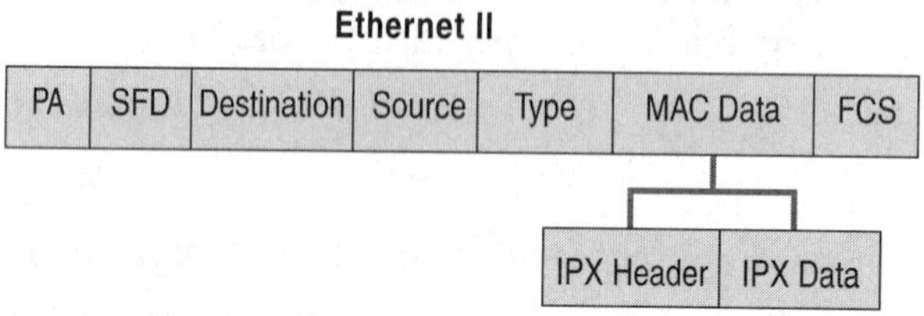

Ethernet II

Figure 12.8   NWLink and Supported IPX Frame Types

Ethernet II

The Ethernet II frame includes a 2-byte Type field that immediately follows the source address. The Type field contains a unique value, called an EtherType, which identifies the receiving computer for which the upper-layer protocol should handle the contents of the Data field.

Ethernet 802.2

Several frame types are based on the IEEE 802.3 standards, which define operations for the physical layer and the media access control (MAC) sublayer. NetWare combines the IEEE 802.3 standard for the physical layer and the IEEE 802.2 standard for operations of the Logical Link Control (LLC) sublayer and refers to the combination of these standards as the Ethernet 802.2 frame type.

Ethernet II and Ethernet 802.2 frames can run on the same network. Because the value in the Ethernet II Type field always equals a number greater than 1,500 and the value in the Ethernet 802.2 Length field always equals a number 1,500 or less, network hardware and software can distinguish between these two frame types; therefore, both can co-exist on the same network.

Subnet Access Protocol

The Subnet Access Protocol (SNAP) frame type is derived from the Ethernet 802.2 frame type. The SNAP portion of the frame is carried in the Data field. This frame type was designed to give individual vendors the ability to assign their own unique values for protocols running on their hardware.

Ethernet 802.3

Like the 802.2 frame, the 802.3 frame differs from the Ethernet II frame by using a Length field in the place of the Type field in Ethernet II. It is often called "802.3 raw" because it does not use the 802.2 LLC header in the Data field.

Token Ring 802.5

The Token Ring protocol is composed of two distinct frame subtypes, the MAC frames and non-MAC frames.

The MAC frames carry management information for the Token Ring network. They carry signaling information and are not passed on by bridges and routers. They reside only on the LAN ring where the packets originate.

The non-MAC frames carry data for Token Ring networks. Non-MAC frames carry data between computer stations on the ring and are passed on by bridges and routers.

The content of fields early in a Token Ring frame can redefine the composition of fields later in the frame.

Network Numbers

NWLink can be configured with two distinctly different types of network numbers for routing purposes: the external network number and the internal network number. NWLink uses an IPX external network number to identify the computer's local network segment within the routed environment. NWLink also uses a virtual network number, known as an internal network number, to identify a logical network inside the computer. The logical network inside the computer is used to provide optimal routing to services running on the computer.

In Windows 2000 you can change both the external network number and internal network number in Control Panel. For information about procedures on manually setting network numbers, see "NWLink Auto Detect," earlier in this chapter.

For more information about network numbers see "IPX Routing" in this book.

External Network Number

The external network number is associated with the physical network adapter and the local area network segment (a segment is analogous to a TCP/IP subnet). The external network number identifies the computer's local segment and is used to facilitate communications within the routed environment. Packets transmitted across the network contain the computer's external network number or, if an internal number exists, the internal network number, along with an appended MAC address to identify the individual computer. All computers on the same network segment that use a given frame type must have the same external network number, and that number must be unique for each network segment.

If the external network number on this segment changes, if you replace a network adapter, or if you connect the computer to a different segment, you might not be able to communicate over IPX. If you lose IPX connectivity, you need to reset the external network number and then, if prompted, reboot the computer.

To determine the external network number and frame type that have been set on a computer running Windows 2000, execute the IPXROUTE CONFIG command in the command-line interface.

To determine the external network number and frame type that have been set on a server running NetWare, enter CONFIG in the command-line interface of the NetWare server or inspect the Autoexec.ncf file.

Note It is possible to run multiple IPX networks over the same physical network segment if those networks use different frame types.

Internal Network Number

The internal network number is used for internal routing purposes. Internal network numbers are used by service-supporting hosts; that is, hosts running services that SAP-based clients need to access. Service-supporting hosts use internal network numbers to help clients determine the optimal route for transmitting packets to services running on the service-supporting hosts. If only external network numbers are used, different routers might send a client host multiple routes with the same route metrics, when only one route is actually optimal. However, if you specify an internal network number, you create a virtual network inside the service-supporting host, and packets are always forwarded to the services running on the service-supporting host using an optimal path. For more information about how the internal network number is used to provide optimal routing, see "IPX Routing" in this book.

By default, an internal network number is not specified. When NWLink is installed, the Auto Detect feature does not detect the internal network number automatically. Instead, NWLink sets the internal network number of 00000000 on the computer's network adapter by default. When set to 00000000, the internal network number is not used.

This default behavior works when NWLink is bound to a single network adapter or to multiple network adapters. However, you must have an internal network number when your computer is acting as a server running Windows 2000 for an application that uses NetWare SAP, such as SQL Server, Microsoft Exchange, or SNA Server.

Depending on your configuration, you might already have an internal network number. File and Print Services for NetWare, Routing and Remote Access service, and the SAP agent automatically install a unique internal network number during its setup procedures. If you have previously installed File and Print Services for NetWare, Routing and Remote Access service, or the SAP agent, you might already have a unique internal network number set for your computer's network adapter.

The default value of zero (00000000) for the internal network number is not seen when you enter the IPXROUTE CONFIG command on the command prompt. However, if you have configured such an internal network number, you can later view it by using **ipxroute config**, or in a trace of a RIP or a SAP broadcast from your computer.

Gateway Service and Client Service

Windows 2000 provides two features that enable Windows-based client computers to access NetWare file, print, and directory services that are located on both NetWare bindery-based servers and on Novell Directory Services (NDS). Gateway Service for NetWare acts as a gateway through which multiple clients can access NetWare resources, and Client Service for NetWare provides a client-based NetWare connectivity solution. Both depend on and work with the NWLink protocol, which is automatically installed when Client Service for NetWare or Gateway Service for NetWare are installed. For more information about NWLink, see "NWLink," earlier in this chapter.

Note To make sure you are in compliance with Novell licensing policies, refer to your Novell licensing agreement.

Gateway Service for NetWare is installed on a Windows 2000 Server–based computer. Through the gateway, multiple Windows 2000 Professional, Windows NT Workstation, Windows 95, and Windows 98 clients can access NetWare file, print, and directory services. Because the gateway provides a single access point to NetWare services, you do not need to install and maintain NetWare client software (such as Client Service for NetWare) on each of your workstations. Gateway Service for NetWare also supports direct access to NetWare services from the computer running Windows 2000 Server, in the same way that Client Service for NetWare supports direct access from the client computer.

Client Service for NetWare is installed on individual Windows 2000 Professional clients and gives each client direct, high performance access to NetWare file, print and directory services. Because Windows 2000 clients configured with Client Service for NetWare connect directly to NetWare servers, they do not need to use a gateway running Gateway Service for NetWare as an intermediary service. For client-based connectivity, clients running Windows 2000, Windows NT, Windows 95, or Windows 98 must use the networking client software provided in their software package or comparable NetWare client software.

Both Gateway Service for NetWare and Client Service for NetWare also provide support for NetWare login scripts. For more information, see "Login Scripts" later in this chapter.

Note Windows 2000 contains an upgrade for NetWare client software previously installed with Windows NT, Windows 95, and Windows 98. This upgrade only applies to computers running NetWare client software earlier than version 4.7 and a version of Windows that was upgraded to Windows 2000. For more information, see the Readme file included with Windows 2000.

Computers running Windows 2000 Server with Gateway Service for NetWare and computers running Windows 2000 Professional with Client Service for NetWare can use pass-through authentication. If a user has the same credentials for a Windows 2000 network and a NetWare network, and the password is synchronized, the user can log on to both networks at once.

When the computer running Windows 2000 Server or Windows 2000 Professional with either Gateway Service for NetWare or Client Service for NetWare installed is booted, the **Log on to Windows** dialog box appears. The user then logs on to the Windows 2000–based network as usual, supplying a user account and password for Windows 2000, and is also authenticated on the NetWare network, provided that the password is synchronized. Users can synchronize their password on Windows-based servers, and NetWare 4.*x* servers through Gateway Service for NetWare or Client Service for NetWare, by pressing CTRL+ALT+DELETE and then entering the new password in the dialog box. For information about how to synchronize passwords, see "Additional Resources," later in this chapter.

Choosing Between Gateway Service and Client Service

Consider the following information when determining whether to use Gateway Service for NetWare or Client Service for NetWare on your Windows 2000–based network to access NetWare services. In general, if you intend to create or indefinitely maintain a heterogeneous environment composed of both Windows 2000 and NetWare servers, consider using Client Service for NetWare. If you intend to migrate gradually from NetWare to Windows 2000 or if you want to reduce administration, consider using Gateway Service for NetWare.

Advantages and Disadvantages of Client Service for NetWare

Client Service for NetWare provides the following advantages:

- Client Service for NetWare allows for user-level security

  Client Service for NetWare allows you to establish user-level security rather than share-level security. With Client Service for NetWare, you can allow users access to individual user home directories (directories where individual user data resides) that are stored on a NetWare volume. Users can then map to their home directory plus any additional volumes to which they have been granted user-level security. On the other hand, to allow users access to individual home directories with Gateway Service for NetWare, you would need to give each user a separate drive letter.

- Client Service for NetWare might perform better than Gateway Service

  Client Service for NetWare communicates directly with NetWare servers, avoiding the potential bottleneck caused by excessive traffic moving through a single network connection.

However, Client Service for NetWare has the following disadvantages:

- Client Service for NetWare requires you to manage multiple user accounts for each user

  For each user, you must create and manage separate user accounts for both Windows 2000 and NetWare. However, you do not need to manage the accounts separately if you are using an additional product. For Windows NT 4.0, Directory Service Manager eliminated the need to create separate user accounts on bindery-based servers. At this writing, this tool works only with Windows NT 4.0 and supports only bindery-based servers. For information about updates, see "Additional Resources" later in this chapter.

- Client Service for NetWare requires more installation and management overhead

  With Client Service for NetWare, you must install and maintain additional Client Service for NetWare software on each Windows 2000 Professional workstation.

- Client Service for NetWare requires you to add IPX to your entire network

  Servers running Windows 2000 and servers running NetWare 5.0 use TCP/IP as the native protocol. However, Client Service for NetWare requires you to use IPX (through NWLink) and does not enable you to restrict IPX to a certain portion of your network. Even if you have clients on only one subnet running the IPX protocol, you might need to route IPX throughout your network.

Advantages and Disadvantages of Gateway Service for NetWare

Gateway Service for NetWare provides the following advantages:

- Gateway Service for NetWare allows you to manage a single user account for each user

   With Windows 2000 Gateway Service for NetWare, the gateway service becomes the central interface for user access to NetWare Service for NetWare and you can perform all Windows 2000 user account management within the Gateway Service for NetWare user interface. You can secure regular share-level permissions and assign users or groups to the access control list (ACL) of each share.

- Gateway Service for NetWare reduces installation overhead

   With Gateway Service for NetWare, you can give clients access to NetWare resources without installing NetWare client software. Thus, you do not need to deploy and maintain network client software (such as Client Service for NetWare) on multiple client computers.

- Gateway Service for NetWare provides protocol isolation for IPX

   With Gateway Service for NetWare, you can isolate the IPX protocol to your local area network, so you do not have to route IPX throughout your network.

However, Gateway Service for NetWare has the following disadvantages:

- Gateway Service for NetWare allows limited user-level security

   With Gateway Service for NetWare, all Windows 2000 users access NetWare resources as if they were the same NetWare user. Gateway Service for NetWare assigns drive letters to separate NetWare files or directories, and then Windows 2000 share-level access is applied to the entire share. Therefore, the only way to provide user-level security using Gateway Service for NetWare is to assign separate drive letters for each user. Because users need to reserve some drive letters for local drives, mapped drives, and other applications, user-level security is impractical if you have a large number of users (more than twenty).

- Gateway Service for NetWare might not perform as well as Client Service for NetWare

   Using Gateway Service for NetWare, the Windows 2000 Server–based computer must act as a gateway between client computers and NetWare servers. All requests for NetWare services are processed through a single gateway connection, creating a potential bottleneck. However, in some cases, Gateway Service for NetWare performs better than Client Service for NetWare; for example, if most of your traffic is SMB rather than NCP traffic.

How Gateway Service for NetWare Works

Gateway Service for NetWare acts as a gateway between the Common Internet File System (CIFS) protocol used on Windows networks and the NetWare Core Protocol (NCP) used on NetWare networks. CIFS, formerly known as SMB, is the native file-sharing protocol in Microsoft Windows 2000. When you enable this gateway, Windows network clients can access NetWare services through the Gateway Service for NetWare gateway located on the Windows 2000 Server.

Figure 12.9 shows multiple Windows client computers accessing NetWare services through a Windows 2000 server acting as a gateway. The CIFS-based protocol traffic is translated to NCP protocol, which is then passed to the NetWare server.

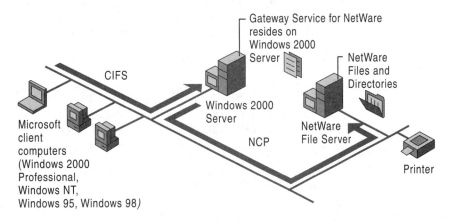

Figure 12.9   Gateway Service for NetWare Access

To give Windows-based clients access to a NetWare volume, the Windows 2000 Server–based computer running Gateway Service for NetWare redirects one of its drives to the NetWare volume and then shares that drive to the Windows-based clients. The Windows 2000 Server gateway uses a NetWare account to create a validated connection to the NetWare server. This connection appears on the computer running Windows 2000 Server as a redirected drive. When you share the redirected drive, it performs like any other shared resource, appearing to users as a Windows 2000 Server resource although it is actually a resource on a NetWare server.

For example, suppose you want to create a gateway from computer A (running Gateway Service for NetWare) to the Data volume on the NetWare bindery-based server B. When activating the gateway, you specify \\B\Data in the **Configure Gateway** dialog box as the NetWare resource, and then you specify a share name for Windows 2000–based clients, such as Nw Data. Windows clients then refer to this resource as \\A\Nw_Data.

After the gateway connection is established, it is disconnected only if the computer running Windows 2000 Server is turned off, if the administrator disconnects the shared resource or disables the gateway, or if a network problem prevents access to the NetWare server. Logging off the computer running Windows 2000 Server does not, by itself, disconnect the gateway.

Note Because requests from Windows-based networking clients are processed through a single connection between the Windows 2000 gateway server and the NetWare server, access is slower with Gateway Service for NetWare than direct access from the Windows client to the NetWare network using Client Service for NetWare. Windows clients that require frequent access to NetWare resources should use local client software (such as Client Service for NetWare or Novell Client for Windows 2000) to achieve higher performance. For more information about deciding between Gateway Service for NetWare and Client Service for NetWare, see "Choosing Between Gateway Service and Client Service" earlier in this chapter.

Gateway Service for NetWare Packet Translation

When you use Gateway Service for NetWare to transmit data between the Windows 2000 CIFS protocol and the Novell NCP protocol, conversion occurs within the gateway by means of the Nwrdr.sys redirector.

Figure 12.10 shows how a CIFS packet is translated to an NCP packet and sent to the NetWare server. First, a Windows client sends a CIFS request. A CIFS request can come from a variety of Windows-based networking clients over a variety of network transport protocols. For example, a CIFS request might come from a Windows client dialing into the network using Routing and Remote Access service, or it might come from a Windows client attached directly to the network using TCP/IP, IPX/SPX, or NetBEUI.

When the networking client sends out the CIFS request to the Windows 2000 Server–based computer running Gateway Service for NetWare, it is initially picked up by the Server service (Srv.sys).

Next, if the request is a file manipulation request (a request that requires a file handle to be returned), the Server service passes the share name, file path, and file name enclosed within the packet, to the Windows 2000 I/O manager.

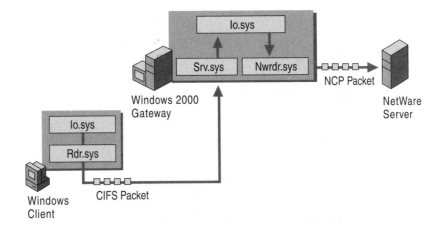

Figure 12.10   Gateway Service for NetWare Packet Translation

Next, the Windows 2000 I/O manager (Io.sys) uses the file object name to call into Nwrdr.sys redirector, passing Nwrdr.sys information on the security token of the object that sent the CIFS request. Based on the security token, Nwrdr.sys determines if the request was from a local account or was a remote request. If the request was a remote request, Nwrdr.sys uses the gateway credentials (established upon gateway entry when sending the file manipulation NCP to the NetWare file server.

Next, Nwrdr.sys returns the file handle to the Windows 2000 I/O manager, which then returns the file handle to Server service. CIFS traffic related to this file manipulation request (for example, if the file manipulation request was to open a file for reading) is sent directly to Nwrdr.sys by the Server service using the file handle.

From Nwrdr.sys, the request is passed to the NetWare server.

How Client Service for NetWare Works

Client Service for NetWare uses a subset of Gateway Service for NetWare code. You install it on Windows 2000 clients so that they can access NetWare services directly. Unlike Gateway Service for NetWare, clients using Client Service for NetWare do not use the Windows 2000 Gateway to translate CIFS protocol to NCP protocol.

Instead, a Windows 2000 Professional computer running Client Service for NetWare creates NCP protocol packets and passes them directly to the network, as shown in Figure 12.11. The packet is then picked up by the NetWare server.

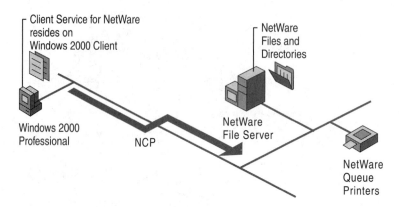

Figure 12.11   Client Service for NetWare Access

When a drive is mapped to a NetWare volume, the computer running Windows Professional uses a NetWare account to create a validated connection to the NetWare server. This connection appears on the computer running Windows 2000 Professional as a redirected drive.

For example, suppose you want to create a connection from computer A (running Client Service for NetWare) to the NetWare \\B\Server1\Org_Unit.Org\Data volume on the NetWare NDS-based server B. You would simply create the connection by using **Map Network drive** or the **net use** command-line utility and specifying the path \\B\Server1\Org_Unit.Org\Data for the NetWare resource. For information about mapping drives, see the Windows 2000 Professional Help.

After the mapped connection is established, it is disconnected only if a network problem prevents access to the NetWare server, if the drive is manually disconnected, or if the computer running Windows 2000 Professional is turned off. The mapped drive is then reestablished when the user logs on to the network.

Note Because requests from Windows Professional client using Client Service for NetWare are processed through a dedicated single connection to the NetWare server, access is faster than with shared access through a Gateway Service for NetWare gateway. For more information about deciding between Gateway Service for NetWare and Client Service for NetWare, see "Choosing Between Gateway Service and Client Service" earlier in this chapter.

Client Service for NetWare Packet Translation

Packets are redirected to NetWare file and print servers through Client Service for NetWare similarly to Gateway Service for NetWare, except that they are executed on the Windows 2000–based client. As Figure 12.12 shows, the packets pass through Io.sys, then through the Nwrdr.sys redirector, and then they are transmitted onto the LAN using the NCP protocol.

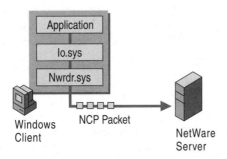

Figure 12.12   Client Service for NetWare Packet Translation

Configuring Gateway Service and Client Service

Because connectivity is a cross-platform issue, whether you choose to use Gateway Service for NetWare or Client Service for NetWare to establish and maintain connectivity between Windows 2000 and NetWare, it is necessary to configure both the Windows 2000–based network and the NetWare network.

Preparing the NetWare Server for Gateway Service and Client Service

For both Gateway Service for NetWare and Client Service for NetWare, it is necessary to create accounts and set up access rights on the NetWare network. You can use the NetWare Syscon utility or the NetWare NDS NWadmin utility to do so.

Important   Neither Gateway Service for NetWare nor Client Service for NetWare support access to the NetWare NWAdmin utility. To use the NetWare NWAdmin utility you need to log on to the NetWare NDS server through a client-based computer that has NetWare client software installed, such as Novell Client for Windows 2000.

The following sections explain which accounts you need to set up.

Preparing the NetWare Server for Gateway Service for NetWare

To establish connectivity to NetWare resources for a Windows 2000 Server–based computer running Gateway Service for NetWare, you need to create user and group accounts.

You must first create a unique user account on the NetWare network to serve as the NetWare interface for the Windows 2000 Server–based gateway computer running Gateway Service for NetWare. The password for the NetWare user account must be identical to the password used to enable the Windows 2000 Server gateway, described in "Configuring a Gateway on the Windows 2000 Server–Based Computer" later in this chapter.

You must also create a unique NetWare group account named NTGATEWAY. You must create this account on the NetWare network. The NTGATEWAY group account acts as a common access point to NetWare resources for all Windows 2000 Server gateway users; therefore, you must set appropriate trustee access rights on the NTGATEWAY group account for all the NetWare resources that the group must access.

Finally, make the NetWare user account that you created a member of the NTGATEWAY group account.

Preparing the NetWare Server for Client Service for NetWare

To establish connectivity to NetWare resources for a Windows 2000 Professional computer running Client Service for NetWare, you need to create a unique user account on the NetWare network and set the necessary rights for the user's resource needs. You or the user must also synchronize the passwords.

Configuring a Gateway Service on the Windows 2000 Server–Based Computer

Once the NetWare user account is a member of the NetWare NTGATEWAY group account, and you have administrative permission to create a share on the local Windows 2000 Server–based computer, you can create a Windows 2000 Server gateway.

Caution   Before you install Windows 2000 Gateway Service for NetWare, you must remove any existing NetWare redirectors installed previously on your Windows NT–based server computer, such as Novell Client for Windows 2000. If prompted, restart your computer.

Installing Gateway Service for NetWare

Install Gateway Service for NetWare on the Windows 2000 Server–based computer in order to use it as a gateway.

▶ **To install Gateway Service for NetWare**

1. In the properties for your connection, on the **General** tab, click **Install**.

2. In the **Select Network Component Type** dialog box, click **Client**, and then click **Add**.

   Click **Gateway (and Client) Services for NetWare** if you are installing a server gateway, and then click **OK**.

3. In the **Select NetWare Logon** dialog box, enter the name of the preferred server to which the Windows 2000 Server–based computer is to attach if you are running a bindery-based server version of NetWare.

   –Or–

   Click the **Default Tree and Context** button and type the correct tree and context names, if you are running an **NDS** version of NetWare. Select the **Run Login Script** option if you are running a login script, and then click **OK**.

Note   Although Gateway Service for NetWare and Client Service for NetWare enable access to NetWare file, print, and directory services from Windows 2000, the correct user accounts, necessary rights for resources, appropriate group rights, and associated login scripts need to be configured on the NetWare servers. Contact your NetWare administrator or see your NetWare documentation for more information.

For more information about the preferred server, the default tree, and context and how to choose between them, see "Selecting the Default Tree and Context or the Preferred Server" later in this chapter.

After you have installed Gateway Service for NetWare, you can change your configuration from the Gateway Service for NetWare icon in Control Panel. The **Gateway Service for NetWare** dialog box, as shown in Figure 12.13, appears.

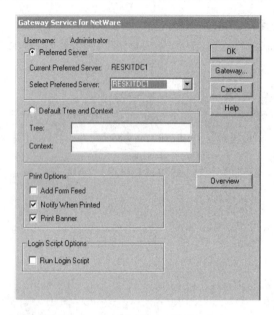

Figure 12.13   Gateway Service for NetWare Dialog Box

Within this dialog box, you can also specifyprint options. You can also select **Run Login Script** if you choose to execute a NetWare login script when you log on to the NetWare network through Gateway Service for NetWare.

Configuring the Windows 2000 Gateway

To enable the Windows 2000 Server gateway, click **Gateway** on the **Gateway Service for NetWare** dialog box. The **Configure Gateway** dialog box, shown in Figure 12.14, is displayed. Select **Enable Gateway** in the **Configure Gateway** dialog box. Enter the gateway account name you wish to call this gateway connection and enter the password. The password must be identical to the password for the user account that you previously created on the NetWare server. You need to do this only once for each server that acts as a gateway.

Note If your account is an NDS account, you must enter the full distinguished name for the user account. For example, you would need to add Jdoe.Sales.Milan.Eu.Reskit rather than Jdoe.

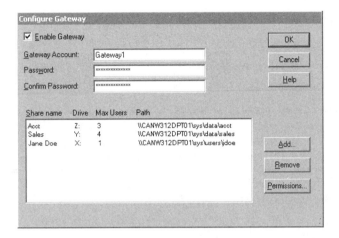

Figure 12.14   Configure Gateway Dialog Box

Establishing Shares and Permissions

After you have installed Gateway Service for NetWare and configured the gateway, you can establish shares and permissions. To create a share, click **Add** in the **Configure Gateway** dialog box. In the appropriate text boxes, type the share name, network path, drive mapping, and the user limit for that particular share. To complete the configuration, set user permissions on the share for an appropriate access level to NetWare resources.

In the **Configure Gateway** dialog box you can set up multiple shares to accommodate user access needs. By setting appropriate shares and permissions on the Windows 2000–based gateway, you can control which directories, files, and print queues a user can access on the NetWare server.

Configuring a Gateway Printer

When the appropriate user and group accounts are established, the necessary rights are set on the NetWare servers, and Gateway Service for NetWare is installed correctly on the Windows 2000–based server, you can configure and establish a connection to a NetWare-based printer through the Windows 2000 Server–based gateway. For more information about setting up a gateway printer share, click the **Overview** button on the **Gateway Service for NetWare** dialog box.

Configuring Client Service for NetWare on Windows 2000 Professional

When you have set up the NetWare user account, you can install and configure Client Service for NetWare on the Windows 2000 Professional computer.

Caution Before you install Windows 2000 Client Service for NetWare, you must remove any existing NetWare redirectors, such as Novell Client for Windows 2000, and then restart your computer.

Installing Client Service for NetWare

Install Client Service for NetWare on the computer running Windows 2000 Professional.

▶ **To install Client Service for NetWare**

1. In the properties for your connection, on the **General** tab, click **Install**.

2. In the **Select Network Component Type** dialog box, click **Client**, and then click **Add**.

3. In the **Select Network Client** dialog box, highlight **Client Service for NetWare**.

4. In the **Select NetWare Logon** dialog box, enter the name of the preferred server to which the Windows 2000 Server–based computer is to attach if you are running a bindery-based server version of NetWare.

   –Or–

   Click the **Default Tree and Context** button and type the correct tree and context names, if you are running an **NDS** version of NetWare. Select the **Run Login Script** option if you are running a login script, and then click **OK**.

Note Although Gateway Service for NetWare and Client Service for NetWare enable access to NetWare file, print, and directory services from Windows 2000, the correct user accounts, necessary rights for resources, appropriate group rights, and associated login scripts need to be configured on the NetWare servers.

Contact your NetWare administrator or see your NetWare documentation for more information.

After you have installed Client Service for NetWare, you can change your configuration from the Client Service for NetWare icon in Control Panel. The **Client Service for NetWare** dialog box appears.

Within this dialog box, you can also specify print options. You can also select **Run Login Script** if you choose to execute a NetWare login script when the gateway service is initiated.

Selecting the Default Tree and Context or the Preferred Server

To access NetWare services through Gateway Service for NetWare or Client Service for NetWare, you must specify either the correct default tree and context for the user or workgroup or the correct preferred server.

If users need to connect to NDS resources, you should specify the tree and context.

–Or–

If users need to connect to bindery-based resources, you should specify a preferred server.

Specifying the Default Tree and Context in an NDS Environment

In Novell Directory Services (NDS), tree refers to the NDS hierarchical Directory structure, and context refers to the location of an object in the Directory tree. If there is only one tree in an organization, the tree is easy to select and specify. The context, on the other hand, is not so obvious. However, in order to locate the necessary network resources for the particular user object, you must define the context correctly when accessing NDS servers through Client Service for NetWare or Gateway Service for NetWare.

Note When accessing an NDS environment, the most frequent problem with accessing files or services results from setting an incorrect context. If you set an incorrect context, you cannot authenticate.

As shown in Figure 12.15, for example, **Reskit**, located at the top of the NDS Directory tree, is the actual name of the root object.

You specify the context in the **Client Service for NetWare** or **Gateway Service for NetWare** dialog box. You can type in either the typefull name or typeless name formats.

Within the tree, the context in typefull name format for the user JDOE is ou=sales.ou=milan.ou=eu.o=reskit, and the context in the typeless name format is sales.milan.eu.reskit.

Both the typefull name and the typeless name formats are valid entries in the **Client Service for NetWare** or **Gateway Service for NetWare** dialog box.

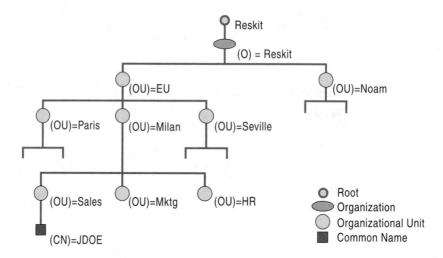

Figure 12.15   NDS Directory Tree

Setting a Preferred Server in a Bindery-Based Server Environment

In a NetWare bindery-based server environment, you must direct the Windows 2000–based computer running Gateway Service for NetWare or Client Service for NetWare to the NetWare server where the Windows 2000 user and group accounts with the appropriate rights are located. To direct the Windows 2000–based computer to the NetWare server, select the appropriate NetWare server as the preferred server. Your computer can then log on to the NetWare server. Once you are logged on to a bindery server, you can attach to another server.

If you do not want to set a preferred server in the **Client Service for NetWare** dialog box, click **None**. Your computer sends out a get nearest server request, and the first server that responds becomes a SAP agent. You are not authenticated to this server, but you can use it for browsing (viewing other servers attached on the network), as when you enter the NetWare slist command.

Installing Multiple Gateways

If you use Gateway Service for NetWare and you have a high volume of traffic, you can install multiple gateways, as shown in Figure 12.16, to balance the traffic load. However, the NTGATEWAY group account is still the only access point on the NetWare network. To administer each gateway account separately, you must create individual NetWare user accounts for each gateway, then make those user accounts members of the NetWare NTGATEWAY group account.

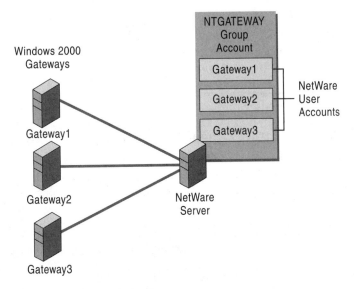

Figure 12.16   Multiple Windows 2000 Gateways

Establishing Security

When you install Gateway Service for NetWare on a computer running Windows 2000 Server and connect it to the NetWare NTGATEWAY group account, you can control security for that connection at two different locations:

- You can add trustee rights on the NTGATEWAY group account on the NetWare network server.

- You can set permission restrictions on the Windows 2000 Gateway.

For simplest management, consider adding trustee rights on the NTGATEWAY group account. Because the NTGATEWAY group account is the single interface to the NetWare network, trustee rights set up on NTGATEWAY apply to all users using that account. Therefore, you must set up trustee rights that satisfy the access needs of all users going through that account. For additional security, you can then set all security restrictions by adjusting access permissions at the Windows 2000 gateway.

Suppose you have several different users who want to have home directories on the NetWare server, and each user wants to limit access for the home directory. The best way to provide separate security is to use a client such as Client Service for NetWare. However, you could provide separate security for a few users by creating a separate share for each user on the Windows 2000 gateway server, then assigning trustee rights for each share.

Keep in mind that each share uses one drive letter, as shown in Figure 12.14. Thus, each share you create uses at least one drive letter. To determine how many gateways you can create, determine the number of available drive letters.

For information about how to add trustee rights to the NetWare server, consult your NetWare documentation or contact Novell.

Files Installed with Gateway Service, Client Service, and NWLink

Table 12.3 describes the files that are installed when Gateway Service for NetWare is installed on a computer running Windows 2000 Server or when Client Service for NetWare is installed on the computer running Windows 2000 Professional.

When Gateway Service for NetWare or Client Service for NetWare is installed on a Windows 2000 computer NWLink is installed automatically.

Table 12.3   Gateway Service and Client Service Files

File Names	Description	Location
Nwlnkipx.sys, Nwlnknb.sys, and Nwlnkspx.sys	Basic drivers that provide NetWare Link Protocol support.	%windir%\system32\drivers
Ipxroute.exe	Diagnostic tool.	%windir%\system32
Nwlnkflt.sys, Nwlnkfwd.sys	Routing and Remote Access service filter driver and forwarder table manager (installed if the Routing and Remote Access service feature is installed).	%windir%\system32\drivers
Nwrdr.sys	Client for NetWare servers.	%windir%\system32\drivers
Nwnks.dll, Nwapi32.dll, Nwapi16.dll	Client, service, and redirector.	%windir%\system32
NetWare.drv,Nw16.exe, Vwipxspx	Provide support for older 16-bit applications.	%windir%\system32
Nwscript.exe	Login script processor.	%windir%\system32
Nwc.cpl	Control Panel.	%windir%\system32
Nwdoc.hlp, Nwdocgw.hlp	Help files.	%windir%\system32\help
Nwcfg.dll	For client installation and uninstallation.	%windir%\system32
Perfnw.dll	Performance counters.	%windir%\system32
Nwevent.dll	Event log strings.	%windir%\system32

NetWare Administration Through Windows 2000

When access to NetWare is established on the Windows 2000–based computer either through Gateway Service for NetWare or Client Service for NetWare, you can administer most NetWare server functions and manipulate NetWare resources.

Administering NetWare Servers

You cannot administer NetWare servers directly through servers running NetWare 3.*x* or 4.*x*. Although you can perform some administrative tasks, you cannot set up users, user rights, and so on. Instead, you can use a networked Windows 2000–based computer to act as the system console and control the administration of the NetWare server.

When you configure a Windows 2000 server with Client Service for NetWare or Gateway Service for NetWare, you can use it to access bindery-based NetWare utilities, such as System Console (syscon), Remote Console (rconsole), and Printer Console (pconsole). In a NetWare bindery-based server environment, use syscon, the primary administration tool, to set up user accounts, define policies, and grant user access permissions to the NetWare network.

Note Although Windows 2000 Gateway Service for NetWare and Client Service for NetWare support connections to NDS servers, you cannot use Virtual Loadable Modules (VLM) or other utilities specific to NDS. To access these utilities, you need to install the Novell Client for Windows 2000.

Table 12.4 lists the most commonly used 16-bit NetWare administrative utilities that you can run from a Windows 2000–based computer. Not all versions of NetWare support all these utilities. Novell has replaced some utilities and updated others. Even if NetWare supports these utilities, they might not perform consistently from version to version when you run them from Windows 2000.

Table 12.4   16-Bit NetWare Utilities

Utility	Functions	Notes
Chkvol	Provides information about any volume on the NetWare server.	NetWare 4.x and later do not support this utility. Use the **ndir [path] /vol** command.
Colorpal	Provides ability to modify NetWare's default color scheme.	
Dspace	Limits the disk space a user can use on a volume.	NetWare 4.x and later do not support this utility. Use the **filer** command.
Fconsole	Broadcasts messages, views current user connections, and alters status of file server.	Windows 2000 does not support all menus. Down File Server does not function properly.
Filer	Modifies the directory's owner, creation date, and timestamps.	
Flag	Views and changes attributes of files in a given directory.	You might have problems with NetWare 5.0.
Flagdir	Views and changes attributes of subdirectories in a given directory.	NetWare 4.x and later do not support this utility. Use the **flag path attributes /do** command.
Grant	Grants trustee rights to users or groups in a given file or directory.	NetWare 4.x and later do not support this utility. Use the **rights path attributes /name=l/group=usernames** command.
Help	Provides online information about NetWare utilities, system messages, and concepts.	Normal syntax is *<utility name>* **/help**
Listdir	Views directories, subdirectories, and their inherited rights mask, effective rights, and creation dates.	NetWare 4.x and later do not support this utility. Use **ndir [path] /do** command.
Ncopy	Provides ability to copy one or more files from one network directory to another.	You might have problems with NetWare 4.x and NetWare 5.0.
Ndir	Views information on file names, sizes, and their modification, access, creation, and archive dates.	You might have problems when using Windows 2000 with NetWare 5.0.
Pconsole	Provides the administrator with the tools necessary to manage print servers.	Change Current Server does not work

continued

Table 12.4   16-Bit NetWare Utilities *(continued)*

Utility	Functions	Notes
Psc	Views status on and controls print servers and network printers.	NetWare 5.0 does not support this utility.
Rconsole	Provides a remote view of the NetWare system console. The console functions can be performed on the remote console.	
Remove	Provides ability to delete a user or group from the trustee list of a file or directory.	NetWare 4.x and later do not support this utility. Use the **rights** command.
Revoke	Provides ability to revoke trustee rights from a user or group in a file or directory.	NetWare 4.x and later do not support this utility. Use the **rights** command.
Rights	Views the effective rights in a file or directory.	You might have problems with NetWare 5.0.
Send	Sends a brief message from one workstation to another, or to multiple workstations.	Send command is not supported when connected to an NDS server. You might have problems using this command with Windows 2000 and NetWare 4.x or NetWare 5.0.
Session	Performs temporary drive mappings, create, change, and delete search drives, view groups on network, or send messages.	Search mapping option not supported because it always maps as root. Novell replaced session with the **netuser** command in NetWare 4.x.
Setpass	Sets or changes passwords on one or more file servers.	Use this command only for bindery servers. Use CTRL+ALT+DEL to change NDS passwords.
Settts	Provides ability to verify that the Transaction Tracking System (TTS) is tracking transactions.	NetWare 5.0 does not support this utility.
Slist	Provides a list of file servers on the internetwork.	NetWare 4.x and later do not support this utility. Use the **nlist server** command.
Syscon	Used to set up user accounts, define policies, and grant user access permissions to the NetWare network.	NetWare 4.x and later do not support this utility.

continued

Table 12.4   16-Bit NetWare Utilities *(continued)*

Utility	Functions	Notes
Tlist	Provides ability to view the trustee list of a directory or a file.	NetWare 4.*x* and later do not support this utility. Use the **rights** command.
Userlist	Views list of current users for given file server, each user's connection number, time at which the user logged on, and network address.	Novell does not support this utility in NetWare 4.*x* or greater. Use the **nlist /A /B** command.
Volinfo	Views information about each volume on NetWare file servers.	If update interval equals 5, command executes very slowly. NetWare 4.*x* and later do not support this utility. Use the **filer** command.
Whoami	Views information on logged-on users, user name on each server, file servers to which users are attached, groups to users belong, and rights.	Displays only bindery connection when connected to an NDS server.

Note For information about NetWare administration utilities, see your NetWare documentation.

Many Windows 2000 commands are provided as equivalents to NetWare commands and can perform functions on the NetWare server through Windows 2000. Table 12.5 shows NetWare utilities and their Windows 2000 equivalents.

Table 12.5   NetWare Utilities and Their Windows 2000 Equivalents

NetWare Utility	Windows 2000 Equivalent
Slist	net view /network:nw
Attach, capture, login, and logout	net use
Map	net use
Map root	net use \server\share\
Capture (to make MS-DOS and Windows applications print to a specific port)	net use

Additionally, you can use the Printers folder to manipulate and connect to a printer.

> **Caution** The NetWare **attach**, **capture**, **login**, and **logout** utilities are not
> supported in Windows 2000 and can cause errors when executed through a
> computer running Windows 2000.

To simplify network management, you can run multiple sessions of the
administration tools on a single Windows 2000–based computer. You can open
separate windows on one computer to monitor multiple NetWare servers at once.

▶ **To connect to additional NetWare servers**

1. Click **Start**, point to **Programs**, click **Accessories**, and click **Windows
   Explorer**.
2. On the **Tools** menu, click **Map Network Drive**.
3. In the **Drive** text box, enter a drive letter, if necessary.
4. In the **Folder** text box, type the path to the NetWare server.
5. Click **Finish**.

Windows 2000 and NetWare Security

Although Windows 2000 and NetWare security structures are not directly
equivalent, you can maintain security from one security structure to another when
transmitting data from one security structure to the other.

The following sections describe how Microsoft permissions are translated to
NetWare rights in a heterogeneous environment composed of Windows 2000
servers and workstations and NetWare servers.

Windows 2000 Permissions

You can protect Windows 2000 FAT partitions and partitions using the version of
NTFS file system included with Windows 2000 against network access using
share level security. However, you can protect Windows NT file system NTFS
partitions only with user-level security.

NetWare Trustee Rights

NetWare file security is similar to NTFS security because you can control group and user abilities to access files, called *rights* in NetWare. A NetWare trustee right, which is equivalent to a Windows 2000 permission is a rule associated with an object (usually a folder, file, or printer) that regulates which users can gain access to the object and in what manner. Most often the creator or owner of the object sets the permissions for the object.

The primary design difference between Windows 2000 permissions and NetWare trustee rights are that Windows 2000 permissions are subtractive while NetWare trustee rights are additive. When you create folders and files in Windows 2000, full access is granted and then access rights can be subtracted or restricted, whereas in NetWare when you create a directory or file, access is denied and then access rights need to be added.

NetWare uses a combination of trustee assignments and inherited rights masks or filters to establish security settings. The intersection of these two access control mechanisms determine the actual access rights, known as NetWare effective rights, that a user or group has for a particular directory or file. There are eight NetWare directory rights settings: Read, Write, Create, Erase, Modify, File Scan, Access Control, and Supervisor.

The individual NetWare directory rights, their abbreviations, and their descriptions are listed in Table 12.6.

Table 12.6   NetWare Directory Rights

Directory Rights	Description
Read (R)	Read data from an existing file.
Write (W)	Write data to an existing file.
Create (C)	Create a new file or subdirectory.
Erase (E)	Delete an existing files or directory.
Modify (M)	Rename and change attributes of a file.
File Scan (F)	List the contents of a directory.
Access Control (A)	Control the rights of other users to access files or directories.
Supervisor (S)	Automatically allowed all rights.

Windows 2000 Folder Permissions and NetWare Directory Rights

Table 12.7 compares Windows 2000 folder permissions to NetWare directory rights.

Table 12.7   Windows 2000 Folder Permission to NetWare Directory Rights

Windows 2000 Folder Permissions	Corresponding NetWare Directory Rights
List Folder Contents	File Scan (F)
Read	Read, File Scan (RF)
Write	Write, Create, Modify (WCM)
Modify	Read, Write, Create, Erase, Modify, File Scan (RWCEMF)
Full Control	Supervisor (S)

Windows 2000 File Permissions and NetWare File Rights

Table 12.8 compares Windows 2000 file permissions to NetWare file rights.

Table 12.8   Windows 2000 File Permissions to NetWare File Rights

Windows 2000 File Permissions	Corresponding NetWare File Rights
Read	Read (R)
Modify	Read, Write, Erase, Modify (RWEM)
Full Control	Supervisor (S)

Windows 2000 and NetWare File Attributes

NetWare file attributes, also known as flags, are not exactly the same as Windows 2000 file attributes. Table 12.9 shows how Windows 2000 file attributes correspond to NetWare file attributes when you open a NetWare file through Gateway Service for NetWare or Client Service for NetWare. The four attributes below are actually a subset of many attributes supported by NetWare. Windows 2000 does not support any additional NetWare file and directory attributes.

Table 12.9   Windows 2000 and NetWare File Attributes

Windows 2000 File Attributes	NetWare File Attributes
A (Archive)	A (Archive needed)
S (System)	Sy (System file)
H (Hidden)	H (Hidden)
R (Read-only)	Ro (Read-only), Di (Delete inhibit), Ri (Rename inhibit)

Gateway Service for NetWare does not support the following NetWare file attributes: Dc (Don't Compress), Ci (Copy Inhibit), Dm (Don't Migrate), Ic (Immediate Compress), P (Purge), Ri (Rename Inhibit), Ra (Read Audit), Rw (Read Write), S (Sharable), T (Transactional), I (Index), and X (Execute Only). These attributes vary between different NetWare versions.

When you copy a file from a Windows or Windows 2000 Professional–based network client to the NetWare file server by means of Client Service for NetWare or Gateway Service for NetWare, the A, S, H, and R attributes are assigned the corresponding NetWare A, Sy, H, and Ro attributes.

When you use a computer running Client Service for NetWare or Gateway Service for NetWare to access NetWare servers and you need to set attributes that are not supported in Client Service for NetWare or Gateway Service for NetWare, you can use NetWare utilities, such as **filer**, **rights**, or the **flag** command from a command prompt to set those attributes.

NDS Object and Property Rights

The NetWare NDS security structure adds NDS object and NDS property rights to the directory and file rights that exist in the NetWare bindery-based server security structure. In NDS, a network structure is organized through the use of NDS objects. Objects are components of the NDS hierarchical tree structure. The tree structure includes the following:

- Root objects at the top of the tree.
- Container objects, which are composed of various organizational units.
- Leaf objects such as users, groups, servers, and volumes.

The following NDS object settings exist: Supervisor, Browse, Create, Delete, and Rename.

Properties are contained within an object and are attributes that represent that object. For instance a user object can contain properties, such as a user telephone number, office location, and title. Property rights are implemented as a separate security structure than object rights in the NetWare NDS security structure. Therefore, you can configure security separately for objects and object properties. The following five object properties exist: Supervisor, Compare, Read, Write, and Add/Delete Self.

Note NDS object and property rights apply only to NetWare NDS volumes, and you can manipulate them only by using the NetWare network operating system software.

Accessing NetWare Volumes

You can access NetWare volumes either through the Windows 2000 graphical user interface or through the Windows 2000 command-line interface.

▶ **To connect to a NetWare volume using the graphical user interface**

1. On the desktop, double-click **My Network Places**.

2. If only Windows 2000–based or Windows NT–based network resources are shown, double-click **Entire Network**, and if you still do not see NetWare resources, on the left pane click **Entire contents,** and then double-click **NetWare or Compatible Network**. Tree icons for NDS trees and computer icons for individual NetWare computers appear.

3. Double-click a tree or computer to see its contents; you can double-click the resulting object, computer, or volume to see volumes or folders.

4. When you find the volume or folder you want to access, double-click it to expand it.

   –Or–

   To map a local drive to the volume or folder, click the volume or folder, and then click **Map Network Drive**.

Note When you map a network drive, by default you are connected under the user name and password you used to log on. To connect under a different user name, type the user name in the **Connect As** box.

The following procedures illustrate how to connect to a NetWare volume using the command-line interface.

▶ **To connect to a volume to which you are not authenticated**

- At the command prompt, type:

`net use <drive>: <UNCpath or NetWarepath> /user:.cn.ou.ou.o password`

where *cn* is the NDS common name, *ou* is the organizational unit, and *o* is the organization. The tree location, user name, and context can be typed in either the name type or the typeless name format at the command prompt.

▶ **To connect to a volume to which you are authenticated**

- At the command prompt, type:

```
net use <drive>: <UNCpath or NetWarepath>
```

For example, to redirect the G drive to the folder \Data\Mydata of the A volume on server B using UNC naming syntax, type:

```
net use G: \\B\A\data\mydata
```

If you see the error message, "The password is invalid for *<server name>**<volume name>*[*<directory name>*...]," then your user name and password are not valid and you cannot be authenticated. Follow the procedure "To connect to a volume to which you are authenticated," earlier in this section.

Note When you connect to NetWare file resources using the command-line interface, you can use the next available drive letter by replacing the drive letter with an asterisk (*) in the syntax. For example,

```
net use * <UNCname or NetWarename>
```

If you prefer to be prompted for a password, you can replace the password in the command line with an asterisk (*). When you type your password at the command prompt, it does not appear on the screen.

Using the Net View Command

At the command prompt, use the **net view** command to view NetWare file resources or view the list of network servers. The **net view** command is similar to the NetWare slist utility.

▶ **To display a list of NetWare file servers**

- At the command prompt, type:

```
net view /network:nw
```

▶ **To display volumes on a specific NetWare file server**

- At the command prompt, type:

  `net view \\`*`<nwservername>`*` /network:nw`

  For example, to view the volumes on NetWare server B, type:

  `net view \\B /network:nw`

▶ **To display the contents of a directory on a NetWare file server running NDS**

- At the command prompt, type:

  `dir \\<directory path>`

Login Scripts

A NetWare login script is a list of commands that are executed each time the user logs on to the NetWare network. Login scripts can create settings for user defaults such as drive mappings, search drive mappings, printer configurations, and other variable settings that define the user's environment configuration on the NetWare network. Thus, they enable you to create a consistent user environment.

Login scripts reside on NetWare servers and execute when you access NetWare networks through Client Service for NetWare or Gateway Service for NetWare. If you want to use a NetWare login script to set up variables on the NetWare network each time a user connects to the NetWare network, you must enable the **Login Script** option in the **Client Service for NetWare** or the **Gateway Service for NetWare** dialog box. When you enable the **Login Script** option in Gateway Service for NetWare, the NetWare login script is executed when you log on to the computer. The variables in the NetWare login script then apply for all users that access the NetWare network through Gateway Service for NetWare. When you enable the **Login Script** option in Client Service for NetWare, the NetWare login script is executed when the user is authenticated to the NetWare network and the NetWare login script variables only apply to the individual user.

Bindery-based and NDS versions of NetWare enable you to use different login scripts. The bindery-based server version provides system and user login scripts that are executed at the system-wide level and at the user level, respectively. The system login script sets variables for all users on a server.

NDS enables you to use four types of login scripts that work in sequence to set users rights to services at the container, profile, and user level. NDS enables you to use the following login scripts:

- The NDS container login script is similar to the system login script in the NetWare bindery-based server version but sets global variables at the container level so that you can set variables for different organizations.
- The NDS profile login script allows you to set variables for users who need common access to specific applications or members of workgroups.
- The user login script allows you to set variables for individual users.
- The default login script is executed when a user login script is not available.

For detailed information about setting up a NetWare login script, see your NetWare documentation. For information about troubleshooting login scripts accessed through Gateway Service for NetWare or Client Service for NetWare, see "Troubleshooting NetWare Login Scripts" later in this chapter.

Troubleshooting Windows 2000 and NetWare Connectivity

The following sections explain how to troubleshoot common problems, including incorrect setup and login scripts, and describe the tools you can use to do so.

Windows 2000 Troubleshooting Tools

Windows 2000 has several tools that allow you to determine computer settings and perform diagnostic tests to resolve communication problems.

Ipxroute Config

This command-line utility enables you to troubleshoot IPX connectivity problems and provides information about the current state of the stack. It displays the current IPX status, including the network number, media access control (MAC) address, interface name, and frame type. To use this utility, type **ipxroute config** at the command prompt.

Ipxroute Ripout

This command uses RIP to determine if there is connectivity to a specific network. To use this command, type **ipxroute ripout** *<network number>* at the command prompt.

Network Monitor

Network Monitor enables you to detect and troubleshoot problems on LANs and on WANs, including RAS links. With Network Monitor you can identify network traffic patterns and network problems. For example, you can locate client-to-server connection problems, find a computer that makes a disproportionate number of work requests, capture frames (packets) directly from the network, display and filter the captured frames, and identify unauthorized users on your network.

Windows 2000 Server includes a version of Network Monitor that allows you to capture traffic coming to or going from the local computer. This version of Netmon is not available with Windows 2000 Professional. For more information about network monitoring, see "Monitoring Network Performance" in the *Server Operations Guide*.

Troubleshooting Common Problems

Most connectivity problems between Windows 2000 and NetWare are caused by an incorrect setup. Without proper setup, access to NetWare resources is either inconsistent or nonexistent.

If you experience any of the following symptoms when connecting to the NetWare network, you probably have an incorrect setup:

- Access is denied to applications residing on NetWare servers.
- Programs fail to run and display error messages.
- Data throughput is slow.
- Users see the error message "Server not found."
- Users are denied access to network resources located on NetWare servers.
- Access to NetWare resources is limited.
- Some clients have some access to NetWare services, but others have no access.
- Users can connect to servers running Windows 2000 and Windows NT, but not to NetWare servers.
- Users can connect to some NetWare servers but not to others.

Because connectivity involves resources on both Windows 2000 and NetWare computer resources must be set up correctly on both Windows 2000–based computers and NetWare computers.

First, verify that access to NetWare resources is correctly configured on the NetWare file servers. You must check a variety of parameters, depending on the problem and its severity. Consider the following questions when resolving connectivity problems:

- Are user accounts set up correctly on the NetWare file server?
- Are the appropriate groups set up?
- Is group membership set up correctly?
- Are the correct rights set for the required resources?

Note Contact your NetWare administrator or consult your NetWare documentation for information on proper NetWare configuration procedures.

When you have verified that the necessary configurations and rights are set up on the NetWare file servers and the problem has still not been resolved, test the configuration on the Windows 2000–based computer. For best results, follow the steps in Figure 12.17. Each step is discussed later in this section.

Start

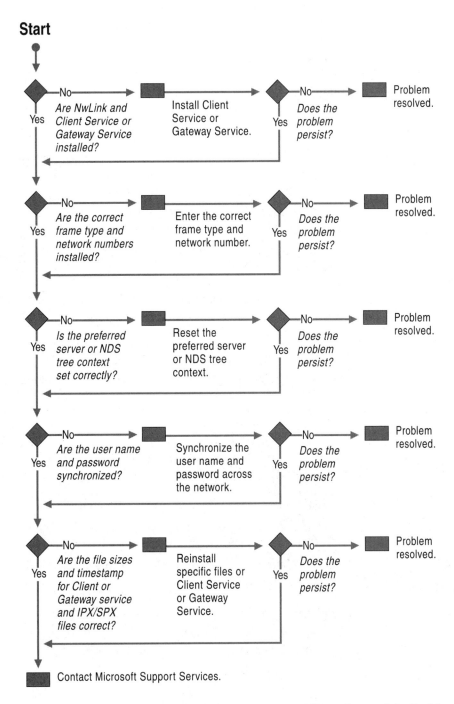

Figure 12.17   Troubleshooting Windows 2000 and NetWare Connectivity Problems

Are NWLink and Gateway Service for NetWare or Client Service for NetWare installed?

For a client or server running Windows 2000 to access NetWare servers, NWLink and Gateway Service for NetWare or Client Service for NetWare must be installed on the computer running Windows 2000. When Gateway Service for NetWare or Client Service for NetWare is installed, NWLink is installed automatically.

▶ **To verify NWLink and Gateway Service/Client Service installation**

1. Double-click **My Computer**, double-click **Control Panel,** and then double-click **Network and Dial-up Connections**.

2. In the **Network and Dial-up Connections** window, right-click the connection you want to configure, and then click **Properties**.

3. In the properties for your connection, verify that NWLink and either **Gateway Service for NetWare** or **Client Service for NetWare** is listed.

For more information about how to install Client Service for NetWare or Gateway Service for NetWare, see "Configuring Gateway Service and Client Service" earlier in this chapter.

Are the correct frame type and network number installed?

When you install Gateway Service for NetWare or Client Service for NetWare and NWLink, the Auto Detect feature is enabled. For more information about Auto Detect, see "NWLink Auto Detect" earlier in this chapter. In most cases, Auto Detect detects the correct frame type and network number. However, problems can occur when a network is using multiple frame types or when an incorrect frame type is set manually. If NWLink detects no network traffic, NWLink sets the frame type to 802.2.

▶ **To verify that the frame type is set to Auto Detect**

1. In the properties box for your connection, double-click **NWLink IPX/SPX/NetBIOS Compatible Transport Protocol**.

2. On the **General** tab, verify that **Auto frame type detection** is selected as the adapter method.

▶ **To determine the frame type set on the NetWare server**

1. Connect to the NetWare server system console locally or connect to it remotely by using the NetWare **Rconsole utility**.

2. At the console, type:

```
Config
```

The frame type is displayed.

▶ **To determine the installed frame type and network number on the Windows 2000 Server–based computer**

1. Click **Start**, point to **Programs**, and then click **Command Prompt**.

2. At the command prompt, type:

   ```
   ipxroute config
   ```

   Verify that the frame and network number in the **Frame** and **Network** columns are correct for your installation.

   If you have multiple network adapters, examine the Node MAC address column to determine the network number that is associated with the specified card.

To manually set the correct frame type and network number, follow the procedures in "Frame Types and Network Numbers," earlier in this chapter.

Is the computer set to the correct bindery server or to the correct NDS tree and context?

When Gateway Service for NetWare or Client Service for NetWare is configured with an incorrect bindery server or an incorrect context within the NDS tree, users have problems accessing network resources.

▶ **To reset the current preferred server or default tree and context**

1. Double-click **My Computer**, then double-click **Control Panel**.

2. In **Control Panel**, double-click the Gateway Service for NetWare or the Client Service for NetWare icon.

3. The preferred bindery server or default tree and context is displayed.

4. If the default tree and context or preferred server is incorrect, select the correct default tree and context or preferred server, and then click **OK**.

Note   If you do not want to set a preferred server, click **None**. You then connect to NetWare through the nearest available NetWare bindery-based server. However, you are not actually logged on to this server; you can use it only for browsing.

Are the user name and password the same across the LAN servers?

If a user running Windows 2000 Professional cannot gain access to certain servers on the network, the user name and password might not be synchronized across the network.

▶ **To determine whether the user name and password is synchronized**

1. Log on to the network on the Windows 2000 Professional–based computer that is having a problem, using a user name and password combination that is known to work.

2. If you can access the desired network resources using this alternate account, the original account needs to be synchronized across the network. Set the password on the client running Windows 2000 to propagate the password across the network.

Tip Use the **Change Password** option on the client running Windows 2000 Professional to automatically modify the password on both the servers running Windows 2000 and the NetWare servers. If you modify the password only on the NetWare servers, it does not propagate to the servers running Windows 2000.

Are the file sizes and timestamps for Gateway Service or Client Service and IPX/SPX files correct?

In some instances files do not copy correctly, or they become corrupt during the file copy process.

▶ **To determine if the file sizes and timestamps are correct**

1. Examine the file sizes and timestamps for the files created when NWLink, Gateway Service for NetWare, or Client Service for NetWare is installed on the Windows 2000–based client or server that is having a problem.

   For a list of files that are installed when Gateway Service for NetWare or Client Service for NetWare is installed on a computer running Windows 2000 see "NWLink" and "Gateway Service and Client Service" earlier in this chapter.

2. Make sure that they are the same as the identical files on a working Windows 2000–based client or server.

   If the file sizes and timestamps are not identical, your files could be corrupt.

▶ **To correct a problem with file corruption**

1. In the properties for your network connection, select **Client Service for NetWare** on a Windows 2000 Professional computer or **Gateway (and Client) Services for NetWare** on a Windows 2000 Server computer, click **Uninstall**, and then click **OK**.

2. Check whether all of the Gateway Service for NetWare or Client Service for NetWare and NWLink files have been deleted. If any files remain, rename them rather than deleting them, in case you need them later. To rename the files, replace each file name extension with .bak (for example, rename file Nwlknb.sys to Nwlknb.bak, and so forth).

3. Reinstall Gateway Service for NetWare or Client Service for NetWare.

Troubleshooting NetWare Login Scripts

Login scripts set the user environment on NetWare servers and are used when the servers are accessed. Therefore, they need to be set correctly for optimal performance. You might experience the following problems when login scripts are activated through Client Service for NetWare or Gateway Service for NetWare.

CX Command

The user receives the following error message when the NetWare login script attempts to change context using a relative path: "The context you want to change to does not exist."

Nwscript.exe parses the NetWare login script. The CX command changes the context and can be used as follows: "cx ..". This should move the user's context one level up within the NDS hierarchy. Instead, the user receives an error message.

To correct this problem, use absolute paths in login scripts. For example, type:

```
cx .somecontainer
```

Capture Command

Error 255 is reported in line 668 of Spool.c when the login script containing the following line is run:

```
#COMMAND /c CAPTURE /S=servername /Q=quename
```

To correct this problem, replace the preceding line with the following:

```
#CAPTURE /S=<servername> /Q=<queuename>
```

Note Capture.exe is not a supported application and often fails when run from the command-line interface. The login script processor does not actually run Capture.exe. Instead, it parses the command #CAPTURE and works in the background. Therefore, when you use the #CAPTURE command, you are running the actual Capture.exe file.

Troubleshooting Other Common Problems

In addition to potential NetWare and Windows 2000 connectivity problems related to setup and login scripts, you might experience the following problems.

Gateway Service or Client Service creates multiple licensed connections to NDS servers

If you have a NetWare NDS tree that includes more than one NetWare server, you could be using multiple licensed connections by connecting to one server for authentication and login, then mapping connections through a login script to another server. If you do this, you could be using twice the number of Novell-licensed connections as necessary.

For information about how to correct this problem, see the Microsoft Knowledge Base link on the Web Resources page at http://windows.microsoft.com/windows2000/reskit/webresources. Search the knowledge base using the keywords "connect to multiple servers" and "NDS."

Windows 2000–based computers cannot connect to other Windows clients

By default, Windows 95–based and Windows 98–based computers use client and server-side direct hosting for the IPX/SPX protocol. Direct hosting is a feature that allows computers to communicate over IPX, bypassing the NetBIOS layer.

Windows 2000 supports server-side direct hosting but does not support client-side direct hosting. Therefore, although a Windows for Workgroups, Windows 95, or Windows 98–based client running only the IPX/SPX protocol can connect to a Windows 2000–based server, a Windows 2000–based client cannot connect to a Windows 2000–based server running only the IPX/SPX protocol. To resolve this problem you need to enable NetBIOS on the Windows 2000–based client and the Windows 2000–based server.

For information and instructions about how to enable NetBIOS on the Windows client version running on your computer, see the documentation provided with your Windows operating system.

Additional Resources

- For more information about how to synchronize passwords for NetWare 4.*x* servers, see the Novell link on the Web Resources page at http://windows.microsoft.com/windows2000/reskit/webresources or contact Novell.

- For more information about updates on Windows NT 4.0 Directory Service Manager, see the ResourceLink link on the Web Resources page at http://windows.microsoft.com/windows2000/reskit/webresources.

CHAPTER 13

Services for Macintosh

Microsoft® Windows® 2000 Services for Macintosh provides an integration platform for mixed Windows 2000–based and Macintosh-based networks. Services for Macintosh is an integrated component of Windows 2000 that makes it possible for computer and Macintosh clients to share files and printers. With Services for Macintosh, Windows 2000 and Macintosh users can share files on Transmission Control Protocol/Internet Protocol (TCP/IP) or AppleTalk networks, share printers, and gain access to remote networks with the Routing and Remote Access service feature in Windows 2000.

In This Chapter

Related Information in the Resource Kit

- For more information about remote access, see "Remote Access Server" in this book.

- For more information about routing, see "Routing and Remote Access Service" in this book.

- For more information about TCP/IP, see "Introduction to TCP/IP" in the *Microsoft® Windows® 2000 Server Resource Kit TCP/IP Core Networking Guide*.

Overview

Windows 2000 Services for Macintosh provides a powerful integration platform for Macintosh and Windows 2000 internetworking. It enables Windows 2000 and Apple Macintosh clients to share files over Transmission Control Protocol/Internet Protocol (TCP/IP) networks and gives them access to the printer server over an AppleTalk network. It also offers AppleTalk-based services for Macintosh clients, such as AppleTalk Routing. Macintosh users can dial in to a server running Windows 2000 and gain access to the AppleTalk network by using a Point-to-Point Protocol (PPP) client that supports the AppleTalk Control Protocol (ATCP). Services for Macintosh also supports varying degrees of encryption and security. Installation of the Microsoft User Authentication Method (MS-UAM) is an option on the Macintosh client; when it is installed, the Macintosh client can log on to the server running Windows 2000 in a manner consistent with other Windows 2000 clients.

Services for Macintosh provides a complete AppleTalk Phase 2 protocol and router in support of AppleTalk networks. The AppleTalk protocol stack is the underlying mechanism that permits communication between the File Services for Macintosh and the Print Server for Macintosh and the Macintosh network.

Windows 2000 Services for Macintosh provides the features listed in Table 13.1.

Table 13.1   Windows 2000 Services for Macintosh Features

Feature	Description
File Services for Macintosh	Offers support for AppleTalk Filing Protocol over TCP/IP and over AppleTalk.
Print Server for Macintosh	Provides access to AppleTalk network–connected PostScript printers or any printer connected to a Windows 2000–server.
Secure Logon (Microsoft-User Authentication Module [MS-UAM])	Enforces network security for Macintosh users in the same way it is enforced for Windows 2000 users.
Apple Standard User Authentication Method (UAM)	Supports clear or encrypted passwords.
Support for AppleTalk Phase 2	The latest version of the AppleTalk protocol.

continued

Table 13.1   Windows 2000 Services for Macintosh Features *(continued)*

Feature	Description
Remote Access (Support for AppleTalk Control Protocol [ATCP])	Macintosh clients can use PPP to dial in to servers and gain remote access to AppleTalk and TCP/IP networks simultaneously.
Support for Plug and Play	Changes made to Services for Macintosh through the user interface, such as enabling or re-enabling a guest account or changing network configurations, is implemented automatically. There is no need to restart the computer to implement the change.
Administrative tools fully integrated into an MMC snap-in	Provides centralized administration.
Disk Quotas	Used to monitor and limit disk space use for volumes formatted for the version of NTFS included with Windows 2000. If this feature in enabled, the system administrator can configure the server so that the disk storage space of individual users is limited.
Enhanced performance and robustness	Provides increased reliability.

AppleTalk

AppleTalk is a network system developed by Apple Computer. It is based on the AppleTalk protocol architecture, which is concerned with the way the connectivity of the network system is implemented. AppleTalk Phase 2 supports AppleTalk networks with more than 254 nodes, multiple zones per network, the AppleTalk internet router, and extended Ethernet and token ring support. The features supported by AppleTalk Phase 2 are discussed in more detail later in this chapter.

In Figure 13.1, the AppleTalk protocol architecture is shown as a layered configuration.

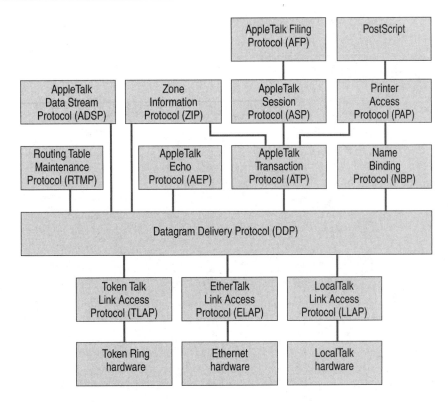

Figure 13.1   AppleTalk Protocol Architecture

The protocols shown in each level of Figure 13.1 receive services from the protocols shown in the lower-level layers. In turn, the protocols in each layer provide services to the protocols in the layers above them. These services, listed in Table 13.2, include connectivity, routing, internetworking, reliable end-to-end data transfer, message exchange between two processes or applications, and data value representation.

Table 13.2 AppleTalk Protocols

Protocol	Description
Datagram Delivery Protocol (DDP)	Provides for data delivery in discrete packets. Neither the order of the data nor its actual delivery is guaranteed.
Routing Table Maintenance Protocol (RTMP)	Used by routers to exchange routing information. Concerned with the establishment and maintenance of routing tables.
AppleTalk Echo Protocol (AEP)	Used to test a system's responsiveness and to establish round-trip transmission times.
AppleTalk Transaction Protocol (ATP)	Provides reliable data transmission.
Name Binding Protocol (NBP)	Provides a name translation service that converts a device name to an AppleTalk network address.
AppleTalk Data Stream Protocol (ADSP)	Provides reliable, full-duplex data transmission between two sockets on an AppleTalk network.
Zone Information Protocol (ZIP)	Maintains the internet-wide mapping of network number ranges to zone names.
AppleTalk Session Protocol (ASP)	Provides for reliable transmission without duplication. Establishes a session between two programs and terminates the session.
Printer Access Protocol	Provides for the reliable transmission of messages. Handles connection setup, maintenance, and termination.
AppleTalk Filing Protocol (AFP)	Provides the interface between an application and a file server. It allows a workstation on an AppleTalk network to access files as an AFP file server.

AppleTalk Networking and Routing

Before setting up Services for Macintosh on a computer that is running Microsoft® Windows® 2000 Server, consult this section for information about planning your network.

Important File Services for Macintosh can run over a TCP/IP network, so you can run a network without using the AppleTalk protocol and with Windows 2000 Server instead. TCP/IP is the standard data transmission protocol, and it provides excellent performance. For information about setting up a TCP/IP network, see the *TCP/IP Core Networking Guide*.

Windows 2000 supports an AppleTalk protocol stack and AppleTalk routing software so that the Windows 2000–based server can connect to and provide routing for AppleTalk-based Macintosh networks.

Most large AppleTalk networks are not single physical networks in which all computers are attached to the same network cabling system. Instead, they are AppleTalk internets, which are smaller, physical networks connected by routers.

A Windows 2000–based server can provide routing and seed routing support. You can install an unlimited number of network adapters on a computer that is running Windows 2000 Server to add an AppleTalk network, which consists of multiple smaller physical networks connected by routers. Routers are necessary for communication between computers on different physical networks. They also reduce traffic on the network by isolating the physical networks.

Some routers on the network are seed routers. A seed router initializes and broadcasts routing information about one or more directly connected physical networks. This information tells routers where to send each packet of data. Each physical network must have one or more seed routers that broadcast the routing information for that network.

Not all routers must be seed routers. Routers that are not seed routers maintain a map of the physical networks on the network, forward information such as network addresses to the correct physical network, and keep track of and direct data packets on AppleTalk networks. Seed routers perform these functions as well, but they also initialize the routing information (such as network numbers and zone lists) for one or more physical networks.

The network number or network range is the address or range of addresses assigned to the network. A network number is unique and identifies a particular AppleTalk physical network. By keeping track of network numbers and network ranges, routers can send incoming data to the correct physical network. A network number can be any number between 1 and 65,279.

LocalTalk networks can only have a single network number; EtherTalk, TokenTalk, and Fiber Distributed Data Interface (FDDI) networks can have network ranges. For more information about routing, see "Routing and Remote Access Service" in this book.

AppleTalk Phase 2 Features

AppleTalk supports the following Phase 2 features:

- LocalTalk networks, which have a single network number and can have as many as 254 nodes. (They are actually limited to 32 or fewer nodes because of media capacity.)

- EtherTalk and TokenTalk networks, which can be assigned a network range so that the network can have more nodes. EtherTalk and TokenTalk networks can have as many as 253 nodes for every number in the network range, for a maximum of 16.5 million nodes.

- LocalTalk networks, which each must be in a single zone. Each EtherTalk and TokenTalk network can have multiple zones, and individual nodes on a network can be configured to be in any one of the network's associated zones.

Network Design

Before you set up AppleTalk on a computer that is running Windows 2000 Server, it is a good idea to create a plan for your network. One major consideration with this type of network—one that includes both Windows 2000 and Macintosh computers—is how to plan the physical setup of the network, including the network media. Use the following guidelines to develop your plan:

- Determine which router is to seed each network.
- Decide how to assign network numbers and network ranges.
- Decide how to assign zones.
- Create a router plan and a router record.

Seed Routers

When you install a Windows 2000–based server and set up AppleTalk, you must specify whether the server computer is to seed each physical network to which it is attached. For example, a computer that is running Windows 2000 Server and is attached to three physical AppleTalk networks might serve as a seed router on two of the networks, but not on the third.

For networks that the server is to seed, specify the routing information. The server computer then functions as a seed router, seeding the routing information that you provide. If you specify that a server is a non-seed router, the port must be seeded by another AppleTalk router that is attached to the same network.

Using Multiple Seed Routers on a Network

To make your network more reliable, install multiple seed routers on the same physical network.

When you install multiple seed routers for a particular network, all of the seed routers must seed the same information for that network. When the network starts, the first seed router to start on the network becomes the actual seed router for the network.

If the first seed router to start on the network has different routing information than other seed routers that start later, the information established by the first seed router is used. If a seed router started subsequently has different information and is a Windows 2000–based server, the conflicting information is ignored, an event is written to the event log, and the subsequent server ceases to be a seed router. Non-Microsoft routers might behave differently.

Determining Seed Router Placement on a Network

When you plan a large mixed network, it is helpful to make a diagram of your AppleTalk network, including the physical network layout and connecting points. Figure 13.2 shows an example of an AppleTalk network.

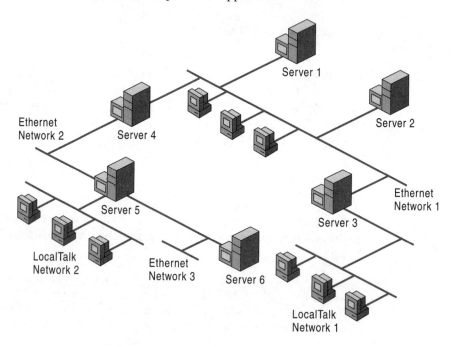

Figure 13.2   Example of an AppleTalk Network

For example, if you have an existing network with six computers that are running Windows 2000 Server, you must determine which server is to seed each network.

- The seed router for Ethernet network 1 must be Server 1, Server 2, Server 3, or Server 4.

- The seed router for Ethernet network 2 must be Server 4 or Server 5.

- The seed router for Ethernet network 3 must be Server 5 or Server 6.

- The seed router for LocalTalk network 2 must be Server 5 because the router on Server 5 is the only router available for this network. Similarly, Server 3 must seed LocalTalk network 1.

Assigning Network Numbers and Network Ranges

Setting the network range is part of seeding a network. Each AppleTalk network within a mixed network is assigned a range of numbers. Each node is identified to the network by one of those numbers, which is combined with a dynamically assigned AppleTalk node identification number. As a result, no two networks on a mixed network should have overlapping ranges of identification numbers.

Use the following guidelines to decide how to assign network numbers and network ranges:

- Use network numbers that leave room for expansion.

- Base network ranges on the number of nodes you expect to have in the future for each network.

- For a LocalTalk network, you can only assign a single network number. For each Ethernet or token ring network, you can assign a network range. The range can be either m–m (a single number) or m–n (a range of numbers). It cannot be zero.

- The network number or range of network numbers must be unique for a given physical network.

- The network numbers in a range must not overlap with numbers contained in other ranges.

- Base the extent of a network range on the number of AppleTalk nodes you expect to have on the physical network. The total number of possible AppleTalk nodes is 253 times the number of network numbers in the range.

Zones

A zone is a logical grouping of nodes (a network entity with an address) that simplifies browsing the network for resources, such as servers and printers. In LocalTalk networks, each physical network can be associated with only one zone. However, for EtherTalk, TokenTalk, or FDDI, you have more flexibility in assigning zones. Each EtherTalk, TokenTalk, or FDDI network can have one or more zones associated with it, and each zone can include servers and printers on one or more physical networks. Servers and printers can group logically into zones so that users can easily locate and gain access to them, no matter where and on which physical networks they are located.

Each Macintosh computer has access to servers and printers in any zone on the network, even though the client itself resides in only one zone. Zones make access to network resources easier for users. When users use the Chooser to view the network, they see only the resources in a single zone at a time, which prevents them from having to navigate through large numbers of resources on large networks to find the resources they need. The clients, servers, and printers that are used by a single group can be included in a single zone; that is, users can view which resources are used most frequently and still have access to resources in other zones when necessary.

A zone list includes all of the zones that are associated with that network. One of these zones is the network's default zone, to which the Macintosh clients are assigned by default. Users can configure the client to be in a different zone, however.

Assigning Zones

Setting zone information is also part of seeding a network. AppleTalk zones are identified by zone names. You can view the current list of zones, add and remove zones, and set the default zone. The default zone is the zone to which all AppleTalk devices appear if a zone has not previously been specified for the device.

Use the following guidelines to decide how to assign zone names:

- Assign one zone name to each physical LocalTalk network. You can assign one or more zone names to each Ethernet and token ring network. A zone name can be up to 31 characters long. You cannot use an asterisk for a zone name.

- For each Ethernet and token ring network, decide what zone is to be the default zone.

- The number of zones your internet has depends on the size of the internet you are planning. If your internet is small, a single zone can be adequate. If you have a single Phase 2 Ethernet or token ring network that spans a large geographic area or contains a large number of AppleTalk devices, use several zones to make it easier for a user to find a device.

Making a Router Plan

After you have designed your network, make a router plan that shows the location and type of each seed router for the network. The seed router examples are based on its corresponding network diagram.

To make a router plan, determine the following:

- The expected number of AppleTalk devices on present and projected Ethernet and token ring networks.

- The quantity of network numbers sufficient to satisfy capacity requirements. (Up to n x 253 devices can be supported, where n is the number of network numbers in the range.)

- Table 13.3 shows an example of a router seeding plan.

Table 13.3   Example of a Router Seeding Plan

Cable ID	Network Range	Zone List	Seed Devices[1]
Ethernet #1	16-25	Finance[2]	
		Accounts Payable	Server 1
		Accounts Receivable	Server 3
Ethernet #2	32-37	Marketing[2]	
		Marketing Exec	Server 5
Ethernet #3	768	Engineering[2]	Server 6
LocalTalk #1	1024	Finance	Server 3
LocalTalk #2	1280	Marketing	Server 5

[1] Seed device information can indicate the server name, the type of dedicated hardware router, or the location, as needed

[2] Indicates the network's default zone.

Keep information about your network for maintenance purposes. Create a record from your router seeding plan, and include the following information:

- Router location:
  - Physical location.
  - Computer name of the server, if the router is a computer that is running Windows 2000 Server with AppleTalk.
- Router type and version.
- The physical networks connected to the router, with the following information for each:
  - Cabling identification
  - Network media type
  - Network numbers
  - Zone names
  - Default zone
  - Whether this router is a seed router for the networks that are attached to it

Planning the Physical Setup

As you plan how to physically connect your Windows 2000 and Macintosh computers, the first thing to consider is network media. Each network media type has its own method of cabling and network topology, and each requires different network hardware.

A Windows 2000–based server supports six types of media:

- Ethernet
- Token ring
- FDDI (Fiber Distributed Data Interface)
- LocalTalk
- CDDI (Copper Distributed Data Interface)
- ATM

Ethernet, token ring, and FDDI are common network media. LocalTalk is used in AppleTalk networking. Every Macintosh computer includes hardware and software that enables it to be a client on a LocalTalk network. If Ethernet is being used, no changes are necessary. If LocalTalk is being used, a LocalTalk card must be installed. If the Macintosh client is using LocalTalk and Ethernet, routing must be turned on.

Suppose your server and Windows 2000 clients use Ethernet, and your Macintosh clients are not currently attached to a network (that is, they have built-in LocalTalk hardware and software). To enable communication between the computers that are running Windows 2000 Server and the Macintosh computers, use one of the options described in the following sections.

Installation of Ethernet Cards

Install Ethernet cards on each Macintosh computer, and then attach these cards to your existing Ethernet network. The server uses its existing Ethernet card to communicate with both Windows 2000 and Macintosh clients, all of which can attach to a single Ethernet network. Figure 13.3 is an example of this type of network.

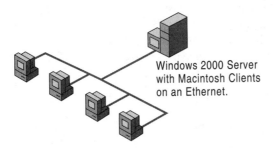

Windows 2000 Server with Macintosh Clients on an Ethernet.

Figure 13.3   Ethernet Network with a Windows 2000–Based Server and Macintosh Clients

Installation of LocalTalk Card

Install a LocalTalk network adapter card on the server (in addition to the Ethernet card that is already installed). You can then set up the Macintosh computers on a LocalTalk network that is attached to the server's new LocalTalk card. The server communicates with the Macintosh computers by means of LocalTalk. Figure 13.4 is an example of this type of network.

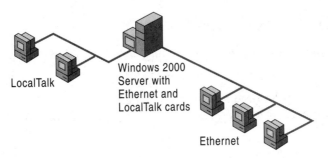

LocalTalk

Windows 2000 Server with Ethernet and LocalTalk cards

Ethernet

Figure 13.4   Windows 2000–Based Server with Ethernet and LocalTalk Cards

This solution requires only one additional network card. However, LocalTalk is not as fast as Ethernet, so network performance is affected. Because the number of Macintosh computers on a LocalTalk network is limited, this solution is impractical if your network has a large number of Macintosh computers.

Installation of an Ethernet/LocalTalk Router

Install an Ethernet/LocalTalk router, which translates data on the network between the two media. A Windows 2000–based server that is running Services for Macintosh also can act as a router between Ethernet and LocalTalk. A Windows 2000–based server, however, must have both an Ethernet and a LocalTalk card installed.

By using an Ethernet/LocalTalk router, the server can still use its Ethernet card. You can put the Macintosh clients on a LocalTalk network and attach the router to both the Ethernet and the LocalTalk networks. All data that is transferred between the server and the Macintosh computers passes through the router. To the server, all Macintosh computers appear to be on the Ethernet network. Figure 13.5 illustrates this type of network.

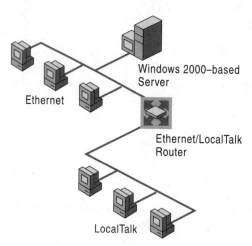

Figure 13.5   Ethernet LocalTalk Router

To use the Ethernet/LocalTalk router, you must be able to bind the AppleTalk protocol on the server to an Ethernet card on the server.

This solution is useful if you want to make printers on the Ethernet available to Macintosh clients; however, a LocalTalk router degrades performance.

Note Because a computer that is running Windows 2000 Server can function as a router, it can also function as an Ethernet/LocalTalk router — as long as it has both an Ethernet network adapter card and a LocalTalk card. To connect one physical network of Macintosh computers to several servers, you can install a LocalTalk card on one server, which then functions as a router and enables the Macintosh computers to reach the other servers on the Ethernet network.

Advanced Examples of a Physical Network

Depending on which clients you have on your network, the issues you face when deciding how to connect them can be more complex than the issues that were discussed earlier in this chapter. The following two examples address advanced issues and proposed solutions:

- The Windows 2000–based server uses Ethernet, but some of your Macintosh computers use Ethernet and others use LocalTalk.

  You can install a LocalTalk card on the computer that is running Windows 2000 Server to communicate with the Macintosh computers that use LocalTalk, install Ethernet cards on all the Macintosh computers, or use an Ethernet/LocalTalk router.

- The Windows 2000–based server uses Ethernet, but some of your Macintosh computers use either Ethernet or LocalTalk. In addition, you have some Macintosh computers that have token ring network cards.

  In addition to implementing the first solution, install a token ring network card on the computer that is running Windows 2000 Server to communicate with these Macintosh computers.

These solutions also work with FDDI.

File Services for Macintosh

File Services for Macintosh provides Macintosh users with access to files that are stored on the Windows 2000–based server. The file server is accessible over TCP/IP networks and over AppleTalk networks.

File Server Accessibility over TCP/IP

File Server for Macintosh is available over TCP/IP networks, so it can be run on a network without using the AppleTalk protocol. To use AFP over TCP/IP networks, AppleShare client version 3.7 or later must be installed on the Macintosh client.

The file server works with either AppleTalk or TCP/IP installed. When both are installed on the client and the server, the Macintosh client attempts to start a connection by using TCP/IP. If the server has multiple IP addresses, the list of all IP addresses is sent to the client.

If a user wants to browse the AppleTalk network to connect to the server, AppleTalk must be installed. If the user knows either the IP address or the Domain Name System (DNS) name, this information can be entered into the dialog box in place of selecting the server from the Chooser list. If the DNS name or the IP address is known, you do not have to run AppleTalk on the server.

File Server Accessibility over AppleTalk

Even though the Windows 2000 file system differs from that of the Macintosh file system, both Windows 2000 clients and Macintosh clients can use the files that are stored on the Windows 2000–based server. Services for Macintosh works in the background to make this possible. For both Macintosh and Windows 2000 users, files appear as they usually do. A Windows 2000 user sees files located in a directory tree structure. A Macintosh user sees files located in a Macintosh folder structure. The files on a Windows 2000–based server that is running Services for Macintosh are stored in shared directories or in Macintosh volumes, which are Macintosh file storage units. If a Macintosh volume is shared out, it is not seen by the Windows 2000 client. Each server can have one or more shared directories. Each shared directory on a server is assigned a unique name, called a share.

Macintosh users cannot gain access automatically to all shared folders by using Services for Macintosh. Only Macintosh users have access to folders that are designated by the administrator as "Macintosh-accessible volumes."

Within a folder that is both a share and a Macintosh-accessible volume, networked Windows 2000 users see folders and files that are stored on the server's hard disk. To Macintosh users, the volume appears to contain Macintosh files and folders. When Macintosh users browse through the list of files that are available on the server, they see icons that represent each file and folder.

Macintosh files and folders can have Macintosh file names, including long names and names containing spaces and other characters. They are not limited to the 8.3 naming convention of the file allocation table (FAT) file system used with the Microsoft® MS-DOS® system. The file server and the NTFS translate the names so that users can see them.

AppleTalk Filing Protocol

The AppleTalk Filing Protocol (AFP) enables file sharing across a network. Clients can gain access to files on remote servers by using native file system commands. AFP also provides user authentication and file access control. On Macintosh computers, the AFP server is implemented as AppleShare. AFP is built on top of the AppleTalk Session Protocol (ASP), if AppleTalk is being used, or on top of the Data Stream Interface (DSI), if TCP/IP is being used.

AFP is concerned with file system components, such as files, Macintosh folders, volumes, and forks, and AFP calls, which are used by the client to access information about the file server and services as well as make changes to files and directories.

NTFS Streams

The Windows 2000–based server uses NTFS streams to store Macintosh-specific file and directory information, Macintosh Finder information, various AFP attributes, and indexing information. The data and resource forks are maintained in two different streams for the corresponding file on the NTFS volume. The data fork stores most of the file's information and is shared between Macintosh and personal computer clients. The resource fork holds the Macintosh operating system resources, such as code, menu, font, and icon definitions. Resource forks, however, have no relevance to personal computers, so the resource forks of files on the server are never accessed by personal computer clients.

FinderInfo, Indexing, and DesktopInfo are also kept as separate NTFS streams that are stored at the root of the volume. The DesktopInfo and Indexing streams are opened when the volume is first initialized. These streams are deleted when the volume is deleted. The FinderInfo stream, which is per file and per directory, is not deleted. Streams associated with the volume root are created when the volume is created.

The Macintosh Finder uses the information in the resource fork of a file to determine what application was used to create the file and what type of file it is. The Macintosh Finder uses this information to display the correct type of icon for the file and to launch the file by using the correct application.

Macintosh files keep some data in a part of the file called a resource fork. The actual file is stored in the data fork. Windows 2000 allows for the creation of these data and resource forks when a Macintosh file is stored on the Windows 2000–based server, so that a Macintosh client can view and launch files from the server.

Indexing

Whenever a new volume is added to the file system, it must be initialized. New volumes are initialized one at a time and sequentially in the order in which they were created. Initializing includes indexing, in which File Server for Macintosh systematically examines the entire directory structure and creates an image of the entire structure of the volume, which is saved in virtual memory. The indexing stream is updated once at startup and once at shutdown. After indexing is complete, it does not have to be recreated. Instead, the stream is read at startup, and the image is updated with any changes that have occurred to the file since the server was shut down.

During the indexing of the volume, non-paged memory use increases, but this use is temporary. Non-paged memory use depends on the number of directories in the volume (The number of files does not influence use.) The non-paged memory is released after indexing is complete.

The initialization of a volume occurs sequentially. A volume is not available (that is, visible on the network and available for mounting) until it is completely initialized. Therefore, if a large volume is being created before a small one, the small volume does not appear until after the large one.

Virtual memory use is also affected. As a rough estimate, a combination of 10,000 files and directories can take up to 2 MB of virtual memory. It might be useful to tune the Performance System attribute for increased virtual memory in Control Panel to prevent performance degradation with volumes that contain more than 10,000 files and directories. If the indexing information cannot be written to disk at shutdown, a new one is created again at startup.

Disk Storage

Macintosh clients that use OS 7.5 or earlier have access to a maximum of 2 gigabytes (GB) of storage space. Clients that use later versions of the system software have access to a maximum of 4 GB of storage. There is virtually no limitation on storage space for clients that use AFP 2.2.

Network Security

With Windows 2000 Server and Services for Macintosh, network security is enforced for Macintosh users in the same way it is enforced for Windows 2000 users. The same user accounts and passwords are used by Windows 2000 and Macintosh.

Authentication

Macintosh users are logged on to a computer that is running Windows 2000 Server through one of the three following authentication schemes:

- As a guest, if the server is configured to permit guest users.
- As a user with a cleartext password.
- As a valid Windows 2000 account that is using Apple Standard UAM or MS-UAM.

Guest Users

With Services for Macintosh, you can set up guest users and allow users who do not have domain or workgroup accounts to log on to the server that is using a Macintosh. With the Windows 2000 guest account, you can specify what access to resources a guest user is allowed; administrators usually grant guest users fewer permissions than users who have accounts on the server. If the guest logon option is enabled, the server always approves the logon request without requiring a password.

Cleartext Passwords

Cleartext password protection is part of the AppleShare client software on Macintosh computers. It provides less security than encrypted passwords because the password is sent over the network as cleartext, which is vulnerable to detection by sniffers. Cleartext password protection is offered for Macintosh users who use the standard AppleShare client software or System 7 Filing sharing.

Encrypted Passwords

Note If the Windows 2000–based server permits cleartext passwords, as well as encrypted passwords, the Macintosh switches automatically to the encrypted authentication method.

Services for Macintosh offers two encryption methods to Macintosh clients.

- Apple Standard Encryption, in which passwords are up to eight characters long.

- MS-User Authentication Method (UAM), in which passwords are up to 14 characters long. This method requires that AppleShare client version 3.8 be installed.

In both of the encrypted password authentication schemes, the password itself is never sent over the network. Instead, the server provides a random number and the password is applied to the random number as an encryption key. The encrypted random number is sent over the network to the server. The server, which must be configured to store the user's password (or its derivative) in reversibly encrypted form, uses the password to encrypt the same random number. The two results are compared, and if both match, the user is authenticated.

Services for Macintosh does not support Kerberos authentication.

Domains and Trusted Domains

A user can log on in one of two ways:

- Enter the *username*.

- Enter the *domain\username*.

If the user enters *domain\username*, the logon mechanism uses the domain that has been specified to authenticate the user.

If the user enters only *username*, the server first checks the local account; if it finds the correct user name, it logs the user on. If the user name is not found, the server checks the primary domain account (the domain for the server). If this fails, the server checks all trusted domains to find the user name. If the user name occurs in more than one trusted domain, the server logs on to the first domain in which it finds the user name, which might or might not be the wanted account.

Windows 2000 Server Accounts for Macintosh Clients

Services for Macintosh uses the same user accounts database as the Windows 2000–based server or its domain. Therefore, if you already have Windows 2000 Server accounts for the people who are using Macintosh computers on the network, you do not have to create additional accounts. You must create accounts only for users who do not already have accounts on the computer or domain that is running Windows 2000 Server and Services for Macintosh.

One aspect of Windows 2000 Server user accounts, the user's primary group, applies only to Services for Macintosh. The user's primary group is the group the user works with most, and it should be the group with which the user has the most resource needs in common. When a user creates a folder on a server, that user becomes its owner. The owner's primary group is set as the group associated with the folder. The administrator or owner can change the group associated with the folder.

File Permissions

Access to network files and directories is controlled with permissions. With the Windows 2000 security system, you specify which users can use which directories and files and how they can be used. The Macintosh-style permissions differ in that they can be set for volumes and folders only, not files.

The set of permissions available for Windows 2000 users differs from the set of permissions available for the Macintosh. Services for Macintosh automatically translates permissions so that permissions are enforced for both Windows 2000 and Macintosh users.

The Windows 2000 Server Administrator account always has full permissions on Services for Macintosh volumes.

Types of Permissions

Windows 2000 users and administrators use Windows 2000 permissions. Macintosh users set Macintosh-style permissions on the folders they create.

In Windows 2000, new files and new subdirectories inherit permissions from the directory in which they are created.

Macintosh files inherit the permissions set on folders. Any Windows 2000 permissions specified for a file are recognized by File Server for Macintosh, even though the Macintosh user does not see any indication in the Finder that these permissions exist.

Macintosh operating systems prior to OS 8.5 use the following four types of permissions for a folder:

See Files   Allows a user to see what files are in the folder and read those files.

See Folders   Allows a user to see what folders are contained in the folder.

Make Changes   Allows a user to modify the contents of files in the folder, rename files, move files, create new files, and delete existing files.

Cannot Move, Rename, Or Delete   Prohibits these actions on a folder.

The Macintosh OS 8.5 supports the following Windows 2000 access privileges:

Read-Only   Allows a user to see an item, but not delete, change, or replace it.

Write-Only   Allows a user to add items.

Read and Write   Allows a user to add, delete, and save changes to items.

None   Prevents access to, or adding, items.

A Macintosh user cannot give these permissions to multiple users and groups. Instead, permissions are assigned to three categories of users:

Owner   The user who created the folder.

User/Group   Similar to the Windows 2000 Server group associated with the folder. Every folder on a server can have one group associated with it at any one time. The group can be a special group, such as users or administrators, or it can be any other group on the server.

Everyone   All other users of the server, including user accounts with guest access.

The Macintosh security scheme is based on the idea that every folder on a server falls into one of three types: private information (accessible only by the owner of the folder); group information (accessible by a single workgroup); and public information (accessible by everyone).

For example, consider a folder containing information that all members of a certain group should see, but that only one person can change. The person allowed to change the information should be the Owner of the folder and should have See Files, See Folders, and Make Changes permissions. The workgroup that users the folder should be the group associated with the folder and should have only See Files and See Folders permissions. Because no one else has a need to see the folder's contents, the Everyone category should not be selected.

Although a folder's owner is often a member of the group associated with the folder, this is not required.

With both Macintosh-style and Windows 2000 Server–style permissions, users' access to folders can be defined differently for each directory and subdirectory within a directory tree. For example, you could give a user See Files, See Folders, and Make Changes permissions for one folder, only the See Files permission for a subfolder of that folder, and no permissions at all for another subfolder.

Handling File-Level Permissions

With Windows 2000 Server, Windows 2000 users can assign permissions separately for each file within a directory. The Macintosh, however, does not support file-level permissions. When a file has file-level permissions, those permissions apply to Macintosh users only if the permissions are more restrictive than those assigned for the directory that contains the file.

For example, if a Macintosh user has See Files, See Folders, and Make Changes permissions for a directory (which appears as a folder), the user can read and make changes to files in the directory. However, if the user has only Read permission for a particular file in a directory, the user can only read the file, not make changes to it.

Translating Permissions

Services for Macintosh translates permissions so that those set by a Windows 2000 user are translated into the equivalent Macintosh permissions, and vice versa. When a Windows 2000 user sets permissions for a directory or a Macintosh user sets permissions for a folder, permissions are translated as shown in Table 13.4.

Table 13.4   Translations of Directory and File Permissions

Windows 2000 Permissions	Macintosh Permissions
Read	See Files, See Folders (or both)
Write, Delete	Make Changes

The following guidelines apply:

- When a Windows 2000 user sets Read permissions on a directory or file, users have both See Files and See Folders permissions when they use a Macintosh computer.

- When a Windows 2000 user sets Write and Delete permissions on a directory or file, users then have Make Changes permissions when they are using a Macintosh.

- When a Macintosh user sets See Files or See Folders (or both) permissions, users have Read permissions when they are using Windows 2000.

- When a Macintosh user sets the Make Changes permissions, users have Write and Delete permissions when they are using Windows 2000.

Setting Permissions from a Macintosh or a Windows 2000 Computer

A folder's owner can set permissions for the folder. Both the folder's owner and the server administrator can also use Windows 2000 to set permissions for folders on the server. The folder's owner can set permissions for the folder (directory) from Windows 2000 because the owner of every folder (directory) has the P (Change Permission) permission on that folder.

Volume Passwords

Services for Macintosh provides an extra level of security through Macintosh-accessible volume passwords. A volume password is a password you can assign to a Macintosh-accessible volume when configuring it. Any Macintosh user who wants to use the volume must type the volume password in addition to the user logon password. Windows 2000 users do not have to know the volume password to gain access to the directory that corresponds to the Macintosh-accessible volume.

Volume passwords are case-sensitive. When you create a new Macintosh-accessible volume, the default is to have no volume password. Volume passwords are optional.

Because of a constraint with the Macintosh System 6 and Macintosh System 7 Finder, you cannot automatically mount a volume with a volume password at startup or by double-clicking an alias. You also cannot automatically mount a volume if the user originally connected to the volume using Microsoft UAM.

Macintosh File Name Translation

Services for Macintosh allows a Windows 2000 and a Macintosh computer to share files; however, conflicts can arise because of the different file naming conventions that are supported by each system.

As shown in Table 13.5, Windows 2000, Macintosh, and MS-DOS systems each follow different file-naming conventions.

Table 13.5   File-Naming Conventions

Operating System	File System	Character Limit
MS-DOS/Windows 2000	FAT	8.3 (8 characters, plus an optional extension, signaled by a period and up to 3 characters)
Macintosh	System software	31 characters
Windows 2000	NTFS	256 characters

When a file with a long name (any name over 8.3 MS-DOS standard) is saved on an NTFS partition, the long name is maintained and a short name is created so that MS-DOS users can gain access to the file if they have permission to do so. For example, Macintosh users who create folders or files on an Services for Macintosh volume and use the 31-character limit see the original long names. MS-DOS users, however, see a shortened version of the file name. Furthermore, Windows 2000 system users see the longer Macintosh file names because NTFS has a 256-character file name limit.

Even though NTFS translates long names to short names, it is a good idea for users of systems that do not recognize large file names to name shared files following the 8.3 convention that is used by the FAT file system in MS-DOS. This simplifies file identification for users working on different platforms. This section explains how file translations work on Windows 2000–based servers that are running Services for Macintosh. For more information about file name translation, see Windows 2000 Server Help.

Naming Differences

In general, the FAT file naming system, which is used on MS-DOS systems, is more restrictive than the Macintosh system. The two systems differ in the following ways:

- Macintosh file names and folder names can have as many as 31 characters and can include blank spaces. FAT file names and directory names can have as many as eight characters, followed by an optional extension (signaled by a period and up to three additional characters), and they cannot include blank spaces.

- Macintosh file names and folder names can include any Macintosh character except a colon. MS-DOS file names and directory names have more exceptions, such as the following:

  / [ ] ; = " \ : | , * .

- Both Macintosh and MS-DOS file names and folder names (or directory names) can include extended characters; however, the Macintosh and MS-DOS extended character sets are different.

FAT file names and directory names are acceptable as Macintosh file names and folder names unless they contain extended characters not found in the Macintosh character set. In such cases, Macintosh users see valid characters substituted for the invalid ones.

Overview of Macintosh-to-8.3 Translation

When a file is created on a Macintosh and saved on a computer that is running Windows 2000 Server, the File Server for Macintosh first checks it for illegal NTFS characters. Then NTFS takes over the file translation process.

Services for Macintosh Functionality

When a Macintosh file name is saved on a computer that is running Windows 2000 Server, File Server for Macintosh component of Services for Macintosh does the following:

- If required, File Server for Macintosh changes illegal NTFS characters to the available range of Unicode characters, which are then mapped to the ANSI default character, a question mark (?). The result is that the file can be seen, but a use or client does not have access to it.

  - The following are the illegal NTFS characters:

    " / \ * ? < > | :

NTFS Functionality

When NTFS receives a legal NTFS name from File Server for Macintosh, it translates the name as follows:

- Macintosh names that are valid MS-DOS names do not change: The long name and short name are the same. For example, "Sample.art" remains "Sample.art."
- Long names are truncated to six characters, followed by a tilde and a unique number, for a total of eight characters (not including any extension).
- The last period (if any) in a long name signals the extension, which is retained.
- If the short name is a duplicate of another name (long or short), NTFS automatically modifies the short name of the new file or folder by truncating the name to six characters and adding a tilde an a number until it creates a unique name.

Note If a Macintosh user gives a file or a folder a valid MS-DOS name, which makes translation to a short name unnecessary, the user might see a message that states that the name already exists and that the user must choose a new name. For example, this message appears if the user creates a file named Sales.dat when another file in the folder already has that name.

Mapping of Extended Characters

If Macintosh extended characters are used in file names or folder names that are saved to the computer that is running Windows 2000 Server by Macintosh users, the File Server for Macintosh translates these extended characters to the equivalent Unicode characters so that Windows 2000 users can see them.

If MS-DOS extended characters are used in file names or directory names that are saved to the computer that is running Windows 2000 Server by Windows 2000 users, the File Server for Macintosh also translates these extended characters to the equivalent Macintosh ANSI characters so that Macintosh users can see them.

Cross-Platform Applications on Macintosh and Windows 2000 Computers

For many applications that have versions for Windows 2000 and for Macintosh computers, users of both versions can work on the same data file by using Services for Macintosh. When Macintosh users view directories on the server that contains these data files, they see the files represented by the appropriate icon.

For example, a person who is using a Windows 2000 version of Microsoft® Excel® can create a spreadsheet file and then store it on the server in a shared directory that also is configured as a Macintosh-accessible volume. A Macintosh user who opens that folder sees the file represented by the Macintosh icon that represents a Microsoft Excel spreadsheet. The Macintosh user can double-click the file icon, and Microsoft Excel for Macintosh starts and opens the file. The Macintosh user can modify the file and then save it. When the Windows 2000 user opens the file, the modified version of the file appears.

Services for Macintosh uses extension-type associations to display Windows 2000 files with the correct icon when the Macintosh user sees a Microsoft Excel for Macintosh document icon for a Microsoft Excel for Windows 2000 file.

Extension-Type Associations

With extension-type associations, users of both the Windows 2000 and the Macintosh version of an application can work on the same data file. The extension-type associations provided with Services for Macintosh tell the Finder which MS-DOS file name extensions correspond with which Macintosh file types and file creators. When a file on the server has a file name extension associated with a Macintosh file type and file creator, the Finder displays the appropriate icon for that file when a Macintosh user browses the files available on the server. If a Macintosh user chooses the file, the appropriate application starts and opens the file.

The extension-type associations shown in Table 13.6 are already defined. Others can be added to Services for Macintosh. For a comprehensive list, click the **Association** tab in the **Configure File Server for Macintosh** dialog box, in the File Services Management snap-in.

Table 13.6   Extension-Type Associations

Windows 2000 Application/File Format	Macintosh Application	MS-DOS Extension	Macintosh Type	Macintosh Creator
Adobe Encapsulated PostScript II	Adobe Illustrator '88	EPS	EPSF	ARTZ
AldusPageMaker for Microsoft Windows version 2.0, Aldus PageMaker for OS/2 version 2.0	Aldus PageMaker for Macintosh version 2.0	PUB	PUBF	ALD2
Aldus PageMaker for Microsoft Windows version 3.0	Aldus PageMaker for Macintosh version 3.0			
Publication	Publication	PM3	ALB3	ALD3
Template	Template	PT3	ALT3	ALD3
Template	Template	TEM	ALT3	ALD3
Template	Template	TPL	ALT3	ALD3
TIFF graphics file	TIFF graphics file	TIF	TIFF	ALD3
Aldus PageMaker for Microsoft Windows version 4.0	Aldus PageMaker for Macintosh version 4.0			
Publication	Publication	PM4	ALB4	ALD4
Template	Template	PT4	ALT4	ALD4
Template	Template	TEM	ALT4	ALD4
Template	Template	TPL	ALT4	ALD4
TIFF graphics file	TIFF graphics file	TIF	TIFF	ALD4
Borland dBASE	Microsoft® FoxBASE® / FoxBASE+® for Macintosh	DBF	F+DB	FOX+
Lotus 1-2-3 for Microsoft Windows version 2.0	Lotus 1-2-3 for Macintosh version 2.0	WK3	LWK3	L123
Microsoft Excel for Microsoft Windows version 3.0, Microsoft Excel for OS/2 version 3.0	Microsoft Excel for Macintosh version 3.0			
Chart	Chart	XLC	XLC3	XCEL
Spreadsheet	Spreadsheet	XLS	XLS3	XCEL
Macro sheet	Macro sheet	XLM	XLM3	XCEL
Workspace	Workspace	XLW	XLW3	XCEL
Add-in macro file	Add-in macro file	LA	XLA	XCEL
Template file	Template file	XLT	SLM3	XCEL

continued

Table 13.6   Extension-Type Associations *(continued)*

Windows 2000 Application/File Format	Macintosh Application	MS-DOS Extension	Macintosh Type	Macintosh Creator
Microsoft Excel for Microsoft Windows version 4.0, Microsoft Excel for OS/2 version 4.0	Microsoft Excel for Macintosh version 4.0			
Chart	Chart	XLC	XLC4	XCEL
Spreadsheet	Spreadsheet	XLS	XLS4	XCEL
Macro sheet	Macro sheet	XLM	XLM4	XCEL
Workspace	Workspace	XLW	XLW4	XCEL
Add-in macro file	Add-in macro file	XLA	XLA	XCEL
Template file	Template file	XLT	SLM3	XCEL
Microsoft® Multiplan®/SYLK	Microsoft Excel for Macintosh version 3.0	SLK	TEXT	XCEL
Microsoft® PowerPoint® version 2.0	Microsoft PowerPoint for Macintosh version 2.0	PPT	SLD2	PPT2
Microsoft PowerPoint version 3.0	Microsoft PowerPoint for Macintosh version 3.0			
Slides	Slides	PPT	SLD3	PPT3
Microsoft® Project for Windows version 1.*x*	Microsoft Project for Macintosh version 1.*x*			
Projects	Projects	MPP	MSPF	MSPJ
Exchange format	Exchange format	MPX	MSPF	MSPJ
Calendars	Calendars	MPC	MSPJ	MSPJ
Views	Views	MPV	MSPJ	MSPJ
Workspaces	Workspaces	MPW	MSPF	MSPJ
Microsoft® Word for Windows version 2.0	Microsoft Word for Macintosh version 5.1			
Document	Document	DOC	WDBN	MSWD
Text Document	Document	WRD	TEXT	MSWD
Rich Text	Rich Text	RTF	TEXT	MSWD
Style Sheet	N/A	STY	TEXT	MSWD
Glossary	N/A	GLY	TEXT	MSWD
N.A./Comma-Separated Values	Microsoft Excel for Macintosh version 4.0	CSV	TEXT	XCEL
N.A./SIT files	Alladin Stuffit	SIT	SIT!	SIT!
N.A./Text (TXT files)	Teachtext	TXT	TEXT	TTXT

continued

Table 13.6   Extension-Type Associations *(continued)*

Windows 2000 Application/File Format	Macintosh Application	MS-DOS Extension	Macintosh Type	Macintosh Creator
Windows Program	N/A	EXE	DEXE	LMAN
		COM	DEXE	LMAN
		CMD	DEXE	LMAN
		BAT	DEXE	LMAN
Symantec Ready!	Symantec MORE	RDY	TEXT	MORE
Unknown File	N/A	All others	TEXT	LMAN
VisiCalc (DIF)	Microsoft Excel for Macintosh version 4.0	DIF	TEXT	XCEL

You can also add extension-type associations. You can add new associations for an application not listed in the preceding table, or you can add extra associations for any of the listed applications. For example, if your company has a custom of saving Microsoft Word documents with a .wrd file name extension, you can add one of the extensions listed in Table 13.7.

Table 13.7   Additional Extension-Type Associations

Application	Extension
MS-DOS extension	.wrd
Macintosh file type	WDBN
Macintosh file creator	MSWD

When you add a new extension-type association, it affects only files that are subsequently created on the server, not the currently existing files. Moreover, you can associate multiple extensions with a Macintosh file type and creator. However, the reverse is not true. Only one file type and creator can be associated with an extension.

Note The WKS and WK1 formats allow a single data file to be used by users of Microsoft Excel, Lotus 1-2-3, and Informix Wingz. However, you can set up an extension for only one Macintosh application for this format. For example, if you map the WKS and WK1 extensions to the file type and file creator values for Microsoft Excel for Macintosh and then a Macintosh user double-clicks the file's icon, the file is loaded into Microsoft Excel for Macintosh.

▶ **To make new extension-type associations**

1. Open Computer Management.

2. Right-click **Shared Folders**.

3. Click **Configure File Server for Macintosh**.

4. In the **Files with MS-DOS Extension** box of the **File Association** tab, type an extension or select one from the list.

    If the extension is already associated with a file type and a file creator, it is highlighted in the **With Macintosh Creator and Type association list**.

5. In the **With Macintosh Creator and Type association list**, select a creator and type to which you want to associate this extension.

6. Click **Associate**.

▶ **To add file creators and types**

1. Open Computer Management.

2. Right-click **Shared Folders**. Then select **Configure File Server for Macintosh**.

3. In the **Properties** dialog box, select the **File Association** tab, then click **Add**.

4. Type the **Creator** and **File Type** and a description (optional).

The new creator and type now appear in the **File Association** list.

▶ **To edit a description of a file type**

1. Open Computer Management.

2. Right-click Shared Folders. Then select **Configure File Server for Macintosh**.

3. In the **File Association** tab, type an extension or select one from the list.

4. Click **Edit** and type the new description.

▶ **To remove a file type and associations**

1. Open Computer Management.

2. Right-click Shared Folders. Then select **Configure File Server for Macintosh**.

3. In the **File Association** tab, select the creator you want to delete.

4. Click **Delete**.

5. Click **Yes** to confirm that you want to remove the selected file type and associated extensions.

Print Server for Macintosh

Services for Macintosh allows you to configure the Windows 2000–based server to provide either of the two types of printing services, as shown in Figure 13.6. Windows 2000 clients can use the server to gain access to the services of AppleTalk network–connected PostScript printers with LaserWriter drivers. Any printer connected to the communication port of the Windows 2000–based server or over the network can be accessed by a Macintosh client.

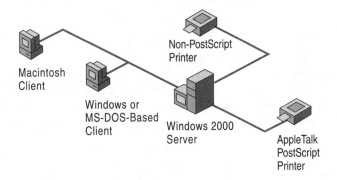

Figure 13.6   Print Services

Services for Macintosh provides additional benefits for Macintosh users who use AppleTalk printers, such as spooling. With spooling, Macintosh users can start other tasks as soon as they send a print job to the computer that is running Windows 2000 Server, where print jobs are stored until a printer becomes available. Without spooling, users must wait until the print job completes before doing anything else.

The Print Services require AppleTalk, which is installed automatically during the installation of the Services for Macintosh Print Services.

Printing Protocol

Print Server for Macintosh uses the Printer Access Protocol, a session-level protocol that provides reliable data transfer between a client and a server. It is a session-level protocol that is responsible for starting, maintaining, and terminating the (possibly multiple) connections between a workstation and a printer server.

A printing request is sent by an application to the Printing Manager. This discussion assumes the existence of a spooler, but the process is the same regardless of the existence of a spooler. A spooler allows the client to continue working without waiting for the print job to complete. However, to the protocol, the printer and the server or spooler look the same.

Printing Authentication

Native Macintosh networking does not support authentication for printers. Users do not need to be authenticated to use the print service; therefore, it is not possible to restrict use of network printers by Macintosh clients. If a Macintosh client is physically capable of sending a print job to a print device or a print server, it has implicit permission to do so. However, it is possible, if a print server is started from a user account, to attach an Access Control List (ACL) to a specific printer so that a user has access to the spooler but not to the printer itself. In this case, the Macintosh user is not able to print to that specific printer.

In addition, it is possible for a system administrator to enforce one set of user-level print permissions for all Macintosh print clients as a group. The Macintosh client must start the MacPrint service by logging on as the System account, which has Print permission on all local print devices. To limit the permissions for Macintosh clients, create a new user account and give it the printer permissions you want the group to have. Then, set the Macintosh client MacPrint service to log on with this account.

Note The System account on one computer does not have access permission for resources on other computers. Macintosh clients that start the MacPrint service by logging on as System user cannot send jobs to printers that forward jobs to other print servers. The solution is to configure the Macintosh client MacPrint service to log on as another user, one which has permission to print on all the print servers to which print jobs are forwarded.

Macintosh Port Monitor

The Macintosh port monitor transmits jobs over a network by using the AppleTalk protocol to network-attached print devices. It also lets you send jobs to AppleTalk spoolers, regardless of the print device to which the spooler is attached.

The port monitor is available on Windows 2000 and enables any Windows 2000–based computer to send local print jobs to AppleTalk print devices. The port monitor enables Windows 2000 to send print jobs to an AppleTalk print device regardless of how the print job was sent to the server.

Some print devices process non-PostScript print jobs incorrectly if they receive those jobs over AppleTalk. Also, some print devices process PostScript jobs incorrectly if those jobs contain binary data and arrive over any protocol other than AppleTalk. These problems usually result from restrictions in those print devices.

Services for Macintosh Print Processor

The Services for Macintosh print processor, installed with Print Server for Macintosh, assigns either of two data types, RAW or PSCRIPT1, to a document. Both data types and their use are described in Table 13.8.

Table 13.8   Print Processor Data Types

Data Type	Spooler Instructions	Use
RAW	Print document without changes.	All documents targeted to PostScript printers.
PSCRIPT1	Convert document to rasterized images or bitmaps.	All documents targeted to non-PostScript printers.

The PSCRIPT1 data type indicates that the job is a Level 1 PostScript code from a Macintosh client, but the target printer is not a PostScript printer. The spooler sends the PostScript code through a Microsoft® TrueImage® raster image processor, supplied with Services for Macintosh. The raster image processor creates a series of one-page, monochrome bitmaps at a maximum of 300 dpi. The Windows 2000 print spooler sends the rasterized images, or bitmaps, to the print driver for the target printer. The print driver returns a job that prints the bitmaps on the page.

Because the bitmaps are monochrome and no more than 300 dpi, the target print driver produces final output that is monochrome and not more than 300 dpi, even if the target printer driver supports color or higher resolutions. The restrictions are in the raster image processor software itself, not in the Windows 2000 printer drivers.

Several third-party Microsoft® Win32® raster image processor packages are commercially available if a higher-end raster image processor is needed.

Note If binary PostScript print jobs are sent to a server that is running Windows 2000, the output might be garbled because different protocols are being used

Setup of Printing Devices for Network Printing

The following list shows the three scenarios for printing on a network:

- Windows clients send print requests to printers representing printing devices attached to a computer that is running Windows 2000 Server.

- Macintosh clients send print requests to printers representing printing devices on an AppleTalk network.

- Macintosh and Windows 2000 clients send print requests to printers representing printing devices attached to a computer that is running Windows 2000 Server (for example, to a non-PostScript printing device such as the HP DeskJet 500) and to printing devices on an AppleTalk network (for example, a PostScript printing device such as the Apple LaserWriter).

Printing in these scenarios happens as follows. Windows 2000 users specify printers on a computer that is running Windows 2000 Server and send print jobs to them as usual, whether the printing device is attached to the server itself or located elsewhere on the network. Similarly, Macintosh users can use the Chooser interface for connecting to printers that are set up for AppleTalk printing devices and those available to a computer that is running Windows 2000 Server.

With Services for Macintosh, installing and setting up printing devices and creating printers is no different than the process you use with Windows 2000 Server with one exception: the print server and the file server must appear in the same zone. All Windows 2000 print queues are automatically shared out for Macintosh computers. However, consider the following performance issues as part of your planning.

In Windows 2000 networks, printing devices traditionally have attached to a server through serial or parallel ports, whereas printing devices that are used on Macintosh networks have been attached to the network by using a LocalTalk connection. With Services for Macintosh, you can either attach a printing device to a computer that is running Windows 2000 Server or put it on the AppleTalk network. Either way, both types of clients can send print jobs to the printing device. (For AppleTalk, the printer must be a PostScript printer that uses the LaserWriter driver.)

To obtain fastest performance, attach printing devices to the network rather than to a port. The following attachment options are listed in order from slowest to fastest:

1. The printing device is connected to a serial port attached to the computer that is running Windows 2000 Server. (Some older models of the Apple LaserWriter can be attached only to a serial port, not to a parallel port.)

2. The printing device is connected to a parallel port attached to the computer that is running Windows 2000 Server.

3. The printing device is connected to the AppleTalk network through LocalTalk, which is the typical Macintosh network attachment.

4. The printing device is connected to AppleTalk through the token ring or Ethernet media.

Printing devices with built-in Ethernet interfaces offer the best performance. These printing devices attach directly to the network and do not have to be physically close to the computer that is running Windows 2000 Server. In addition, they print at faster network transmission speeds than printers that rely on parallel or serial connections.

Avoiding LaserPrep Wars

With some AppleTalk networks, a condition known as LaserPrep Wars causes slow printing performance. Services for Macintosh solves this problem.

LaserPrep Wars occur when a network has Macintosh clients that use two or more versions of Chooser Packs (a collection of files, some of which contain PostScript information). When a Macintosh computer sends a print job to a PostScript printer, the printer uses a Chooser Pack to interpret PostScript commands in the print job, which include a PostScript preparation file (also called a LaserPrep file) and a PostScript driver. A printer can use only one version of the LaserPrep file at a time. When a Macintosh user sends a print job to the printer, the Macintosh checks for the printer's version of the LaserPrep file. If the printer currently has a different version than the Macintosh client uses, the Macintosh client sends its version of the LaserPrep file along with the print job and instructs the printer to load that file as the printer's resident LaserPrep file. Because Macintosh computers with different LaserPrep file versions send print jobs to a printer, different versions of the LaserPrep file are loaded and unloaded on the printer.

Performance problems arise because the printer must load and unload versions of the LaserPrep file and then print a startup page each time a different LaserPrep file becomes resident. This can also reduce the life cycle of the printer.

For example, suppose a Macintosh user whose client uses Chooser Pack version 6.0 sends a document to the printer. The LaserPrep version 6.0 file is made resident on the printer. Then, if the next document sent to the printer comes from a client that is using Chooser Pack version 7.0, the printer must reset, load LaserPrep 7.0, and print a new startup page before printing the document.

Services for Macintosh solves the LaserPrep Wars problem by sending the LaserPrep file with each job. This extra effort actually improves overall performance: the printer never has to spend time making a LaserPrep resident or printing a startup page.

For printers on an AppleTalk network, LaserPrep Wars are guaranteed to be avoided only if the printer is captured. If the printer is not captured, users who send print jobs directly to the printer, bypassing the print server, can initiate LaserPrep Wars.

LaserPrep Wars are always prevented when printers are attached directly to a computer that is running Windows 2000 Server that is set up with Services for Macintosh.

Advanced Printing Topics

Whether printing devices are attached to the computer that is running Windows 2000 Server or are located elsewhere on the AppleTalk network, the Printers folder displays a list of print jobs for the printers you created to represent the devices. Each list, by default, presents jobs on a first-come, first-serve basis. You can change the priority of jobs, however, and specify permissions for the printer and times for print jobs to run. For example:

- Set up multiple printers that all send print jobs to a single printing device. You might want to assign the printers a priority number or assign times for the printer to spool its jobs. Figure 13.7 illustrates this approach.

- Set up a single printer that sends print jobs to a pool of printing devices. Doing this can make printing more efficient because print jobs are sent to the first available printing device in the pool.

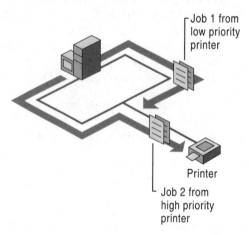

Figure 13.7   Multiple Printers with a Single Printing Device

Creating Multiple Printers for a Single Printing Device

You might want to create multiple printers, all of which send print jobs to a single printing device. Each printer has a print-priority level associated with it. If you create two printers and associate them with a single printing device, jobs routed to the printer with the highest priority print first.

For Windows 2000 users, it is a good idea to create a group that corresponds to each printer. For example, users in Group 1 might have access rights to a priority 1 printer, users in Group 2 might have access rights to a priority 2 printer, and so on. This allows you to prioritize print jobs according to the users who are submitting them.

For Macintosh users, however, one user account must be created for all incoming print jobs to the computer that is running Windows 2000 Server. Consequently, all Macintosh users who are sending print jobs through the computer that is running Windows 2000 Server have the same access rights.

▶ **To specify priorities for printers sending jobs to a single printing device**

1. If necessary, create two or more printers and share them.
2. Open **Printers**.
3. Right-click a printer, and click **Properties**.
4. In the **Advanced** tab, select a priority.

Creating Printing Pools

When you create a printer, you can associate it with more than one printing device in order to form a printing pool. A printing pool consists of two or more similar printing devices associated with one printer name. To set up a pool, you create a printer and assign it as many output ports as you have identical printing devices. Printing pools have the following characteristics:

- All devices in the pool share the same print property settings and act as a single unit. For example, stopping one device stops them all.
- Print destinations can be of the same type, or they can be mixed (serial, parallel, and network).
- When a job arrives for the printing pool, the spooler on the computer that is running Windows 2000 Server checks the destinations to see which device is idle. The first port that is selected gets checked first, the second port second, and so on. If your pool consists of a different type of port, make sure you select the fastest port first (network, then parallel, then serial).
- A printing pool can contain a mixture of printer interface types, but the printing devices must all use the same printer driver.

Remote Access

Windows 2000 supports remote access, which permits remote clients to connect transparently to corporate networks or the Internet over the protocols that are listed in Table 13.9.

Table 13.9   Supported Remote Access Protocols

Protocol Name	Description
Layer Two Tunneling Protocol (L2TP)	A protocol used in conjunction with IPSec to create secure virtual private networks (VPNs).
Point-to-Point Protocol (PPP)	A protocol used for dial-up connections. PPP encapsulates IP, IPX, AppleTalk, and NetBEUI packets.
Point-to-Point Tunneling Protocol (PPTP)	A protocol extension to PPP that permits remote access to VPNs over TCP/IP.

The Point-to-Point Protocol (PPP) defines a method for encapsulating network layer protocol information over point-to-point links. The AppleTalk Control Protocol (ATCP) (RFC 1378) defines the Network Control Protocols (NCPs) used by the AppleTalk Protocol over PPP. ATCP follows the Link Control Protocol (LCP) for packet exchange, with some exceptions related to frame modification, the use of the data link layer protocol and code fields, timeouts, and configuration options.

ATCP is installed automatically if remote access and the AppleTalk Protocol (ATP) are installed. ATP is installed automatically when the file server and print server are installed. You can also install ATP separately.

ATCP supports the following:

- Addresses are dynamically allocated.
- Users do not have to change their passwords.
- Client callback provided.
- Guest account authentication and access authorization are the same as for other dial-up methods.
- User passwords must be saved in reversibly encrypted cleartext format on the dial-up server.
- For ATCP clients, the administrator must configure encrypted cleartext password storage for each user.

Troubleshooting

The following sections provide solutions for problems that users and administrators might encounter on a computer that is running Windows 2000 Server with Services for Macintosh installed.

Administrator and User Issues and Solutions

When a Macintosh user is unable to gain access to a Services for Macintosh resource, first check the Macintosh and ensure that the following are true:

- The Macintosh client is using System version 6.0.7 or later of the Macintosh operating system.
- The Macintosh client is using current versions of its network drivers, and these versions are compatible with the version of the operating system on that Macintosh.

To determine whether the issue is with the Macintosh computer, try to gain access to a network entity other than the computer that is running Windows 2000 Server or a printer (for example, an AppleShare server or a printer that is not used by Services for Macintosh). If the Macintosh computer has no access to any network entity, the problem might be with the Macintosh computer.

If a computer that is running Windows 2000 Server fails to start and Event Viewer is filled with AppleTalk error messages, see whether your network has a bridge that is filtering packets. It might be filtering out the server's request to find a unique address.

The following sections address common user problems and their solutions.

Macintosh-accessible volume is unavailable to a user

The volume might be configured as a private volume. A private volume is any volume for which the owner, primary group, or categories have no access permissions; only the volume's owner has permissions. In this case, only the owner has access to the volume.

To make the volume accessible to users, the owner should use the **Permissions** dialog box, available from the **MacFile** menu, to give the primary Group or Everyone categories at least one permission for the volume.

If the Macintosh-accessible volume is on a CDFS (CD-ROM File System)volume and it appears in the Chooser but cannot be selected, the CD-ROM on which it was created might not be in the disk drive.

Make sure that the correct CD-ROM is in the disk drive and that the drive door is closed.

Macintosh user's password has expired without notification

Users are notified that their passwords have expired only if MS-UAM files are installed on their clients. If they are using the standard UAM for Apple, they are told only that their logon attempts failed and that they should try again later. For more information about installing the Macintosh client software, see the Teachtext Readme file in the MS-UAM volume.

To correct this problem, install the MS-UAM files on the user's client computer.

User has forgotten his or her password

Assign the user a new password.

Incorrect password message appears, although it was entered correctly

The user might have two accounts on separate domains, each with a different password. Have the user enter the domain name and then the account name in the **Name** box when they log on. For example, type:

Domain1\alex02A

Computer that is running Windows 2000 Server and Services for Macintosh appears in the Chooser for Macintosh clients and then disappears

Two physical AppleTalk networks have been given the same network numbers. The server that started first works fine. When the second server is started, it appears in the Chooser on one Macintosh client, and then disappears and appears in the Chooser on a different client. The order of appearance is unpredictable.

Use the **Configure** button, available when you choose **Network** to check the network numbers used for each physical network. When you find the duplicates, change one so that all physical networks are using unique network numbers. After you make the change, restart the AppleTalk Protocol on the server on which you made the change.

If you find no duplicates, see if your network has a bridge that is filtering packets. It might be filtering out the second server's requests to find a unique address.

Computer that is running Windows 2000 Server and printers intermittently appears and disappears in the Chooser

Zones and network numbers are no longer in correspondence. When you change the name of a zone, you must shut down the routers that are directly connected to the networks in question for 10 to 15 minutes before restarting. This allows the other routers to discard old zone information. If you have not changed zone names recently, this situation could occur if an AppleTalk network number is duplicated on your AppleTalk network.

Cannot find a file or folder

The user might not have the necessary permissions for the folder that contains the file or folder in question. The administrator or the owner of the folder can reset permissions to allow the user access to the folder.

Cannot save a file with an 8.3 file name from the Macintosh computer

A short name might already exist with the 8.3 file name; however, Macintosh users cannot see it. Give the 8.3 file name a different name.

Cannot find a server

Follow these steps:

1. Make sure AppleTalk is installed.

2. Make sure the cable system between the client and the server is correct. Make sure the network connection, layout, and cable termination conform to the specifications of the cable system you are using.

3. Start with the client that cannot find the server. If the cable system is LocalTalk, check whether the LocalTalk connector box is attached firmly to the printer port, not the modem port on the back of the Macintosh client.

   If the cable system is not LocalTalk, ensure that the network connector is securely connected to its port. Click **Network** to review other network settings.

4. Determine whether other clients are having the same problem.

   If they are, check the cables and connections at the server. Ensure that the server is operating properly. If the server is not the source of the problem, proceed to step 5.

5. Check for breaks in the cable system. If the missing server is on a local network, check each client between the client that cannot find the server and the server, until you find the server in the Chooser. The break in the cable system is between the client that shows the server in the Chooser and the client that does not.

   If the missing server is on a different physical network in the internet, use your router seeding plan and server information table to determine which client is the first one beyond the router that links the two networks. Test that client, and then test each client beyond it (in the direction of the server) until the server appears in the Chooser.

   If the server was visible at the first client, work backward toward your own network and test the client adjacent to each router until the server fails to appear in the Chooser. Isolate the break by testing the clients on this network.

6. When you have isolated the network break, check the network cables and connection at that location to make sure all are securely attached. Try again to display the server in the Chooser. If necessary, try replacing cables or connectors.

Cannot see any zones within the Chooser on a Macintosh computer

Make sure AppleTalk is active in the Chooser. Click **Network**. Make sure the correct network port is selected.

There might be network problems, so check for the following:

- The Macintosh might be running on an AppleTalk Phase 2 Network without the correct Ethernet driver.
- The router might be using Phase 1, although the rest of the internet is using Phase 2.
- The Macintosh is configured for one type of network media but is actually on a network that uses a different media type.

If the problem persists, make sure all routers are configured properly.

The Microsoft UAM volume cannot be found

When the computer running Windows 2000 Server was installed, there might have been insufficient disk space for the Microsoft UAM volume. Or the computer running Windows 2000 Server might have been installed without an NTFS partition.

You can create a volume by typing and entering the following at the command prompt:

setup /i oemnxpsm.inf /c uaminstall

This command line copies UAM files to the AppleShare folder in the first NTFS partition and sets up registry values for this volume in the registry editor.

View of a folder is erased or does not match the view selected in the view menu

The folder owner must log on to the server, connect to the Macintosh-accessible volume and select a view (such as **View By, View By Name**) from the **View** menu. The selected view then remains in effect.

The Finder occasionally cannot show the correct view of a folder. Having the folder owner log on and select the view resolves the situation.

File is now displayed with the default Windows 2000 icon instead of the correct icon

The application that uses that type of data file might have been removed from the Macintosh.

If the file had no resource fork, use the Apple ResEdit tool to reset the file type and file creator of the file. Use this tool only if you are experienced in using it.

The Windows 2000 user does not have sufficient permissions to view the contents of the folder. Use the computer that is running Windows 2000 Server to make sure the user has Read permission, or the folder owner can use a Macintosh to give both the See Files and See Folders permissions. (A Windows 2000 user must have both these permissions to get the Windows 2000 Server Read permission.)

Macintosh user did not receive a server message

Only Macintosh clients that are running version 2.1 (or later) of the AppleTalk Filing Protocol can see server messages. Make sure the client has installed version 3.0 of AppleShare, which uses later versions of this protocol.

User cannot automatically connect to a Macintosh-accessible volume by using an alias

Macintosh clients can be configured to automatically connect to volumes when the client is started or when the user double-clicks an alias to an object on a volume. However, automatic connection to volumes is not supported by the Macintosh system software if the volume is configured with a volume password or if the user originally connected to the volume by using MS-UAM.

If the volume has a password, you can mount it through the Chooser and then use the alias. Or you can specify that it be opened at system startup time when you mount the volume.

If you are using MS-UAM to log on to the server, you must mount the volume through the Chooser and then use the alias.

Printing Issues and Solutions

The following are common issues and solutions involving printers or printing devices.

AppleTalk printers do not show up in the printers folder available from the AppleTalk Printers dialog box

Clicking the AppleTalk zone name does not display the printers in that zone. You must double-click the **Zone** name from the **Available AppleTalk Printers** dialog box.

Printing error messages consistently appear when the printing device prints documents

- Reset the printing device by turning it off and then on again.

The PostScript error "Offending command" appears at the end of the printed document or elsewhere

A user or administrator might have canceled the print job while it was spooling. No action is necessary, and you can reprint the file as desired.

A user is spooling to a PSTODIB printing device, and it has PostScript level 2 elements or is a PostScript level 2 document.

Print jobs fail to print

Check each printing device that prints jobs for these printers. If one of the printing devices is turned off, all printing devices can stop printing.

Macintosh extended characters (such as bullets, smart quotes, and copyright and trademark symbols) are changed into other characters on the LaserWriter II

Set the communications port for the LaserWriter correctly, referring to the owner's manual for the printing device. If the LaserWriter has not been set correctly, printing problems can occur, regardless of how you set the COM port in **Control Panel** in Windows 2000 Server. This problem affects Macintosh computers more frequently than Windows 2000 computers because Macintosh computers use extended characters more often than other clients do.

For more information about troubleshooting, see the link to the Microsoft Technet Web site at http://windows.microsoft.com/windows2000/reskit/webresources.

Additional Resources

- For more information about AppleTalk, see *Inside AppleTalk*, Second Edition by G.S. Sidhu, R. F. Andrews, and A. B. Oppenheimer, 1990, Massachusetts: Addison-Wesley.

P A R T   4

Media Integration

The successful implementation and efficient use of multimedia applications on a network continue to be important issues for network managers and administrators. Part 4 examines Microsoft® Windows® 2000 features that support and enhance multimedia networking.

In This Part

C H A P T E R   1 4

Asynchronous Transfer Mode

Microsoft® Windows® 2000 provides native Asynchronous Transfer Mode (ATM) services, which integrate ATM functions with the Microsoft® Windows® family of operating systems. Windows 2000 supports ATM applications in a variety of networking situations, including ATM LANE and IP over ATM, all of which are detailed throughout this chapter.

In This Chapter

Related Information in the Resource Kit

- For more information about telephony integration, see "Telephony Integration and Conferencing" in this book.

- For more information about other types of QoS, see "Quality of Service" in the *Microsoft® Windows® 2000 Server Resource Kit TCP/IP Core Networking Guide*.

Introduction to ATM

Asynchronous Transfer Mode (ATM) describes several related, standards-based technologies that provide high-speed communication over a broad range of media. The International Telecommunication Union (ITU-T) defines ATM as "a high-speed, connection-oriented multiplexing and switching method specified in international standards utilizing fixed-length cells to support multiple types of traffic." Before you can decide whether to deploy ATM in your network, you need to understand how it integrates with current networking environments and how it functions in new networking environments.

Asynchronous Transfer Mode (ATM) is a wide array of services and concepts. At this time, ATM technologies are used selectively in local and wide area networks. Some networks have been completely transformed into native ATM networks, with software, end-station hardware, and network fabric all made up of ATM devices and drivers. In other networks, ATM is used only in the network backbone, shuttling data from one local area network (LAN) to another. In some instances, ATM is deployed in small pockets intermixed with standard LAN components and other networking technologies.

ATM is continually evolving. In some cases, its usefulness is judged by how well it emulates legacy networks; that is, how it compares with traditional LAN technologies such as Ethernet and Token Ring. In other cases, ATM provides so many clear advantages in terms of speed, manageability, and accuracy that it has quickly been recognized as the only viable solution.

To clarify ATM and to define the terms and concepts that are essential to any understanding of ATM, this chapter begins with an overview of ATM and its related technologies. It then describes how ATM is supported and integrated into current networks. The final section includes details on Microsoft Windows 2000 ATM support, how the support is achieved, and how you can maximize the new, native ATM services provided in Windows 2000.

The most important features of Windows 2000 ATM support are easy to list: it provides native support of LAN emulation, IP over ATM, TAPI, Direct Streaming, and other services. Each of these is further detailed in "Windows 2000 ATM Services" later in this chapter.

ATM Overview

Asynchronous Transfer Mode (ATM) is a connection-oriented, unreliable, virtual circuit packet switching technology. ATM technology includes:

- Scalable performance — ATM can send data across a network quickly and accurately, regardless of the size of the network. ATM works well on both very low and very high-speed media.

- Flexible, guaranteed Quality of Service (QoS) — ATM allows the accuracy and speed of data transfer to be specified by the client. This feature distinguishes ATM from other high-speed LAN technologies such as gigabit Ethernet. The QoS feature of ATM also supports time dependent (or isochronous) traffic. Traffic management at the hardware level ensures that the level of service exists end-to-end. Each virtual circuit in an ATM network is unaffected by traffic on other virtual circuits. Small packet size and a simple header structure ensure that switching is done quickly and that bottlenecks are minimized.

- Speed — ATM imposes no architectural speed limitations. Its pre-negotiated virtual circuits, fixed-length cells, message segmentation and re-assembly in hardware, and hardware-level switching all help support extremely fast forwarding of data.

- Integration of different traffic types — ATM supports integration of voice, video, and data services on a single network. ATM over ADSL enables residential access to these services.

Most importantly, unlike most connectionless networking protocols, ATM is a deterministic networking system — it provides predictable, guaranteed quality of service. From end to end, every component in an ATM network provides a high level of control.

Basic Components

ATM contains two basic components: an endstation, a computer connected to the ATM network; and an ATM switch, the device responsible for connecting endstations and making sure data is transferred successfully.

The scalability of ATM means that connections made from an ATM endstation can be made using a single protocol to any other endstation attached to the ATM network, without requiring additional protocol layers.

Traditional LAN and ATM LAN

The following sections examine how a traditional LAN operates, and contrast the two networking systems in order to clarify the strengths of ATM.

Connectionless vs. Connection-Oriented

Traditional local area networks, such as Ethernet and Token Ring, use a connectionless, unreliable approach when sending information across the network. Likewise, TCP/IP data transfers between networks are connectionless and unreliable. These traditional approaches are very different from that employed by ATM, which is a connection-oriented, circuit-based technology. The following section describes the differences between these two approaches to networking.

Traditional LAN

In a traditional LAN, each client is connected to the network by an adapter card, which has a driver. Above that driver is a protocol driver, such as TCP/IP. The protocol driver bundles information into frames of varying size and gives each bundle an appropriate header. As a result, when the adapter gains access to the media, the data packets are sent on the media to a destination hardware address. Traditional LAN technologies do not guarantee that data arrives on time or in the proper order. While Ethernet and Token Ring can detect errors, they provide no service guarantees and are not responsible for the recovery of missing or corrupted data packets.

Because they are joined by a common medium, each station on the traditional LAN sees the frames of data put on the wire by each of the others, regardless of whether the frame is passed sequentially from one station to the next (as in a ring topology) or broadcast to all stations simultaneously (as with Ethernet). Each station has an adapter card, which processes the frame and examines the destination address. If the address applies to that computer, the frame is checked for errors and if there are no errors, the adapter initiates a hardware interrupt and passes the frame to the network adapter driver. Figure 14.1 shows an example of a traditional LAN.

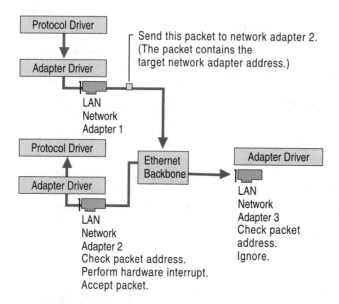

Figure 14.1   Traditional LAN: Connectionless Data Transmittal of a Packet

Because a traditional LAN is connectionless, it cannot provide guarantees or similar features. For example, it cannot determine the status of the destination adapter to ensure that it can receive a frame. It cannot ensure that bandwidth is available throughout the transmission. Unanticipated bottlenecks due to the media access control scheme of shared access technologies can hinder a traditional LAN technology's ability to support time-sensitive applications such as video or voice traffic. Traditional LANs can use upper-level protocol drivers to verify packet transmission (retransmitting, if necessary), partition big messages into smaller ones, use time stamps for synchronization, and so forth. However, these services add time to the transmission, and none of them provide end-to-end Quality of Service (QoS) guarantees.

Traditional Internetworking

If the destination address is remote rather than local, the differences increase. If a router on an Ethernet network detects a broadcast meant for another network, the router accepts the packet and passes it on using TCP/IP. A TCP/IP datagram is packet-switched to its destination individually. Each frame's header contains a globally significant switching address; this address allows a routing decision to be made each time the packet is forwarded — and packets to the same destination might follow completely different paths to get there, jumping over networks employing different underlying technology. No connection is required, but no delivery is guaranteed. Figure 14.2 shows an example of two packets taking different routes through a traditional LAN.

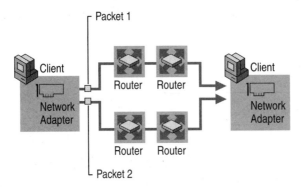

Figure 14.2   Two Packets Taking Different Routes Through a Traditional LAN

Like an Ethernet data transfer, a routed data transfer cannot offer guarantees because bandwidth is never reserved ahead of time. The packets being sent over TCP/IP are simply put on the wire and routed. While this allows flexibility in routing around obstructions, network performance can vary a great deal depending on conditions at the routers and on the degree of network traffic at any given time.

ATM Networks

On the other hand, ATM is connection-oriented. An ATM endpoint establishes a defined path known as a virtual circuit (VC) to the destination endpoint prior to sending any data on the network. It then sends a series of same-size frames called cells along the virtual circuit towards the destination.

While establishing the connection, the ATM endpoint also negotiates a Quality of Service (QoS) contract for the virtual circuit. The QoS contract spells out the bandwidth, maximum transit delay, acceptable variance in the transit delay, and so forth, that the VC provides, and this contract extends from one endpoint to the other through all of the intermediate ATM switches.

The path of ATM traffic is established at the outset, and the switching hardware merely needs to examine a simple header to identify the proper path. Beyond specifying a path, ATM allows a location to establish a full duplex connection (that is, traffic can travel in both directions) with multiple locations at the same time. Note, however, that ATM is an unreliable transmission protocol. It does not acknowledge the receipt of cells sent. As with LANs, missing or corrupted information must be detected and corrected by upper-layer protocols.

Figure 14.3 illustrates ATM virtual circuit and packet transmission.

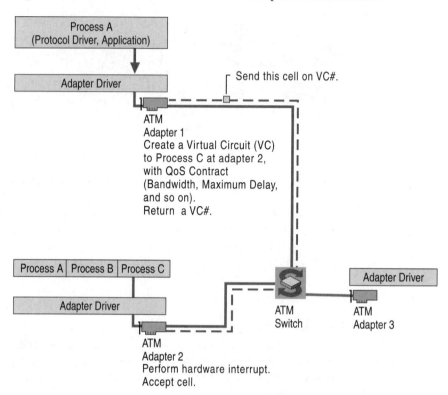

Figure 14.3   ATM Virtual Circuit and Packet Transmission

Network Speed

Unlike Ethernet networks, ATM has no inherent speed limit, and its efficiency is not affected by the distance that the data has to travel. In addition, ATM establishes the pathway for a particular series of packets at the outset and ATM switches make minimal switching decisions thereafter. To travel across the ATM network, data is segmented into same-size cells, and encapsulated with a header that contains switching, congestion, and error-checking information.

Cells are transmitted in order, and the ATM network uses Virtual Path Identifier and Virtual Channel Identifier (VPI/VCI) numbers in the ATM header to forward them efficiently. A switch reads the header, compares the VPI/VCI to its switching table to determine the correct output port and new VPI/VCI, and then forwards the cell. All of the addressing information the ATM switch needs is contained in the header and is always found in the same place. This makes the forwarding task simple to implement in hardware, reducing latency. Moreover, with ATM from end to end, there is no data translation required if a packet must travel from a LAN through a WAN to reach a destination LAN.

ATM virtual paths and virtual channels and the ATM cell structure are explained in more detail later in this chapter. Figure 14.4 shows two ATM endstations sending fixed-length cells from A to B (although ATM traffic is bi-directional).

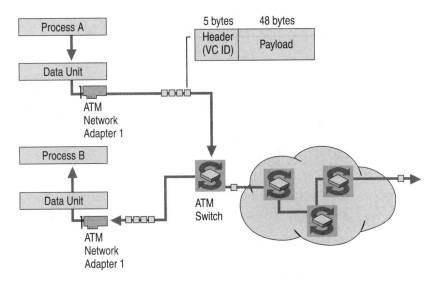

Figure 14.4   ATM Fixed-Length Cells (Bi-Directional Traffic)

Because ATM uses small (53-byte), fixed-length cells that require less logic to process, the network spends no time determining where a particular cell begins and ends. The small cell size ensures that delays in forwarding cells are minimized. Because the cell size is so predictable, buffer usage and analysis algorithms can be simplified and optimized.

Traditional LAN technologies, such as Ethernet, have inherent speed limitations; either the underlying infrastructure (the cable) or the segment length must be changed to support fast traffic. However, unlike Ethernet and Token Ring, ATM has no such imposed limitations. If you can invent a faster physical layer — if you can design a quicker method of transmitting data from one place to another over one wire or many wires — ATM can work over that physical layer and at those new speeds. In addition, ATM allows information with different requirements and from different nodes to be transmitted nearly simultaneously without contention.

ATM places fixed-length cells on the media when the data is produced according to the parameters of a negotiated connection. ATM can simultaneously handle the needs of isochronous (time-dependent) traffic, such as voice and video, and non-isochronous traffic, such as LAN data.

The next section describes the hardware components that connect an endstation to an ATM network, and the software that establishes, manages, and maintains the network connections.

ATM Architecture

ATM is a combination of hardware and software that can provide either an end-to-end network or form a high-speed backbone for older protocols. The structure of ATM and its software components comprise the ATM architecture.

ATM Model

The ATM model's primary layers are the physical layer, the ATM layer, and the ATM Adaptation layer. Each layer and sublayer is described in more detail in the following sections.

Physical Layer

The physical layer provides for the transmission and reception of ATM cells across a physical medium between two ATM devices; this can be a transmission between an ATM endpoint and an ATM switch, or it can be between two ATM switches. The physical layer is subdivided into a Physical Medium Dependent sublayer and Transmission Convergence sublayer.

PMD Sublayer

The Physical Medium Dependent (PMD) sublayer is responsible for the transmission and reception of individual bits on a physical medium. These responsibilities encompass bit timing, signal encoding, interacting with the physical medium, and the cable or wire itself.

ATM does not rely on any specific bit rate, encoding scheme or medium and various specifications for ATM exist for coaxial cable, shielded and unshielded twisted pair wire, and optical fiber at speeds ranging from 64 kilobits per second to 9.6 gigabits per second. In addition, the ATM physical medium can extend up to 60 kilometers or more using single-mode fiber and long-reach lasers, so it can readily support campus-wide connectivity and even private metropolitan area networks (MANs). The independence of ATM from a particular set of hardware constraints has allowed it to be implemented over radio and satellite links.

Transmission Convergence Sublayer

The Transmission Convergence (TC) sublayer functions as a converter between the bit stream of ATM cells and the Physical Medium Dependent sublayer. When transmitting, the TC sublayer maps ATM cells onto the format of the Physical Medium Dependent sublayer (such as DS-3 or SONET frames). Because a continuous stream of bytes is required, unused portions of the ATM cell stream are "filled" by idle cells. These idle cells are identified in the ATM header and are silently discarded by the receiver. They are never passed to the ATM layer for processing.

The TC sublayer also generates and verifies the Header Error Control (HEC) field for each cell. On the transmitting side, it calculates the HEC and places it in the header. On the receiving side, the TC sublayer checks the HEC for verification. If a single bit error can be corrected, the bit is corrected and the results are passed to the ATM layer. If the error cannot be corrected (as in the case of a multi-bit error) the cell is silently discarded.

Finally, the TC sublayer delineates the ATM cells, marking where ATM cells begin and where they end. The boundaries of the ATM cells can be determined from the Physical Medium Dependent layer formatting or from the incoming byte stream using the HEC field. The PMD performs the HEC validation per byte on the preceding 4 bytes. If it finds a match, the next ATM cell boundary is 48 bytes away (corresponding to the ATM payload). The PMD performs this verification several times to ensure that the cell boundaries have been determined correctly.

The ATM Layer

The ATM layer provides cell multiplexing, demultiplexing, and VPI/VCI routing functions. The ATM layer also supervises the cell flow to ensure that all connections remain within their negotiated cell throughput limits. If connections operate outside their negotiated parameters, the ATM layer can take corrective action so the misbehaving connections do not affect connections that are obeying their negotiated connection contract. The ATM layer also maintains the cell sequence from any source.

The ATM layer multiplexes and demultiplexes and routes ATM cells, and ensures their sequence from end to end. However, if a cell is dropped by a switch due to congestion or corruption, it is not the ATM layer's responsibility to correct the dropped cell through retransmission or to notify other layers of the dropped cell. Layers above the ATM layer must sense the lost cell and decide whether to correct it or disregard it.

In the case of interactive voice or video, a lost cell is typically disregarded because it would take too long to resend the cell and place it in the proper sequence to reconstruct the audio or video signal. A significant number of dropped cells in time-dependent services, such as voice or video, results in a choppy audio or video playback, but the ATM layer cannot correct the problem unless a higher Quality of Service is specified for the connection.

In the case of data (such as a file transfer), the upper layer application must sense the absence of the cell and retransmit it. A file with missing 48-bytes chunks here and there is a corrupted file that is unacceptable to the receiver. Because operations such as file transfers are not time dependent, the contents of the cell can be recovered by incurring a delay in the transmission of the file corresponding to the recovery of the lost cell.

ATM Layer Multiplexing and Demultiplexing

ATM layer multiplexing blends all the different input types so that the connection parameters of each input are preserved. This process is known as traffic shaping.

ATM layer demultiplexing takes each cell from the ATM cell stream and, based on the VPI/VCI, either routes it (for an ATM switch) or passes the cell to the ATM Adaptation Layer (AAL) process that corresponds to the cell (for an ATM endpoint).

ATM Adaptation Layers

The ATM Adaptation Layers (AAL) are responsible for the creation and reception of 48-byte payloads through the lower layers of ATM on behalf of different types of applications. Though there are five different types of AALs, Windows 2000 supports only AAL5. ATM Adaptation is necessary to link the cell-based technology at the ATM Layer to the bit-stream technology of digital devices (such as telephones and video cameras) and the packet-stream technology of modern data networks (such as Frame Relay, X.25 or LAN protocols such as TCP/IP or Ethernet).

The five different AALs each provide a distinct class of service:

AAL0 AAL0 is user-defined, or No AAL, meaning that no AAL layer is used. In all other AAL types, some delineation of the data segment is included at the AAL level before the segment is made into cells. This affects how the data is passed up to the ATM layer. With AAL5, the data is not passed up until a complete AAL segment is received. With AAL0, for example, there is no delineation or synchronization, so individual cells are passed up as they are received, or the adapter might optimize and accrue a certain amount before indicating that a cell can be passed along.

AAL1 AAL1 provides circuit emulation over an ATM network. This requires constant bit rate, time-dependent service. To provide this, AAL1 adds timestamps, error checking and sequencing to the data payload. Additional functionality is provided in AAL1 to load the 48-byte cell payload with multiple smaller-than-48-byte samples, as is usually required with voice streams. Due to its high overhead, AAL1 is used only when these features are required. This format is most commonly used with voice or video applications.

AAL2 AAL2 is a mechanism that allows the transfer of high-speed, variable bit rate information in an isochronous, connection-oriented manner. Unlike AAL1, AAL2 is designed to use bandwidth only when data is sent. AAL2 has never been fully defined by the standards committee and did not gained wide acceptance. It has largely been supplanted by AAL5.

AAL3/4   AAL3/4 combines two once-separate AAL specifications. AAL3 was intended for the framing of connection-oriented protocols, while AAL4 was intended for the framing of connectionless protocols. While pursuing these two standards, the ATM standards bodies learned that there was no difference in the framing between the two types of protocols; therefore, they combined the two separate framing methods to create AAL3/4. This AAL adds information to the payload regarding segment size, sequencing, and ordering control. However, AAL 3/4 is rarely used because of the high overhead required; AAL5 provides the same services with minimal overhead.

AAL5   AAL5 provides a way for non-isochronous, variable bit rate, connectionless applications to send and receive data. AAL5 was developed as a way to provide a more efficient transfer of network traffic than AAL3/4. AAL5 merely adds a trailer to the payload to indicate size and provide error detection. AAL5 is the AAL of choice when sending connection-oriented or connectionless LAN protocol traffic over an ATM network. Windows 2000 supports AAL5.

AAL5 in Detail

AAL5 provides a straightforward framing at the Common Part Convergence Sublayer (CPCS) that behaves more like existing LAN technologies, such as Ethernet. Figure 14.5 shows a detailed breakdown of an AAL5 Cell Header and Payload.

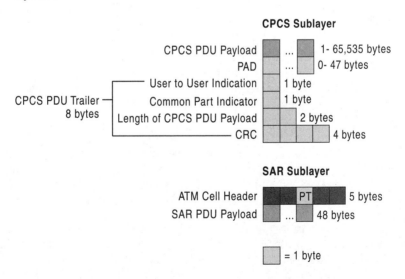

Figure 14.5   Breakdown of an AAL5 Cell Header and Payload

With AAL5, there is no longer a dual encapsulation. The service class frames cells at the CPCS, but not at the Segmentation and Reassembly (SAR) sublayer to minimize overhead. It also uses a bit in the Payload Type (PT) field of the ATM header rather than a separate SAR framing.

AAL5 is the AAL of choice when sending connection-oriented (X.25 or Frame Relay) or connectionless (IP or IPX) LAN protocol traffic over an ATM network.

AAL5 CPCS Sublayer

Figure 14.5 shows the framing that occurs at the AAL5 CPCS sublayer. (Note that only a trailer is added.)

CPCS PDU Payload

The block of data that an application sends. The size can vary from 1 byte to 65,535 bytes. The PAD consists of padding bytes of variable length (0-47 bytes), which create a whole number of cells by making the CPCS PDU payload length a multiple of 48 bytes.

User-to-User Indication

Transfers information between AAL users.

Common Part Indicator

Currently used only for alignment processes so that the AAL5 trailer falls on a 64-bit boundary.

Length of CPCS PDU Payload Field

Indicates the length of the CPCS PDU payload in bytes. The length does not include the PAD.

Cyclic Redundancy Check (CRC)

A Cyclic Redundancy Check, or CRC, is a 32-bit portion of the trailer that performs error checking on the bits in the CPCS PDU. The AAL5 CRC uses the same CRC-32 algorithm used in 802.x-based networks such as Ethernet and Token Ring.

AAL5 SAR Sublayer

Byte-by-byte, Figure 14.5 shows the framing that occurs at the AAL5 SAR sublayer. There is no SAR header or trailer added. On the transmitting side, the AAL5 SAR sublayer merely segments the CPCS PDU into 48-byte units and passes them to the ATM layer for the final ATM header.

On the receiving side, the sublayer reassembles a series of 48-byte units and passes the result to the CPCS. The AAL5 SAR uses the third bit in the Payload Type (PT) field to indicate when the last 48-byte unit in a CPCS PDU is being sent. When the ATM cell is received with the third bit of the PT field set, the ATM layer indicates this fact to the AAL; the AAL then begins a CRC and length-checking analysis of the full CPCS PDU.

ATM Cell Structure

At either a private or a public user-network interface (UNI), an ATM cell always consists of a 5-byte header followed by a 48-byte payload. The header is composed of six elements, each detailed in Figure 14.6.

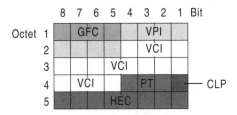

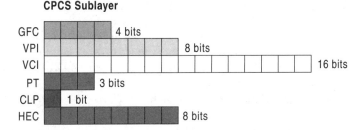

Figure 14.6   ATM Cell Header Structure

Generic Flow Control

The Generic Flow Control (GFC) field is a 4-bit field that was originally added to support the connection of ATM networks to shared access networks such as a Distributed Queue Dual Bus (DQDB) ring. The GFC field was designed to give the User-Network Interface (UNI) 4 bits in which to negotiate multiplexing and flow control among the cells of various ATM connections. However, the use and exact values of the GFC field have not been standardized, and the field is always set to 0000.

Virtual Path Identifier

The Virtual Path Identifier (VPI) defines the virtual path for this particular cell. VPIs for a particular virtual channel connection are discovered during the connection setup process for switched virtual circuit (SVC) connections and manually configured for permanent virtual circuit (PVC) connections. At the UNI, the VPI length of 8 bits allows up to 256 different virtual paths. VPI 0 exists by default on all ATM equipment and is used for administrative purposes such as signaling to create and delete dynamic ATM connections.

Virtual Channel Identifier

The Virtual Channel Identifier (VCI) defines the virtual channel within the specified virtual path for this particular cell. Just as with VPIs, VCIs are also discovered during the connection setup process for switched virtual circuit (SVC) connections and manually configured for permanent virtual circuit (PVC) connections. The VCI length of 16 bits allows up to 65,536 different virtual channels for each virtual path. VCIs 0 to 15 are reserved by the ITU and VCIs from 16 to 32 are reserved by the ATM Forum (for each virtual path). These reserved VCIs are used for signaling, operation and maintenance, and resource management.

The combination of VPI and VCI values identifies the virtual circuit for a specified ATM cell. The VPI/VCI combination provides the ATM forwarding information that the ATM switch uses to forward the cell to its destination. The VPI/VCI combination is not a network layer address such as an IP or IPX network address.

The VPI/VCI combination acts as a local identifier of a virtual circuit and is similar to the Logical Channel Number in X.25 and the Data Link Connection Identifier (DLCI) in Frame Relay. At any particular ATM endpoint or switch, the VPI/VCI uniquely identifies a virtual circuit to the next ATM endpoint or switch. The VPI/VCI pair need not match the VCI/VPI used by the final destination ATM endpoint.

The VPI/VCI combination is unique for each transmission path (that is, for each cable or connection to the ATM switch). However, two different virtual circuits on two different ports on an ATM switch can have the same VPI/VCI without conflict.

Payload Type Indicator

The Payload Type Indicator (PTI) is a 3-bit field. Its bits are used as follows:

The first bit indicates the type of ATM cell that follows. A first bit set to 0 indicates user data; a bit set to 1 indicates operations, administration & management (OA&M) data.

The second bit indicates whether the cell experienced congestion in its journey from source to destination. This bit is also called the Explicit Forward Congestion Indication (EFCI) bit. The second bit is set to 0 by the source; if an interim switch experiences congestion while routing the cell, it sets the bit to 1. After it is set to 1, all other switches in the path leave this bit value at 1.

Destination ATM endpoints can use the EFCI bit to implement flow control mechanisms to throttle back on the transmission rate until cells with an EFCI bit set to 0 are received.

The third bit indicates the last cell in a block for AAL5 in user ATM cells. For non-user ATM cells, the third bit is used for OA&M functions.

Cell Loss Priority

The Cell Loss Priority (CLP) field is a 1-bit field used as a priority indicator. When it is set to 0, the cell is high priority and interim switches must make every effort to forward the cell successfully. When the CLP bit is set to 1, the interim switches sometimes discard the cell in congestion situations. The CLP bit is very similar to the Discard Eligibility (DE) bit in Frame Relay.

An ATM endpoint sets the CLP bit to 1 when a cell is created to indicate a lower priority cell. The ATM switch can set the CLP to 1 if the cell exceeds the negotiated parameters of the virtual channel connection. This is similar to bursting above the Committed Information Rate (CIR) in Frame Relay.

Header Error Check

The Header Error Check (HEC) field is an 8-bit field that allows an ATM switch or ATM endpoint to correct a single-bit error or to detect multi-bit errors in the first 4 bytes of the ATM header. Multi-bit errored cells are silently discarded. The HEC only checks the ATM header and not the ATM payload. Checking the payload for errors is the responsibility of upper layer protocols.

Virtual Paths and Virtual Channels

Key to understanding how ATM transfers information through an ATM network are the concepts of the transmission path, virtual path and virtual channel, illustrated in Figure 14.7.

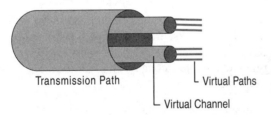

Figure 14.7   **Channels Within a Path Within the Transmission Medium**

Transmission Path

The transmission path consists of the physical cable connected to a particular port of an ATM switch. The cable has a defined bandwidth, such as 155 megabits per second for an Optical Carrier-3 (OC-3) optical fiber link.

Virtual Path

The bandwidth of the transmission path is logically divided into separate virtual paths and identified using the VPI in the ATM header. Each virtual path is allocated a fixed amount of bandwidth. Virtual paths do not dynamically vary their bandwidths beyond what has been allocated.

Virtual Channel

The bandwidth of a virtual path is logically divided into separate virtual channels using a virtual channel identifier in the ATM header. Unlike virtual paths, virtual channels share the bandwidth within a virtual path dynamically.

Switching Hierarchy

The transmission path to virtual path to virtual channel hierarchy is the basis for ATM switching. ATM can switch cells at the transmission path, virtual path and virtual channel level.

Switching at the Transmission Path Level

Switching at the transmission path level allows an ATM switch to determine which output port to use to forward the cell.

Switching at the Virtual Path Level

Switching at the virtual path level allows entire groups of virtual channels to be switched at the same time. Virtual path switching is similar to the telephone system cross-connect switching of entire groups of telephone calls based on the area code of the phone number. The switching occurs based on the area code, not the 7-digit individual phone number.

When performing virtual path switching, an ATM switch looks only at the virtual path identifier in the ATM cell header. This ability to ignore the rest of the header makes virtual path switching faster than virtual channel switching.

ATM virtual path switching most often occurs within the public networks of ATM service providers, because this virtual path switching allows ATM service providers to aggregate bundles of virtual channels along high speed backbone links. These aggregate channels create trunk line structures very similar to those used in telephone networks.

Switching at the Virtual Channel Level

Switching at the virtual channel level allows for a granularity of switching and bandwidth allocation. Virtual channel switching resembles switching a phone call to its final 7-digit location; that is, ATM switching is based on the entire VPI/VCI, just as the final phone switching is based on the entire 10-digit phone number (3-digit area code and 7-digit individual phone number).

ATM virtual channel switching occurs within both private and public networks. A switch must analyze both the virtual path identifier and the virtual channel identifier to make a switching decision.

Quality of Service

As part of the negotiated connection, ATM endpoints establish a service contract that guarantees a specific quality of service. These Quality of Service (QoS) guarantees are not offered by traditional LAN technologies.

With a traditional LAN, any notion of service guarantee is based on priority, where one transmission receives delivery preference over others. Because the sending station does not know the condition of the network or the data recipient prior to transmission (traditional LANs are connectionless), traffic is subject to delay at routers and elsewhere. These unforeseen delays make bandwidth availability and delivery times difficult to predict. While higher-priority traffic generally reaches its destination prior to lower-priority traffic, it is possible that the higher priority traffic arrives too late for isochronous traffic.

Note The term "QoS" applies to several forms of quality guarantees, including ATM QoS, RSVP, and Generic QoS. Of the three, only ATM QoS is implemented at the hardware level.

For more information about other types of QoS, see "Quality of Service" in the *TCP/IP Core Networking Guide*.

ATM offers granular, explicit service guarantees that are not based on a relative structure (such as priority). With ATM, a data supplier can request a specific bandwidth, maximum delay, delay variation tolerance, and so forth. Each ATM switch then determines whether or not it can meet the request after taking current allocations into consideration. If it can accommodate the transmission, it guarantees the service level and allocates the necessary resources. With ATM, the service contract is enforced and the bandwidth is allocated at the hardware level; all of the switches between the sender and receiver know and agree to the service level before the contract is granted. The source station hardware, also having agreed to the contract, is responsible for shaping the traffic to fit the connection contract before it enters the network.

ATM offers the following five service categories:

- Constant Bit Rate (CBR)

  Specifies a fixed bit rate. Data is sent in a steady stream with low cell loss. This is an expensive service because the granted bandwidth must be allocated, regardless of whether or not it is actually used. CBR is typically used for circuit emulation. This category is supported in Windows 2000.

- Variable Bit Rate (VBR)

  Specifies a throughput capacity over time, but data is not sent at a constant rate. This also specifies low cell loss. It is available in two varieties, real-time VBR for isochronous applications and non-real-time VBR for all others.

- Available Bit Rate (ABR)

  Ensures a guaranteed minimum capacity but allows data to be sent at higher capacities when the network is free. ABR adjusts the rate of transmission based on feedback. This specifies low cell loss. ABR provides better throughput than VBR, but is less expensive than CBR. It is important to note that ABR has only recently been fully defined and not all hardware and software support this service category. It is part of the UNI 4.0 specification.

- Unspecified Bit Rate (UBR)

  Does not guarantee bandwidth or throughput; cells can be dropped. A UBR connection does not have a contract with the ATM network. This category is supported in Windows 2000.

- Weighted Unspecified Bit Rate (WUBR)

  The newest service category put forward by the ATM Forum, and it functions by assigning different processing priorities to different types of traffic, similar to a traditional connectionless LAN. Each such type of traffic is carried across a different connection; cells in connections with lower priority are dropped before those with higher priority.

Guaranteed QoS allows ATM to support time-sensitive (isochronous) applications, such as video and voice, as well as more conventional network traffic. While 100-megabit Ethernet and other high speed networks can provide comparable bandwidth, only ATM can provide the QoS guarantees required for real-time telephony, VCR-quality video streaming, CD-quality sound, smooth videoconferencing, and other delay-sensitive voice and video applications.

QoS is so vital to the industry that several initiatives are underway to provide QoS support for connectionless TCP/IP–based networks. While these solutions are useful, they require that all nodes on the network participate — which can be difficult to guarantee on heterogeneous networks. Because these solutions shape the traffic in software, latency and variations in delay are sometimes introduced. This is not the case with ATM.

Most importantly, the acceptance of ATM as a common standard for both LANs and WANs enables enterprise deployment of QoS applications and integrated services. The deployment of ATM/Asymmetric Data Subscriber Line (ADSL) to the home enables residential access to these services. ADSL uses existing copper twisted pair telephone lines to transmit broadband data to the home, without requiring recabling or a new telephone infrastructure. This extends the reach of ATM networks from the home desktop to the business desktop and everywhere in between.

ATM Addresses

ATM addresses are needed to support the use of virtual connections through an ATM network. At the simplest level, ATM addresses are 20 bytes in length and composed of three distinct parts. Figure 14.8 shows the three parts of the 20-byte ATM address.

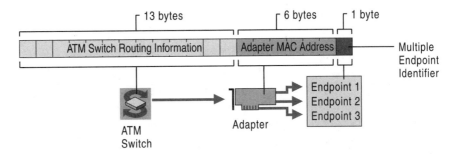

Figure 14.8   Simplified View of ATM Addressing

This ATM address breaks down into the following three basic parts:

ATM switch identifier   The first 13 bytes identify a particular switch in the ATM network. The use of this portion of the address can vary considerably depending on which address format is in use. Each of the three major ATM addressing schemes in use provides information about ATM switch location differently. The three formats are the data country/region code (DCC) format, international code designator (ICD) format, and the E.164 format proposed by the ITU-T for international telephone numbering use in broadband ISDN networks.

Adapter MAC address   The next 6 bytes identify a physical endpoint, such as a specific ATM adapter, using a media access control (MAC) layer address that is physically assigned to the ATM hardware by the manufacturer. The use and assignment of MAC addresses for ATM hardware is identical to MAC addressing for other Institute of Electrical and Electronic Engineers (IEEE) 802.*x* technologies, such as Ethernet and Token Ring.

Selector (SEL)   The last byte is used to select a logical connection endpoint on the physical ATM adapter.

Although all ATM addresses fit this basic three-part structure, there are significant differences in the exact format of the first 13 bytes of any given address, depending on the addressing format that is being used or whether the ATM network is for public or private use.

In summary, the 20-byte ATM address is in the hierarchical format starting with the switch at the highest level, down to the adapter, and then down to the logical endpoint.

All of the three ATM address formats that are currently in widespread use (DCC, ICD, and E.164) include the following characteristics:

- Compliance with the Network Service Access Point (NSAP) addressing plan as proposed by the Open Standards Interconnection (OSI) protocol suite of the International Standards Organization (ISO).

- Each can be used to establish and interconnect privately-built ATM networks that support switched virtual circuits (SVCs).

Addressing in Detail

The type of ATM address used depends on whether the addresses are for a public or private ATM network. ATM addresses are used to establish virtual circuit connections between ATM endpoints. Figure 14.9 shows the three primary address formats.

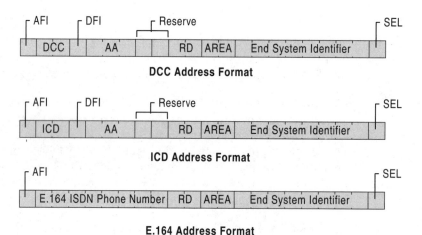

Figure 14.9   Primary ATM Address Formats

The three formats are known as data country/region code (DCC), International Code Designator (ICD), and E.164 addresses. The E.164 address format is designed specifically for public ATM networks. While a detailed explanation of each field is beyond the scope of this chapter, the most important fields from these address formats are listed in Table 14.1.

Table 14.1   Primary ATM Address Format Fields

Address Fields	Function
AFI	The single-byte authority and format identifier (AFI) identifies the type of address.
DCC	The defined values are 45 for E.164, 47 for ICD and 39 for DCC addresses.
AA	This single byte identifies the domain -specific part (DSP) of the address.
Reserve	Reserved for future use
RD	2 bytes of routing domain information
Area	2 bytes of area identifier
ESI	6 bytes of end system identifier, which is an IEEE 802.*x* media access control (MAC) address.
SEL	1 byte of NSAP selector
ICD	2 bytes of international code designator
E.164	8 bytes (16 digits) of the Integrated Services Digital Network (ISDN) telephone number

Incorporating the MAC address into the ATM address using the End System Identifier field makes it easier to adapt ATM addresses into existing LAN technologies that use IEEE 802.*x* address types.

Important   For long term success, it is important to plan for E.164 Public Network Integration.

Although Bellcore administers the area code and address assignment of PSTN telephone numbers used throughout North America, assignment and registration of unique E.164 ISDN telephone numbers is still relatively new.

If you are building a private ATM network and intend to eventually link it with public ATM networks, consider obtaining a public E.164 address to use when configuring and implementing ATM on your internal network.

Applying for an E.164 phone number is similar to acquiring a reserved set of phone numbers for a private business to use with traditional telephone service. For example, a large business could apply for and obtain a set of local dialing extensions or thousands group (such as 555-5000), and then assign phone numbers for PBX configuration as direct inbound dial (DID) numbers to individual phones or handsets. To find out who is responsible for registering public E.164 addresses in your area, check with your local ATM network service provider.

ATM Connection Types

ATM connections between endpoints are not distinguished only by their various Quality of Service parameters and the formats of their addressing schemes. They also fall into one of two larger categories: point-to-point connections and point-to-multipoint connections. Which of these connection types any particular ATM connection uses depends on how ATM signaling builds its connection.

Signaling

Signaling components exist at the endstation and at the ATM switch. The signaling layer of ATM software is responsible for creating, managing, and terminating switched virtual circuits (SVCs). The ATM standard wire protocol implemented by the signaling software is called the User Network Interface (UNI). The way one ATM switch signals another ATM switch comprises a second signaling standard, called the Network Network Interface (NNI).

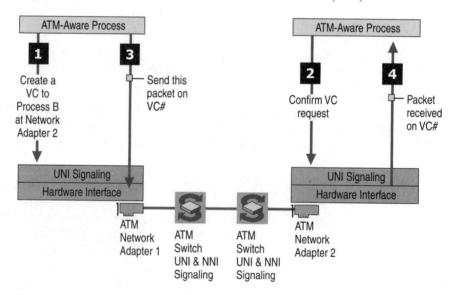

Figure 14.10   ATM Signaling

Point-to-Point Connection

When an ATM-aware process seeks to connect to another process elsewhere on the network, it asks the signaling software to establish an SVC. To do this, the signaling software sends an SVC creation request to the ATM switch using the ATM adapter and the reserved signaling VC. Each ATM switch forwards the request to another switch until the request reaches its destination. An ATM switch determines which switch to send the request to next based on the ATM address for the connection and the switch's internal network database (routing tables). Each switch also determines whether or not the request's service category and Quality of Service needs can be met. At any point in this process, a switch can refuse the request.

If all the switches along the path can support the virtual circuit as requested, the destination endstation receives a packet that contains the VC number. From that point on, the ATM-aware process can communicate with the destination process directly by sending packets to the VPI/VCI that identify the specified VC.

The ATM adapter shapes data traffic for each VC to match the contract made with the ATM network. If too much data is sent for any reason, the ATM switch can ignore — and lose — the data in favor of providing bandwidth to another contract or set of contracts. This is true for the entire breadth of the network; if bandwidth or speed exceeds the limits established by the contract, any device, including the ATM adapter, can simply drop the data. If this happens, the endstations concerned are not notified of the cell loss.

Point-to-Multipoint Connection

Unlike a standard LAN environment, ATM is a connection-oriented medium that has no inherent capabilities for broadcasting or multicasting packets. To provide this ability, the sending node can create a virtual circuit to all destinations and send a copy of the data on each virtual circuit. However, this is highly inefficient. A more efficient way to do this is through point-to-multipoint connections. Point-to-multipoint connects a single source endpoint, known as the root node, to multiple destination endpoints, known as leaves. Wherever the connection splits into two or more branches, the ATM switches copy cells to the multiple destinations.

Point-to-multipoint connections are unidirectional; the root can transmit to the leaves, but the leaves cannot transmit to the root or to each other on the same connection. Leaf-to-node and leaf-to-leaf transmission requires a separate connection. One reason for this limitation is the simplicity of AAL5 and the inability to interleave cells from multiple payloads on a single connection.

LAN Emulation

LAN emulation (LANE) is a group of software components that allows ATM to work with legacy networks and applications. With LAN emulation, you can run your traditional LAN-aware applications and protocols on an ATM network without modification.

LAN emulation makes the ATM protocol layers appear to be an Ethernet or Token Ring LAN to overlying protocols and applications. LAN emulation provides an intermediate step between fully exploiting ATM and not using ATM at all. LANE can increase the speed of data transmission for current applications and protocols when ATM is used over high speed media; unfortunately, LANE does not take advantage of native ATM features such as QoS. However, LANE does allow your current system and software to run on ATM, and it facilitates communication with nodes attached to legacy networks.

LANE Architecture

LANE consists of two primary components: the LAN emulation client and the LANE services. The LANE client allows LAN protocols and LAN-aware applications to function as if they were communicating with a traditional LAN. It exposes LAN functionality at its top edge (to users) and native ATM functionality at its bottom (to the ATM protocol layers).

The LANE services are a group of native ATM applications that hide the connection-oriented nature of ATM from connectionless legacy protocols. These services maintain the databases necessary to map LAN addresses to ATM addresses, thus allowing the LANE clients to create connections and send data.

The LANE services components can reside anywhere on an ATM network, but most ATM switches are included with LANE services components installed. Therefore, for practical purposes, LANE services reside on an ATM switch or group of switches.

The three primary LANE services are the LAN emulation configuration server (LECS), the LAN emulation server (LES), and the Broadcast and Unknown server (BUS). The LECS distributes configuration information to clients, allowing them to register on the network. The LES manages one or more Emulated LANs (ELANs); it is responsible for adding members to the ELAN, maintaining a list of all the ELAN's members, and handling address resolution requests for the LANE clients. The BUS handles broadcast and multicast services, as shown in Figure 14.11.

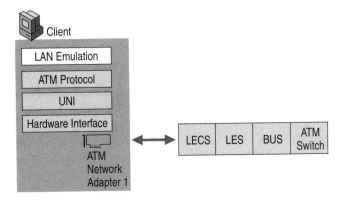

Figure 14.11   LANE Client, LECS, LES, and BUS

The following section describes how a LANE client joins and navigates an ATM network running LANE services.

When the LANE client seeks to join the network, the first thing it must do is find the LECS because the LECS gives the client the address of the LES managing the ELAN that it seeks to join. Without the LES address, the client cannot communicate with other members of the ELAN. Unfortunately, at initialization the client has not established a connection to any ATM switch, let alone to the switch or other entity containing the LECS. The client must establish an ATM connection, preferably a connection directly to the configuration server.

If the ATM network only has a single ATM switch, and the switch contains all the LANE services, then finding the LECS is easy. However, if the network has multiple switches, the local switch to which the LANE client has immediate access might not have LANE services running on it. Fortunately, LANE includes several established mechanisms for a LANE client to discovery the LECS.

LECS Discovery

The LANE client can use any of the following techniques when attempting to connect to the LECS:

- It can try a well-known ATM address, defined in the ATM protocol.
- It can use a well-known VC.
- It can query using the Integrated Local Management Interface (ILMI).

Both the well-known ATM address and the well-known VC are standardized. Most switches and clients are preconfigured with this information. In most cases, the LANE client can find the LECS using one of these methods. However, if the well-known values have been changed at the endstation or at the switch, either type of discovery becomes unsuccessful.

If this happens, the LANE client can fall back on ILMI, a protocol standard (similar to Simple Network Management Protocol) designed for ATM administrative and configuration purposes. ILMI provides a query function that the LANE client can use to find the LECS address, and then set up a VC to it.

After the client has discovered the LECS and connected to it, the client asks the LECS to provide configuration information to allow it to connect to a particular ELAN. It does this by sending one or more pieces of information about the desired ELAN, such as the LAN type (Ethernet or Token Ring), the maximum packet size, and the name of the LAN.

The LECS takes the information from the LANE client and looks in its table of ELANs, trying to find a match. When it locates the correct ELAN, it returns that address to the LANE client.

LES Address Matching

With the information provided by the LECS, the LANE client can now join the ELAN. To do this, it sends an emulated LAN address and its true ATM address to the LES. The LES registers this information. From this point on, the LANE client can send and receive data over the ATM network as if it were using a normal LAN.

When the LANE client receives a request from a protocol (such as TCP/IP, IPX, or NetBEUI) to send information to another point in the ELAN, it sends the destination LAN address to the LES. The LES looks for a match in its database, and then returns the true ATM address to the LANE client. The client then sets up a normal VC between itself and the destination, and subsequent data traffic is sent directly on this VC without any further intervention by the LES or the other LANE services. While this address resolution request is being processed, interim traffic is sent to the BUS and copied from there to all stations in the ELAN.

If the LES does not find a match for the destination address, the data is sent to the Broadcast and Unknown server (BUS). The BUS attempts to deliver the data to the unknown client, as described in the following section.

BUS Distribution

The BUS does two different things: it handles distribution of data to unknown clients and it emulates LAN broadcast services. If the LES cannot find a particular ELAN client, the data is sent to the BUS for distribution, and the BUS forwards it to all the clients of the ELAN.

The BUS also handles broadcasts; it registers its address with the LES identical to any other client. It registers under the address of F (x16), which is the normal LAN address for a broadcast message. When a LANE client protocol wants to broadcast a message to the entire LAN, it addresses the message to F (x16) and passes it on. The LEC sends this address to the LES for resolution, and the LES returns the ATM address of the BUS. The LEC can then send the message to the BUS. The BUS maintains a list of all clients on the ATM network and sends the message to all clients. The BUS service is usually co-located (in the same piece of equipment) with the LES.

Integrated Local Management Interface

The Integrated Local Management Interface (ILMI) resides on an ATM switch and provides diagnostic, monitoring, and configuration services to the User-Network Interface. The ILMI is defined by the ATM Forum, and uses the Simple Network Management Protocol (SNMP) and a management information base (MIB). It runs over AAL3/4 or AAL 5 with a default VPI/VCI of 0/16.

The ILMI MIB contains data describing the physical layer, the local VPCs and VCCs, network prefixes, administrative and configuration addresses, ATM layer statistics, and the ATM layer itself. The most common client-oriented function of the ILMI is to assist a client during LECS discovery. For more detailed information about the specifics of the ILMI MIB, see RFC 1695.

LANE Operation

ATM often serves as an efficient, high-speed backbone for an emulated LAN. Here are a few tips to set up an ELAN's clients and keep them operating.

Configuring the LANE Client

Complete information about configuring an ATM adapter card and LANE client can be found in Windows 2000 Server Help. The information provided there describes the step-by-step process required to add a new client to an existing ELAN.

Avoiding Loss of Client-Side Information when Upgrading from Windows NT 4.0

Before upgrading from Microsoft® Windows NT® version 4.0 to Windows 2000, it is important to note the following configuration information for each of the LAN emulation clients you plan to upgrade:

- The ELAN name.

  In **Control Panel,** double-click **Network.** Next, in the **Network and Dial-Up Network Connections** dialog box, click the **Identification** tab. Record the ELAN name from the **Domain Name** field.

- The LAN media to be emulated on the LAN, either Ethernet or Token Ring.

- ATM addresses for the LES and BUS associated with the ELAN.

  To find these addresses, open **Control Panel** and double-click **Network.** Next, in the **Network and Dial-Up Network Connections** dialog box, click the **Adapters** tab. Open the **Hardware Properties** dialog box, the same place that lists the Ethernet network adapter.

- The maximum allowable packet size for the ELAN.

  To view this listed information, in **Control Panel**, double-click **Network,** and then click the **Adapters** tab. Open the **Windows NT 4.0 Properties** dialog box.

After you note these configuration parameters, use the LECS interface on your ATM switch to configure ELANs and their associated parameters. This includes the ELAN name, media type, LES and BUS addresses, and maximum packet size.

Next, install Windows 2000 and configure the ELAN name for each LEC. For information about configuring the ELAN name, see "Configure a LAN Emulation Client" in Windows 2000 Server Help. Windows 2000 LANE clients are preconfigured with the "default" or "unspecified" ELAN, and this (ELAN) is usually enabled and configured in ATM switches sold today. This eases the configuration for small networks.

LANE Client Fault Tolerance

If the LECS or LES fails, the Windows LANE client completely restarts its initialization at the point of LECS discovery. Therefore, if the LANE servers fails and then restarts, the LANE client automatically reregisters itself properly without any interaction from users. Ultimately the fault tolerance responsibility lies primarily with the LECS and LES. The LANE client only detects a fault and restarts.

Some switches allow a backup LECS or LES to be ready and waiting to come online if the current server goes down. If this happens, the backup LECS can register at the same well-known address as the failed LECS, and all clients can find it.

TCP/IP Over ATM

The protocol for classical IP over ATM (sometimes abbreviated as CLIP/ATM) is a well-established standard spelled out in RFC 1577 and subsequent documents. Windows 2000 provides a full implementation of this standard.

The IP over ATM approach provides several attractive advantages over ELAN solutions. The most obvious advantages are its ability to support QoS interfaces, its lower overhead (as it requires no MAC header), and its lack of a frame size limit. All of these features are discussed in the following sections.

IP over ATM Architecture

IP over ATM is a group of components that do not necessarily reside in one place, and, in this case, the services are not usually on an ATM switch. In some cases, switch vendors provide some IP over ATM support, but not always. (For the purposes of this discussion, it is assumed the IP over ATM server services reside on a Windows 2000 server.)

The core components required for IP over ATM are roughly the same as those required for LANE, as both approaches require the mapping of a connectionless medium to a connection-oriented medium, and vice versa. In IP over ATM, these services are provided by an IP ATMARP server for each IP subnet. This server maintains a database of IP and ATM, and provides configuration and broadcast services, as described in the following section.

IP over ATM Components

IP over ATM is a very small layer between the ATM protocol and the TCP/IP protocol. As with LANE, the client emulates standard IP to the TCP/IP protocol at its top edge while simultaneously issuing native ATM commands to the ATM protocol layers underneath.

IP over ATM is often preferred to LANE because it is faster than LANE. One key reason for this performance advantage is that IP over ATM adds almost no additional header information to packets as they are handed down the stack. Once it has established a connection, the IP over ATM client can generally transfer data without modification.

As with LANE, IP over ATM is handled by two main components: the IP over ATM server and the IP over ATM client. The IP over ATM server is composed of an ATMARP server and Multicast Address Resolution Service (MARS). The ATMARP server provides services to map network layer IP unicast addresses to ATM addresses, while MARS provides similar services for broadcast and multicast addresses. Both services maintain IP address databases just as LANE services do.

The IP over ATM server can reside on more than one computer, but the ATMARP and MARS databases cannot be distributed. You can have one IP over ATM server handle ATMARP traffic, and one handle MARS. If, however, you divided the ATMARP Server between servers, it would effectively create two different IP networks. All IP over ATM clients in the same logical IP subnet (LIS) need to be configured to use the same ATMARP server. Traditional routing methods are used to route between logical IP subnets, even if they are on the same physical network.

Windows 2000 includes fully integrated ATMARP and MARS servers. These services are described in more detail in the following sections.

ATMARP Server

The IP over ATM client and ATMARP server go through a process similar to the LANE client and the LECS when a client joins the network and discovers other network members. As with LANE, once an address is found, native ATM takes over and TCP/IP packets are sent across a VC from endstation to endstation. There is, however, a major difference in how the IP over ATM client discovers the ATMARP server.

ATMARP Server Discovery

Because the ATMARP server usually resides on a server rather than on an ATM switch, it is not possible to use ILMI or a well-known VC to discover its address. In fact, there is no default IP over ATM mechanism for server discovery. To start using IP over ATM, an administrator must find the ATM address of the appropriate ATMARP server and manually configure each IP over ATM client with this address. In a single ATM switch network, this is not much of a problem, but in larger networks it can become a demanding job. To ease configuration in smaller networks, Windows 2000 ATM ARP/MARS services and ATM ARP/MARS clients use a default address. For more information about deployment issues, see Windows 2000 Server Help.

After the ATMARP server has been discovered, the IP over ATM client can use this server to resolve IP to ATM address mappings and communicate with other computers. The ATMARP server supports only unicast traffic. To send packets to a broadcast address or multicast list, the IP over ATM client goes to the MARS.

MARS

Mimicking the role of the BUS in LAN emulation, MARS handles distribution of broadcast and multicast messages to all the members of the network or to all members of a multicast group. Because of the potential for bottlenecks, MARS provides two modes of operation. When an ATMARP client receives a request to send a packet to a multicast or broadcast IP address, it sends a request to the MARS to resolve this address to a list of clients that are members of that group.

In one mode of operation, the MARS return a list of all ATM addresses to which the group address resolves. The client then creates a point-to-multipoint (PMP) ATM connection to all of these addresses and forwards the packet on that connection.

The other mode of operation involves a multicast server (MCS). The MCS registers interest in one or more multicast groups with the MARS. The MCS receives information describing the membership of that group, as well as updates when clients join or leave that group. When a client requests a group address resolution from the MARS, the MARS simply returns the single address of the MCS. The packet is then sent to the MCS, which creates the PMP connection and distributes the packet to all members of the group.

See Figures 14.12 and 14.13 for examples of the VCs that are created in each of these modes.

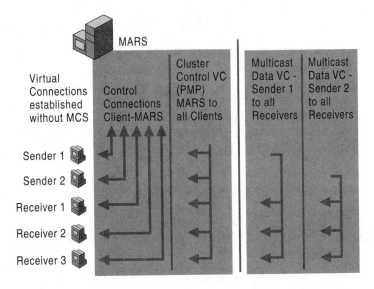

Figure 14.12   IP Multicast over ATM Connections Without MCS

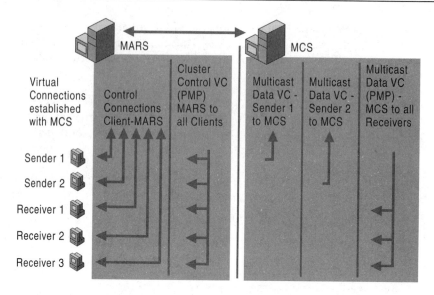

Figure 14.13   IP Multicast over ATM Connections with MCS

The disadvantage of the first method, in which each client sending packets to the group creates its own PMP connection to all other members of the group, is the large number of virtual circuits required. The disadvantage of the second method, which uses the MCS, is that the MCS becomes both a central point of failure and a potential bottleneck because it distributes all multicast packets for all of the groups it serves.

IP over ATM Operation

IP over ATM faces the same problems, and relies on the same basic tools and fixes as LANE. In particular, it faces the issues of address resolution and broadcasting.

In normal ATM, SVC connections are established by sending a connection request containing the ATM address of the destination endpoint to the ATM switch. Before an IP endpoint can create an SVC in this manner, the endpoint must resolve the IP address of the destination to an ATM address.

Normally, when an Ethernet host needs to resolve an IP address to an Ethernet MAC address, it uses an ARP broadcast query frame. As explained earlier, hardware broadcasting is not done in ATM. The Address Resolution Protocol (ARP) of the ATMARP server resolve IP addresses to ATM addresses.

An ATM endpoint wishing to resolve an IP address sends an ATMARP request to the ATMARP server for their LIS. The ATMARP request contains the sender's ATM address and IP address and the requested IP address. If the ATMARP server knows the requested IP address, it sends back an ATMARP response containing the requested ATM address. If the requested IP address is not found, the ATMARP servers send back a negative ATMARP reply, unlike the procedure in an ELAN, which would send an unresolved address to the LANE BUS. This behavior allows an ARP requestor to distinguish between an unknown address and non-functioning ATMARP server.

The end result is a three-way mapping from the IP address to an ATM address to a VPI/VCI pair. The IP address and ATM address are required to create a VC. The IP address and VPI/VCI then are required to send the subsequent cells containing data across the VC.

An ATM endpoint creates SVCs to other ATM endpoints within its LIS. For an ATM endpoint to resolve an arbitrary IP address, it must be configured with the ATM address of the ATMARP server in its LIS.

Upon startup, an ATM endpoint establishes a VC with the ATMARP server using ATM signaling. As soon as the VC is opened with the server, the server sends the ATM endpoint an InATMARP request. When the ATM endpoint sends the response, the ATMARP server has the ATM and IP address of the new ATM endpoint. In this way, the ATMARP server builds its table of ATM to IP address mappings.

IP over ATM Client Initialization

In Windows 2000, IP over ATM does not require the use of an Inverse ARP. Instead, the client goes directly to the server to register itself on the network. Since the process is automatic, no human intervention is required to initialize the client. Depending on whether the client address is mapped to a static address or a dynamic address, the procedure varies between the following two approaches.

With a Static IP Address

The following example details each step in establishing an IP over ATM connection for a single IP over ATM client with a static IP address. First, the client initializes and gets an ATM address from the ATM switch. The client then connects to the ATM ARP/MARS server and joins the broadcast group. The client's IP to ATM address mapping is also added to the ATMARP server database. The client is now ready to contact other hosts and begin data transfer.

With DHCP

Establishing an IP over ATM connection for a single IP over ATM client using Dynamic Host Configuration Protocol (DHCP) is similar but not identical. First the client initializes and gets an ATM address from the ATM switch. Then the client connects to the ATM ARP/MARS server and joins the broadcast group. The client connects to the multicast server (MCS) and sends a DHCP request. The MCS broadcasts the DHCP request to all members of the broadcast group.

When the DHCP server receives the request, it sends a DHCP reply to the MCS. The MCS then broadcasts the reply to the broadcast group. The client receives the DHCP reply and then registers its IP and ATM addresses with the ATM ARP/MARS server. The client is now ready to contact other hosts and begin data transfer. For more information about DHCP, see "Dynamic Host Configuration Protocol" in the *TCP/IP Core Networking Guide*.

Logical IP Subnets

A LAN-based IP internetwork consists of a series of cabling plants separated by IP routers. The cabling plants connect the hosts of an IP network or subnet together and the routers connect the networks and subnets to each other. An IP host on a particular network can send IP packets directly to a host on the same network by addressing the packet to the media access control (MAC) address of the destination host. An IP host can send IP packets to hosts on other networks by addressing the packet to the router's MAC address. This paradigm can connect hundreds (or thousands) of hosts on the same network to hundreds (or thousands) more on other networks. While this configuration works well for connectionless, broadcast-based technologies such as Ethernet and Token Ring, it is important to exercise care when attempting to create the same situation with ATM. Figure 14.14 shows two LISs running on a single switch.

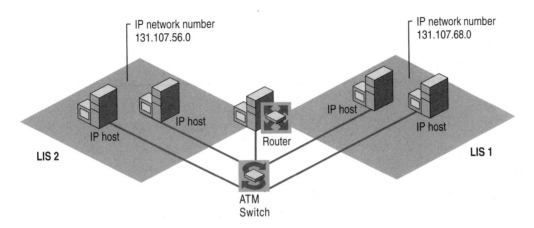

Figure 14.14   Two LISs Running on a Single Switch

Before a single IP packet can be sent, a connection must be created between the source and destination at the ATM layer. On an ATM network using SVC, the path must be negotiated between switches so that the sender has a valid VPI/VCI address to which to send the ATM cells. While possible, it is not very practical to have hundreds (or thousands) of ATM endpoints on the same IP network. A host such as a network server cannot have an arbitrarily large number of VCs to the other hosts in the network. More VCs mean more overhead and resources for the both the IP network's operating systems and its hardware (ATM adapters and switches). If connecting across an ATM service provider, more VCs also mean more cost.

The logical IP subnet (LIS) is a way of constraining the number of ATM endpoints in an IP network or subnet. The LIS is a group of IP hosts that share a common IP network number; these hosts communicate with each other directly using ATM virtual circuits. Different logical IP subnets can be created on the same ATM switch to create a virtual IP internetwork.

Note the example in the diagram above. When hosts in LIS 131.107.56.0/24 want to communicate among themselves, they establish a VC with each other (direct delivery). When hosts in LIS 131.107.56.0/24 want to communicate with hosts in LIS 131.107.68.0/24, they establish a VC with the router and send an IP packet to the router (indirect delivery). The router then establishes its own VC with the destination host and forwards the IP packet.

An IP router belongs to multiple LISs and is configured with multiple IP addresses and subnet masks. If the router has a single ATM interface (and therefore a single ATM address), it can either use the single ATM address (with the unique End System Identifier) or use multiple ATM addresses by varying the last byte in the 20-byte ATM address (the SEL field). It uses multiple addresses primarily in the case of a server failure, when a route is no longer functional, to give clients a secondary point of access.

For more information about creating a LIS, see "ATMARP Utility" later in this chapter.

Services at an ATM Switch

The overall scheme of ATM protocols, hardware, and interconnections comes together in Figure 14.15. The hardware includes ATM clients, ATM switches, and the blades that function as edge devices between an ATM-aware device or application and another protocol or environment. The connections include SVCs and permanent virtual circuits (PVCs), all handled by the local switch shown at the center of the diagram.

In addition, Figure 14.15 shows LANE clients joining the local switch, as well as a client being redirected from Local Switch 2 by the LECS to the BUS and LES services on Local Switch 1. The bottom layer is the client section, showing all the ARP, ATM, and other clients of the local switch. (With the exception of a remote access client, which is shown dialing into the switch at the top of the diagram). The various forms of edge devices are shown in the central section, and remote connections are shown at the top.

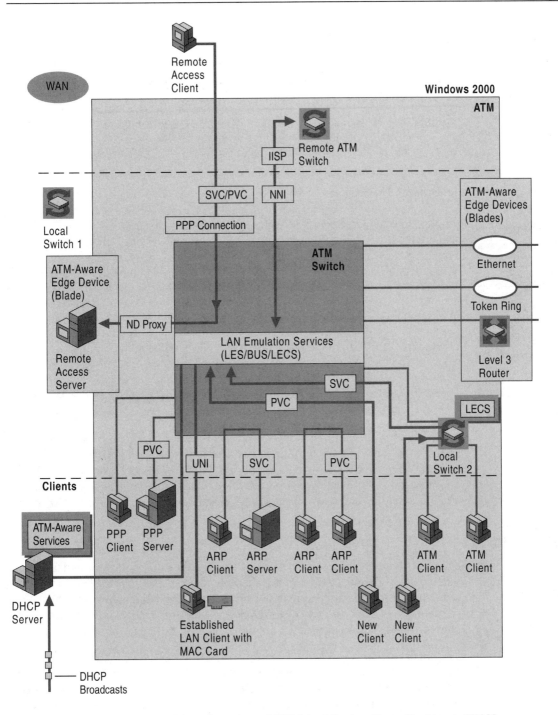

Figure 14.15   Overview of ATM Architecture From Desktop to WAN

Windows 2000 ATM Services

This section describes ATM support in Windows 2000, which includes a high level of integrated ATM support. This section also describes some of the major advantages afforded by this integration.

Windows 2000 provides high levels of support for ATM in three main areas:

- APIs and integrated network services for direct access to ATM.
- Support for existing network protocols.
- Broad ATM adapter support.

Applications can access ATM services directly through a new set of ATM APIs that are made available through established operating system components, including Network Device Interface (NDIS), Windows Sockets, and TAPI/Direct Show. These interfaces support access to ATM services in both kernel and user mode.

Windows 2000 also contains a higher level of integrated support for existing network protocols over ATM. Microsoft has implemented a universal LANE client, IP over ATM components, PPP over ATM components, a Windows Sockets Service Provider, and UNI signaling modules for endstations.

Because of this integration and extensive testing, hardware vendors can focus on their hardware and can largely ignore LANE, IP over ATM, PPP over ATM, Windows Sockets support, and UNI. Hardware vendors must write only the small NDIS miniport driver to interface with their hardware because the components formerly required in the monolithic driver are now all folded into the operating system. With driver development simplified, the cost of ATM adapters can fall. In addition, the simplification of driver development can improve adapter reliability and increase the number of supported ATM adapters.

Components

The cost of maintaining separate, specialized networks for computer, voice, and video is high. Fortunately, current technology enables integration of all of these services on a single network and the combination of existing networks into a single infrastructure. In particular, Windows operating systems provide rich connectivity using ATM while maintaining support for legacy systems.

To support native ATM, Microsoft updated NDIS with native ATM commands. Because many applications do not yet use native ATM services, Microsoft added LANE support for LAN applications (Ethernet and so forth). Similarly, Microsoft has added IP over ATM support, thereby eliminating the additional header cost of LAN packets. Microsoft also added Winsock 2.0 native ATM to support the many applications that use Windows Sockets (Winsock).

Furthermore, Microsoft has added circuit connectivity to TAPI (connection management protocol) in order to provide complete ATM support. TAPI can now make and receive calls and can redirect them to ATM circuits or from circuits into devices or other network types. Examples include Microsoft® DirectShow®, as well as PPP over ATM as the dial-up remote access protocol on ATM. Using the raw channel access (RCA) kernel streaming filter, TAPI can be used to connect a data stream to the RCA filter containing video, and send it over an ATM circuit, as shown in Figure 14.16.

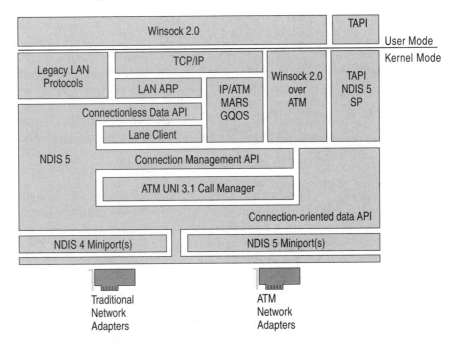

Figure 14.16   Windows ATM Services

These enhancements allow applications to exploit ATM services (such as QoS), and with the use of TAPI, achieve a high level of integration between established multimedia features and network protocols.

The next section describes the ATM call manager and other Windows ATM services components.

ATM Call Manager

The ATM signaling component, also known as the UNI call manager, handles virtual circuit creation and management. This section describes how the ATM call manager does its job, specifically with regard to the handling of both permanent and switched virtual circuits.

How the Call Manager Differentiates PVCs and SVCs

Permanent virtual circuits (PVCs) are almost identical to switched virtual circuits (SVCs), but each PVC must be manually configured, device by device, by an administrator. In contrast, SVCs are dynamically configured when they are established. Each device — from a starting endstation through switches to another endstation — independently determines its role in supporting a virtual circuit, what device to forward the request to, and whether or not it can guarantee the requested Quality of Service at that time. PVC resource allocations are set aside the moment they are first configured, whether or not they are used immediately. SVC resource allocations are allocated dynamically.

The SVC and PVC values are both stored in the internal tables of the ATM call manager, the ATM adapter, and the ATM switch, and the kind of values stored in those tables are identical. The difference between the two kinds of circuits lies in how the circuit values are handled at initialization. At that time, the ATM call manager checks the registry for any PVCs. If it finds one, it stores its VC number, along with other VC information such as quality of service, the process ID (or more generically, the service access point), and the source and destination addresses. It uses a single bit to designate that it is a PVC and not an SVC.

During initialization, the ATM adapter does not know about PVCs. Until someone (usually an administrator) configures an application to use a PVC, applications are not aware of PVCs either. When an application wants to use a PVC, it issues an ATM command through its provided interfaces. The request specifies the destination address, the Quality of Service, and the virtual circuit number (among other information). Up to this point, the PVC is handled exactly as if it were a request for an SVC. The call manager receives the request and checks the information received against the entries in its internal table of VCs. If it finds a match and the match is designated as a PVC in the PVC field in its table, the call manager then handles the rest of the process a little differently than it would for an SVC request.

A normal SVC request initiates two commands; the first determines whether the adapter can handle another VC, and the second activates the VC along the path of network components. A PVC request, however, works a little differently. When the call manager receives a request specifying a PVC, it assumes that the PVC has already been established end-to-end. Therefore, it sends the two initiating calls in rapid succession to the ATM adapter. The ATM adapter never knows that it is working with a PVC. It obtains the Quality of Service and other information from the setup commands and determines how to shape the traffic. From that point, the PVC functions identically to an SVC.

ATM LAN Emulation Module

LAN emulation client services are included in the Windows 2000 operating system. When Plug and Play detects an ATM adapter and installs the appropriate driver, the LANE client is also installed by default. This permits full LANE connectivity without the need for configuration, provided that:

- The switch has LANE services available and turned on.
- The LANE services configuration has a default ELAN enabled.

For centralized administration and ease of configuration, this LANE client implementation allows configuration of the ELAN name only. All other ELAN configuration information — such as the Maximum Transmissible Unit (MTU), ELAN type, and LES — is obtained from the LECS. If a default ELAN is enabled in the LECS, no configuration is required.

For more information about configuring the LANE client, see Windows 2000 Server Help.

ATMARP and ARP MARS

IP over ATM support is included with Windows 2000. In fact, in many ways the IP over ATM support provides more efficient network services than those provided through LANE. IP over ATM is faster than LANE for a variety of reasons, but the key difference between the two is that IP over ATM adds almost no additional header information to packets as they are handed down the protocol stack to the physical medium. The IP over ATM client, once it has established a connection, can generally transfer data without touching it. As a result, IP over ATM is a very small — and very fast — layer between the ATM protocol and the TCP/IP protocol.

IP over ATM exposes many features of ATM so that TCP/IP can make use of them directly. With this support, applications written to use TCP/IP, either through Windows Sockets or otherwise, can also make use of ATM. Applications written to use Generic QoS (GQoS) under Windows Sockets also benefit from this QoS being mapped to ATM-specific QoS parameters in IP over ATM.

In addition, the Windows 2000 ATMARP (IP over ATM) client supports multicast address resolution through MARS. This client contains an ATM ARP/MARS service that enables Windows to act as both an ATMARP server and a MARS with integrated multicast server (MCS). The MARS setup allows configuration of a ranges of addresses; the service acts as an MCS for all those addresses. For deployment and configuration information about IP over ATM, see Windows 2000 Server Help.

API Support: Winsock 2.0, TAPI, and NDIS 5.0

All of these enhancements are possible due to extensions to the operating system. The chief extension is a connection-oriented service added to NDIS version 5.0. NDIS 5.0 includes connection-oriented NDIS, or CoNDIS, a new NDIS API extension for the support of connection oriented media. These new APIs enable applications and protocols to create virtual circuits and specify Quality of Service for those virtual circuits. CoNDIS supports multiple call managers to enable different media-specific signaling needs, including an ATM-specific call manager. In addition, CoNDIS supports point-to-multipoint connections for efficient multicast services, as shown in Figure 14.17.

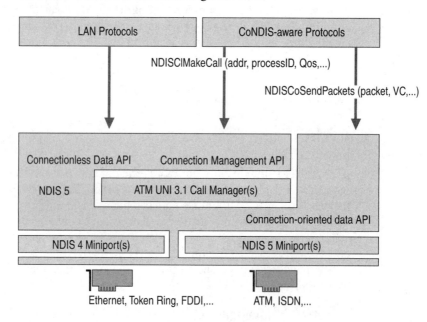

Figure 14.17   Supported CoNDIS Multicast Services

Two components operate on top of NDIS, integrating ATM services with the rest of the operating system and exposing ATM services through well-known APIs. Windows Sockets 2.0 now has direct ATM support through the Windows Sockets ATM Service Provider. Windows Sockets support through the Windows Sockets ATM Service Provider provides direct access to ATM services from user mode applications. With the addition of IP over ATM support, Windows Sockets applications that use TCP/IP as a transport protocol can be run over ATM networks and inter-operate with standard LAN-based IP clients.

NDIS 5.0 ATM Miniport Drivers

Although NDIS 5.0 supports both connectionless and connection-oriented network adapter drivers, only the connection-oriented drivers are of use in an ATM network.

Connection-oriented miniport drivers are always deserialized; that is, they serialize the operation of their own miniport functions and queue all incoming packets internally rather than relying on NDIS to perform the same functions. This results in better full-duplex performance, provided that the driver's critical sections are kept small.

While NDIS library continues to support legacy NDIS 3.0 network adapter drivers, only NDIS 4.0 and 5.0 miniport drivers can take advantage of the enhanced functionality and performance characteristics of the current and future NDIS library support for network adapter drivers.

NDIS has several connection-oriented features; it also contains additional features of general utility to networks, such as binary compatibility, improved power management through Wake On LAN support (which enables a network adapter to power up a client from a low power state based on packet receipt), and checksum performance in hardware rather than in software. As a result, driver performance is improved over all network types.

TAPI

Telephony Application Programming Interface, also known as Telephony API (TAPI), is responsible for connection setup and other operating system functions related to telephony. In Windows 2000, TAPI has been expanded to support telephony-like things over connection-oriented media such as ATM. While TAPI does not handle data directly, it can create a circuit and connect that circuit to another device.

By redirecting calls, TAPI provides more than just high bandwidth and good throughput. The TAPI component of CoNDIS maps (or proxies) the TAPI call management functions to NDIS 5.0 call management functions, allowing a connection from another medium to be redirected directly to or from ATM. For example, TAPI can redirect calls to a data handler such as the raw channel access filter, or DirectShow components. For another example of the ability of TAPI to act as a redirector, see "PPP over ATM and NDISWAN" later in this chapter.

PPP over ATM

With the advent of Digital Subscriber Line (xDSL) technologies, high-speed network access from the home and small office environment is becoming more of a reality. Several standards are being developed in these areas, including Asymmetric DSL (ADSL) and Universal ADSL (UADSL or DSL Lite). These technologies operate over a local loop, that last run of copper wire between the public telephone network and the home. In most areas, this local loop connects directly to an ATM core network run by a telephone company.

ATM over the xDSL service preserves the high-speed characteristics and QoS guarantees available in the core, without changing protocols. This creates the potential for an end-to-end ATM network to the residence or small office. This network model provides several advantages, including:

- Protocol transparency
- Support for multiple classes of QoS with service guarantees
- Bandwidth scalability
- An evolution path to newer DSL technologies

Adding the Point-to-Point Protocol (PPP) over this end-to-end architecture adds functionality and usefulness. PPP provides the following additional advantages:

- Authentication
- OSI Layer 3 address assignment
- Multiple concurrent sessions to different destinations
- OSI Layer 3 protocol transparency
- Encryption and compression

These enhancements provide high bandwidth, even over a telephone line with an ATM adapter and this new level of integrated ATM support. In addition, with the adoption of PPP over ATM, little change is required at the ISP level, as telephone companies and ISPs both generally use PPP.

Finally, if each VC carrying a PPP session carries only one session, each destination has its own authenticated PPP session, providing per-VC authentication. This provides an extra measure of security. Using Null Encapsulation over AAL5 (because the protocol multiplexing is provided in PPP) can further reduce overhead.

PPP over ATM and NDISWAN

Windows 2000 supports PPP dial-up connections over ATM; however, a complete description of this process requires a discussion of TAPI and its function as a universal connection manager and redirector.

In earlier versions of Windows operating systems, the NDISWAN component both supported operation of standard protocol stacks over WAN media and acted as the PPP engine. As explained earlier, in Windows 2000 the NDISWAN component has been extended and the TAPI proxy component added to provide this same support over NDIS 5.0 connection-oriented media, such as ATM.

At initialization, the NDISWAN component, acting as a client to the TAPI proxy, registers itself as the stream handler for PPP data. When the user starts dial-up networking to connect to a network, the dial-up networking module communicates with TAPI to make the phone call. When the request is made on an ATM device, TAPI does two things:

1. Through the TAPI proxy and NDIS 5.0, it uses a call manager to make the telephone call through the ATM adapter.

2. When the call goes through, it redirects the connection from the adapter, through NDIS 5.0, to NDISWAN.

NDISWAN then handles further network (PPP) negotiation, and ultimately, through the LAN and TCP/IP stacks, it connects the user's computer to the remote network. The important thing to note here is that TAPI makes the call and then feeds the resulting connection to another process, in this case NDISWAN.

This connectability enables several new types of applications, such DVD quality streaming video, real-time process control, a common standard for both LAN and WAN, and integrated software that pulls together aspects of TV, telephony, and data streams. Many of these make use of the raw channel access filter and DirectShow technology, both described in the following section.

Support for Raw Channel Access Filtering: DirectShow

Microsoft developed DirectShow technology to better integrate multimedia services and to enable multimedia developers to more easily customize the operating system to their needs. DirectShow allows hardware and software vendors to create individual multimedia modules called filters. Multiple filters can be connected by the use of pins and a filter graph. (The language used here is identical to that used to describe the Component Object Model [COM], a high-level specification for designing fully independent and object-oriented software.) TAPI connects different components, and DirectShow uses the same approach to enable filters and devices to connect to each other.

Figure 14.18 illustrates Windows COM-based DirectStreaming. A
Windows 2000–based application can handle many categories of real-time inputs,
as shown in Figure 14.18.

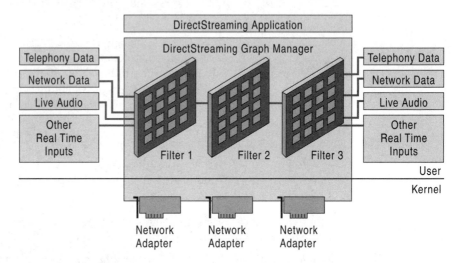

Figure 14.18   Windows COM-Based DirectStreaming

DirectShow has an RCA filter — a simple module that exposes the raw data,
whether it is voice, video, or other, to any device that wants to handle it. With
NDIS 5.0, the RCA filter can be connected to TAPI. NDIS 5.0 can export ATM
VCs as DirectShow pins.

Raw Channel Access Filtering

The Windows 2000 support for raw channel access filtering comes through the
CoNDIS 5.0 driver. The NDIS proxy sets up a call at the ATM layer, running
from the proxy through the call manager to the client. Unlike many voice or video
feeds, this connection is made using AAL5, rather than AAL1. The analog data
transferred through the filter becomes digital data, which is packaged and handled
identically to any other data over an AAL5 connection.

Weather Report Application

An example of using DirectShow and raw channel access support in Windows
ATM services is a video streaming application that delivers up-to-date weather
information over the telephone. Customers can simply dial a number and hear a
recorded message.

The following steps outline this process:

1. At initialization, the raw channel access filter registers as the stream handler for voice data.

2. A user calls a number to get the current weather information.

3. TAPI receives the call. TAPI redirects the incoming call to the raw channel access filter, because it is a voice call.

4. NDIS 5.0 maps the DirectShow pin to the VC number.

5. DirectShow searches the filter graph, and the stream starts.

Figure 14.19 shows an example of a weather report application using the DirectShow raw channel access filter. The path shows how the data is routed through the various protocols from telephony data to the application layer.

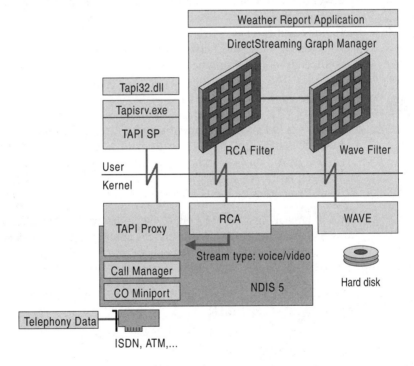

Figure 14.19   Weather Report Application Using DirectShow RCA Filter

IP Phone Access

Similarly, a user can make a telephone call that would be routed across a traditional LAN. This can enable such things as IP-based telephones. Again, TAPI handles the incoming call and uses NDIS 5.0 to connect it to a pin. DirectShow then reformats the data using a real-time protocol filter that goes through UDP/IP to ultimately reach an Ethernet card. The resulting connection allows a telephone user to talk to a computer user. This ATM-based network integration blurs the boundaries between telephone and computer networks considerably.

Best Practices

Like any other network, an ATM network or LANE network performs best when it is properly deployed. While many of the critical functions of managing an ATM network require managing the switch itself, many basic tasks can be handled from the client side in an emulated LAN or IP over ATM network. This section provides details on how to best use Windows 2000 features to keep your ATM end-to-end or backbone network operating smoothly. It also explains the use of resource kit tools to examine the network.

Using the Default ELAN

Windows ATM services are configured with LANE installed, and are configured to use the default ELAN. As a result, the LANE client automatically attempts to join this ELAN unless another is configured. The default ELAN is referred to as <unspecified ELAN name>, and this name must always appear in the **ATM LAN Client Properties** dialog box when configuring a LAN Emulation client.

When purchasing an ATM switch, check the product specifications to make sure it is preconfigured with LANE services enabled and with a default ELAN. This is the ELAN to which a client is assigned if no ELAN is specified when contacting LANE services.

If the switch is not preconfigured, check the manufacturer's specifications for how to add clients to an ELAN.

Using Multiple ELANs for Security

If you implement LAN emulation for several groups of clients with differing security needs, the preconfigured default ELAN might not be enough. In this case, you should consider establishing multiple ELANs. For instance, you can divide a corporate network into multiple ELANs for different departments, with Finance and Human Resources on a high-security ELAN, a lower-security ELAN for Production, Marketing, Sales, Shipping, and Facilities, and a second lower-security ELAN for an overseas branch office.

This use of multiple ELANs requires additional work to set up, but it enhances security because anyone who does not know the specified names of these ELANs cannot join them as a client.

Enable Event Logging

Logging of significant events, such as call setup and teardown, can be enabled in ATMUNI. Non-localized English strings are written to the specified file. These settings are global; that is, across all ATM adapters.

Under the registry subkey:

HKEY_LOCAL_MACHINE\System\CurrentControlSet\Services\AtmUni
\Parameters

add the following entries:

- **LogFlags** - REG_DWORD Bit mask indicating events to be logged.
- **LogFileName** - REG_SZ File name into which ATMUNI writes events.

If the **LogFlags** entry is missing (the default), ATMUNI does not log any events. The **LogFlags** value is made up as a logical bitwise OR of the following:

- 1: Log failed calls
- 2: Log successful calls
- 4: Log abnormal call terminations
- 8: Log normal call terminations

To turn on all events, set **LogFlags** to 8+4+2+1=0xf. **LogFileName** is a fully qualified file name as in "C:\atm\logs\log2.txt." This file is created (or truncated if it already exists) when ATMUNI starts.

Proper ELAN Names

When naming an ELAN, use proper naming procedures. ELAN names cannot exceed 32 alphanumeric characters in length. Special characters and blank spaces cannot be part of an ELAN name; the names are also case-sensitive.

Using Supported ATM Adapters

Before you buy an ATM adapter for use with Windows 2000, check to make sure it is on the Hardware Compatibility List. For more information, see the Hardware Compatibility List link at http://windows.microsoft.com/windows2000/reskit/webresources.

ATM Utilities

To access the tools included with the *Windows 2000 Resource Kit*, click **Start**, point to **Programs**, and then click **Command Prompt**. From this prompt, you can use the ATMADM, ATMLANE, and ATMARP utilities to diagnose and resolve network problems, or simply to monitor the state of network usage. Each utility is described in greater detail in the following sections.

ATMADM Utility

The ATMADM utility is provided with Windows ATM services to assist in troubleshooting. It monitors connections and addresses registered by the ATM Call Manager on an ATM network. You can use the utility to display statistics for incoming and outgoing calls on ATM adapters.

Parameters

ATMADM can retrieve information about ATM's the operation of ATM in your system. It displays ATM address information, ATM statistics, and the current state of all ATM connections.

Note To learn what options are available for any Windows 2000 command-line utility, type the utility name followed by a /?. After typing the following string:

```
atmadm /? <enter>
```

the utility returns a list of the available options for that utility.

The three main options available for ATMADM are A, S, and C. ATMADM -C displays call information for all current connections to the ATM network adapter installed on this computer. ATMADM -S displays statistics for monitoring the status of active ATM connections.

ATMADM -A displays the registered ATM network service access point address for each adapter installed in this computer. These ATM addresses indicate only the client's own address, and not the address of other ATM endpoints that it has called. The first 26 hexadecimal characters (13 bytes) of the 40-character string represent the switch address, the next 12 hexadecimal characters (6 bytes) indicate the MAC address of the hardware in question, and the last two hexadecimal characters represent the selector value. This selector value allows the call manager to distinguish between two different logical addresses that are addressed with the same hardware.

Addresses for Multiple Adapters

If the client contains two ATM adapters or devices, both are listed in the ATMADM-A report, but the friendly name is identical for identical devices. For instance, if a client contains two MAC adapters made by the same manufacturer, they both return the same name, though not the same address. This is illustrated in Figure 14.20, which shows a client with two ForeRunner adapters installed.

Figure 14.20   ATM Addresses for a Computer Configured with Two ATM Adapters

```
C:\users>atmadm -a

Windows ATM Call Manager Statistics

ATM Addresses for Interface : [003] ForeRunner PCA-200EPC ATM AdapterNNf

    47009181000000000613E5BFE0100204808119B00

ATM Addresses for Interface : [002] ForeRunner PCA-200EPC ATM Adapter

    47009181000000000613E5BFE010020480811F300
```

The second option, ATMADM -S, provides a set of useful statistics describing the performance of the ATM client: the number of connections it has created, received, and dropped since being added to the ATM network by a switch, and the number of virtual circuits that it is currently maintaining. In addition, this utility tracks the number of overhead cells sent for signaling and ILMI. Figure 14.21 shows an example of a typical report, with 10 active calls and a short history of successful incoming and outgoing calls.

Figure 14.21   Statistics for a Client with a Single ATM Adapter

```
C:\users>atmadm s

Windows ATM Call Manager Statistics

ATM Call Manager statistics for Interface : [002] ForeRunner PCA-200EPC
ATM Adapter

            Current Active Calls            = 10
            Total successful Incoming calls  = 19
            Total successful Outgoing calls  = 19
            Unsuccessful Incoming calls      = 0
            Unsuccessful Outgoing calls      = 0
            Calls Closed by Remote           = 20
            Calls Closed Locally             = 8
            Signaling and ILMI Packets Sent    = 1488
            Signaling and ILMI Packets Received = 1506
```

These statistics are invaluable in diagnosing connection problems. For example, if ATMADM-S indicates that incoming calls have been successful but outgoing calls have all failed. Knowing which calls are getting through reduces the number of potential problems to investigate. In the case of failed outgoing calls, the client might be attempting to contact a client that is no longer available, but which is still listed in the ARP server cache of available addresses. Alternately, the desired endpoint might be unable to handle the call due to a lack of resources. Finally, the failure of outgoing calls could result from a compatibility problem. For example, the requested service category (such as UBR or real-time CBR) is not supported by the client.

If no incoming calls have been successful, the problem is more likely a result of the client's lack of ability to meet the incoming calls QoS requirements. This is especially possible if the client has provided a heavy allocation of resources to other connections.

If there are no successful incoming or outgoing calls and LAN emulation is in use, but signaling and ILMI packets continue to increment, the problem might be compatibility with the switch. As a result, the client fails to register with the LECS. Alternately, the services are available and the client has registered, but the desired endpoint is unavailable or overloaded.

If all fields return a result of 0 except for a signaling and ILMI Packet result of 1, the client probably has no physical connection to the switch. Check the integrity of cables and other physical connections.

The last option for this utility is ATMADM -C. This option provides a set of parameters describing all the computer's ATM connections, such as those to the BUS, to the LES, and to other ATM devices. Figure 14.22 shows a sample result after running this option.

Figure 14.22   Typical ATMADM -C Report

```
C:\users>atmadm -c

Windows ATM Call Manager Statistics

ATM Connections on Interface : [003] ForeRunner PCA-200EPC ATM
AdapterNNf

Connection        VPI/VCI Remote Address/
                          Media Parameters (rates in bytes/sec)


In  P-P SVC    0/285   4700918100000000613E5BFE01002048082C3C01
                       Tx: UBR, Peak 16953984, Avg 16953984, MaxSdu 9188
                       Rx: UBR, Peak 16953984, Avg 16953984, MaxSdu 9188
In  P-P SVC    0/47    4700918100000000613E5BFE0100204808119B01
                       Tx: UBR, Peak 16953984, Avg 16953984, MaxSdu 9188
                       Rx: UBR, Peak 16953984, Avg 16953984, MaxSdu 9188
Out PMP SVC    0/37    4700000000003C0001A00000000000C11082B601 (11)
                       4700918100000000613E5BFE01002048082C3C01 (10)
                       39840F8001BC3C0000010016640060A000088B01 (8)
                       4700918100000000613E5BFE0100204808119B01 (7)
                       39840F8001BC3C0000010016640060A00008DC01 (6)
                       39840F8001BC61DF00072045000020480EB4EB01 (5)
                       39840F8001BC61DF00072045000000778FE73E01 (4)
                       39840F8001BC61DF00072045000000D10F4FAD01 (1)
                       39840F8001BC61DF00072045000020480E06E301 (0)
                       Tx: UBR, Peak 16953984, Avg 16953984, MaxSdu 9180
                       Rx: UBR, Peak 0, Avg 0, MaxSdu 0
In  P-P SVC    0/58    39840F8001BC61DF00072045000000D10F4FAD01
                       Tx: UBR, Peak 16953984, Avg 16953984, MaxSdu 9188
                       Rx: UBR, Peak 16953984, Avg 16953984, MaxSdu 9188
Out P-P SVC    0/51    39840F8001BC3C0000010016640060A000088B01
                       Tx: UBR, Peak 16953984, Avg 16953984, MaxSdu 9188
                       Rx: UBR, Peak 16953984, Avg 16953984, MaxSdu 9188
Out P-P SVC    0/45    4700790001020000000000000000A03E00000200
                       Tx: UBR, Peak 16953984, Avg 16953984, MaxSdu 9188
                       Rx: UBR, Peak 16953984, Avg 16953984, MaxSdu 9188
Out P-P SVC    0/44    39840F8001BC3C0000010016640060A00008DC01
                       Tx: UBR, Peak 16953984, Avg 16953984, MaxSdu 9188
                       Rx: UBR, Peak 16953984, Avg 16953984, MaxSdu 9188
In  PMP SVC    0/48    4700918100000000613E5BFE0100204808119B00
                       Tx: UBR, Peak 0, Avg 0, MaxSdu 0
                       Rx: UBR, Peak 16953936, Avg 16953936, MaxSdu 9180
Out P-P SVC    0/46    4700918100000000613E5BFE0100204808119B00
                       Tx: UBR, Peak 16953984, Avg 16953984, MaxSdu 9188
                       Rx: UBR, Peak 16953984, Avg 16953984, MaxSdu 9188
```

Several of the connections listed in Figure 14.22 can be traced to standard components. For instance, the entry for VCI/VPI pair 0/45 is the default ATMARP server address. The entry for 0/48 is the actual adapter address, as you can see by comparing it with the results of the ATMADM -A query. The entry for 0/37 is clearly a multicast connection with 12 endpoints.

In general, all VPI/VCI values of 0/0 to 0/32 are reserved for signaling and management functions. For example, 0/0 and 0/5 are reserved for UNI signaling, 0/16 is an ILMI channel, and 0/17 indicates ILMI for LANE. VPI/VCI values above 0/32 are endstation-to-endstation data direct or multicast connections.

The media parameters portion of each of the connection ends with the maximum service data unit. These indicate the type of connection operating, as shown in Table 14.2.

Table 14.2   Standard MTUs for Common Network Types

MTU Size	Network Type
9234	Ethernet option
18190	Typical Token Ring
4544	Token Ring option
1516	Ethernet default
9188	IP over ATM

ATMLANE Utility

This utility allows you to examine the various aspects of the Microsoft LAN emulation client. When it is run from the command line, it displays the ATM adapter device name, the ELANs configured on that ATM adapter, the ELAN's number (since an adapter can be configured with multiple ELANs), and the ELAN's state.

The ELAN state can be one of the following.

Table 14.3   Common ELAN States

ELAN State	Description
INITIAL	The ELAN has just begun to operate.
LECS CONNECT ILMI	The ELAN is attempting to connect to the LECS using the ATM address obtained from ILMI.
LECS CONNECT WKA	The ELAN is attempting to connect to the LECS using the well-known LECS ATM address.
LECS CONNECT PVC	The ELAN is attempting to connect to the LECS using the LECS PVC.
LECS CONNECT CFG	The ELAN is attempting to connect to the LECS using a specially configured LECS address.
CONFIGURE	The ELAN has connected to the LECS and is exchanging configuration data with the LECS.
LES CONNECT	The ELAN is connecting to the LES using the address returned from the LECS.
JOIN	The ELAN is exchanging join data with the LES.
BUS CONNECT	The ELAN is discovering and connecting to the BUS.
OPERATIONAL	The ELAN is fully operational.
SHUTDOWN	The ELAN is shutting down.

Following the ELAN state three sets of parameters are displayed, as shown in Figure 14.24. The first set describes some of operating parameters of the LANE client. The parameters C1, C2, and up to C28 all have values that are either defaults, spelled out in the LANE specification from the ATM Forum, or parameters obtained from the LECS and LES.

The second set of parameters (C16) describes the current Ethernet address to ATM address mappings. All of these parameters are shown in Figure 14.23, which shows a normal report from an LEC.

Figure 14.23   Results of an ATMLANE Query

```
Windows ATM LAN Emulation Client Information

Adapter: \DEVICE\{11DC1752-1B17-11D2-A8E5-853DAA694C23}

ELAN: \Device\{FDEBFE5E-1B55-11D2-A8E6-000000000000}

          ELAN Number:          0
          ELAN State:           OPERATIONAL
     C1   ATM Address:          47.0091.81.000000.0061.3e5b.fe01.0020480811f3.00
     C2   LAN Type:             Ethernet/802.3
     C3   MaxFrameSize:         1516
     C4   Proxy:                Off
     C5   ELAN Name:            Collage740ElanEth
     C6   MAC Address:          00.20.48.08.11.f3
     C7   ControlTimeout:       300 sec
     C8   RouteDescriptors:     None
          LECS Address:         47.0079.00.000000.0000.0000.0000.00a03e000001.00
     C9   LES Address:          39.840f.80.01bc61.df00.0720.4500.00006f072045.03
          BUS Address:          39.840f.80.01bc61.df00.0720.4500.00006f072045.04
     C10  MaxUnkFrameCount:     5
     C11  MaxUnkFrameTime:      1 sec
     C12  VccTimeout:           1200 sec
     C13  MaxRetryCount:        1
     C14  LEC ID:               27
     C15  multicastMacAddrs:    Broadcast,All_multicast
     C16  LE_ARP Cache:         See below
     C17  AgingTime:            300 sec
     C18  ForwardDelayTime:     15 sec
     C19  TopologyChange:       Off
     C20  ArpResponseTime:      16 sec
     C21  FlushTimeout:         4 sec
     C22  PathSwitchingDelay:   6 sec
     C23  LocalSegmentId:       4080
     C24  McastSendVcType:      Best Effort
     C25  McastSendVcRate:      0 cps
     C26  McastSendPeakRate:    0 cps
     C27  RemoteMacAddrs:       None
     C28  ConnComplTimer:       4 sec

C16 LE_ARP Cache

00.00.c1.00.02.8b -> 39.840f.80.01bc61.df00.0720.4500.0000c100028b.00
00.20.48.0e.06.e3 -> 39.840f.80.01bc61.df00.0720.4500.0020480e06e3.00
00.a0.24.b3.3c.20 -> 47.0005.80.ffe100.0000.f219.19a5.00a024b33c20.00
00.00.d1.0f.4f.ad -> 39.840f.80.01bc61.df00.0720.4500.0000d10f4fad.00
00.00.d1.0f.5f.aa -> 47.0000.00.00003c.0000.a000.0000.0000d10f5faa.00
00.00.d1.0f.9f.66 -> 47.0000.00.00003c.0000.a000.0000.0000d10f9f66.00
ff.ff.ff.ff.ff.ff -> 39.840f.80.01bc61.df00.0720.4500.00006f072045.04
```

```
Connection Cache

PEER 47.0000.00.00003c.0000.a000.0000.0000d10f9f66.00 DataDirect
PEER 47.0000.00.00003c.0001.a000.0000.0000d100083c.00 DataDirect
PEER 47.0000.00.00003c.0001.a000.0000.0000d10f9f5e.00 DataDirect
PEER 39.840f.80.01bc61.df00.0720.4500.0000c100028b.00 DataDirect
PEER 47.0000.00.00003c.0000.a000.0000.0000d10f5faa.00 DataDirect
PEER 47.0005.80.ffe100.0000.f219.19a5.00a024b33c20.00 DataDirect
PEER 39.840f.80.01bc61.df00.0720.4500.0020480e06e3.00 DataDirect
PEER 39.840f.80.01bc61.df00.0720.4500.0000d10f4fad.00 DataDirect
BUS  39.840f.80.01bc61.df00.0720.4500.00006f072045.04 McastSend +
McastFwd
LES  39.840f.80.01bc61.df00.0720.4500.00006f072045.03 CtrlDirect +
CtrlDistr
```

The third set of parameters shows the current ATM connections used by the
ELAN. The first column shows the class of the connection, a Peer, BUS, or LES.
The second column lists the destination ATM address of the connection, and the
third column describes the specific connection type for that VC (DataDirect for a
Peer, Mcast for the BUS, and Ctrl for the LES). The six types of VCs are
described in the following section.

Configuration Direct A bi-directional VC established between the LEC and the
LECS as part of the LECS Connect process; it is used by the client to obtain
configuration information such as the ATM address of the LES.

Control Direct A bi-directional, point-to-point VC that carries control information
between a LANE client and the LES. Used, for example, during address
resolution.

Control Distribute A point-to-multipoint VC from the LES to one or more LECs.

Data Direct The most common type of VC, a bi-directional, point-to-point
connection that carries data between two LECs.

Multicast Send A bi-directional, point-to-point VC between a LEC and the BUS.
Used for sending multicast frames to the BUS.

Multicast Forward A unidirectional point-to-point or point-to-multipoint VC from
the BUS to one or more LECs, used for forwarding multicast data frames to
members of an ELAN.

ATMARP Utility

This utility describes the Address Resolution Protocol (ARP) server or Atmarmps.sys used in an IP over ATM network. However, since the Windows 2000 IP over ATM service combines the functions of ARP, MARS, and MCS servers, it provides more information than its name might first imply. While the tool is named ARP, it also describes MARS and MCS statistics, such as packets received, forwarded, members joining the multicast list of clients, attempts to add new clients, registrations, leaf joins, and so on.

The utility includes two primary options, ATMARP -C and ATMARP -S, as well as an ATMARP /reset option. This last option works as might be expected; it resets the values of all ARP and MARS statistics to zero. The default is ATMARP -S; simply typing **ATMARP** or **ATMARP -S** brings up a report similar to the example shown in Figure 14.24, describing the current state and the history of the ATMARP server:

Figure 14.24   Typical ATMARP -S Report

```
C:\>atmarp

Windows ATM ARP Server Information

Adapter: {BA021C4A-8475-11D2-9FC7-95AE3A1F5FF7}

Arp Server Statistics
     Elapsed Time: 71763 seconds
     Recvd. Pkts.: 14869 total          (0 discarded)
          Entries: 13    current        (13 max)
        Responses: 11    acks           (909 naks)
       Client VCs: 6     current        (11 max)
   Incoming Calls: 4582  total

Mars Server Statistics
     Recvd. Pkts.: 13949 total          (13 discarded)
     MCData Pkts.: 49069 total          (0 discarded, 49069 reflected)
          Members: 6     current        (8 max)
          Promis.: 0     current        (1 max)
        Add Party: 24    total          (0 failed)
     Registration: 4142  requests       (0 failed)
            Joins: 9323  total          (36 failed, 9286 dup's)
           Leaves: 31    total          (0 failed)
         Requests: 453   total
        Responses: 440   acks           (0 naks)
          VC Mesh: 1     joins          (0 acks)
           Groups: 0     current        (1 max)
       Group Size: 1     max
```

Elapsed Time notes the seconds elapsed since the ARP/MARS/MCS service was started, or since **ATMARP /reset** was run. All the statistics that total up a value over time are reset to zero by the **/reset** command. "Received Packets" indicates the total number of ATP and MARS control packets received by the server on this adapter, as well as the number discarded. A high number of discarded packets indicates a communications or resource-related problem. "Entries" lists both the number of ARP entries currently in the internal ARP table and the maximum number that it has held since the start of statistics collection. "Responses" simply lists the number of ARP ACK and NACK response sent. **"Client VCs"** lists the current number of incoming client VCs, while "Incoming Calls" lists the aggregate total number of client VC calls.

Next come the MARS server statistics. These begin with the total number of packets received and discarded. A high number of discarded packets indicates a communications or resource-related problem. Next, "MCData Pkt" represents the total number of multicast packets received from clients, discarded, and reflected on the cluster control VC. "Members" describes the current number of multicast clients, as well as the maximum number of clients at any one time since the start of data collection. "Promis" just lists the number of current (and maximum) number of clients that have requested promiscuous joins. "Add Party" tracks the number of times the ARP server has attempted to add a client to the cluster control VC, and how many of them have failed. "Registration" lists the number of clients that have attempted to register with the MCS, and how many have failed. "Joins" and "Leaves" list the number of requests by clients to join and to leave a multicast group, the number of requested that failed, and the number that duplicated an earlier join. These include promiscuous join and leave requests.

"Requests" lists the total number of MARS requests, that is requests asking for ATM addresses associated with a particular IP multicast group address. "Responses" lists the number of ACKs (indicating a successful response containing at least one address) and NAKs (indicating no ATM addresses were associated with the IP multicast address in question).

"VC Mesh" shows the total number of successful joins involving VC Mesh IP multicast group addresses. ACKs list the number of MARS requests for a VC Mesh–served IP multicast group address. "Groups" tracks the number of VC-Mesh IP multicast group addresses, both current and the maximum number at any time. The last ATMARP -S entry, "Group Size" provides the maximum number of clients that requested the same VC Mesh IP multicast address group at any one time.

The MARS server (based on a user-modifiable configuration) determines which addresses are MCS-served. VC Mesh group addresses are all the addresses that are not served by the MCS. When an address is MCS-served, the MARS server return its own ATM address in response to clients' requests for information about that set of multicast addresses. For all others — that is, for VC Mesh group addresses — the MARS returns a list of ATM addresses of those clients who have joined the specific address.

The term "VC Mesh" derives from the fact that communication between clients end up creating a "mesh" of point-to-multipoint VCs. Each client that hopes to send data to a particular VC Mesh group address must create a point-to-multipoint VC; all the clients receiving data sent on that address make up the leaves of that VC.

In contrast to the default server information the ATMARP -C report provides a look at the address cache. A sample output is provided in Figure 14.25, containing four address mappings:

Figure 14.25   Results of ATMARP -C

```
Windows ATM ARP Server Information
Adapter: {EB535D2A-8044-11D2-AFE3-A9CC1F4296B4}
Arp Cache
192.168.74.20 -> 47.0000.00.00003c.0000.a000.0000.0000c1100879.01
192.168.74.23 -> 47.0000.00.00003c.0000.a000.0000.0020480811da.01
Mars Cache
promiscuous -> 47.0000.00.00003c.0000.a000.0000.0020480811da.01
236.1.2.3 -> 47.0000.00.00003c.0000.a000.0000.0000c1100879.01:q
```

Each entry in the ARP cache shows the mapping of one IP unicast address to an ATM address. There is no hard-coded limit to the number of addresses that can be stored in this cache, and the list entries are not in any particular order.

Each entry in the MARS caches shows the mapping of one IP multicast group address to one or more ATM addresses. The special IP multicast group address known as "promiscuous," lists the ATM addresses of clients that have joined in promiscuous mode.

Only VC Mesh IP multicast group addresses show up in the cache. This is significant because a network can easily have active multicast sessions going on between several clients using several IP multicast group addresses (all of which happen to be MCS-served). In this case, the MARS cache remains empty.

IP over ATM

Setting up and maintaining an IP over ATM network provides real benefits, but it also requires additional start-up work to configure an optimally efficient network. Logical IP subnets and PVCs are just some of the tools available to system administrators to keep a network performing; both are described in more detail in the following sections.

Enhancing Security through Logical IP Subnets

A logical IP subnet (LIS) prevents communication between other IP hosts except through a router. (The term is defined in RFC 1577).

Adding clients to a LIS is performed at the client level by establishing an SVC to the ARP server and using a static or DHCP-assigned IP address within the same IP subnet and having the same subnet mask. A LIS can also be established by using a PVC between clients in the same IP network or subnet and subnet mask.

For instance, an IP over ATM network can be set up to contain two LISs, one for users on site, and a second in another department or group or PVCs. The ATM ARP server examines all users who call it to join the CLIP network. All those who access the same IP over ATM server address with DHCP share the same IP network or subnet number and subnet mask are members of the same LIS. The LIS members have full network access to each other. Security is enforced simply by the inability of other networks connecting to the LIS or its members.

The security feature works to prevent others from accessing the network. To extend the example further, a second LIS can be formed using the same ATMARP server address but with a different IP network/ subnet number and subnet mask by static addressing or through a DHCP server on the second LIS. For a member of the second LIS to gain access to the secured servers in LIS 1, they must cross a router, which can enforce the desired security protocol. Routing is required even though both LISs are logically served by the same ATMARP server since the LISs do not share the same IP network.

Combining PVCs and a LIS reveals another useful property of IP over ATM. ATM ARP clients can be pointed to one another through the ATM Call Manager and IP over ATM to utilize a common PVC that has been set up on the ATM switch and that operates without the use of ATM addresses. You can then use IP addresses within the same IP network or subnet and subnet mask to form a small and secure LIS. The LIS is completely secure between the systems on the subnet and unavailable to other LISs, even through the ATM switch, without routing the IP packets from one of the systems. Additional uses for PVCs are described below.

Using PVCs Effectively

PVCs are similar to LISs as they are also useful in private ATM networks in certain situations. For instance, a large campus LAN might need to migrate to a higher-speed ATM backbone. In backbone configurations, the connections required are just a few static configurable switch paths that change infrequently. Permanent configuration of an ATM circuit serves this function well.

As another example, consider a small WAN with a limited number of sites that require a continuous dedicated high-speed connection to guarantee a fixed Quality of Service between site locations. With a circuit permanently established, the ATM switches at both WAN sites do not suffer the added latency and overhead of call signaling, or connection setup and teardown, each time ATM cell traffic data is sent on the network. When data is sent it is forwarded directly over the PVCs established between sites.

In Windows 2000, PVCs are set up from the **Network Connections** interface. PVCs are used for special situations, such as custom connections (like raw channel access), PPP over ATM server & client, and ATMARPC over PVCs. To configure them, go to the advanced properties of the ATM Call Manager.

Setting Up IP over ATM for a PVC-Only Environment

It is possible to configure Windows 2000 Professional or Windows 2000 Server computers to use IP over ATM using just PVCs. Doing so, however, requires some preparation.

First, allocate IP addresses for each computer. Each computer requires an IP address. You also need a PVC (that is, a VPI/VCI pair) for each pair of communicating computer. Write down the VPI/VCI values at each end of the PVC; each direction uses the same value for the PVC, but those values must be entered at both endpoints. Set up your switches with the PVC and port information; the PVCs can all be set up as UBR (line rate) virtual circuits.

Follow these steps:

▶ **To enable IP over ATM**

1. From **Control Panel**, click **Network**.

2. In the **Network Connections** dialog box, select the **Properties** tab and then double-click on the **ATM adapter** to display all protocols bound to the ATM adapter.

3. Select **TCP/IP Protocol**, and then click **Enable**.

▶ **To assign the IP address to the computer**

1. Right-click **Internet Protocol (TCP/IP)** on the **ATM Connection Properties** page.

2. In the **TCP/IP Properties** dialog box, select your ATM adapter name in the **Connect Using** field.

3. Click **Use the following IP Address**, and then enter the appropriate information in the **IP Address**, **Subnet Mask**, and **Default Gateway** fields.

   Optionally, click **WINS Address** and complete the corresponding fields.

▶ **To configure the ATMARP Client on each computer for PVC-only**

1. In **Control Panel**, click **Network and Dial-Up Connections**, and then right-click **ATM Connection**.

2. Click the **Properties** tab, and select **ATM Call Manager**; click the **Properties** tab from the **ATM Call Manager** dialog box.

3. Click **Add**.

4. In the **ATM PVC Configuration** dialog box, enter the PVC's name and VCI number, and then change the **Application Type** from **Custom** to **Default**.

Important The **Application Type** defaults to the **Custom** value on the ATM PVC Configuration page. You must change the **Application Type** to **ATMARP** every time you enter a new PVC value.

Once you have configured all the PVCs you need for the IP Mesh, the IP over ATM protocol uses this information along with the Inverse ARP to populate the address mapping cache (ARPCache) of the ARP server. This happens automatically; once the PVCs are configured, the network is ready for operation.

Modifying ATM Defaults

It is possible to modify the default performance parameters of an ELAN (other than the ELAN name), but doing so reduces the chances of making a successful JOIN request. All such modifications must be made at the switch rather than in the operating system. Contact your switch manufacturer for details.

Security: Preventing Unauthorized Access to a Switch

ATM is intrinsically secure, since under normal circumstances you cannot connect to the ATM services themselves from the outside. Anyone attempting to connect to LANE services from outside the emulated LAN must first contact a bridging entity (such as Ethernet and Token Ring edge device bridges or an ATM-to-Ethernet router). This means that the easiest way for you to control access to LANE connections from the outside is by not connecting any legacy components to your ATM switch.

From the inside, access can be controlled by changing the ELAN name and the ARP server address from the default values to more secure specific names and numbers. You can make these changes as part of a larger effort to create a set of multiple ELANs that are transparent to one another, but that provide different levels of security. Since ATMARP must be used between components of the network, the entire network can be secured by changing the ATMARP server address; the new name acts as a form of password for any client seeking to log on to the network and register itself with the ATM switch.

The VPI/VCI join (sometimes called an ILMI join) is the first option that almost all LECs try when seeking to join an ELAN. This ability can be secured by setting up MAC address filters, usually in the LECS but sometimes in the ELAN/VLAN level that disallow a join for an unknown MAC address. This type of join is secured on some switches by turning off the use of ILMI by the LECS. The next most common method is by Well Known Address (WKA) which uses a fixed ATMF NSAP (47.00.79.00.00.00.00.00.00.00.00.00.00.a0.3e.00.00.01.00).

Troubleshooting

Troubleshooting all ATM connections follows a similar pattern because the greatest strength in ATM, its connection-oriented nature, is also a source of difficulty when those connections fail to materialize.

Because connections are central to successful operation of an ATM network, successful troubleshooting always involves the use of the ATMADM tool. Three steps can lead to a diagnosis of most problems. First, use ATMADM -C to find out whether the connections the computer has are correct.

Second, use ATMADM -A to check that the UNI connection is working correctly. If ATMADM -A returns an address, it proves that you have communicated with the switch, and the switch is aware of the LEC. In rare cases, it is possible to gain an address but still be unable to access any services at the switch; this is due to a very poor quality connection between LEC and switch, and generally indicates a cabling problem.

Finally, if you have no UNI address, use ATMADM -S to determine whether ILMI is operating correctly. If it is, the bottom two entries of the utility report (shown in Figure 14.21) show two incrementing and approximately equal values. "Received" does not increment at quite the same rate as "Sent."

Initialization Failure

One of the most common sources of problems in ATM function is during the initialization of a new ATM client. Most commonly, the problem stems from an inability of the LANE client to find the LECS. There are a number of possible reasons why: the LANE services are not enabled on the switch, the LEC is attempting to join an ELAN that does not exist, or the LEC specifies parameters for an ELAN it wants to join that the switch does not support. Each of these is examined in more detail below.

If the switch's LANE services are not enabled, the ATMADM -C utility shows outgoing cells incrementing slowly. The same utility shows an attempt to contact the switch on the VPI/VCI pair 0/17. If the LEC is specifying a bad ELAN name in its attempt to join the network, the attempt to contact the switch generates a message in the Event Log. If the LANE services are not enabled on the switch, the Event Log contains no such a message.

For more information about troubleshooting connection failures, see "ATMADM Utility" earlier in this chapter.

Parameters Unsupported

The QoS levels on the switch do not have any affect on UBR traffic unless traffic shaping is in effect on the switch. You might notice that your connection has different up and down rates, or per VC bandwidth is much lower than the overall bandwidth of the connection. This can result in a loss of connections that would otherwise have gone through. To correct the problem, you must change the QoS parameters at the switch. See the manufacturer for details.

PVC Not Forwarding Cells

Sometimes you establish a PVC or series of PVCs (as described in "IP over ATM" earlier in this chapter) and then discover that the PVC is not forwarding cells from one endpoint to another as expected. The roots of the problem can be diagnosed by comparing the results of ATMADM -C and ATMADM -A.

The ATMADM -A utility shows the UNI address of the ATM adapter negotiated with the switch and proofs the UNI connection.

ATMADM -C shows the addresses of both inbound and outbound calls. It also shows the attributes for SVC point-to-point and point to multipoint calls. However, in the case of PVCs, ATMADM -C shows an inbound PVC with an assigned path and channel — but without an address. ATMADM -C shows no address because no call is made to establish a PVC. To establish the connection, the UNI simply opens the PVC. The UNI attributes of the connection — including the VPI/VCI values, and the inbound and outbound bit rates — are established on the switch as part of the signaling and VP/VC setup. Once a PVC connection has been established, it remains active at the UNI level even if information is not passing through it.

Figure 14.26 shows a sample ATMADM -C result for a working PVC connection:

Figure 14.26   ATMADM -C Results for a Normal PVC Connection

```
D:\>atmadm c
Windows ATM Call Manager Statistics
ATM Connections on Interface : Interphase 5525/5575 PCI ATM Adapter

Connection    VPI/VCI    Remote Address/
                          Media Parameters (rates in bytes/sec)

In  P-P PVC    0/51      Tx: UBR, Peak 16932864, Avg 16932864, MaxSdu 9188
                         Rx: UBR, Peak 16932864, Avg 16932864, MaxSdu 9188
```

Note The sample shown in Figure 14.26 is at full bandwidth and settings for an ATM ARP client over PVCs with no shaping as an example. Establishing traffic shaping through QoS levels at the switch can provide different up and down transmission rates, or it can lower bandwidth per VC to a much lower level than the overall bandwidth of the connection.

If ATMADM -C shows no connection but ATMADM -A and -S look okay, check your PVC settings in ATMUNI. You can do this by going to the Control Panel to the Network Connections and Local Area Connections windows; compare the values you see there for the PVC settings with the switch PVC settings. If these two VP and VC pair does not match exactly, no PVC connection can be made.

If ATMADM -A returns no address then the UNI has not established a link. If ATMADM -S is negative then the problem is probably a connection issue.

ATMADM -A results in a printout of the ATM address acquired from the switch (ILMI interaction) which is composed of 20 bytes of info. The first thirteen bytes are the switch address, the next six are the MAC address of the adapter and the last two are the selector bytes. Acquiring the address proves that you have interaction at the UNI level with the switch.

If ATMADM -A does not provide an ATM address but the ATMADM utility itself does not return an error in its output, this indicates that the utility program could not contact the call manager. The next step in this case is to dig a little deeper using ATMADM -S. In particular, study the last two figures from the ATMADM -S report, which describe transmission and reception. If only transmit is working, the adapter is up but has either no connection or only a half duplex connection. This indicates that the system has been wired improperly. Check whether the system is wired with the wrong cable (Ethernet twist instead of straight through, for instance), whether a length of bad fiber is fouling up the transmission medium, or whether some other instance of reversed polarity is plaguing the wiring. To correct the problem, check the cable type, seating, and connection.

If both transmission and reception figures are incrementing but you have no address is returned, the system is suffering from one of two possible problems: either ILMI has been disabled at the switch or the switch is running in UNI 3.0. In either case, the solution is to check the switch configuration.

If ATMADM -A indicates that you have an address and ATMADM -S indicates that ILMI is working, the next place to look is still in ATMADM -S report. In particular, check for unsuccessful outgoing calls. In LANE unsuccessful calls generally mean that the LEC cannot contact the LECS by VPI/VPI or by the well-known address — the repeated attempts to do so increment the outgoing calls.

There are several possible suspects for any failure to connect the outgoing call: LANE is not running on the switch, the switch has nodefault ELAN on the switch, or the ELAN name specified in the **ATM LAN Emulation Client Properties** dialog box does not exist. The last of these problems generates a warning in the event log.

IP over ATM Troubleshooting

IP over ATM indications are approximately the same. From the IP over ATM client side, failed calls generally mean that there is no IP over ATM Server at the ATM address you are trying to call. If this is true for IP over ATM Server, it is possible that the switch you are connected to is an early UNI 3.1 version and does not allow you to register two addresses on the same connection. In this case, you must use the actual ATM address of the server for the server's onboard client and disseminate it to all the clients you plan to connect.

Additional Resources

- For more information, see the ATM Forum Signaling Specifications link on the Web Resources page at http://windows.microsoft.com/windows2000/reskit/webresources.

C H A P T E R   1 5

Telephony Integration and Conferencing

Microsoft® Windows® 2000 is an advanced platform for telephony applications encompassing conventional computer telephony integration (CTI) features, as well as upgrades in Internet Protocol (IP)–based Internet telephony and Internet conferencing functionality.

In This Chapter

Related Information in the Resource Kit

- For more information about Quality of Service (QoS), see "Quality of Service" in the *Microsoft® Windows® 2000 Server Resource Kit TCP/IP Core Networking Guide*.

- For more information about remote access servers, see "Remote Access Server" in this book.

Introduction to Windows 2000 Telephony and Conferencing

Telephony applications use Telephony Application Programming Interface function calls, also known as Telephony API (TAPI), to provide various types of telephony services to users. This set of Win32 function calls is processed internally by TAPI, resulting in corresponding calls to Telephony Service Providers (TSPs) and Media Service Providers (MSPs) that communicate with their associated hardware and software to provide various types of telephony services to users.

These applications can also use other features of the Windows environment, such as the directory service, databases, and e-mail. TAPI uses standard mechanisms to retrieve and manipulate information offered by telephone systems, such as identification of calling parties, in order to automate the process of associating data with telephone calls. TAPI also provides IP telephony and video-conferencing infrastructure, allowing the deployment of applications that integrate conventional and IP telephony functionality.

A key advantage of using TAPI is that telephony applications can work with any hardware for which a TSP or MSP is available. The abstraction of hardware by TAPI reduces difficulty for developers, and provides flexibility to network administrators. For example, TAPI abstracts the underlying hardware of the telephone system, allowing developers to create telephony applications that work with a variety of telephone systems. Without hardware abstraction, a developer might have to significantly rewrite code to match each type of telephony hardware that their program could be used for. As more developers create applications that can work across an array of hardware, network administrators have more choice in deploying CTI, conferencing, and IP telephony solutions.

Computer-Telephony Integration Overview

Windows 2000 builds upon the support for computer-telephony integration (CTI) that was first introduced in previous versions of Windows operating systems. This is in response to an increasing interest by developers in creating CTI and conferencing applications, and a need on the part of network administrators to deploy CTI and conferencing solutions on their networks.

With TAPI applications, users perform telephone operations from the user interface of the computer using integrated computer-based information, such as personal directories or databases. Computer-telephony integration (CTI) applications range from Phone Dialer programs, which allow a user to click a number on the computer screen, to programs that manage conference calls. TAPI provides standard programming interfaces and delivery mechanisms, such as speed dialing, transferring calls, and integrating Caller ID functions, that simplify the delivery of telephony operations.

Additional examples of CTI include:

Integrated Services

Moving voice mail to the computer enables the creation of a universal inbox containing e-mail, voice mail, and fax messages.

Call Center Applications

TAPI offers two ways to integrate:

- Through an interface to the hardware-based system, such as a Public Branch Exchange (PBX) or an external Automatic Call Distribution (ACD) system.

- Through an entirely software-based system, such as an IP telephony network or an IDC built entirely on the Windows 2000–based server.

Historically, call center applications that direct calls based on information gathered from a database have been built on relatively expensive, proprietary systems that are challenging to customize and to integrate with existing information systems. By making these applications entirely software-based, call center applications can be developed more quickly at a decreased cost, and become more tightly integrated with computer-based information systems.

Predictive Dialing   In an outbound telemarketing environment, a telephony server with the appropriate hardware can rapidly dial a list of chosen numbers. When a connection is detected with a live person, the call is immediately routed to a customer service agent. Because only a fraction of calls result in connections with people, as opposed to those that are busy, have no answer, or are picked up by an answering machine, this application can dramatically improve the efficiency of outbound telemarketing by limiting time spent on non-productive calls.

Interactive Voice Response   Interactive Voice Response (IVR) allows developers to create voice menus that callers can obtain with the telephone keypad, using them to access information or execute transactions. Auto attendants handle initial routing of incoming telephone calls with outgoing messages, such as "For sales, press one."

Computer PBX   TAPI can provide an interface to single-box, personal computer–based PBXs. In these environments, sophisticated call processing services can be implemented entirely within Windows 2000 using comprehensive, connection control and media API.

IP Telephony and Conferencing   TAPI includes IP telephony service providers, which enable video conferencing over IP networks.

Microsoft Support of CTI

TAPI support is also built into clients running Microsoft® Windows® 95 and Microsoft® Windows® 98.

The telephony and conferencing infrastructure of Windows 2000 consists of the following elements:

- Phone Dialer Application
- Telephony Application Programming Interface 3.0
- Telephony Service Providers

Phone Dialer Application

Phone Dialer, which is a TAPI application, is included with Windows 2000. Phone Dialer can be used for basic telephony functions, as well as audio and video conferencing services.

The Phone Dialer makes TAPI function calls to utilize the Telephony Service Providers (TSPs), including the H.323 and the Multicast Conferencing Service Providers. In addition, the Phone Dialer can be used with TSPs supplied by other vendors.

▶ **To launch the Phone Dialer**

1. From the **Start** menu, point to **Programs, Accessories**, and **Communications**.
2. Click **Phone Dialer**.

TAPI 2.1 and 3.0

Versions of the Microsoft Windows family of operating systems prior to Windows 2000 were supplied with TAPI 2.1 or earlier. (For instance, TAPI 1.4 was included with Windows 95 and can be upgraded to TAPI 2.1 through a free download; TAPI 2.1 was included with Windows 98.) These versions of TAPI provided a Microsoft® C-based procedural application programming interface (API).

Version 3.0 of TAPI is included with Windows 2000, but Windows 2000 continues to support previous versions of TAPI. TAPI 3.0 adds support for the Microsoft Component Object Model. A set of COM objects are provided to enable the use of any COM-compatible programming language, including Microsoft® Visual Basic®, Java, and Microsoft® Visual C++®, as well as scripting languages, such as Visual Basic® Scripting Edition (VBScript) or JavaScript, for writing telephony applications. The existing C API continues to be available under TAPI. Telephony applications written using the older version of C API are also still usable.

In addition to COM support, TAPI 3.0 also provides functionality for H.323-based IP telephony and IP multicast–based multiparty audio and video conferencing over TCP/IP data networks, by means of service providers included with the operating system.

Service Providers

A Telephony Service Provider (TSP) is a dynamic-link library (DLL) that supports communications to one or more specific hardware devices through a set of exported service functions. The service provider responds to telephony requests, sent to it by TAPI, by carrying out the low-level tasks necessary to communicate over the network. In this way, the service provider, in conjunction with TAPI, shields applications from the service-dependent and technology-dependent details of the network communication.

Developers write service providers to extend telephony services for existing hardware or to provide telephony services for new hardware. Each service provider supports at least one hardware device, such as a fax board, an ISDN card, a telephone, or a modem. The installation utility for a service provider associates that service provider with its hardware devices.

TAPI 3.0 supports two classes of service providers: telephony and media. Telephony Service Providers provide the implementation of signaling and connection control features, and Media Service Providers (MSPs) provide access to media content associated with those connections.

TSPs are mandatory service providers, and might optionally be associated with their own TSP-specific access to media content. MSP functionality is a new feature of TAPI 3.0, and is not supported on previous versions of TAPI.

Windows 2000 includes a set of service providers, which are described in greater detail later in this chapter. Windows 2000 Telephony Service Providers include:

- H.323 Service Provider
- Multicast Conferencing Service Provider
- NDIS Proxy Service Provider
- Remote Service Provider
- TAPI Kernel-Mode Service Provider
- Unimodem 5 Service Provider

Note   To install TSPs and MSPs from third-party vendors, follow the instructions they provide. To verify the installation, use the Telephony snap-in from the Start menu.

TAPI Architecture

All components of Win32 Telephony (other than components provided for backward compatibility), including service providers, are implemented in 32 bits.

Existing 16-bit applications link to Tapi.dll. In Microsoft® Windows® 3.1 and Windows 95, Tapi.dll is the core of Windows Telephony, but with TAPI 2.0 and later, Tapi.dll is simply a thunk layer (or translation layer) to map 16-bit addresses to 32-bit addresses, and pass requests along to Tapi32.dll.

Existing 32-bit applications link to Tapi32.dll. In Windows 95, Tapi32.dll is a thunk layer to TAPI. With TAPI 2.0 and later, Tapi32.dll is a thin marshaling layer, that transfers function requests to Tapisrv.exe and, when needed, loads and invokes service provider user interface DLLs in the application's process.

Tapisrv.exe is the core of TAPI. It runs as a separate service process, in which all Telephony Service Providers execute. Service providers can create threads in the TAPISRV context as needed to do their work.

Key components of TAPI 3.0 architecture include:

- TAPI 3.0 COM API
- TAPI Server Process
- Telephony Service Providers
- Media Service Providers

TAPI 3.0 COM API

The TAPI 3.0 COM API is implemented as a suite of Component Object Model (COM) interfaces. This allows developers to write TAPI-enabled applications in any COM-aware language, such as Java, Visual Basic®, or Microsoft® Visual C/C++®.

TAPI Server Process

The TAPI Server provides a process context that is independent of the application, under which Telephony Service Providers can execute. TAPI API functions communicate with the TAPI Server to send service requests to Telephony Service Providers.

Telephony Service Providers

Two new IP Telephony Service Providers, and their associated Media Stream Providers (MSPs), are included as part of TAPI 3.0.

H.323 Service Provider

The Microsoft H.323 Telephony Service Provider and its associated Media Service Provider allow TAPI-enabled applications to engage in multimedia audio/video sessions with any H.323-compliant terminal (such as Microsoft NetMeeting) on a local area network (LAN) or the Internet.

Specifically, the H.323 TSP and MSP implement the H.323 signaling stack. The H.323 TSP accepts a number of different address formats, including user name, computer name, and e-mail address.

The H.323 MSP is responsible for constructing the Microsoft® DirectShow® filter graph, including the Real-Time Transport Protocol (RTP), codec, sink, and render filters, for an H.323 connection.

Multicast Conferencing Service Provider

The multicast conferencing service provider uses IP multicast to provide efficient multiparty audio and video conferencing facilities over the IP network, intranets and the Internet. Due to large bandwidth usage by video streams, multiparty video conferencing services have been difficult to achieve. By using IP multicast, the TSP makes it possible to reduce the number of video streams.

NDIS Proxy Service Provider

The NDIS Proxy Service Provider offers a TAPI interface to wide area network (WAN) devices, such as ISDN or ATM. As such, these devices (written to the Microsoft Network Driver Interface Service (NDIS) interface version 5.0) can be used by TAPI applications. The NDIS Proxy is a generic service provider, meaning that it supports all such WAN devices—without those devices needing to be individually TAPI-aware.

An important feature of the NDIS Proxy Service Provider is that underlying NDIS 5 components need not be aware of TAPI in order to be provided with a proxied TAPI interface. In this way, TAPI applications, such as the Routing and Remote Access service, can use NDIS 5 drivers to establish connections across wide area networks.

Remote Service Provider

TAPI includes a Remote Service Provider to support client/server telephony. The Remote SP exposes TAPISRV telephony service extensions for client access to TAPI devices that reside on networked server computers. Remote SP resides on the client, where it appears as just another service provider to TAPI. When a TAPI request is made through Remote SP, it communicates with a remote telephony server in order to service the request. The service provider on the server that ultimately services the request need not be aware that it is operating in this client/server environment. An example of such a service provider would be a CTI link installation, whereby client applications communicate with a server, which in turn is connected through a CTI link to a PBX. In this way, those applications gain third-party control of telephones on the attached PBX.

TAPI Kernel-Mode Service Provider

The TAPI Kernel-Mode Service Provider communicates with NDIS 4 components in order to provide a TAPI interface for backward compatibility to NDIS 4 WAN drivers. An example of the sorts of driver that can take advantage of the NDIS Proxy would be an ISDN driver offering connection-oriented services. Using such a driver, TAPI applications such as Routing and Remote Access service can use the TAPI Kernel-Mode Service Provider in order to establish PPP connections across wide area networks.

Unimodem 5 Service Provider

Unimodem 5 is a Telephony Service Provider that provides an abstraction for modem devices such that applications can operate transparently across a wide variety of types and makes of modems. In addition, modem installation is greatly simplified since Unimodem is aware of the operating characteristics of these modems, and their drivers are already available in the operating system. Unimodem 5 also adds support for voice modems.

Third-Party Service Providers

Independent hardware and software vendors can write their own Telephony Service Providers, compatible with TAPI.

Media Service Providers

TAPI 3.0 ships with two Media Service Providers, including the H.323 Conferencing MSP and the IP multicast conferencing MSP. These MSPs use the DirectShow API for efficient control and manipulation of streaming media.

Figure 15.1 shows the architecture of TAPI.

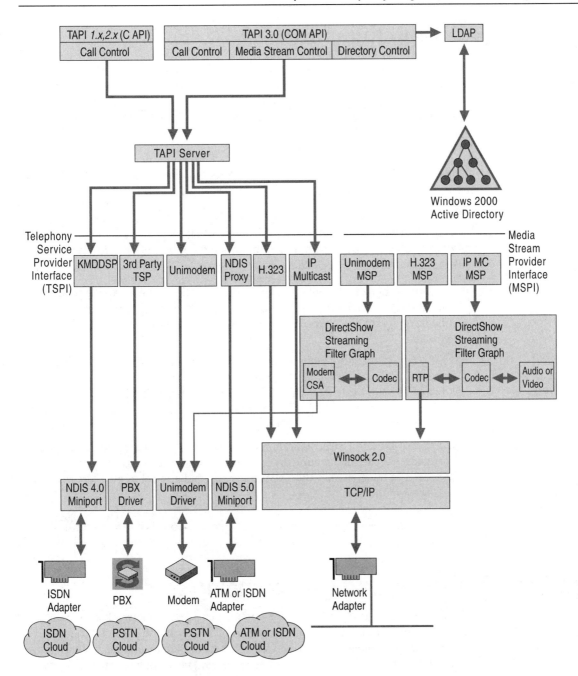

Figure 15.1   TAPI Architectural Diagram

Client/Server Telephony

In a client/server environment, TAPI provides distributed access to shared telephony resources. For example, a LAN-based server might have multiple telephone-line connections to a local telephone switch or PBX. TAPI operations invoked at any associated client are forwarded over the LAN to the server. The server uses third-party call control between the server and the PBX to implement the client's call-control requests.

This model offers a lower cost per computer for call control if the LAN is already in use.

The server can be connected to the switch using a switch-to-host link. It is also possible for a PBX to be directly connected to the LAN on which the server and associated clients reside. Within these distributed configurations, different subconfigurations are possible:

- To provide personal telephony to each desktop, the service provider could model the PBX line associated with the computer (on a desktop) as a single line device with one channel. Each client computer would have one line device available.

- Each third-party station can be modeled as a separate line device to allow applications to control calls on other stations. (In a PBX, a station is anything to which a wire leads from the PBX.) This enables the application to control calls on other stations. This solution requires that the application open each line it wants to manipulate or monitor.

- The set of all third-party stations can be modeled as a single line device with one address (one phone number) assigned to it per station. Only a single device is to be opened, providing monitoring and control of all addresses (all stations) on the line.

A major advantage of such client/server implementations is a lowered cost of telephony services per client application.

Internet Telephony and Conferencing

Conventional telephony is based on switched circuit voice networks, which are integrated with computer-based data networks to varying degrees. The need for dual networks in enterprises has been the subject of debate, and the need to unify voice and data applications into a single integrated network has come to the forefront.

At their core, IP telephony and conferencing technologies are built around very simple concepts. A personal computer (or other device) is used to capture audio and video signals from the user (for example, by using a microphone attached to a sound card, and a video camera connected to a video capture card). This information is compressed and sent to the intended receivers over the local area network or the Internet. At the receiving end, the signals are restored to their original form and played back for the recipient. Audio can be rendered by using speakers attached to a sound card, and video, by creating a window on the display of the computer.

Windows 2000 includes two different sets of technologies that enable the unification of voice and data networks.

Internet Telephony with H.323

H.323 is an ITU-T protocol that is used to provide voice and video services over data networks. At the most basic level, H.323 allows users to make point-to-point audio and video phone calls over the intranet. The Microsoft implementation also allows voice-only calls to be made to conventional phones using IP-PSTN Gateways, and audio-video calls to be made over the Internet. For more information about H.323, see the link to the International Telecommunication Union Web site on the Web Resources page http://windows.microsoft.com/windows2000/reskit/webresources.

Placing H.323 Calls with the Dialer

The TAPI Phone Dialer application can be used to place H.323 audio and video calls over IP networks. The dialing user interface allows called parties to be identified in numerous ways. Frequently called users can be added to speed dial lists. The **Dial** dialog box can also be used to place calls by specifying the computer name or IP address of the computer on which the called party's H.323 application is running.

After resolving the caller's identification to the IP address of the computer on which he/she is available, the dialer makes TAPI calls, which are routed to the Microsoft H.323 Telephony Service Provider. The service provider then initiates H.323 protocol exchanges to set up the call. The Media Service Provider associated with the H.323 TSP uses audio and video resources available on the computer to connect the caller and party receiving the call in an audio or audio/video conference.

The Windows Address Book can also be used to place H.323 Internet Telephony calls using the dialer.

▶ **To place H.323 Internet Telephony calls using the dialer**

1. Run WAB. Create a new contact and fill in the information fields.

2. Click **Properties**, and then click the **Business** tab; enter the user's name, e-mail address, computer name, or IP address.

3. To place a call to a user, click **Start** and point to **Programs**, **Accessories**, and **Address Book**.

4. Right-click on the entry in the **Windows Address Book**.

5. Select **Action**, and then select **Dial**.

This invokes the Phone Dialer, which places the call.

Receiving H.323 Calls

The TAPI Phone Dialer also has the capability to listen for incoming H.323 IP Telephony calls, notify the user when such calls are detected, and accept or reject the calls based upon the user's choice. To enable this functionality, the Phone Dialer application must always be running. The dialer can be minimized into an icon on the system tray for ease of use.

Using Windows 2000 Directory Services

Windows 2000 provides a set of directory services that allow telephone calls to be made by specifying individuals by name rather than their phone numbers or IP addresses. TAPI provides services that search the Windows 2000 directory to translate user names or e-mail addresses into respective telephony addresses, and then places calls to those addresses.

Two different directory services can be used with TAPI applications running on Windows 2000.

Active Directory™ directory service is a recent Windows 2000 feature that provides scalable, centrally administered, automatically replicated, and persistent storage. It is used to store various attributes of information in a set of objects that represent the resources available on the network. TAPI utilizes the IPPhone attribute of User objects to store information about the computer name or IP Address on which the specific user is available for H.323 Internet telephony calls.

The Phone Dialer application automatically locates the user object for the logged in user, and updates the IPPhone attribute. When other users attempt to place calls to the user, the Rendezvous object inside TAPI performs a directory search to translate the user's name or e-mail address to his computer name or IP address. The application can then use the H.323 TSP, and specify the IP address to place the call.

The Microsoft® Site Server ILS Service is another directory service that can be used with TAPI applications on Windows 2000–based computers. This service is distinct from Active Directory in that it is less scalable, and does not provide persistent, centrally-administered data storage. The TAPI Phone Dialer creates a user object on the Site Server ILS Service when the application starts up, and places the user's IP address inside it in a form that is compatible with NetMeeting. This can be used by the Phone Dialer and other TAPI applications to place calls to the user by specifying his name or e-mail address. The advantage of using the Site Server ILS Service is that it allows NetMeeting users to view users of TAPI applications and place calls to them by simply double-clicking their names from the directory view pane of NetMeeting.

H.323 Protocol

The Microsoft H.323 TSP and MSP together implement an H.323 version 1.0 protocol stack. The protocol consists of three layers of individual signaling protocols:

- Registration, Admission, and Status
- Q.931
- H.245

Registration, Admission, and Status

Registration, Admission, and Status uses UDP ports 1718 and 1719 for discovery, registration, and call admission requests between Gatekeepers and H.323 applications. This layer is optional, and is not currently implemented by the Microsoft H.323 Telephony Service Provider in Windows 2000.

Q.931

Q.931 uses TCP port 1720 for call setup, alerting, tear down, and other connection oriented signaling. This signaling layer relies on the knowledge of caller's IP address, which is provided by the TAPI Rendezvous control COM object using Windows 2000 directory services. This layer is supported by the Microsoft H.323 Telephony Service Providers.

H.245

H.245 uses dynamic TCP ports for media-oriented signaling, such as negotiating media types and setting up media channels. This layer is supported by the Microsoft H.323 Telephony Service Providers.

Media Streams with RTP

H.323 makes use of the IETF Real-Time Transport Protocol (RTP)for transferring digitized audio and video data between the various parties participating in a call. This protocol utilizes dynamic UDP ports negotiated between the sender and receiver of specific media streams. Each RTP packet contains one or more media payloads, and other relevant information such as timestamps and sequence numbers. TAPI 3.0 incorporates an implementation of the RTP protocol stack.

Audio and Video Codecs

Audio and video codecs are used to compress digitized audio and video signals before transmission by the sender, and then decompress them on the receiving computer before they are played for the user. The effect of this compression-decompression operation is that network bandwidth utilization is reduced and traffic load on the network is minimized.

The Microsoft H.323 Media Service Provider uses G.711 and G.723.1 codecs for audio signals, and H.261 and H.263 codecs for video signals.

Figure 15.2 illustrates how codecs are used for video compression and decompression.

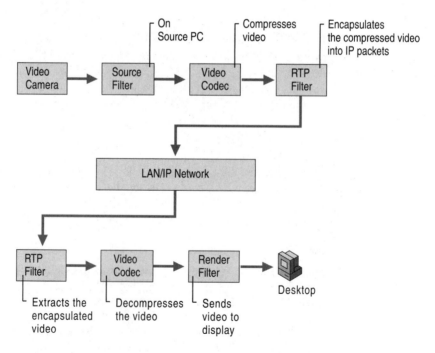

Figure 15.2   Codecs Used for Video Compression and Decompression

Calling Through IP-PSTN Gateways

The H.323 protocol incorporates support for placing calls from data networks to the switched circuit PSTN network, and vice versa. The main advantage is that the long-distance portion of the call can be carried on private or public data networks, and the call can then be placed onto the switched voice network to bypass long-distance toll charges.

For example, a user in a Seattle branch office could call Boston, with the phone call going across the corporate network from branch office Seattle to a branch office in Boston, where it would then be switched to a PSTN network to be completed as a local call. This is especially effective in cases where enterprises own private WAN links to their subsidiaries and branch offices. These can be used to carry audio signals in addition to data, and result in lower long-distance telephone bills paid by the company.

The H.323 TSP provides support for Gateway (a bridge from IP to PSTN) calling through the use of a static configuration option, accessible through **Phone and Modem Options** in **Control Panel**.

▶ **To specify the IP address of the IP-PSTN Gateway**

1. From the **Start** menu, point to **Settings**, and then click **Control Panel**.

2. Double-click **Phone and modem options**.

3. Click the **Advanced** tab, and then select the Microsoft H.323 Telephony Service Provider.

4. Click **Configure**. Select the **Use H.323 Gateway** check box and type the computer name or IP address of the IP-PSTN Gateway in the text box.

Users can specify the IP address or computer name of an IP-PSTN Gateway through which all IP-PSTN calls are routed by the H.323 TSP. The IP-PSTN Gateway is expected to be running an ITU-T H.323 v1.0 interoperable H.323 application.

Figure 15.3 provides an example of a PSTN Gateway.

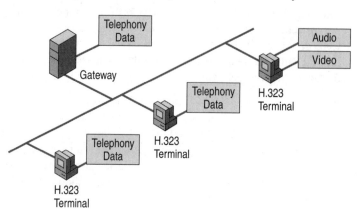

Figure 15.3   PSTN Gateway

Calling Through Firewalls

H.323 calls cannot pass through firewalls based on simple network address translation (NAT) solutions due to the complexity of H.323. Special application layer proxy servers are required in order to make and receive calls between computers on networks separated by firewalls.

Many enterprises choose to erect firewalls between their private corporate intranets and the Internet for security reasons. This has the effect of complicating the passage of H.323 based Internet telephone calls across the Internet.

The Microsoft H.323 TSP incorporates support for firewall traversal. **Phone and Modem Options** (in Control Panel) can be used to specify the inner IP address of the firewall computer. This allows calls to be made and received across the Internet.

▶   **To specify the IP address of the H.323 Proxy**

1. From the **Start** menu, point to **Settings**, and then select **Control Panel**.

2. Double-click **Phone and modem options**.

3. Click the **Advanced** tab, and select the Microsoft H.323 Telephony Service Provider.

4. Click **Configure**. Select the **Use H.323 Proxy** check box and type the computer name or IP address of the inner edge of the H.323 proxy/firewall computer in the text box.

Calling Through Gatekeepers

Gatekeepers are useful tools for managing IP Telephony clients and providing address resolution, call routing, call logging, and other services. The current implementation of H.323 Service Provider does not include support for making H.323 calls using Gatekeepers.

Quality of Service Support

TAPI includes quality of service (QoS) support to improve conference quality and network manageability. QoS can be supported on ATM networks as well as on packet-based networks such as the Internet.

QoS information in TAPI is exchanged between applications and service providers in FLOWSPEC structures that are defined in Windows Sockets 2.0. Support for QoS is not restricted to ATM transports; any service provider can implement QoS features.

QoS in TAPI 3.0 is handled through the DirectShow RTP filter, which negotiates bandwidth capabilities with the network based on the requirements of the DirectShow codecs associated with a particular media stream. These requirements are indicated to the RTP filter by the codecs through its own QoS interface. The RTP filter then uses the COM Winsock2 GQoS interfaces to indicate its QoS requirements to the Winsock2 QoS service provider (QoS SP). The QoS SP, in turn, invokes a number of varying QoS mechanisms appropriate for the application, the underlying media, and the network, in order to guarantee appropriate end-to-end QoS. These mechanisms include:

- The Resource Reservation Protocol (RSVP) for providing QoS over non-ATM networks. RSVP is a signaling protocol which enables the sender and receiver in a communication session to set up a reserved QoS highway between them. The RSVP message carries the reservation request to each router and switch along the communication path between the sender and receiver.

- Local Traffic Control, a QoS mechanism for reducing delay and latency in the transmission of network traffic, and for providing traffic control for networks which do not comply with RSVP such as legacy networks, broadcast networks or over-provisioned networks.

- Packet Scheduling, which manages the queues set up by the packet classifier. It retrieves the packets from the queues and sends them across the QoS-reserved highway.

- 802.1p, which defines a mechanism by which traffic can be handled at a certain priority within LANs. It includes an implicit signaling mechanism and special traffic handling mechanisms in the LAN devices. Typically, hosts or routers which are sending traffic into a LAN mark submitted packets with the appropriate priority values. Thus, the hosts or routers use 802.1p to signal a priority to LAN devices. LAN devices, such as switches, bridges and hubs are expected to treat the packets accordingly.

For more information about QoS, see "Quality of Service" in the *TCP/IP Core Networking Guide*.

Multiparty Conferencing with IP Multicast

The Multicast Conferencing Service Provider included with TAPI 3.0 provides support for IP multicast-based audio and video conferencing between multiple participants. The TAPI 3.0 rendezvous control provides additional COM interfaces that TAPI applications can use to access directory services such as Active Directory, and the Site Server ILS Service.

Conferences

The call model for multi-person conferences differs from conventional one-on-one calls. The conference is hosted by one of the participants, who takes the step of determining the conference name, its start and end times, and the list of participants. The host then publishes the conference on a server using his TAPI application (such as the Phone Dialer), and notifies the prospective participants that a conference is available for their participation.

Other participants might use their TAPI applications to visit the server and browse the list of conferences that are available for participation. At the designated time, participants use their TAPI applications to join the conference. TAPI provides all the infrastructure for audio and video streams to be transmitted and received using IP multicast.

IP Multicast

IP multicast is an extension of IP that allows for efficient conferencing. Without the use of IP multicast, a user wishing to broadcast data to N users must send data through N connections, as shown in Figure 15.4.

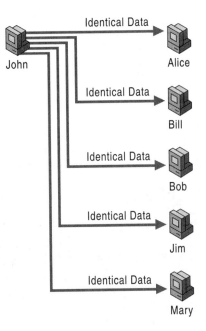

Figure 15.4   Sending Data Without IP Multicasting

Without IP multicasting, network bandwidth is wasted as the same data is transmitted individually to each recipient.

The total bandwidth required for multiparty recipient conferences in which all users are sending data goes up exponentially with the number of parties involved. This prevents widespread deployment of conferences involving multiple participants.

IP multicast takes advantage of the actual network topology to eliminate the transmission of redundant data through the same communications links. To reach a multicast group, a user sends a single copy of the data to a single group multicast IP address that reaches all recipients. No knowledge of other users in a group is necessary. To receive data, users register their interest in a particular multicast IP address with a multicast-aware router.

Multicast conferences are inherently more scalable because conference participants are not required to send additional audio and video copies as more participants are added.

Single Group IP Address

IP multicast uses a single group IP address to reduce network traffic. The value of this is illustrated in Figure 15.5, where six users who wish to participate in a conference are connected together by a number of routers.

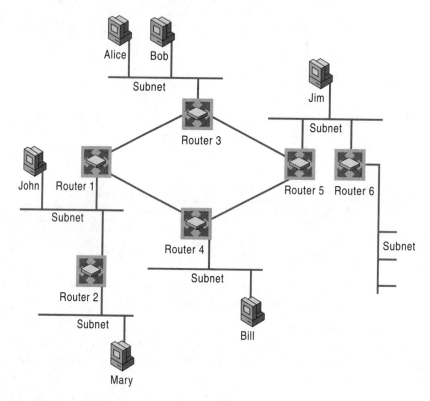

Figure 15.5   Actual Network Topology

Without the use of multicast conferencing, all six users would send out five copies each of their audio and video data, resulting in 30 audio and 30 video streams which could potentially cause traffic congestion at some locations on the network.

IP multicast eliminates this volume of packets by using a single group IP address that can be joined by all six participants. Multicast aware routers route these one-to-many data streams efficiently by constructing a spanning tree in which there is only one path from one router to any other. Copies of the stream are made only when paths diverge, as shown in Figure 15.6.

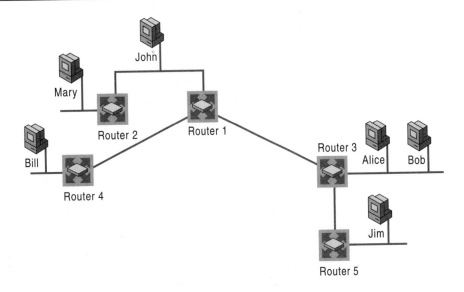

Figure 15.6   IP Multicasting Spanning Tree

IP multicasting uses a spanning tree algorithm to minimize network traffic while ensuring that all multicast recipients receive the data stream.

Without multicasting, the same information must either be carried over the network multiple times, one time for each recipient, or broadcast to everyone on the network, consuming unnecessary bandwidth and processing.

Allocating Multicast Addresses

IP multicast uses Class D Internet Protocol addresses to specify multicast host groups, ranging from 224.0.0.0 to 239.255.255.255. Both permanent and temporary group addresses are supported. Permanent addresses are assigned by the Internet Assigned Numbers Authority (IANA) and include 224.0.0.1, the all-hosts group used to address all multicast hosts on the local network, and 224.0.0.2, which addresses all routers on a LAN. The range of addresses between 224.0.0.0 and 224.0.0.255 is reserved for routing and other low-level network protocols. Other addresses and ranges have been reserved for applications, such as 224.0.13.000 to 224.0.13.255 for NetNews. For more information, see RFC 1700.

Windows 2000 includes a Multicast Address Dynamic Client Protocol (MADCAP) server that can be used to allocate a unique multicast IP address for the duration of the conference. TAPI provides an API that allows applications to make such 'lease' requests to the server and obtain a multicast address without intervention from the user. Such requests can be made automatically while the host is creating the conference, ensuring the availability of a unique IP address that other participants can join to participate in the conference.

> **Note** A MADCAP server must be running somewhere on an organization's network to enable TAPI applications to obtain multicast IP addresses. For more information about MADCAP and its support in Windows 2000, see "Dynamic Host Configuration Protocol" in the *TCP/IP Core Networking Guide*.

Publishing Conference Objects

Once a host has determined the details of a conference, there are several possible ways to disseminate this information to potential participants. TAPI provides the means to publish these conferences on the Site Server ILS Service running on a centralized server, where all participants who have been granted access to the conference by the host are able to access this information. These conference objects are based on RFC 2327.

TAPI also provides the means for applications to access the Site Server ILS Service running on remote servers and allow users to browse the published conference objects and join conferences described in them.

The Phone Dialer application contains appropriate user interface elements to facilitate the creation, browsing, and joining of conferences.

> **Note** A Site Server ILS Service must be running on a server somewhere on an organization's network to enable TAPI applications to create conference objects.

Site Server ILS Service uses Active Directory to publish its own location on the network. TAPI also provides facilities to enable TAPI applications to locate Site Server ILS servers by querying Active Directory. This eliminates the need for individual users to know the specifics about the location of ILS servers on which conferences might be published by conference hosts.

Session Description Protocol

Session Description Protocol (SDP) is an IETF standard for announcing multimedia conferences. The purpose of SDP is to publicize sufficient information about a conference (time, media, and location information) to allow prospective users to participate if they so choose. Originally designed to operate over the Internet MBONE, SDP has been integrated with Active Directory and Site Server ILS service by TAPI 3.0, thereby extending its functionality to LANs.

An SDP descriptor advertises the following attribute information about a conference:

- Conference Name and Purpose
- Conference Time
- Conference Contact Information
- Media Type (video, audio, and so on)
- Media Format (H.261 Video, MPEG Video, and so on)
- Transport Protocol (RTP/UDP/IP, H.320, and so on)
- Media Multicast Address
- Media Transport Port
- Conference Bandwidth

A Session Description is broken into three main parts: a single Session Description, zero or more Time Descriptions, and zero or more Media Descriptions. The Session Description contains global attributes that apply to the whole conference or all media streams. Time Descriptions contain conference start, stop, and repeat time information, while Media Descriptions contain details that are specific to a particular media stream.

While traditional IP multicast conferences operating over the MBONE have advertised conferences using a push model based on the Session Announcement Protocol (SAP), TAPI 3.0 utilizes a pull-based approach using Windows 2000 Active Directory. This approach offers numerous advantages, among them bandwidth conservation and ease of administration.

Conference Security Model

The conference security system in TAPI 3.0 controls who can create, delete, and view conference announcements. Each object in Active Directory can be associated with an access control list (ACL) specifying object access rights on a user or group basis. By associating ACLs with SDP conference descriptors, as shown in Figure 15.7, conference creators can control who can enumerate and view conference announcements. User authentication is provided through Windows 2000 security.

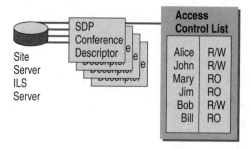

Figure 15.7   SDPs and ACLs

Session descriptors are transmitted from the Site Server ILS server to the user using the LDAP protocol on port 1002. Windows 2000 IP Security connections can be used to secure this transmission, ensuring that the SDP conference descriptors are safe from eavesdroppers.

Important Current implementations do not support encryption of media streams to prevent unauthorized eavesdropping of multicast packets during transit on the network.

Routing and Remote Access Service Considerations

Routers and dial-up Routing and Remote Access service connection servers must be explicitly configured to route or forward multicast packets and Internet Group Management Protocol (IGMP) requests made by clients wishing to join multicast conferences. IGMP enables clients to make requests for joining multicast group addresses in which they are interested).

For information about how to configure the Windows 2000 remote access server to enable multicast routing on a network, see "Remote Access Server" in this book.

Troubleshooting

The following information can be of assistance when troubleshooting telephony deployments.

Troubleshooting PSTN Telephony

The following sections outline common problems and solutions for conventional (non-IP) Public Switched Telephone Network (PSTN) telephony deployment.

One or more client computers cannot "see" the telephony server

If the telephony server cannot be reached through the network, for example, a user cannot 'ping' the telephony server, it is possible that:

1. The telephony server has not been correctly set up. Consult Windows 2000 Server Help for how to manage telephony servers.

2. The Unicast IP protocol is not installed. Consult Windows 2000 Server Help for installing and troubleshooting Unicast IP.

3. A Windows 2000 domain has not been correctly established. Consult Windows 2000 Server Help for installing a domain controller.

One or more client computers cannot "see" lines on the telephony server

If one or more client computers cannot see the lines of a telephony server, it could be because they are unable to be authorized for access to lines on the telephony server. When a TAPI application accesses lines on the telephony server, the user context associated with the application process is first authenticated. This means that those lines must have been configured on the server to allow access by that client. If client cannot see lines on the telephony server, it is possible that:

1. The lines have not been configured on the server to allow access by the client. Consult Windows 2000 Server Help on how to set up and manage telephony servers.

2. The user process context in which the application is running has not been associated with lines. Consult Windows 2000 Server Help on how to manage TAPI clients and users on the server.

For information about Active Directory domains and trusts, and authorizing users, see Windows 2000 Server Help.

An application fails to start after you have cancelled the Location Information dialog box

If an application fails to start after you have cancelled out of the **Location Information** dialog box, the problem might be that address translation required by TAPI applications has not been specified. This can be solved by using the **Local Information** dialog box to enter your country/region code, local area code, and pulse or tone and external line access settings.

A client cannot "see" a new line appearance on the server, even though the server administrator has assigned the client to the line

When you assign a currently running client to a line on the telephony server, the new settings are not available until TAPI on the client computer restarts. The solution is to stop all client TAPI applications so that TAPI shuts down. When the client applications restart, they are able to see the newly allocated lines.

For information about how to manage TAPI clients and users, see Windows 2000 Server Help.

Troubleshooting H.323 Calls and Multicast Conferencing

Users of H.323 or multicast conferences might encounter problems connecting with other users or receiving audio or video.

If audio problems occur

If audio problems occur in H.323 or multicast video conferences, the microphones or sound cards on the client computers might be incorrectly configured or malfunctioning.

To diagnose sound hardware on client computers, start the Sound Recorder application by clicking **Start**, pointing to **Programs**, **Accessories**, **Entertainment**, and then clicking **Sound Recorder**, or by typing **sndrec32** at the command prompt. Make a recording of your own voice using Sound Recorder, and then play it back. If there is no sound, check if the microphone is properly plugged in.

If the Sound Recorder test works properly but you continue to have audio problems, verify that the sound settings are correct on all client computers.

▶   **To verify sound settings through Volume Control**

1. Click **Start** and point to **Programs**, **Accessories**, **Entertainment**, and select **Volume Control**.

2. In the **Volume Control** dialog box, select **Options**, **Properties**, and then click **Playback**. Make sure that the **Wave** and **Microphone** checkboxes are selected. You might have to scroll the window in order to see these settings.

3. Click **OK**.

4. Select the **Mute** checkbox in the **Microphone** column if it is not checked. This will prevent speech from being echoed locally (played back on the speaker's computer).

5. If the voices of all other conference participants are too loud or too quiet, adjust the **Volume Control** and/or **Wave** sliders downwards or upwards as needed.

6. Select **Options**, **Properties** and then click **Recording**. Select all of the checkboxes in the window at the bottom of the dialog box. (You might have to scroll the window in order to see these settings.)

7. Click **OK**.

8. Select the **Mute** checkboxes in all of the columns except for the **Microphone** column if they are not already checked. Make sure that the **Mute** checkbox in the **Microphone** is left unchecked. This will allow your speech to be sent to the conference, but will prevent other sounds, including those of other conference participants, from being transmitted from your computer.

9. If other conference participants are dissatisfied with the level of sound, adjust the **Microphone** slider downwards or upwards as needed.

Note A single incorrectly configured computer can cause audio problems or echoes for all other conference participants.

If you continue to encounter audio problems after adjusting the sound settings, check if the affected computers have full-duplex sound cards. Full-duplex sound cards are capable of capturing and playing audio simultaneously, while half-duplex sound cards can only do one at a time. Most modern sound cards are full-duplex, but many older sound cards are only half-duplex.

To check if the sound card on your computer supports full-duplex audio, start Sound Recorder and record a speech sample for approximately thirty seconds. After this is complete, open a second instance of Sound Recorder. Play the sample you recorded using the first instance of Sound Recorder, and while this is playing, attempt to record a sample using the second instance of Sound Recorder. If the second instance of Sound Recorder is unable to properly record a sample while the first instance is recording, the sound card does not support full-duplex audio, and thus will not work with TAPI.

If sound is distorted or otherwise continues to malfunction after you attempt the above procedures, there is most likely a problem with the microphone, sound card hardware, or sound card driver. Check with the manufacturer of your sound cards to ensure that you are using the most recent Windows 2000 drivers. Also, replace the microphones and sound cards on affected computers and attempt these tests again.

If audio echo occurs

Audio echo is a common problem with audio conferencing systems. It originates in the local audio loop-back that happens when a user's microphone picks up sounds from their speakers and transmits it back to the other participants. Normal conversation can become impossible for other participants in the conference when very sensitive microphones are used, speaker level is high, or the microphone and speakers are placed in close proximity to each other.

One of the easiest ways to completely eliminate audio echo is to use audio headsets. These work by eliminating the possibility of a user's microphone picking up sound that is being received from other conference participants.

A more expensive solution is to use special microphones with built-in echo-canceling capabilities. These microphones detect and cancel out echo. The main advantage to these is that users do not have to wear headsets. Echo-canceling microphones are also a necessity for conference rooms because using headphones is not a practical solution.

If video problems occur

If the video image of an H.323 conference participant cannot be seen by the other party, or if the image of a multicast conference participant cannot be see by all of the other endpoints, the computer's video capture device might not be working properly. When using Phone Dialer, participants should be able to see their own video image whenever they participate in videoconferences. If this is not the case, run the camera troubleshooter included in Windows 2000 Professional Help.

Audio and video problems in multicast conferences can also be caused by multicast issues. The following sections describe how to diagnose and resolve these problems using the MCAST tool included in the Resource Kit.

Verifying router configuration for multicast

Problems in multicast conferences can be caused by incorrect network configuration.

▶ **To verify router configuration for multicast**

1. Enable multicast from a global context.

2. Determine the interfaces for which multicast is to be enabled.

3. Enable the use of multicast routing protocols on the selected interfaces. For example:

   - Protocol Independent Multicast (PIM) Sparse Mode for links that have limited bandwidth.

   - PIM Dense mode for links that have a large amount of bandwidth.

   - Distance Vector Multicast Routing Protocol (DVMDP).

4. If access lists are required, consult your router documentation.

Detailed router configuration data is usually available from the router vendor. Certain publications also contain information describing the configuration of routers and how the underlying protocols work.

Verifying network is configured for multicast packets

If you are uncertain whether your network is configured to send and receive multicast packets, use the MCAST diagnostic tool. MCAST can send and receive multicast packets, helping you to determine which parts of your network are enabled for transmission of IP multicast packets. You can use this tool in send mode to set up multicast sources at different locations on your network, and in receive mode to determine the locations at which multicast traffic from these sources is being received.

To run MCAST as a multicast sender, use the following command-line on your Windows 2000–based computer:

```
MCAST /SEND /INTF:172.31.253.55 /GRPS:230.1.1.1 /INTVL:1000
/NUMPKTS:3600
```

MCAST will start sending multicast packets from the IP address 172.31.255.255 to the multicast group IP address 230.1.1.1 at the rate of 1 packet per every 1000 milliseconds. A total of 3600 packets will be sent over a one-hour period.

To run MCAST as a multicast receiver, use a command-line as follows:

```
MCAST /RECV /INTF: 172.31.255.255/GRPS:230.1.1.1
```

MCAST will start listening for multicast packets on its IP address 172.31.255.255 for the multicast group IP address 230.1.1.1. Received packets are displayed on the screen:

```
Started.... Waiting to receive packets...
Received [1]: [GOOD] SRC- 172.31.253.55 GRP- 230.1.1.1    TTL- 5 Len-
256
Received [2]: [GOOD] SRC- 172.31.253.55 GRP- 230.1.1.1    TTL- 5 Len-
256
Received [3]: [GOOD] SRC- 172.31.253.55 GRP- 230.1.1.1    TTL- 5 Len-
256
Received [4]: [GOOD] SRC- 172.31.253.55 GRP- 230.1.1.1    TTL- 5 Len-
256
Received [5]: [GOOD] SRC- 172.31.253.55 GRP- 230.1.1.1    TTL- 5 Len-
256
```

If unable to publish multicast conference invitations

If you are unable to publish multicast conference invitations, set up Site Server ILS Service. The Site Server ILS Service is an essential component of TAPI IP Multicast Conferencing. This server represents the meeting place where conference creators and participants go through their client software application to find the information they need to participate in a conference.

When a conference originator creates a new conference, the Windows Phone Dialer software automatically creates a conference object on the selected ILS server. Participants who are granted access to this conference by the conference originator can see the conference from their Phone Dialer's view pane, and join it by double-clicking the conference name.

For documentation about installing ILS, refer to Windows 2000 Server Help.

If Windows 2000 Phone Dialer cannot see ILS

The Windows 2000 Phone Dialer application must know the location of the Site Server ILS Service to provide conference creation and joining facilities.

The Phone Dialer application can locate this information in Active Directory if the following conditions are fulfilled:

- The computer running the Phone Dialer application is part of a Windows 2000 domain.
- The user is logged on using a Windows 2000 domain account.
- The ILS server location is published in Active Directory.

Using Active Directory in this way means that users do not need to know the location of the ILS server on their network or manually enter that information into their Phone Dialer application. This makes using IP Multicast Conferencing with Windows 2000 easier for client.

For more information about installing domain controllers and the Active Directory, see Windows 2000 Server Help.

If a computer or user cannot access Active Directory

All of the Windows 2000 components required to support TAPI Multicast Conferencing on a client computer are installed, by default, in Windows 2000 Professional and Windows 2000 Server. However, in order for a computer or a user to use TAPI Multicast Conferencing, they need to be added to a Windows 2000 domain. If machine or user accounts for Windows 2000 domain are not created, users cannot access Active Directory and will need to add their ILS servers to the Phone Dialer application manually.

Additional Resources

- For more information about IP multicast, see *Deploying IP Multicast in the Enterprise* by Thomas A. Maufer, 1998, Upper Saddle River, NJ: Prentice Hall PTR.

P A R T   5

Other Protocols

Part 5 examines additional Microsoft® Windows® 2000 protocols that support networking on smaller networks and interoperability between Windows 2000 and non-Windows operating systems.

In This Part

C H A P T E R   1 6

NetBEUI

Microsoft® Windows® 2000 continues to support NetBIOS Extended User Interface (NetBEUI) to provide backwards compatibility with legacy protocols. Windows 2000–based NetBEUI works with the architecture of Windows 2000 to support network sessions (logical connections between networked computers), as well as connection-oriented and connectionless communication.

In This Chapter

Related Information in the Resource Kit

- For information about the architecture of Microsoft® Windows® 2000 Server, see "Windows 2000 Networking Architecture" in the *Microsoft® Windows® 2000 Server Resource Kit TCP/IP Core Networking Guide*.

- For information about the architecture of Microsoft® Windows® 2000 Professional, see the *Microsoft® Windows® 2000 Professional Resource Kit*.

Overview of Windows 2000 NetBEUI

NetBIOS Extended User Interface (NetBEUI) was one of the earliest protocols available for use on networks composed of personal computers. It was designed around the Network Basic Input/Output System (NetBIOS) interface as a small, efficient protocol for use in department-sized local area networks (LANs) of 20 to 200 computers, which would not need to be routed to other subnets. At present, NetBEUI is used almost exclusively on small, non-routed networks composed of computers running a variety of operating systems, including:
Microsoft® Windows NT® Server 3.5 and later, Microsoft® Windows NT® Workstation version 3.5 and later, Microsoft® LAN Manager, Microsoft® Windows® for Workgroups, Microsoft® Windows® version 3.1, Microsoft® Windows® 95, Microsoft® Windows® 98, Microsoft® Windows NT® version 3.1, and LAN Manager for UNIX, as well as IBM PCLAN and LAN Server.

Windows 2000–based NetBEUI, known as NetBIOS Frame (NBF), implements the NetBEUI version 3.0 specification. NBF is the underlying implementation of the NetBEUI protocol installed on a computer running Windows 2000. It provides compatibility with existing LANs using the NetBEUI protocol, and is compatible with the NetBEUI protocol driver included with previous versions of Microsoft networking products. In addition, NBF:

- Uses the Windows 2000–based Transport Driver Interface (TDI), which provides an emulator for interpretation of NetBIOS network commands.

- Uses the Windows 2000–based Network Device Interface Specification (NDIS) with improved transport support and a full 32-bit asynchronous interface.

- Uses memory dynamically to provide automatic memory tuning.

- Supports dial-up client communications with a remote access server.

- Provides connection-oriented and connectionless communication services.

- Removes the NetBIOS session number limit.

The following definitions are provided to clarify terms used later in this chapter:

- Network Basic Input/Output System (NetBIOS) is software developed by IBM; provides the interface between a computer's operating system, the I/O bus, and the network; a de-facto network standard.

- NetBIOS Extended User Interface (NetBEUI) is the original personal computer networking protocol and interface designed by IBM for their LAN Manager server. NetBEUI implements the OSI LLC2 protocol and has a limitation of 254 session connections.

- Windows 2000 NetBEUI 3.0, also known as NetBIOS Frame Format Protocol (NBFP), is the Microsoft implementation of the IBM NetBEUI protocol. It eliminates the previous NetBEUI limitation of 254 sessions to a server and uses the Microsoft TDI layer as an interface to NetBIOS.

Interoperability Using NBF

NetBIOS Frame (NBF) provides compatibility with computers running on the previous versions of operating systems, such as Microsoft LAN Manager, MS-Net, and IBM LAN Server. NBF can be used to connect LAN workstation and server computers, and to connect remote and dial-up clients, including portable computers, to computers running Windows 2000 Server.

NBF can be used with programs that implement a variety of services based on the following application programming interfaces (APIs):

- NetBIOS
- Named Pipes
- Mailslot
- Network dynamic data exchange (DDE)
- Remote Procedure Call (RPC) over NetBIOS
- RPC over Named Pipes

NBF is most efficient when used for computers connecting to small or medium-sized, single-location networks. NBF is not a routable protocol like Transmission Control Protocol/Internet Protocol (TCP/IP) or Internetwork Packet Exchange (IPX), although NBF does support Token Ring routing — available only on IBM Token Ring networks. Additionally, NBF uses a single part naming scheme that does not support network segmentation used in most large networks.

Architecture of NBF

NBF is a transport driver that is composed of the following layers:

- LLC802.2 Protocol

  LLC802.2 Protocol (LLC) corresponds to the Open Systems Interconnection (OSI) Data Link layer. It performs code, address, control frame flow, and provides connection-oriented and connectionless communications.

- NetBIOS Frame Format Protocol

  NetBIOS Frame Format Protocol (NBFP) corresponds to the OSI Transport layer. It performs session establishment, multiplexing, and termination. It also performs message segmentation, delimiting, assembly, and acknowledgment.

Figure 16.1 compares the OSI model to the NBF architecture.

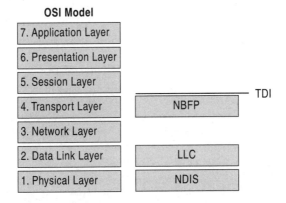

Figure 16.1   OSI Model and NBF Architecture

NBFP connects with TDI, which provides a common interface to multiple transport driver protocols, while the LLC component connects to the Network Driver Interface Specification (NDIS), which in turn provides the interface to the network adapter. Since NBF is not a routable protocol, it does not have a component that corresponds to the OSI model Network layer.

Note In Token Ring networks, NetBEUI uses IBM Token Ring source routing to perform Network layer functions. Token Ring source routing conforms to the Institute of Electrical and Electronics Engineers (IEEE) 802.5 standard and corresponds to the OSI Physical layer, not the OSI Network layer.

TDI Interface

Software programs that rely on NBFP for network communication require a transport driver that exposes the NetBIOS interface. However, instead of exposing the NetBIOS interface, the Windows 2000–based transport drivers expose the more flexible Windows 2000 TDI interface, which in addition to supporting NBF, also serves as a common interface to support protocols such as IPX and TCP/IP.

Figure 16.2 shows how NBFP is exposed through the Transport Driver Interface (TDI).

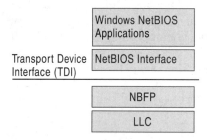

Figure 16.2   Transport Driver Interface (TDI) and NBF

Windows 2000 TDI provides a NetBIOS emulator that maps NetBIOS commands to TDI commands to support applications designed for use with NBFP. NetBIOS commands are formatted as network control blocks (NCBs). When a program running on a Windows 2000–based computer creates an NCB, the NetBIOS command is first processed by the Windows 2000–based NetBIOS driver (Netbios.sys). Netbios.sys processes the NCB by mapping it to the corresponding TDI commands, and sends the TDI command to the Windows 2000–based NetBEUI driver (Nbf.sys). TDI calls implement the same general semantics as NetBIOS NCBs, but are optimized for a 32-bit kernel interface.

Note   Legacy 16-bit Windows 2000 and Microsoft® MS-DOS® transport clients send NCBs directly to the NetBEUI driver.

NDIS Interface

The NBF transport driver processes the TDI requests as frames to be sent out on the network by the logical link control (LLC) layer. The LLC layer is the NBF layer that receives and sends frames from and to a remote computer on the network.

NBF conforms to the IEEE 802.2 LLC protocol standard and performs the following functions:

- Link establishment for connection-oriented communications

- Maintenance and termination of connections

- Frame sequencing and acknowledgment

- Frame flow control

- Connection-oriented and connectionless communications

At the LLC layer, NBF binds, receives, and sends packets to the underlying network adapter drivers by using the NDIS interface.

Communication within the LLC layer is based on service access points, links, and link stations. A link station is a logical point within a service access point that enables an adapter to establish connection-oriented communication with another adapter. Each LLC client program identifies itself by registering a unique service access point. A *service access point* is a mechanism by which the layer above can programmatically access a particular service implemented by the layer below. There are well-known service access points, similar to the well-known ports of TCP/IP. Because NBF is a NetBIOS implementation, it uses the well-known NetBIOS service access point (0xF0).

Figure 16.3 shows the NetBIOS service access point, other access points, and their relationships to the LLC layer.

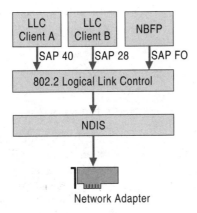

Figure 16.3   NBF LLC Layer and NDIS Interface to the Service Access Points

When a network client program uses LLC to send a frame on to the network, LLC specifies the client or source service access point (SSAP), as well as the destination service access point (DSAP) in the header of the LLC frame.

Network Communication Methods

NBF supports two types of network communication methods: unreliable connectionless communications and reliable connection-oriented communications.

Connectionless Network Communications

With unreliable connectionless communications, NBF transmits the message once or a specified number of times and is responsible only for ensuring that the frame is properly transmitted on the network medium. The message can only be a single frame. The SSAP, DSAP, and the network adapter address of the destination client are all that is needed for unreliable connectionless communications, and no acknowledgment from the destination client is required.

Note Connectionless communications can be either unreliable or reliable. NBF provides only unreliable connectionless communications. Reliable connectionless communication is like a registered letter whose sender is notified that the letter arrived. If reliable connectionless communication is required, NBF can be configured for certain communication commands to send a number of frames that allow time for the destination computer to respond to the message. The number is based on setting a retry value for the registry entry **NameQueryRetries**. The time between sending each frame is determined by time-out registry entry **NameQueryTimeout**.

Three types of NetBIOS commands generate connectionless communications:

- Name claim and resolution
- Datagrams
- Miscellaneous commands

These commands are sent as Unnumbered Information frames at the LLC layer.

To understand how Windows 2000 uses retry and time-out values, consider what happens when a Windows 2000–based computer running NBF registers its NetBIOS computer name. The Windows 2000–based computer sends a multicast message containing an ADD_NAME_QUERY frame on the network. Other computers on the network running NBF can retrieve and process the ADD_NAME_QUERY message. The multicast frames are sent as many times as is specified by **AddNameQueryRetries** at time intervals specified by **AddNameQueryTimeout.** This allows computers on the network enough time to inform the sending computer if the name is already registered as a unique computer name or as a group name on the network.

All registry values discussed in this chapter are found under the following registry path:

HKEY_LOCAL_MACHINE\SYSTEM\CurrentControlSet\Services\Nbf

Warning Do not use a registry editor to edit the registry directly unless you have no alternative. The registry editors bypass the standard safeguards provided by administrative tools. These safeguards prevent you from entering conflicting settings, or settings that are likely to degrade performance or damage your system. Editing the registry directly can have serious, unexpected consequences that can prevent the system from starting, and require that you reinstall Windows 2000. To configure or customize Windows 2000, use the programs in the Microsoft Management Console (MMC) or Control Panel whenever possible.

Connection-Oriented Network Communications

With reliable connection-oriented communications, NBF transfers the frame from the source computer to the destination computer using a link between the sending and receiving LLC computers. The frame is composed of the sending SSAP, the DSAP, and the network adapter address of the destination computer. The frame can be addressed as:

- An individual computer's network adapter address where the LLC frame is received by a single LLC computer that registered the DSAP.

- A NetBIOS multicast address where the LLC frame is received by all LLC computers that have registered the multicast DSAP.

Reliable connection-oriented communication (also called session, or Type 2 operation) requires more overhead than connectionless communication. For example, an acknowledgment from the destination client that the frame is received is required. The transport protocol driver assumes responsibility for transferring the entire message from source to destination, within an acceptable time period. Sequencing is provided; a message that is larger than the maximum transmit frame size can be broken down into multiple frames, sent across the network, and properly reassembled at the receiving computer.

The following procedure uses the **net use** command as an example to describe the signaling process in connection-oriented communication.

1. When you type **net use** at the command prompt to connect to a shared resource, NBF must first locate the server by sending Unnumbered Information frames, and then initialize the link. This is handled by the redirector when it makes a connection to the NBF drivers by using the TDI interface.

2. NBF begins the sequence by generating a NetBIOS Find Name frame.

3. When the server is found, a session is set up with Class-II frames that contain timing parameters following the 802.2 protocol standard (802.2 governs the overall flow of data).

4. The client sends a Set Asynchronous Balance Mode Extended frame, and the server returns an Unnumbered Acknowledgment frame.

5. The client sends a Receive Ready (RR) frame, notifying the server that it is ready to receive Informational (I) frames, which have sequence numbers starting at 0. The server acknowledges this frame.

6. When the LLC-level session is established, additional NetBEUI-level information is exchanged. The client sends a Session Initialize frame, and then the server responds with a Session Confirm frame. At this point, the NetBEUI-level session is ready to handle application-level frame Server Message Blocks (SMBs).

Reliable transfer is achieved with link-oriented frames by numbering the I-frames. This allows the receiving computer to determine whether the frames were lost and in what order they were received.

NBF improves performance for connection-oriented traffic using two techniques: adaptive sliding windows and link timers, which are described in the following sections.

Adaptive Sliding Windows

NBF uses an adaptive sliding window algorithm to improve performance while reducing network congestion and providing flow control. An adaptive sliding window algorithm allows the Windows 2000–based computer using NBF to dynamically tune the number of LLC frames sent before an acknowledgment is requested.

If the sending computer can send only one frame on the network and then has to wait for an acknowledgment (ACK), the sending computer is underused. The frames travel forward, and then ACKs for the received frames have to travel back to the sending computer before it can send another frame. The number of frames that the sender is allowed to send before it must wait for an ACK is referred to as the send window.

The number of frames that a receiving computer is allowed to receive before sending an ACK to the sending computer is referred to as a receive window. In general, NBF has no receive window, unless it detects that the remote sending computer is running a version of IBM NetBEUI that does not support polling (polling is accomplished by sending a frame to check the status of the peer); in this case, NBF uses a receive window based on the value of **MaximumIncomingFrames** in the registry.

The default value for **MaximumIncomingFrames** is 2 and this value does not change dynamically. It must be changed manually by using the Registry Editor.

Limiting the send window size can improve performance by reducing network traffic. The adaptive sliding window tries to determine the best size for the send window based on current network conditions. Ideally, the window is big enough for maximum throughput. However, if the window gets too big, the receiving computer can become overloaded and drop frames, which then have to be retransmitted. This can result in significant network traffic on slow links, or when frames have to pass over multiple hops to find the destination computer.

Link Timers

NBF uses three timers to help regulate network traffic: the response timer (T1), the acknowledgment timer (T2), and the inactivity timer (Ti). These timers are controlled by the values of the registry entries DefaultT1Timeout, DefaultT2Timeout, and DefaultTiTimeout, respectively.

The response timer is used to determine an interval, after which the sender assumes that the I-frame is lost. In this event, NBF sends an RR frame and doubles the value for the response timer (T1). If the RR frame is not acknowledged after the number of retries (defined by the value of LLCRetries), the link is dropped.

When an I-frame cannot be sent within the specified time period, the acknowledgment timer (T2) begins, and an ACK message is sent. The default T2 value is 150 milliseconds. To avoid delays over slow links, and other possible timing issues, NBF is optimized so that the last frame from the sender has the Poll bit turned on. This forces the receiver to send an ACK immediately.

The inactivity timer (Ti) is used to detect whether the link has gone down. The default value Ti value is 30 seconds. If Ti milliseconds pass without activity on the link, NBF sends an I-frame for polling. An ACK is then sent, and the link is maintained.

Note   T2 is less than or equal to T1, which is less than or equal to Ti.

The T1 entry is tuned dynamically per link, based on link conditions and throughput. The value of the T1 entry as specified in the registry is used as the starting value for the time period that the process waits for a response. This entry can be changed. For example, if you know that the computer connects to the network on a slow link, the T1 value can be increased. However, even if this value is not changed, NBF can detect the slow link quickly and automatically tune the T1 value. T2 and Ti are not adapted dynamically.

NBF Dynamically Allocates Memory

A Windows 2000–based computer running NBF allocates the memory necessary to process the requests made by session clients. This means that NBF uses memory only when needed. For example, on a Windows 2000–based computer that does not have an active network connection, very little memory is used by the NBF protocol stack. Because of this dynamic memory management, the installation of NBF on a Windows 2000–based computer does not require additional configuration for number of sessions, packets, or buffers.

NBF Supports Remote Access Clients

NBF is used by remote computers that need to connect to a computer running Windows 2000 Server. Because NBF dynamically allocates memory and is self-tuning, no configuration is required on the computer using the Routing and Remote Access service. To restrict the number of times a query is sent, change the **WanNameQueryRetries** entry by using the Registry Editor. (This entry is the WAN equivalent of the **NameQueryRetries** entry.)

Warning Do not use a registry editor to edit the registry directly unless you have no alternative. The registry editors bypass the standard safeguards provided by administrative tools. These safeguards prevent you from entering conflicting settings or settings that are likely to degrade performance or damage your system. Editing the registry directly can have serious, unexpected consequences that can prevent the system from starting and require that you reinstall Windows 2000. To configure or customize Windows 2000, use the programs in Microsoft Management Console (MMC) or Control Panel whenever possible.

NBF Session Limit

Previous versions of NetBIOS used a 1-byte (8-character binary) number with a maximum decimal value of 256 to identify NetBIOS sessions. Session numbers were assigned per computer. Therefore, a computer using previous versions of NetBEUI can support a maximum of 254 network connections, since NetBIOS reserves session numbers 0 and 255.

NBF breaks the 254-session barrier by using a combination of two matrices, one maintained by NBF and one maintained by NetBIOS. NBF is not constrained by the session limitation of earlier versions of NetBEUI. NBF uses the TDI and a TDI 32-bit handle composed of the session number and the network adapter address of the remote computer. This allows a virtually limitless range of unique numbers that can be used to uniquely identify sessions.

Figure 16.4 illustrates the additional sessions provided by the addition of the NBF matrix.

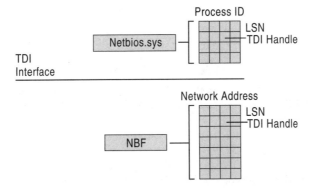

Figure 16.4   Additional Sessions from NBF Matrix

Along the side of the NBF matrix are the Local Session Numbers (LSNs) from 0 to 255. Across the top are the network adapter addresses for the different computers that it has sessions with. In the cell defined by the intersection of the LSN and network address, is the TDI handle. For more information about LSNs, see "Establishing Sessions" later in this chapter.

Note The matrix concept and its contents are for illustration purposes only. The physical storage algorithm and exact contents are beyond the scope of this chapter.

Using NBF, it is possible for a Windows 2000 server with a single network adapter to support simultaneous sessions that exceed the previous NetBEUI session limit of 254. For example, a Windows 2000 server running NBF with a single network adapter is able to support sessions with more than 1,000 clients.

Although NBF breaks the 254-session barrier of previous NetBIOS versions, a limitation is still present when connecting to a remote client with a group NetBIOS name.

Consider the following three scenarios:

A client connecting to a Windows 2000 computer running NBF

When a client connects to a computer running NBF, NBF can inspect the incoming frame to determine the remote adapter's address and assign a session number for that adapter.

NBF connecting to a remote client with a NetBIOS name

When NBF is connecting to a remote client, it first sends a FindName frame. A response from the remote client means that the name is a unique name. NBF can then assign a session number for that remote adapter address because only that remote client owns that name.

NBF connecting to a remote client with a group NetBIOS name

If the FindName response indicates that the connection is being made to a group name, NBF has no way to determine which adapter belonging to the group responds when it tries to connect. In this case, NBF has to assign a session number on a global basis, just as NetBEUI does for all connections.

NBF has no limit on sessions, unless it is establishing connections to group names. In this case, the old NetBEUI limit still applies. For instance, if you have n group name connections, then you can have 254-n connections to any particular remote client. If n is 0, then you can have a full 254 connections to a remote. If n is 253, you can still have one connection to each remote, but if n is 254, then no more connections can be made until one of the existing connections is disconnected.

Establishing Sessions

When two computers initiate a session using NBF, there is an exchange of LSNs.

Initially a frame is sent from the originating computer with an LSN of 0. LSN 0 is a reserved LSN used for the FindName frame of the NameQuery frame.

Figure 16.5 shows this session-creation frame exchange.

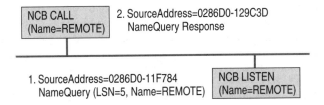

Figure 16.5   Multicast of NameQuery

All computers read the frame and check to see if they have the name in their console tree and if there is a LISTEN NCB frame pending on the name. If there is a LISTEN NCB pending, the computer assigns a new LSN for itself. It adds the LSN to the response frame, satisfying the LISTEN NCB, which now contains just the LSN used on that computer. The LSNs used by individual computers might be different. They do not have to match, but each computer always uses the same LSN for a particular session. This number is assigned when a program issues a call for a network control block (NCB). Even though each computer knows the LSN of the other, the information is not used. The more important information for the two communicating partners is the network adapter addresses that are part of the frames. As the frames are exchanged, each partner picks up the address of the other in the source address component of the frame received. The NBF protocol keeps the network adapter address of the remote partner so that subsequent frames can be addressed directly.

Note   This process applies only to NBF connections. NetBIOS connections established by using NetBIOS over TCP/IP (NetBT) are handled differently.

For information about NetBIOS over TCP/IP, see "Introduction to TCP/IP" and "Windows 2000 TCP/IP" in the *TCP/IP Core Networking Guide*.

Windows 2000 has to use the same NameQuery frame to establish connections with remote computers using NBF. The NameQuery frame transmitted must contain the 1-byte-wide LSN to be used.

For example, suppose a computer running Windows 2000 Server and NBF assigns a session number of 1 to identify the session between itself and computer A and also assigns the number 1 for the simultaneous session with computer B. The computer running Windows 2000 Server can identify the different sessions because it uses the computer network adapter address as part of the TDI handle to further identify each session. When the computer running Windows 2000 Server sends a session frame to either computer A or computer B, it uses the network adapter address to direct the frame across the network. Therefore, computer A does not receive the frames addressed to computer B, and vice versa. However, if the computer running Windows 2000 Server and NBF establishes another session with computer A, it must use a session number other than 1 to uniquely identify the second session.

The NameQuery frame from Windows 2000 contains the LSN associated with the TDI handle that satisfies either the NCB CALL or the LISTEN NCB. In the case of an NCB CALL, it is not multicast but is addressed directly to the remote computer.

The Local Session Number (LSN) from the NBF matrix cannot be the one returned to the process issuing the NCB CALL or LISTEN NCB commands. NBF might have established connections with multiple remote computers with LSN=5, for example. Windows 2000 must return an LSN that uniquely defines its session.

As stated earlier, NBF uses the TDI handle to determine to which LSN and network address to send frames, and each process has its own set of LSNs available to it. Therefore, a component called Netbios.sys is used between the originating process and the TDI interface of NBF to translate a process ID and an LSN into a TDI handle.

Figure 16.6 illustrates an NCB CALL processed through the NetBIOS and NBF matrices. The Netbios.sys matrix has 254 LSNs per LAN adapter number per process. In Windows 2000, the LAN adapter number identifies a unique binding of a protocol driver and one network adapter driver. Each process can have up to 254 sessions per LAN adapter number, not just a total of 254 sessions.

Figure 16.6 shows how the NCB CALL is processed through the NetBIOS and NBF matrices.

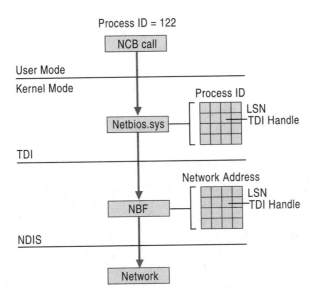

Figure 16.6   NCB Call Processed Through the NetBIOS and NBF Matrices

Netbios.sys builds a matrix that has LSNs down the side, process IDs along the top, and TDI handles in the cells. It is the LSN from this table that is passed back to the originating process.

To further understand how Netbios.sys uses this matrix, suppose a process needs to establish a session with a remote computer. Before the process can issue the CALL NCB, it must issue a Reset NCB frame. This command signals Netbios.sys to allocate space in its TDI handle table, among other things. When the Reset NCB is satisfied, the process issues a CALL NCB to make a connection with a specific remote computer. This NCB is directed down to the Netbios.sys device driver. The driver opens a new TDI handle to NBF and sends the command to NBF.

NBF issues the first NameQuery with LSN=0 to find the remote computer. When the remote computer responds, the network adapter address is extracted from the frame, and a column in the NBF table is created. The second NameQuery with an LSN is sent directly to the remote computer. When that frame is returned successfully, NBF returns a successful status code from the TDI call to the Netbios.sys driver.

Netbios.sys then fills in the LSN from its table into the NCB and sends it back to the calling process.

Limited Network Routing Using NBF

Multi-location networks, such as a wide area network (WAN), require routing capabilities, while single-location, small to medium-sized local area networks (LANs) generally do not require the overhead of a routing protocol.

NBF is not a routable protocol. It uses a single-part naming scheme that cannot be used to differentiate between computers belonging to multiple interconnected networks. NBF can provide a simple form of routing known as Token Ring source routing, which can only be implemented on Token Ring networks using bridges.

Token Ring source routing occurs when NBF broadcasts a NameQuery frame on a local Token Ring; if it does not receive a response in a set period of time, it enables source routing fields in the NameQueryRing frame that force source routing bridges to receive and process the frame. The source routing bridges add additional routing information to the frame and send it to all other rings to which the bridge is connected. When the name query frame reaches the desired computer, that computer sends its computer name in the return message frame, using the routing information from the query to send the message directly to the originating computer. The originating computer caches the routing information and uses the cache to address subsequent frames.

Plug and Play

NBF is Plug and Play–aware and can support all network adapters complying with the IEEE specifications that are currently on the market. For more information about Plug and Play, see "Windows 2000 Networking Architecture" in the *TCP/IP Core Networking Guide*.

Troubleshooting NetBEUI

The following sections discuss problems that you might encounter on a Windows 2000–based computer on which the NetBEUI (or NetBIOS Frame) protocol is installed and running.

Tuning NetBEUI using registry entries

When NetBEUI is installed on a Windows 2000-based computer, because it is largely self-tuning, no configuration is required during installation.

If desired, however, you can change the default values for NetBEUI registry entries. The NetBEUI startup entries are found under the following subkey:

HKEY_LOCAL_MACHINE\SYSTEM\Services\NBF\Parameters

Warning Do not use a registry editor to edit the registry directly unless you have no alternative. The registry editors bypass the standard safeguards provided by administrative tools. These safeguards prevent you from entering conflicting settings or settings that are likely to degrade performance or damage your system. Editing the registry directly can have serious, unexpected consequences that can prevent the system from starting and require that you reinstall Windows 2000. To configure or customize Windows 2000, use the programs in Microsoft Management Console (MMC) or Control Panel whenever possible.

Changing a NetBEUI binding

You can make the following status changes to NetBEUI bindings:

- Enable a binding.
- Disable a binding.
- Move the order (priority) of the bindings up or down.

▶ **To change a NetBEUI binding positions**

1. From the **Start** menu, point to **Settings**, and then click **Control Panel**.
2. Double-click **Network and Dial-up Connections**.
3. Click **Advanced**, and then select **Advanced Settings**.
4. In the **Advanced Settings - Connections** dialog box, select the **Local Area Connection**.
5. In the **Bindings for Local Area Connections** dialog box, select the appropriate binding.
6. Scroll through the **Bindings for Local Area Connections** list to adjust priority.

Attempting to bind NetBEUI to multiple network adapters

Do not bind NetBEUI to multiple adapters on the same physical network or on bridged Ethernet segments. If NetBEUI is bound to multiple adapters on the same physical network or on bridged networks, each adapter attempts to register the same NetBIOS name on the network, causing a conflict to be generated. This might result in disabled adapters and any NetBEUI network connectivity to be lost.

Source routing not supported in FDDI network

Source routing is only supported for Token Ring networks. A network using a Fiber Data Distributed Interface (FDDI) for network communications cannot use NBF for source routing. To correct this problem, use transparent source routing or transparent bridging.

No Session Alive frames

NBF does not use NetBIOS Session Alive frames to determine if the remote client is present; instead, it sends LLC poll frames, which perform the same function. NBF, however, responds to Session Alive frames, so no interoperability problems with other implementations of NetBEUI should be expected.

Using Windows 2000 NetBEUI in IBM LAN Server networks

In general, NBF has no receive window, unless it detects that the remote sending computer is running a version of IBM NetBEUI that does not use network polling — for example, a computer running IBM LAN Server. NBF initiates a link with a remote computer in the same manner as IBM NetBEUI; however, NBF looks for a poll bit in received frames. If a frame is received that does not have the poll bit set, the Windows 2000–based computer waits until T2 expires before sending a frame ACK. For more information about T2, see "Connection-Oriented Network Communications" earlier in this chapter.

Note   When the poll bit is set in a received frame, NBF ignores the receive window and immediately sends an ACK.

For example, an IBM LAN Server computer is a nonpolling system that might have a send window set to 1. If this is the case, the registry parameter **MaxIncomingFrames** need to be decreased to 1 from its default of 2. If not, the non-Windows 2000–based computer waits for an ACK from the Windows 2000–based computer, which in this case is sent only when the T2 time limit expires.

NBF uses a receive window based on the value of **MaximumIncomingFrames** in the registry. The default value for **MaximumIncomingFrames** is 2, and this value does not dynamically change. The default value must be manually changed in the registry.

Note   When a Windows 2000–based computer is using the **MaxIncomingFrames** receive window, it might not always send an Acknowledgment frame after receiving **MaxIncomingFrames** packets. This is because NBF also waits until it receives an NDIS **ProtocolReceiveComplete** packet before sending the ACK. However, when the Windows 2000–based computer receives Poll frames, it sends the ACK immediately (typically on return from **NdisTransferData** [synchronous communications] or within **ProtocolTransferDataComplete** [asynchronous communications]).

NetBEUI browser does not see TCP/IP clients

Browsing (viewing other computers on the network) on a computer running Windows 2000 is done per protocol. In other words, there is a master browser for each protocol. Computers running only the NetBEUI protocol register with the master browser computer running the NetBEUI protocol. Computers running only NetBEUI get the master browser list from the master browser running NetBEUI. Because computers running only the TCP/IP protocol register with a master browser running TCP/IP, these computers are not on the master browser list of a computer running only NetBEUI. For information about browsing, see "Browser Service" in the *TCP/IP Core Networking Guide*.

C H A P T E R   1 7

Data Link Control

Data Link Control (DLC) protocol, as implemented in
Microsoft® Windows® 2000, provides connectivity to IBM mainframes and to
local area network (LAN) print devices attached directly to the network. DLC is a
non-routable protocol used only on computers performing these tasks and is not
configured as a primary protocol for use between workstation computers. A
device driver for the DLC protocol interface is also included with Windows 2000.

In This Chapter

Related Information in the Resource Kit

- For more information about DLC and network printing, see "Network Printing" in the *Microsoft® Windows® 2000 Server Resource Kit Server Operations Guide.*

- For more information about IBM interoperability, see "Interoperability with IBM Host Systems" in this book.

Overview of Data Link Control

The DLC protocol driver is provided with Microsoft® Windows® 95, Microsoft® Windows® 98, Microsoft® Windows NT® version 4.0 and earlier, and Windows 2000. This driver enables the computer to communicate with other computers running the DLC protocol stack, such as IBM mainframes; and network peripherals, such as print devices that use a network adapter to connect directly to the network. The DLC protocol driver provides access to Institute of Electrical and Electronics Engineers, Inc. (IEEE) 802.2 class I and class II services. It also provides a direct interface to send and receive 802.3 and other Ethernet-type network frames, as well as raw 802.5 frames.

The interface consists of a dynamic-link library (DLL) and a device driver. These services are available with network cards that use Windows network driver interface specification (NDIS)–compliant drivers. Windows 2000–based DLC works with either Token Ring or Ethernet Media Access Control Drivers, and can transmit and receive Digital Intel Xerox (DIX) format frames when bound to Ethernet Media Access Control.

Windows 2000–based DLC contains an 802.2 logical link control (LLC) finite state machine, which is used when transmitting and receiving type 2 connection-oriented frames. DLC can also transmit and receive type 1 connectionless frames, such as unnumbered information frames. Type 1 and 2 frames can be transmitted and received simultaneously.

The DLC interface can be accessed from 32-bit Windows 2000–based programs as well as from 16-bit MS-DOS-based and 16-bit Windows-based programs. The 32-bit interface conforms largely to the Command Control Block (CCB) 2 interface, in which the segmented 16-bit pointers are replaced with flat 32-bit pointers. The 16-bit interface conforms to the CCB1 interface.

Windows 2000–based DLC does not support the transport driver interface (TDI) as other Windows 2000–based transport protocols do. Because of this, DLC cannot be used for communication with TDI client applications such as the Windows 2000 redirector and server. Because the redirector cannot use DLC, this protocol is not used for normal session communication between Windows 2000–based computers.

Installing the DLC Protocol

The DLC protocol is installed separately after the Windows 2000 Setup is complete.

▶ **To install DLC**

1. From the **Start** menu, point to **Settings**, and then double-click **Control Panel**.
2. Double-click **Network Connections**.
3. Right-click **Local Area Connections** and select **Properties**.
4. Click **Add**.
5. Select **Protocols**, and then click **Add**.
6. Select **DLC Protocols**, and then click **Add**.

Configuring Network Bindings

Network bindings consist of connections between network cards, protocols, and services. You can make the following status changes to network bindings for DLC:

- Enable or disable a binding.
- Move the order (priority) of the bindings up or down.

The order of the bindings is significant to DLC because an adapter is specified at the DLC interface as a number—typically 0 or 1, although Windows 2000 DLC can support up to 16 physical adapters at one time. The number corresponds to the index of the adapter in the DLC bindings section.

If you have only one network adapter installed, DLC applications use a value of 0 to refer to this adapter, and you do not need to make any changes to the bindings. If you have more than one network adapter, you might want to modify the bindings.

▶ **To change a DLC binding position**

1. Click **Start**, point to **Settings**, and then double-click **Control Panel**.
2. Double-click **Network Connections**.
3. Click **Advanced**, and then select **Advanced Settings**.
4. In the **Advanced Settings - Connections** window, select **Local Area Connection**.
5. In the **Bindings for Local Area Connections** window, select the item whose binding position you want to adjust.
6. Use the up and down arrows on the left of the **Bindings for Local Area Connections** window to adjust priority.

DLC Driver Parameters in the Registry

When an adapter is opened for the first time, the DLC protocol driver writes default values into the Windows registry for that adapter. These values control the various timers that DLC uses, whether DIX frames should be used over an Ethernet link, and whether bits in a destination address should be swapped (used) when traversing a bridge that swaps destination addresses.

The timer entries in the registry are supplied because program-supplied timer values might not be sufficient. There are three timers used by DLC link communication:

- T1—The response timer.
- T2—The acknowledgment delay timer.
- Ti—The inactivity timer.

Warning Do not use a registry editor to edit the registry directly unless you have no alternative. The registry editors bypass the standard safeguards provided by administrative tools. These safeguards prevent you from entering conflicting settings or settings that are likely to degrade performance or damage your system. Editing the registry directly can have serious, unexpected consequences that can prevent the system from starting and require that you reinstall Windows 2000. To configure or customize Windows 2000, use the programs in Microsoft Management Console (MMC) or Control Panel whenever possible.

Each timer is split into two groups, **TxTickOne** and **TxTickTwo**, where x represents "1," "2," or "i." Typically, these timer values are set when a program opens an adapter or creates a Service Access Point. The registry contains entries used to modify timer values. Registry entries for DLC are found in the following location:

HKEY_LOCAL_MACHINE\SYSTEM\CurrentControlSet\Services\DLC \Parameters\<*Adapter Name*>

When you edit the value of a timer entry, the change takes effect only when the adapter is re-opened.

Communicating with SNA Hosts Using DLC

A major use of the DLC protocol is connecting personal computers to Systems Network Architecture (SNA) hosts, such as IBM mainframes or midrange computers such as the AS/400.

SNA provides functionality that is equivalent to the Open System Interconnection (OSI) Model Network, Transport, Session, and Presentation layers (although functionality might differ at each level). The DLC layer and the OSI Data Link layer are almost identical in functionality, and a programming interface is available for programmers who want to work with the interface at the DLC layer level. The interface is described in the IEEE 802.2 standard.

Note DLC is not robust enough to handle multithreaded programming.

Figure 17.1 shows a comparison of the SNA and OSI models.

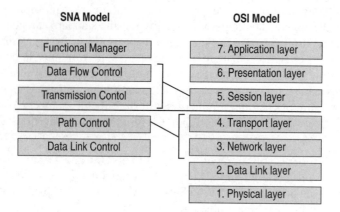

Figure 17.1   Comparison of SNA and OSI Models

Microsoft® SNA Server uses the DLC protocol device driver when communicating to mainframes.

Changing the Locally Administered Address

When using the DLC protocol, it might be necessary to change or override the network address of the network adapter. For example, some configurations of mainframe software require that the network addresses of devices follow a set format. You can change the network address of the network adapter using the registry editor (Regedt32.exe).

The following procedure is supported for IBM Token Ring adapters. To verify that you can override the network address on a specific network adapter, consult the documentation provided with the network adapter.

Warning Do not use a registry editor to edit the registry directly unless you have no alternative. The registry editors bypass the standard safeguards provided by administrative tools. These safeguards prevent you from entering conflicting settings or settings that are likely to degrade performance or damage your system. Editing the registry directly can have serious, unexpected consequences that can prevent the system from starting and require that you reinstall Windows 2000. To configure or customize Windows 2000, use the programs in Microsoft Management Console (MMC) or Control Panel whenever possible.

▶ **To change the address of an adapter card**

1. Click **Start**, and then click **Run**.

2. Type the following:

   regedt32

3. Click **OK**.

4. When the registry editor starts, select the following key:

   HKEY_LOCAL_MACHINE\SYSTEM\CurrentControlSet\Services\ibmTOK MC01

5. In the **Edit** menu, click **Add Value**.

6. Type <*network address*> in the **Value** text box, select **REG_SZ** for data type, and then click **OK**.

7. Type the 12-digit Locally Administered Address (LAA) that you need to communicate to the mainframe.

   If you do not know this address, see your network administrator or operations group.

8. Close the registry editor and restart your computer for the modification to take effect.

9. At the command prompt, type the **net config rdr** command to report the active media access control (MAC) address.

   If the media access control address is the same as the LAA you typed in the registry editor, the LAA has taken effect.

For more information about the registry editors, see Windows 2000 Help.

Using DLC to Connect to Print Devices

You can also use DLC to provide connectivity to LAN print devices that are attached directly to the network.

Note The DLC protocol is not used for printers attached locally to workstations through parallel or serial ports.

To install the DLC protocol, follow the procedure in "Installing the DLC Protocol" earlier in this chapter.

To connect to and configure a Hewlett-Packard print device, you must first install the Hewlett-Packard Network Port monitor on the Windows 2000–based print server. You can then use the Add Printer Wizard to install the Hewlett-Packard Network Port to configure the print device.

Before starting the Add Printer Wizard:

- Run a self-test on the Hewlett-Packard print device to obtain the network adapter address. The network adapter address is a unique 12-byte number that is supplied by the card manufacturer.

- Choose a logical name for the printer. This logical name is used to identify the printer and is associated with the card address.

▶ **To configure a Hewlett-Packard print device that is directly connected to the network**

1. From the **Start** menu, point to **Settings**, and then double-click **Printers**.

2. Double-click **Add Printer**.

3. Click **Next** in the Add Printer Wizard.

4. Select **Network Printer**, and then click **Next**.

5. Select the network that the printer is to be added to, and type the printer name in the **Printer** text box.

6. Click **OK**.

   The Add Printer Wizard completes the configuration of the print device.

Note When configuring Hewlett-Packard network printers, or printers from manufacturers other than Hewlett-Packard, please refer to the manufacturer's installation manual. For more information about configuring printers, see Windows 2000 Help.

Additional Resources

- For more information about DLC, see *IBM Local Area Network Technical Reference (IBM part number SC30-3383)* by IBM, Armonk, NY.

P A R T   6

Appendixes

The Appendixes provide detailed information on interoperability concepts. The additional technical information in this section is a useful source for network administrators when troubleshooting interoperability issues.

In This Part

APPENDIX A

IBM SNA Interoperability Concepts

The Microsoft solution for integration with IBM host systems is Microsoft® SNA Server. To effectively use SNA Server, you need to understand the IBM mainframe and AS/400 host networking environments. IBM Systems Network Architecture (SNA) and Advanced Peer-to-Peer Networking (APPN) define the protocols used in traditional IBM host networks. SNA Server embraces these IBM networking protocols and additional technologies and standards that allow interoperability between Microsoft® Windows® 2000–based networks and IBM host data, applications, and network management systems.

In This Appendix

Related Information in the Resource Kit

- For more information about SNA Server and interoperability with IBM host systems, see "Interoperability with IBM Host Systems" in this book.

IBM Host Integration

Many large organizations run their line-of-business applications on specialized IBM mainframe, midrange, and AS/400 computer systems. Consequently, Systems Network Architecture (SNA), the native networking architecture of IBM host systems, continues to be one of the most widely used networking protocols today.

To leverage the value of information that resides in IBM host systems, information technology architects must find ways to seamlessly integrate their Windows 2000–based networks and intranets with SNA-based host systems and the associated data, applications, and network services.

Microsoft SNA Server

SNA Server is a Microsoft® BackOffice® application that runs on the Microsoft® Windows® 2000 Server operating system. SNA Server provides you with a comprehensive solution to integrate Windows 2000–based networks and intranets with IBM SNA or TCP/IP-based mainframe, midrange, and AS/400 host systems.

Clients connect to SNA Server through standard networking protocols such as TCP/IP, IPX/SPX, NetBEUI, Banyan VINES IP, AppleTalk, and Windows 2000 Routing and Remote Access service. If the IBM host system runs SNA networking protocols, SNA Server completes the network connection to the host system using standard IBM SNA protocols, as shown in Figure A.1.

When network connectivity is established, clients can use SNA Server's advanced host integration features to gain access to IBM host data, applications, and network services. Using SNA Server, Information Technology departments can build applications that allow users to maximize the value of IBM host data and applications without leaving their familiar desktop or Web browser interface.

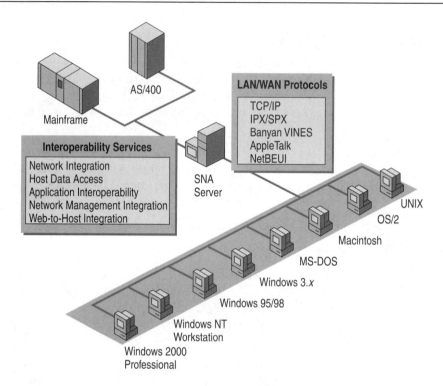

Figure A.1   SNA Server Provides Seamless Access to IBM SNA Host Systems

SNA Server provides the full range of host integration services.

Network Integration Cross-platform network connectivity and protocols, directory utilization, security integration, and single sign-in.

Host Data Integration Transparent file transfer services, Universal Data Access technologies such as OLE DB-based and Open Database Connectivity (ODBC)–based solutions, and host data replication for access to IBM DB2, DB2/400, VSAM, AS/400 flat files, and ORACLE database files.

Application Integration Terminal access, integration with IBM transaction services, and integration between IBM MQSeries and Microsoft Message Queue Services asynchronous messaging environments.

Network Management Integration Integration between Windows 2000 network management services and IBM NetView–based management services.

To understand how you can use SNA Server to integrate Windows 2000–based networks with IBM mainframe and midrange system networks, first you need to understand the basic components of IBM SNA.

The remainder of this appendix provides essential background information. If you are already familiar with IBM SNA and IBM mainframe and midrange systems, you can bypass this material and proceed to "Interoperability with IBM Host Systems" in this book.

IBM Systems Network Architecture

SNA is a computer networking architecture developed by IBM to provide a network structure for IBM mainframe, midrange, and personal computer systems. SNA defines a set of proprietary communication protocols and message formats for the exchange and management of data on IBM host networks.

SNA defines methods that accomplish the following:

- Terminal access to mainframe and midrange computer applications.
- File transfer of data between computer systems.
- Printing of mainframe and midrange data on SNA printers.
- Program-to-program communications that allow applications to exchange data over the network.

SNA can be implemented in the following two network models:

Hierarchical The hierarchical SNA networking model, also called subarea networking, provides geographically disparate terminal users access to centralized mainframe processing systems. In the hierarchical networking model, centralized host-based communication systems must provide the networking services for all users on the network.

Peer-to-Peer The more recently developed Advanced Peer-to-Peer Networking (APPN) model makes use of modern local area network (LAN) and wide area network (WAN) resources and client/server computing. APPN networking enables a form of distributed processing by allowing any computer on the network to use SNA protocols to gain access to resources on any other computer on the network. Computers on an APPN network do not have to depend on mainframe-based communication services.

Because of the large installed base of legacy applications that run on IBM mainframe and midrange systems, both of these SNA networking models continue to be widely used in enterprise networks.

> **Note** SNA is gradually evolving into a more of a peer-to-peer networking structure. As part of that evolution, APPN networking is often combined with hierarchical SNA networking. APPN is described in "Advanced Peer-to-Peer Networking" later in this appendix.

Hierarchical SNA Networks

In the SNA hierarchical model, also called subarea networking, communication begins with the mainframe at the top of the hierarchy and proceeds down the hierarchy to the end user.

> **Note** In SNA terminology, an end user represents either a person or an application program.

SNA defines several classes of components to support communications between the mainframe, or host system, and the end user.

Hardware Components or Nodes Hardware that provides the computing platforms and network devices that implement specific SNA communications and management functions.

Connection Types Hardware and communication standards that provide the data communication paths between components in an SNA network.

Physical Units (PUs) A combination of hardware and software that provide the configuration support and control of the SNA network devices, connections, and protocols.

Logical Units (LUs) Protocols that provide a standardized format for delivery of data for specific applications, such as terminal access and printing.

These components provide the basis for IBM SNA. Thus, integrating Windows 2000–based networks and intranets with IBM host systems begins with an understanding of these SNA components. The following sections describe each of these components and how they interact in a hierarchical SNA environment.

Hardware Components on Hierarchical Networks

The construction of a hierarchical SNA network begins with its hardware components. Each hardware component is distinguished by a node type, which corresponds to a position in the SNA hierarchy and identifies its relationships to other hardware components on the network. Table A.1 defines SNA hardware components. Figure A.2 illustrates the hierarchical relationships between these components.

Table A.1   Hardware Components on a Hierarchical SNA Network

Hardware Component	Node	Function
Mainframe	Type 5 host node	Core component of a hierarchical network. Runs the centralized processing applications that are made available to users on the SNA network.
Front-end processor (FEP)	Type 4 node	Generally dedicated to the control of communication from the network to the mainframe. Offloads many network communication processes that would otherwise consume valuable mainframe processing resources. Also called a communications controller.
Cluster controller	Type 2 node	Controls a group, or cluster, of end-user terminals and printers. Often located at remote sites, connecting to the FEP over WAN links.
End-user components	Peripheral nodes	Terminals and printers attached to the cluster controller that are used to access, display, and print mainframe application data.

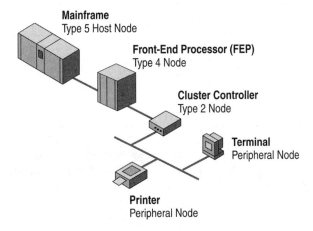

Mainframe
Type 5 Host Node

Front-End Processor (FEP)
Type 4 Node

Cluster Controller
Type 2 Node

Terminal
Peripheral Node

Printer
Peripheral Node

Figure A.2   Hierarchy of SNA Hardware Components

Note Some modern mainframe host systems can also support peer-to-peer networking functions. In such environments, type 2.1 (peer-oriented) end-user nodes can also be used.

Connection Types in Hierarchical Networks

Connections provide the lower-level data path between hardware components on an SNA network. These connections include paths from the mainframe to the FEP and from the FEP to the cluster controller.

Connections from the Mainframe to the FEP

FEPs can be connected to mainframes with either an IBM Channel connection or an Open Systems Adapter.

An IBM Channel connects components to a mainframe using a proprietary, high-speed communication link. The channel connection includes a microprocessor within the mainframe that is dedicated to a single purpose, such as directing input/output (I/O) from a mainframe hard disk drive or managing an FEP communications line. Fast and efficient communications through dedicated channel microprocessors represent the native method of connecting to IBM mainframes. Table A.2 describes two common types of IBM Channel connections.

Table A.2   IBM Channel Connections

Cable Type	Composition	Transmission Rate
Bus & Tag	Two heavy-gauge multiple lead copper cables with large multiple-pin connectors at each end.	3.0 or 4.5 megabytes per second.
Enterprise System Connectivity (ESCON)	Fiber-optic cable.	Up to 17 megabytes per second.

An Open System Adapter, placed in the host, provides a direct network connection to Token Ring, Ethernet, and Fiber Distributed Data Interface (FDDI) networks.

Connections from the Front-End Processor to the Cluster Controller

Several connection types, also known as links, are available for connecting an FEP to a cluster controller or other components operating lower in the SNA hierarchy. Each connection type uses a different method to gain access to an FEP. Three of the most common links are:

Synchronous Data Link Control (SDLC)   Enables a cluster controller to communicate with an FEP over standard (switched) telephone lines or leased (dedicated) telecommunication lines. SDLC has been available for many years and is widely used in the SNA networking environment.

802.2 Data Link Control (DLC)   Enables a cluster controller to communicate with an FEP over standard networking topologies, such as Token Ring, Ethernet, or FDDI. Although DLC has not been available as long as SDLC, its efficiency and flexibility are making it very popular for new installations.

X.25/QLLC   Enables a cluster controller to communicate with an FEP over standard packet-switching networks. X.25/QLLC is an International Telecommunications Union (ITU) standard for global packet-switching network communications that uses the qualified logical link control (QLLC) protocol, also known as X.25. An X.25 connection is slower than an 802.2-type connection but is comparable to an SDLC connection.

For more information about connection types, see "Interoperability with IBM Host Systems" in this book.

Physical Units in Hierarchical Networks

The creation of an SNA network requires the installation of specific networking software on SNA hardware components. Network software programs are available for each of the three primary hardware components: mainframes, FEPs, and cluster controllers. The combination of software and hardware installed in a device on an SNA network is referred to as a physical unit (PU), as shown in Figure A.3.

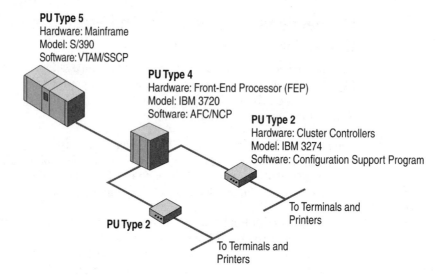

Figure A.3   A PU Is a Combination of Software and Hardware

In the preceding figure, note that the PU is the component that represents the hardware device (node) to the SNA network. Each PU type is identified by a number, with the highest number representing the top of the SNA hierarchy.

Note   The concept of a physical unit (PU) can be confusing. Please keep in mind that a PU is not an actual hardware device; it is a combination of software and hardware that represents a device to the SNA network.

Table A.3 identifies the PU types, the hardware component with which each PU type is associated, and typical IBM model numbers for each PU type.

Table A.3   PU Types

PU Type	Hardware Component	Model Number
PU 5	Mainframe (type 5 host node)	Type S/370, S/390
PU 4	FEP (type 4 node or communications controller)	IBM 3745, 3720
PU 2	Cluster controller (type 2 node)	IBM 3174, 3274

Note PU type 3 has not been implemented. An additional PU type, PU 2.1 is identified in the section that describes peer-to-peer SNA networks, later in this appendix.

The following sections outline the software options for each hardware component, or node, and the resulting PU.

Mainframe Software

Virtual Telecommunications Access Method (VTAM) is the IBM mainframe program that controls communications between mainframe applications and the terminals and computers that connect to the mainframe.

VTAM contains the system services control point (SSCP), which is the networking focal point for a hierarchical network. The SSCP activates, controls, and deactivates network resources, such as FEPs, cluster controllers, terminals, and printers. The SSCP also monitors and logs the status of SNA components.

With the activation of VTAM and the SSCP, the mainframe becomes a PU 5.

Traditionally, VTAM and the SSCP communicate directly with the next lower level in the hierarchy, a PU 4 FEP. In an increasing number of cases however, the PU 5 communicates directly with a PU 2 that is either channel-attached or connected with an Open System Adapter.

FEP Software

The front-end processor (FEP), also called a communications controller or PU 4, runs a communications management program called Advanced Communication Function/Network Control Program (ACF/NCP). The FEP uses this software to manage the routing and communications on a hierarchical SNA network, offloading these tasks from the mainframe system. ACF/NCP is configured on the mainframe and then downloaded to the FEP. The FEP, as a PU 4, supports bi-directional communications with the next lower level in the hierarchy.

Cluster Controller Software

The cluster controller, or PU 2, contains administration software called the Configuration Support program, which controls the connections from the cluster controller to terminals and printers.

Note A computer running SNA Server can be used in place of a traditional SNA cluster controller.

Logical Units in Hierarchical Networks

In an SNA network, type 5 and type 2 PUs transmit and control SNA networking protocols, called logical units (LUs).

An LU is the end user's entry point into the SNA network. In SNA terminology, the end user can be a person or an application. For example, when an end user enters information into an SNA terminal, the data is passed to an LU for routing over the network to a host node. When the data reaches the host node, another end user passes it to an LU within the host for processing. In this example, the end user at the terminal is an actual person but the end user at the host node is the host application program.

In hierarchical networks, all LUs depend on the mainframe SSCP to establish and manage communications with other LUs, and are therefore referred to as dependent logical units.

As with PU types, each type of LU is identified by a number. Table A.4 identifies the LU types used in hierarchical networks, the hardware component with which each is associated, and the function of each in an SNA network.

Table A.4   LU Types Used in Hierarchical Networks

LU Type	Component	Function
LU 0	Nonstandard, user-defined component interface.	Enables the development of specialized applications. LU 0 is a general purpose LU.
LU 1	IBM 3287–type printers.	Handles transmission of printer data to system and network printers. LU 1 uses SNA character string format (SCS).
LU 2	IBM 3278 (3270) monochrome terminals; 3279/3179 color terminals; graphics terminals.	Defines how terminal data streams are formatted and transmitted.
LU 3	IBM 3270–type printers.	Uses SNA 3270 data stream format to control the transmission of data to system and network printers. LU 3 is the most often used printing LU type.

Note Peer-oriented LU types, including LU 6.2, are described in "Advanced Peer-to-Peer Networking" later in this appendix.

SNA Functional Layers

The functionality of each SNA layer operating in the context of a hierarchical network model is summarized in Table A.5. The transaction services layer and the physical layer are both outside of the original scope of SNA specifications but are included here to show the full range of IBM host networking.

Table A.5   Functional Layers in Hierarchical SNA Networks

SNA Functional Layers	Description
Transaction Services	A conceptual layer to represent host applications that establish and terminate SNA user-to-user sessions.
Functional Management	Formats data streams and converts character codes for presentation (for example, 3270 data streams). Also controls active sessions.
Data Flow Control	Provides protocols for managing data integrity in sessions, synchronizing data exchange, and packaging data units.
Transmission Control	Uses VTAM and NCP to manage active end-to-end sessions. Controls data sequencing and pacing. Optionally supports data encryption and decryption.
Path Control	Routes data between hierarchical SNA nodes using VTAM and NCP.
Data Link Control	Manages data transmissions between nodes and performs error detection and recovery. Manages transmissions over standard WAN (including SDLC), LAN (Token Ring, Ethernet, FDDI, Asynchronous Transfer Mode (ATM)) and channel interfaces.
Physical Control	Transmits bits over industry standard physical/electrical circuits. SNA generally relies on industry standard LAN and WAN specifications at this layer, although specifications for channel attachments are unique to SNA.

Note APPN uses different methods to accomplish networking functions at some layers.

Because many networking professionals are familiar with the Open Systems Interconnection Reference Model (OSI model), it is sometimes helpful to describe the SNA functional layers within the context of the OSI model.

SNA functional layers define protocols and services that are similar in scope to layers in the OSI model. In fact, the OSI model was developed in response to SNA and was influenced by SNA functions. Originally, SNA did not include specifications for layers that correspond to the physical and applications services layers in the OSI model. However, recent descriptions of SNA include all seven layers, including the physical and transaction services layers (equivalent to the application layer in the OSI model). The transaction services layer plays an important role in IBM host system networking because transaction-based applications often initiate SNA networking sessions.

While the scope of the networking layers described by the SNA and OSI models are similar, the methods SNA uses to perform networking functions within each hierarchical networking layer are quite different from methods described by the OSI model, as is made apparent in Figure A.4.

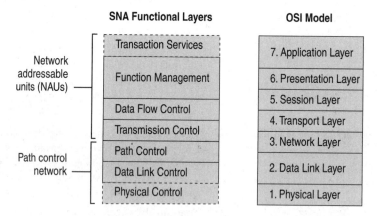

Figure A.4   SNA Functional Layers Mapped to the OSI Model

Path Control

The three lower SNA functional layers comprise the SNA path control network components, also called the SNA transport network. These layers control the routing and flow of messages through the network and provide the interfaces to physical media that carry transmissions between network devices.

Network Addressable Units

The four upper SNA functional layers provide end-to-end communication protocols between network addressable units (NAUs). NAUs include the following SNA components:

- Physical units
- Logical units
- Control points (such as SSCP in VTAM)

SNA nodes might each contain several NAUs to manage specific networking functions. Each NAU has a unique address so data can be routed to the NAU during an SNA session.

SNA Sessions

SNA communications are based on the establishment and termination of logical sessions between NAUs. Logical sessions are communication paths that support the operation of network devices and the flow of traffic through the network.

In SNA networks, routing information is dynamically determined when a session is established and only remains fixed until the session is terminated. During sessions, all SNA packets follow the same logical path from the source NAU to the destination NAU.

SNA packet transmissions are also time sensitive. If communication in an SNA session is interrupted, even for a short time, SNA terminates the session. As such, networks that tunnel SNA protocols across standard wide area network (WAN) connections must use routers that support Data Link Switching (DLSw), Frame Relay Assembler/Disassemblers (FRADs) that support frame relay (RFC 1490), or specialized Asynchronous Transfer Mode (ATM) switches.

Table A.6 summarizes the types of sessions that are used in hierarchical SNA networks.

Table A.6   Hierarchical SNA Session Types

Hierarchical SNA Session Type	Description
SSCP to SSCP	Supports communications between SSCPs in multidomain, hierarchical networks.
SSCP to PU	Used by system administrators to communicate with network devices.
SSCP to LU	Used by logical units in hierarchical networks to obtain session services that are controlled by the SSCP, such as logon or logoff services.
LU to LU	Supports communications between end users and applications in both hierarchical and peer-to-peer networks.

Note SNA APPNs support control point to control point (CP to CP) sessions in addition to LU to LU sessions. CP to CP sessions allow a peer-to-peer SNA network to manage all of its functions without relying on a mainframe SSCP.

Hierarchical Domains and Subareas

Hierarchical SNA networks organize nodes into *domains* and *subareas*. In a hierarchical SNA network, an SNA domain represents a set of network resources that are managed by a SSCP implemented within the host system VTAM. Each domain has only one SSCP.

Some large SNA networks contain hundreds of domains. When end users in different domains need to communicate through an LU to LU session, the SSCPs in each domain must first establish communications through an SSCP to SSCP session.

SNA domains typically include several subareas. A subarea is composed of one subarea node (a type 5 host node or a type 4 node [an FEP]) and the resources it controls, including type 2 nodes, as illustrated in Figure A.5.

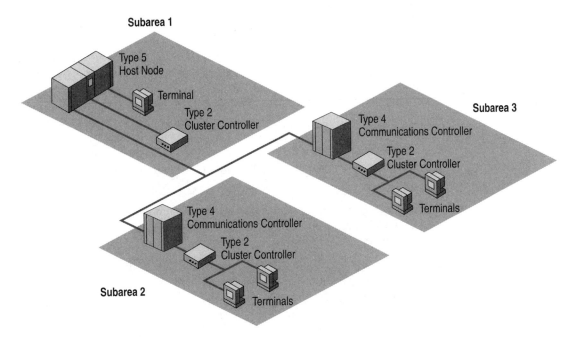

Figure A.5   Single Hierarchical SNA Domain with Three Subareas

Subarea nodes can communicate with the peripheral nodes in its subarea and can also establish one or more links with other subarea nodes. Links between subarea nodes are called transmission groups. The capability to establish transmission groups allows subarea nodes to create routing tables of other subareas, which are used for SNA network addressing and routing sessions.

Maintaining multiple links in a transmission group maximizes network availability and performance. If one link should fail, SNA reroutes the data over one of the other links in the transmission group.

Note In SNA peer-to-peer networks, domains and routing functions are defined differently than in SNA hierarchical networks. Peer-oriented networks are described in the following section.

Advanced Peer-to-Peer Networking

In 1981, IBM began to introduce communication standards that developed into a peer-oriented network architecture called Advanced Peer-to-Peer Networking (APPN). The development of APPN marks a significant change from the traditional top-down hierarchical SNA model because APPN supports a form of distributed processing. That is, all computers on an APPN network can communicate directly with each other, without having to depend on centralized type 5 hosts or type 4 communications controllers. This model provides an environment that is more flexible than the traditional top-down hierarchical model.

APPN defines how peer-oriented components communicate with each other, as well as the level of network services, such as routing sessions, that are supplied by each computer on the network.

The SNA APPN model defines its own standards for the following components:

Hardware Components or Nodes Hardware that provides the computing platforms and network devices that implement specific SNA APPN communications and management functions.

Connection Types Hardware and communication standards that provide the data communication paths between components in an SNA APPN network.

Physical Units (PUs) Hardware and software that provide the configuration support and control of the SNA APPN network devices, connections, and protocols.

Logical Units (LUs) Protocols that provide a standardized format for delivery of data for specific applications, such as terminal access and printing.

Note Although the SNA APPN network model is organized into the same component classes as the hierarchical SNA network model, the components themselves are often quite different from the components used in the hierarchical model.

The following sections describe each of these components and how they interact in an SNA APPN environment.

Hardware Components on Peer-to-Peer Networks

A typical APPN network is composed of several different devices, such as IBM host computers or personal computers connected to one or more LANs, as illustrated in Figure A.6.

The peer-oriented model can be employed within many different environments. The AS/400 midrange computer, because of its popularity and primary use of APPN, is the host that is most often associated with APPN and the peer-oriented networking model. Modern mainframe systems are beginning to support APPN as well.

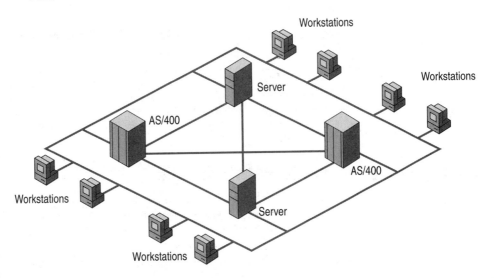

Figure A.6   APPN Network Components

An APPN hardware component can be any device on the APPN network that can function as a PU type 2.1 node. PU 2.1, described later in this appendix, is an upgrade and extension of PU type 2 used in hierarchical networks. With the appropriate software, the following hardware components can be configured as PU 2.1 nodes:

- AS/400 computers
- Mainframes
- Workstation computers
- Routers

Connection Types in Peer-to-Peer Networks

The most common connection types, also called links, used to connect APPN devices are listed in Table A.7. For more detailed information about these connection types, see "Interoperability with IBM Host Systems" in this book.

Table A.7   Connection Types

Connection Type	Method of Connection
802.2 DLC	Token Ring
	Ethernet
	FDDI
SDLC	Public and private switched telephone lines
Twinax	Twinax protocols

Note The Twinax link represents the native method for accessing AS/400 computers.

Physical Units in Peer-to-Peer Networks

As with the hierarchical network model, the type of software that is implemented in an APPN hardware component determines how it functions on an APPN network. Also, just as in an hierarchical network, the combination of hardware and software that is implemented in an APPN network device is called a PU. A PU represents a device, often called a node, to the SNA network.

In a pure APPN network, all nodes are PU type 2.1 nodes. PU type 2.1 is an upgrade of the PU type 2.0 standard used in hierarchical SNA networks. Like PU type 2.0 nodes in hierarchical SNA networks, peer-oriented type 2.1 nodes can communicate with type 5 host nodes. However, type 2.1 nodes provide the added capability to establish peer-to-peer communications with other type 2.1 nodes. As such, type 2.1 nodes do not require the use of mainframe system services control points (SSCPs) or communications controllers used in hierarchical SNA networks.

This capability allows SNA APPN networks to be constructed entirely of type 2.1 nodes, such as those implemented in IBM AS/400 systems and personal computers.

Node Types

There are three types of PU 2.1 nodes in APPN networks, as shown in Figure A.7:

- APPN network nodes
- APPN end nodes
- Low Entry Network (LEN) nodes

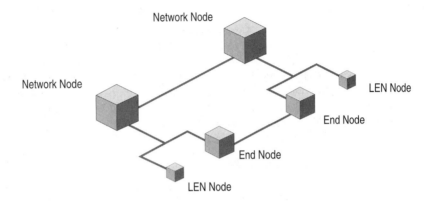

Figure A.7   PU 2.1 Node Types in an APPN Network

APPN Network Nodes

APPN network nodes contain the highest level of functionality of the three APPN node types. APPN network nodes can perform all the basic functions supported by the other APPN PU type 2.1 nodes. These basic functions include the ability to establish sessions with other APPN PU type 2.1 nodes. To maintain compatibility with hierarchical networks, APPN PU type 2.1 nodes can also establish sessions with type 5 (mainframe) host nodes. However, APPN network nodes (such as those implemented in IBM AS/400 computers) can provide the following additional services for the other PU type 2.1 node attached to it:

- LU to LU session control
- Routing
- Full directory services
- CP to CP sessions (to support APPN management functions)

An APPN network node and the other PU type 2.1 nodes attached to it comprise an APPN domain. The APPN network node acts as a server for the other PU type 2.1 nodes in its domain. It can also act as an intermediate node, supporting routing functions in APPN networks that contain multiple APPN network nodes.

An APPN network node contains a control point (CP) that provides directory database updates and directory search services. The CP can establish sessions with CPs in adjacent APPN network nodes to keep the network structure and directory information up-to-date, without relying on the presence of a mainframe SSCP.

For example, when a new APPN end node is added to the APPN network, its APPN network node server automatically updates its directory and routing tables and propagates that information to the other APPN network nodes.

Note APPN directory services differ from most other directory services that use non-SNA network protocols. Because no fixed addresses are assigned to APPN resources, APPN directories respond to LU directory requests by providing the location and route to the destination LU, rather than the address of the destination resource. Consequently, APPN network nodes must dynamically create route identifiers when LU to LU sessions are established.

APPN End Nodes

Like all PU type 2.1 nodes, APPN end nodes can establish peer-to-peer sessions with other PU type 2.1 nodes (and with PU type 5 mainframe host nodes used in hierarchical SNA networks).

Unlike APPN network nodes, APPN end nodes cannot perform routing functions and cannot function as intermediate nodes in APPN networks. However, APPN end nodes can provide a subset of APPN session services and directory services for its own LUs.

APPN end nodes can also be attached to an APPN network node, which acts as the server for routing, session, and directory services. An end node can have links to more than one network node, but only one network node acts as the server for the end node at any given time.

Low Entry Network End Nodes

Like APPN network nodes and APPN end nodes, LEN nodes can establish peer-to-peer sessions with other PU type 2.1 nodes (and with PU type 5 mainframe host nodes used in hierarchical SNA networks).

However, to communicate with APPN nodes that are controlled by other APPN network nodes, LEN nodes, must communicate through the APPN network node that is acting as its server. LEN nodes do not provide any APPN routing or session services for other nodes.

Logical Units in Peer-to-Peer Networks

LUs are SNA protocols that provide a standardized format for delivery of data for applications. APPN networks typically use type 6.2 LUs, also known as Advanced Program-to-Program Communications (APPC) LUs. LU 6.2 is the most recently developed and the most advanced LU type. Unlike dependent LUs that are used in hierarchical SNA networks, LU 6.2 does not depend on centralized mainframe communications software. Rather, LU 6.2 provides a foundation for distributed computing in which programs on separate computers can communicate directly with each other across the network.

Although LU 6.2 provides the foundation for APPN communications, APPN can use additional LU types for AS/400 printers and display terminals as described in Table A.8. However, LU 6.2 is the only widely implemented APPN LU type.

Table A.8   APPN LU Types

APPN LU Type	Description
LU 6.2	Supports APPC for a broad range of SNA nodes and includes functions to support any type of SNA-based application. The most recent and advanced LU type.
LU 4	Supports printers that use the IBM 5250 data stream. Not widely implemented because it does not provide the broad functionality of LU 6.2.
LU 7	Supports display terminals that use IBM 5250 data streams, such as AS/400 display stations. Not widely implemented because it does not provide the broad functionality of LU 6.2.

Advanced Program-to-Program Communications

LU 6.2 forms the basis for IBM's Advanced Program-to-Program Communications (APPC), the network communications protocol most commonly associated with APPN. APPC is a general purpose network access method that supports applications such as:

- 5250 terminal access (to AS/400 systems)
- TN5250 terminal access
- File transfer
- Network services

The programs that use APPC LU 6.2 to communicate are called transaction programs (TPs). Figure A.8 illustrates TPs communicating through APPC sessions.

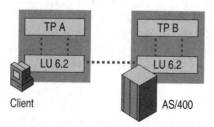

Figure A.8   Transaction Programs Communicating Through APPC Sessions

APPC LU 6.2 serves as a translator between TPs and the network. When a TP on one computer passes information to the APPC software, APPC establishes a session and sends it to the destination node. On the receiving end, APPC translates the information back into its original format and passes it to the corresponding partner TP. APPC can be used across any of the standard types of connections supported by SNA.

Dependent and Independent LUs

APPC generally uses a local APPC LU and one or more remote APPC LUs. Local APPC LUs can be dependent or independent.

Dependent LUs are used to provide backward compatibility with hierarchical networks. As such, dependent LUs require a host VTAM SSCP to establish and manage LU to LU sessions. Dependent LUs can support only a single session between a given pair of LUs.

A dependent LU must be used when an APPC TP needs to communicate with a mainframe that uses a version of VTAM earlier than V3R2. Independent LUs are not supported by earlier versions of VTAM. Also, dependent LUs cannot be used to communicate with AS/400 systems.

In full peer-oriented APPN networks, typically implemented in AS/400 environments, independent APPC LUs are used. Independent APPC LUs can establish and manage LU to LU sessions without the aid of a mainframe VTAM SSCP. Independent LUs provide the ability to run multiple, concurrent, parallel sessions between a single pair of LUs. Support for independent LUs is one of the main advantages of APPN networks.

SNA in Transition

SNA is a legacy networking model that was created decades ago. However, it has never been a static networking environment. What began as a hierarchical model has evolved into a more flexible peer-to-peer environment. Recently, IBM has been making efforts to combine the SNA hierarchical and APPN models and to integrate both models with modern LAN and WAN protocols.

Hierarchical and Peer-to-Peer Integration

Although SNA hierarchical and APPN environments differ in many ways, IBM provides the means to integrate the two SNA networking models. As described in the previous section, APPN PU type 2.1 nodes can establish sessions with PUtype 5 mainframe host nodes used in hierarchical networks. APPN networks can also serve as interchange networks to connect hierarchical network domains.

More recently, IBM is upgrading hierarchical network components to perform APPN functions. For example, VTAM can now support its own native hierarchical networking model and APPN simultaneously. VTAM can also act as an interchange node to connect APPN networks.

IBM is currently working to provide a migration path to upgrade traditional hierarchical SNA networks to the APPN network model.

IBM Networking Blueprint

IBM is also implementing a networking blueprint that seeks to integrate protocols and standards beyond the traditional SNA networking model. The IBM Networking Blueprint specifies standards for network protocols, application services, and systems management services. As part of this model, IBM is seeking to further integrate IBM host systems and SNA models with standard network protocols such as TCP/IP, IPX, and NetBIOS.

Note   Because Microsoft SNA Server is fully integrated with Windows 2000 Server, it supports these and other protocols and services that permit authorized Windows and non-Windows clients to connect to IBM SNA host systems. For more information about integrating heterogeneous networks with IBM hierarchical SNA and APPN networks, see "Interoperability with IBM Host Systems" in this book.

Host Application Standards

The purpose of any networking model is to efficiently and reliably support applications that automate an organization's business processes. In an SNA networking environment, these applications often rely on terminal access methods, relational and nonrelational database standards, transaction processing services, and network management systems that are provided by the IBM host system.

The following sections describe these host services and identify the standards that are essential for integrating heterogeneous networks with IBM host data, application, and network management services.

Terminal Access

Although SNA Server provides features that support advanced database integration and transaction oriented Web-to-host applications, traditional terminals and terminal emulation applications continue to play an important role in many organizations.

Users can use one of two types of terminal access, depending on the type of IBM host system that controls the session, 3270 terminal access to mainframe systems or 5250 terminal access to AS/400 systems.

Terminal Access to IBM Mainframes

Users who need access to IBM SNA–based mainframe computers generally use the 3270 data stream, a protocol that defines how components in hierarchical SNA networks can gain access to IBM mainframe computers. The 3270 data stream uses LUs to support 3270 Display Devices such terminals and terminal emulators (LU 2), 3270 Printer Devices (LU 1 or LU 3), and applications (LUA). A 3270 LU is known as a dependent LU because it requires a mainframe to function.

Clients can use several variations of 3270 type display terminals and terminal emulators (LU 2) to gain access to SNA resources:

- 3270 terminals and terminal emulators.
- 3278 terminals and terminal emulators (models 2, 3, 4, and 5).
- Telnet-based (TN3270) terminal emulation types, including TN3270E (extended TN3270) and Web browser–based terminal emulators.

Telnet terminal emulators allow TCP/IP-based computers to gain access to host systems that support TCP/IP access or through gateways that convert TCP/IP communications to native SNA.

Note SNA Server supports both 3270 and TN3270 access methods.

Terminal Access to AS/400 Systems

Users who need access to IBM AS/400 systems use the 5250 data stream. This protocol supports terminal emulation only. Variations include standard 5250 terminal emulators and TN5250 terminal emulators, including Web browser–based TN5250 terminal emulation services.

Note SNA Server supports both of the AS/400 terminal access methods. For more information about terminal access, see "Interoperability with IBM Host Systems" in this book.

Host Database Standards

Although terminal access provides an appropriate interface to a wide range of host applications, most organizations also require applications that seamlessly integrate host data and applications with modern client/server and Internet-based information systems. Achieving this level of integration with IBM host systems begins with an understanding of the standards that support IBM host database applications.

IBM host applications often rely on an underlying database architecture provided by the host system. IBM uses the Distributed Data Management (DDM) architecture to provide a common language and set of rules for host data access. Programs adhering to this architecture can share data across multiple platforms.

Record-Level Data Access

Record-level access using DDM enables an application to go directly to the wanted record within a physical file. For host data access, DDM supports two record-level protocols, shown in Figure A.9:

Distributed Relational Database Architecture (DRDA). DRDA is a DDM protocol that provides access to relational data on host platforms, including Multiple Virtual Storage (MVS) and AS/400 systems that use the IBM DB2 relational database program.

Record Level Input/Output (RLIO). RLIO is a DDM protocol that supports record-level access to nonrelational data on various host operating systems, including MVS, OS/390, and OS/400.

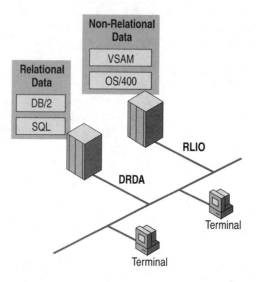

Figure A.9   IBM Relational and Non-relational Data Formats

File-Level Data Access

DDM also supports the Stream Input/Output (Stream I/O) file-level protocol for host data access. Stream I/O provides access to IBM host data one file at a time, as opposed to one record at a time, such as with Structured Query Language (SQL). This process provides the basis on which to build fast bulk-data file transfer solutions, such as moving files from one host region to another or transferring entire files from a workstation computer to the host.

Note   Microsoft SNA Server includes the ODBC Driver for DB2 and the Microsoft OLE DB Provider for AS/400 and virtual storage access memory (VSAM) to support access to relational and nonrelational host data. SNA Server can also support applications that replicate host database information to Windows 2000 Server–based database applications such as Microsoft® SQL Server™. For more information about how to use SNA Server host database drivers and replication methods, see "Interoperability with IBM Host Systems" in this book.

Host Transaction Processing

Organizations often use IBM host systems for online transaction processing (OLTP) applications that automate real-time business activities. These applications consist of transaction programs (TPs) that must maintain data integrity and security in line-of-business environments such as banking and financial services, insurance, reservation systems, and retail applications.

Reliable Transaction Standards

To ensure that these transactions are processed correctly, a TP must adhere to four key transaction properties known as ACID. An ACID-compliant TP ensures that each transaction is:

Atomic Each transaction must be carried out completely or not at all.

Consistent Data must be processed in a way that maintains the structural integrity of the database.

Isolated Transactions must be carried out sequentially so that a transaction cannot access data that is already involved in a transaction.

Durable Completed transactions must be stored in a way that enables recovery of the transaction results even if the system fails.

Transaction Processing Components

In the online transaction processing (OLTP) distributed environment, data can become corrupt if it is not managed correctly. A TP monitor manages the operating environment of the OLTP application by optimizing the use of operating system resources and the network. The TP monitor provides a management platform for the system administrator that supports:

- Load balancing
- Fault tolerance
- Performance monitoring
- Security

TP monitors typically include a software component known as a TP manager. TP managers use the two-phase commit (2PC) protocol to ensure the reliable execution of transactions by enabling the TP manager to execute a transaction only if all systems carry out the transaction.

Note   On the Windows 2000 platform, Microsoft® Component Services is the native TP monitor. MTS includes a TP manager called the Distributed Transaction Coordinator. IBM provides different TP managers for different TP monitors.

For a TP to communicate directly with another TP by using SNA APPC, the two programs must first establish a logical unit (LU) 6.2 session with each other. LU 6.2 is the standard for distributed transaction processing in the mainframe environment.

Transaction Processing Synchronization

One program can interact with another program by using one of three levels of synchronization, as shown in Figure A.10:

- Sync Level 0 has no message integrity.
- Sync Level 1 supports limited data integrity.
- Sync Level 2 uses the two-phase commit (2PC) protocol to ensure the reliability of a transaction.

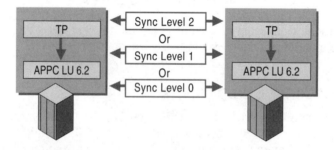

Figure A.10   Host TPs Synchronizing Over an APPC Session

Of the three sync levels, only Sync Level 2 guarantees a true ACID-compliant transaction. Thus, in the host environment, the term transaction program might or might not imply the use of Sync Level 2 and the 2PC protocol.

Note   In the Component Object Model (COM) environment, any mention of transactions refers to true ACID-compliant, 2PC transactions.

IBM Host Transaction Processing Standards

IBM uses different transaction processing standards for different operating environments. The following are the two most popular host-based systems used to monitor and manage OLTP programs.

Customer Information and Control System (CICS)   This system was developed to run OLTP programs on the IBM MVS operating system. It is a proprietary system that supports host-based transaction processing using a TP monitor with an integrated TP manager.

Information Management System (IMS)   This system provides a TP monitor with an integrated TP manager and a hierarchical database. The TP monitor and the database can both coordinate transactions with non-IMS TP monitors and databases. Because CICS and IMS are so widely used, the Windows platform and COM programs must support interoperability with CICS and IMS data and transactions to effectively support OLTP.

Note   Microsoft SNA Server provides a feature called COM Transaction Integrator (COMTI) for CICS and IMS to enable COM-based programs to interact with IBM host–based CICS and IMS programs. Organizations can use COMTI with other SNA Server host integration technologies to build robust, multi-tier applications that make IBM host data and applications available to heterogeneous networks and intranets. For more information about SNA Server integration with host data and applications, see "Interoperability with IBM Host Systems" in this book.

IBM NetView Network Management System

The integration of Windows 2000–based networks with other network computing platforms is not complete until network administrators can monitor and control the integrated network environment. In IBM host environments, network managers often use proprietary network management products that are compatible with the IBM NetView management system.

This section introduces the IBM NetView management system to provide a context for understanding SNA Server network management integration features that are described in "Interoperability with IBM Host Systems" in this book.

IBM NetView is a network management system that was originally designed to monitor and control SNA networks. Subsequent updates extended the NetView architecture to provide integrated management services for non-SNA network resources. The NetView approach to network management is implemented in IBM's NetView product and in compatible third-party products.

NetView Functions

Table A.9 summarizes the four major functions of IBM NetView.

Table A.9   IBM NetView Management Functions

Management Function	Description
Problem Management	Manages hardware, software, and communication problems from detection through resolution.
Configuration Management	Monitors the relationships between physical and logical network components.
Performance and Accounting Management	Monitors network availability and performance, and tracks network usage charges.
Change Management	Assists with the process of planning, tracking, and controlling changes to network software, hardware, and microcode.

NetView Management Architecture

As shown in Figure A.11, in a traditional SNA management environment, NetView is a centralized management model that specifies three points of network management control:

- The Focal Point
- Entry Points
- Service Points

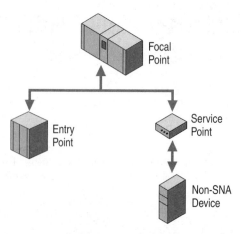

Figure A.11   NetView Network Management Control Points

Focal Point Serves as the central point in the network that collects, analyzes, and stores network management data. This is also the point where network administrators can issue commands in response to network management issues. IBM NetView and compatible network management products can serve as the SNA network focal point. In hierarchical SNA networks, the focal point is typically implemented in a mainframe system. In APPN networks, one or more nodes can serve as focal points.

Entry Points Implemented in SNA devices to serve as distributed points of control for SNA resources. An entry point gathers information about itself (the SNA device) or about a group of SNA devices, and forwards that information to the focal point. Most IBM SNA network devices can function as entry points.

Service Points Serve as distributed points of control for hardware or software resources that are not specifically designed for the SNA environment. Service points gather information about non-SNA resources and forward that information to the focal point. Service points can also receive commands from a focal point to be executed on non-SNA resources. As such, service points act as gateways, translating network management information between SNA resources and non-SNA resources.

Since introducing the original version of NetView, IBM has expanded the NetView management model to include hierarchies of nested focal points and distributed collection points. In recent years, IBM has made efforts to upgrade its network management strategy to a more open, enterprise-wide approach that embraces modern, distributed computing platforms such as Windows 2000.

For information about how SNA Server communicates with IBM NetView, see "Interoperability with IBM Host Systems" in this book.

Additional Resources

- For more information about SNA Server and related host integration technologies, see the SNA Server link on the Web Resources page at http://windows.microsoft.com/windows2000/reskit/webresources.

A P P E N D I X   B

Unix Interoperability Concepts

The UNIX operating system, written primarily in C language, consists of a library of functions that are used to access the system resources. Many interfaces to these functions are available, including C itself, the various shells, and Perl. Almost all UNIX commands and programs are executable files.

In This Appendix

Hierarchical File Structure

The UNIX file system is arranged in a hierarchical tree of directories divided into subdirectories, beginning with the root (/) directory. These directories and subdirectories contain files.

The root directory, which is the parent of all other directories, typically contains some or all of the following directories.

Table B.1   Root Subdirectories

Subdirectory	Description
/bin	Contains the binary files used by programs within /usr.
/sbin	Contains system administration utilities.
/usr	Contains most of the operating system files and programs. Typical subdirectories include /bin, /sbin, and /lib.
/etc	Contains configuration files and directories. The /etc directory contains a number a significant files, including the /etc/shadow/ and the etc/passwd files.
/var	Contains files whose contents change frequently, such as temporary files, spooled files, and mailbox files.
/dev	Contains device files.
/tmp	Contains temporary files.
/home	Contains users' home directories.
/lib	Contains shared libraries.
/boot	Contains static boot files.
/man	Contains online manual pages.

Every file and directory has a name. Within a directory, the names of files and subdirectories must be unique among themselves and between each other. Files in different directories can have identical names. Naming is case sensitive; thus, Members, members, and MEMBERS are unique names. File names can have extensions, such as .doc or .c. Files beginning with a period are called invisible because the **ls** command does not list them by default. Every directory contains two files "." and ".." created by the **mkdir** command. These represent, respectively, the current working directory and its parent directory. Files are addressed using paths. You can use either the absolute or the relative path when referring to a file. The absolute path shows the path to the file, beginning with root. For example, for the file members in the directory documentation in the home directory for jane, the absolute path is /usr/jane/documentation/members. The relative path shows the path to the file relative to the current working directory. The current working directory is the directory in which you are currently (use the **pwd** command to see the path of the directory).

You use the **cd** command to change the current working directory. The following table contains examples of using the **cd** command.

Table B.2   Various Uses of the cd Command

Command	Description
cd	No argument; changes to the user's home directory.
cd .	Changes to the current working directory.
cd ..	Changes to the parent of the current working directory.
cd *./directoryname*	Changes to a specified subdirectory of the current working directory.
cd *../directoryname*	Changes to a specified subdirectory in the parent of the current working directory.

Each user has a personal, home directory, which is the working directory used by the shell when a user first logs on. In your home directory is a startup file (.profile if you are using Korn or Bourne; .login if you are using C shell). This file contains information that determines such environment settings as the paths that the shell searches to find executable files, the shell prompt you see on your terminal, your terminal type, and your terminal settings, such as the line kill key, which deletes the entire current line, and the erase key.

Kernel

The kernel, which is the heart of the UNIX system, controls the computer's resources and allocates them among users. It enables users to run programs, which communicate with the kernel through system calls. It controls peripheral devices and provides the file structure used for storage.

The kernel allocates memory, controls processes, manages system resources, runs shell programs, manages multitasking, handles interrupts (signals to terminate running of processes), handles errors, provides input and output services, and manages the file system. The kernel does this by providing an interface between the programs under its control and the system hardware, using the system call interface, which is an application programming interface (API).

Root

Every UNIX system has a special user, called *root* or *superuser*, who has unique and powerful privileges associated with system administration. Root can access all files, regardless of access permissions. Root can read, write, or run any file; search any directory; and add or delete a file in any directory. Root can change a user's password without knowing the original password. Root can halt the system and change ownership of files. Because root privileges are so powerful, they can be destructive, intentionally or not. Root privileges should be used carefully.

There are two ways to log on as root: by logging on at the logon prompt with the user name **root** and the root password; and, while logged on as another user, by typing the command **su** and the root password.

UNIX Implementations

UNIX, first developed at AT&T Bell Laboratories, has evolved over the years. Berkeley Software Distribution (BSD), which was developed by the Computer Systems Research Group at the University of California, offers enhancements to the Bell Labs operating system, including C Shell and the vi editor. UNIX System V from Bell Labs incorporates BSD features. Solaris, from Sun, provides System V for use on Sparc workstations and 486-based and Pentium-based computers. This operating system runs on multiple and single-CPU-based systems. SunOS in a BSD-based operating system is offered by Sun for use on Sparc workstations but only runs on single-CPU-based systems. Linux is UNIX freeware that is compatible with System V and BSD and is POSIX compliant.

Table B.3   UNIX Implementations Supported by Services for UNIX

UNIX product	Based on
HP-UX (Hewlett-Packard)	System V with some BSD features
IRIX (Silicon Graphics)	Incorporates functionality from System V R4.1 and R4.2.
Linux	GNU; Posix compliant; no proprietary source code used.
Digital UNIX	Compliant with System V R3.2 and R4.
Solaris (Sun Microsystems)	A renaming of SunOS 4.1.x (BSD with some System V R4 features). Solaris 2.x includes SunOS 5.x, which is derived from System V R4.

UNIX Printing

UNIX provides commands to send files to the printer. If no printer is specified, the default printer is assumed. The /etc/printcap file contains a list of printer definitions. The default printer can also be specified using an environment variable (LPDEST for System V and PRINTER for BSD). Table B.4 lists common printer commands for UNIX.

Table B.4   UNIX Print Commands

UNIX command	Based on	Description
cancel	System V	Cancels a request to the LP print service.
lpstat	System V	Prints information about the status of the LP print service.
lp	System V	Sends a request to the LP print service.
lpq	BSD	Displays the queue of printer jobs.
lpr	BSD	Sends a job to the printer (provided with Windows 2000).
lprm	BSD	Removes a job from the print queue.

UNIX Man Pages

UNIX provides online documentation, which explains commands and procedures, in the form of manual pages. To access a particular man page, type **man** *command_name* at the shell prompt.

A P P E N D I X   C

Windows 2000 Resource Kit Deployment Lab

The Microsoft® Windows® 2000 Resource Kit Deployment Lab was created to test and document Windows 2000 deployment scenarios. These deployment scenarios show you how to design and configure Windows 2000 in an enterprise network environment. This appendix describes the Windows 2000 Resource Kit Deployment Scenarios Web site and the equipment used in the Windows 2000 Deployment Scenarios Resource Kit lab.

In This Appendix

Windows 2000 Resource Kit Deployment Scenarios Web Site

The Windows 2000 Resource Kit team is currently constructing the Windows 2000 Deployment Scenarios Web site to document the Windows 2000 deployment scenarios that are configured and tested in the Resource Kit Deployment lab. These scenarios were created in cooperation with the Windows 2000 development and test teams. Leading networking companies, including Cisco®, Compaq®, and Intel®, contributed advanced networking technologies to the deployment lab. The Windows 2000 Resource Kit Deployment Scenarios Web site is located at http://windows.microsoft.com/windows2000/reskit/webresources.

The lab was designed as an enterprise network that includes multiple sites and domains, heterogeneous operating systems, enterprise network applications, the Internet, and secure network extensions to business partners. The Web site describes the infrastructure (equipment and software), how it works, and setup instructions for each Windows 2000 deployment scenario. With this information, you can reproduce these scenarios in your test lab and deploy Windows 2000 in your organization.

Resource Kit Deployment Lab Partners

The following Microsoft partners have contributed hardware, software, and support services to the Windows 2000 Resource Kit Deployment Lab:

- Cisco
- Compaq
- Intel
- Windows 2000 program managers, developers, software testers, technical support engineers, and the Microsoft Information Technologies Group.

Routers

The following sections contain information about the contributed hardware.

Cisco 7500 Series Routers

The Cisco 7500 series of routers are strategic routers for both collapsed backbone local area network (LAN) and enterprise wide area network (WAN) applications. The Cisco 7500 series supports multiprotocol routing and multiple-media networks including Fiber Distributed Data Interface (FDDI), Token Ring and Asynchronous Transfer Mode (ATM) using Fast Ethernet, Fast Ethernet Channel, and Gigabit Ethernet technologies.

For more information about Cisco technology, visit the Cisco Web site at http://www.cisco.com.

Table C.1   Cisco 7513 Router

Resource Kit lab location	Seattle site, OSPF Area 0
Quantity	1
Operating system	Cisco Internet Operating System (IOS) V.12.0.4T Enterprise Edition
Hardware configuration	Cisco 7513 Router 13-Slot Chassis and Power Supply, 2 CyBus, 1 RSP2
	Cisco 7513 Route Switch Processor
	RSP Flash Credit Card: 20 MB Option
	RSP 128 MB DRAM Option
	6-Port Ethernet Interface Processor
	2-Port Fast Ethernet Interface Processor (100TX)
	HSSI Interface Processor
	8-Port Serial Interface Processor
	Gigabit Ethernet Interface Processor
	128 MB DRAM Option for VIP2-50/xIP-50
	8 MB SRAM Option for VIP2-50/xIP-50
	Gigabit Interface Converter For 1000BASE-SX (Short Wavelength)
	Dual Serial Ports
Windows 2000 interoperability	Multiprotocol Routing, Multicast, IP Security, Quality of Service, SNMP, Cisco Network Services for Active Directory™ directory service.

Table C.2   Cisco 7507 Router

Resource Kit lab location	Milan site, OSPF Area 2
Quantity	1
Operating system	Cisco Internet Operating System (IOS) V.12.0.4T Enterprise Edition
Hardware configuration	Cisco 7507 7-Slot, 2 CyBus, 1 RSP2
	RSP Flash Credit Card: 20 MB Option
	RSP 128 MB DRAM Option
	7507 Chassis and AC Power
	Cisco 7507/7513 Route Switch Processor
	6-Port Ethernet Interface Processor
	2-Port Fast Ethernet Interface Processor (100TX)
	HSSI Interface Processor
	4-Port Serial Interface Processor
	Dual Serial Ports
Windows 2000 interoperability	Multiprotocol Routing, Multicast, IP Security, Quality of Service, SNMP, Cisco Network Services for Active Directory.

Table C.3   Cisco 7505 Router

Resource Kit lab location	Hong Kong SAR site, OSPF Area 4
	Seattle, OSPF Area 0
	Supplier.com, OSPF Area
Quantity	4
Operating system	Cisco Internet Operating System (IOS) V.12.0.4T Enterprise Edition
Hardware configuration	
Milan site, OSPF Area 2	7507 Chassis and AC Power
	RSP Flash Credit Card: 20 MB Option
	RSP 128 MB DRAM Option
	Cisco 7507/7513 Route Switch Processor
	6-Port Ethernet Interface Processor
	2-Port Fast Ethernet Interface Processor (100TX)
	HSSI Interface Processor
	4-Port Serial Interface Processor
	Dual Serial Ports

continued

Table C.3   Cisco 7505 Router *(continued)*

Hong Kong SAR site, OSPF Area 4	Cisco 7505 5-Slot, 1 CyBus, 1RSP1
	RSP Flash Credit Card: 20 MB Option
	RSP 128 MB DRAM Option
	Cisco 7505 Route Switch Processor
	2-Port Ethernet Interface Processor
	4-Port Serial Interface Processor
	Dual Serial Ports
	ATM Interface, SONET/SDH Multimode, 155 megabits per second (Mbps)
Seattle, OSPF Area 0	Cisco 7505 5-Slot, 1 CyBus, 1RSP1
	7505 Chassis and Power Supply
	RSP Flash Credit Card: 20 MB Option
	RSP 128 MB DRAM Option
	Cisco 7505 Route Switch Processor
	6-Port Ethernet Interface Processor
	2-Port Fast Ethernet Interface Processor (100TX)
	HSSI Interface Processor
	Multi-Channel Interface Processor T1/PRI 2-Port
San Jose, OSPF Area 6	Cisco 7505 5-Slot, 1 CyBus, 1RSP1, 1
	7505 Chassis and AC Power
	Cisco 7505 Route Switch and Processor
	RSP Flash Credit Card: 20 MB Option
	RSP 128 MB DRAM Option
	6-Port Ethernet Interface Processor
	2-Port Fast Ethernet Interface Processor (100TX)
	HSSI Interface Processor
	4-Port Serial Interface Processor
	Dual Serial Ports
Windows 2000 interoperability	Multiprotocol Routing, Multicast, IP Security, Quality of Service, SNMP, Cisco Network Services for Active Directory.

Cisco 3600 Router

The Cisco 3600 Router is a multifunction platform that supports branch/enterprise, hybrid dial-access applications, ATM, LAN to LAN or routing applications, and multi-service applications.

Table C.4   Cisco 3600 Router

Resource Kit lab location	Atlanta, OSPF Area 5
	San Jose, OSPF Area 6
Quantity	2
Operating system	Cisco Internet Operating System (IOS) V.12.0.4T Enterprise Edition
Hardware configuration	
Atlanta, OSPF Area 5	Cisco 3600 2-slot Modular Router with IP Software
	8-to-32MB Flash Factory Upgrade for Cisco 3600
	32-to-64 MB DRAM Factory Upgrade for Cisco 3620
	2 Ethernet 2 WAN Card Slot Network Module
	1-Port Serial WAN Interface Card
	1-Port T1/Fractional T1 DSU/CSU WAN Interface Card
	1-Port T1/Fractional T1 DSU/CSU WAN Interface Card
	1-Port Fast Ethernet Network Module (TX Only)
San Jose, OSPF Area 6	Cisco 3600 2-slot Modular Router with IP Software
	8-to-32MB Flash Factory Upgrade for the Cisco 3600
	32-to-64 MB DRAM Factory Upgrade for the Cisco 3620
	1-Port Fast Ethernet Network Module (TX Only)
	32 Port Asynchronous Module
Windows 2000 interoperability	Multiprotocol Routing, Multicast, IP Security, Quality of Service, SNMP, Cisco Network Services for Active Directory

Switches

The following sections contain information about the contributed switches.

Cisco Catalyst 6000 L3 Switch

The Cisco 6000 switch is a multilayer switching platform for campus networks. It is designed to address the increased requirements for gigabit scalability, high availability and multi-layer switching in backbone/distribution, and server aggregation.

Table C.5   Cisco Catalyst 6000 L3 Switch

Resource Kit lab location	Seattle site 3 units, Milan 1 unit
Quantity	4
Operating system	Cisco Internet Operating System (IOS) V.12.0.4T Enterprise Edition
Hardware configuration	Catalyst 6006 Chassis
	Catalyst 6006 with 2 x 8 port Gigabyte Ethernet
	Catalyst 6000 Supervisor Flash Image, Release 5.2(1)
	Catalyst 6000 Supervisor Engine 1, 2 Gigabyte Ethernet
	Catalyst 6000 Supervisor PCMCIA Flash Memory Card, 24MB Option
	Catalyst 6000 8-port Gigabit Ethernet Module
	Catalyst 6000 48-port 10/100 MBs RJ-45 Module
	1000BASE-SX "Short Wavelength" (Multimode only)
	Catalyst 6000 Multilayer Switch Module
	Catalyst 6000 MSM IP/IP-Multicast Routing Feature Set
Windows 2000 interoperability	Support for 802.1P

Cisco Catalyst 3500 Switch Series

The Cisco Systems Catalyst 3500 Series XL Switch is a scalable 10/100 and gigabyte switch that delivers premium performance, manageability, and flexibility. It allows management of all Cisco switched ports from a single IP address and provides interconnected switches with an independent high-speed stacking bus that preserves computer ports.

Table C.6   Cisco Catalyst 3508G XL Switch

Resource Kit lab location	Tokyo, Vancouver, Boston, Seville
Quantity	4
Operating system	Cisco Internet Operating System (IOS) V.12.0.4T Enterprise Edition
Hardware configuration	8 port stackable, scalable 10, 100, Gigabyte Ethernet Switches
	4 MB shared memory architecture
	8 MB DRAM and 4 MB Flash memory onboard
	Gigabyte Interface Card (GBIC)
Windows 2000 interoperability	Support for 802.1P, 802.1Q

Servers

The following sections contain information about the contributed servers.

Compaq ProLiant 5500 LAN Server

The Compaq ProLiant 5500 Series Server is designed for enterprise applications in mission-critical environments. This server is designed for a branch office or Datacenter applications. It can be rack-mounted or used in a tower installation. The ProLiant 5500 server provides enhanced fault tolerance capabilities and rapid recovery features, which provide high server availability.

For more information about Compaq technology, visit the Compaq Web site at http://www.compaq.com.

Table C.7   Compaq ProLiant 5500 LAN Server

Quantity	6
CPU	Dual Intel Pentium Pro 200 MHz
Memory	128 MB ECC Protected EDO
Storage	RAID Array Level 5
Host Bus Adapter	Wide Ultra SCSI, Wide-Ultra SCSI-3
Slots	3 EISA/5 PCI
	2 Serial 1 Parallel Ports

Compaq ProLiant 2500 LAN Server

The Compaq ProLiant 2500 series server is designed for departmental and remote office networks that require high levels of availability. The ProLiant 2500 server can be rack-mounted and has extensive manageability features. It offers automatic server recovery (ASR-2) to monitor server performance and returns the server to full operation in the event of critical failure.

Table C.8   Compaq ProLiant 2500 LAN Server

Quantity	6
CPU	Intel Pentium II 200 MHz
Memory	128 MB
Storage	RAID Array Level 5
Host Adapter	32 Bit Fast-Wide SCSI-2/E Controller, 1 with Fiber Array
Slots	4 EISA/PCI 2 PCI

Compaq ProLiant 850R LAN Server

The Compaq ProLiant 850R Series server is designed for medium-to-large businesses requiring a rack mounted server for Internet/Intranet, gateway or file and printer sharing applications. It offers automatic server recovery (ASR-2) to monitor server performance and returns the server to full operation in the event of critical failure.

Table C.9   Compaq ProLiant 850R LAN Server

Quantity	28
CPU	Intel Pentium 200 MHz
Memory	128 MB
Storage	RAID Array Level 1
Host Adapter	Embedded Wide-Ultra SCSI-3, Wide Ultra SCSI
Slots	2 ISA, 5 PCI

Intel Quad Pentium LAN Server

The Intel Quad Pentium LAN Servers contain 4 Intel Pentium 200 MHz processors. These servers provide enterprise solutions for mission-critical environments. The servers can handle branch office or Datacenter applications because of high levels of availability. Applications such as Microsoft® SQL Server™ and Microsoft® Exchange Server® are good candidates for this enterprise server.

For more information about Intel technology, visit the Intel Web site at http://www.intel.com.

Table C.10   Intel Quad Pentium LAN Server

Quantity	2
CPU	Quad Intel Pentium 200 MHz
Memory	1 GB
Storage	RAID Array Level 5

Intel Dual Pentium LAN Server

The Intel Dual Pentium LAN Server contains 2 Intel Pentium 200 MHz processors. These servers provide enterprise solutions for mission-critical environments. The servers is capable of high levels of availability. Applications such as SQL Server and Exchange Server are good candidates for this enterprise server.

Table C.11   Intel Dual Pentium LAN Server

Quantity	18
CPU	Dual Pentium 200 MHz
Memory	128 MB
Storage	RAID Array Level 5

Desktop Computers

The following sections contain information about the contributed desktop computers.

Compaq Deskpro 4000 Series

The Compaq Deskpro 4000 series is designed to be a dependable computer for a networked environment. The Compaq Deskpro 4000 has an integrated network adapter and has enhanced Intelligent Manageability features. It includes new fault predicting capabilities and added security features, which make these computers easy to manage and integrate in any computing environment.

Table C.12   Compaq Deskpro 4000

Quantity	10
CPU	Intel Pentium 233 MHz
Memory	128 MB
Storage	3.2 GB Hard Drive ATA/IDE
Host Adapter	Embedded IDE
Slots	1 ISA, 1 ISA/PCI, 2 PCI

Compaq Deskpro 6000 Series

The Compaq Deskpro 6000 meets the needs of power users. The Deskpro 6000 series has error checking and correction (ECC) SDRAM for optimal performance and fault-tolerance. It also includes new fault predicting capabilities and added security features, which make these computers easy to manage and integrate in any computing environment.

Table C.13   Compaq Deskpro 6000CDS

Quantity	5
CPU	Intel Pentium 300 MMX
Memory	128 MB
Storage	4.3 GB Hard Drive ATA/IDE
Host Adapter	Embedded ATA/IDE and SCSI 32 bit Fast-SCSI-2
Slots	3 ISA/PCI

Table C.14   Compaq Deskpro EN 6400

Quantity	10
CPU	Intel Pentium II 400 MHz
Memory	64 MB
Storage	3.2 GB Hard Drive
Host Adapter	Embedded ATA/IDE
Slots	1 AGP, 2 ISA/PCI, 2 PCI

Table C.15   Compaq Deskpro EN 6300

Quantity	11
CPU	Intel Pentium 300 MHz
Memory	64 MB
Storage	3.2 GB
Host Adapter	Embedded ATA/IDE
Slots	2 ISA/PCI, 2 PCI

Portable Computers

The following sections contain information about the contributed portable computers.

Compaq Armada 4000 Series

The Compaq Armada 4000 has an Intel Pentium processor with MMX up to 266 MHz, up to 4 GB Hard Drive, a 12.1 inch, 800 x 600 CTFT display supporting up to 16 million colors, and 32 MB Synchronous Dynamic RAM (SDRAM). The Armada 4000 series has 64 bit PCI local bus video.

Table C.16   Compaq Armada 4210

Quantity	3
CPU	Intel 233 MHz MMX
Memory	64 MB
Storage	3.2 GB Hard Drive
Host Adapter	Embedded ATA/IDE

Compaq Armada 1700 Series

The Compaq Armada 1700 series has up to a 400 MHz Intel Mobile Pentium II processor. A 14.1 inch CTFT displays up to a 10 GB SMART hard drive 24x CD-ROM 64 MB SDRAM. The Armada 1700 features an integrated AC adapter, integrated modem and hard drive, and both a CD-ROM and diskette drive.

Table C.17   Compaq Armada 1700

Quantity	3
CPU	Pentium II 233MHz MMX
Memory	64 MB
Storage	4 GB Hard Drive
Host Adapter	Embedded ATA/IDE

Compaq Armada 7700 Series

The Compaq Armada 7700 series includes an Intel Mobile Pentium MMX processor up to 266 MHz, up to 13.1 inch 1024 x 768 CTFT display supporting up to 16.8 million colors with local bus graphics, which is standard on the 7770 model, up to 32MB MB EDO RAM.

Table C.18   Compaq Armada 7770 DMT

Quantity	3
CPU	Intel Pentium 233 MHz MMX
Memory	64 MB
Storage	3.0 GB Hard Drive
Host Adapter	Embedded ATA/IDE

Compaq Armada 7800 Series

The Compaq Armada 7800 series includes an Intel Mobile Pentium II processor up to 400 MHz, up to a 14.1 inch 1024 x 768 CTFT display supporting up to 16.8 million colors, a standard DVD-ROM drive, 64 MB SDRAM, AGP (Accelerated Graphic Port) implementation with a high-performance 66 MHz graphic bus, and a S3ViRGE/MX graphics controller with 4 MB.

Table C.19   Compaq Armada Model 7800

Quantity	3
CPU	Intel Pentium II 266 MHz
Memory	64 MB
Storage	5.0 GB Hard Drive
Host Adapter	Embedded ATA/IDE

Glossary

3

3270 A class of IBM Systems Network Architecture terminal and related protocol used to communicate with IBM mainframe host systems.

5

5250 A class of IBM Systems Network Architecture terminal and related protocol used to communicate with IBM mainframe host systems.

8

802.1p A protocol that supports the mapping of RSVP signals to Layer 2 signals using 802.1p priority markings to enable the prioritization of traffic across Layer 2 devices, such as switches, on a network segment. IEEE 802 refers to the Layer 2 technology used by LANs including the data-link layer and the media access control layer.

A

AAL See ATM Adaptation Layer.

access control The security mechanism in Windows NT and Windows 2000 that determines which objects a security principal can use and how the security principal can use them.

access control entry (ACE) An entry in an access control list (ACL) containing a security identifier (SID) and a set of access rights. A process with a matching security identifier is either allowed access rights, denied rights, or allowed rights with auditing.

access privileges Permissions set by Macintosh users that allow them to view and make changes to folders on a server. By setting access privileges (called permissions when set on a computer running Windows 2000 Server), administrators control which Macintosh computers can use folders on a volume.

access token An object containing the security information for a logon session. Windows 2000 creates an access token when a user logs on, and every process executed on behalf of the user has a copy of the token. The token identifies the user, the user's groups, and the user's privileges. The system uses the token to control access to securable objects and to control the ability of the user to perform various system-related operations on the local computer. There are two kinds of access token: primary and impersonation. See also impersonation token; primary token; process; security identifier.

accessibility The quality of a system incorporating hardware or software to engage a customizable user interface, alternative input and output methods, and greater exposure of screen elements to make the computer usable by people with cognitive, hearing, physical, or visual disabilities.

account domain A Windows NT domain that holds user account data. Also known as a master domain.

account lockout A Windows 2000 security feature that locks a user account if repeated failed logon attempts occur within a specified amount of time, based on security policy lockout settings. (Locked accounts cannot log on.)

ACE See access control entry.

Active Directory The directory service included with Windows 2000 Server. It stores information about objects on a network and makes this information available to users and network administrators. Active Directory gives network users access to permitted resources anywhere on the network using a single logon process. It provides network administrators with an intuitive hierarchical view of the network and a single point of administration for all network objects. See also directory; directory service.

ActiveX A set of technologies that enables software components to interact with one another in a networked environment, regardless of the language in which the components were created.

ActiveX control A reusable software component that incorporates ActiveX technology.

address pool A group of IP addresses in a scope. Pooled addresses are then available for dynamic assignment by a DHCP server to DHCP clients.

Address Resolution Protocol (ARP)
In TCP/IP, a protocol that uses limited broadcast to the local network to resolve a logically assigned IP address. The IP address is conferred in software for each IP network host device to its physical hardware or media access control layer address. In ATM the ARP protocol is used two different ways. For CLIP, ARP is used to resolve addresses to ATM hardware addresses. For ATM LAN emulation, ARP is used to resolve Ethernet/802.3 or Token Ring addresses to ATM hardware addresses. See also media access control; Transmission Control Protocol/Internet Protocol.

adjacency A relationship formed between selected neighboring OSPF routers for the purpose of exchanging routing information. When the link state databases of two neighboring routers are synchronized, the routers are said to be adjacent. Not every pair of neighboring routers becomes adjacent. See also link state database.

Advanced Peer-to-Peer Networking (APPN)
An upgrade to IBM Systems Network Architecture that supports distributed session control services and dynamic routing, avoiding dependencies on centralized mainframe network services.

Advanced Program-to-Program Communication (APPC)
An IBM Systems Network Architecture communications method that uses the LU 6.2 protocol to establish, manage, and terminate network communication between programs in a distributed computing environment.

Advanced Program-to-Program Communication File Transfer Protocol (AFTP)
A file transfer protocol used in IBM host systems, the IBM Advanced Program-to Program Communications equivalent to the TCP/IP File Transfer Protocol.

agent An application that runs on a Simple Network Management Protocol (SNMP) managed device. The agent application is the object of management activities. A computer running SNMP agent software is also sometimes referred to as an agent.

algorithm A rule or procedure for solving a problem. Internet Protocol security uses cryptographically-based algorithms to encrypt data.

AppleTalk The Apple Computer network architecture and network protocols. A network that has Macintosh clients and a computer running Windows 2000 Server with Services for Macintosh functions as an AppleTalk network.

AppleTalk Control Protocol (ATCP)
The Network Control Protocol for AppleTalk-based PPP connections. ATCP negotiates AppleTalk-based parameters to dynamically configure an AppleTalk-based PPP peer across a point-to-point link.

AppleTalk Phase 2 The extended AppleTalk Internet model designed by Apple Computer that supports multiple zones within a network and extended addressing capacity. See also AppleTalk.

AppleTalk Protocol The set of network protocols on which the AppleTalk network architecture is based. The AppleTalk Protocol stack must be installed on a computer running Windows 2000 Server so that Macintosh clients can connect to it. See also AppleTalk.

application layer The layer at which applications access network services. This layer represents the services that directly support applications, such as software for file transfers, database access, and e-mail.

application programming interface (API)
A set of routines that an application uses to request and carry out lower-level services performed by a computer's operating system. These routines usually carry out maintenance tasks such as managing files and displaying information.

APPN See Advanced Peer-to-Peer Networking.

APPN domain An APPN network node and the other physical unit (PU) type 2.1 nodes attached to it.

area A group of contiguous networks within an OSPF autonomous system. OSPF areas reduce the size of the link state database and provide the ability to summarize routes. See also autonomous system; link state database.

area border router (ABR) A router that is attached to multiple areas. Area border routers maintain separate link state databases for each area. See also link state database.

ARP See Address Resolution Protocol.

ARP cache A table of IP addresses and their corresponding media access control address. There is a separate ARP cache for each interface.

Asynchronous Transfer Mode (ATM)
A high-speed connection-oriented protocol used to transport many different types of network traffic.

ATCP AppleTalk Control Protocol

ATM See Asynchronous Transfer Mode.

ATM adaptation layer (AAL) The layer of the ATM protocol stack that parses data into the payload portion of the ATM cell for transport across an ATM network. See also Asynchronous Transfer Mode (ATM).

attribute (object) In Active Directory, a single property of an object. An object is described by the values of its attributes. For each object class, the schema defines what attributes an instance of the class must have and what additional attributes it might have.

authentication In network access, the process by which the system validates the user's logon information. A user's name and password are compared against an authorized list. If the system detects a match, access is granted to the extent specified in the permissions list for that user. When a user logs on to an account on a computer running Windows 2000 Professional, the authentication is performed by the client. When a user logs on to an account on a Windows 2000 Server domain, authentication can be performed by any server of that domain. See also server; trust relationship.

authentication The IPSec process that verifies the origin and integrity of a message by assuring the genuine identity of each computer. Without strong authentication, an unknown computer and any data it sends is suspect. IPSec provides multiple methods of authentication to ensure compatibility with earlier systems running earlier versions of Windows, non-Windows-based systems, and shared computers.

authenticator A data structure used by one party to prove that another party knows a secret key. In the Kerberos authentication protocol, authenticators include timestamps, to prevent replay attacks, and are encrypted with the session key issued by the Key Distribution Center (KDC). See also Kerberos authentication protocol; Key Distribution Center; replay attack; secret key.

Automatic Private IP Addressing (APIPA)
A feature of Windows 2000 TCP/IP that automatically configures a unique IP address from the range 169.254.0.1 to 169.254.255.254 and a subnet mask of 255.255.0.0 when the TCP/IP protocol is configured for dynamic addressing and a Dynamic Host Configuration.

Automation A Component Object Model (COM) based technology that allows for interoperability among ActiveX components, including OLE components. Formerly referred to as OLE Automation. See also ActiveX; object linking and embedding.

autonomous system (AS) A group of routers exchanging routing information by using a common routing protocol.

availability A measure of the fault tolerance of a computer and its programs. A highly available computer runs 24 hours a day, 7 days a week. See also fault tolerance.

available bit rate (ABR) An ATM service type that supports available-bit-rate traffic, minimum guaranteed transmission rate, and peak data rates. ABR also allows bandwidth allocation depending on availability, and it uses flow control to communicate bandwidth availability to the end node.

B

B channel One of the 64 Kbps communications channels on an ISDN circuit. A BRI (Basic Rate Interface) ISDN has two bearer channels and one data channel. A PRI (Primary Rate Interface) ISDN line has 23 bearer channels (in North America) or 30 bearer channels (in Europe) and one data channel. B channel is also called bearer channel. See also Integrated Services Digital Network (ISDN).

backbone In OSPF, an area common to all other OSPF areas that is used as the transit area for inter-area traffic and for distributing routing information between areas. The backbone must be contiguous. See also Open Shortest Path First (OSPF).

backbone router In OSPF, a router that is connected to the backbone area. This includes routers that are connected to more than one area (area border routers). However, backbone routers do not have to be area border routers. Routers that have all networks connected to the backbone are internal routers. See also area border router; Open Shortest Path First (OSPF).

backup designated router (BDR) An OSPF router that forms adjacencies with all other routers on a multiple access network and becomes the designated router when the designated router becomes unavailable.

backup domain controller In Windows NT Server 4.0 or earlier, a computer running Windows NT Server that receives a copy of the domain's directory database (which contains all account and security policy information for the domain). The copy synchronizes periodically with the master copy on the primary domain controller. A backup domain controller also authenticates user logon information and can be promoted to function as primary domain controllers as needed. Multiple backup domain controllers can exist in a domain. Windows NT 3.51 and 4.0 backup domain controllers can participate in a Windows 2000 domain when the domain is configured in mixed mode. See also mixed mode; primary domain controller.

bandwidth In communications, the difference between the highest and lowest frequencies in a given range. For example, a telephone line accommodates a bandwidth of 3,000 Hz, the difference between the lowest (300 Hz) and highest (3,300 Hz) frequencies it can carry. In computer networks, greater bandwidth indicates faster data-transfer capability and is expressed in bits per second (bps).

Bandwidth Allocation Control Protocol (BACP) A PPP Network Control Protocol that negotiates the election of a favored peer for a multiprocessing connection. If both ends of the multiprocessing connection issue a connection request at the same time, then the connection request of the favored peer is performed.

Bandwidth Allocation Protocol (BAP) A PPP control protocol that is used on a multiprocessing connection to dynamically add and remove links.

binary A base-2 number system in which values are expressed as combinations of two digits, 0 and 1.

bindery A database in Novell NetWare 2.*x* and 3.*x* that contains organizational and security information about users and groups.

binding A process by which software components and layers are linked together. When a network component is installed, the binding relationships and dependencies for the components are established. Binding allows components to communicate with each other.

bit stuffing A technique used by PPP on synchronous links, such as T-Carrier, ISDN, or other digital links, to prevent the occurrence of the Flag character within the PPP frame.

bits per second (bps) The number of bits transmitted every second, used as a measure of the speed at which a device, such as a modem, can transfer data. A character is made up of 8 bits. In asynchronous communication, each character is preceded by a start bit and terminates with a stop bit. So for each character, 10 bits are transmitted. If a modem communicates at 2,400 bits per second (bps), then 240 characters are sent every second.

bonding The combining of ISDN B channels through hardware support.

boot To start or reset a computer. When first turned on or reset, the computer executes the software that loads and starts the computer's operating system, which prepares it for use.

Border Gateway Protocol (BGP) A routing protocol designed for use between autonomous systems. See also autonomous system.

Bourne shell A UNIX command processor developed by Steven Bourne.

broadcast and unknown server (BUS)
A multicast service on an emulated local area network (ELAN) that forwards broadcast, multicast, and initial unicast data traffic sent by a LAN emulation client. See also emulated local area network (ELAN).

broadcast message A network message sent from a single computer that is distributed to all other devices on the same segment of the network as the sending computer.

broadcast network A network that supports more than two attached routers and has the ability to address a single physical message to all of the attached routers (broadcast). Ethernet is an example of a broadcast network.

browser A client tool for navigating and accessing information on the Internet or an intranet. In the context of Windows networking, "browser" can also mean the Computer Browser service, a service that maintains an up-to-date list of computers on a network or part of a network and provides the list to applications when requested. When a user attempts to connect to a resource in a domain, the domain's browser is contacted to provide a list of available resources.

brute force attack See key search attack.

buffer An area of memory used for intermediate storage of data until it can be used.

BUS See broadcast and unknown server.

C

C shell A UNIX command processor whose programming constructs are similar to those of the C language.

cache For DNS and WINS, a local information store of resource records for recently resolved names of remote hosts. Typically, the cache is built dynamically as the computer queries and resolves names; it helps optimize the time required to resolve queried names. See also cache file; naming service; resource record.

cache file A file used by the Domain Name System (DNS) server to preload its names cache when service is started. Also known as the "root hints" file because resource records stored in this file are used by the DNS service to help locate root servers that provide referral to authoritative servers for remote names. For Windows DNS servers, the cache file is named Cache.dns and is located in the %SystemRoot%\System32\Dns folder. See also cache; systemroot.

Call Manager A software component that establishes, maintains and terminates a connection between two computers.

Callback Control Protocol (CBCP)
The Network Control Protocol for negotiating the use of callback over PPP links.

Challenge Handshake Authentication Protocol (CHAP)

A challenge-response authentication protocol for PPP connections documented in RFC 1994 that uses the industry-standard Message Digest 5 (MD5) one-way encryption scheme to hash the response to a challenge issued by the remote access server.

character stuffing A technique used by PPP on asynchronous links, such as analog phone lines, to prevent the occurrence of the Flag character within the PPP frame.

child object An object that resides in another object. For example, a file is a child object that resides in a folder, which is the parent object. See also object; parent object.

Chooser The Macintosh desk accessory with which users select the network server and printers they want to use.

cipher The method of forming a hidden message. The cipher is used to transform a readable message called plaintext (also sometimes called cleartext) into an unreadable, scrambled, or hidden message called ciphertext. Only someone with a secret decoding key can convert the ciphertext back into its original plaintext. See also ciphertext; plaintext; cryptography.

ciphertext Text that has been encrypted using an encryption key. Ciphertext is meaningless to anyone who does not have the decryption key. See also decryption; encryption; encryption key; plaintext.

Class D IP address The Internet address class designed for IP multicast addresses. The value of the first octet for Class D IP addresses and networks varies from 224 to 239.

class-based IP addressing or routing that is based on the internet address classes.

classical IP over ATM (CLIP) A proposed Internet standard, described in RFC 2225 and other related RFCs, that allows IP communication directly on the ATM layer, bypassing an additional protocol (such as Ethernet or Token Ring) in the protocol stack. See also Asynchronous Transfer Mode; Internet Protocol.

Classless Interdomain Routing (CIDR)

A method of allocating public IP addresses that is not based on the original internet address classes. Classless Interdomain Routing (CIDR) was developed to help prevent the depletion of public IP addresses and minimize the size of Internet routing tables.

cleartext Data transmitted without encryption.

client Any computer or program connecting to, or requesting services of, another computer or program. See also server.

Client Service for NetWare A service included with Windows 2000 Professional that allows clients to make direct connections to resources on computers running NetWare 2.*x*, 3.*x*, 4.*x*, or 5.*x* server software.

CLIP See Classical IP over ATM.

cluster A set of computers that work together to provide a service. The use of a cluster enhances both the availability of the service and the scalability of the operating system that provides the service. Network Load Balancing provides a software solution for clustering multiple computers running Windows 2000 Server that provides networked services over the Internet and private intranets. See also availability; scalability.

Cluster controller An IBM Systems Network Architecture component that manages input/output operations for clusters of terminals or attached network devices.

cn (Common-Name) The name of the class belonging to the class attributeSchema. The Common-Name property is unique across all Common-Names for all classSchema and attributeSchema objects in the Schema container.

command control block (CCB) A specifically formatted information set used in the IBM Token Ring environment that is transmitted from the application program to the adapter support software to request an operation.

common gateway interface (CGI) A server-side interface for initiating software services. For example a set of interfaces that describe how a Web server communicates with software on the same computer. Any software can be a CGI program if it handles input and output according to the CGI standard.

Common Internet File System (CIFS)
A protocol and a corresponding API used by application programs to request higher level application services. CIFS was formerly known as SMB (Server Message Block).

Common Programming Interface for Communications (CPIC)
A platform-independent API developed by IBM to provide portability for APPC LU 6.2-based applications.

Component Object Model (COM) An object-based programming model designed to promote software interoperability; it allows two or more applications or components to easily cooperate with one another, even if they were written by different vendors, at different times, in different programming languages, or if they are running on different computers running different operating systems. COM is the foundation technology upon which broader technologies can be built. Object linking and embedding (OLE) technology and ActiveX are both built on top of COM.

computer name A unique name of up to 15 uppercase characters that identifies a computer to the network. The name cannot be the same as any other computer or domain name in the network.

confidentiality An Internet Protocol security service that ensures that a message is disclosed only to intended recipients by encrypting the data.

connection establishment delay The delay encountered when forwarding a packet across an on-demand demand-dial connection. The delay is due to the connection establishment process, consisting of creating a physical connection and/or a logical connection and a PPP connection.

connection-oriented A type of network protocol that requires an end-to-end virtual connection between the sender and receiver before communicating across the network.

connection-oriented communication
Network transmission service where a link is established prior to packet transmission and an acknowledgment of the data transmission received is returned to the originating source.

Connection-Oriented NDIS (Co-NDIS)
A Network Driver Interface Specification that supports connection-oriented data transfer.

connectionless A network protocol in which a sender broadcasts traffic on the network to an intended receiver without first establishing a connection to the receiver.

console tree The tree view pane in a Microsoft Management Console (MMC) that displays the hierarchical namespace. By default it is the left pane of the console window, but it can be hidden. The items in the console tree (for example, Web pages, folders, and controls) and their hierarchical organization determines the management capabilities of a console. See also Microsoft Management Console (MMC); namespace.

constant bit rate (CBR) An ATM service type that supports constant bandwidth allocation. CBR ensures that all cells in a transmission are maintained from end to end. This service type is used for voice and video transmissions that require little or no cell loss and rigorous timing controls during transmission.

container object An object that can logically contain other objects. For example, a folder is a container object. See also noncontainer object; object.

convergence The process of stabilizing a system after changes occur in the network. For routing, if a route becomes unavailable, routers send update messages throughout the internetwork, reestablishing information about preferred routes. For Network Load Balancing, a process by which hosts exchange messages to determine a new, consistent state of the cluster and to elect the host with the highest host priority, known as the default host. During convergence, a new load distribution is determined for hosts that share the handling of network traffic for specific TCP or UDP ports. See also cluster; default host; host; User Datagram Protocol (UDP).

convergence time The time it takes for the internetwork to achieve convergence. See convergence.

CryptoAPI (CAPI) An application programming interface (API) that is provided as part of Windows 2000. CryptoAPI provides a set of functions that allow applications to encrypt or digitally sign data in a flexible manner while providing protection for private keys. Actual cryptographic operations are performed by independent modules known as cryptographic service providers (CSPs). See also cryptographic service provider; private key.

cryptographic key See encryption key.

cryptographic service provider (CSP) An independent software module that performs cryptography operations such as secret key exchange, digital signing of data, and public key authentication. Any Windows 2000 service or application can request cryptography operations from a CSP. See also CryptoAPI.

cryptography The art and science of information security. It provides four basic information security functions: confidentiality, integrity, authentication, and nonrepudiation. See also confidentiality; integrity; authentication; nonrepudiation.

current directory The directory being worked in currently. Also called current folder.

current working directory The directory that a user is associated with at any given time.

D

daemon A networking program, usually associated with UNIX systems, that runs in the background performing utility functions such as housekeeping or maintenance without user intervention or awareness. Pronounced "demon."

Data Encryption Standard (DES) An encryption algorithm that uses a 56-bit key, and maps a 64-bit input block to a 64-bit output block. The key appears to be a 64-bit key, but one bit in each of the 8 bytes is used for odd parity, resulting in 56 bits of usable key.

Data Link Control (DLC) A protocol used primarily for IBM mainframe computers and printer connectivity.

data stream All information transferred over a network at any given time.

data-link layer A layer that packages raw bits from the physical layer into frames (logical, structured packets for data). This layer is responsible for transferring frames from one computer to another, without errors. After sending a frame, the data-link layer waits for an acknowledgment from the receiving computer.

datagram An unacknowledged packet of data sent to another network destination. The destination can be another device directly reachable on the local area network (LAN) or a remote destination reachable using routed delivery through a packet-switched network.

decryption The process of making encrypted data readable again by converting ciphertext to plaintext. See also ciphertext; encryption; plaintext.

default gateway A configuration item for the TCP/IP protocol that is the IP address of a directly reachable IP router. Configuring a default gateway creates a default route in the IP routing table.

default host The host with the highest host priority for which a drainstop command is not in progress. After convergence, the default host handles all of the network traffic for TCP and UDP ports that are not otherwise covered by port rules. See also convergence; host priority; port rule; User Datagram Protocol.

default printer The printer to which a computer sends documents if the Print command is selected without first specifying which printer to use with a program.

default route A route that is used when no other routes for the destination are found in the routing table. For example, if a router or end system cannot find a network route or host route for the destination, the default route is used. The default route is used to simplify the configuration of end systems or routers. For IP routing tables, the default route is the route with the network destination of 0.0.0.0 and netmask of 0.0.0.0.

default zone The zone to which all Macintosh clients on a network are assigned by default.

defragmentation The process of rewriting parts of a file to contiguous sectors on a hard disk to increase the speed of access and retrieval. When files are updated, the computer tends to save these updates on the largest continuous space on the hard disk, which is often on a different sector than the other parts of the file. When files are thus fragmented, the computer must search the hard disk each time the file is opened to find all of the parts of the file, which slows down response time. In Active Directory, defragmentation rearranges how the data is written in the directory database file to compact it. See also fragmentation.

demand-dial connection A connection, typically using a circuit-switched wide area network link, that is initiated when data needs to be forwarded. The demand-dial connection is typically terminated when there is no traffic.

demand-dial filter An IP packet filter that specifies what types of TCP/IP traffic either creates the connection or ignores it for the purposes of creating the connection.

demand-dial interface A logical interface that represents a demand-dial connection (a PPP link) that is configured on the calling router. The demand-dial interface contains configuration information such as the port to use, the addressing used to create the connection (such as a phone number), authentication and encryption methods, and authentication credentials.

demand-dial routing Routing that makes dial-up connections to connect networks based on need. For example, a branch office with a modem that dials and establishes a connection only when there is network traffic from one office to another.

demultiplexing The action of forwarding a packet to the proper process, such as when an IPX packet arrives at its destination and is handed to the IPX protocol.

designated router (DR) An OSPF router that forms adjacencies with all other routers on a multiple access network.

DHCP relay agent A routing component that transfers messages between DHCP clients and DHCP service located on separate networks.

dialog box A window that is displayed to request or supply information. Many dialog boxes have options which must be selected before Windows NT can carry out a command.

dictionary attack An attack in which an attacker tries known words in the dictionary and numerous common password names in an attempt to "guess" the password. Because most users prefer easily remembered passwords, dictionary attacks are often a shortcut to finding a password in significantly less time than key search (brute force) attacks would take to find the same password. See also key search attack.

direct delivery The delivery of an IP packet by an IP node to the final destination on a directly attached network.

direct hosting A feature that allows computers to communicate over IPX, bypassing the NetBIOS layer.

directory An information source that contains information about computer files or other objects. In a file system, a directory stores information about files. In a distributed computing environment (such as a Windows 2000 domain), the directory stores information about objects such as printers, applications, databases, and users.

directory service Both the directory information source and the service that make the information available and usable. A directory service enables the user to find an object given any one of its attributes. See also Active Directory; directory.

directory tree A hierarchy of objects and containers in a directory that can be viewed graphically as an upside-down tree, with the root object at the top. Endpoints in the tree are usually single (leaf) objects, and nodes in the tree, or branches, are container objects. A tree shows how objects are connected in terms of the path from one object to another. A simple tree is a single container and its objects. A contiguous subtree is any unbroken path in the tree, including all the members of any container in that path.

disabled user account A user account that does not permit logging on. The account appears in the user account list of Local Users and Groups or Active Directory Users and Computers and can be re-enabled by a member of the Administrators group at any time. See also user account.

discovery A process by which the Windows 2000 Net Logon service attempts to locate a domain controller running Windows 2000 Server in the trusted domain. Once a domain controller has been discovered, it is used for subsequent user account authentication. For SNMP, dynamic discovery is the identification of devices attached to an SNMP network.

discretionary access control list (DACL)
The part of an object's security descriptor that grants or denies specific users and groups permission to access the object. Only the owner of an object can change permissions granted or denied in a DACL; thus access to the object is at the owner's discretion. See also access control entry; object; system access control list; security descriptor.

disjointed subnet Subnets of a subnetted IP network ID that are not contiguous (connected by the same routers).

distance vector A routing protocol technology in which routing information is advertised as a series of network IDs and their distance in hops from the advertising router. Routing information exchanged between typical distance vector–based routers is unsynchronized and unacknowledged.

Distributed Data Management (DDM)
an underlying database architecture provided by the host system, used by IBM.

Distributed Relational Database Architecture (DRDA)
An IBM distributed database protocol that provides access to IBM DB2 relational database programs on IBM host platforms including IBM Multiple Virtual Storage (MVS) and AS/400 systems.

distribution point In Systems Management Server, a site system with the distribution point role that stores package files received from a site server. Systems Management Server clients contact distribution points to obtain programs and files after they detect that an advertised application is available from a client access point.

DNS server A computer that runs DNS server programs containing name-to-IP address mappings, IP address-to-name mappings, information about the domain tree structure, and other information. DNS servers also attempt to resolve client queries.

domain For Windows NT and Windows 2000, a networked set of computers running Windows NT or Windows 2000 that share a Security Accounts Manager (SAM) database and that can be administered as a group. A user with an account in a particular domain can log on to and access his or her account from any computer in the domain. A domain is a single security boundary of a Windows NT computer network. For DNS, a branch under a node in the DNS tree.

domain controller For a Windows NT Server or Windows 2000 Server domain, the server that authenticates domain logon requests and maintains the security policy and the master database for a domain. Both servers and domain controllers are capable of validating a user's logon request, but password changes must be made by contacting the domain controller.

domain local group A Windows 2000 group only available in native mode domains and can contain members from anywhere in the forest, in trusted forests, or in a trusted pre-Windows 2000 domain. Domain local groups can only grant permissions to resources within the domain in which they exist. Typically, domain local groups are used to gather security principals from across the forest to control access to resources within the domain.

domain name In Windows 2000 and Active Directory, the name given by an administrator to a collection of networked computers that share a common directory. For DNS, domain names are specific node names in the DNS namespace tree. DNS domain names use singular node names, known as "labels," joined together by periods (.) that indicate each node level in the namespace. See also Domain Name System (DNS); namespace.

Domain Name System (DNS) A hierarchical naming system used for locating domain names on the Internet and on private TCP/IP networks. DNS provides a service for mapping DNS domain names to IP addresses, and vice versa. This allows users, computers, and applications to query the DNS to specify remote systems by fully qualified domain names rather than by IP addresses. See also domain; Ping.

domain tree In DNS, the inverted hierarchical tree structure that is used to index domain names. Domain trees are similar in purpose and concept to the directory trees used by computer filing systems for disk storage. See also domain name; namespace.

dotted decimal notation The format of an IP address after it is converted from binary format. (Example: 192.168.3.24)

duplex A system capable of transmitting information in both directions over a communications channel. See also full-duplex; half-duplex.

DWORD A data type composed of hexadecimal data with a maximum allotted space of 4 bytes.

Dynamic Host Configuration Protocol (DHCP) A networking protocol that provides safe, reliable, and simple TCP/IP network configuration and offers dynamic configuration of Internet Protocol (IP) addresses for computers. DHCP ensures that address conflicts do not occur and helps conserve the use of IP addresses through centralized management of address allocation.

dynamic router A router with dynamically configured routing tables. Dynamic routing consists of routing tables that are built and maintained automatically through an ongoing communication between routers. This communication is facilitated by a routing protocol. Except for their initial configuration, dynamic routers require little ongoing maintenance, and therefore can scale to larger internetworks.

dynamic routing The use of routing protocols to update routing tables. Dynamic routing responds to changes in the internetwork topology.

dynamic update An updated specification to the Domain Name System (DNS) standard that permits hosts that store name information in DNS to dynamically register and update their records in zones maintained by DNS servers that can accept and process dynamic update messages.

dynamic-link library (DLL) A feature of the Microsoft Windows family of operating systems and the OS/2 operating system. DLLs allow executable routines, generally serving a specific function or set of functions, to be stored separately as files with .dll extensions, and to be loaded only when needed by the program that calls them.

E

EAP See Extensible Authentication Protocol.

EAP type A specific EAP authentication scheme. Once the use of EAP is determined, the specific EAP type must be negotiated and performed.

emulated local area network (ELAN)
A logical network initiated by using the mechanisms defined by LAN emulation. This could include ATM and previously attached end stations.

encapsulation See tunneling.

encrypted password A password that is scrambled. Encrypted passwords are more secure than plaintext passwords, which are susceptible to network sniffers.

encryption The process of disguising a message or data in such a way as to hide its substance.

Encryption Control Protocol (ECP)
The Network Control Protocol for negotiating the use of encryption over PPP links. ECP is documented in RFC 1968.

encryption key A value used by an algorithm to encode or decode a message.

end system A network device without the ability to forward packets between portions of a network. See also host.

end-to-end encryption Data encryption between the client application and the server hosting the resource or service being accessed by the client application.

environment variable A string consisting of environment information, such as a drive, path, or filename, associated with a symbolic name that can be used by Windows NT and Windows 2000. Use the System option in Control Panel or the set command from the command prompt to define environment variables.

error detection A technique for detecting when data is lost during transmission. This allows the software to recover lost data by requesting that the transmitting computer retransmit the data.

event logging The Windows 2000 process of recording an audit entry in the audit trail whenever certain events occur, such as services starting and stopping or users logging on and off and accessing resources. You can use Event Viewer to review Services for Macintosh events as well as Windows 2000 events.

everyone category In the Macintosh environment, one of the user categories to which permissions for a folder are assigned. Permissions granted to everyone apply to all users who use the server, including guests.

export In NFS, to make a file system available by a server to a client for mounting.

Extensible Authentication Protocol (EAP)
An extension to PPP that allows for arbitrary authentication mechanisms to be employed for the validation of a PPP connection.

extension-type association The association of an MS DOS file name extension with a Macintosh file type and file creator. Extension-type associations allow users of the personal computer and Macintosh versions of the same program to share the same data files on the server. Services for Macintosh has many predefined extension-type associations.

external network number A 4-byte hexadecimal number used for addressing and routing purposes. The external network number is associated with physical network adapters and networks. To communicate with each other, all computers on the same network that use a given frame type must have the same external network number. All external network numbers must be unique to the IPX internetwork. See also internal network number; Internetwork Packet Exchange (IPX).

extranet A limited subset of computers or users on a public network, typically the Internet, that are able to access an organization's internal network. Typically the computers or users belong to partner organizations.

F

fault tolerance The assurance of data integrity when hardware failures occur. On the Windows NT and Windows 2000 platforms, fault tolerance is provided by the Ftdisk.sys driver.

Fiber Distributed Data Interface (FDDI)
A type of network media designed to be used with fiber-optic cabling. See also LocalTalk; Token Ring.

file allocation table (FAT) A file system based on a file allocation table (FAT) maintained by some operating systems, including Windows NT and Windows 2000, to keep track of the status of various segments of disk space used for file storage.

file creator A four-character sequence that tells the Macintosh Finder the name of the program that created a file. In Services for Macintosh, extension-type associations can be created that map personal computer file name extensions to Macintosh file creators and file types. These associations allow both Windows and Macintosh users to share the same data files on the server. See also extension-type association.

file server A server that provides organization-wide access to files, programs, and applications.

File Server for Macintosh A Services for Macintosh service that allows Macintosh clients and Windows clients to share files. Also called MacFile.

file system In an operating system, the overall structure in which files are named, stored, and organized. NTFS, FAT, and FAT32 are types of file systems.

File Transfer Protocol (FTP) A protocol that defines how to transfer files from one computer to another over the Internet. FTP is also a client/server application that moves files using this protocol.

filtering mode For Network Load Balancing, the method by which network traffic inbound to a cluster is handled by the hosts within the cluster. Traffic can either be handled by a single server, load balanced among the hosts within the cluster, or disabled completely. See also server.

filters In IP and IPX packet filtering, a series of definitions that indicate to the router the type of traffic allowed or disallowed on each interface.

finite state machine A computer, or operating system, in which a set of inputs determine not only the set of outputs but also the internal state of a computer, so that processing is optimized.

firewall A combination of hardware and software that provides a security system, usually to prevent unauthorized access from outside to an internal network or intranet. A firewall prevents direct communication between network and external computers by routing communication through a proxy server outside of the network. The proxy server determines whether it is safe to let a file pass through to the network. A firewall is also called a security-edge gateway.

flat routing infrastructure A routing infrastructure where each network segment is represented individually by a network route in the routing table. The network IDs in a flat routing infrastructure have no network/subnet structure and cannot be summarized.

flow A stream of data sent or received by a host. Also called network traffic.

Flowspec A traffic parameter that specifies the type of QoS requested. Flowspec is used to set parameters in the QoS packet scheduler.

forest A collection of one or more Windows 2000 Active Directory trees, organized as peers and connected by two-way transitive trust relationships between the root domains of each tree. All trees in a forest share a common schema, configuration, and Global Catalog. When a forest contains multiple trees, the trees do not form a contiguous namespace.

forwarder A DNS server designated by other internal DNS servers to be used to forward queries for resolving external or offsite DNS domain names.

forwarding address A field in a routing table entry that indicates the address to which a packet is forwarded. The forwarding address can be a physical address or an internetwork address.

forwarding IP address The IP address to which a packet is being forwarded based on the destination IP address and the contents of the IP routing table.

fragmentation The scattering of parts of the same disk file over different areas of the disk. Fragmentation occurs as files on a disk are deleted and new files are added. It slows disk access and degrades the overall performance of disk operations, although usually not severely. See also defragmentation.

frame In synchronous communication, a package of information transmitted as a single unit from one device to another. Frame is a term most often used with Ethernet networks. A frame is similar to the packet used on other networks. See also packet.

front-end processor (FEP) A dedicated computer that controls communications between an IBM mainframe and the network devices that communicate with it, offloading communication processing overhead from the mainframe.

full-duplex A system capable of simultaneously transmitting information in both directions over a communications channel. See also duplex; half-duplex.

G

gateway A device connected to multiple physical TCP/IP networks, capable of routing or delivering IP packets between them. A gateway translates between different transport protocols or data formats (for example, IPX and IP) and is generally added to a network primarily for its translation ability. See also IP address; Internet Protocol router.

Gateway Service for NetWare A service that creates a gateway in which Microsoft clients can access NetWare core protocol networks, such as NetWare file and print services, through a Windows 2000 server.

Gigabit Ethernet The Ethernet standard that transmits data at 1billion bits per second or more.

global group For Windows 2000 Server, a group that can be used in its own domain, in member servers and in workstations of the domain, and in trusting domains. In all those places a global group can be granted rights and permissions and can become a member of local groups. However, a global group can contain user accounts only from its own domain. See also group; local group.

graphical user interface (GUI) A display format, like that of Windows, that represents a program's functions with graphic images such as buttons and icons. GUIs allow a user to perform operations and make choices by pointing and clicking with a mouse.

group A collection of users, computers, contacts, and other groups. Groups can be used as security or as e-mail distribution collections. Distribution groups are used only for e-mail. Security groups are used both to grant access to resources and as e-mail distribution lists. In a server cluster, a group is a collection of resources, and the basic unit of failover. See also domain local group; global group; native mode; universal group.

group account A collection of user accounts. By making a user account a member of a group, the user obtains all the rights and permissions granted to the group. See also user account.

group address An IP multicast address in the Class D range of 224.0.0.0 to 239.255.255.255 as defined by setting the first four high order bits of the IP address to 1110.

Group Policy An administrator's tool for defining and controlling how programs, network resources, and the operating system operate for users and computers in an organization. In an Active Directory environment, Group Policy is applied to users or computers on the basis of their membership in sites, domains, or organizational units.

guest account A built-in account used to log on to a computer running Windows 2000 when a user does not have an account on the computer or domain or in any of the domains trusted by the computer's domain.

H

h-node A NetBIOS implementation that uses a hybrid of b-node and p-node to register and resolve NetBIOS names to IP addresses. An h-node computer uses a server query first and reverts to broadcasts only if direct queries fail. Windows 2000-based computers are h-node by default.

half-duplex A system capable of transmitting information in only one direction at a time over a communications channel. See also duplex; full-duplex.

Hardware Compatibility List (HCL)
A list of the devices supported by Windows 2000, available from the Microsoft Web site.

hardware failure A malfunction of a physical component, such as a disk head failure or memory error.

hardware router A router that performs routing as a dedicated function and has specific hardware designed and optimized for routing.

hash See message digest.

hash message authentication code (HMAC)
An Internet Protocol security function providing a way to verify that information received is exactly the same as the information that was sent.

hashing algorithm See message digest.

header error check (HEC) The fifth byte in the ATM cell header used to detect and correct errors in the ATM header.

hexadecimal   A base-16 number system whose numbers are represented by the digits 0 through 9 and the letters A (equivalent to decimal 10) through F (equivalent to decimal 15).

hierarchical routing infrastructure

A routing infrastructure where groups of network IDs can be represented as a single routing table entry through route summarization. The network IDs in a hierarchical internetwork have a network/subnet/sub-subnet structure.

hop count   The value in the Transport Control field that indicates the number of IPX routers that have processed the IPX packet.

host   A Windows 2000 computer that runs a server program or service used by network or remote clients. For Network Load Balancing, a cluster consists of multiple hosts connected over a local area network.

host address   See host ID.

host group   The set of hosts listening for IP multicast traffic sent to a specific multicast group address.

host ID   A number used to identify an interface on a physical network bounded by routers. The host ID should be unique to the network.

host name   The name of a computer on a network. In the Windows 2000 Server Resource Kit, host name is used to refer to the first label of a fully qualified domain name. See also hosts file.

host priority   For Network Load Balancing, a host's precedence for handling default network traffic for TCP and UDP ports. It is used if a host within the cluster goes offline, and determines which host within the cluster will assume responsibility for the traffic previously handled by the offline host. See also User Datagram Protocol (UDP).

host route   A route to a specific internetwork address (network ID and host ID). Instead of making a routing decision based on just the network ID, the routing decision is based on the combination of network ID and host ID. Host routes allow intelligent routing decisions to be made for each internetwork address. Host routes are typically used to create custom routes to control or optimize specific types of internetwork traffic. For IP routing tables, a host route has a netmask of 255.255.255.255.

Hosts file   A local text file in the same format as the 4.3 Berkeley Software Distribution (BSD) UNIX/etc/hosts file. This file maps host names to IP addresses. In Windows 2000, this file is stored in the \%SystemRoot%\System32\Drivers\Etc folder. See also systemroot.

hub   A network-enabled device joining communication lines at a central location, providing a common connection to all devices on the network.

Hypertext Transfer Protocol (HTTP)

The protocol used to transfer information on the World Wide Web. An HTTP address (one kind of Uniform Resource Locator [URL]) takes the form: http://www.microsoft.com

I

idempotent   An initialization subroutine that completes an action only once, even if the routine is called more than once.

impersonation   A circumstance that occurs when Windows NT or Windows 2000 allows one process to take on the security attributes of another.

impersonation token   An access token that has been created to capture the security information of a client process, allowing a service to "impersonate" the client process in security operations. See also access token; primary token.

independent software vendors (ISVs)
A third-party software developer; an individual or an organization that independently creates computer software.

indirect delivery   The delivery of an IP packet by an IP node to an intermediate router.

inode   A UNIX system data structure that contains unique identifying information about a file.

input filter   A filter that defines the incoming traffic on a given interface that is allowed to be routed or processed by the router.

integrated local management interface (ILMI)
A set of functions used to exchange configuration data in an ATM network. The ATM Call Manager in Windows ATM Services uses ILMI for many tasks, such as exchanging ATM addresses. By default, the ATM Call Manager uses ILMI on all ATM network adapters.

Integrated Services Digital Network (ISDN)
A type of phone line used to enhance WAN speeds. ISDN lines can transmit at speeds of 64 or 128 kilobits per second, as opposed to standard phone lines, which typically transmit at 28.8 kilobits per second. An ISDN line must be installed by the phone company at both the server site and the remote site. See also wide area network (WAN).

integrity   An Internet Protocol security property that protects data from unauthorized modification in transit, ensuring that the data received is exactly the same as the data sent. Hash functions sign each packet with a cryptographic checksum, which the receiving computer checks before opening the packet. If the packet-and therefore signature-has changed, the packet is discarded.

interface   In networking, a logical device over which packets can be sent and received. In the Routing and Remote Access administrative tool, it is a visual representation of the network segment that can be reached over the LAN or WAN adapters. Each interface has a unique name. See also network adapter; local area network (LAN); routing; wide area network (WAN).

Interior Gateway Routing Protocol (IGRP)
A distance vector IP routing protocol developed by Cisco Systems, Inc.

intermediate system   A network device with the ability to forward packets between portions of a network. Bridges, switches, and routers are examples of intermediate systems.

internal network number   A 4-byte hexadecimal number used for addressing and routing purposes. The internal network number identifies a virtual network inside a computer. The internal network number must be unique to the IPX internetwork. Internal network number is also called virtual network number. See also external network number; Internetwork Packet Exchange (IPX).

Internet   A worldwide public TCP/IP internetwork consisting of thousands of networks, connecting research facilities, universities, libraries, and private companies.

internet Two or more network segments connected by routers. Another term for internetwork. With Services for Macintosh, an internet can be created by connecting two or more AppleTalk networks to a computer running Windows 2000 Server. With TCP/IP, an internet can be created by connecting two or more IP networks to a multihomed computer running either Windows 2000 Server or Windows 2000 Professional. IP forwarding must be enabled to route between attached IP network segments.

Internet address class The original Internet design of dividing the IP address space into defined classes to accommodate different sizes of networks. Address classes are no longer used on the modern Internet. See Class A IP address, Class B IP address, and Class C IP address.

Internet Assigned Numbers Authority (IANA)
An organization that delegates IP addresses and their allocation to organizations such as the InterNIC.

Internet Control Message Protocol (ICMP)
A required maintenance protocol in the TCP/IP suite that reports errors and allows simple connectivity. ICMP is used by the Ping tool to perform TCP/IP troubleshooting.

Internet Engineering Task Force (IETF)
An open community of network designers, operators, vendors, and researchers concerned with the evolution of Internet architecture and the smooth operation of the Internet. Technical work is performed by working groups organized by topic areas (such as routing, transport, and security) and through mailing lists. Internet standards are developed in IETF Requests for Comments (RFCs), which are a series of notes that discuss many aspects of computing and computer communication, focusing on networking protocols, programs, and concepts.

Internet Group Management Protocol (IGMP)
A protocol in the TCP/IP protocol suite that is responsible for the management of IP multicast group membership.

Internet Information Services (IIS)
Software services that support Web site creation, configuration, and management, along with other Internet functions. Internet Information Services include Network News Transfer Protocol (NNTP), File Transfer Protocol (FTP), and Simple Mail Transfer Protocol (SMTP). See also File Transfer Protocol (FTP); Simple Mail Transfer Protocol (SMTP).

Internet Multicast Backbone The portion of the Internet that supports multicast routing and forwarding of Internet-based IP multicast traffic. The MBone structure consists of a series of multicast-enabled islands, collections of contiguous networks, connected together using tunnels. Multicast traffic is passed from one island to another by tunneling - encapsulating the IP multicast packet with an additional IP header addressed from one router in a multicast island to another router in another multicast island.

Internet Protocol (IP) A routable protocol in the TCP/IP protocol suite that is responsible for IP addressing, routing, and the fragmentation and reassembly of IP packets.

Internet Protocol Control Protocol (IPCP)
The Network Control Protocol for IP-based PPP connections. IPCP negotiates IP-based parameters to dynamically configure a TCP/IP-based PPP peer across a point-to-point link. IPCP is documented in RFCs 1332 and 1877.

Internet Protocol router A system connected to multiple physical TCP/IP networks that can route or deliver IP packets between the networks. See also packet; router; routing; Transmission Control Protocol/Internet Protocol.

Internet Protocol security (IPSec)
A set of industry-standard, cryptography-based protection services and protocols. IPSec protects all protocols in the TCP/IP protocol suite and Internet communications using L2TP. See also Layer 2 Tunneling Protocol (L2TP).

internet router A device that connects networks and directs network information to other networks, usually choosing the most efficient route through other routers. See also router.

Internet service provider (ISP) A company that provides individuals or companies access to the Internet and the World Wide Web. An ISP provides a telephone number, a user name, a password and other connection information so users can connect their computers to the ISP's computers. An ISP typically charges a monthly and/or hourly connection fee.

internetwork At least two network segments connected using routers.

internetwork address The combination of the network ID and the host ID that uniquely identifies a host on an internetwork. An example is an IP address, which contains a network ID and a host ID.

Internetwork Packet Exchange (IPX)
A network protocol native to NetWare that controls addressing and routing of packets within and between LANs. IPX does not guarantee that a message will be complete (no lost packets). See also Internetwork Packet Exchange/Sequenced Packet Exchange (IPX/SPX).

Internetwork Packet Exchange Control Protocol (IPXCP)
The Network Control Protocol for IPX-based PPP connections. IPXCP negotiates IPX-based parameters to dynamically configure an IPX-based PPP peer across a point-to-point link. IPXCP is documented in RFC 1552.

Internetwork Packet Exchange/Sequenced Packet Exchange (IPX/SPX)
Transport protocols used in Novell NetWare and other networks.

internetwork-level broadcasts Broadcast packets with a special destination internetwork address that informs the router that the packet is to be forwarded to all other network segments except the network segment on which it was received.

intranet A network within an organization that uses Internet technologies and protocols, but is available only to certain people, such as employees of a company. An intranet is also called a private network.

IP address A 32-bit address used to identify a node on an IP internetwork. Each node on the IP internetwork must be assigned a unique IP address, which is made up of the network ID, plus a unique host ID. This address is typically represented with the decimal value of each octet separated by a period (for example, 192.168.7.27). In Windows 2000, the IP address can be configured manually or dynamically through DHCP. See also Dynamic Host Configuration Protocol (DHCP); node.

IP multicast group See host group.

IP source routing The practice of specifying the list of router interfaces corresponding to the path through an IP internetwork that a packet must travel. IP source routing is used in network testing and debugging situations.

IP-in-IP interface A logical interface that sends IP packets in IP-in-IP tunneled mode.

IP-in-IP tunnels A tunneling technology used to forward information between endpoints that are acting as a bridge between portions of an IP internetwork that have differing capabilities. A typical use for IP-in-IP tunnels is the forwarding of IP multicast traffic from one area of the intranet to another area of the intranet, across a portion of the intranet that does not support multicast forwarding or routing.

IPX packet filtering Filtering that provides a way to precisely define the type of IPX traffic allowed to cross a router.

ISDN See Integrated Services Digital Network.

J

join latency The time it takes for the first member of an IP multicast host group on a subnet to begin receiving group traffic.

K

Kerberos authentication protocol
An authentication mechanism used to verify user or host identity. The Kerberos v5 protocol is the default authentication service for Windows 2000. Internet Protocol security and the QoS Admission Control Service use the Kerberos protocol for authentication. See also Internet Protocol security (IPSec); QoS Admission Control Service.

kernel The core of layered architecture that manages the most basic operations of the operating system and the computer's processor for Windows NT and Windows 2000. The kernel schedules different blocks of executing code, called threads, for the processor to keep it as busy as possible and coordinates multiple processors to optimize performance.

The kernel also synchronizes activities among Executive-level subcomponents, such as I/O Manager and Process Manager, and handles hardware exceptions and other hardware-dependent functions. The kernel works closely with the hardware abstraction layer.

kernel mode A highly privileged mode of operation where program code has direct access to all memory, including the address spaces of all user-mode processes and applications, and to hardware. Kernel mode is also known as supervisor mode, protected mode, or Ring 0.

key A secret code or number required to read, modify, or verify secured data. Keys are used in conjunction with algorithms to secure data. Windows 2000 automatically handles key generation. For the registry, a key is an entry in the registry that can contain both subkeys and entries. In the registry structure, keys are analogous to folders, and entries are analogous to files. In the Registry Editor window, a key appears as a file folder in the left pane. In an answer file, keys are character strings that specify parameters from which Setup obtains the needed data for unattended installation of the operating system.

Key Distribution Center (KDC) A network service that supplies session tickets and temporary session keys used in the Kerberos authentication protocol. In Windows 2000, the KDC runs as a privileged process on all domain controllers. The KDC uses Active Directory to manage sensitive account information such as passwords for user accounts. See also Kerberos authentication protocol; session ticket.

key exchange Confidential exchange of secret keys online, which is commonly done with public key cryptography. See also public key cryptography.

key management Secure management of private keys for public key cryptography. Windows 2000 manages private keys and keeps them confidential with CryptoAPI and CSPs. See also private key; CryptoAPI; cryptographic service provider.

key search attack An attack to find a secret password or a symmetric encryption key by trying all possible passwords or keys until the correct password or key is discovered. Also called a brute force attack.

kilobits per second (Kbps) Data transfer speed, as on a network, measured in multiples of 1,024 bits per second.

Korn shell (ksh) A command shell which provides the following functionality:

file input and output redirection
command line editing using vi
command history
integer arithmetic
pattern matching and variable substitution
command name abbreviation (aliasing)
built-in commands for writing shell programs

L

L2TP client A tunnel client using the L2TP tunneling protocol and IPSec.

L2TP server A tunnel server using the L2TP tunneling protocol and IPSec.

LAN emulation (LANE) A set of protocols that allow existing Ethernet and Token Ring LAN services to overlay an ATM network. LANE allows connectivity among LAN- and ATM-attached stations. See also Asynchronous Transfer Mode (ATM).

LAN emulation client (LEC) The client on an emulated local area network (ELAN) that performs data forwarding, address resolution, and other control functions. The LEC resides on end stations in an emulated local area network (ELAN). See also Asynchronous Transfer Mode (ATM); emulated local area network (ELAN); LAN emulation.

LAN emulation configuration server (LECS)
The service that assigns individual LANE clients to particular emulated local area networks (ELANs) by directing them to the LAN emulation service (LES). See also emulated local area network (ELAN); LAN emulation; LAN emulation server.

LAN emulation server (LES) The central control point for an emulated local area network (ELAN). Enables LANE clients to join the emulated local area network (ELAN) and resolves LAN addresses to ATM addresses. See also Asynchronous Transfer Mode (ATM); emulated local area network (ELAN); LAN emulation (LANE).

latency See replication latency.

Layer 2 Tunneling Protocol (L2TP)
A tunneling protocol that encapsulates PPP frames to be sent over IP, X.25, Frame Relay, or ATM networks. L2TP is a combination of the Point-to-Point Tunneling Protocol (PPTP) and Layer 2 Forwarding (L2F), a technology proposed by Cisco Systems, Inc.

leave latency The time between when the last host on a subnet has left an IP multicast host group and when no more multicast traffic for that group is forwarded to the subnet.

Lightweight Directory Access Protocol (LDAP)

A directory service protocol that runs directly over TCP/IP and the primary access protocol for Active Directory. LDAP version 3 is defined by a set of Proposed Standard documents in Internet Engineering Task Force (IETF) RFC 2251. See also Lightweight Directory Access Protocol application programming interface (LDAP API).

Lightweight Directory Access Protocol application programming interface (LDAP API)

A set of low-level C-language APIs to the LDAP protocol.

limited broadcast address

The broadcast address of 255.255.255.255.

line kill

In UNIX, an assigned key that deletes the entire current line.

Link Control Protocol (LCP)

A PPP control protocol that negotiates link and PPP parameters to dynamically configure the data-link layer of a PPP connection.

Link State Advertisements (LSAs)

A advertisement of an OSPF router that contains its attached networks and their configured costs.

link state database (LSDB)

A map of an area maintained by OSPF routers. It is updated after any change in the network topology. The link state database is used to compute IP routes, which must be computed again after any change in the topology. See also Open Shortest Path First (OSPF).

link station

Hardware and software components within a node that represent a connection to an adjacent node over a specific link.

listening mode

The way that the network adapter analyzes the destination media access control address of incoming frames in order to decide to process them further.

local area network (LAN)

A communications network connecting a group of computers, printers, and other devices located within a relatively limited area (for example, a building). A LAN allows any connected device to interact with any other on the network. See also wide area network (WAN).

local computer

A computer that can be accessed directly without using a communications line or a communications device, such as a network adapter or a modem. Similarly, running a local program means running the program on your computer, as opposed to running it from a server.

local group

For computers running Windows 2000 Professional and member servers, a group that is granted permissions and rights from its own computer to only those resources on its own computer on which the group resides. See also global group.

locally administered address (LAA)

Internal network address on a network adapter that is specifically written to accommodate an organization's adapter naming standard.

LocalTalk

The Apple networking hardware built into every Macintosh computer. LocalTalk includes the cables and connector boxes to connect components and network devices that are part of the AppleTalk network system. LocalTalk was formerly known as the AppleTalk Personal Network.

lock

To make a file inaccessible. When more than one user can manipulate a file, that file is locked when a user accesses it in order to prevent more than one user from modifying the file simultaneously.

log file A file that stores messages generated by an application, service, or operating system. These messages are used to track the operations performed. For example, Web servers maintain log files listing every request made to the server. Log files are usually ASCII files and often have a .log extension. In Backup, a file that contains a record of the date the tapes were created and the names of files and directories successfully backed up and restored. The Performance Logs and Alerts service also creates log files.

log on To begin using a network by providing a user name and password that identifies a user to the network.

logical IP subnet (LIS) A group of IP hosts/members belonging to the same IP subnet and whose host ATMARP server ATM address is the same.

logical link control (LLC) A protocol standard developed by the IEEE 802 committee, which governs the exchange of transmission frames between data stations independently of how the transmission medium is shared on the local area network.

logical unit (LU) An IBM Systems Network Architecture protocol that allows end users to communicate with each other and gain access to IBM network resources.

long name A folder name or file name longer than the 8.3 file name standard (up to eight characters followed by a period and an extension of up to three characters) of the FAT file system. Windows 2000 supports long file names up to the file-name limit of 255 characters. Macintosh users can assign long names to files and folders on the server and, using Services for Macintosh, long names to Macintosh-accessible volumes can be assigned when created. Windows 2000 automatically translates long names of files and folders to 8.3 names for MS DOS and Windows 3.x users. See also name mapping.

M

Macintosh-accessible volume Storage space on the server used for folders and files of Macintosh users. A Macintosh-accessible volume is equivalent to a shared folder for personal computer users. Each Macintosh-accessible volume on a computer running Windows 2000 Server will correspond to a folder. Both personal computer users and Macintosh users can be given access to files located in a folder that is designated as both a shared folder and a Macintosh-accessible volume.

Macintosh-style permissions Folder and volume permissions that are similar to the access privileges used on a Macintosh.

Management Information Base (MIB)
A collection of formally described objects, each of which represents a particular type of information, that can be accessed and managed by the Simple Network Management Protocol (SNMP) through a network management system.

maximum receive unit (MRU)   The maximum size of a PPP frame. The MRU is determined during the negotiation of the logical link.

media access control   A layer in the network architecture of Windows NT and Windows 2000 that deals with network access and collision detection.

member server   A computer that runs Windows 2000 Server but is not a domain controller of a Windows 2000 domain. Member servers participate in a domain, but do not store a copy of the directory database.

message digest   A fixed-size result obtained by applying a one-way mathematical function called a message digest function (sometimes called a "hash function" or "hash algorithm") to an arbitrary amount of data. Given a change in the input data, the resulting value of the message digest will change. Message digest is also called a hash.

metacharacter   A character that is assigned a special meaning that is recognized by the shell.

metric   A number used to indicate the cost of a route in the IP routing table to enable the selection of the best route among possible multiple routes to the same destination.

Microsoft Challenge Handshake Authentication Protocol version 1 (MS-CHAP v1)
An encrypted authentication mechanism for PPP connections similar to CHAP. The remote access server sends a challenge to the remote access client that consists of a session ID and an arbitrary challenge string. The remote access client must return the user name and a Message Digest 4 (MD4) hash of the challenge string, the session ID, and the MD4-hashed password.

Microsoft Challenge Handshake Authentication Protocol version 2 (MS-CHAP v2)
An encrypted authentication mechanism for PPP connections that provides stronger security than CHAP and MS-CHAP v1. MS-CHAP v2 provides mutual authentication and asymmetric encryption keys.

Microsoft Management Console (MMC)
A framework for hosting administrative consoles. A console is defined by the items on its console tree, which might include folders or other containers, World Wide Web pages, and other administrative items. A console has one or more windows that can provide views of the console tree and the administrative properties, services, and events that are acted on by the items in the console tree. The main MMC window provides commands and tools for authoring consoles. The authoring features of MMC and the console tree might be hidden when a console is in User Mode. See also console tree.

miniport drivers   A driver that is connected to an intermediate driver and a hardware device.

mixed mode   The default mode setting for domains on Windows 2000 domain controllers. Mixed mode allows Windows 2000 domain controllers and Windows NT backup domain controllers to co-exist in a domain. Mixed mode does not support the universal and nested group enhancements of Windows 2000. You can change the domain mode setting to Windows 2000 native mode after all Windows NT domain controllers are either removed from the domain or upgraded to Windows 2000. See also native mode.

multicast   Network traffic destined for a set of hosts that belong to a multicast group. See also multicast group.

multicast address dynamic client allocation protocol (MADCAP)
An extension to the DHCP protocol standard used to support dynamic assignment and configuration of IP multicast addresses on TCP/IP-based networks.

multicast address resolution service (MARS)
A service for resolving multicast IP addresses to the ATM addresses of the clients that have joined that multicast group. The MARS can work in conjunction with the multicast server MCS and clients to distribute multicast data through point-to-multipoint connections.

multicast DHCP (MDHCP) An extension to the DHCP protocol standard that supports dynamic assignment and configuration of IP multicast addresses on TCP/IP-based networks.

multicast forwarding table The table used by IP to forward IP multicast traffic. An entry in the IP multicast forwarding table consists of the multicast group address, the source IP address, a list of interfaces to which the traffic is forwarded (next hop interfaces), and the single interface on which the traffic must be received in order to be forwarded (the previous hop interface).

multicast group A group of member TCP/IP hosts configured to listen and receive datagrams sent to a specified destination IP address. The destination address for the group is a shared IP address in the Class D address range (224.0.0.0 to 2239.255.255.255). See also datagram.

multicast heartbeat The ability of the Windows 2000 router to listen for a regular multicast notification to a specified group address.

multicast promiscuous mode A listening mode that passes up for processing all frames that have the IEEE-defined multicast bit set to 1.

multicast routing protocol Protocols such as Distance Vector Multicast Routing Protocol (DVMRP), Multicast Open Shortest Path First (MOSPF), or Protocol Independent Multicast (PIM) used to exchange IP multicast host membership information. Group membership is either communicated explicitly, by exchanging [group address, subnet] information, or implicitly, by informing upstream routers that there either are or are not group members in the downstream direction from the source of the multicast traffic.

multicast scope A range of IP multicast addresses in the range of 239.0.0.0 to 239.254.255.255. Multicast addresses in this range can be prevented from propagating in either direction (send or receive) through the use of scope-based multicast boundaries.

multicast static route A static route used to determine the previous hop interface for IP multicast forwarding table entries and the previous hop neighbor used for multicast diagnostic utilities such as mtrace.

multihomed A computer that has multiple network adapters installed.

multilink protocol (MP) An extension to PPP that is used to aggregate multiple physical links into a single logical link. MP is defined in RFC 1990.

multimaster replication A replication model in which any domain controller accepts and replicates directory changes to any other domain controller. This differs from other replication models in which one computer stores the single modifiable copy of the directory and other computers store backup copies. See also domain controller; replication.

multipath routing infrastructure A routing infrastructure where multiple paths exist between network segments in the internetwork.

mutual authentication The process when the calling router authenticates itself to the answering router and the answering router authenticates itself to the calling router. Both ends of the connection verify the identity of the other end of the connection. MS-CHAP v2 and EAP-TLS authentication methods provide mutual authentication.

N

name management Registering, querying, and releasing NetBIOS names.

name mapping A Windows 2000 feature that enables file system access by MS DOS and Windows 3.x users to NTFS and FAT volumes, and enables user account assignments for Kerberos users from non-Windows 2000 Kerberos realms or for external (non-enterprise) users with X.509 certificates. For file system access, Windows 2000 allows share names of up to 255 characters, as opposed to MS DOS and Windows 3.x, which are restricted to eight characters followed by a period and an extension of up to three characters. Each file or folder with a name that does not conform to the MS DOS 8.3 standard is automatically given a second name that does. MS DOS and Windows 3.x users connecting to the file or directory over the network see the name in the 8.3 format; Windows 2000 users see the long name.

name query A query broadcast to a local network or to a NetBIOS name server in order to resolve the IP address when one NetBIOS application wants to communicate with another NetBIOS application.

name registration The process of registering a computer name with a name server, such as a DHCP or WINS server, when a client computer joins a computer network. This process of name registration creates a database entry that other network services use to locate that computer.

name resolution The process of having software translate between names that are easy for users to work with, and numerical IP addresses, which are difficult for users but necessary for TCP/IP communications. Name resolution can be provided by software components such as the Domain Name System (DNS) or the Windows Internet Name Service (WINS). In directory service, the phase of LDAP directory operation processing that involves finding a domain controller that holds the target entry for the operation. See also Domain Name System (DNS); Transmission Control Protocol/Internet Protocol (TCP/IP); Windows Internet Name Service (WINS).

name resolution service A service required by TCP/IP internetworks to convert computer names to IP addresses and IP addresses to computer names. (People use "friendly" names to connect to computers; programs use IP addresses.) See also internetwork; IP address; Transmission Control Protocol/Internet Protocol (TCP/IP).

name server In the DNS client/server model, a server authoritative for a portion of the DNS database. The server makes computer names and other information available to client resolvers that are querying for name resolution across the Internet or an intranet. See also Domain Name System (DNS).

Named Pipe A portion of memory that can be used by one process to pass information to another process, so that the output of one process is the input of the other process. The second process can be local (on the same computer as the first) or remote (on a networked computer).

namespace A set of unique names for resources or items used in a shared computing environment. The names in a namespace can be resolved to the objects they represent. For Microsoft Management Console (MMC), the namespace is represented by the console tree, which displays all of the snap-ins and resources that are accessible to a console. For Domain Name System (DNS), namespace is the vertical or hierarchical structure of the domain name tree. For example, each domain label, such as "host1" or "example," used in a fully qualified domain name, such as "host1.example.microsoft.com," indicates a branch in the domain namespace tree. For Active Directory, namespace corresponds to the DNS namespace in structure, but resolves Active Directory object names.

naming service A service, such as that provided by WINS or DNS, that allows friendly names to be resolved to an address or other specially defined resource data that is used to locate network resources of various types and purposes.

NAT editor A component of a network address translator that performs additional translation and payload adjustment beyond the IP, TCP, and UDP headers. A NAT editor is an installable component that can properly modify otherwise non-translatable payloads so that they can be forwarded across a NAT.

native mode The condition in which all domain controllers within a domain are Windows 2000 domain controllers and an administrator has enabled native mode operation (through Active Directory Users and Computers). See also mixed mode.

nested groups A Windows 2000 capability available only in native mode that allows the creation of groups within groups. See also domain local group; forest; global group; universal group.

NetBIOS Enhanced User Interface (NetBEUI)
A network protocol native to Microsoft Networking, that is usually used in local area networks of one to 200 clients. NetBEUI uses Token Ring source routing as its only method of routing. It is the Microsoft implementation of the NetBIOS standard.

NetBIOS Frames Control Protocol (NBFCP)
The Network Control Protocol for NetBEUI-based PPP connections. NBFCP negotiates NetBEUI-based parameters to dynamically configure a NetBEUI-based PPP connection across a point-to-point link. NBFCP is documented in RFC 2097.

NetBIOS name A name recognized by WINS, which maps the name to an IP address.

NetBIOS name query A packet sent to either a NetBIOS name server, such as a WINS server, or as a broadcast to resolve the IP address of a NetBIOS name.

NetBIOS name server A computer that resolves NetBIOS names to IP addresses. A WINS server is a NetBIOS name server.

NetBIOS Node Type A designation of the exact mechanisms by which NetBIOS names are resolved to IP addresses.

NetBIOS over TCP/IP (NetBT) A feature that provides the NetBIOS programming interface over the TCP/IP protocol. It is used for monitoring routed servers that use NetBIOS name resolution.

netsh A command-line and scripting utility for Windows 2000 networking components for local or shared computers.

NetWare Novell's network operating system.

NetWare Core Protocol (NCP) The file-sharing protocol that governs communications about resource (such as disk and printer), bindery, and NDS operations between server and client computers on a Novell NetWare network. Requests from client computers are transmitted by the IPX protocol. Servers respond according to NCP guidelines. See also bindery; Internetwork Packet Exchange (IPX); Novell Directory Services (NDS).

NetWare Link Services Protocol (NLSP)
A link state routing protocol developed by Novell and used on IPX internetworks.

network access server (NAS) The device that accepts PPP connections and places clients on the network that the NAS serves. NAS is also called Terminal server.

network adapter A software or hardware plug-in board that connects a node or host to a local area network. If the node is a member of a server cluster, the network adapter is a server cluster object (the network interface object).

network address See network ID.

network address translation (NAT)
A protocol that allows a network with private addresses to access information on the Internet through an IP translation process. With NAT, you can configure your home network or small office network to share a single connection to the Internet.

network address translator An IP router defined in RFC 1631 that can translate IP addresses and TCP/UDP port numbers of packets as they are being forwarded.

network basic input/output system (NetBIOS)
An application programming interface (API) that can be used by applications on a local area network or computers running MS DOS, OS/2, or some version of UNIX. NetBIOS provides a uniform set of commands for requesting lower level network services.

network bridge A device that connects networks by using the same communications protocols so that information can be passed from one to the other. Also, a device that connects two local area networks, whether or not they use the same protocols. A bridge operates at the ISO/OSI data-link layer.

Network Control Protocol (NCP) A protocol within the PPP protocol suite that negotiates the parameters of an individual LAN protocol such as TCP/IP or IPX.

Network Device Interface Specification (NDIS)
A software component that provides Windows 2000 network protocols a common interface for connection to network adapters. NDIS allows more than one transport protocol to be bound and operate simultaneously over a single network adapter card.

network file system (NFS) A service for distributed computing systems that provides a distributed file system, eliminating the need for keeping multiple copies of files on separate computers.

network ID A number used to identify the systems that are located on the same physical network bounded by routers. The network ID should be unique to the internetwork.

network layer A layer that addresses messages and translates logical addresses and names into physical addresses. It also determines the route from the source to the destination computer and manages traffic problems, such as switching, routing, and controlling the congestion of data packets.

network media The type of physical wiring and lower-layer protocols used for transmitting and receiving frames. For example, Ethernet, FDDI, and Token Ring.

Network Monitor A packet capture and analysis tool used to view network traffic. This feature is included with Windows 2000 Server; however, Systems Management Server has a more complete version.

network name In server clusters, the name through which clients access server cluster resources. A network name is similar to a computer name, and when combined in a resource group with an IP address and the applications clients access, presents a virtual server to clients.

network number In the Macintosh environment, the routing address or range of addresses assigned to the physical network that Phase 2 AppleTalk routers use to route information to the appropriate network. Network number is also called network range and cable range. See also routing.

network prefix The number of bits in the IP network ID starting from the high order bit. The network prefix is another way of expressing a subnet mask.

network range See network number.

network route A route to a specific network ID in an internetwork.

NFS See network file system.

node In tree structures, a location on the tree that can have links to one or more items below it. In local area networks (LANs), a device that is connected to the network and is capable of communicating with other network devices. In a server cluster, a server that has Cluster service software installed and is a member of a cluster. See also local area network (LAN).

nonce A randomly generated value used to defeat replay attacks. See also replay attack.

noncontainer object An object that cannot logically contain other objects. A file is a noncontainer object. See also container object; object.

nonrepudiation A basic security function of cryptography. Nonrepudiation provides assurance that a party in a communication cannot falsely deny that a part of the communication occurred. Without nonrepudiation, someone can communicate and then later deny the communication or claim that the communication occurred at a different time. See also cryptography; authentication; confidentiality; integrity.

Novell Directory Services (NDS) On networks running Novell NetWare 4.x and NetWare 5.x, a distributed database that maintains information about every resource on the network and provides access to these resources.

NVRunCmd service A service that allows commands issued from a host system NetView console to be carried out on the computer running Windows 2000 and SNA Server. The NVRunCmd service also returns the command results to the host NetView console in standard character or number formats.

NWLink An implementation of the Internetwork Packet Exchange (IPX), Sequenced Packet Exchange (SPX), and NetBIOS protocols used in Novell networks. NWLink is a standard network protocol that supports routing and can support NetWare client/server applications, where NetWare-aware Sockets-based applications communicate with IPX/SPX Sockets-based applications. See also Internetwork Packet Exchange (IPX); network basic input/output system (NetBIOS).

O

object An entity, such as a file, folder, shared folder, printer, or Active Directory object, described by a distinct, named set of attributes. For example, the attributes of a File object include its name, location, and size; the attributes of an Active Directory User object might include the user's first name, last name, and e-mail address. For OLE and ActiveX objects, an object can also be any piece of information that can be linked to, or embedded into, another object. See also attribute; container object; noncontainer object; parent object; child object.

object linking and embedding (OLE)
A method for sharing information among applications. Linking an object, such as a graphic, from one document to another inserts a reference to the object into the second document. Any changes you make in the object in the first document will also be made in the second document. Embedding an object inserts a copy of an object from one document into another document. Changes you make in the object in the first document will not be updated in the second unless the embedded object is explicitly updated. See also ActiveX.

octet In programming, an octet refers to eight bits or one byte. IP addresses, for example, are typically represented in dotted-decimal notation; that is, with the decimal value of each octet of the address separated by a period. See also IP address.

off-subnet addressing The allocation of IP addresses from remote access servers to remote access clients that are not in a range defined by a subnet to which the remote access server is attached.

OLE See object linking and embedding.

on-demand connection A demand-dial connection made over dial-up links when the cost of using the communications link is time-sensitive. For example, long distance analog phone calls are charged on a per-minute basis. With on-demand connections, the connection is made when traffic is forwarded, and the connection is terminated after a configured amount of idle time.

on-demand router-to-router VPN connection
A router-to-router VPN connection that is made by a calling router who has a dial-up connection to the Internet.

on-subnet addressing The allocation of IP addresses from a remote access server to remote access clients that are in a range defined by a subnet to which the remote access server is attached.

open database connectivity (ODBC)
An application programming interface (API) that enables database applications to access data from a variety of existing data sources.

Open Shortest Path First (OSPF) A routing protocol used in medium-sized and large-sized networks. This protocol is more complex than RIP, but allows better control and is more efficient in propagating routing information.

OSPF See Open Shortest Path First.

output filters Filters which define the traffic that is allowed to be sent from that interface.

owner In Windows 2000, the person who controls how permissions are set on objects and can grant permissions to others. In the Macintosh environment, an owner is the user responsible for setting permissions for a folder on a server. A Macintosh user who creates a folder on the server automatically becomes the owner of the folder. The owner can transfer ownership to someone else. Each Macintosh-accessible volume on the server also has an owner.

P

packet A transmission unit of fixed maximum size that consists of binary information. This information represents both data and a header containing an ID number, source and destination addresses, and error-control data.

packet filtering Prevents certain types of network packets from either being sent or received. This can be employed for security reasons (to prevent access from unauthorized users) or to improve performance by disallowing unnecessary packets from going over a slow connection. See also packet.

page-description language (PDL) A computer language that describes the arrangement of text and graphics on a printed page. See also printer control language (PCL); PostScript.

parent object The object in which another object resides. A parent object implies relation. For example, a folder is a parent object in which a file, or child object, resides. An object can also be both a parent and a child object. See also child object; object.

pass-through VPN connection A less common combined Internet and intranet virtual private network (VPN) connection.

password authentication protocol (PAP) A simple, plaintext authentication scheme for authenticating PPP connections. The user name and password are requested by the remote access server and returned by the remote access client in plaintext.

path A sequence of directory (or folder) names that specifies the location of a directory, file, or folder within the Windows directory tree. Each directory name and file name within the path must be preceded by a backslash (\). For example, to specify the path of a file named Readme.doc located in the Windows directory on drive C, type C:\Windows\Readme.doc.

performance counter In System Monitor, a data item associated with a performance object. For each counter selected, System Monitor presents a value corresponding to a particular aspect of the performance that is defined for the performance object. See also performance object.

performance object In System Monitor, a logical collection of counters that is associated with a resource or service that can be monitored. See also performance counter.

permanent virtual circuit (PVC) A virtual circuit assigned to a preconfigured static route.

persistent connection A connection that is always active. For instance, the WINS servers in Windows 2000 use persistent connections to constantly update their WINS databases.

persistent demand-dial connection
A demand-dial connection that uses a dial-up WAN technology when the cost of the link is fixed. A persistent demand-dial connection can be active 24 hours a day. Examples of WAN technologies for persistent demand-dial connections include local calls that use analog phone lines, leased analog lines, and flat-rate ISDN. If a persistent connection is lost, the calling router immediately attempts to reestablish the connection.

persistent route Routes that are not based on the TCP/IP configuration, that are automatically added to the IP routing table when the TCP/IP protocol is started. Routes added to the IP routing table using the route utility with the "-p" command line option are recorded.

persistent router-to-router VPN connection
A scenario in which both the calling and answering routers are permanently connected to the Internet.

physical layer A software layer that transmits bits from one computer to another and regulates the transmission of a stream of bits over a physical medium. This layer defines how the cable is attached to the network adapter and which transmission technique is used to send data over the cable.

physical media A storage object that data can be written to, such as a disk or magnetic tape. A physical medium is referenced by its physical media ID (PMID).

physical unit (PU) An IBM Systems Network Architecture component that monitors and manages the resources of a network node as requested by the systems services control point.

Ping A tool that verifies connections to one or more remote hosts. The ping command uses the ICMP echo request and echo reply packets to determine whether a particular IP system on a network is functional. Ping is useful for diagnosing IP network or router failures. See also Internet Control Message Protocol (ICMP).

ping of death A denial of service attack where malicious users send one or multiple 64-KB ICMP Echo Request messages. The 64-KB messages are fragmented and must be reassembled at the destination host. For each separate 64-KB message, the TCP/IP protocol must allocate memory, tables, timers, and other resources. With enough fragmented messages, a host can become bogged down so that the servicing of valid information requests is impaired.

PKI See public key infrastructure.

plaintext Data that is not encrypted. Sometimes also called clear text. See also ciphertext; encryption; decryption.

PMTU black hole router A router that silently discards IP datagrams that require fragmentation when the Don't Fragment (DF) flag in the IP header is set to 1.

point of presence (POP) The local access point for a network provider. Each POP provides a telephone number that allows users to make a local call for access to online services.

point-to-LAN remote access connectivity
In internetworking, when remote access clients are transparently connected to the network to which the remote access server is attached.

Point-to-Point Protocol (PPP) An industry standard suite of protocols for the use of point-to-point links to transport multiprotocol datagrams. PPP is documented in RFC 1661.

point-to-point remote access connectivity In internetworking, when remote access clients connect to remote access servers and are connected only to the remote access server.

Point-to-Point Tunneling Protocol (PPTP) A tunneling protocol that encapsulates Point-to-Point Protocol (PPP) frames into IP datagrams for transmission over an IP-based internetwork, such as the Internet or a private intranet.

poison reverse A process that, used with split horizon, improves RIP convergence over simple split horizon by advertising all network IDs. However, the network IDs learned in a given direction are advertised with a hop count of 16, indicating that the network is unavailable. See also split horizon.

port monitor A device that controls the computer port that provides connectivity to a local or remote print device.

port rule For Network Load Balancing, a set of configuration parameters that determine the filtering mode to be applied to a range of ports. See also filtering mode.

PostScript A page-description language (PDL) developed by Adobe Systems for printing with laser printers. PostScript offers flexible font capability and high-quality graphics. It is the standard for desktop publishing because it is supported by imagesetters, the high-resolution printers used by printing services for commercial typesetting. See also printer control language (PCL); page-description language (PDL).

PPP See Point-to-Point Protocol.

PPTP client See Point-to-Point Tunneling Protocol client.

PPTP server See Point-to-Point Tunneling Protocol server.

preferred server The NetWare bindery-based (NetWare 2.*x*, and 3.*x*) server to which you connect by default when you log on to your computer. The preferred server validates your user credentials and is queried when you request information about resources available on the NetWare network.

presentation layer A network layer that translates data from the application layer into an intermediary format. This layer also manages security issues by providing such services as data encryption, and compresses data so that fewer bits need to be transferred on the network.

primary domain controller A Windows NT 4.0 and 3.51 domain controller that is the first one created in the domain and contains the primary storehouse for domain data. Within the domain, the primary domain controller periodically replicates its data to the other domain controllers, known as backup domain controllers. See also backup domain controller.

primary server An authoritative DNS server for a zone that can be used as a point of update for the zone. Only primary masters have the ability to be updated directly to process zone updates, which include adding, removing, or modifying resource records that are stored as zone data. Primary masters are also used as the first sources for replicating the zone to other DNS servers.

primary token The access token assigned to a process to represent the default security information for that process. It is used in security operations by a thread working on behalf of the process itself rather than on behalf of a client. See also access token; impersonation token; process.

print server A computer that is dedicated to managing the printers on a network. The print server can be any computer on the network.

print sharing The ability for a computer running Windows 2000 Professional or Windows 2000 Server to share a printer on the network.

print spooler Software that accepts a document sent to a printer and then stores it on disk or in memory until the printer is ready for it. This collection of dynamic-link libraries (DLLs) receives, processes, schedules, and distributes documents for printing. The term spooler is an acronym created from "simultaneous print operations online." See also spooling.

printer control language (PCL) The page-description language (PDL) developed by Hewlett Packard for their laser and inkjet printers. Because of the widespread use of laser printers, this command language has become a standard in many printers. See also page-description language (PDL); PostScript.

printer driver A program designed to allow other programs to work with a particular printer without concerning themselves with the specifics of the printer's hardware and internal language. By using printer drivers that handle the subtleties of each printer, programs can communicate properly with a variety of printers. See also printer control language (PCL); PostScript.

private addresses IP addresses that are designed to be used by organizations for private intranet addressing within one of the following blocks of addresses: 10.0.0.0/8, 172.16.0.0/12, 192.168.0.0/16.

private key The secret half of a cryptographic key pair that is used with a public key algorithm. Private keys are typically used to digitally sign data and to decrypt data that has been encrypted with the corresponding public key. See also public key.

privileged mode Also known as kernel mode, the processing mode that allows code to have direct access to all hardware and memory in the system.

process An operating system object that consists of an executable program, a set of virtual memory addresses, and one or more threads. When a program runs, a Windows 2000 process is created. See also thread.

promiscuous mode A feature of the network adapter that supports the detection of all frames sent over the network segment.

protocol A set of rules and conventions by which two computers pass messages across a network. Networking software usually implements multiple levels of protocols layered one on top of another. Windows NT and Windows 2000 include NetBEUI, TCP/IP, and IPX/SPX-compatible protocols.

protocol number A field in the IP packet which identifies the next level higher in the protocol stack.

public addresses IP addresses assigned by the Internet Network Information Center (InterNIC) that are guaranteed to be globally unique and reachable on the Internet.

public key The non-secret half of a cryptographic key pair that is used with a public key algorithm. Public keys are typically used to verify digital signatures or decrypt data that has been encrypted with the corresponding private key. See also private key.

public key cryptography　A method of cryptography in which two different keys are used: a public key for encrypting data and a private key for decrypting data. Public key cryptography is also called asymmetric cryptography.

public key infrastructure (PKI)　The laws, policies, standards, and software that regulate or manipulate certificates and public and private keys. In practice, it is a system of digital certificates, certification authorities, and other registration authorities that verify and authenticate the validity of each party involved in an electronic transaction. Standards for PKI are still evolving, even though they are being widely implemented as a necessary element of electronic commerce.

Q

QoS Admission Control Service　A software service that controls bandwidth and network resources on the subnet to which it is assigned. Important applications can be given more bandwidth, less important applications less bandwidth. The QoS Admission Control Service can be installed on any network-enabled computer running Windows 2000.

quantization noise　The noise introduced on an analog dial-up connection due to an analog to digital conversion.

queue　A list of programs or tasks waiting for execution. In Windows 2000 printing terminology, a queue refers to a group of documents waiting to be printed. In NetWare and OS/2 environments, queues are the primary software interface between the application and print device; users submit documents to a queue. In Windows 2000, however, the printer is that interface; the document is sent to a printer, not a queue.

R

Record Level Input/Output (RLIO)
An IBM distributed database protocol that provides record level access to nonrelational data on IBM host operating systems, including MVS, OS/390, and OS/400.

redirector　See Windows 2000 Redirector.

registry　In Windows 2000, Windows NT, Windows 98, and Windows 95, a database of information about a computer's configuration. The registry is organized in a hierarchical structure and consists of subtrees and their keys, hives, and entries.

remote access policy　A set of conditions and connection parameters that define the characteristics of the incoming connection and the set of constraints imposed on it. Remote access policies determine whether a specific connection attempt is authorized to be accepted.

Remote Access Service (RAS)　A Window NT 4.0 service that provides remote networking for telecommuters, mobile workers, and system administrators who monitor and manage servers at multiple offices.

remote access VPN connection　A connection made by a remote access client, a single user, that connects to a private network. The VPN server provides access to the resources of the VPN server or to the entire network to which the VPN server is attached. The packets sent from the remote client across the VPN connection originate at the remote access client computer.

remote computer　A computer that is accessible only by using a communications line or a communications device, such as a network adapter or a modem.

remote procedure call (RPC) A message-passing facility that allows a distributed application to call services that are available on various machines in a network. Used during remote administration of computers.

replay attack An attempt to circumvent an authentication protocol by copying authentication messages from a legitimate client and then resending them during the impostor's own authentication to the server. See also nonce.

replication The process of copying data from a data store or file system to multiple computers that store the same data for the purpose of synchronizing the data. In Windows 2000, replication of Active Directory occurs through the Directory Replicator Service and replication of the file system occurs through Dfs replication.

replication latency In Active Directory replication, the delay between the time an update is applied to a given replica of a directory partition and the time it is applied to some other replica of the same directory partition. Latency is sometimes referred to as propagation delay. See also multimaster replication.

Request for Comments (RFC) A document that defines a standard. RFCs are published by the Internet Engineering Task Force (IETF) and other working groups.

resource record (RR) Information in the DNS database that can be used to process client queries. Each DNS server contains the resource records it needs to answer queries for the portion of the DNS namespace for which it is authoritative.

Resource Reservation Protocol (RSVP) A signaling protocol that allows the sender and receiver in a communication to set up a reserved highway for data transmission with a specified quality of service.

RFC See Request for Comments.

RIP See routing information protocol.

root The highest or uppermost level in a hierarchically organized set of information. The root is the point from which further subsets are branched in a logical sequence that moves from a broad or general focus to narrower perspectives.

root directory The top-level directory (or folder) on a computer, a partition or volume, or Macintosh-accessible volume. See also directory tree.

root domain The beginning of the Domain Name System (DNS) namespace. In Active Directory, the initial domain in an Active Directory tree. Also the initial domain of a forest.

route flapping A condition on an internetwork in which a network segment becomes intermittently available.

route summarization The practice of combining multiple network IDs into a single route in the routing table. With proper planning, hierarchical routing infrastructures can use route summarization.

routemon utility A scripting utility for the Routing and Remote Access service that is intended as a command-line alternative to the router administration user interface available through the Routing and Remote Access Manager.

router A network server that helps LANs and WANs achieve interoperability and connectivity and that can link LANs that have different network topologies, such as Ethernet and Token Ring.

router-to-router VPN connection A connection made by a router that connects two portions of a private network. The VPN server provides a routed connection to the network to which the VPN server is attached. On a router-to-router VPN connection, the packets sent from either router across the VPN connection typically do not originate at the routers.

routing The process of forwarding a packet based on the destination IP address.

routing domain A collection of contiguous network segments connected by routers that share the routing information for the routes within the domain.

Routing Information Protocol (RIP)
A suite of networking protocols that provides communications across interconnected networks made up of computers with diverse hardware architectures and various operating systems. TCP/IP includes standards for how computers communicate and conventions for connecting networks and routing traffic. See also protocol; Transmission Control Protocol.

routing infrastructure The structure and topology of the internetwork.

routing loop A path through an internetwork for a network ID that loops back onto itself.

routing protocol A series of periodic or on-demand messages containing routing information that is exchanged between routers to exchange routing information and provide fault tolerance. Except for their initial configuration, dynamic routers require little ongoing maintenance, and therefore can scale to larger internetworks.

routing table A database of routes containing information on network IDs, forwarding addresses, and metrics for reachable network segments on an internetwork.

routing table maintenance protocol (RTMP)
A distance vector routing protocol used on AppleTalk internetworks.

S

SAP table The service and IPX internetwork address information is collected in a database called a SAP table by IPX routers and Novell NetWare servers.

scalability A measure of how well a computer, service, or application can expand to meet increasing performance demands. For server clusters, the ability to incrementally add one or more systems to an existing cluster when the overall load of the cluster exceeds its capabilities.

scaling The process of adding processors to a system to achieve higher throughput.

secret key An encryption key that two parties share with each other and with no one else. See also symmetric key encryption.

Secure Sockets Layer (SSL) A proposed open standard developed by Netscape Communications for establishing a secure communications channel to prevent the interception of critical information, such as credit card numbers. Primarily, it enables secure electronic financial transactions on the World Wide Web, although it is designed to work on other Internet services as well.

Security Accounts Manager (SAM)
A protected subsystem of Windows NT and Windows 2000 that maintains the security accounts management database and provides an API for accessing the database. In Windows NT 4.0, both local and domain security principals are stored by SAM in the registry. In Windows 2000, workstation security accounts are stored by SAM in the local computer registry, and domain controller security accounts are stored in Active Directory.

security context The security attributes or rules that are currently in effect. For example, the rules that govern what a user can do to a protected object are determined by security information in the user's access token and in the object's security descriptor. Together, the access token and the security descriptor form a security context for the user's actions on the object. See also access token; security descriptor.

security descriptor A set of information attached to an object that specifies the permissions granted to users and groups, as well as the security events to be audited. See also discretionary access control list (DACL); object; system access control list (SACL).

security identifier (SID) A unique name that identifies a user who is logged on to a Windows NT or Windows 2000 security system. A security identifier can represent an individual user, a group of users, or a computer.

Security Parameters Index (SPI) A unique, identifying value in the SA used to distinguish among multiple security associations existing at the receiving computer.

seed router In the Macintosh environment, a router which initializes and broadcasts routing information about one or more physical networks. This information tells routers where to send each packet of data. On an AppleTalk network, a seed router initially defines the network numbers and zones for a network. Services for Macintosh servers, and third-party hardware routers can function as seed routers.

Sequenced Packet Exchange (SPX)
A transport layer protocol built on top of IPX.

server A computer that provides shared resources to network users.

Server Message Block (SMB) A file-sharing protocol designed to allow networked computers to transparently access files that reside on remote systems over a variety of networks. The SMB protocol defines a series of commands that pass information between computers. SMB uses four message types: session control, file, printer, and message.

Server service A software component that provides RPC (remote procedure call) support and file, print, and Named Pipe sharing. See also Named Pipe; remote procedure call (RPC).

service access point A logical address that allows a system to route data between a remote device and the appropriate communications support.

session key A key used primarily for encryption and decryption. Session keys are typically used with symmetric encryption algorithms where the same key is used for both encryption and decryption. For this reason, session and symmetric keys usually refer to the same type of key. See also symmetric key encryption.

session layer A network layer that allows two applications on different computers to establish, use, and end a session. This layer establishes dialog control between the two computers in a session, regulating which side transmits, as well as when and how long it transmits.

session ticket A credential presented by a client to a service in the Kerberos authentication protocol. Because session tickets are used to obtain authenticated connections to services, they are sometimes called service tickets. See also Kerberos authentication protocol; Key Distribution Center (KDC).

sessions Multiple packets sent with acknowledgments between two endpoints.

share name A name that refers to a shared resource on a server. Each shared folder on a server has a share name used by personal computer users to refer to the folder. Users of Macintosh computers use the name of the Macintosh-accessible volume that corresponds to a folder, which may be the same as the share name. See also Macintosh-accessible volume.

shell The command interpreter that is used to pass commands to the operating system.

Shiva Password Authentication Protocol (SPAP)
A two-way, reversible encryption mechanism for authenticating PPP connections employed by Shiva remote access servers.

short name A valid MS DOS or OS/2 8.3 file name (with up to 8 characters followed by a period and an extension of up to 3 characters) that a computer running Windows 2000 Server creates for every Macintosh folder name or file name on the server. Personal computer users refer to files on the server by their short names; Macintosh users refer to them by their long names. See also name mapping.

silent discard When a packet is discarded and the sending host is not informed as to why the packet was discarded.

silent RIP The capability of a computer to listen for and process Routing Information Protocol (RIP) announcements but without announcing its own routes.

Simple Mail Transfer Protocol (SMTP)
A protocol used on the Internet to transfer mail. SMTP is independent of the particular transmission subsystem and requires only a reliable, ordered, data stream channel.

Simple Network Management Protocol (SNMP)
A network management protocol installed with TCP/IP and widely used on TCP/IP and Internet Package Exchange (IPX) networks. SNMP transports management information and commands between a management program run by an administrator and the network management agent running on a host. The SNMP agent sends status information to one or more hosts when the host requests it or when a significant event occurs.

single-path routing infrastructure
A routing infrastructure where only a single path exists between any two network segments in the internetwork.

site server A computer running Windows NT Server on which Systems Management Server (SMS) site setup has been run. When SMS is installed on a computer, that computer is assigned the site server role. The site server, which hosts SMS components needed to monitor and manage an SMS site, typically performs several additional SMS roles, including component server, client access point, and distribution point.

Small Office/Home Office (SOHO)
An office with a few computers that can be considered a small business or part of a larger network.

smart card A credit card-sized device that is used with a PIN number to enable certificate-based authentication and single sign-on to the enterprise. Smart cards securely store certificates, public and private keys, passwords, and other types of personal information. A smart card reader attached to the computer reads the smart card. See also authentication.

SNMP See Simple Network Management Protocol.

socket A bidirectional pipe for incoming and outgoing data between networked computers. The Windows Sockets API is a networking API used by programmers to create TCP/IP-based sockets programs.

software router A router that is not dedicated to performing routing but performs routing as one of multiple processes running on the router computer.

source routing The practice of specifying the list of networks or routers in the network layer header to forward a packet along a specific path in an internetwork.

split horizon A route-advertising algorithm that prevents the advertising of routes in the same direction in which they were learned. Split horizon helps prevent routing loops. See also poison reverse.

spooling A process on a server in which print documents are stored on a disk until a printer is ready to process them. A spooler accepts each document from each client, stores it, and sends it to a printer when the printer is ready.

standard error (STDERR) In UNIX, the defined receiver of error messages about a process. By default, the standard error goes to the terminal.

standard input (STDIN) In UNIX, the defined source of input for a process. By default, standard input comes from the terminal.

standard output (STDOUT) In UNIX, the defined receiver for output from a process. By default, the standard output goes to the terminal.

static router A router with manually configured routing tables. A network administrator, with knowledge of the internetwork topology, manually builds and updates the routing table, programming all routes in the routing table. Static routers can work well for small internetworks but do not scale well to large or dynamically changing internetworks due to their manual administration.

static routing Routing limited to fixed routing tables, as opposed to dynamically updated routing tables. See also dynamic routing; routing; routing table.

static services An IPX service that is permanently stored in a SAP table. Static services are advertised using normal SAP processes. Static SAP services are typically used to define the services that are available across a demand-dial connection.

Stream Input/Output (Stream I/O)
A protocol that provides access to IBM host data one file at a time, as opposed to one record at a time, such as with Structured Query Language (SQL).

structured query language (SQL)
A widely accepted standard database sublanguage used in querying, updating, and managing relational databases.

stub area An OSPF area that does not advertise individual external networks. Routing to all external networks in a stub area is done through a default route (destination 0.0.0.0 with the network mask of 0.0.0.0).

subarea An area composed of one subarea node (a type 5 host node or a type 4 node [a Front End Processor]) and the resources it controls, including type 2 nodes

subkey   In the registry, a key within a key. Subkeys are analogous to subdirectories in the registry hierarchy. Keys and subkeys are similar to the section header in .ini files; however, subkeys can carry out functions. See also key.

subnet   A subdivision of an IP network. Each subnet has its own unique subnetted network ID.

subnet mask   A 32-bit value expressed as four decimal numbers from 0 to 255, separated by periods (for example, 255.255.0.0). This number allows TCP/IP to distinguish the network ID portion of the IP address from the host ID portion. The host ID identifies individual computers on the network. TCP/IP hosts use the subnet mask to determine whether a destination host is located on a local or a remote network.

subnetted network ID   A network ID for a subnetted network segment that is the result of a subdivision of a TCP/IP network ID.

subnetting   The act of subdividing the address space of a TCP/IP network ID into smaller network segments, each with its own subnetted network ID.

supernetting   The practice of expressing a range of IP network IDs using a single IP network ID and subnet mask. Supernettting is a route aggregation and summarization technique.

switch   A computer or other network-enabled device that controls routing and operation of a signal path. In clustering, a switch is used to connect the cluster hosts to a router or other source of incoming network connections. See also routing.

switched virtual circuit (SVC)   A connection established dynamically between devices on an ATM network through the use of signaling.

symmetric key encryption   An encryption algorithm that requires the same secret key to be used for both encryption and decryption. This is often called secret key encryption. Because of its speed, symmetric encryption is typically used rather than public key encryption when a message sender needs to encrypt large amounts of data.

system access control list (SACL)
The part of an object's security descriptor that specifies which events are to be audited per user or group. Examples of auditing events are file access, logon attempts, and system shutdowns. See also access control entry (ACE); discretionary access control list (DACL); object; security descriptor.

system call   A routine that makes the operating system available to a program or that requests services from the operating system.

systemroot   The path and folder name where the Windows 2000 system files are located. Typically, this is C:\Winnt, although a different drive or folder can be designated when Windows 2000 is installed. The value %systemroot% can be used to replace the actual location of the folder that contains the Window 2000 system files. To identify your systemroot folder, click Start, click Run, and then type %systemroot%.

Systems Management Server   A part of the Windows BackOffice suite of products. Systems Management Server (SMS) includes inventory collection, deployment, and diagnostic tools. SMS can significantly automate the task of upgrading software, allow remote problem solving, provide asset management information, manage software licenses, and monitor computers and networks.

Systems Network Architecture (SNA)

A communications framework developed by IBM to define network functions and establish standards for enabling computers to share and process data.

T

T1 A wide-area carrier that transmits data at 1.544 Mbps.

TCP Transmission Control Protocol.

TCP connection The logical connection that exists between two processes that are using TCP to exchange data.

TCP segment The quantity consisting of the TCP header and its associated data. TCP segments are exchanged using a TCP connection.

TCP/IP See Transmission Control Protocol/Internet Protocol.

TCP/IP filtering A feature of Windows 2000 TCP/IP that allows you to specify exactly which types of incoming non-transit IP traffic are processed for each IP interface.

Telephony API (TAPI) An application programming interface (API) used by communications programs to communicate with telephony and network services. See also Internet Protocol.

Telnet A terminal-emulation protocol that is widely used on the Internet to log on to network computers. Telnet also refers to the application that uses the Telnet protocol for users who log on from remote locations.

Telnet 3270 (TN3270) Terminal emulation software, similar to Telnet, that allows a personal computer to log on to an IBM mainframe over a TCP/IP network.

Telnet 5250 (TN5250) Terminal emulation software, similar to Telnet, that allows a personal computer to log on to an IBM AS/400 host system over a TCP/IP network.

terminal A device consisting of a display screen and a keyboard that is used to communicate with a computer.

thread A type of object within a process that runs program instructions. Using multiple threads allows concurrent operations within a process and enables one process to run different parts of its program on different processors simultaneously. A thread has its own set of registers, its own kernel stack, a thread environment block, and a user stack in the address space of its process.

throughput For disks, the transfer capacity of the disk system.

Tick Count An estimate of the amount of time it takes an IPX packet to reach the destination network.

Time To Live (TTL) A timer value included in packets sent over TCP/IP-based networks that tells the recipients how long to hold or use the packet or any of its included data before expiring and discarding the packet or data. For DNS, TTL values are used in resource records within a zone to determine how long requesting clients should cache and use this information when it appears in a query response answered by a DNS server for the zone.

Token Ring A type of network media that connects clients in a closed ring and uses token passing to allow clients to use the network. See also Fiber Distributed Data Interface (FDDI); LocalTalk.

topology In Windows operating systems, the relationships among a set of network components. In the context of Active Directory replication, topology refers to the set of connections that domain controllers use to replicate information among themselves. See also domain controller; replication.

totally stubby area An OSPF area that does not advertise individual external networks or OSPF inter-area routes. A router's routing table within a totally stubby area contains intra-area routes and a default route (destination 0.0.0.0 with the network mask of 0.0.0.0). The default route summarizes all inter-area routes and all external routes.

tracing A capability of components of the Windows 2000 Routing and Remote Access service that records internal component variables, function calls, and interactions. You can use tracing to troubleshoot complex network problems.

Traffic Control A Windows 2000 mechanism that creates and regulates data flows with defined QoS parameters. The Traffic Control API (TC API) creates filters to direct selected packets through this flow. Traffic control is invoked by the QoS API and subsequently serviced by the RSVP SP.

Transaction Program Monitor A monitor that manages the operating environment of the online transaction processing (OLTP) application by optimizing the use of operating system resources and the network. The TP Monitor provides a management platform for the system administrator that supports: load balancing, fault tolerance, performance monitoring, and security.

transit internetwork The shared or public internetwork crossed by the encapsulated data.

Transmission Control Protocol/Internet Protocol (TCP/IP)
A set of software networking protocols widely used on the Internet that provide communications across interconnected networks of computers with diverse hardware architectures and operating systems. TCP/IP includes standards for how computers communicate and conventions for connecting networks and routing traffic.

Transport Driver Interface (TDI) In the Windows NT and Windows 2000 networking model, a common interface for network layer components that communicate with the session layer of the Open Systems Interconnection model. The TDI is not a single program, but a protocol specification to which the upper bounds of transport protocol device drivers are written. It allows software components above and below the transport layer to be mixed and matched without reprogramming.

transport layer The network layer that handles error recognition and recovery. When necessary, it repackages long messages into small packets for transmission and, at the receiving end, rebuilds packets into the original message. The receiving transport layer also sends receipt acknowledgments.

Transport Layer Security (TLS) A standard protocol that is used to provide secure Web communications on the Internet or intranets. It enables clients to authenticate servers or, optionally, servers to authenticate clients. It also provides a secure channel by encrypting communications for confidentiality.

transport protocol A protocol that defines how data should be presented to the next receiving layer in the Windows NT and Windows 2000 networking model and packages the data accordingly. The transport protocol passes data to the network adapter driver through the network device interface specification (NDIS) interface and to the redirector through the Transport Driver Interface (TDI).

trigger For Network Monitor data captures, a set of conditions defined by a user that, when met, initiate an action such as stopping a capture or executing a program or command file.

triggered update A route advertising algorithm that advertises changes in the network topology as they occur, rather than waiting for the next scheduled periodic advertisement.

trust relationship A logical relationship established between domains that allows pass-through authentication in which a trusting domain honors the logon authentications of a trusted domain. User accounts and global groups defined in a trusted domain can be given rights and permissions in a trusting domain, even though the user accounts or groups do not exist in the trusting domain's directory. See also authentication; domain; two-way trust relationship.

tunnel The logical path by which the encapsulated packets travel through the transit internetwork.

tunneled data Data that is sent through the tunneled, or encapsulated, portion of the connection.

tunneling A method of using an internetwork infrastructure of one protocol to transfer a payload (the frames or packets) of another protocol.

tunneling protocol A communication standard used to manage tunnels and encapsulate private data. Data that is tunneled must also be encrypted to be a VPN connection. Windows 2000 includes the Point-to-Point Tunneling Protocol (PPTP) and Layer 2 Tunneling Protocol (L2TP).

two-way initiated connection A demand-dial connection where either router can be the answering router or the calling router depending on who is initiating the connection. Both routers must be configured to initiate and accept a demand-dial connection. You use two-way initiated connections when traffic from either router can create the demand-dial connection.

two-way trust relationship A link between domains in which each domain trusts user accounts in the other domain to use its resources. Users can log on from computers in either domain to the domain that contains their account. See also trust relationship.

U

unicast An address that identifies a specific, globally unique host.

unicast listening mode A listening mode where the only frames that are considered for further processing are in a table of interesting destination media access control addresses on the network adapter. Typically, the only interesting addresses are the broadcast address (0xFF-FF-FF-FF-FF-FF) and the unicast address, (also known as the media access control address), of the adapter.

Unicode A fixed-width, 16-bit character-encoding standard capable of representing the letters and characters of the majority of the world's languages. Unicode was developed by a consortium of U.S. computer companies.

universal group A Windows 2000 group only available in native mode that is valid anywhere in the forest. A universal group appears in the Global Catalog but contains primarily global groups from domains in the forest. This is the simplest form of group and can contain other universal groups, global groups, and users from anywhere in the forest. See also domain local group; forest; Global Catalog.

UNIX A powerful, multiuser, multitasking operating system initially developed at AT&T Bell Laboratories in 1969 for use on minicomputers. UNIX is considered more portable—that is, less computer-specific—than other operating systems because it is written in C language. Newer versions of UNIX have been developed at the University of California at Berkeley and by AT&T.

user account A record that consists of all the information that defines a user to Windows 2000. This includes the user name and password required for the user to log on, the groups in which the user account has membership, and the rights and permissions the user has for using the computer and network and accessing their resources. For Windows 2000 Professional and member servers, user accounts are managed by using Local Users and Groups. For Windows 2000 Server domain controllers, user accounts are managed by using Microsoft Active Directory Users and Computers. See also domain controller; group.

User Datagram Protocol (UDP) A TCP component that offers a connectionless datagram service that guarantees neither delivery nor correct sequencing of delivered packets.

user network interface (UNI) The interface between ATM users or end stations and an ATM switch or network. The UNI interface is defined in the ATM Forum UNI documents.

V

variable bit rate (VBR) An ATM service type that guarantees service based on average and peak traffic rates. VBR is used for traffic that requires little or no cell loss. It transmits data in spurts, or bursts, rather than in a continuous stream.

variable length subnet masks (VLSM) Subnet masks used to produce subnets of an IP network ID of different sizes.

variable length subnetting The practice of subdividing the address space of an IP network ID into subnets of different sizes.

virtual channel identifier (VCI) A section of the ATM cell header that contains the virtual channel address over which the cell is to be routed.

Virtual Circuit (VC) A point-to-point connection for the transmission of data. This allows greater control of call attributes, such as bandwidth, latency, delay variation, and sequencing.

virtual link A logical link between a backbone area border router and an area border router that is not connected to the backbone.

virtual memory The space on the hard disk that Windows 2000 uses as memory. Because of virtual memory, the amount of memory taken from the perspective of a process can be much greater than the actual physical memory in the computer. The operating system does this in a way that is transparent to the application, by paging data that does not fit in physical memory to and from the disk at any given instant.

virtual network A logical network that exists inside Novell NetWare and NetWare-compatible servers and routers but is not associated with a physical adapter. The virtual network appears to a user as a separate network. On a computer running Windows 2000 Server, programs advertise their location on a virtual network, not a physical network. The internal network number identifies a virtual network inside a computer. See also internal network number; external network number.

virtual path identifier (VPI) A section of the ATM cell header that contains the virtual path address over which the cell is to be routed.

virtual private network (VPN) The extension of a private network that encompasses links across shared or public networks, such as the Internet.

virtual private network connection
A link in which private data is encapsulated and encrypted.

VPN See virtual private network.

VPN client A computer that initiates a VPN connection to a VPN server. A VPN client can be an individual computer that obtains a remote access VPN connection or a router that obtains a router-to-router VPN connection.

VPN connection The portion of the connection in which your data is encrypted.

VPN server A computer that accepts VPN connections from VPN clients. A VPN server can provide a remote access VPN connection or a router-to-router VPN connection.

W

Web server A server that provides the ability to develop COM-based applications and to create large sites for the Internet and corporate intranets.

wide area network (WAN) A communications network connecting geographically separated computers, printers, and other devices. A WAN allows any connected device to interact with any other on the network. See also local area network (LAN).

wildcard In DNS, a character that can be substituted for another character during a query.

Windows 2000 Redirector A software component that intercepts network requests and redirects them to network servers, workstations, printers and directory shares.

Windows Internet Name Service (WINS)
A software service that dynamically maps IP addresses to computer names (NetBIOS names). This allows users to access resources by name instead of requiring them to use IP addresses that are difficult to recognize and remember. WINS servers support clients running Windows NT 4.0 and earlier versions of Windows operating systems. See also Domain Name System (DNS).

Windows Sockets (Winsock) An industry-standard application programming interface (API) used on the Microsoft Windows operating system that provides a two-way, reliable, sequenced, and unduplicated flow of data.

WINS proxy A computer that listens to name query broadcasts and responds for those names not on the local subnet. The proxy communicates with the name server to resolve names and then caches them for a specific time period. See also Windows Internet Name Service (WINS).

Z

zone In a DNS database, a zone is a contiguous portion of the DNS tree that is administered as a single separate entity by a DNS server. The zone contains resource records for all the names within the zone. In the Macintosh environment, a logical grouping that simplifies browsing the network for resources, such as servers and printers. It is similar to a domain in Windows 2000 Server networking. See also domain; Domain Name System (DNS); DNS server.

zone list In the Macintosh environment, a list that includes all of the zones associated with a particular network. Not to be confused with Windows 2000 DNS zones. See also zone.

Index

H

Comprehensive
information and tools—
straight from the
Windows 2000 Server team!

Deploy, manage, and optimize Microsoft's next-generation operating system with expertise from those who know the technology best—the Microsoft Windows 2000 Server development team. This RESOURCE KIT gives you seven comprehensive guides—thousands of pages packed full of technical details—plus hundreds of tools and utilities on CD. It's the complete kit you need to help maximize system performance and reduce ownership and support costs. Get seven volumes of authoritative Windows 2000 Server drill down, straight from the source!

Microsoft® Windows® 2000 Server Resource Kit
ISBN: 1-57231-805-8

Also available in
separate volumes!

These powerhouse guides—available separately and distilled from the MICROSOFT WINDOWS 2000 SERVER RESOURCE KIT— make it easy to find the exact technical information you need to optimize system performance and reduce costs.

Microsoft® Windows® 2000 Server Deployment Planning Guide
ISBN: 0-7356-1794-5

Microsoft Windows 2000 Server Distributed Systems Guide
ISBN: 0-7356-1795-3

Microsoft Windows 2000 Server Operations Guide
ISBN: 0-7356-1796-1

Microsoft Windows 2000 Server Internetworking Guide
ISBN: 0-7356-1797-X

Microsoft Windows 2000 Server TCP/IP Core Networking Guide
ISBN: 0-7356-1798-8

microsoft.com/mspress

Ready solutions *for the* IT administrator

Keep your IT systems up and running with the ADMINISTRATOR'S COMPANION series from Microsoft. These expert guides serve as both tutorials and references for critical deployment and maintenance of Microsoft products and technologies. Packed with real-world expertise, hands-on numbered procedures, and handy workarounds, ADMINISTRATOR'S COMPANIONS deliver ready answers for on-the-job results.

Microsoft® SQL Server™ 2000 Administrator's Companion

U.S.A. $59.99
Canada $86.99
ISBN   0-7356-1051-7

Microsoft Exchange 2000 Server Administrator's Companion

U.S.A. $59.99
Canada $86.99
ISBN   0-7356-0938-1

Microsoft Windows® 2000 Server Administrator's Companion

U.S.A. $ 69.99
Canada $ 107.99
ISBN   1-57231-819-8

Microsoft Systems Management Server 2.0 Administrator's Companion

U.S.A. $59.99
Canada $92.99
ISBN   0-7356-0834-2

Microsoft®

mspress.microsoft.com

In-depth. Focused.
And
ready for work.

Get the technical drilldown you need to deploy and support Microsoft products more effectively with the MICROSOFT TECHNICAL REFERENCE series. Each guide focuses on a specific aspect of the technology—weaving in-depth detail with on-the-job scenarios and practical how-to information for the IT professional. Get focused—and take technology to its limits—with MICROSOFT TECHNICAL REFERENCES.

Data Warehousing with Microsoft® SQL Server™ 7.0 Technical Reference
U.S.A. $49.99
Canada $76.99
ISBN 0-7356-0859-8

Microsoft SQL Server 7.0 Performance Tuning Technical Reference
U.S.A. $49.99
Canada $76.99
ISBN 0-7356-0909-8

Building Applications with Microsoft Outlook® 2000 Technical Reference
U.S.A. $49.99
Canada $72.99
ISBN 0-7356-0581-5

Microsoft Windows NT® Server 4.0 Terminal Server Edition Technical Reference
U.S.A. $49.99
Canada $72.99
ISBN 0-7356-0645-5

Microsoft Windows® 2000 TCP/IP Protocols and Services Technical Reference
U.S.A. $49.99
Canada $76.99
ISBN 0-7356-0556-4

Active Directory™ Services for Microsoft Windows 2000 Technical Reference
U.S.A. $49.99
Canada $76.99
ISBN 0-7356-0624-2

Microsoft Windows 2000 Security Technical Reference
U.S.A. $49.99
Canada $72.99
ISBN 0-7356-0858-X

Microsoft Windows 2000 Performance Tuning Technical Reference
U.S.A. $49.99
Canada $72.99
ISBN 0-7356-0633-1

Microsoft®

mspress.microsoft.com

Get a **Free**
e-mail newsletter, updates,
special offers, links to related books,
and more when you

register on line!

Register your Microsoft Press® title on our Web site and you'll get a FREE subscription to our e-mail newsletter, *Microsoft Press Book Connections.* You'll find out about newly released and upcoming books and learning tools, online events, software downloads, special offers and coupons for Microsoft Press customers, and information about major Microsoft® product releases. You can also read useful additional information about all the titles we publish, such as detailed book descriptions, tables of contents and indexes, sample chapters, links to related books and book series, author biographies, and reviews by other customers.

Registration is easy. Just visit this Web page and fill in your information:

http://www.microsoft.com/mspress/register

***Microsoft*®**

Proof of Purchase

Use this page as proof of purchase if participating in a promotion or rebate offer on this title. Proof of purchase must be used in conjunction with other proof(s) of payment such as your dated sales receipt—see offer details.

Microsoft® Windows® 2000 Server Internetworking Guide
0-7356-1797-X

CUSTOMER NAME

Microsoft Press, PO Box 97017, Redmond, WA 98073-9830

END-USER LICENSE AGREEMENT FOR MICROSOFT SOFTWARE

Microsoft WINDOWS 2000 RESOURCE KIT

IMPORTANT-READ CAREFULLY: This Microsoft End-User License Agreement ("EULA") is a legal agreement between you (either an individual or a single entity) and Microsoft Corporation for the Microsoft software identified above, which includes computer software and may include associated media, printed materials, additional computer software applications, and "online" or electronic documentation ("SOFTWARE"). By downloading, installing, copying, or otherwise using the SOFTWARE, you agree to be bound by the terms of this EULA. If you do not agree to the terms of this EULA, do not install or use the SOFTWARE. This print EULA supercedes any End User License Agreement found on the CD.

SOFTWARE LICENSE

The SOFTWARE is protected by copyright laws and international copyright treaties, as well as other intellectual property laws and treaties. **The SOFTWARE is licensed, not sold.**

1. **GRANT OF LICENSE.** This EULA grants you the following rights:

   a. **SOFTWARE.** Except as otherwise provided herein, you, as an individual, may install and use copies of the SOFTWARE on an unlimited number of computers, including workstations, terminals or other digital electronic devices ("COMPUTERS"), provided that you are the only individual using the SOFTWARE. If you are an entity, you may designate one individual within your organization to have the right to use the SOFTWARE in the manner provided above. The SOFTWARE is in "use" on a COMPUTER when it is loaded into temporary memory (i.e.. RAM) or installed into permanent memory (e.g., hard disk, CD-ROM, or other storage device) of that COMPUTER.

   b. **Client/Server Software.** The SOFTWARE may contain one or more components which consist of both of the following types of software: "Server Software" that is installed and provides services on a COMPUTER acting as a server ("Server"); and "Client Software" that allows a COMPUTER to access or utilize the services provided by the Server Software. If the component of the SOFTWARE consists of both Server Software and Client Software which are used together, you may also install and use copies of such Client Software on COMPUTERS within your organization and which are connected to your internal network.

Such COMPUTERS running this Client Software may be used by more than one individual.

2. **DESCRIPTION OF OTHER RIGHTS AND LIMITATIONS.**

   a. **Limitations on Reverse Engineering, Decompilation, and Disassembly.** You may not reverse engineer, decompile, or disassemble the SOFTWARE, except and only to the extent that such activity is expressly permitted by applicable law notwithstanding this limitation.

   b. **Rental.** You may not rent, lease, or lend the SOFTWARE.

   c. **Support Services.** Microsoft does not support the SOFTWARE, however, in the event Microsoft does provide you with support services related to the SOFTWARE ("Support Services"), use of such Support Services is governed by the Microsoft policies and programs described in the user manual, in "online" documentation, and/or in other Microsoft-provided materials. Any supplemental software code provided to you as part of the Support Services shall be considered part of the SOFTWARE and subject to the terms and conditions of this EULA. With respect to technical information you provide to Microsoft as part of the Support Services, Microsoft may use such information for its business purposes, including for product support and development. Microsoft will not utilize such technical information in a form that personally identifies you.

   d. **Software Transfer.** You may permanently transfer of all of your rights under this EULA, provided you retain no copies, you transfer all of the SOFTWARE (including all component parts, the media and printed materials, any upgrades, this EULA, and, if applicable, the Certificate of Authenticity), **and** the recipient agrees to the terms of this EULA. If the SOFTWARE is an upgrade, any transfer must include all prior versions of the SOFTWARE.

   e. **Termination.** Without prejudice to any other rights, Microsoft may terminate this EULA if you fail to comply with the terms and conditions of this EULA. In such event, you must destroy all copies of the SOFTWARE and all of its component parts.

3. **UPGRADES.** If the SOFTWARE is labeled as an upgrade , you must be properly licensed to use a product identified by Microsoft as being eligible for the upgrade in order to use the SOFTWARE. SOFTWARE labeled as an upgrade replaces and/or supplements the product that formed the basis for your eligibility for the upgrade. You may use the resulting upgraded product only in accordance with the terms of this EULA. If the SOFTWARE is an upgrade of a component of a package of software programs that you licensed as a single product, the SOFTWARE may be used and transferred only as part of that single product package and may not be separated for use on more than one computer

4. **INTELLECTUAL PROPERTY RIGHTS.** All title and intellectual property rights in and to the SOFTWARE (including but not limited to any images, photographs, animations, video, audio, music, text and "applets" incorporated into the SOFTWARE), and any copies you are permitted to make herein are owned by Microsoft or its suppliers. All title and intellectual property rights in

and to the content which may be accessed through use of the SOFTWARE is the property of the respective content owner and may be protected by applicable copyright or other intellectual property laws and treaties. This EULA grants you no rights to use such content. If this SOFTWARE contains documentation which is provided only in electronic form, you may print one copy of such electronic documentation. You may not copy the printed materials accompanying the SOFTWARE.

5. **U.S. GOVERNMENT LICENSE RIGHTS**. SOFTWARE provided to the U.S. Government pursuant to solicitations issued on or after December 1, 1995 is provided with the commercial license rights and restrictions described elsewhere herein. SOFT-WARE provided to the U.S. Government pursuant to solicitations issued prior to December 1, 1995 is provided with "Restricted Rights" as provided for in FAR, 48 CFR 52.227-14 (JUNE 1987) or DFAR, 48 CFR 252.227-7013 (OCT 1988), as applicable.

6. **EXPORT RESTRICTIONS**. You agree that you will not export or re-export the SOFTWARE (or portions thereof) to any country, person or entity subject to U.S. export restrictions. You specifically agree not to export or re-export the SOFTWARE (or portions thereof): (i) to any country subject to a U.S. embargo or trade restriction; (ii) to any person or entity who you know or have reason to know will utilize the SOFTWARE (or portion thereof) in the production of nuclear, chemical or biological weapons; or (iii) to any person or entity who has been denied export privileges by the U.S. government. For additional information see http://www.microsoft.com/exporting/.

7. **DISCLAIMER OF WARRANTIES. To the maximum extent permitted by applicable law, Microsoft and its suppliers provide the SOFTWARE and any (if any) Support Services *AS IS AND WITH ALL FAULTS*, and hereby disclaim all warranties and conditions, either express, implied or statutory, including, but not limited to, any (if any) implied warranties or conditions of merchantability, of fitness for a particular purpose, of lack of viruses, of accuracy or completeness of responses, of results, and of lack of negligence or lack of workmanlike effort, all with regard to the SOFTWARE, and the provision of or failure to provide Support Services. ALSO, THERE IS NO WARRANTY OR CONDITION OF TITLE, QUIET ENJOYMENT, QUIET POSSESSION, CORRESPONDENCE TO DESCRIPTION OR NON-INFRINGEMENT, WITH REGARD TO THE SOFTWARE. THE ENTIRE RISK AS TO THE QUALITY OF OR ARISING OUT OF USE OR PERFORMANCE OF THE SOFTWARE AND SUPPORT SERVICES, IF ANY, REMAINS WITH YOU.**

8. **EXCLUSION OF INCIDENTAL, CONSEQUENTIAL AND CERTAIN OTHER DAMAGES. TO THE MAXIMUM EXTENT PERMITTED BY APPLICABLE LAW, IN NO EVENT SHALL MICROSOFT OR ITS SUPPLIERS BE LIABLE FOR ANY SPECIAL, INCIDENTAL, INDIRECT, OR CONSEQUENTIAL DAMAGES WHATSOEVER (INCLUDING, BUT NOT LIMITED TO, DAMAGES FOR LOSS OF PROFITS OR CONFIDENTIAL OR OTHER INFORMATION, FOR BUSINESS INTERRUPTION, FOR PERSONAL INJURY, FOR LOSS OF PRIVACY, FOR FAILURE TO MEET ANY DUTY INCLUDING OF GOOD FAITH OR OF REASONABLE CARE, FOR NEGLI-GENCE, AND FOR ANY OTHER PECUNIARY OR OTHER LOSS WHATSOEVER) ARISING OUT OF OR IN ANY WAY RELATED TO THE USE OF OR INABILITY TO USE THE SOFTWARE, THE PROVISION OF OR FAILURE TO PROVIDE SUPPORT SERVICES, OR OTHERWISE UNDER OR IN CONNECTION WITH ANY PROVISION OF THIS EULA, EVEN IN THE EVENT OF THE FAULT, TORT (INCLUDING NEGLIGENCE), STRICT LIABILITY, BREACH OF CONTRACT OR BREACH OF WARRANTY OF MICROSOFT OR ANY SUPPLIER, AND EVEN IF MICROSOFT OR ANY SUPPLIER HAS BEEN ADVISED OF THE POSSIBILITY OF SUCH DAMAGES.**

9. **LIMITATION OF LIABILITY AND REMEDIES. Notwithstanding any damages that you might incur for any reason whatsoever (including, without limitation, all damages referenced above and all direct or general damages), the entire liability of Microsoft and any of its suppliers under any provision of this EULA and your exclusive remedy for all of the foregoing shall be limited to the greater of the amount actually paid by you for the SOFTWARE or U.S.\$5.00. The foregoing limitations, exclusions and disclaimers shall apply to the maximum extent permitted by applicable law, even if any remedy fails its essential purpose.**

10. **NOTE ON JAVA SUPPORT**. THE SOFTWARE MAY CONTAIN SUPPORT FOR PROGRAMS WRITTEN IN JAVA. JAVA TECHNOLOGY IS NOT FAULT TOLERANT AND IS NOT DESIGNED, MANUFACTURED, OR INTENDED FOR USE OR RESALE AS ONLINE CONTROL EQUIPMENT IN HAZARDOUS ENVIRONMENTS REQUIRING FAIL-SAFE PERFOR-MANCE, SUCH AS IN THE OPERATION OF NUCLEAR FACILITIES, AIRCRAFT NAVIGATION OR COMMUNICATION SYSTEMS, AIR TRAFFIC CONTROL, DIRECT LIFE SUPPORT MACHINES, OR WEAPONS SYSTEMS, IN WHICH THE FAILURE OF JAVA TECHNOLOGY COULD LEAD DIRECTLY TO DEATH, PERSONAL INJURY, OR SEVERE PHYSICAL OR ENVIRONMENTAL DAMAGE. Sun Microsystems, Inc. has contractually obligated Microsoft to make this disclaimer.

11. **APPLICABLE LAW.** If you acquired this SOFTWARE in the United States, this EULA is governed by the laws of the State of Washington. If you acquired this SOFTWARE in Canada, unless expressly prohibited by local law, this EULA is governed by the laws in force in the Province of Ontario, Canada; and, in respect of any dispute which may arise hereunder, you consent to the jurisdiction of the federal and provincial courts sitting in Toronto, Ontario. If this SOFTWARE was acquired outside the United States, then local law may apply.

12. **ENTIRE AGREEMENT. This EULA (including any addendum or amendment to this EULA which is included with the SOFTWARE) is the entire agreement between you and Microsoft relating to the SOFTWARE and the Support Services (if any) and it supersedes all prior or contemporaneous oral or written communications, proposals and representations with respect to the SOFTWARE or any other subject matter covered by this EULA. To the extent the terms of any Microsoft policies or programs for Support Services conflict with the terms of this EULA, the terms of this EULA shall control.**

SI VOUS AVEZ ACQUIS VOTRE PRODUIT MICROSOFT AU CANADA, LA GARANTIE LIMITÉE SUIVANTE VOUS CONCERNE :

RENONCIATION AUX GARANTIES. Dans toute la mesure permise par la législation en vigueur, Microsoft et ses fournisseurs fournissent le PRODUIT LOGICIEL et tous (selon le cas) Services d'assistance TELS QUELS ET AVEC TOUS LEURS DÉFAUTS, et par les présentes excluent toute garantie ou condition, expresse ou implicite, légale ou conventionnelle, écrite ou verbale, y compris, mais sans limitation, toute garantie (selon le cas) garantie ou condition implicite ou légale de qualité marchande, de conformité à un usage particulier, d'absence de virus, d'exactitude et d'intégralité des réponses, des résultats, d'efforts techniques et professionnels et d'absence de négligence, le tout relativement au PRODUIT LOGICIEL et à la prestation ou à la non-prestation des Services d'assistance. DE PLUS, IL N'Y A AUCUNE GARANTIE ET CONDITION DE TITRE, DE JOUISSANCE PAISIBLE, DE POSSES- SION PAISIBLE, DE SIMILARITÉ À LA DESCRIPTION ET D'ABSENCE DE CONTREFAÇON RELATIVEMENT AU PRODUIT LOGICIEL. Vous supportez tous les risques découlant de l'utilisation et de la performance du PRODUIT LOGICIEL et ceux découlant des Services d'assistance (s'il y a lieu).

EXCLUSION DES DOMMAGES INDIRECTS, ACCESSOIRES ET AUTRES. Dans toute la mesure permise par la législation en vigueur, Microsoft et ses fournisseurs ne sont en aucun cas responsables de tout dommage spécial, indirect, accessoire, moral ou exemplaire quel qu'il soit (y compris, mais sans limitation, les dommages entraînés par la perte de bénéfices ou la perte d'information confidentielle ou autre, l'interruption des affaires, les préjudices corporels, la perte de confidentialité, le défaut de remplir toute obliga- tion y compris les obligations de bonne foi et de diligence raisonnable, la négligence et toute autre perte pécuniaire ou autre perte de quelque nature que ce soit) découlant de, ou de toute autre manière lié à, l'utilisation ou l'impossibilité d'utiliser le PRODUIT LOGICIEL, la prestation ou la non-prestation des Services d'assistance ou autrement en vertu de ou relativement à toute disposition de cette convention, que ce soit en cas de faute, de délit (y compris la négligence), de responsabilité stricte, de manquement à un contrat ou de manquement à une garantie de Microsoft ou de l'un de ses fournisseurs, et ce, même si Microsoft ou l'un de ses fournisseurs a été avisé de la possibilité de tels dommages.

LIMITATION DE RESPONSABILITÉ ET RECOURS. Malgré tout dommage que vous pourriez encourir pour quelque raison que ce soit (y compris, mais sans limitation, tous les dommages mentionnés ci-dessus et tous les dommages directs et généraux), la seule responsabilité de Microsoft et de ses fournisseurs en vertu de toute disposition de cette convention et votre unique recours en regard de tout ce qui précédé sont limités au plus élevé des montants suivants: soit (a) le montant que vous avez payé pour le PRODUIT LOGICIEL, soit (b) un montant équivalant à cinq dollars U.S. (5,00 $ U.S.). Les limitations, exclusions et renonciations ci-dessus s'appliquent dans toute la mesure permise par la législation en vigueur, et ce même si leur application a pour effet de priver un recours de son essence.

LÉGISLATION APPLICABLE. Sauf lorsqu'expressément prohibé par la législation locale, la présente convention est régie par les lois en vigueur dans la province d'Ontario, Canada. Pour tout différend qui pourrait découler des présentes, vous acceptez la compétence des tribunaux fédéraux et provinciaux siégeant à Toronto, Ontario.

Si vous avez des questions concernant cette convention ou si vous désirez communiquer avec Microsoft pour quelque raison que ce soit, veuillez contacter la succursale Microsoft desservant votre pays, ou écrire à: Microsoft Sales Information Center, One Microsoft Way, Redmond, Washington 98052-6399.